DAVID H. BENNETT

★ ★

The Party of Fear

David H. Bennett, author of *Demagogues in the Depression: American Radicals and the Union Party, 1932–1936*, is a professor of history in the Maxwell School at Syracuse University.

DAVID H. BENNETT

★ ★

The Party of Fear

FROM NATIVIST MOVEMENTS

TO THE NEW RIGHT IN

AMERICAN HISTORY

Vintage Books

A Division of Random House, Inc.

New York

Library of Congress Cataloging-in-Publication Data
Bennett, David Harry, 1935–
The party of fear : from nativist movements to the New
Right in American history / David H. Bennett.
p.   cm.
Reprint. Originally published: Chapel Hill: University of
North Carolina Press, © 1988.
Includes bibliographical references.
ISBN 0-679-76721-5
1. Radicalism—United States.   2. Nativism—History.
3. Anti-communist movements—United States—
History.   4. United States—Politics and government.
5. United States—Social conditions.   I. Title.
[E183.B43   1990]
320.5′3—dc20   89-405000
CIP

Manufactured in the United States of America

For

Matthew and Steven

and for Gerda

CONTENTS

★ ★

ACKNOWLEDGMENTS

★ ★

THIS BOOK has been years in the making. It started as a study of right-wing politics in modern United States history, and at first I did not plan an extensive treatment of the early nativists. But it soon was clear that any consideration of such movements in America must begin with a careful exploration of developments in the nineteenth century and before. It became a larger project than I had intended.

As the work was nearing completion, the emergence of new movements on the Right again raised questions about the nature of antialien activities in America and about the viability of the old slogans and attitudes in the new world of the 1980s. What was to be an epilogue became the last chapter.

The staffs of several libraries were helpful in the search for materials on various movements studied in this volume. Much of the work on the early nativists was done at the New York Public Library. The resources of its History of Americas collections and its Manuscripts Division are invaluable for any student of nineteenth- and early twentieth-century nativism. In pursuing the story of antialien activities, I have profited from visits to the Library of Congress, the Regenstein Library at the University of Chicago, the University of California at Berkeley, the University of California at Los Angeles, Butler Library and the Oral History Project at Columbia University, the Van Pelt Library at the University of Pennsylvania, the Chicago Historical Society, and the Olin Library at Cornell University. Of course, I have made extensive use of the facilities at Bird Library at Syracuse University. Staff members at Bird have been most generous in responding to requests for help in securing obscure materials.

Time to pursue this study was made available by Syracuse University in the form of research leaves and a summer research grant. I am indebted to the dean of the Maxwell School and the vice-president for research and graduate study for their support. Jane Frost and Gretchen Morris rendered invaluable help in typing the

manuscript. Matthew Bennett and Steven Bennett povided important research assistance in the final stage of revision.

Some of the findings were presented in papers delivered at the
American Historical Association and at the State University of
New York Health Science Center. Early versions of part of this
manuscript were read by Professors J. Roger Sharp of the History
Department and Michael Barkun of the Political Science Department at Syracuse. Professor Stephen Saunders Webb also has heard
material from the first part of the work. The comments of these
friends and colleagues have been both insightful and supportive.
Professor Otis Graham of the University of North Carolina has
made helpful suggestions about all sections of the work. Of course,
these readers bear no responsibility for any errors of fact or for questionable judgments.

Many other friends—faculty members, family members, students, and others—have been gracious in responding to questions
and listening to discussions of these movements since the project
began some time ago. I hope the finished product justifies the faith
they have shown in it.

My greatest debt is to my sons, Matthew and Steven. Their affec-
tion and support have been constant; they are the most important
people in my life. The book is dedicated to them.

To the acknowledgments noted above, I add thanks to several in-
dividuals and organizations graciously responding to my request for
materials that proved useful in preparing Chapter 16: Danny Welch,
Director of Klanwatch, a special project of the Southern Poverty Law
Center; Alan M. Schwartz and Gail L. Gans of the Anti-Defamation
League; Jonathan Mozzochi of the Coalition for Human Dignity; and
Kenneth S. Stern of the American Jewish Committee. Annie Barker
shared with me her fascinating materials on the militia movement.
Staff members at the Center for Democratic Renewal and Political
Research Associates also provided information.

Special thanks go to my friend, Roger Sharp, for suggesting the new
chapter, and to editor Edward Kastenmeier of Vintage Books, who has
been most helpful in shaping the project. My sons, Matthew and
Steven, have been supportive as always and made useful suggestions
about the work in progress. Gerda, as always, has been an understanding and sensitive companion.

★ ★

THE RETURN OF
THE PARTY OF FEAR

A BUMPER STICKER marketed by a militia in Missouri read, "I Love My Country, But I Fear My Government." The commander of the Michigan Militia Corps said, on national television, "it is not anger we feel, it is fear," fear "of the federal government."

Spring 1995. The party of fear had emerged in a new guise. Clad in camouflage "uniforms," bedecked with badges and medals, and toting assault rifles and other arms, militia members who had organized across the land in the previous few months insisted that they were the true defenders of America, the first groups to recognize and confront the menacing federal government that imperiled their freedom. Small business proprietors, including gun shop owners, farmers of modest means, displaced factory workers, and a sprinkling of professionals, they proclaimed that they were just ordinary citizens.

When asked what it was that they feared from "the government," the answers—beyond constant references to gun control—lost focus. Some pointed to high taxes, others to environmental regulation which threatened their "property rights," some even protested the need to carry social security cards. Brief mention of violations of "the Constitution" or the abridgment of the rights of "the states" or of "the counties" suggested a more complex story, but the vague responses seemed all out of proportion to the action taken. How could such pallid complaints about issues in contemporary politics be the reason for the creation of private armies?

To the militia recruits, their paramilitary groups were to be compared to the Minutemen of the revolutionary past, and the specific nature of the issues was less important than the intensity of their fears. Like political extremists of the right throughout American history, they proclaimed themselves patriots brave enough to confront a sinister enemy, a conspiracy of power that could destroy the nation. The only relatively new theme for many in this party of fear was that their enemy was not an "alien" religion, "alien" peoples, or an "alien" ideology which might capture the government. It was the government itself. Its reemergence in the form of these new militias reminds us that while some older tensions that provided the setting for earlier movements may have disappeared, new (or continuing) dissonances in American life still produce versions of the phenomenon, albeit in a slightly different form.

Extremism of the right manifesting itself in the party of fear is as old as America. It began before the birth of the United States. In colonial America, when the Catholic population was only a tiny fraction of the whole, there were fears of a conspiracy led by Catholics, which would take over the government, bringing "slavery, poverty, superstition, and wretchedness" in its wake. This early nativist reaction seemed to diminish with the revolution, but it would return with increased immigration from Catholic Europe.

In the early 1830s, the sacking and burning of the Ursuline convent was the work of "ordinary Americans," truckers, bricklayers and volunteer firemen. They seemed convinced, as in the title of Samuel F. B. Morse's book, that there was a *Foreign Conspiracy Against the Liberties of the United States.*

With the vast migrations from Ireland and Germany changing the nation and transforming its port cities in the next decade, nativism— fear of "foreign" religions and "foreign" peoples—found political expression. First came the American Republican party, whose followers took up arms against their un-American enemies in the extraordinary street battles of Philadelphia in 1845. Shortly thereafter, emerging from secret societies such as the Order of the Star Spangled Banner, came the American party. Most members of these nativist fraternities were "ordinary Americans," a cross section of nineteenth-century Protestant urbanites: masons and painters, machinists and seamen, butchers and grocers, shipwrights and carpenters. But so convinced were their organizers that immigrant Catholic conspirators would penetrate and undermine the party, its members were instructed to respond "I Know Nothing" when asked about it. Swollen by recruits from mainstream parties fractured by the abolitionist and free soil issues, the Know Nothings briefly became the second largest party in the nation.

The Civil War crisis pushed aside the nativist movement, but the "new immigration" from southern and eastern Europe at the end of the nineteenth century would give it new life. With millions of Italian

Catholics, Jews, Russians, and southern Slavs entering the nation came the return of the nativist fraternities. Like the proliferating militias of the 1990s, there were dozens of such groups. Representatives from many of them, including the Patriotic Order of the Sons of America, the American Patriotic League, and the Red, White and Blue Organization, gathered for a national meeting in 1890.

The largest of these new movements, with chapters spread across the continent and a membership of one-half million, was the American Protective Association. The A.P.A., like its progenitors composed of "ordinary people" who talked of conspiracies against America, grew in a setting of growing fear of Catholic control of city halls, state legislatures, and Congress, what they called "political Romanism."

The Progressive Era early in the twentieth century was unfertile ground for this party of fear and it would take World War I and the postwar Red Scare to give it renewed strength. During the war the American Protective League recruited ordinary citizens to trace and check "the Teutonic hand" behind any opponents of the war effort.

After the war, the Palmer raids of 1919 seemed to make the federal government itself the instrument for protecting America from a new conspiracy of power. This time, it was the communists and other radicals who represented not only un-American ideas imported from Europe but "aliens" who were propagating them at home. "Where Do the Reds Come From: Chiefly Imported and So Are Their Red Theories," explained one magazine. This fear of foreign conspiracy soon evaporated, but nativist fears would endure into the roaring twenties.

It was a new organization with an old title, the Ku Klux Klan, which recruited millions to an anti-Catholic, anti-Semitic, antialien, antiblack crusade. A Klan spokesman explained that "against us are all the forces of the mixed alliance composed of alienism, Romanism, hyphenism, Bolshevism, and un-Americanism." The recruits were "ordinary Americans" and—like those in earlier and later organizations—they were concerned about defending traditional family values imperiled by the un-American conspirators. But along with poor farmers, blue-collar workers, mechanics, and day laborers were lawyers, doctors, ministers, and prosperous businessmen.

The bonding theme was fear of sinister enemies, but there were other appeals, as well. They found a community in the KKK, just as some militia members seemed to find one in their new organizations seventy years later. Local Klans sponsored Sunday dinners, square dances, and basketball tournaments; it was comforting to be in the movement, it was fun, and it could be good for business. Still, the sexual and financial scandals which ravaged the Klan by mid-decade ended the appeal. And after the death of the great Ku Klux Klan of the twenties, traditional nativism would not rise again.

There was a form of inverted nativism which found a mass following in the crisis decade of the thirties. Father Charles E. Coughlin, the famous "radio priest" who recruited part of his vast listening audience into membership in his National Union for Social Justice, offered a hyperinflationary monetary panacea to cure the depression. Father Coughlin pointed to the remote plutocrats in the East as "a modern band of exploiters," men who were "the rulers of the world, dominating and controlling the social life of this nation." It was a theme that would be repeated in the 1990s by another religious leader who had become a media celebrity. And like Pat Robertson, Coughlin's conspirators of power were members of the social and economic elites: "the Wall Street attorney . . . the erudit[e] of Harvard and Yale . . . the bankers with their grouse hunting estates."

Later, Coughlin's archvillains would be Jews and communists, and his anti-Semitic speeches from 1938 to 1941 are replete with phrases similar to those used by antialien and neo-Nazi fringe group leaders of the nineties. But while his N.U.S.J. was recruiting hundreds of thousands of followers, this Catholic priest was offering part of his membership, those who were heirs to the pain and suffering of America's nativist past, a measure of revenge by characterizing WASP elites—not American Catholics—as the real un-Americans. The devastating defeat suffered by Father Coughlin when he challenged Franklin D. Roosevelt with a third party in 1936 effectively ended this movement.

Why nativism declined as a source for truly mass movements of the extreme Right, which could recruit hundreds of thousands or millions of followers, is a complex question that is addressed in chapter 14. There were several forces at work in this process, but perhaps the final blow to traditional nativism was the impact of World War II.

The war was a bonding experience for most Americans; not only did it provide the setting for a postwar prosperity that would remove some of the economic anxieties in which the old antialienism had taken root, but it also left America alone at the pinnacle of Western power. The Cold War had its origins in the emerging international conflicts of the postwar years, and these conflicts were centered not on tensions involving ethnic or religious enemies but on ideological enemies. Disloyal Americans now were identified not by religion or ethnicity but by their dangerous, un-American views.

The new Red Scare, which had begun in 1945 but gained vigor with the advent of Senator Joseph R. McCarthy in 1950, provided a different arena for a party of fear. Here was a movement of people who feared communists and sought explanations for any American setbacks in the Cold War in the machinations of "domestic Reds and pinkos"— sinister enemies within. But like earlier recruits to organizations on the far Right, they saw themselves as patriots on the front line of a struggle to save America.

The sources and meaning of McCarthyism are the subject of debate, but there is little doubt that millions of ordinary Americans—this time from many ethnic and religious groups—were affected by the themes of the movement. There may have been no powerful groups with membership rolls promoting the program of the Red Scare activists, but for a time there was a massive response by those who said they feared "Red" conspirators, this new menace to their country.

The demise of McCarthy in 1954 fatally weakened the crusade against "alien" ideology. The John Birch Society would be organized in 1958 and endures today, but the bizarre teachings of its founder, who characterized even Dwight D. Eisenhower as a "pro-Communist," kept it from finding a real following. The Christian Anti-Communist Crusade of the sixties also had limited appeal. Communism remained the source of fear in many parts of America, but long before the end of the Cold War and breakup of the Soviet Union it was clear that the communist enemy within would not be the impetus for significant new movements.

What would replace the fear of alien and un-American religions, ethnic groups and ideologies as the source for new parties of fear?

In the seventies and eighties came the emergence of televangelists of the new religious Right. Soon Jerry Falwell, Pat Robertson, Jimmy Swaggart, and others were reporting audiences in the millions (and yearly revenues approaching $100 million). When key figures in this movement made an alliance with political operatives of the "hard Right"—Richard Viguerie, Paul Weyrich, Terry Dolan, Howard Phillips—the Moral Majority was born.

Secular Humanists became the new enemies menacing America. Influential theorists in the movement saw an enormous conspiracy in which the atheistic enemies of "America as a Christian nation" gained control over public schools, the movie industry, publishers, academia, the courts, the unions, important foundations and—as one writer put it—"to a large degree, the government."

Not all the media celebrities of the new electronic church or their political allies completely accepted this assessment. Some have offered other conspiratorial visions. In 1991, Pat Robertson's book *The New World Order* resurrected tales of a series of monetary conspiracies and hinted at sinister plots affecting America from revolutionary times to the Gulf War. They may differ in their characterization of the foe, but most leaders and followers of this new movement do share a vision of themselves as patriots and a resolve to confront enemies they fear: those who threaten "the American Way of Life" and "traditional family values."

Are there links between the emerging militia groups and such leaders and movements of the New Right? There surely are common political grounds, and they are rooted in support of what have become mainstream Republican policies. Hostility to most government social programs and regulatory agencies is found in both camps; anger at gun control, gay rights, and the freedom to have abortions are unifying themes. They share a general distaste for government efforts to promote equality of opportunity and to strengthen the bonds of national community, if this entails use of federal tax dollars.

But many Americans outside the ranks of the New Right or the militia movement embrace these views. And the activists of the New Right, who had such success in influencing elections and helping to shape the legislative agenda of the victorious Republican party in the 1994 Congressional elections, would not tell interviewers that they "fear the government" in the same way as the militia leaders of 1995.

In fact, spokesmen for the new paramilitary groups have given no sign of any formal or informal alliance with religious or political leaders of the New Right. Yet both these strands of the party of fear represent important recent developments in the history of the far Right in America.

Less clear in 1995 was the linkage between some of the militias and various "Christian Patriot," white supremacist, "Constitutionalist," or neo-Nazi groups. Many of these organizations are loosely tied to the most formidable element on this remotest fringe of the far Right, Christian Identity. (These extremist movements will also be considered in the new final chapter.) Christian Identity, a strange twentieth-century phenomenon, is built on the belief that Jews are not Israelites but are children of the Devil and represent the evil enemy which will confront Aryan Christians in an apocalyptic final struggle.

In the eighties, several Identity groups emerged to briefly capture national attention. There was the terrorist cell in the Pacific Northwest known as The Order; an armed survivalist sect in the Ozarks called The Covenant, The Sword and The Arm of the Lord; and the Posse Comitatus, which was responsible for violent confrontations with law enforcement officers in the upper Midwest. All of these groups were defunct by the early nineties. But the most prominent Identity organization, Aryan Nations/Church of Jesus Christ Christian, with its headquarters compound in Hayden Lake, Idaho, would endure and by 1995 would be growing in strength and influence in extremist circles.

There appear to be ties between Identity and tiny fragments of the contemporary Ku Klux Klan, various collections of American skinheads organized in the previous half-decade, several disparate survivalist or self-styled "Christian Patriot" bands, and other minuscule units proclaiming white Aryan supremacy. Of course, members of all these groups make use of new means of electronic communication unavailable to yesterday's extremists, who had to be satisfied with newspapers and crude pamphlets. With shortwave radio, fax, e-mail, and the computer internet, contemporary activists of the radical Right reach a larger audience.

Are such activists at work in the militia movement? It seems clear that they have been influential in some of the paramilitary groups organized in the early nineties. But there have been strenuous denials of such links by many militia members willing to breach secrecy and make public statements.

The Identity sects and their allies are small fringe groups located, for the most part, in sparsely populated sections of the country. They do not represent a mass movement. They cannot be compared to the large organizations on the nativistic and anticommunist Right of the past or today's New Right. In the size of their membership—at least thus far—as well as in the themes of violence in their literature and the speeches of their spokesmen, they are closer to numerous tiny extremist cells on the radical Right in earlier years of this century: the Silver Shirt Legion of America, the Khaki Shirts, the Defenders of the Christian Faith, and other quasifascist and millenarian groups of the thirties, or the National Renaissance Party, the American Nazi Party, and the Minutemen of the fifties and sixties.

If the militia movement succeeds in recruiting large numbers of Americans with its curious new appeal to "fear of the federal government," it could take its place with the mass movements on the far Right in American history. But it is unlikely to find a real mass following if it embraces the rhetoric of white supremacist, anti-Semitic or quasifascist sects of the past and present.

In 1995, it remains unclear how successful the several right-wing movements in the United States which have emerged in the eighties and nineties will be, but all of these new parties of fear can be understood better if viewed in the context of the long history of the far Right. In assessing their origins, activities, goals and membership as well as in addressing the critical question of why they appear in the form they take at this time, the historical setting remains a critical variable. That is the reason for producing this second edition of *The Party of Fear*, with a new chapter (Chapter 16) on developments from 1987 to 1995.

THE PARTY OF FEAR

★ ★

PROLOGUE

★ ★

A CHOSEN PEOPLE,
A THREATENED PARADISE

BITS OF WHITE PAPER strewn across a prearranged site announced the meeting of the brotherhood. Held at night, in keeping with the secrecy that shrouded its early years, the sessions of the local chapters of the Order of the Star Spangled Banner were open only to initiates and those about to join them in the ranks. The ritual for admission to the lodge seemed endless. But instead of irritating men tired after a long day's work, the elaborate raps and special handclasps, the passwords between brothers, and the sentinels sent to escort candidates long known to the membership seemed to heighten the feeling of camaraderie, the sense of special excitement at the dangerous but essential mission they were privileged to share. For they were there to save and cleanse the nation, to preserve for themselves that abstraction which some would later call the American dream.[1]

The ceremony for administering the oath of membership was found, seven decades later, at the ritualized heart of another powerful American secret society. But in the 1850s, for the movement emerging under its informal name of Know Nothings, it seemed fresh enough. "A sense of danger," the lodge leader or sachem read, "has struck the heart of the nation. The danger has been seen and the alarm sounded. True men have devised this order as a means of disseminating patriotic principles, of keeping alive the fire of national virtue, of furthering America and American interests."[2]

In dozens of books, pamphlets, and broadsides the theme was repeated and refined: "Our mission is to restore America to the Americans, to purify and strengthen this nation . . . to keep it clean from corruption." For Americans were specially blessed. Europeans were "ignorant and servile, passionate children governed by fear and deformed by vices," yet America had imbued her native-born with "mutual confidence, social friendship and good fellowship," which were the cement of a nation set apart. In *The Great American Battle*, one Know Nothing propagandist explained that "America has done and is doing the world's work, establishing the only true principles of liberty the world has ever known. . . . The hand that guides this light is a Divine one. It is the hand of God. America has a mission to teach the world."[3]

The picture of the United States as a unique and gifted land, a garden of Eden that must be preserved against the encroachment of sinners, informed the work of the most important nativist movement of the nineteenth century. But as the Know Nothing fires burned throughout large sections of America in the pre–Civil War years, dominating the political scene in major cities and states and coloring the social life of a decade, the movement marked neither the beginning nor the end of the image of America as a threatened paradise.[4]

The colonial experience of an immigrant people was not free of the fear of "foreign influences." The specter of an alien religion, penetrating and poisoning the New World garden, made anti-Catholicism a recurring theme in early American history. And long after the crusade against immigration and papism of the 1850s had disappeared, the concerns that energized it lived on. In the proliferation of patriotic societies organized in the years before the turn of the century, particularly in the American Protective Association, the same arguments were repeated, the same villains excoriated. Three decades later, in the post–World War I era of the 1920s, the attack on un-American peoples continued in the bizarre ritual of the new Ku Klux Klan.

What tied these movements to one tradition was the common vision of alien intruders in the promised land—people who could not be assimilated in the national community because of their religion or ethnicity. This concern with alien peoples, always a paradox in the multiethnic, multiracial world of America, faded slowly in the period following the legislation restricting immigration at the end of the Great War. But the image of a threatened paradise did not fade away. Even before the Klan rose to prominence, a new enemy within had been identified and battle lines were being drawn. Foreign ideologies had frightened Americans in the past, but with the Bolshevik revolution and the rise of communism in 1919, the danger of alien ideas soon matched traditional nativist concerns. Because some of those advocating these "corrosive" ideas were foreigners, many of whom could not speak English, the first Red Scare was a product of both converging streams of antialien activity. But in the depression decade of the 1930s, there were other efforts to identify the "un-Americans" through the ideas they held, and by the time of the anticommunist eruption of the Cold War years, it was clear that the great internal threat to the American dream was seen primarily as emanating from the head and not the blood.

If there has been political extremism of the Right in American history, it is found in large measure in these efforts to combat peoples and ideas that were seen as alien threats to a cherished but embattled American "way of life." The passionate men and women who joined the right-wing groups that sought to check various alien enemies became extremists when they violated democratic procedures and moved outside the norms of a democratic society. Seeing a vast conspiracy behind the invasion of strange and unpromising immigrants, the growth of an "authoritarian" church, and the appearance of an ideology dedicated to destroying traditional arrangements, they insisted that desperate times called for extraordinary measures, that saving America was worth paying any price. They were the leaders and members of the party of fear. As politicians of morality, they refused to treat those whom they feared with tolerance or civility. As moralists of the Right, they were idealists whose vision of utopia was in the past. They sought, as had other rightists, to preserve the old, idyllic order by purging the corrupting elements that menaced its values and perverted its institutions.[5]

"America" is a dream from the past imperiled; it needs protectors to preserve its promise for future generations. Only idealists who see themselves as supreme patriots are willing to rise to its defense. That, at least, is what they seemed to be saying to anyone who would listen. But to many who would study these matters in later years, as well as to critical contemporaries, it was only the plight of the "alien enemy" that seemed poignant.

Who were these sinister aliens? For the Know Nothings, most of them were Irish Catholics, newly arrived emigrants from a hopelessly blighted land of famine and despair. The risks these "aliens" ran, the terrible, disrupting experience they faced at every stage of the journey, would be eloquently described by chroniclers in another century. But in the pitiless anger of the antialiens, whether it be the Know Nothings or those who followed them, there was rarely a hint of concern for the newcomers or an appreciation of the problems they confronted.[6]

The same was true for the crusade against alien ideas. On a cold day in early January 1920, hundreds of men were rounded up and imprisoned in major cities across the nation. Newspapers labeled them "Bolsheviks, Anarchists, Terrorists." For those who conducted or supported the attacks on the "Reds," the end justified the means and excused any incidental abuses. Alien ideas, like alien peoples, were so dangerous that they must be checked no matter what the costs.[7]

But scholars never accepted the heroic self-portrait of these "protectors" of America, never viewed them as chosen people defending a threatened paradise. Many early studies of these movements focused on the "history of American bigotry." The antialiens were seen as vicious authoritarians, terrorizing the vulnerable, the sensitive, and the innocent.[8]

Other writers, more detached and analytic, focused on economic determinants, suggesting that social disorder led to fears of displacement in the marketplace—to increased competition for jobs and advancement. Although a radical interpretation might picture both antialiens and their adversaries as the marginal people of a capitalist culture, struggling over the crumbs as the rich and powerful look on from the sidelines, it seemed sufficient to note the nagging self-interest of the attackers as they tried to make their way in an uncertain world of prosperity and decline. Not applicable to all movements, this view helped explain the motives of many nativists of the nineteenth and twentieth centuries.[9]

But in dealing with the long tradition of antialien activity, some other analysts sought explanations in the social and psychological problems of the activists. "Any society is liable at times to collective emotion," H. R. Trevor-Roper observed in his study of the European witch craze of the sixteenth and seventeenth centuries. Other nations have had different "great fears." In the "paranoid style" of the spokesmen and their movements and in the "status resentments" of members and fellow travelers there was offered another explanation for a "great fear" in America.[10]

"The paranoid spokesman in politics," Richard Hofstadter noted in an influential essay, "tends to be overheated, oversuspicious, overaggressive, grandiose, and apocalyptic." Believing that hostile and conspiratorial forces motivate historical events, the paranoid makes a curious leap in imagination and abandons "sensible judgment." He may feel that he has "no access to the making of decisions," and as he experiences helplessness, his original conception of the world of power as "omnipotent, sinister and malicious" is confirmed. In fact, loss of place and position in society was seen by many social scientists as the critical element in the growth of antialien movements. In their view, the social strains in American life led to the relative loss of social and economic power for some groups and, in turn, to growing resentment and anger and a "splenetic politics of frustration." Unable to adjust to a world of power dispersal or to handle life in a complex society, the ignorant or the powerless abandoned themselves to apocalyptic fantasies. They embraced what two writers called a "politics of unreason," striking out against certain perceived villains, who often themselves were innocent victims of a society in flux.[11]

A persuasive statement of the methods and motives of the extremists of the Right, this was an effort to link antialien extremism to alienation, then to "status politics" and to its unhappy, unreasoning consequences. But like the other interpretations, it was far from sympathetic. The antialiens were seen as mean, narrow, and cruel, or as unbalanced, irrational, and ill-equipped to function in a world of change. In each case, there was little sympathy for the men and women of the past who saw themselves as sublime patriots, the most deserving of all the chosen people.

If one spends any time with the written records left by members of various right-wing movements, it is clear why critical opinion never has been positive. In books, articles, pamphlets, newspapers, and speeches, the style is always the same: graceless, florid, and self-serving. There is no irony here, no sense of paradox, no sense of humor. The authors seem incapable of making distinctions. They not only call for separation of law and morality but insist on the primacy of their vision of morality, asking that "conspiratorial" religions (Catholicism) or political ideologies (communism) be excluded from America lest they destroy its tolerant institutions. But they show no tolerance themselves. With absurd rituals and frenetic fraternalism, with the hint of violence lurking in back of the claims of strength and programs for change, with overt anti-intellectualism a common theme, the rightists are not people who will receive a warm response from intellectuals. They appear what their angriest critics have called them: repressed, repressive, and repulsive.

The extremists of the Right have seemed much less attractive than those of the Left. The men and women of the Left can be pictured as heroic losers, persevering but not prevailing in the struggle for justice and equality, fighting to help the poor, the powerless, and the alienated; those on the Right often appear only as the deranged or malevolent enemies of American freedom. The vision of those on the Left is of the future, not the past; the ideal America is yet to be created, and it will be better than any that existed before. Their language may be as graceless as that of their adversaries, but as one writer noted, it is "graceless by choice, written on a drumhead to be read to an impatient army." Those who respond to its appeal reject not only traditional political arrangements but also the values of the society. For those who believe that the much celebrated individualist ethos brings only alienation and loneliness, the traditional arrangements can never work, no matter how carefully cultivated the reforms of the day. The real idealists, they seem to say, must reject both past and present. Theirs is a dream based on hope and not on memory. Only tomorrow will bring an America worth preserving.[12]

"Send flowers to the rebels failed," Bartolomeo Vanzetti said, and there are many failed rebels of the Left throughout the nation's history, men and women who hoped to bring justice to the "people," men and women easier to like, love, and mourn than the activists of the Right. Although the historical literature is replete with critical studies of various movements in both camps—including many describing the ugly strain of authoritarian control in some parties of the Left—images of the radical as heroic victim and the antialien only as disturbed or malevolent victimizer die hard.

But the extremists of the movements of the Right do deserve a measure of dispassionate attention, not because of services they have rendered America but because they have reflected tensions endemic in the entire population and in the very structure of American life. For all their overbearing language and grandiose plans, conspiratorial fears and repressive programs, they have been themselves the victims of conflicts and contradictions built into the nature of the society for which they were self-proclaimed protectors.

Of course, a straight line cannot be drawn from the early nativists of the nineteenth century to the anticommunists of the post-

World War II period and to a new generation of activists who emerged in the 1970s. The passing years brought striking new concerns; different issues recruited new followers and disappointed some of the old. The antialien cause often attracted political opportunists, people without a party or in search of an audience. It attracted greedy moneymakers, people hoping to exploit a climate of fear for their own advantage. It attracted people who could use the apologias of an organization or the secrecy it provided as a screen behind which to practice private vendettas and to even old personal scores. But the movements did not depend upon the manipulators, the charlatans, or the thugs. Their presence may have swollen the ranks and given the cause an image of strength that would prove illusory, but antialienism had much deeper roots.

What was this American dream the "protectors" claimed to defend? What was "the mission America had to teach the world"? The stirring words that filled even the early nativist oratory provide part of the answer: freedom, opportunity, individualism, equality for all true Americans. Mankind's most compelling myth concerns the chosen people and the Garden of Eden, which they are privileged to inhabit, and more than a century ago, as R. W. B. Lewis noted, the image embodying the most important contemporary idea was that the authentic American was "a figure of heroic innocence and vast potentialities, poised at the start of a new history." The Know Nothings and their heirs believed this to be so. Behind their broad and uplifting generalities lay the composite of truth and fantasy that became a living and fighting faith. They would have embraced John Locke's romantic assertion that "in the beginning all the world was America"; edenic imagery filled their writing. They saw America as a unique civilization, rejecting the feudal traditions and accompanying rigid class and caste lines that marked European cultures. It was a vast and virgin land, sparsely settled and overflowing with unmatched resources. In such a land, they believed, every man had a chance to start even, to be judged on his own merits, talents, and efforts. Liberated from the dead hand of the past, from the sins or failures of ancestors, each man had the opportunity to achieve as much as possible in his own lifetime, to be a participant in a democratic polity of equals.[13]

If their beliefs seem conventional, part of the received truths of generations, it should not be surprising. The Americans of the Right were never monarchists, dreaming of a new aristocracy of the estates. They were not fascists, plotting to overthrow the nation's institutions and replace them with some sinister new order. They were, instead, Americanists par excellence. Their ideal society was the one they had been taught to believe existed in their own country. Like most other citizens, they rejected challenges to these sacred beliefs. Future writers, like contemporary opponents, would insist that their vision of American history as a unique and seamless web was overstated. Class differences and economic, racial, and sexual exploitation marred the New World as they did the old. Individualism was not an American invention. Opportunity and mobility surely were not available for all Americans. But those who held fast to a belief in the United States as the New Jerusalem were not dissuaded from insisting upon their own uniqueness, adding to it a feeling of superiority.[14]

Their most striking feature was their personal identification with the nation. They were special and superior because they were part of the great nation; if its perfection was tarnished, their lives would be diminished. From the very start it was "America: love it or leave it," and most of the activists seemed to believe the things they told their children. The need to act on these beliefs led to a passionate commitment reminiscent of the Red Guard, but it was made in the name of the American way of life. Some have argued that the New World was from the start a disproving ground for utopias, that its formless, pragmatic, abundant social structure belied the need for ideology. Yet the myth of a freedom-filled American paradise became an ideology itself, which created its own brand of protectors.[15]

But did the country need protecting at the times the antialiens made their bids for power? Their movements took shape in periods of great social and political disorder, when those who did not share their views also feared for the future of America. Objective conditions did warrant serious concern. The immigrants of the mid-nineteenth century appear as innocent victims from the perspective of later generations, but to many people living among the newcomers, only the terrible problems they brought to America seemed important. Spiraling crime rates, growing poverty rolls, and terrifying epidemics were the only characteristics many natives saw as being associated with them. Cities generally blighted from their inception became grim and dangerous, and for most there was no suburban escape route. Social disorder was a haunting specter, most often connected to the "alien." How could these strange, unhappy people with a religion long denounced in native churches as un-American to the core ever be assimilated? How many such strangers could enter the garden before it ceased to bear fruit?

The fears of nativists in the 1890s and 1920s echoed the themes of their progenitors in the decades before the Civil War. All groups were reacting to the upheavals of the age. The brutal industrial revolution before the turn of the century was fueled by waves of new immigrants flooding into eastern seaports even as the frontier was closing in the West, raising unsettling questions about the future of a "unique" America. The newest arrivals were not necessarily the objects of many a nativist's wrath, but these newcomers were threatening by their sheer numbers and by the social disorder they helped create. Social disorder colored the "roaring twenties" as well, when the new consumer economy of the post–World War I expansion raised expectations and ruptured traditional social relationships, creating confusion in the expanding urban areas and despair in the rural communities, which seemed increasingly isolated from the alien world of the big city.

Those who joined the nativist movements did not invent the crises of values they saw developing around them. The disruption of American life was not the product of their overheated imaginations but of objective conditions. Their "solutions" to these problems may have been irrelevant, inappropriate, and destructive, but their fears were rooted in reality.

The antialiens were protectors, responding to true crises. But the objects of their attacks—"alien" peoples and "alien" ideas—were often only incidentally related to the disorder that seemed to call for defensive action. By their reactions in these movements, the protectors of the "American dream" were revealing how difficult it was to live that cherished way of life in the world of their threatened paradise. In the end many sought refuge from the dream in the antialien cause. The protectors were also fugitives; the defenders sought succor outside the walls of the promised land.

The men and women who flocked to the movements insisted that they subscribed to American values—individualism, egalitarianism, and all the rest. It was easy enough for them to scoff at the Thoreaus and Emersons, romantic dissidents on the margins of events, who insisted that freedom should be used for self-fulfillment beyond the imperatives of the competitive struggle. But they could not avoid paying a price for embracing the values of a society that, as Robert K. Merton observed, "placed highest premium on economic affluence and social ascent for all its members . . . a patterned expectation regarded as appropriate for everyone, regardless of station in life."[16] The anxiety and stress in such a society fascinated Alexis de Tocqueville, and almost twenty years before the rise of the Know Nothings he wrote:

> He who has set his heart exclusively upon the pursuit of worldly welfare is always in a hurry, for he has but a limited time at his disposal to reach it. . . . This thought fills him with anxiety, fear and regret, and keeps his mind in ceaseless trepidation . . . men easily attain a certain equality of conditions; they can never attain the equality they desire. It perpetually retires from before them, yet without hiding itself from their sight and in retiring draws them on. At every moment they think they are about to grasp it; it escapes at every moment from their hold. They are near enough to see its charms, but too far off to enjoy them; and before they have fully tasted its delights they die.[17]

Tocqueville remarked time and again on the paradox of a nation of self-conscious individualists whose greatest desire was for equality. Without equality there would be no chance of success, and failure carried with it moral damnation. This American dream had no room for losers.

Of course, at times when economic and social disorder raised the levels of anxiety to even greater heights, Americans could take comfort in being part of a national community of those who shared belief in a common system of values. Or could they? Almost from the beginning, there was a lack of traditional moral authority. The reduced influence of crown and class was obvious enough in a country that celebrated its democratic and egalitarian ethos, but the influence of family and church was reduced as well. For all the power of evangelical Protestantism, it never could provide the authority of a Catholic church that was hated for the influence it was supposed to have on all aspects of its parishioners' lives. The search for a sanction-source in the United States led more directly to "the people" than in societies in which traditional institutions carried greater weight. Yet the question remained, who were "the people," the Americans? Could those who subscribed to religions or ideologies that appeared secretive to outsiders be trusted as free citizens in an open society? Could all the newcomers in this nation of immigrants, even the poorest and most credulous, earn the right to share the political and moral authority which the creed invests in the majority?[18]

The search for an authoritative community faced other obstacles. Most important was the very mobility of the American people. The vagueness and limitless expanse of territory, the common language, the freer temperament of people long uprooted from ancestral homes created a setting for mobility unmatched on the planet. In this nation, a house or farm was "an investment and not a home" and social and physical movement created constant disorder. It was, therefore, a forbidding territory in which to build a sense of community.[19]

Denied the rigid standards and simple verities of a class society, many Americans turned to the antialien movements in their search for closeness, community, and authority. Self-conscious individualists in the nineteenth century denied their longing for group solidarity and group strictures but it was not in mid-twentieth century that Americans ceased to be "inner directed." Fierce competition and clear acquisitive goals may have been facts of life for many, but there was also a lack of individualism, as James Bryce observed, in the "inner life of men." The myth of the chosen people helped to justify sacrifices in a society that offered so much at such great cost, but it was not enough. The "chosen people" must be clearly defined so as to provide a shelter behind which the losers or battle-weary in the competitive environment might find comfort. In "true Americanism" there could be unity and community for all who needed authority in an amorphous social structure. In crusades against alien peoples or alien ideas, there could be fraternity for those who needed some sanctuary in times of troubles.[20]

There is only a superficial paradox in the excessive concern with religious, ethnic, sectional, and ideological differences by people who celebrated the uniqueness and superiority of their entire nation. For failure carried high costs, and if things went wrong, many of the most vulnerable people could not take comfort in being merely "Americans." If social mobility and social disorder became too acute and too discomforting, if changes in the environment—new waves of immigration, new tensions between sectional or interest groups, new upheavals in the economic order—became threatening to the notion of a superior and unique promised land, then many men and women would seek community within a subculture and call it "America." In assailing the "un-Americans" around them they could solve both problems. As self-styled defenders of the American paradise they could feel a special pride at defining the boundaries in the battle against the evil outsiders. But as members of a "movement," they could escape the loneliness of an individualism they glorified and find fellowship in the ranks of a manageable brotherhood. For many nativists, there was an additional attraction. Their movements were dedicated to preserving the ascendancy of certain subgroups—the most "American" ethnic and religious sets— and so they might protect their own positions in a competitive culture in which social ascendancy carried with it somber implications.

Antialiens have been both protectors and fugitives. As protectors, their bizarre and ugly solutions to the problems of their time make them the repository and embodiment of the dark side of that American dream they shared with most of their fellow citizens. But in protecting their image of an American eden, they also sought to escape from its problems and its harsh realities. Like most other Americans, they rejoiced at what they considered their good fortune but suffered at the price they paid for it. Only in the extremity of some of the social and political programs did they differ.

The campaigns against alien people and alien ideologies are found in every period of American history. What follows is an effort to examine some of the major movements and the settings in which they rose, prospered, and declined.

This is not an intellectual history of racism, anti-Catholicism, anti-Semitism, or anticommunism. Numerous theorists who called for exclusion or repression are not considered or cited. Some developments in social and intellectual history that contributed to the emergence of right-wing groups are not described in any detail. Many mainstream political figures have used the rhetoric or adopted the arguments of such groups from time to time; these individual political actors also are not the subject of this book. The focus here is on movements. It is on the particular organizations— and their leaders—that have found a following by promising to defend America and its values from the un-American people, un-American ideologies, and destructive tendencies seen as menacing it.

These are the movements which constitute the party of fear. They have inspired fear among those they have defined as enemies. But more important, they have been organized out of the fear that their America was threatened by powerful, sinister, and conspiratorial adversaries.

Of course, not every such organization of the Right can be included here. There have been thousands of them, many consisting of little more than a dreamer or a schemer and a few handbills. My concern is with the major movements and the more significant smaller groups.

Part I will assess the activities of the nineteenth-century nativists and the reasons for the growth of their crusades against "alien" people and an "alien" church. Part II begins with the return of the nativist fraternities in post–Civil War America and then discusses the rise of the modern Ku Klux Klan, traditional nativism's last stand, in the 1920s. But the Red Scare of 1919 clearly signaled growing concern with a different crusade, one against alien ideologies. In the depression decade of the 1930s, new groups and new leaders rose, some suggesting the reasons why nativism would disappear as the driving force in America's right-wing movements.

By the end of World War II, nativism was no longer viable. The cessation of unlimited immigration and its attendant social disorder some two decades earlier had blunted the cutting edge of nativist hostility. Further weakened by the transforming social and political developments of the interwar years, this oldest source of right-wing passion was visibly on the decline. At the same time, it had become obvious that the scientific case for Anglo-Saxon superiority was finally demolished and with it the remaining shred of intellectual respectability for nativism. The old animus could not survive in an America celebrating a new pluralism in the postwar years. This was modern America, the land in which managerial and professional advancement increasingly was unconnected to the themes nativists had promoted in the past.

The old antialienism, the source of the early right-wing movements, was replaced by the new, the fear of communism, that un-American ideology which had served as a source for right-wing anxiety in the past and loomed large in the Cold War years. But with the end of the McCarthy era and the decline of the anticommunist activists of the 1960s, the crusade against radical ideas imported from foreign soil also began to fade away. Communist "conspiracy" could not explain the social upheavals of the late 1960s or the shattering defeats of the 1970s.

The concluding chapter will address the reappearance of old themes in the 1980s, in the form of various small sects. But the most significant story of recent years is how new developments have made the rise of a "New Right" a major departure in the history of such movements in America. The growth of the religious Right and the political "hard" Right suggests that in the future important right-wing movements will find their energizing themes in very different "threats" to the American way than had their predecessors on the old antialien Right.

The central concerns in Part I are nineteenth-century activities, but any consideration of a topic that stretches across the breadth of the American experience must begin with the colonial heritage.

PART I

★ ★

NATIVISM IN
EARLY AMERICAN
HISTORY

CHAPTER 1

★ ★

A COLONIAL HERITAGE

IN 1782 A REMARKABLE BOOK was published in London and Dublin. J. Hector St. John de Crèvecoeur's *Letters from an American Farmer* won instant celebrity. Within a year a second English and Irish edition had been issued along with numerous reviews and extracts. Crèvecoeur wrote: "There is no wonder that this country has so many charms and presents to Europeans so many temptations to remain in it. A traveller in Europe becomes a stranger as soon as he quits his own kingdom; but it is otherwise here. We know, properly speaking, no strangers; this is every person's country. . . . No sooner does a European arrive, no matter of what condition, than his eyes are opened upon the fair prospect . . . he meets with hospitality, kindness, and plenty everywhere."[1]

This alluring portrait of American life, painted at the end of the colonial period, stimulated the fantasies of many emigrants from the United Kingdom. But for all the merits of the larger work, this "letter" from across the Atlantic was anything but accurate. America was not "every person's country." Many European newcomers found no hospitality or kindness waiting to greet them. Conflict raged between the "chosen people" and the outsiders long before the Know Nothing crusaders of the mid-nineteenth century. Antialien enmity was part of the heritage of the colonial experience.

The earliest target was Roman Catholicism. Anti-Catholicism was rampant in England many years before the first colonists sailed for America. It took root in the nationalism of a state threatened by the rival imperial ambitions of Catholic Spain and France. It was fed by the quasi-historical post-Reformation propaganda used by the enemies of church-state ties within the island empire.

The first white men to settle the Western shores were Spaniards and Roman Catholics, who planted missions in Florida and New

Mexico in the sixteenth century. When Richard Hakluyt prepared his *Discourse of Western Planting,* an elaborate treatise on the advantages of American colonization for Queen Elizabeth I, he laid great stress on the need to combat the Spaniards, to counteract the "spread of their superstitious worship" in the New World. But English settlers needed little encouragement in their struggle against Catholicism. The Elizabethan Acts of Supremacy and Uniformity in 1559 had put the kingdom permanently in the Protestant camp, fulfilling the demands of Henry VIII, who insisted that England not be bound to Rome and that the king be the supreme head of the church in England. In the agonizing conflicts that followed the religious rupture, a series of real or imagined Catholic conspiracies had a devastating impact on the British mind. The folly of Guy Fawkes and his associates, who sought to advance the Catholic cause by blowing up king, lord, and commons in November 1605 in the Gunpowder Plot, was followed by the imaginary Popish Plot reported by Andreas ab Habernfeld in 1640. The Irish Massacre of 1641, the baseless story that it was the papists who had burned London in 1666, and the so-called Popish Plot of Titus Oates in 1678 all aroused hatred of Catholicism. For many Englishmen, to be a Catholic was to be accomplice to a sinister conspiratorial organization that had declared holy war on Protestant England. The defeat of the Spanish armada in 1588 might have been a sign that God was on the side of the Reformation, but the Antichrist remained formidable and menacing. When the pioneers at last arrived in the wilderness across the great ocean, their sense of isolation and loneliness only exacerbated the bigotry felt by those who had spent their lives with "No-Popery" laws proscribing the social and political role of Catholics.[2]

Still, it was not a crime to be a Catholic in colonial America. Proscription occurred not because of English law but through local legislative action or, in a few cases, the specific intervention of the crown. But most colonies were not unwilling to restrict the freedom of the church. There could be only limited sanctuary for those who subscribed to an "authoritarian," "secretive," "conspiratorial" religion. Particularly in the Puritan Zion of Massachusetts Bay, the American garden was contrasted with the fallen world of Roman Catholic Europe, a cesspool of murderers, fornicators, sorcerers, and idolators. The Calvinists would build a City Upon a Hill, a church "purged of Romish corruptions," a model for the world. These colonists had as their goal the redemption of man for the sins of the Old World, and they depicted Catholicism as a kind of Hell. These first settlers despised the Anglican church because they insisted it was the mirror image of the church of Rome.[3]

In the seventeenth century, the mass could not be publicly celebrated anywhere except in relatively tolerant Pennsylvania, home of the Quaker experiment. In the Bay Colony, there were few Catholics to be banished, but priests or Jesuits who returned did so on pain of execution. John Cotton wrote of "the carnall and sinfull pity that is found in any state that shall be sparing spilling the . . . blood of the Priests and Jesuits. . . . The Lord loathes this kind of leniency and gentleness." In New Hampshire, all Englishmen save Roman Catholics enjoyed the franchise; North Carolina provided liberty of conscience for all save Roman Catholics; and New York was the scene of repeated anti-Catholic demonstrations. Even Maryland, founded by a Catholic, who encouraged Catholic settlement (Sir George Calvert, Lord Baltimore), had trouble with neighboring Virginia and with a restive Protestant majority. One important group within the colony organized as the Association in Arms for the Defense of the Protestant Religion. Finally, William and Mary voided the proprietor's charter following the Glorious Revolution and established Maryland as a royal colony with an Anglican established church.[4]

Indeed, the Glorious Revolution of 1689 was another ill omen for American Catholics. John Locke, its great apologist and the philosopher of English democracy, considered Catholics dangerous participants in any civil government. Even the most egalitarian colonies, Rhode Island and Pennsylvania, seemed to agree—disfranchising and ruling them ineligible for any "office of trust and honor." Rhode Island was founded, of course, by Roger Williams, that great enemy of religious persecution, the man who had demanded freedom of worship for Quakers. But in his private papers, Williams wrote of the "Romish wolf gorging herself with huge bowls of the blood of saints," filled his correspondence with references to the "popish leviathan," and conducted his dispute with the Puritan divines of Massachusetts in the terminology of antipapal rhetoric.[5]

There was no setting for toleration in colonial America. The eighteenth century brought only new assaults on religious freedom. In the former Catholic haven of Maryland, in 1704, Governor John Seymour complained that most of the incoming white indentured servants "are generally Irish Papists . . . induced to come hither by the false tho' specious Pretences, of the free Exercise of their Superstitious Worship." By the 1740s, in the outpouring of Protestant fundamentalist religious fervor known as the Great Awakening, there was fiery hatred of Rome and a warning that Catholicism was a deadly threat to America. George Whitfield preached of the "swarms of monks . . . and friars like so many locusts . . . overspreading and plaguing the nation." Elisha Williams, a member of New England's leading family of divines, one of the most widely trained men of his generation, wrote in support of religious conscience, but his *Essential Rights and Liberties of Protestants* provided little comfort for Catholics: "The Pope, who has deluged the Earth with the Blood of Christians [is] the most detestable Monster the Earth ever had upon it . . . the true Spirit of Popery is to impose their Determinations on all within their Power by any Methods . . . those civil Magistrates that suffered and Helped that Beast . . . did therein commit Fornication with her . . . instead of proving Fathers to their People proved the cursed Butchers of them." In a land where wars against France and Spain had led to new rumors of a Catholic conspiracy and images of phantom Catholic armies mobilizing in Canada and Florida, it was not difficult to see the papist as an enemy agent. Nativism already was firmly rooted in both the religious and the political conventional wisdom.[6]

In the years before the birth of the United States, social as well as political custom made a mockery of the declaration that "all men are created equal" even for white America. Almanacs, tracts, sermons, and periodicals vilified Catholicism. Public school primers instructed children to "abhor that arrant Whore of Rome and all her Blasphemies." "Pope Night" festivals depicting the Devil in league with the Catholics and fireside games like "Break the Pope's Kneck" were standard fare. With the outbreak of the French and Indian War, word spread in some areas of a wicked alliance: Indians, Negroes, and Catholics combining to overthrow the government and give Catholic France and her Indian allies a victory that would bring, in Jonathan Mayhew's words, "slavery, poverty, superstition and wretchedness" in its wake.[7]

But the coming of the Revolution undercut some of this hostility. If one of the functions of anti-Catholic activity in colonial days was to unite a disparate people in a lonely land, creating a sense of community for those in search of a new national identity, the conflict with the mother country suddenly made all this irrelevant and counterproductive. The Revolution was a great unifier for "true" Americans. In the end, the real test of loyalty was whether a person supported the new government or the crown, not whether he or she practiced Catholicism or some other religion. There was no time or place for traditional bigotry in the great crucible of the War for Independence; every man and ally was needed, and General George Washington quashed the Pope Day festivals in 1775 because American Catholics were useful in the revolutionary army and Catholic France was essential as an ally in the field against the British.[8]

Although there was hostility in Pennsylvania and upstate New York to Catholics who adopted the Loyalist cause, perhaps in response to persecution suffered at the hands of neighbors supporting the uprising, nativism soon became an instrument of the Loyalists and not their American opponents. This was magnified when anti-secessionist Tories tried to manipulate the old anti-Catholic symbols in attacking the alliance between the revolutionary government and France.[9]

By the conclusion of the war, a new spirit of tolerance was felt everywhere. At the beginning of the Revolution, pamphleteers still evoked the old specter of conspiratorial power, as with Jonathan Mayhew's famous *Discourse Concerning Unlimited Submission,* which exposes the English Episcopal clergy for cherishing the memory of a tyrannical king who "was very well affected to . . . that true mother of harlots . . . to all the follies and superstitions and hierarchy of Rome." But by 1790, President Washington would tell the clerical and lay leaders of Maryland Catholicism that he expected America to become one of the foremost nations in advancing justice and freedom; "and I presume that your fellow-citizens will not forget the patriotic part which you took in the accomplishment of their Revolution and the establishment of their Government; or the important assistance which they received from a nation in which the Roman Catholic faith is professed."[10]

So strongly rooted was the new tolerance that the Constitutional Convention imposed no religious test for officeholders. Some state constitutions created established churches and proscribed Catholic activity; Thomas Jefferson and James Madison, however, made great efforts on behalf of religious liberty in Virginia, offering a different and more hopeful model for state and local constituencies. There were only thirty-five thousand Roman Catholics, one-half of them in Maryland, among the 3 million citizens of the new United States in 1790. Suddenly, the most paranoid nativist seemed incapable of seeing the dangers these few people posed to national institutions. The Founding Fathers had been heirs to the Protestant hatred of Rome; John Adams earlier wrote of the "fraud, Bigotry, Impudence and Superstition, on which the Papal Usurpations are founded . . . of all the ridiculous Nonsense, Delusion, and Frenzy that . . . ever passed into the Mind of Man, none had ever been more glaring and extravagant than the notions of Canon Law." But the Founders had overcome this heritage in forming their more perfect Union. Anti-Catholic activity would not be seen again until a new wave of Catholic immigration began three decades later.[11]

★★★

Antialienism in the New Nation

Still, hostility to foreigners continued to boil beneath the surface of events even during the first years of relative religious tolerance. Anti-Catholicism was not the only source of nativist frenzy. In the nation of immigrants, political and ideological differences at home and upheavals and conflicts abroad raised again the enduring question: Who are the real Americans? As the Federalist government's hostility to revolutionary France reached a peak with the undeclared naval war near the turn of the century, the Alien Act of 1798 became another monument to America's endemic nativism. It was inspired by the Adams administration's distrust of alien support for the hated Jeffersonian opposition; Alexander Hamilton hinted darkly of a "Gallic faction" and "subaltern mercenaries," and John Jay was convinced that American "Jacobins" were "numerous, desperate, active." But it was inspired as well by the isolation felt in a new and fragile nation far removed from European struggles. The act extended the probationary period for the naturalization of citizens from five to fourteen years. It foreshadowed later efforts to preserve the American "way of life" by withholding citizenship from those considered unfit or untrustworthy. But it heralded no general assault against foreign peoples. The election of Thomas Jefferson to the presidency in 1800 helped to dissipate antialien sentiment. Only in the Federalist-inspired Hartford Convention a few years later—when dissident New Englanders desperately opposed the Jeffersonian commercial embargo against the warring Continental powers—was an echo of nativism heard again. With their shipping and export businesses reeling under the embargo and their Anglophile sentiments ablaze at this declaration of hostility to England, the Hartford delegates raged at Jefferson's appeal to foreign and Irish support and called for the exclusion of naturalized citizens from all elective offices. But this was a rump meeting of men whose political power and influence were decaying. The reemergence of nativism in such a setting seemed only to suggest again that it was no longer an effective theme in postrevolutionary America.[12]

With the end of the War of 1812 and the exploitation of new frontier resources in the West, "foreigners" had more reason than ever to hope that ethnic and religious differences would no longer lead to exclusion and discrimination. In a land of enormous potential wealth, much of it only recently discovered, might there not be riches enough for everyone, equality of opportunity for all without the hostilities which in the past had set one group against another? But those who recalled the curious outburst of hysteria over the Bavarian Illuminati in the late 1790s might have known that there would be no final solution to the problem of a heterogeneous immigrant population living at peace in what so many proudly considered the new Garden of Eden. Fear of un-American ideas paralleled and exacerbated hostility to alien peoples even in these earlier years. In the paradoxical antialienism of the Illuminati affair much that came later would be illuminated.

The secret societies known as the Illuminati had passed from the European scene some time before their transplantation in the American republic. Rooted in the liberal reaction to Catholic religious intolerance and clerical political influence, the Illuminati organizations, founded in 1776 by Adam Weishaupt, a professor of law at the University of Ingolstadt, had spread from Bavaria across the Continent in the 1770s and 1780s. They attracted Freemasons and other anti-Catholics willing to take a secret pledge to battle for utopian goals of human equality and fraternity. Although Illuminism seemed to be just another manifestation of widespread Enlightenment rationalism, conservatives fixated on the "conspiratorial" nature of a secret society marked by various ranks and grades and accused it of plotting against all established institutions. The Illuminati disbanded before 1787 on the Continent. Nevertheless, they were seen as responsible for the French Revolution and the widespread disorder of the contemporary world, for the corruption of women, the cultivation of sensuality, the violation of property rights, and the assault on organized religion. The basic texts in the attack on the movement were Scotsman John Robison's *Proofs of a Conspiracy Against All the Religions and Governments of Europe* and Abbé Barruel's *Memoirs, Illustrating the History of Jacobinism.* Robison wrote: "Nothing is more clear than that the design of the Illuminati was to abolish Christianity . . . and we now see how effectual this would be for the corruption of the fair sex, a purpose they eagerly wished to gain that they might corrupt the men."[13]

In the United States, the reaction against the Illuminati fit perfectly in the social and political climate of New England at the turn of the century. Establishment clergymen were alarmed at the challenge to their authority in a revolutionary age. Efforts at repression (such as temperance) had failed, and their traditionally pessimistic world view was repeatedly rejected by many hopeful and mobile parishioners convinced by their success of their own worth. Establishment political figures within the Federalist party were alarmed at the proliferating Democratic societies of the Jeffersonian opposition, which threatened the older party's hold on the national government and long-standing sociopolitical relationships everywhere. They were furious at the Francophile orientation of the opposition, coming as it did at a moment when the French revolutionary leadership seemed to enjoy insulting the American government in the infamous XYZ affair. What better time to see, in Hamilton's words, "a league . . . between the apostles and disciples of irreligion and anarchy," originating overseas but threatening to spread to the New World and destroy all that had been built here?[14]

The Reverend Jedidiah Morse would receive a serious hearing when he announced, in May 1798, that a conspiracy to undermine political and religious institutions in America had been hatched in Europe by secret societies. These Illuminati were anti-Catholic, he reminded his readers, and they might be praised if all they did was to fight popery and despotism, but they were atheistic men, "artful and wicked," opposed to private property and chastity, advocating everything from adultery to assassination in their plot to undermine America "by secret and systematic means." Morse's fantasy was shared in many quarters. President-elect Timothy Dwight of Yale College warned of the "malice of atheism and the sins of the enemies of Christ" in a sermon on "the duty of Americans in the Present Crisis." Newspapers accused Illuminati of sedition, even tied them to the yellow fever epidemic. Attacks on "foreign influences" were heard throughout the region, and numerous tracts were published warning of this dire threat. *A Discovery of a Clan of Conspirators Against All Religions and Governments in the Whole World* by "A Citizen of the United States" noted the poisonous spread of alien ideas: "The French hold up to other nations a fearful . . . example of the dreadful and inevitable consequences of irreligion and vice . . . beware the arch villain Weishaupt . . . and the wretch Marat."[15]

But the "Illuminism conspiracy" thesis could not endure serious scrutiny. Within a year, newspapers and journals, with those friendly to the Jeffersonian opposition in the lead, were attacking the "evidence" of secret designs to overthrow the government. When Robison's book finally was exposed as fraudulent, an embarrassed and humiliated Jedidiah Morse, unable to prove his charges, retired in silence. By the end of 1799, the Illuminati affair was over.[16]

Its lessons lived on. Again and again some Americans were to accuse their countrymen influenced by "foreign" ideas of threatening the nation in times of crisis. It is paradoxical that later antialien crusaders would assail the Catholic church and organize in secret societies just as the victims of this outburst—the Illuminati—were known to do, but perhaps the paradox is resolved by recalling that the fear of a secret Jesuitical conspiracy would be used to justify the creation of these underground patriotic movements in succeeding years. It is the nagging anxiety that "conspirators" are at work in the shadows, Edward Shils suggested in *The Torment of Secrecy*, that leads some to desperate efforts to uncover the enemy, to emulate him if necessary, to counterpose the "good" secret order against the bad. Hofstadter called the protectors "paranoid" because they attribute superhuman qualities to the enemy conspirator; they see him as "a kind of amoral superman . . . ubiquitous, cruel . . . deflecting the normal course of history in an evil way." The injunction to fight fire with fire to save America from secret plotters was heard in the Know Nothings' activities and, more than a century later, in the John Birch Society's call to emulate the secret cell tactics of "successful" communist infiltrators. It is not surprising to find echoes of Robison and Morse in one of the basic books of the Birch movement. Robert Welch wrote in 1966 that the Illuminati "tried to reach and control collectivist activities after 1776" and that this old order "has now been absorbed into the top echelons of the communist conspiracy."[17]

The opponents of Illuminism were significant not only because they were self-styled protectors of national institutions but because of the ways in which they manipulated the antialien theme to serve their personal political and ideological causes. Conservative clergymen and Federalist politicians were trying to stem the tide of change that threatened to engulf their careers. In the struggle against foreign influence they might find a way of holding on a while longer, as well as an explanation for their potential failures. It would not be the last time that Americans would embrace a conspiracy theory of alien activity to explain events that menaced both their personal lives and their vision of a cherished national order.

The fear of alien peoples and alien ideas was a heritage of the colonial period and the years of revolution and nation building that followed. After the turn of the nineteenth century, some thought that a new climate of tolerance had come to the New World and that Crèvecoeur's romantic promise of "hospitality, kindness and plenty" might at last be fulfilled for all newcomers in God's American Israel. But within three decades of the Alien Act and the Illuminati controversy, rapid social and economic changes would raise new hopes and present new problems for Americans. The pressures of an age of change and flux would dramatically intersect with a swelling wave of immigration. Soon the old specter of foreign influence endangering the unique quality of American life would loom large again in the imaginations of many.

★ ★

CHAPTER 2

FEAR AND HATRED IN
AN AGE OF EQUALITY

ON A WARM EVENING in the late summer of 1834, an angry mob of Protestant workmen in Charlestown, Massachusetts, attacked the Ursuline Convent, an imposing red brick building set atop a commanding hill known as Mount Benedict. The convent had become a symbol of hated Catholic power. The crowd of truckers and bricklayers, aided by volunteer firemen, ransacked it from top to bottom, smashing the furniture and piling combustible materials in the center of rooms. Amid cheers and jeers, the ornaments of the altar and the cross were hurled on the pyre just after midnight, and the building—"the first fruit of Catholic educational enterprise in New England," a church historian would later write— went up in a roar of flames.[1]

The burning of the Ursuline Convent is a landmark in the record of intergroup violence in America. But in the 1830s it was only the most dramatic of many confrontations between Catholics and Protestants—the "aliens" and their adversaries. Forty years later, the magazine *Catholic World*, reviewing the history of anti-Catholic movements in the United States, was puzzled by the violent eruptions of this decade. The editors concluded that such "un-American activity" could come only at the point when "the whole generation . . . of the great founding fathers passed away," allowing mindless mobs to feel free to challenge the "solemn guarantees of our federal compact."[2]

To see nativism as the enemy of the egalitarian ethos of a "real" America was an exemplary error. The setting for the new violence suggested instead that conditions of American life nourished the ugly developments. Heroic figures from the past could not have changed the course of events without changing the institutions they had helped to build. The growing ranks of emigrants from Catholic Europe, embarking for the New World in these years in huge numbers, would land in a nation experiencing social disorder and political change—the "age of Jackson," filled with promise and unrest. Violent hostility to Roman Catholicism would flourish once more in the "era of the common man."

★★★

Immigration Resumes

Immigration to the United States increased dramatically in 1827–28 after years in which America had been in disfavor with potential settlers. From 1820 to 1825 the recorded arrivals ranged from but six to ten thousand because of the bitter autumn of economic disaster in 1819 and the difficult conditions following the panic. The trouble had begun in the West, where an overvalued real estate market led to the collapse of local banks. As the panic spread to the East, more financial institutions were destroyed and, in their wake, factories shut down, commercial houses were imperiled, and farmers—discovering prices dropping and European markets closing to them—could find no place to borrow money against a better tomorrow. Cotton mills in Philadelphia that had employed 2,325 men in 1816 had laid off all but 149 by October of 1819. Agents collecting data for the federal census the next year noted of various enterprises: "Flourishing in 1816 but now useless to the owners"; "Stopped by the pressure of the times"; "Ceased operation in 1819." Jobless aliens seemed to fill many of the small cities of the new nation, and one homesick immigrant carved on a bridge in Pennsylvania the words, "England, with all thy faults, I love thee still." There was no lack of potential emigrants in Europe. If the United States had lost its appeal, however, Russia experienced vast German migrations to the Caucasus and to the czar's Kingdom of Poland in these years. Brazil, too, became a magnet for many, a new household word on the Continent.[3]

But America soon regained its charms. The depression following 1819 came to an end, and projects for canals, turnpikes, warehouses, and mills were launched. In the Old World, bitter winters plagued the poor, with food shortages to follow in the spring. The winter of 1829–30 was one of the coldest on record; and there were agonized complaints of lack of fuel and alarming rises in prices of all necessities. In Ireland, there was greater distress than in the famine summer of 1822, and it was compounded by the disfranchisement act of 1829, which abolished the poor freeholder's status as an elector by raising the qualification to vote to ten pounds. This act was Parliament's response to the assertion of class and religious feeling by an awakened Catholic peasantry under the leadership of Daniel O'Connell. When tenant farmers refused to heed the commands of their proprietors at the polls, the incentive for landlords to encourage subdivision and create more captive voters disappeared, and the new legislation led to the "clearing" of parcels into larger holdings and the dispossession of thousands. The Irish poor were forced to take refuge with relatives, to squat on the wastelands and the bogs, or to become beggars or laborers in the cities. By 1837, an English poor law commissioner would write, "Nothing can exceed the miserable appearance of the cottages in Donegal, or the desolate aspect of a cluster of these hovels, always teeming with an excessive population. . . . But what could you do: There was no employment for the young people nor relief for the aged."[4]

Many of the dispossessed in Ireland lacked the means to migrate. But the social disorder they engendered increased tensions during an era of a stupendous increase in population. The first census in 1821 had surprised even pessimistic experts when the numbers reached almost 7 million, and America seemed a more attractive goal to thousands every year in this unhappy corner of the Old World.

Immigration to the United States grew rapidly. Sixty thousand foreigners arrived in 1832 and at least as many in each succeeding year, with the exception of a mild decline in the recession of 1835 and a sharp but brief reversal following the crash of 1837. A growing proportion of these newcomers were Catholic. The Irish alone accounted for one-third of American immigration in the 1830s. Their numbers swelled to almost a quarter of a million between 1840 and 1844—before the coming of the famine—most of them from predominantly Catholic districts. In an America where there were but 70,000 Roman Catholics in 1807, this was a striking change. By 1830 there were 74,000 Catholics in New England alone; by 1840 the church numbered its American membership at 660,000 and would almost triple its size in the next decade. In Ohio, where there had been no Catholic churches at all, twenty-two were established within fourteen years, along with a newspaper, a seminary, and a college. The new growth brought opportunities and obligations. Even before the sharp upturn of the 1830s, the Papal Jubilee was celebrated widely in 1827, and a provincial council met in 1829 to issue a call for new parochial schools.[5]

The new immigrants were coming to a land that was undergoing breathtaking changes. The striking social and political upheavals of the years from 1824 to 1840 would later be chronicled as the "age of Jackson," but at the time they seemed to signify once more the virtues of a unique civilization. It was separate from and superior to Europe, its glory—as Noah Webster put it—beginning "at the dawn" of a new era. Growth was everywhere. The population leaped ahead and spread to the West. Indiana's population doubled between 1830 and 1840, and Illinois's tripled. By 1840 almost 6.5 million, or more than one out of three Americans, lived in the trans-Appalachian region. The development of urban communities was even more dramatic. Cities in the East and West quadrupled in numbers between 1820 and 1850 until New York's population was at half a million and Pittsburgh, Cincinnati, Boston, and other gateway centers were substantial even by the standards of the Continent. Accompanying this urban growth was a marked trend toward industrialization. By 1830 household manufactures had declined noticeably and factory methods soon were applied to watchmaking and woolens, copper and wire manufacturing, and ready-made clothing. A spectacular "transportation revolution" was both cause and effect of the pattern of growth—from but 73 miles of railroad track in the United States in 1830, mileage increased to over 3,300 in 1840 and almost 9,000 by 1850. "Life consists in motion," wrote Francis Grund, an Austrian who had settled in America in the late 1820s, "the United States present certainly the most animated picture of universal bustle and activity of any country in the world. . . . This state of incessant excitement gives to the Americans an air of busy inquietude which, in fact, constitutes their principal happiness."[6]

The celebration of American progress and the belief in its happy destiny dominated the literature of the age, and the optimistic words reached across the Atlantic. Calvin Colton, editor, essayist, and quintessential booster, wrote in the *Manual for Emigrants to America* in 1832 that "I have no objection that America should present the first example . . . to dissolve the dark and gloomy spell of evil boding to man. . . . America presents an open field for a mighty and incalculable population. The providence of God has set up a state of society of hopeful and high promise." The message was picked up and relayed by European visitors. John Robert Godley exclaimed: "In energy, enterprise, perseverance, sagacity, activity and varied resources—in all the faculties, in short, which contribute to produce what is technically called material civilization . . . there is no disputing the superiority of the Americans to ourselves. There is no competing with them." Another Englishman told the House of Commons, "I could not fail to be impressed . . . with the extraordinary energy of the people, and their peculiar aptitude in availing themselves of the immense natural resources of the country. . . . They leave no means untried to effect what they think it is possible to accomplish."[7]

The vision of an Edenic America, filled with self-reliant individuals, did not square with the harsh realities confronting many poor farmers and laborers in the new factories. Nor did it undo the haunting anxieties that would accompany their way of life. But there was enough truth in the vision of fresh opportunities to draw tens of thousands of immigrants yearly to the port cities and to persuade perceptive foreign observers that here was not only a pastoral garden of the world, a new agrarian lifestyle different from that of postfeudal, aristocratic Europe, but also a "workshop in the wilderness" that could serve as a standard for all industrial societies. Charles Dickens passed through Lowell, Massachusetts, and compared American factories with those in England: "The contrast would be . . . between the Good and Evil, the living light and deepest shadow . . . the difference between this town and those great haunts of desperate misery." American spokesmen agreed, insisting on the distinction between "virtuous" American factories set in rural areas and their corrupting European counterparts, emphasizing the relationship between moral progress and material progress, which freed men to live a fuller and richer life. Everywhere the climate seemed one of optimism and excitement. Daniel J. Boorstin observed of this period that "the young nation flourished not in discovery but in search. It prospered not from the perfection of its ways but from their fluidity. It lived with the constant belief that something else or something better might turn up. . . . When before had men put so much faith in the unexpected?"[8]

★★★

The Age of Jackson

The central political figure of this remarkable age was Andrew Jackson. Frontier judge, general and hero, powerful president and party builder, he was a man with charismatic authority. Scholars disagree on the nature and meaning of his following, on the very question of who the Jacksonians were. But the debate suggests another dimension to the brilliant period of opportunity symbolized by Jackson's person and manifest in the ambience of his presidency, another reason why this period of hope was laced with anxiety.

The most influential early interpretation of the age was Frederick Jackson Turner's famous thesis that Andrew Jackson represented the changing of the guard in American politics, symbolized by the western farmers, the "democrats of the American forest," who marched with muddy feet through the White House on Inaugural Day in 1829 after their man had wrenched power from the leaders of the effete East and the decadent South. Later writers offered other explanations. Some saw Jackson as the champion of the underprivileged and depressed laboring classes of the East, spearheading a movement of workingmen and reformers against exploitive capitalists who had manipulated the money system for their own benefit. Others argued that middle-class entrepreneurial groups were his main supporters—an ambitious and proliferating class of businessmen ("new" capitalists for old), who had been thwarted by government-sponsored monopolies that left them at a disadvantage in the competitive struggle. Still others suggested that Jacksonians and anti-Jacksonians used essentially the same language, that the "Old Hero" was merely the dominant manipulator of the vocabulary of an "Age of Egalitarianism."[9]

The disparate concerns of various groups portrayed as Jacksonians reduces the credibility of any theory relating Jacksonian politics to a traditional interest or regional coalition. But these various groups did all share one desire. Large numbers of hopeful farmers, laborers, and businessmen, sensing an opportunity for advancement in the whirlpool that was American life, could agree that their common enemy was vested interests of the old order. Many people would respond to leadership that did not try to divide groups by emphasizing diverse interests but would offer instead an amorphous and unifying theme. That theme was equal rights. Those who were anxious to make their mark and contemptuous of the Virginia and New England gentlemen who had controlled establishment politics could see in Andrew Jackson and his crusade against the "hydra-headed monster" of the National Bank—that Greek temple in Philadelphia, which was described as favoring the rich and powerful allies of its cultured director—a new wind blowing in their direction. The bank was the classic symbol around which Jackson could build an alliance of the upwardly mobile. It could be pictured as denying opportunity to the majority, as malevolent because it did not afford equal rights to all. If poor or demoralized farmers in older communities of the Middle States and New England also voted Democratic, in an effort to redress the balance of economic power they believed the "interests" had turned against them, it only indicated that equal treatment was a compelling theme to men moving up or down the socioeconomic ladder.[10]

Jackson and his associates returned again and again to this theme. Presidential adviser William M. Gouge noted in 1835 that "unequal political and commercial institutions . . . take much of the capital of a country from those whose industry produced it and give it to those who neither work nor save." In his famous message vetoing extension of the National Bank, Andrew Jackson exclaimed:

> It is to be regretted that the rich and powerful too often bend the acts of government to their selfish purposes. Distinctions in society will always exist . . . but when the laws undertake to add to these natural and just advantages artificial distinctions, to grant titles, gratuities and exclusive privileges to make the rich richer and the potent more powerful . . . the farmers, mechanics and laborers who have neither the time nor the means of securing like favors to themselves have a right to complain of the injustice of their Government.[11]

Jackson and his followers have been accused of underestimating the strains of a rapidly expanding economy and mischievously undermining the financial institutions that served as broker for a growing nation. But there is no doubt that they understood Tocqueville's dictum that "the passion for equality . . . is the chief and constant object of Americans." In subscribing to a value system that had endured across the years, the Jacksonians accepted the competitive matrix and asked only that all people be given an equal chance, that they be free to search after that achievement which alone seemed to bring a sense of self-mastery.[12]

Henry David Thoreau understood this ethic and despised it. In *Life without Principle*, he observed of this period that "if a man walk in the woods for love of them half of each day he is in danger of being regarded as a loafer; but if he spends his whole day as a speculator . . . he is esteemed as an industrious and enterprising citizen." Thoreau was speaking for the men and women in the Transcendentalist movement, who renounced the competitive world and mourned the spread of its spirit throughout America. Thomas Jefferson, writing earlier of the soul-destroying nature of urban-industrial society, had noted that such a setting made men dependent on the "caprice of customers" and that "dependence begets subservience and venality, suffocates the germ of virtue and prepares fit tools for the designs of ambition." These new romantic idealists of the Jacksonian age called on their countrymen to abandon a lifestyle that could only bring alienation. The leader of Transcendentalism, Ralph Waldo Emerson, hopefully observed that "it is a sign of our times that many intelligent and religious persons withdraw themselves from the common labors and competitions of the market and the caucus and betake . . . a certain solitary and critical way of living. . . . They are striking work and crying out for something worthy to do."[13]

Few Americans deserted the marketplace and the "common labors" in the 1830s. Relatively few have ever done so, although the setting for such an "inner emigration" seemed more attractive for awhile 140 years later. But in pointing to the tension between the romanticized ideal of Jeffersonian individualism and the realities of competitive culture in the rapidly changing world of Jacksonian times, Transcendentalists pointed to another source of widespread anxiety. They suggested another reason for the enormous appeal of President Andrew Jackson and the curious way in which the egalitarian ethos he celebrated would serve as prelude to a new outburst of nativist hostility.

Some writers have noted that the figure of Jackson served to allay fears of many contemporaries that their lives might be at variance with a "golden age of the past in which liberty and progress were joined inseparably with simple yeoman virtues," the ideal of a "chaste republican order, resisting the seductions of risk and novelty, greed and extravagance, rapid motion and complex dealings." Unable or unwilling to desert contemporary opportunities for the alternative culture offered by Emerson and his circle, many who responded to Jackson's leadership might have seen him as a symbolic and heroic figure, the embodiment of an individualism of a less complex age. As symbol of past virtue and articulator of the values of contemporary competitive culture, the president could not fail to be a figure of enormous importance. For in a time when "men put so much faith in the unexpected," anxiety would be a concomitant of optimism. It was anxiety lest the virtues of the pastoral past be lost, lest "equal rights" lead to failure rather than success.[14]

★★★

The Reemergence of Anti-Catholicism

With the retirement of Andrew Jackson, the advent of the Panic of 1837, and the subsequent economic turmoil marking the administration of his successor, Martin Van Buren, another dramatic setting was created for rifts in the American community. The decline of opportunity intensified the fear of failure in a mobile society. If it was fashionable before to ask only for "equal rights," it soon seemed clear that the very "individualism" equated with American freedom left its adherents alone and vulnerable in a time of crisis. If this was the American dream, something more tangible than status concerns or vague feelings of unease present in more prosperous times must be wrong with it. In the late 1830s, the egalitarian ethos of the Jacksonian years exacerbated problems wrought by depression.[15]

As many Americans grappled with economic and social insecurity, they began to notice that the increasing pace of immigration seemed to add to disorder and uncertainty. Many of these newcomers were Roman Catholics from poverty-stricken Ireland. They seemed clannish and often truculent, speaking with an alien brogue, organizing strange clubs, gangs, and societies. Most significant, by not sharing the Protestant faith of the vast majority, they introduced yet another discontinuity in an age of change. From colonial times propaganda had taught Americans to mistrust Catholics, and now they were arriving in record numbers.

gan players and similar practitioners." But the papists represented more than just a covert threat. Nativist leaders reminded the faithful that in 1834, mobs of Roman Catholics attacked speakers and sacked the hall at a public meeting sponsored by the New York Protestant Association on the question "Is Popery Compatible with Civil Liberty?" These association programs had become popular with New Yorkers. At the biweekly sessions, attendance spurted from three hundred to fifteen hundred, and always the themes were the same, as in the title of the first discussion: "Is Popery That Babylon the Great Which John the Evangelist Has Described in the Apocalypse?"[17]

The clash between Protestant and Catholic, native and "foreigner," grew rapidly through confrontations both verbal and violent in the decade of the 1830s. Early in these years, public debates on the lecture platform or in print were a favorite polemic exercise. In Philadelphia, the Reverend John Breckenridge took on Father John Hughes (later to win fame as bishop of New York) in a series of rambling evening meetings before raucous audiences. In New York, the anti-Catholic editor and minister William C. Brownlee assailed a number of priests until the Catholics announced that they refused further debate: "To continue polemic discussion with you cannot add to reputation. Your substitutes for arguments are falsehood, ribald words, gross invective, disgusting calumny." More significant than the war of words was the use of force. In 1833, after a drunken Irishman had killed a native on a Charlestown street, houses were smashed and burned in the Irish section as troops stood by and watched. Within a year, the same town in Massachusetts was the scene of the convent fire, preceded by days of public unrest, rumors of immorality behind the "Nunnery Walls," and posted notices reading "To Arms! To Arms! Ye brave and free. The avenging sword unshield!!" This was a particularly complex event, pitting not only "Irish" against "American" and Catholic against Protestant but lower-class fundamentalist against wealthy liberal. The mob raged through the building on Mount Benedict, shouting "No Popery" and "Down with the Cross" and shocked the leadership of the New England Protestant community. Prominent men, some whose daughters had attended the convent school, met in Faneuil Hall in Boston to denounce destruction of property and threats to life. Even a few of the incendiary religious newspapers called for a moratorium in the struggle against Catholicism. But any truce was temporary. The acquittal of the convent burners presaged another round of violence.[18]

Of course, these were violent times in America. Mobs attacked abolitionist leaders in 1835 and 1837, burning their Philadelphia headquarters in 1838. There were vicious attacks on Mormons in Ohio in 1832 and 1833; they were tarred and feathered, beaten and shot, their homes destroyed. In Missouri in 1838, a mob led by three state militia companies fell upon a small colony of Mormons at Haun's Mill, killing or wounding most residents. Major urban riots exploded in New York, Boston, Baltimore, and Philadelphia. In the fetid slums of the Bowery and Five Points districts in lower Manhattan, powerful gangs controlled the neighborhoods. Their murderous battles were marked by barricades of carts and hurled paving stones, assaults with knives, brickbats, bludgeons, teeth, and fists, the leaders blazing away with muskets and pistols. These encounters led to large-scale civil disturbances in the depression winter of 1837, when mobs desperate for food stormed wheat and flour stores. This was a time of widespread disorder, and in their study *The Rebellious Century*, Charles, Louise, and Richard Tilly suggest that such "competitive collective violence" frequently occurred in Europe in the years before agencies of state control could exercise claims to complete authority, when one group seemed free to try to maintain the status quo through intimidation. But the election riots in New York in 1834 suggest the extent to which such violence and nativism were interconnected in America. The most important gangs of the early days in the Bowery district—the True Blue Americans, the Bowery Boys, and the O'Connell Guards—were mostly Irish and intensely chauvinistic. The True Blue Americans dressed in stovepipe hats and long frock coats and spent much time on the streets cursing England's treatment of Erin. The O'Connell Guards built up a bitter enmity to a rival group whose members prided themselves on their native ancestry. The fighting between the O'Connells and these American Guards finally erupted in a wild riot in 1835, which forced the mayor and sheriff to call out every watchman in the city. In Boston, there were countless feuds between North Enders and South Enders, truckmen and sailors, but the biggest disturbances involved Irish Catholics and natives. The Charlestown burnings were the most dramatic, but there was also the Broad Street riot of June 1837, when a collision between a volunteer fire company and an Irish funeral procession was quelled only by the militia.[19]

In such a setting, new anti-Catholic papers appeared, ever more militant, responsive to the call to arms of Irish activists. In Philadelphia, a former speaker for the New York Protestant Association who claimed to be "late a Popish priest," Samuel B. Smith, offered the sensational *Downfall of Babylon, or the Triumph of Truth over Popery*. In New York, Reverend Brownlee issued the more influential *American Protestant Vindicator and Defender of Civil and Religious Liberty against the Inroads of Popery*. "Our object," he explained, "is to warn our Protestant friends of the insidious Jesuitical workings of that abomination, showing its demoralizing, debasing character." Brownlee argued that Europe had been "chained in mental slavery by Popery for over one thousand years." He warned of the "demoralizing influence of saint worship" and reminded his readers that the "pope considers all Roman Catholics his subjects, bound by his commands. . . . It is this double character, the union of the civil and the ecclesiastical, which renders Popery so dangerous." He asserted that the holy alliance of Catholic monarchs was seeking to destroy the United States by exporting excess Catholic populations across the seas. There was, Brownlee insisted, a reactionary papal conspiracy at work throughout the world. It had destroyed the French Revolution through mobocracy, and had led to sinister counterrevolutions, which destroyed freedom in Latin America. If present in the American colonies, we would never have had "independence or even the potent influence of the founding fathers." Immigration must be stopped. "The enemy is at our gates!"[20]

The *American Protestant Vindicator* was so popular that it soon had emulators in different parts of the country. New missionary groups were organized as well; the Protestant Reformation Society used Brownlee's newspaper to solicit funds and advertise meetings, establishing branches in three major cities and many smaller communities within a year of its birth in 1836. The whole constellation of concerns, fears, and frustrations that would fuel the Know Nothing flame two decades later emerged in an early form at this time. Catholicism was the prime target, but the dominant theme was that the "papists" were aliens, immigrants with foreign accents or language, newcomers who subscribed to an "authoritarian" church and came from lands in which democracy was nonexistent. These people were unassimilable. As members of an ancient religious conspiratorial organization, they could overwhelm and despoil the blessed American nation.[21]

The curious mixture of rational concern for the nation's future and invention of wild conspiracy theories is apparent in the reports of an alleged plot between the pope and the "foreigners" (European monarchs) to infiltrate the Mississippi Valley through Catholic settlement and then wrench it away from the United States. A central figure in this affair was that New England renaissance man Samuel F. B. Morse, the distinguished painter and inventor of the telegraph, a nativist almost by inheritance as son of the Reverend Jedidiah Morse, scourge of the Bavarian Illuminati. In two books, *Imminent Dangers to the Free Institutions of the United States* and *Foreign Conspiracy against the Liberties of the United States*, Morse attacked Catholic immigration and "exposed" the society of St. Leopold, an Austrian-based group dedicated to strengthening the church in the American West.[22]

Morse enlisted Thomas Jefferson in his diatribes against foreigners. In *Notes on the State of Virginia*, the great Founding Father had written that "to the principles of our government nothing can be more opposed than the maxims of absolute monarchies. Yet from such we are to expect the greatest number of immigrants . . . a heterogeneous, incoherent, distracted mass. I doubt the expediency of inviting them by extraordinary encouragements." What Jefferson foresaw and Samuel Morse insisted was that America and its way of life could be insidiously destroyed from within. The disturbances of the 1830s were a case in point. Because the "tendency of democracy is not naturally turbulent," the real source of contemporary distress must lie with "foreign immigration which brings moral chaos." One cannot throw mud into pure water and not disturb its cleanliness.[23]

Morse's rhetoric was vintage nativism: "We are the dupes of our hospitality. The evil of immigration brings to these shores illiterate Roman Catholics, the tools of reckless and unprincipled politicians, the obedient instruments of their more knowing priestly leaders." In this way, "our very institutions are at the mercy of a body of foreigners," people who might boast of being Americans but who talk of Ireland as home, people who bring "mob violence to our cities." In their present state of depravity they were entitled to no natural rights. There was only the "social right" of a nation that

As the Catholic population expanded in the Jacksonian years, the Protestant churches were shaken by one of their periodic "awakenings." The Second Great Awakening began around 1795. By 1825 to 1835 revivalism was in vogue—American Protestantism's weapon in the battle against religious indifference and infidelity. Revivalist camp meetings often lasted for days, while professional evangelists produced "conversions" and reawakened guilt of sin, desire for salvation, and fear of damnation. The great preachers of the period, in particular Charles G. Finney, led an assault on the tenets of Calvinism. They minimized or denied the arbitrary grace of God—which elected some to heaven but most to hell—emphasizing instead the assumption that every individual had the free will and moral ability to work out his own salvation. In keeping with the spirit of Jacksonian individualism, this doctrine also encouraged the growth of movements endorsing American nationalism and castigating the misled or the wicked who willfully threatened American institutions. Congregationalists, Baptists, and Methodists all took part in the new religious excitement and in the mushrooming organizational activity that paralleled it. The missionary zeal that characterized the American Bible Society and the American Tract Society, inspiring the creation of a series of religious newspapers and the founding of the New York Protestant Association and similar groups, was thoroughly nativist in both form and content.[16]

Leaders of the American Bible Society argued that Catholics were opposed to the true Word of God found in the Protestant Bible. Anti-Catholic newspapers sprang up in major eastern communities to spread that message. A prospectus distributed before the first issue of the *Protestant* (New York) in 1830 declared: "The sole objects of this publication are to inculcate Gospel doctrines against Romish corruptions, to maintain the purity and sufficiency of the Holy Scriptures against Monkish traditions . . . to defend that revealed truth against the creed of Pope Pius IV." Later, papers would put their views directly on the masthead: the *Anti-Romanist, Priestcraft Unmasked, Priestcraft Exposed.* These new journals told strange tales of Catholic treachery. In 1834, the *Protestant Vindicator* revealed "the ascertained fact that Jesuits are prowling about all parts of the United States in every possible disguise to disseminate Popery"; the disguises included "puppet show men, dancing masters, music teachers, peddlers of images and ornaments, barrel or-has an obligation to defend itself. If we remember only Jefferson's felicitous phrase "all men are created equal" but forget his fears concerning foreigners, Morse warned, true Americans might discover aliens "obtruding themselves into private clubs" or even "family circles." It was a theme that would be repeated on many occasions throughout American history.[24]

Samuel F. B. Morse tied the domestic problems caused by Catholic immigrants to an international conspiracy, arguing that a "war of principles" was under way between despotism and liberty. The leaders of the holy alliance were dedicated to destroying America. Their instrument was the sinister society of St. Leopold, which Metternich had devised to inject popery into the United States to protect the Hapsburg monarchy and its allies from the democratic ideas that threatened these despotic great powers. Sly and dedicated Jesuits were strategically positioning themselves throughout the great Mississippi Valley, calling forth Catholic immigrants and controlling them through outpost missions. The American West, American freedoms, the Protestant church, and the United States itself were in deadly peril. The great frontier estate that guaranteed national strength and ensured America's future as the world's dominant nation was endangered by the alien conspirators.[25]

Morse's volumes touched sensitive nerves. Reverend Lyman Beecher, father of Harriet Beecher Stowe and Henry Ward Beecher, a major Protestant figure who had established his nativist credentials in speeches before the Boston riots, published a powerful sermon entitled *Plea for the West*. The American Home Missionary Society, frightened by the colonizing efforts of German Catholics, renewed its efforts. The *Home Missionary* declared in 1839 that "the cause is the cause of the West. There the great battle is to be fought . . . between Christianity . . . and the combined forces of Infidelity and Popery." Nativists hurried to protect their mythic West, while publications in the East continued to print Catholic immigration statistics, sounding the alarm at an influx of foreign criminals and paupers.[26]

But the literature of anti-Catholicism contained one important theme that had little to do with problems of the West or the specter of alien social disorder. It was not by accident that the symbolic burning of a Catholic institution occurred at a famous convent. A bizarre spate of books about the sexual underground of Roman Catholicism revealed another dimension of nativist fury. Published in

New York in 1836 was a slim volume that would become an immediate sensation. *The Awful Disclosures of Maria Monk as Exhibited
in a Narrative of Her Sufferings during a Residence of Five Years as
a Novice and Two Years as a Black Nun in the Hotel Dieu Nunnery
at Montreal* sold twenty thousand copies within a few weeks; sales
surpassed three hundred thousand in subsequent years as *Awful
Disclosures* became the best-selling book in American history until
Uncle Tom's Cabin.[27]

Maria Monk claimed to be a Protestant girl who converted to
Catholicism and entered a convent to be educated, only to be
abused by both nuns and priests, one of whom was the father of her
baby, born after her escape. Her mother later testified that Maria
was mentally unstable—the victim of a brain injury—and that she
was a prostitute who probably had conceived in an insane asylum.
Some researchers suggested that she was the dupe of several nativist ministers who shared profits from the book that they had written and/or edited. There is dispute about the authorship, and it has
been attributed to the Reverend J. J. Slocum as well as to Theodore
Dwight.[28]

Whatever the truth about Maria Monk, there is no question that
the book bearing her name had instant celebrity and that it helped
create a new genre of American literature. Convent exposés would
be a staple for booksellers in subsequent years. Whenever lawsuits
or official investigations flowed from the charges they contained,
the stories were revealed as fraudulent. But the nature of those tales
says much about the sources of anti-Catholic activity.

One of the first of the nunnery books was Rebecca Reed's *Six
Months in a Convent*. Published a year after the great fire, it pur-
ported to be the story of life in the Ursuline Convent in the early
1830s and served as an apologia for the destruction of the buildings
on Mount Benedict. The author painted a picture of brutal authoritarianism and sinister conspiracy behind convent walls, of starvation and humiliation, of physical abuse and intimidation. Reed
claimed to have heard the local Catholic bishop reveal plans for
a triumphant papal visit to the United States after the Romanist
plot had succeeded and the pope had become "spiritual director of
America . . . which rightfully belonged to him."[29]

Six Months in a Convent was basically a nativist political tract.
Awful Disclosures, published a few months later, focused almost

wholly on sex and sadism. It told a story of corrupt priests living in the nunnery day and night, terrorizing innocent young women who believed claims that Jesuits could read minds and would "strike dead at any moment" the girl who struggled against their "abominable deeds." Moving through secret passageways between seminary and convent, priests were in league with evil mother superiors to arrange "criminal intercourse." Deep in the cellars were the bleaching bones of infants born of these illicit affairs, strangled immediately after baptism. The descriptions of the sexual assaults were graphic; more than a century after publication, versions of *Awful Disclosures* would reappear in "adult" bookstores. A rival convent exposé was issued in 1836, *Rosamond: A Narrative of Captivity and Sufferings of an American Female under the Popish Priests in the Island of Cuba.* Some of this book's most obscene passages were printed in Spanish or Latin, for Samuel B. Smith, the man who discovered "poor, broken-hearted" Rosamond Culbertson and matched her against poor Maria, explained that certain things were too shocking for the average reader. But such sensibilities were the exception; in most places the books were clear enough in their descriptions of priests "seizing and satiating their appetites . . . only on the young and pretty" women.[30]

Mixed with and often dominating the tales of sexual conquests were revelations of sadistic behavior in the inner sanctums of the convents. Maria Monk wrote of "secret places of internment. . . . Hear the shrieks of helpless females in the hands of atrocious men." The reader is told of young, fair girls dragged to dimly lit rooms, where they are "beaten and stomped to death by superior and priests." Again and again the same images appear: girls "crushed to death" or "maimed" or "garroted" or "trampled to death," while in the background is heard the laughter of brutal clerics. But torture, not murder, is the mainstay of these stories, and the descriptions echo the "velvet underground" of a later day. Innocents are "branded with hot irons" or "whipped on naked flesh with rods before private altars." Leather apparatus of various kinds are described in careful detail: straps binding arms and mouth, belts "sinking into the very flesh." The torturers stick pins in victims' cheeks for penance, force them to go barefoot in the cold dungeons for months, flagellate and punch and choke them as a matter of course. "Well paid" priests slaughter girls and rob passersby for no apparent reason. "Old, cruel and cold blooded superiors" are in it for sheer pleasure. No scenarist for Hollywood horror films could create more despicable villains; they are caricatures of Catholic deviltry.[31]

What can be said of these incredible books, which had such a wide currency in their day? Of course, they did not picture reality. The famous Nunnery Committee in Massachusetts failed to find even a scintilla of supporting evidence when the state legislature commissioned its curious investigation of the "secret places" in the convents. The political position of the anti-Catholic editor-authors, as well as their obvious financial interests, suggest that they were motivated by more than informing public opinion and rooting out hidden evils.

Certainly such "exposés" did not appear for the first time in the 1830s. Long a staple of anti-Catholic literature, some of the more lurid European contributions to the genre were reprinted earlier by nativist editors as part of their concerted assault on the church. Two particular favorites were Scippio de Ricci's *Female Convents: Secrets of Nunneries Disclosed* and Englishman Richard Baxter's *Jesuit Juggling: Forty Popish Frauds Detected and Disclosed.*[32]

In these shocking journeys behind convent walls, enemies of "popery" could play upon their favorite themes—the dangers of secrecy and secret organizations and the un-American nature of Roman Catholicism. Through the "exposure" of the inner workings of the convent and seminary they could destroy the image of morality, rectitude, and service associated with religious orders. Smash down the doors to these sinister repositories of dark secrets, Theodore Dwight demanded in *Open Convents: Or Nunneries and Popish Seminaries Dangerous to the Morals, and Degrading to the Character of a Republican Community.* For if they operate in private, who will believe verbal denials made in public? The way was clear for defenses of the most notable exposés, as in the publication of *Decisive Confirmation of the Awful Disclosures of Maria Monk* and *Further Disclosures by Maria Monk Concerning the Hotel Dieu Nunnery of Montreal; also, Her Visit to Nuns' Island, and Disclosures Concerning That Secret Retreat.*[33]

The gross deviance described in these volumes served to unite militant Protestants and recruit others to their cause. Kai T. Erikson has noted that deviant outsiders create a sense of community by supplying a focus for group feeling: "The excitement generated by the crime . . . quickens the tempo of interaction in the group," producing a climate in which private sentiments of many individuals can be "fused together into a common sense of morality." This was a central goal of a movement that sought to unify "real" Americans so they might effectively meet the threat posed by the enemy within.[34]

It was no coincidence that women were the victims of crimes perpetrated by this enemy. David B. Davis has suggested that the literature was issued in a period of "increasing anxiety and uncertainty over sexual values and the proper role of woman." Anti-Catholics shared with anti-Mormon and anti-Masonic authors a feeling that one of the greatest threats to Christian civilization lay in the desexing and abuse of women; they shared as well a "romantic belief that morality can be secured only by sanctification of women." Woman's role as moral authority was accentuated in an age of socioeconomic upheaval, when national values were under pressure and traditional relationships threatened. Were women offered their sanctified role as a sop for being denied access to opportunity in the competitive marketplace, as one writer implies of southern women? Did the first stirrings of a revived women's consciousness, expressed in Lydia Maria Childs's *History and Condition of Women* (1832) and Sarah Grimké's *Letters on the Equality of Sexes and the Condition of Women* (1837), lead male spokesmen to an even greater insistence on female delicacy, sensitivity, and sensibility unsuited for the rugged, individualistic life of conflict? Women, invested with moral authority, were pictured as abused, degraded, and shamefully cast away by the enemy. What a heroic setting for the true patriot. How better to defend the American way. If the symbolic woman is being raped by "them," certainly she must be saved by "us" in a crusade against the lustful monsters of conspiracy. One of Maria Monk's patrons wrote of the particular danger of the convent system: "It is destructive of female intelligence and usefulness."[35]

Awful Disclosures and its emulators were well designed to bring anti-Catholics to the banners of militancy. But perhaps these books served another and latent function for their readers. This was a time, after all, of religious awakening, when ministers pointed with alarm at the breakdown of moral standards and called for a return to more temperate behavior. This was a period of rapid mobility and economic opportunity, when people poured energy and hope into their jobs, farms, businesses. Could the repression of sexual energies—called for by authoritative religious figures and perhaps necessitated by the demands of a workaday world in crisis—lead to a peculiar fascination with a pornographic literature legitimized only because it damned the sexual activity it described in such exciting detail? Steven Marcus in *The Other Victorians* (a study of sexuality and pornography in mid-nineteenth-century England) observed that "literature is, after all, as much a deflection of impulses as it is a representation of them and of action. We cannot let it pass as an accident that a great age of concerted and organized social growth and social action should also have produced such a literature. . . . That may, among other things, demonstrate part of the price we pay for social advancement." A nineteenth-century writer, a doctor named David M. Reese, agreed that Catholicism was a world conspiracy but loathed the convent books because they were corrupting and had a "deplorable moral influence upon the young." He may have correctly understood their effect but misinterpreted their function.[36]

But what of the role of sadism in these startling books? The appalling violence coloring almost every chapter in them is replete with picture images, finely detailed in the descriptions of the instruments and techniques of torture. They are not merely indictments of a mythical Catholic bestiality. Why did so many rush to purchase books that would take a permanent place in the literature of sadomasochism? It is perilous even to speculate on the fantasies of men and women long dead, but a tentative exploration of this question is in order.

Just as the tantalizing tales of sexual appetites of ostensibly celibate priests may have served as a perverse but acceptable projection of the hidden fantasies of some contemporaries constrained in their own activities, perhaps the reading of lurid narrations of pain (and pleasure through inflicting pain) in the sinister cellars of the nunneries may have served a purpose to some men grappling with the guilt, frustration, fear, and anger accompanying opportunity in the Jacksonian age. There were, of course, other outlets for violent feelings, and not a little of the destructive rage was channeled into overt anti-Catholic displays. But there were enormous burdens borne by those who struggled with the paradox of a competitive ethos which they embraced yet which carried with it a high price in tension and disappointment. Accounts of brutality made acceptable through attribution to the enemy provided another outlet for hostile feelings.

The victims of the sadists always were women. No young priests were brutalized in these volumes; no innocent young seminarians confronted the leather thongs or felt the lash of the sadist's whip. The displacement of shame and guilt onto women in a time of troubles is not a unique phenomenon in relations between the sexes. Secretly blaming women for the anxieties that plagued them might have led some men to devour stories of women brutalized beyond belief by other men sufficiently alien in so many ways that no odious connections could be drawn to real life. Psychoanalytic literature suggests an inextricable alliance between sadism and masochism. Both seem to represent means of defense against castration anxiety; by performing symbolic castration on others, the sadist gains assurance that he is the castrator and not the castrated. There were many reasons why men should seek reassurance that they were still masterful in these years of social and economic challenge and uncertainty. For some, the choice of reading material may have reflected yet another dimension of this need to reaffirm manhood.[37]

In this manner, the convent books could have been one more way in which the early nativists were both protectors of and fugitives from their American dream. In the incredible evils portrayed, they might see more clearly than ever before who was the true enemy of a nation and value system under attack, an America in need of their protection. In the projection of both lusts and fears onto the hated "Romanist" clerics, they might demonstrate again the desire to escape the difficulties their way of life imposed on all its followers.

Fear and hatred in an age of equality found its most curious and perverse expression in the nunnery literature. The verbal violence of this literature seems not unrelated to the physical violence of the nativists, and it helped ignite the flames that consumed the Ursuline Convent. In this fire, some saw a vision of future antialien activity, when anger would be transmuted from isolated eruptions of rage into a political movement. In fact, there were early stirrings of nativist political activity at this very time.

★ ★

CHAPTER 3

THE POLITICS OF
EARLY NATIVISM

ON 4 JULY 1845, a remarkable procession wound
through the streets of Philadelphia. Mounted men adorned with
blue silk scarfs and red and white hats led the way. Marching men
and women followed, bearing banners emblazoned with sacred pictures: the figure of Liberty imposed on an American shield and the
figure of an eagle bearing a Bible against an outline of a public
school. There were likenesses of Washington and the Founding Fathers. July Fourth, the birthday of the nation, was the great festival
day throughout the chauvinistic years of the nineteenth century,
and for nativists it was a day of particular and symbolic import.
But the parade in Philadelphia was more than just another celebration of nationhood, as the truncheons carried by mounted marshals
demonstrated for all to see. For here was nativistic fervor both militant and organized; at the end of the parade route a meeting hall
was reserved for representatives from twenty-six states who would
plan the national program of the new American Republican party.
William D. Barnes read the Declaration of the American Republicans: "Foreign hearts and lips overflow with insolent impieties toward our constitution. Foreign populations are festering and im-
poisoned with the impulse of disorderly appetites."[1]

In 1844, the new party had played a central role in the wild and
bloody battles between natives and "foreigners" that erupted in
the City of Brotherly Love in May and July. Election day that year
brought striking political victories to those who ran under the nativist standard in many states. The growing antialien activity in the
tumultuous years of the 1830s was capped by the emergence of this
substantial party dedicated to nativist goals. But the American Republicans were not the first ambitious politicians to translate the

language of Protestant and anti-immigrant militancy into the slogans of electoral campaigns.

As early as 1828, nativist themes colored the rhetoric of new parties offering to cleanse and protect the land. The curious phenomenon of the anti-Masonic movement is a case in point. The anti-Masonic party emerged from the welter of hysteria and speculation following the abduction and presumed murder of William Morgan, an itinerant stonemason in Batavia, New York. Morgan's effort to establish a Masonic lodge had been thwarted, and he announced the publication of a book exposing the "secrets of the order." Morgan's *Illustrations of Masonry by One of the Fraternity Who Has Devoted Thirty Years to the Subject* was a literary failure, but the author's disappearance proved a political sensation. Several investigations were launched, and a flock of tracts and broadsides flowed off the presses of those whose fear and suspicion of secret societies now had immediate focus. Opposition developed to Masons running for any and all public offices. Two shrewd young western New Yorkers destined to become powerful party figures, editor Thurlow Weed of Rochester and lawyer William H. Seward of Auburn, helped convert the inchoate feelings of anger into a new political instrument.[2]

The Anti-Masonic party played a role in national politics through 1832 and was active in state affairs in subsequent years. It dominated Vermont political life for a time, elected a governor in Pennsylvania, and was a recognized force in New York, Massachusetts, Rhode Island, and throughout New England. Most leaders and members drifted into the emerging Whig party by the mid-1830s. Because many had supported John Quincy Adams and opposed Andrew Jackson in 1828, their party has been considered a transitional vehicle for the Jacksonian opposition, helping to fill the void left by the decay of the National Republicans until the appearance of Henry Clay's new Whig alternative. Whatever the functional role of anti-Masonry in party development, its ideological component involved themes to become familiar in nativist circles in future years. "Masonry, Roman Catholic Faith, Monks, and the Inquisition" were lumped together in alarmist reports appearing in anti-Masonic papers in Ohio and Pennsylvania in 1829 and 1830. "Popery and Freemasonry are schemes equally inconsistent with republicanism," it was argued. "The trammels of these horrid oath-binding systems are the very fangs of despotism," a dark cloud on the horizon of American freedom. When the New York State Senate appointed a select committee to investigate the abduction of Morgan, the committee's report in February 1829 coupled Masons with Jesuits in awkward but accusatory language: they both "secured unity of design and secrecy of action which used the most solemn sanctions of the most high God to subserve purposes the most selfish and profane." Like Catholic conspiracy, Masonic secrecy represented an unpardonable sin in an age of egalitarianism. "On the one side is a privileged order veiling its proceedings from scrutiny by pledges of secrecy . . . controlled and directed by unseen and unknown hands," insisted anti-Masonic New York legislators in 1831. "On the other side, a portion of your fellow-citizens ask for equal rights and equal privileges among the freemen of this country." Hostility to foreign plotting was such a common theme in reference to both groups that in many communities, as long as anti-Masonry prospered, there was no need for the establishment of nativist councils.[3]

Still, traditional nativism was only one source of the new party's strength. It moved on to social reform before disappearing from the national scene. But even as the anti-Masonic movement was dying, antialiens were founding the first party organizations dedicated solely to their own goals. In 1835, the Native American Democratic Association met in convention in New York, its paper *Spirit of '76* announcing the start of an effort to save the nation. Internal struggles over whether to focus on the evils of Catholicism or the "criminal and pauper immigration" supporting foreign Catholics in office weakened this initial effort, yet by fall there were active nativist political groups in several eastern cities as well as New Orleans. The New York Native Americans polled nine thousand votes in a total of twenty-three thousand in 1835 although they failed in the 1836 election, when Samuel F. B. Morse was rejected in his mayoral bid. The next year brought the depression of 1837 and a nativist ticket with Whig backing did capture city hall and the common council. Its campaign pointed to the dangerous competition of aliens in the labor market. In communities where immigration was affecting social and economic relationships, new groups sprang up, endorsing federal legislation to end the flow of foreigners and supporting new laws to make naturalization more difficult. The preamble to the constitution of the Philadelphia association charged that "Europe is ridding herself of an excess of population.

She sends her paupers, convicts, the outpourings of her almshouses and jails" to the New World. Almost word for word, the same statement was repeated in countless documents prepared by antialiens throughout the next ninety years.[4]

Petitions flooded Congress from various parts of the country. Henry Clay presented one from a citizens' group, which shouted its warning: "A flood of foreign Catholics, guided by crafty and zealous priests, are ominously pouring into our country, and in time the Roman Catholic religion is likely to supplant Protestantism." But legislation introduced to accomplish nativist goals died a lingering death. Representatives were not anxious to alienate the growing immigrant vote, and when the economic crisis had passed, the cutting edge of the antialien movement was temporarily blunted. The pause in the struggle against the foreigner would be short-lived.[5]

★★★

The 1840s: Nativism Finds New Supporters

The 1840s marked an important new turn in nativist affairs. In the first year of the decade, William H. Seward, now governor of New York, sent a message to his state legislature calling for state funding for schools with teachers "speaking the same language, professing the same faith" as the children. Seward was a prominent Whig leader. But despite his early association with the anti-Masons, he was no nativist. A proponent of universal education, he was certain that poor Irish and German Catholic children would be discouraged by their parents from attending schools dominated by nativists. He was unhappy with the influence of anti-Catholicism in his own party and distressed that up to 95 percent of the Catholic vote had gone Democratic in recent elections. Moreover, the governor was a friend and admirer of John Hughes, powerful bishop of New York. His message came at a time when clerical leaders were circling cautiously around the question of political involvement. Bishop Hughes himself had expressed skepticism about the Democratic party, feeling his parishioners were being used for selfish purposes by the politicos. Other Catholic spokesmen tried to steer a course through the thornier issues of the day: the Pastoral Letter of the Fourth Provisional Council of Catholic Bishops in May 1840, referring to the growing abolitionist sentiment, stated,

"We disclaim all right to interfere with your judgment in the political affairs of our community." But the question of the schools catapulted the church directly into politics. The American Bible Society and similar groups were trying to force Protestant Bible reading in classes. Nativists dominated "nonsectarian" school boards and encouraged use of books in which Catholics were branded "papists." Hughes was instrumental in a Catholic campaign for construction of parochial schools, and Seward's message promised financial support from the state. In the end, Catholics did not get public money for their schools, but with the governor's help, they won an elected school board for New York City which ended nativist control of the public institutions.[6]

If Catholic leaders achieved some of their own goals in the New York school controversy, the cause of antialienism was advanced even more as new groups were projected into an active role. The educational conflict led to greater effort to recruit the middle class. Now nativist dogma could be tied to traditional concerns for school reform and the well-being of the young. Certainly there was a change in the tone of the Protestant press at this time. Not only did militant papers such as the *American Protestant Vindicator* moderate their language, but nativism moved into the mainstream of Protestant church life. Anti-Catholic resolutions appeared at the General Assembly of the Presbyterian church in 1841 and at various statewide general associations of the Congregational church. Soon Methodists, Episcopalians, and local branches of Baptist congregations were involved in an expanded inquiry into the question of Catholic villainy. By the mid-1840s, American churches presented a virtually united front against Rome, and the vanguard movements, such as the Protestant Reformation Society, could expect more help than ever before in spreading the anti-Catholic word. In 1842, sixty-one ministers of all sects met in Philadelphia to launch the American Protestant Association, which soon branched locally into many cities. The *American Protestant*, the organ of the new association, offered reprints of "The Secret Instructions of the Jesuits," as well as long stories of the corrupting influence of the confessional and worldwide surveys of popery in the nineteenth century. But the frantic accusations and ugly sadomasochistic tales that had filled older nativist publications were lacking. In exchange for a temporary rhetoric of moderation, the movement had fashioned a new appeal for "respectable" Americans.[7]

In focusing on the threat to educational and moral standards, nativists found friends and allies in the temperance crusade. Temperance, like nativism, had grown rapidly in the 1830s, and many ministers, including Lyman Beecher, who made their mark excoriating the papists, were notable in other circles for exposing the "immense evils of ardent spirits." By the early 1840s, the "ultraist" doctrine of total abstinence from all alcoholic beverages dominated the temperance societies, and heavy drinking by lowly Irish and Germans was used as a warning to those who sought acceptance as members of the middle class. Temperance proselytizers warned that the drinker is not only immoral and sinful in his vice but on the road to certain ruination. He will lose his industrious devotion to work, and then his reputation for reliability, and finally, not only his job but his status in the middle class. If, as some argue, temperance politics was status politics (triumphant in one state, at least, with the passage of the total prohibition act or Maine law in 1846), it also represented an effort to uplift a native population that feared comparison with the immigrants. Temperance and nativism made natural moral partners: foreigners were wasting themselves in drink, deluding themselves in choice of schooling, risking their souls by accepting the authority of sinister and manipulative priests who denied them access to the true Bible. The native American was asked to see in the immigrant a vision of dangers confronting himself and his nation. He must try to save America by damming the tide of immigration and forcing those wretched aliens already here to change the destructive ways that threatened everyone.[8]

★★★

The American Republican Party

This image of nativism as the engine of moderate reform took political shape in the creation of the American Republican party. It was the most important milestone in the 1840s on the road to the creation of the Know Nothing movement.

The party was started in 1841 in New Orleans. A state convention of Louisiana militants calling themselves Native Americans established an organization that spread to New York and Philadelphia, Boston and Newark, St. Louis and Charleston by late 1843. The New York group, energized by forces independent of the west-erners, adopted the name American Republican. A student of the movement notes that although it was started in New York by a group of butchers and marketmen, it soon attracted some of the city's professionals and editors. It appealed most strongly "to masters and journeymen in those trades in which the effects of metropolitan industrialization were slight." The goals of the new party were clearly stated in a series of state and national meetings: restriction of officeholding to native-born citizens, continuation of Bible reading in the public schools, extension of the waiting period for naturalization and citizenship from five to twenty-one years, reformation of political systems abused by corruption, and "usage of every means in our power to diminish foreign influences."[9]

These principles of the American Republican party, insisted its spokesmen, made it clear that this was no instrument of bigotry. It was only good sense to deny the franchise and elected office to those under control of foreign authorities. It was reasonable to fear "men of immoral character . . . ignorant of our laws and institutions." One newspaper published in the name of the new party proclaimed its devotion to liberty of press, speech, and conscience "bequeathed to us by our pilgrim and patriotic fathers." The nativists repeatedly pictured themselves as libertarians and their adversaries as the enemies of freedom: "Neither [of the old parties] can conceive it possible for a new [one] to be governed by pure motives, to introduce honesty and purity in politics."[10]

A case could be made that the American Republicans were political reformers, seeking to clean up corruption that blighted the urban civic landscape of the 1840s. In New York City, particularly, there was the sorry history of a Whig administration riddled by scandal until its defeat in 1843 by Democrats—dependent on the vote of foreign-born Catholics—who promised reform only to deliver their own brand of corruption. Respectable people who had turned to nativism in preceding years to defend their schools and their Bible noted that the new party's mayoral candidate in New York in 1844 was James Harper, successful publisher, philanthropist, and temperance advocate. Here was a fresh new force offering a program of moderate reconstruction of a tarnished system.[11]

Still, there was more than just reformers' zeal in attacks on foreigners and Catholics by the mid-1840s. American Republicans believed their nation in immediate peril from foreign influences, and it was clear that these men had a different world view than cultural pluralists such as Seward, who believed all newcomers were worthy of respect and brotherhood. The nativist as protector demanded more than moderate reform; the alien flood must be stopped. "Privileges" of the alien intruders must be proscribed.

Some objective evidence could be presented in defense of these views. In Washington in 1845, an investigation by the Senate Judiciary Committee, spurred to action by the new party, revealed election fraud, voting by noncitizens, fraudulent citizenship papers issued through political chicanery, machine control of courts and judges, and bloc voting by foreign paupers marched from almshouses to polling places. On election day, handbills had appeared in many eastern cities urging "Irishmen to Your Posts," "Irishmen and all Catholic Voters—In Union Is Our Strength." How could these legions of manipulated strangers, incapable of understanding democracy, bullishly insisting on their identification with alien Ireland, ever play a constructive role in the American community? The second national convention of American Republicans in Philadelphia asked: "How shall the institutions of this country be preserved from the blight of foreign influences insanely legalized through the conflicts of domestic parties?" It responded with the declaration: "America faces a crisis of national emergency. We hereby form ourselves into a national body dedicated to radical reform of abuses and to the preservation of our institutions and our liberties."[12]

The emphasis on "radical reform" was revealing. Those who believed they were protecting America from the alien menace subscribed to a fighting faith that could never be contained by the politics of moderate reform. One newspaper, describing Irish immigrants in Brooklyn, venomously observed that "when they arrive among us, too idle or vicious to clear and cultivate the land, [they] dump themselves in our large towns filling them with wretchedness, filth and diseases. What are they but mere marketable cattle." With so much hostility so close to the surface, it was not surprising that nativists would turn away from moderation and take their conflict out of the political arena and into the streets.[13]

As in the case of politics, the protectors insisted that foreigners were the cause of the trouble in the communities, and again there was some evidence to document their claims. Foreign railroad and canal laborers had rioted in Maryland in 1834 and again in 1839. In Florida and Indiana, Connecticut and Michigan, Irishmen were accused of attacking natives. In upstate New York, Protestants had been beaten by roving gangs of drunken foreigners. In Pennsylvania, a Lutheran church had been sacked. When election time came in the pivotal year of 1844, angry natives in the Williamsburgh section of Brooklyn promised elaborate parades to campaign meetings despite the threat of disruption: "If the Irish attempt to interfere, we'll eat them with salt and pepper." Militant immigrants were prepared to man their barricades, and nativists, furious at the spectacle of "enemy" control of whole sections of "American" cities, prepared to meet them there. In the escalating conflicts in the streets, moderation was washed aside.[14]

The scene of the great riots was Philadelphia, and this time the violence eclipsed anything known in the convent-burning excitement of the 1830s. Natives and Irishmen, Protestants and Catholics clashed in fistfights and knifefights. They exchanged gunfire. They menaced each other with cannons, ready to be loaded with stacks of shot, powder, nails, chains, "anything" as one observer put it, that could be used "to kill and maim the foe." In the ugly two-stage upheavals in May and July, some thirty people were killed, hundreds wounded, dozens of homes burned out.[15]

The school controversy, that perennial nativist issue, was the ostensible cause of it all. Bishop Francis Patrick Kenrick of Philadelphia, emulating the stand of Bishop Hughes in New York, protested the use of the St. James Bible for Catholic schoolchildren. Kenrick agreed that all students should have their daily Bible reading, but he insisted that different versions be available for Catholics. The American Protestant Association quickly grasped the issue. The organization's pamphleteers seemed justified in charging an "interference by foreign ecclesiastical power" when efforts were made in the Irish working-class district in Kensington to stop all Bible study. "The public school linked to the Protestant Bible must be saved from the minions of the Pope." Now the American Republican party entered the conflict, announcing a protest meeting in the Irish ward of the city. It was a deliberately provocative move, of course, but the party's local paper, the *Native American*, explained that no district of the city must be closed to the real citizenry: "Natives must be resolved to sustain [their] rights as Americans, firmly but moderately." Moderation never had a chance. An Irish mob routed the antialiens. When they regrouped a few days later, strengthened in resolve by the inflammatory words of speakers and editors, an even larger group of Irish laborers, supported this time by the Hibernia Hose Company, an Irish fire brigade, attacked with clubs, fists, and guns. At least one marcher in the American Republican procession of several thousand was killed. Now the nativists were outraged. It would be blood for blood. The *Native American* proclaimed, "American citizens have been shot down in the public street by foreign ruffians for exercising guarantees to them by the constitution. . . . These paupers, beggars and naked starvelings have in their hands deadly weapons. Another St. Bartholomew's day is begun on the streets of Philadelphia. We are now free to declare that no terms whatever are to be held with these people." A vast, organized mob of nativists appeared in the streets of Irish Kensington. The few fearful Protestants in the community lettered the words "Native American" on the doors of houses and shops, a vision of later riot practice. Despite the presence of militia, St. Augustine's Church and its library of five hundred Bibles in six languages—some ancient works dating from the third century—was burned to the ground.[16]

The natives had exacted the measure and more of their revenge. Dozens of priests and nuns had been terrorized; Irish refugees were seen fleeing with their belongings throughout the district. The church fire chilled further rioting in the days that followed and even nativist papers in other cities were silenced. But Philadelphia had not seen the end of its violent summer. Two months later brought Independence Day celebrations and on 4 July, seventy thousand mourners escorted the widows and orphans of "American" victims of the battles of May through the streets of the city. The following day an American Republican force battled the Irish once more, and, on the urging of a nativist crowd, the sheriff searched a Catholic church and uncovered a large cache of guns. Here was the perfect setting for more mob violence, and both sides were ready on Sunday. This time an Irish military company, the Hibernia Greens, was assembled and cannon fire was heard in the streets of what seemed now a war-torn city. "For weeks after," a Philadelphian later recalled, "a heavy gloom hung over the city. . . . It was still under martial law and the streets leading to the Catholic churches were being guarded by soldiers." Like Belfast or Beirut in another age, an American city had been literally torn apart by intergroup violence.[17]

The Philadelphia riots soon passed into nativist legend as a defensive response to the "Kensington Massacre," as one party pamphlet called it. "Native Americans were assaulted in the streets, the common method of the lower classes of Irishmen." It was "not a sudden outbreak, but the result of a settled, deliberate, premeditated conspiracy against American citizens." The grand jury investigating the causes of the disorder favored the American Republican side. The disturbances, it concluded, were "due to the efforts of a portion of the community to exclude the Bible from the public schools."[18]

Irish Catholics, naturally, insisted that the nativists were the aggressors. In New York, that powerful advocate of Catholic separatism and militancy, John Hughes, was quoted as saying, "If a single Catholic Church is burned [here] the city will become a second Moscow." Bishop Hughes chided Philadelphia Catholics for leaving their churches exposed and garrisoned his own buildings with more than a thousand armed men. Despite menacing words in the local *American Republican* about "the bloody hand of tyranny . . . the call for revenge," there was relative peace in New York City. Later writers would credit Hughes's defensive arrangements with helping to maintain an armed truce.[19]

Whoever caused the riot—and both sides obviously were ready and eager for a fight—the American Republican party was profoundly affected. By polarizing the country and reacquainting fellow-traveling nativists with the "mailed fist of Papism," the urban violence in one center helped to advertise the antialien cause everywhere. But the riots alarmed many who hoped for moderate political reform. The spectacle of gutted churches and beaten immigrants could not have been what they envisioned when enlisting in the struggle to save their Bible, school, and political system. In New York, voting studies of the party's performance in 1844 and after revealed a large majority of support among skilled workers and mechanics, men of lower-middle-class status who feared competition from Irish newcomers in job and housing markets, who particularly resented the foreign culture appearing in their midst. A Catholic paper sourly referred to them as "fire boys, market men and other irregulars." How many "sober, church-going citizens," one writer asked, now turned away from the party of lawlessness?[20]

In the end, the American Republican run of victories covered only a span of months and the party was dead within four years. In 1844, the signal success was in New York, where James Harper was elected mayor in the spring. He was a former Whig, however, and his promises of lighter taxes and civic reform as well as his pledge of bipartisan appointments to office earned him tacit support from local Whigs, who helped fashion a smashing victory by diverting most votes from their own nominal candidate. In the fall election, the two parties entered a more formal alliance, with Whigs promising to back nativists running for local office in return for American Republican endorsement of the Whig national ticket, headed once more by presidential aspirant Henry Clay. The plan made sense to the antialiens, who noted that Clay had been friendly to part of their program and that Theodore Frelinghuysen, his running mate, was an old friend of Bible associations and evangelical Protestantism. Still, the scheme miscarried. The new party won a slim victory in the minor races, but enough former Democrats in the nativist camp (and it was estimated that 40 percent of nativism's recruits were Democrats against 60 percent Whigs) defected to help give James K. Polk his narrow statewide margin. Polk won the electoral votes that made him president of the United States, denying the greatest prize to Clay still another time. Bitter Whigs such as Daniel Webster argued that the heavy Irish Democratic vote in the election made it "imperative . . . that the naturalization laws" be reformed, but Clay and others concluded that the Democrats had shrewdly used nativism to drive all Roman Catholic votes to them. Within a year, Whigs severed their ties with the American Republicans. William H. Seward, an old adversary, teamed with another antinativist, editor Horace Greeley, and effectively isolated the new party. Harper was soundly beaten in his reelection bid and the new political force was spent.[21]

At its convention in 1845, the American Republican party changed its name to Native American and boasted that it had 110,000 members, almost 50,000 in New York. But congressional and mayoral victories in Pennsylvania, Massachusetts, and New York the preceding year could not mask the decline in support. Six American Republicans had sat in the Twenty-ninth Congress, but only one would be elected to the Thirtieth in 1846. The 141 convention delegates, plied with reprints of Samuel F. B. Morse's conspiracy tracts and tired exposés of the "Pope's Foreign Jesuits," attended a political wake. The rise of new and pressing national issues—territorial expansion in the Northwest, talk of war with Mexico, the slave question and arguments over free soil, the gold strike in California—temporarily eclipsed the cause of nativism. In Washington, Congress refused to act on the Senate Judiciary Committee's report on election abuses. Other nativist proposals also died in both houses. Again, the immigrant and Catholic vote appeared too strong to challenge. The political setting for effective antialien activity had disappeared seemingly overnight. By 1847, the party was no more.[22]

Within half a decade, the American Republican party would be resurrected in the form of the much more formidable party that would bear the name "American." If social and economic problems were severe enough to recruit a constituency to the protectors' cause in 1844, the quantum jump in immigration from Catholic Europe would make the appeal of antialienism overwhelming by 1850. With the huge influx of Irish and German émigrés in the late 1840s and early 1850s, the forces that overshadowed nativist fears in preceding years would be obscured or redirected by a new movement. Massive immigration would make the next episode of nativism something more than a footnote in history.

CHAPTER 4

★ ★

A SWEEPING TIDE
OF IMMIGRATION

IN THE GRAY AUTUMN of 1847, a young Englishman representing the Society of Friends traveled through Ireland, reporting what he saw: "The town of Westport was in itself a strange and fearful sight, its streets crowded with gaunt wanderers sauntering to and fro with hopeless air and hunger-struck look—a mob of starved, almost naked, women around the poorhouse clamouring for soup tickets—our inn beset by a crowd of beggars for work." Later, on a second visit to a rural district, he described a scene rarely matched in the history of medieval plague:

One poor woman whose cabin I had visited said, "There will be nothing for us but to lie down and die." I tried to give her hope of English aid, but, alas! her prophecy had been too true. Out of a population of 240 I found thirteen already dead from want. The survivors were like walking skeletons—the men gaunt and haggard, stamped with the livid mark of hunger—the children crying with pain—the women in some of the cabins too weak to stand. When there before I had seen cows at almost every cabin . . . but now all the cows were gone—all the sheep—all the poultry killed . . . the very dogs which had barked at me before had disappeared; no oats—no potatoes.[1]

"No potatoes." In that simple statement buried in a somber report from Galway lay the central fact in an economic catastrophe. For so many in Ireland, Germany, and elsewhere, no potatoes meant famine, and famine brought with it unspeakable suffering. Some victims, recognizing the inevitable, stopped struggling and passively withdrew to their cottages, awaiting death in patient resignation. Others, in entire family groups, took to the road, shuffling from village to village, leaving the weakened young or helpless old to die by the wayside. Many escaped starvation only to yield to a form of typhus induced by undernourishment; these victims of "famine fever" were buried in unmarked pits. But many others fled, mortgaging everything against the chance of survival in a more fortunate country. Those who chanced the journey would be sailing with history.[2]

From the dawn of the colonial period, when the *Mayflower* and the *Susan Constant* brought the first European settlers across the Atlantic, America had been a land of immigrants. After independence, in a pattern tied to the cycle of boom and bust, the annual influx of foreigners grew slowly until by 1844 more than 75,000 sought entry. But in 1847, a spectacular increase in arrivals eclipsed all figures from the past. In that epic year, 234,000 newcomers reached the ports of entry. By 1851, the number approached 380,000, and immigration continued at this unprecedented rate through 1854. In an eight-year period, almost 2.75 million prospective new Americans disembarked. Most of them were practicing Roman Catholics. Many came from Germany in the period 1852–54 but even more from Ireland, in a swelling stream from 1847 through the early 1850s. More than one-quarter million emigrants sailed from Ireland for the United States in 1851 alone, and the survivors joined over a million of their countrymen and women already resettled. It was no nativist fantasy when spokesmen for emerging "American" parties cried out that a flood of new Catholic aliens was coming from hated Ireland and Germany. They fled from the exigencies of "no potatoes."[3]

★★★

The Potato and the Famine

In the thirty years of peace that followed the end of the Napoleonic Wars in Europe, the potato became indispensable to the Irishman. The wartime prosperity of earlier years became only a happy memory in a period of exploding population and fragile land tenure—often at exorbitant rents—but at least there was the beneficence of nature in the flourishing fields of the potato vine. Irish people did not regard oats, wheat, or barley as food—they were grown to pay the rent, and rent was the first necessity of life in

Ireland. In an estimated population of 9 million in 1845, at least 4 million relied on the "tuber," celebrated in popular culture: "On winter nights, when the storm is sweeping over the hills and the rain pattering furiously . . . how happy to sit in a circle all round a fire, to hear the pot boiling, to see the beautiful roots bursting their coats. Give me a winter night, a turf fire and a mealy potato!" A student of Irish immigration noted Irish indifference to bread and meat: "In amazement captains of emigrant vessels saw their passengers throw overboard the chocolate, cheese and plum pudding, ship's fare for special occasions, and down in steerage sick children cried constantly for potatoes." The root was not so central to the lives of Germans, but this cheap, space-saving, nutritious vegetable had made a revolution in the menus of poor agrarians after the end of the eighteenth century. Even as landholdings were torn apart in a period of "fragmentation"—acreages becoming smaller and smaller in an age of social change—the potato became "half the life of Germany, the foundation of peace and of people's well-being." Some even proposed to erect monuments to Francis Drake, who first introduced the crop on the Continent.[4]

From the start, the potato spelled peril. It could not be preserved from year to year; its bulk made transportation uneconomic and meant that even a local shortage could bring disaster. It was ruinous to the soil and, even when alternated with wheat, gradually wore out the land. But the potato was the staff of life for millions of poor farmers, families living in a state of postfeudal peasantry, when disaster struck in 1845. The potato murrain—the blight fungus—first appeared in Ireland when the crops around Dublin—those stored as well as those in the ground—suddenly perished. The blight spread with stunning swiftness. The crop was universally bad in 1846; the next year it died in July. That young visitor witnessed sheer catastrophe in Counties Mayo and Galway: "Some of the women and children that we saw on the road were abject cases of poverty and almost naked. The few rags they had on were with greatest difficulty held together, in a few weeks they must become absolutely naked . . . as we went along, our wonder was not that the people died, but that they lived." In the black winter of that first year of rot and want, men and women who could not feed their children, who could not imagine surviving the bleak days that lay ahead, had to consider leaving the "old sod" that had regulated the rhythm of their family's lives for centuries. So began the only migratory movement in modern history to lead to a significant and permanent decline in a nation's population. In the eight years from 1846 to 1854, 1.75 million people fled Ireland and the total population was permanently shriveled—by 1901 it still hovered at just over 4 million.[5]

In July and August 1846, the devouring blight led to heavy autumn emigration for the first time in Irish history. By winter the exodus became a mad rush. Papers were filled with stories of those who had not planned to go but who were now on their way—to Britain and Australia, but mostly to the new world of Canada and the United States, the ultimate destination of three-quarters of the émigrés. In some dioceses that winter, more than 15 percent of the Catholic population left for North America. Some Galway villages lost a third of their population in a matter of weeks. And still there was no relief. The 1848 crop was a total debacle and the prospects the next year were hardly better. Country roads were swarming with crowds of migrants who had sold scraps of furniture, retrieved the few coins hidden away in cottage thatches, begged or borrowed passage money. In some cases landlords allowed tenants to fall arrears in rent payments and so assisted the emigrants; many landlords viewed emigration as a cheap way of clearing the land and ridding the country of "crime and distress." In other cases more fortunate neighbors loaned carts to transport belongings from home to sea. The exodus peaked in 1851 in Ireland, not until three years later in Germany, when improving weather, reviving crops, and decreased numbers of mouths to feed made survival possible for those who remained.[6]

Of course, there were other precipitants for the great migration. In Ireland, repeal of the Corn Laws, the goal of free traders and workers hoping for cheaper food prices, induced many landlords to take their holdings out of wheat. This had been the rent-paying crop, but it was noncompetitive without government protection. Now the money was put into cattle. Clearing the land for grazing meant the displacement of hundreds of thousands of cottiers with their tiny plots. Many died in the famine, others starved in the poorhouses, and a host of them joined the flight of 1847. The new Irish poor law passed that same year added to the exodus: small holders leasing a quarter of an acre or more could no longer receive assistance, and many who refused to relinquish their little plots in return for survival and servitude left families in the workhouse and headed for embarkation ports. Again some landlords assisted the émigrés; they were responsible for maintaining the workhouses, and it was cheaper to ship the paupers out. The penniless victims hoped to bring the others across the Atlantic when enough money was saved to send home. In Germany, crop failure was compounded by political upheaval, which sent thousands of failed revolutionaries in search of a more liberal environment. Vastly outnumbering these political refugees were the confused victims of social and economic disorder. There were peasants fearfully in debt to new land banks, an unhappy consequence of "reform" that freed agrarians from traditional donations of part of their harvest to church or landlord. The anxieties of city workers and artisans were made worse by the disruption of trade and business in postrevolutionary times. Famine and fear of famine started the immigrant masses on their way, but even when the agricultural crisis began to recede, other factors sustained the outward flow of those who would be Americans.[7]

★★★

The Flight to America

But why was the United States—to which so many who first arrived in Canada were soon bound on rickety coastal vessels—the goal of so many? Here, after all, was the country that had symbolized hope for displaced Europeans from the first days of white settlement. To the fugitives of the Irish famine it was the promised land. It was no paradox that even the relief shipments of corn and wheat clogging the harbor at Cork in the first season of trouble stimulated emigration. The mixed fleet carrying the surplus from American fields was on a mission of mercy, but it demonstrated to many of the hungry the abundance from which this surplus was skimmed. Contemporary developments made the United States seem more full of promise than ever before: the California gold strike and the Mexican War were proof that worldly riches and territorial estates awaited anyone with the courage to make the journey across the great ocean. The lure of a land of milk and honey had been pictured for years in newspaper stories and guidebooks, in the work of business agents, and in the language of handbills from companies building railroads (earlier, it had been canals). In Germany, emigration, seen as the cure for all ills, private and public, became the craze of the Rhineland. The more Irishmen and Germans who came, the more were enticed to come. Letters back home called relatives away from the bankrupt lands; an anonymous Irish poet wrote in 1851, "Come let us fly to freedom's sky." Some European writers did warn countrymen of the "unhealthy climate" and "what it means to be an alien in a far distant land." They suggested that those with "a weak constitution" or "childless with somewhat advanced age" not make the trip. But all agreed that material prosperity was possible as it was nowhere else. A man could make money in America. Fifty cents or a dollar could be made in a day in the mills or construction camps, where unskilled labor was in demand. The long and hard days were seen by newcomers not as evidence of early capitalist exploitation but as a striking improvement upon cultivating a dead crop for hated, absentee landlords, of struggling against a system that had offered no hope of improvement for generations.[8]

Still it is remarkable that so many came, for rarely in history had there been a more perilous voyage awaiting those freely electing to take it. The conditions in the emigrants' steerage spaces aboard the sailing ships of the mid-nineteenth century could hardly have been worse. Hundreds lay together motionless, like sacks, in lightless, almost airless holds, many with fever and some without food or provisions. The water was rationed, the "berths" almost nonexistent—a typical ship had 36 for every 260 passengers. An engineering officer in Quebec said that conditions aboard his vessel "fully realized the worst state of a slaver." Emigrants were "classed with barrels of pork and bales of cotton"; they were used as ballast, a convenient form of freight. The Liverpool passenger brokers had flooded Ireland with misleading handbills describing the trip and had split their profits with transfer agents and landing houses awaiting the survivors. Only in 1855 was a law passed (riddled with loopholes even then) aimed at improving accommodations in steerage. It was too late to save those who perished in the migration of the mid-nineteenth century.[9]

Dr. John H. Griscom, a member of a committee of the New York Academy of Medicine and later superintendent of the Board of Commissioners of Emigration of New York, visited the ship *Ceylon* when it arrived in port with a large cargo of passengers in 1847:

A considerable number had died upon the voyage, and one hundred and fifteen were then ill with the fever. . . . Before any had yet left the ship we passed through the steerage, making a more or less minute examination of the place and its occupants; but the indescribable filth, the emaciated, half-nude figures, many with petechial eruptions disfiguring their faces, crouching in the bunks, or strewed over the decks, and cumbering the gangways; broken utensils and debris of food spread recklessly about, presented a picture of which neither pen nor pencil can convey a full idea. Some were just rising from their berths for the first time since leaving Liverpool, having been suffered to lie there all the voyage, wallowing in their own filth. It was no wonder to us that, with such total neglect of sanitary supervision, and an entire absence of ventilation, so many of such wretched beings had perished or were then ill; it was only surprising that so many had escaped.[10]

Many did not escape. The mortality rate was appalling. "Ship fever" (like "famine fever," a form of typhus bred by undernourishment), smallpox, cholera, and dysentery took their toll. The *Lark* set out with 440 passengers, of whom 108 died on the passage and 150 were sick, almost all of whom died a short time after landing. The *Virginius* sailed with 496 but 158 died on the passage, 186 were sick, and the remainder landed "feeble and tottering." In 1847, of the 89,738 embarking for St. Lawrence ports, 5,293 died en route and more than 10,000 more aboard ships lying in quarantine or in the desolate shore stations at Grosse Island, Quebec, where there was no shelter or food, and stone and wooden benches received the dead and dying. In Montreal, a mass grave was dug for six thousand migrants—escaping, said the inscription, "to a new life in a new land."[11]

Conditions were better on some ships than others. Those from Bremen and Hamburg were cleaner and healthier, and German port regulations compelled distribution of cooked provisions to emigrants. Those from Liverpool bound for New York were worst of all—crowded to excess, often little more than floating fever wards. Those who survived the eight- to ten-week voyage lived through boredom and terror. The monotony of days-long periods in which the ship was calmed might be broken by awesome storms, and peasant farmers heard sounds never before imagined: howling winds in the rigging, crashing waves, sailors shouting orders. Relatively few ships foundered, but how many aboard could be certain they would arrive safely? Poor and unlettered people who already had endured so much in the famine winters, in efforts to leave the homeland and arrange passage at portside, arrived at last as something less than bright new seekers after the American dream.[12]

The initial response of the Americans was, understandably, fear that the diseases the immigrants carried would ravage port cities and spread across the country. People fled Toronto and Kingston when the epidemic ships arrived. Boston needed receiving rooms for invalids at dockside and transport from ship to hospitals. There were outbreaks of typhus in Philadelphia and Baltimore. Soon river towns, including Albany, refused to allow immigrants to leave steamers. In New England cities, hysteria followed an epidemic that hit Boston, and the Massachusetts legislature temporarily prohibited immigrant landings in 1847. Ship fever and cholera were found in epidemic proportions in all places of disembarkation. The port of New York, which handled one-half of the Irish émigrés, set up emergency facilities on Staten Island and threw together a new quarantine hospital financed by a tax on inbound ships.[13]

But in many cases medical facilities were a grim joke, particularly before the establishment of the Board of Commissioners of Emigration. A New York City alderman told a state legislative committee:

> In a two-story dwelling house at Bloomingdale, 46 by 40 feet, the proprietors admitted that 120 patients had been crowded in this miscalled hospital. So odious did these places become that hundreds of sick and destitute quitted them in terror and disgust, and attempted to obtain admittance in the alms house, or the hospital at Bellevue, frequently representing themselves as citizens or pretending that they had been in the country for a period that rendered the municipal authorities responsible for their support.[14]

The pathetic efforts of these sick and lonely newcomers were seen in a very different light by many natives. The immigrants were guilty of deception and fraud, a malevolent effort to pass themselves off as Americans when hardly off the boat. Who had brought these dread diseases to the New World but immigrants themselves, the fevered human refuse of a ruined Europe? But the very death and sickness they brought from steerage called to mind a threat more sinister than disease. From the moment they touched the promised land, the enfeebled new immigrant masses were living proof of America's need for protection.

For the many survivors who did not need hospitalization, exploiters were waiting at dockside. "It is not uncommon," said a health officer in New York, "after the vessel is cleared from Quarantine, for eight or ten boat-loads of runners to surround it; they are desperate men, and can be kept off only by an armed force." Employed by boardinghouse keepers or forwarding establishments, these notorious "runners"—often bringing along muscular guards to fight off opponents—bullied bewildered emigrants. Through cajolery, intimidation, or lies, the runners brought their prey to the boardinghouses, where they were often charged three or four times the contract price. Some operators of these vulturous welcoming committees became wealthy men, and a majority of them were fellow "aliens." "Your Committee have been shocked to find that a large portion of the frauds committed upon these innocent and ignorant foreigners are committed by their own countrymen," reported a select committee of the New York State legislature. "We find the German preying upon the German, the Irish upon the Irish." Welcome to America.[15]

Beyond the doors of the boardinghouses lay the beginnings of a new life, and for most of the Irish arrivals that meant urban life. At first glance this choice appeared paradoxical. Why would men who had struggled desperately to farm tiny plots rented by families for generations in Ireland not take advantage of the vast acreage available in the American West? It was clear that these peasants barely removed from postfeudal culture came without urban skills. Surely they were warned not to stay in "the crowded cities of the seaboard, reeking with vice and crime," as one spokesman put it. Papers, politicians, and priests back home had told them of the dangers of the city. Emigrant aid societies produced booklets encouraging all newcomers to go inland to good farming country. "Instead of being a despised drudge, his children reared among evil influences," an Irish-American newspaper urged, why doesn't the immigrant "proceed directly westward to the broad green lands that lie there, clothed in flowers and sunshine. In a few years he would possess a pleasant country home and be what he never can be in the back alleys of the city ... an independent man." Another writer exclaimed: "Westward Ho! The great mistake that Irish emigrants make is that they remain in New York and other Atlantic cities till they are ruined, instead of proceeding at once to the Western country, where a virgin soil, teeming with plenty, invites them to its bosom." It was an enticing prospect. But the Irish did not go west. Eighty percent of the newcomers were of rural origins, but less than 10 percent resettled on the land. By the early 1860s, there were half a million Irish-Americans in thirteen key cities—more than two hundred thousand in New York, one hundred thousand in Philadelphia, fifty thousand in Boston.[16]

This was no paradox. Unlike many German émigrés, the new Irish settlers had neither the capital nor the training to manage the large-scale prairie farms of the American interior. In a sense, these men scarcely belonged to the "agricultural class." Often their experience had been confined to the primitive tending of potatoes and root crops on tiny plots. They had been locked into an ancient system of land tenure offering few rewards for initiative and no way of learning skills necessary to handle cash-crop enterprises of one hundred acres or more, the typical western farm. Tied to the soil that fed them at home, they were unequipped to become agricultural businessmen, even if they could find the money for seeds and plows, for equipment and subsistence through the difficult first year. A correspondent of *United Ireland* would write later of his astonishment at the "number of young Irishmen who cannot plough."[17]

Agriculture was never a viable option. The immigrants arrived penniless or misspent their meager savings; they were bilked by the vicious runners and boardinghouse owners if they had any money left. If they attempted to head inland, they would soon be gouged again—this time by forwarding houses that sold deck passage on steamboats at exorbitant rates to greenhorns or passenger agents with scales balanced to give false weight readings. Most stayed in the port cities, where they could find employment, opportunity, and community. In mills, factories, or—as in the refrain from the famous ballad—"to work upon the railway," there were places for unskilled labor at wages five times higher than in Ireland. Wives could also find work in expanding urban centers, where domestic help was often in demand. The remarkably youthful immigrants (over 60 percent were between the ages of fifteen and thirty-five in the 1850s) would discover both greater stimulation and security in the city. It offered a dramatic change from the slow-paced life of the old country and yet was a place where friends and family, church and neighborhood soon offered a measure of warmth in a strange environment.[18]

Many more affluent German newcomers did head for the farmlands of the Northwest, arriving at New Orleans and then sailing up the Mississippi. Others settled in the cities of what would be mid-America, permanently changing the character of Cincinnati, St. Louis, and Milwaukee. But the Irish concentrated in the urban coastal belt from Maine to Maryland and in the cities of upstate New York, Pennsylvania, and—for a few—the Great Lakes. They often took cheap lumber boats to Canada before completing the voyage in New York harbor or New England. Some even found their way to New Orleans on cotton carriers deadheading back to the South after making deliveries to British mills. Whether digging canals or working on wharves, swinging spades on railroad sites or laboring in mill towns in Massachusetts, they made their mark by their sheer numbers. By 1850, the Irish population almost equaled the native-born in Boston; by 1855 they exceeded the natives by ten thousand. In the 1850s, one citizen of Ireland went to the United States for every five who remained behind, and this demographic revolution wrought historic changes in American cities.[19]

As more and more newcomers crowded into the small, ugly industrial towns of the midcentury, they caused serious problems of sewage disposal, road construction, street lighting, and water provision. And they faced terrible living conditions, tolerable if at all only by comparison to the squalor and starvation they had left at home. Rents were exorbitant in the overcrowded Irish wards of New York and Boston, where builders squeezed tenements at every conceivable angle to maximize profits during an enormous real estate boom, a triumph of capitalist shrewdness amid a sea of human misery. In alleys and hillsides the wretched houses went up, and so did the rents. In Boston, underground "dwellings" were carved in cellars—cool in summer, warm in winter, but without plumbing and awash in two feet of water, with little space and less air. Despite pleas that "such holes be outlawed," their number multiplied and without them not all the Irish arrivals could have found any housing. In the late 1840s, a committee of the New York City Board of Aldermen found unbelievable living accommodations; in one room fifty feet square, one hundred sick and dying immigrants lay on straw amid dead bodies. It was clear that these were some of the first slum dwellers in American urban history. They were thrown together in the "Irish Channel" of New Orleans, in Half Moon Place in Boston and similar districts, finding among fellow residents companionship but no relief from hunger and sickness. They got little help from established, wealthier countrymen; the Irish Union Immigration Society, which tried to provide some relief, did not represent this older and richer group. They found out early, in contacts with the boardinghouse hustlers, that benevolence was not linked to Irish nationality in this tough, unsentimental culture.[20]

★★★

The Newcomers and Social Disorder

Many native Americans, feeling crowded by almost four hundred thousand Irish and two hundred thousand Germans landing in urban centers, reacted as they did to the plague ships, not with pity or concern but with shock and anger. Slums and pauperism, drunkenness and illiteracy, crime and illness were facts of immigrant life. And nativists who saw an ignorant, diseased, disordered mob growing in the ethnic slums saw them as destructive forces let loose in the land. Of course, they engaged in categorical national character assassination: the Irish were permanently debased, a population beyond assimilation. Still, many nativists could not simply be dismissed as operating in a "paranoid style" or employing a "politics of unreason." For objective conditions gave confirmation to their worst suspicions.[21]

Aliens contributed most heavily to the cost of welfare and to the toll of lawbreaking. "Immigrant" and "pauper" were inextricably linked together in the public mind. The 1850 census revealed that over 50 percent of the destitute were foreigners, yet foreigners represented only some 10 percent of the total population. Sick from the voyage, susceptible to local economic recessions, accustomed to some paltry public aid at home, newcomers inflated the rolls at almshouses in eastern cities. An angry report, *Foreign Criminals and Paupers*, from the Foreign Affairs Committee of the House of Representatives in 1856 charged that "the disproportion of the foreign born on the public charge is on the increase." According to the report of the New York Board of Commissioners of Emigration for 1852, the number of immigrants arriving at New York was 300,992, and the number supported or "pecuniarly assisted" by the commission was 141,992. The census returns for two years earlier were less dramatic but still revealed the severity of a deepening problem: almost $3 million spent in the public sector on aid to the poor, more than one-half the recipients immigrants. In New York and Massachusetts the burdens were heaviest: in the Empire State there were over 40,000 foreign-born paupers to less than 19,000 natives, and the cost of their support approached $1 million; in Massachusetts there was 1 pauper for 317 natives, 1 for 32 foreigners. There was talk of statewide bankruptcy and incessant appraisals of immigrant "national character." A student of nineteenth-century asylums would write of contemporary attitudes, "If one could not earn his daily bread in a land as prosperous as the United States, then the individual himself was primarily at fault." As state officials asked in 1857: "Why has Massachusetts so many paupers? Because we have a larger proportion of foreigners from which they are made." Other state agencies reported: "Our almshouse paupers are nearly all foreigners. . . . Aliens and their children embrace five-sixths of all who become chargeable . . . the greater proportion are lazy, ignorant, prejudiced, unreasonable, receiving charity of the State as a right rather than a favor, most difficult to deal with."[22]

Crime statistics were equally dismal. Of 27,000 arrested for criminal offenses in 1850, one-half were foreign-born. In the state of New York, an astounding 55 percent of those arrested were Irish, 10 percent German, and 23 percent natives of all ancestry. The U.S. Senate was told of a policy "which prevails amongst several of the States of continental Europe in which convicted and unconvicted criminals and paupers are transported to the United States at the expense and by the direction of their Governments." Although little evidence was presented to substantiate this charge, the appended catalog of criminal convictions added to an unhappy picture of immigrant disorder: in Maine, 460 foreigners to 284 natives; in Massachusetts, 3,884 foreigners to 3,366 natives; in New York, 6,317 to only 3,922 native-born. "Juvenile vagrancy" was another growing evil connected to the vast influx of newcomers, and congressional investigators noted that "an examination of the records of our juvenile delinquent institutions shows but too

plainly from whence this painful increase comes." In the Massachusetts Reform School as early as 1849, one-half the inmates were
"of Irish parentage"; in the New York House of Refuge in 1850, 163
of 278 newly admitted young men were Irish. By 1855, 42 percent of
residents in the Philadelphia refuge had parents born in Ireland and
only one-third came from native American families. In Cincinnati,
less than half the refuge residents were native-born; Irish and Germans accounted for the rest. Frequent drunkenness added to the
Irish reputation for criminality. In Boston, the number of liquor
dealers increased by half to twelve hundred between 1846 and 1849,
most of them concentrated in immigrant districts. Many Irish families sold gin as a sideline, and the number of arrests and short jail
terms for intoxication skyrocketed. As crime rates escalated, the
Irish press complained bitterly of police brutality.[23]

By the early 1850s, state penal institutions were well aware of the
problem of the immigrant. At the beginning of the decade, foreign-
born confined to the Clinton, Auburn, and Sing Sing penitentiaries
in New York accounted for 32 percent of the inmate population;
by 1860 they were 44 percent of the total and native New Yorkers
were a minority. In the Charlestown, Massachusetts, prison, aliens
would make up 40 percent of inmates by 1859. The huge, poverty-
stricken immigrant population dashed the dreams of reformers, for
now neither the penitentiary nor the asylum could be mechanisms
for uplifting the fallen through incarceration in a homogeneous and
insular atmosphere. They would be merely an instrument for criminal punishment or a place to confine the deviant and dangerous.
And it was expensive to house the deviant. By 1851, over 40 percent of the patients at the Worcester (Massachusetts) State Lunatic
Hospital were foreign-born, and because most newcomers had no
legal residence, the state assumed the cost of confinement without
charge to family or town. This was not the case with other inmates.
The Massachusetts Commission on Lunacy sourly observed that
the state "offers a bounty to the foreign population and families for
sending their lunatics to its hospitals, levies a tax upon the native
population for doing the same." The commission noted that 36 percent of "American lunatics" were sent to Worcester within three
months of "supposed attacks," 70 percent of foreigners were sent
within the same period; 43 percent of natives were not sent until
the disease "had been established a year or more," only 11 percent
of the aliens were kept away as long.[24]

"Insanity" was, in fact, seen as another sinister part of the alienization of America. The trustees of the State Lunatic Hospital in Massachusetts complained that "the increase of foreigners is an evil the more to be regretted because there is reason to fear . . . an increase of incurables. Mostly Irish, their misery, their ignorance and their jealousy stand in the way of their improvement." A contemporary physician pointed to the "want of forethought in them to save their earnings," the "indulgence of their appetites for stimulating drinks," and their "strong love for their native land" as inhibiting treatment. "It is difficult to obtain their confidence. They seem jealous of our motives. They do not comprehend our language. . . . It is another obstacle in the way of their recovery." The *Report on Insanity and Idiocy in Massachusetts* charted a rising number of "foreign lunatics." The state asylum at New York City was filled with foreigners, and there were large percentages of immigrants in state institutions in Ohio and Pennsylvania.[25]

Physical illness paralleled aliens' "mental illness." The attending physician at the New York Dispensary, in a report on "destitute foreigners" in 1852, noted that of the per annum average of 40,000 patients, about one-third were emigrants in the country less than four years. Of the total, 28,875 were of Irish nativity. The Boston Committee on Internal Health, alarmed at the rise in reported cases of Asiatic cholera, discovered that of 262 patients in the Cholera Hospital in 1849, 218 were foreigners, mostly Irish. Congress was told that in Cincinnati in 1854, of 520 new admissions to the city hospital, 449 were foreigners. The reporting committee emphasized that "these are stubborn, undeniable facts, showing that a great and rapidly increasing public evil exists in our commercial cities."[26]

Where would it all end? In the early years of the migration, the Massachusetts Sanitary Commission made the following bleak statement, one echoed in many other circles:

> The stream of emigration has continued to increase, and seems to gain a new accession of strength in every passing year. Massachusetts seems to have resolved itself into a vast public charitable association . . . the doors of [her] great institutions have been thrown wide open . . . costing thousands upon thousands of dollars; the managers of the pauper-houses of the old world and the mercenary ship-owners who ply their craft across the Atlantic pour their freight freely in. Each smiles at

the open-handed but lax system of generosity which governs us. . . . And yet a greater calamity attends this monstrous evil. . . . Our own native inhabitants, who mingle with these recipients of their bounty, often become themselves contaminated with diseases, and sicken and die; and the physical and moral power of the living is depreciated, and the healthy, social and moral character we once enjoyed is liable to be forever lost. Pauperism, crime, disease and death stare us in the face.[27]

Could the newcomers overcome their disabilities and their vices, cure their own afflictions before they spread to the native population? Critics pointed out that the illiteracy rate was three times higher for the foreign-born, particularly high in Irish communities, with almost 30 percent of the largely Irish population illiterate in Massachusetts, only 7 percent in heavily German Wisconsin. Intemperance had become such a severe problem that even Catholic writer and champion Orestes Brownson despaired of Irish urbanites and "their habit of exposing, instead of concealing, their vices." If literacy and liquor set limits on the adults, what improvement could be expected in the next generation? The city marshal of Boston estimated that of all truant and vagabond children between ages six and sixteen "who, from neglect and bad habits, were unfit to enter the public schools," over 90 percent were foreigners in 1849. Compounding these problems was the staggering immigrant "population explosion." In 1850 the native birth rate in Boston was one for every forty living, but in Irish wards it was one for every nineteen and for Germans (a particularly youthful group) even larger.[28]

The aliens were creating a bewildering variety of serious and costly social problems. This, at least, was a measurable fact. But many natives insisted that their political behavior was another sign of "un-American depravity." The overwhelming majority of Irish-born naturalized citizens were Democratic. Historically attracted to the party because of its identification with the Jeffersonian opposition to Federalism and its support of the hated British, the Irish responded as well to the charismatic appeal of Jackson and his Democracy, symbol of equal opportunity for all Americans regardless of class or ethnic affiliation. But Anglophobia and egalitarianism were not the only factors at work. Where Democratic machines were building in expanding urban centers, Irish politicians had made a real impact. As in New York City's Tammany Hall, largely

Irish by the 1820s, the party signified "green power"—a road to opportunity and influence for sons of Eire.[29]

Some natives saw this political affiliation as a sinister development. Thousands of ignorant and unlettered newcomers were being used as tools of venal politicos; they were a bloc-voting mob whose influence must be checked. As early as March 1847, one eastern paper shouted, "1,124 Democrats just imported! England and other European powers are landing the refuse of their populations in hordes upon our shores." With the parties so nearly equal in votes, in only a few months "the foreigners will have enough votes to decide the Presidential election." Reformers complained that the Irish seemed emotionally dead to the major crusades of the day and accused them of being reactionary on abolitionism, women's rights, temperance, and free soil. They were seen as obstructing progress because of their own problems: victims of drunkenness, they would not battle intemperance; fearful of social and economic competition from Negroes, they were implacably opposed to changes in the condition of the blacks.[30]

But the most destructive dimension of "alien" political activity, critics feared, was its clannish character. Foreigners seemed to bring the conflicts of corrupt Europe into the national arena. The Irish Repeal Association, the American League for the Redemption of Ireland, the United Friends of Ireland, and the Young America movement all were cited as examples of the immigrant's inability to free himself from past allegiances. There was even an aggressive faction in the Democratic party advocating American rivalry with Great Britain, perhaps another manifestation of the unhealthy, un-American identification with foreign struggles.[31]

The clannishness of the newcomers was in part foisted upon them. Native hostility increased feelings of loneliness and intensified the search for community by those uprooted so suddenly and with such trauma from the Old World. Unequipped to connect to many traditional American institutions, innocent of many forms of social communication binding one group to another, the immigrants looked to each other to keep alive the memory of home. Still, Irish nationalist organizations in the United States represented something more than the communal longings of strangers. A spokesman enlisting support for the Irish Emigrant Aid Society in the struggle against Great Britain announced:

The time has at length arrived for action. Every steamer that crosses the Atlantic to our shores brings intelligence of fresh disasters, distress and difficulty to our old inveterate foe. Let us therefore unite in a bond of brotherhood to aid the cause of Liberty for Ireland. The moment is propitious—the means are in our hands. Let us use them—with . . . the determination of men whose birthright is a heritage of vengeance of seven centuries of wrong, of massacre, of spoilation, of rapine, of tyranny, deceit and treachery. . . . Remember Limerick! Remember Skill and Skibberreen! And oh! remember the long, bitter years of exile and think of that beautiful land, the home of your childhood and your affections; where repose the ashes of your fathers and the martyrs of your race. . . . It is for her exiled children to say, shall this cease and Ireland shall be free or shall the tyrant boast a perpetual tenant right of the country. . . . We ask you to form in each city and town in the United States a branch of the Irish Emigrant Aid Society; assemble in each locality at once . . . go to work . . . and when the Supreme Directory is elected there will be unity of action . . . and when the moment of action comes, our leaders will not be working in darkness.[32]

Chauvinistic and aggressive, the new urban immigrants struggled against a sea of woes and produced a host of problems in the nation they had sacrificed so much to reach. Here was a true American tragedy in the early years of the 1850s—millions of newcomers who suffered deeply while making major contributions to the growth of their adopted land and millions of natives whose fear and anger were rooted in the reality of social statistics.

Many immigrants were damned before they arrived in America, where historic anti-Catholic sentiment and recent experience in intergroup violence predisposed the nativist against the alien. The social disorder surrounding the immigrants seemed to justify a renewed drive to contain and proscribe them. But economic concerns were another factor. The standard fear of many who confront a new population is that they will take away jobs and a chance at prosperity. In cities and towns throughout the East and into the West in the 1850s there were complaints that cheap labor was flooding the market and displacing native workers, that aliens destroyed the apprenticeship system by ignoring the division of labor between journeyman and master. Even as the famine was striking Ireland and the great migration was beginning, a Pennsylvania congressman called for a protective tariff for American labor or an industry tax on immigrant workers. In fact, foreigners often did not displace the native-born. In a burgeoning economy they augmented the labor supply and helped to stimulate industrial expansion and demand. The Irish in Boston and New York, in Philadelphia and New Orleans hardly captured the desirable jobs: as ditchdiggers, stablers, draymen, they took the worst-paying work and helped raise the relative social and economic status of many natives. "None need apply but Americans" was a slogan protecting many better positions, reminding the newcomers once more that they were hated interlopers. But despite the immigrants' contribution to industrialization, enough natives feared displacement to give great weight to this economic argument against the "aliens."[33]

The wave of immigration lasted eight years. After 1851, Irish emigration declined; after 1854, German numbers decreased. Those who opposed the process at first seemed caught in an ideological trap. In the past, they took pride in their own immigrant heritage and the historic role of the United States as a magnet for earlier European migrations. Now they must distinguish between their forefathers, who "came to seek a home, [who] felled the forest, who turned up the virgin soil," and the new "vicious and idle aliens" crowding into the cities. But there was more than enough evidence to support claims that foreigners were disruptive to a peaceable social order. The starving victims of the potato famine were filling the almshouses and the asylums, the prisons and the hospitals. The fantasies of yesterday's bigots had become the real problems of everyday life. For those already armed against the alien danger by the struggles of earlier years, the whole complex of concerns and anxieties now called forth a massive literature of nativism. Here was the explanation for a new political movement, an American party suddenly achieving prominence in many parts of the nation, the most powerful expression of antialienism in American history. The image of the intruder in the work of the nativist writers would become the major recruiting device for the new movement, a key to understanding the growth and development of the Know Nothing phenomenon.[34]

★ ★

CHAPTER 5

THE IMAGE OF
THE INTRUDERS

IN BOSTON IN 1854, several Protestant ministers published a "gift book for natives" called *Our Country or the American Parlor Keepsake*. In it, the Reverend E. H. Chapin described how God made a special gift of America, how "we had a new broad field, clear of all feudal rubbish in which to create a new world."[1]

The image of an Edenic America in which people had an opportunity for the first time to realize their dreams and ambitions, to exercise their best talents, to fulfill themselves became the staple of nativist prose. To Thomas R. Whitney, this was a country "removed by sudden and violent steps from the serf-like conditions of others," a land providing "early entrance into the school of self-reliance." To Alfred B. Ely, in *American Liberty: Its Sources, Its Dangers and the Means of Its Preservation*, this was a nation where "children learned that men were regarded according to the measure of their true worth and that birth and rank and wealth conferred no lasting benefit ... to every aspirant, high or low, rich or poor alike the paths of influence and honor" were ever open. In *A Voice to America* Frederick Saunders and T. B. Thorpe told the story of "young and vigorous America, a field for fair trial of this great experience of man."[2]

The strident voices of nativism's politicians often obscured the idealistic passion of its theoreticians. In an age when many men unblushingly proclaimed their love of country, these writers shared a deep belief in the uniqueness and superiority of their homeland. The patriotic call to defend this charmed and innocent culture required protecting the ideals and values that gave a person's life meaning and purpose.

These nativists looked on America as a threatened paradise. But the struggle in which they had enlisted would decide more than the fate of a nation. It would determine whether true freedom could be preserved anywhere. The Saunders-Thorpe volume was subtitled *The Model Republic, Its Glory or Its Fall,* and the authors wrote of "America as a battlefield," the scene of a "contest waged between the armies of Freedom and Tyranny." "An American," (pseudonym of Frederick R. Anspach) declared in *The Sons of the Sires* that "the great conflict of those everlasting principles now reigning over the earth must unquestionably be decided here. . . . Behold the magnificence of this land in all its features. In this land will the fate of humanity be determined."[3]

The vision of the "redeemer nation" caught in an apocalyptic struggle gave added drama to nativist thought and writing. The millennial role of "true Americans" would be as protectors of the promised land in the climactic battle against alien, destructive forces. It was a battle to preserve the cherished past and to secure the future of the United States. It was a battle on which "the fate of humanity would turn." Who could doubt that the time of crisis had come, for the immigrant masses were now pouring out of steerage. These new aliens were seen as vermin in the garden. One nativist writer reviled the "ignorant and depraved foreigners. . . . Their very coming and mingling with us diminishes the purity and intelligence and piety we had before. Our moral power is weakened, our moral sense blunted, our moral compactness divided and distracted by this foreign influence."[4]

The image of life forces diluted and diseased by contact with the intruders revealed a telling insecurity. How confident were these men in the power of their idealized country or in themselves as its protectors? Where was the tradition of resilience and absorbing strength that their florid rhetoric celebrated at other times? In the very metaphor of infection, the nativists uncovered their fears that "America" was but a fragile essence. Like latter-day "defenders" who saw other alien dangers in communism, they attributed enormous influence to the enemy. Their angry words betrayed the desperation of those who half fear the battle is already lost. Everywhere there was crisis, and J. Wayne Laurens subtitled his book by that name *The Enemies of America Unmasked*: "Foreign influences are making this country a receptacle for the hopelessly bad and disaffected population of Europe."[5]

★★★

The American Way of Life Imperiled

But the dimensions of the social problems imported with the immigrants gave the nativists of 1850 a stronger claim on the attention of countrymen than any antialiens before or since. Underscoring the millenarian tone of conflict between forces of good and evil was the discovery of the repugnant lower-class culture of the newcomers. Their burgeoning crime rates and dependency on almshouses, the disorder and decay, violence and immorality they brought threatened a unified and homogeneous society. The spectacle of a class of men and women set apart by their social and economic disarray presented frightening problems. A House committee reported on "vicious foreigners . . . paupers and criminals without character, morality, religion, industry . . . the dregs and offscourings of alien peoples." The terminology of this report reflected insensitivity and bigotry. But nativists insisted that it was a rational response to a deadly threat to their American way of life. Who would want to live among the dangerous and diseased, the slothful and violent masses creating blight wherever they settled? Dealing in themes that would endure beyond the mid-nineteenth century, they tried to elevate their movement beyond simple bigotry or economic self-interest. They fused the enduring image of a promised land to the fearful image of destructive intruders and fashioned for themselves a role as protectors of the American dream.[6]

The statistics of despair seemed terrifying to nativist analysis. Samuel Busey, in *Immigration: Its Evils and Consequences*, pointed to "the alarming decennial ratio of increase—with the astonishing statistical facts that four-fifths of the beggary and three-fifths of the crime spring from our foreign population; more than half the public charities, more than half the prisons and almshouses, more than half the police and the cost of administering criminal justice are for foreigners." Busey concluded that "the people should demand of their statesmen that National and State legislation control these elements."[7]

"These elements" also could be the harbinger of changes in the value structure of society. Developing among the urban immigrant poor might be a world of "dark satanic mills" that blighted the European cityscape. Earlier, Americanists had lauded their factory towns, but now Boston and New York were filling with Irish slums. The immigrants threatened the vision of pastoral America; they were a warning bell for the perils of the urban future. Nativists, hoping to preserve the idealized past, attacked "aliens" as both the symbol of the process of industrialization and the major evil that accompanied it.

Still, there could be no turning back from urban-industrial growth, and nativists charted the economic and political implications of an influx of "bad and disaffected populations." "Cheap ignorant labor will drive out of the market intelligent and honest competition through underbidding," exclaimed one writer. Another looked at the 1850 census and announced that "half of the arrivals [in the period 1845–54] had no occupation, one-fifth were laborers, and only three-tenths were mechanics, farmers and tradesmen; the effect of this immense influx of immigrants will inevitably depreciate the value of American labor which depends on the law of supply and demand." The danger was most acute in certain industrial areas, for the aggregate number of immigrant workers in 1852–54 exceeded that of natives in New York, Pennsylvania, and Ohio. Busey turned the antialien theme to the politics of egalitarianism: "Is not immigration an evil? To the capitalist it is not. It is the ally of the money power of the country, and this money power is being constantly exerted to depreciate the value of labor." Unchecked, the situation must only worsen in succeeding years, as alien birth rates and early marriages contributed to a fearsome "law of increase." These people were not needed for our expanding economy, Whitney argued. The "now powerful and vigorous" United States "can only be weakened" by rapid population growth.[8]

The political impact of the newcomers was even more alarming. "We might as well send ballot boxes to foreign countries and let them vote there," Alfred Ely told a gathering of the Organization of United Americans in 1850. Immigrant participation in politics reflected plots hatched from overseas, "the design of the monarchs of Europe." Nativist writers feared conspiracy from many quarters. Some reported secret conventions of Irish in major eastern cities with Russian agents playing roles of provocateurs. Others noted the "secret influence" of the English "economic oligarchy," which coveted the United States as a financial colony and hoped to weaken it through proliferating immigration. "Enemies of America, numerous, powerful, subtle, unscrupulous, audacious" were at work among "foreign capitalists and speculators," stimulating the rising tide of Irish emigration.[9]

But if nativists worried about foreigners and flatterers in power in the highest places, they also fretted over the childlike nature of the immigrant electorate. "Boys of 12 and 15 are more informed in duties and responsibilities than foreigners of 12 or 15 years residence," argued Anspach. Many shared Anna Carroll's concern about "poll domination by drunken aliens, the intrigue and rowdyism of raw foreigners," the "ballot box activity of thousands from east of the Rhine, from the bogs and marshes of Ireland." Political danger, it seemed, could come through either the deviousness or the innocence of aliens. Whatever the cause, the cure remained the same.[10]

Although nativist xenophobia could be described as paranoid, these political concerns had some basis in reality. Secret German and Irish orders were indeed at work in America. The oath of the Robert Emmett Club, made public during an investigation in Cincinnati, was reprinted in several nativist tracts: "In the awful presence of God, I do voluntarily declare and promise that I shall use my endeavors to form a brotherhood amongst Irishmen of all persuasions for to uproot and overthrow English government in Ireland; and I furthermore declare that neither hopes, fears, rewards nor punishments shall ever induce me to make known any of the secrets of this order." If one feared foreign influence in politics, the election figures for 1850–54 provided rich statistical material. An analysis of "foreign voters in the cities" showed that in Chicago, St. Louis, and Milwaukee, the foreign-born vote exceeded the native and in New Orleans, Detroit, New York, Boston, and Cincinnati, "they are nearly equal." It revealed that "present political power [1854] in the states of Rhode Island, Massachusetts and New York, shows one-third their electorate listed as alien." In the national arena, a nativist argued that there was "actual and undeniable" representation of the foreign population in the House of Representatives because of concentrations of "alien voters in the States." This situation was intolerable: "They have abused American generosity, having scarcely touched upon American soil, understanding social questions as little as would an imported Hottentot." There must be forbearance toward them no longer. "America for Americans," *The Wide-Awake Gift: A Know Nothing Token for 1855* announced:

"And why not? Is there another country under the sun that does not belong to its own native born people? Why shouldn't Americans shape and rule the destinies of their own land—the land of their birth, their love, their altars and their graves, the land red and rich with the blood and hallowed by the memories of their fathers? Why not rule their own, particularly when the alien betrays the trust that should never have been given him, when the liberties of all are thereby imperiled?"[11]

In the nativist mind the intruder was a bestial presence. Immigrants were a repository of social chaos, a sinister threat to economic well-being, a cancer in the body politic. And the nativists searched for still other offenses committed by these foreigners. Immigrants were accused of "remitting an enormous amount of gold and silver to their friends at home, withdrawn from circulation in this country and exported to foreign nations." They were accused of devouring government jobs, denying the native-born places in the post office and lighthouse, patent office and customhouse, taking one-sixth of the number of available offices. In the end, the protectors declared, "We must return to first principles . . . for if patriotism no longer remains a high sounding name, it must be again. My country everywhere and at all times—America above all things." They looked to the past for validation. Washington was quoted again warning of "the insidious wiles of foreign influence." Madison was remembered for saying, "Foreign influence is a Grecian horse to the republic; we cannot be too careful to exclude its entrance." Jefferson, "were he living at this time," could not more distinctly and unequivocally "express the evils of immigration and its blighting and withering effect upon republican institutions."[12]

★★★

The Catholic Menace

The new aliens bore so many burdens and presented so many problems that they would have been assailed even if every one was a good Protestant. But they were not. The "alien menace" at midcentury was a "Catholic menace," and the heritage of an ancient antipapist tradition was evident throughout nativist literature. Andrew Lipscomb wrote in *Our Country: Its Danger and*

Duty in 1854: "To examine the condition of the chosen nation at the advent of the Redeemer is to discover that a perverted religion was the primary source of all their misfortunes."[13]

Many nativist spokesmen were evangelical ministers and gleefully joined battle against the Romanists. Could anyone doubt that Catholicism was anathema to American democracy? The pope is "as far removed from encouraging Republican ideas as the most bigoted prelate of the dark ages," said the author of *The Model Republic*. Autocratic and centralized, opposed to individual judgment and intolerant of dissent, the church was "a portentious cloud rising in the East . . . growing ever darker," it held its followers "spiritually subject to a foreign prince." In books, pamphlets, and broadsides, thousands of pages were devoted to endless accounts of the "evidence" of antidemocratic practices in papal history, from the Inquisition through the Reformation. But the "startling facts for native Americans," as one of these tracts was called, also focused on contemporary events. There was special attention to political developments in Italy, where "Popish despotism" led in 1849 to an uprising of "those yearning to be delivered from the oppressive yoke they have so long and so unwillingly endured."[14]

The internal organization of the church was described as patently un-American. In a land of freedom, what place is there for the confession box, where the secret thoughts of men's hearts, courts, cabinets, and families are "found out by priests"? What democratic role could be played by the "hierarchy of monks, nuns, Bishops," who were, after all, the "spies and watchmen of the dwelling despot in the Vatican, himself the victim of a clique of Cardinal despots"? The distinctive national character of the United States made the "slave creed" of Catholicism unnecessary here: "The American mind . . . different from the European or South American—fearless, inquisitive, impatient of dictation" rejects a religion that "thrives best with men of inferior intellect." Perhaps the "indolent Italians, lascivious Europeans, ignorant and barbaric peoples" of other, poorer lands might embrace such a faith. But nativists never tired of reminding their readers that this was an Anglo-Saxon nation, and "Anglo-Saxons never endorsed the pretensions and dogmas of the Church."[15]

Of course, the Catholic threat was not limited to its institutional structure. Antialiens saw papist conspiracies in almost every corner by the 1850s. The old specter of a plot to steal control of the

Mississippi Valley was resurrected: "Rome looks with wistful eye to domination of this broad land, a magnificent seat for a sovereign Pontiff," the key to conquest of "a country filled with invaluable treasures." Fears of such plots grew easily in the climate of new concern about political power exercised by millions of Catholic immigrants, controlled from abroad and serving as puppets of the political plotters in Rome. And what of education, where "they denounce the public schools, murder American history and maim and mutilate its literature," where the priestcraft "locks up" the minds of youth? "Romish despots," nativists insisted, were succeeding by subversion. Conspiracy was undermining the foundations of the American state.[16]

The tide of immigration was a Catholic tide. The nightmares of eighteenth-century nativists had become reality. It had all happened so quickly that the majority of true Americans might not have realized the dimensions of the danger. For them Thomas R. Whitney revealed the frightening numbers: in 1808 there had been one Catholic diocese in the United States, by 1855 there were forty-one; in 1808 only 68 priests, by 1855, 1,704; 80 churches in 1808, 1,824 in 1855; 678 missions by midcentury when there had been none fifty years earlier; thirty-seven ecclesiastical institutes and twenty-one colleges in 1855 and there had been but one or two at the beginning of the period. Anna Carroll spoke for many antialiens shocked by these statistics: "Rome has put her paw upon America's great shoulder and is clawing at her vitality." Could Americans as a homogeneous people survive this popish invasion? For those who believed that "we have a national character peculiarly our own," this was the central question.[17]

Nativists were not comforted by the inflammatory rhetoric of the country's leading Catholic cleric. John Hughes, aggressive, arrogant, and insensitive, decided to challenge the growing nativist legions in a counterattack that could only confirm their worst fears. In the summer of 1850 he was named the first archbishop of New York. Later that year he published the text of a remarkable lecture, delivered at St. Patrick's Cathedral in November, *The Decline of Protestantism and Its Causes*: "Everybody should know that we have for our mission to convert the world, including the inhabitants of the United States—the people of the cities, country, officers of the navy, commanders of the army, the legislature, the Senate, the Cabinet, the President and all! We have received from God what

Protestantism never received . . . a command to go and teach all nations . . . to convert all Pagan and Protestant nations."[18]

Hughes explained that this was no secret plot but an open plan to convert everyone—particularly "effete Protestants"—to the true church. This fiery zealot, a man who made his reputation confronting anti-Catholics, had been an Irish émigré, a teenage newcomer from County Tyrone. He fiercely defended the rights of recent immigrants as a matter of principle. But his gratuitous act of defiance on the matter of conversion now would help those evangelical Protestants who were redoubling their efforts to attack the church in the name of protecting nation and faith.[19]

The American Foreign and Christian Union (AFCU) led the way; it had 120 missionaries and lecturing agents on the road by 1854. One estimated that he traveled almost fourteen thousand miles, preached 127 times, and visited eight states in a period of two months. Funds poured into the new society and other evangelical groups. They were helped along by a curious decision taken in 1853 by officials of the Roman Court who decided that Archbishop Cajetan Bedini, newly appointed nuncio to Brazil, should pay a visit to the United States. The announced purposes of Bedini's tour were to explore the possibility of establishing a nunciature in America and to settle a controversy within the Buffalo, New York, diocese. In fact, the Vatican wanted a report on the status of the church and its growing immigrant laity in the United States. In response, the AFCU imported Alessandro Gavazzi, an apostate monk, to expose Bedini and the "machinations of that harlot Rome." A tall, striking man with long black hair and piercing eyes, a speaker of consuming passion and electric presence, Gavazzi helped to incite violent demonstrations along the route of the nuncio's visit. Bedini was insulted, burned in effigy, and confronted by mobs shouting "No Kings, No Priests, No Popery." The militia was called out in several towns to protect him from angry crowds.[20]

"Father" Gavazzi's own audiences rioted on occasion, Catholics and Protestants fighting in the aisles and swarming toward the platform as he exposed the secrets of the nunneries with scathing sarcasm and theatrical gesture and reviled that "Jesuit army— whose only rule is obedience," which had come to America to "infiltrate the schools, teach rebellion, to trample upon your country and its faith." Gavazzi was so effective as an anti-Catholic orator that his success encouraged others. Soon native itinerant "ministers" had followings in several eastern and midwestern towns. John S. Orr, "Angel Gabriel" as he was called, summoned listeners with a brass horn. Attired in a bizarre white robe, he led followers through the streets of New York and Boston. Catholics considered Orr a mad figure, but he was effective. Tough mobs of natives and Irishmen gathered at the scene of his street-corner ministry, and riots followed him across Massachusetts and New York in the spring of 1854. From barrel tops and curbstones the word was spread, and if the "preachers" were periodically jailed, their message that Catholic immigrant hordes were corrupting the America of old was hitting home.[21]

These nativist speakers used old antipapist arguments to check the new threat of Catholic immigration. But as they struck out at the symbols of the "Catholic problem" in America—the school, ballot, and press—they played the role of zealous reformer, for these were also the symbols of subordination of the individual to authority. In attacking the traditional "dangers" posed by Catholicism, they were voicing the concerns of many who feared that these disorderly, unlettered, unsophisticated immigrant masses might be unable or unwilling to withstand manipulation and control in a democratic society. Even the crazy, comic "Angel Gabriel" pointed to a new and more threatening image of the intruder. Behind his riotous scenes were somber new realities.[22]

The old rhetoric often obscured these new realities. Sadomasochistic "convent books" reappeared, offering evidence that the nation needed vigilant protectors against terrible enemies. Josephine Bunkley's *Testimony of an Escaped Novice*, produced by Harper & Brothers in 1855, told tales of "discipline . . . whips with leather thongs struck on naked backs . . . females buried alive," and more. But now diatribes against the authoritarian nature of the church were mixed in with pornographic sensationalism. Detailed descriptions of the evils of a tyrannical system, in which Catholics "have no will of their own . . . only the will of the hierarchy," underscored the subordination of individual to clerical authority in a system particularly dangerous to ignorant immigrants. It was "the Papal Juggernaut vs. the Innocent."[23]

The American party fostered the rebirth of convent literature. A "Native American" (E. Hutchinson) offered *Startling Facts for*

Know Nothings, exposing the "licentiousness and debauchery" of Catholic clergymen. Charles W. Frothingham's *The Convent's Doom*, dedicated to "the Know Nothing fraternity throughout the United States," went through at least five editions, with more than fifty thousand books sold. The subject of evil doings in "Romish institutions" was political dynamite. In 1853, the famous Hannah Corcoran riots erupted in Charlestown, Massachusetts, and nativist writers rushed to the printers with the story. Hannah, a young Irish immigrant, a converted Baptist, was spirited away to Philadelphia by her mother and a Catholic priest. Her Protestant guardians immediately called it kidnapping; they hinted darkly of rape and murder. A huge native mob attacked police and militia companies until she was returned. But abuse of innocent girls was not the main concern of the new literature. The central focus in Frothingham's book was on the conspiratorial nature of the enemy: bishops plotting infiltrations of political parties, priests spying on public men throughout America, the spreading stain of Catholic intrigue everywhere. Here was reason and excuse for nativist secret societies, for "if they keep account of every man in the state who holds office and makes speeches . . . and report to bishops and archbishops from whom they receive orders," what choice did protectors of America have but to meet in secrecy to foil the rapists, sadists, Bible burners, and political conspirators? If the church were really "a Trojan horse in the citadel of our liberties," filled with popish traitors fully armed to do battle against true Americans, no measure taken in resistance was too extreme.[24]

The image of a corrupt, immoral, authoritarian force gaining strength with each new boatload of Catholic immigrants led to outbreaks more violent and more frequent than in any previous age. Churches were burned or blown up by gunpowder in New York and Massachusetts, Maine and Ohio. Priests were threatened, beaten, tarred, and feathered. Convents were vandalized in New Orleans, Galveston, Providence, and Chicago. The early 1850s saw countless mob clashes between Catholic newcomers and native Protestants. Almost every month brought new destruction or desecration of church property.[25]

So widespread was the anti-Catholic animus that at least one Catholic writer, searching for a way to defuse the issue, accepted the validity of attacks on the immigrants and asked only that natives separate their ideas about Catholicism from their fears of the alien intruder. Orestes Brownson thought many Irish Catholics "a miserable rabble unlike anything the country has known . . . noisily drinking and brawling, without the American respect for law, following blindly behind their leaders." Germans tend to become "wild democrats . . . sometimes socialists or anarchists," said *Brownson's Quarterly Review*, and "it must be conceded that the great body of foreigners are not republican in spirit, habit, life or discipline." This Catholic intellectual agreed that foreigners were dangerous. "They look upon themselves as a distinct and separate class in the American community." Perhaps, he seemed to suggest, it would be best to restrict naturalization in the interest of protecting the nation. "It is unwise to force foreigners on America." But he insisted that there was nothing alien about the Catholic church: "It is not a foreign religion . . . whatever foreigners are associated with it is accidental." It was not undemocratic or un-American; the pope had spiritual authority alone, and only "demented Protestants" seeking ascendancy for their faith could believe otherwise.[26]

Brownson's efforts to divide the twin themes of nativism had no audience. The fear of alien peoples now was inextricably intertwined with the fear of alien institutions and ideas. The vast immigration and its dreadful social costs reawakened memories of Romish plots. Behind the paupers and criminals, the sick and the mad, the tools of political bosses and the cheap laborers threatening job security was the evil and mysterious church, whose foreign prince was all the more powerful because immigrant parishioners were untutored in the ways of a democratic state. The image of the intruder was shaped by both the realistic agonies of immigrant disorder and the ancient fantasies of papal conspiracy, given particular definition in these years through impolitic posturings of the clerical leadership.[27]

The nativists were idealists; their America was a unique, nonfeudal, democratic society. This idealism in nativist thought was put in service of political and religious passions, and the message of the movement was that checking the alien intruder would preserve America's golden tomorrows. But the nativist movement would prosper not only because of its clearly defined goals and clearly delineated devils, for other threats to its idealized American dream were gaining new strength in the early 1850s. Nativism's promise to protect the nation from sinister alien forces would have been far less appealing for many if these other dangers, unspoken —perhaps unspeakable—were not at work. The converts to the protectors' creed, while responding to problems confronting their America, were fleeing from other difficulties unconnected to the crusade against the alien.

★ ★

CHAPTER 6

SOCIAL UPHEAVAL
AND THE SEARCH
FOR AMERICA

IN THE FALL OF 1850, as the great wave of Catholic immigration engulfed coastal cities and the nativist movement began to organize around the image of alien intruders, another crisis mobilized passionate chauvinists in a very different cause. Robert Barnwell Rhett, eloquent, mercurial, uncompromising—a well-known South Carolina editor and congressman—proclaimed himself a disunionist:

> Let it be that I am a Traitor. The word has no terrors for me. . . .
> I have been born of Traitors, but thank God, they have been Traitors in the great cause of liberty, fighting against tyranny and oppression. Such treason will ever be mine whilst true to my lineage. . . . No, no, my friends! Smaller states before us struggled successfully, for their independence and freedom against far greater odds; and if it must be, we can make one brave, long, last, desperate struggle for our rights and honor, ere the black pall of tyranny is stretched over the bier of our dead liberties. To meet death a little sooner or a little later can be of consequence to very few of us.[1]

Rhett, fierce defender of slavery and implacable foe of the North, was talking treason and he was urging violence. His constituents were not prepared to follow him that far or fast in 1850. When they elected him to the Senate the next year, they put conservative "cooperationists" in control of the state government. But Senator Rhett resigned before the end of his term, convinced that his place was in the South, preparing his countrymen for the inevitable struggle.

The decade that preceded the firing on Fort Sumter would be filled with foreboding, a climate of pervasive disorder affecting political parties and private organizations, churches and family groups. American history has been seen as a series of "ages of anxiety," "crucial decades," periods of "frustration and aggression," times of crisis of all varieties. But there had been nothing to equal the great rupture of the mid-nineteenth century, prelude to national catastrophe.

The ominous polarization of many American institutions across sectional lines was the gravest sign of political instability in pre–Civil War years. But the deepening split between North and South was not the only threat to national order. Catholic immigration was creating a new world of urban problems, but many northerners would have experienced social upheaval had the potato flourished on the Continent. As America moved toward civil conflict, many natives moved restlessly about the country, caught up in the painful mobility of a society in the early stages of industrialization. And many Americans sensed, through this turmoil, an increasing gap between the rhetoric of American opportunity and the realities of their social and economic life.

The sources of the Know Nothing movement and the great appeal of nativism are found in concerns about immigration and historic fears of Catholicism. Yet beyond the obvious lay a complex of national and personal problems seemingly so intractable that displacement of anxiety and rage against the foreigner became the only available solution for many Americans.

In a nation with few vestiges of the authoritative relationships that survived the decay of feudalism in many European states, traditional carriers of authority lacked force. In a culture without a capital, with no clearly defined "high society," there was no tradition of deferential respect for the leadership of the best families, the "tremendous sureties and . . . exact relations that existed between the classes" which F. Scott Fitzgerald saw at the heart of nineteenth-century Europe. Despite the evangelical fervor of Protestants, even churches lacked the influence wielded in the older world, and there was no established religion in more than the legal sense of the term. In place of class and church there was America; fierce, chauvinistic devotion to atomistic individualism and the "unique" nation born to nurture and preserve it. But a "way of life" can be an insubstantial, fragile concept, easily undermined. A major threat to the values and institutional forms central to the "American way of life" could be intolerable. In the 1850s, men sought to escape from the intolerable.[2]

★★★
Slavery and Sectional Conflict

The greatest upheaval was the clash between the North and South. The issue of slavery, and the sectional conflict it helped to generate and exacerbate, was inextricably connected to territorial expansion. The Missouri Compromise of 1820 temporarily resolved that issue, setting the famous line (36° 30") to the Pacific, north of which the South's "peculiar institution" could not be extended. But the question flared anew with the Mexican War and the prospect of a rich California territory and a new estate in the desert and mountain West available for American settlement and development. This war of expansion did not unify the country as have international conflicts in some tranquil times. Nor did that other jingoistic outburst against the British in the debate over division of the Oregon territory in the far Northwest. For all the calls of "fifty-four forty or fight," the spirit of Manifest Destiny that carried James K. Polk to the White House receded before a compromise agreement with Great Britain. The year of the Oregon Compromise, 1846, was no time of national unity. David Wilmot's proviso outlawing slavery in the new territories failed to carry the Senate after passage in the House of Representatives but was warning enough of the divisive force of the slave issue. In 1848, while Democratic and Whig parties attempted to blur the question, the new Free Soil party mobilized support for the end of slave expansion into the territories. Its motto was "Free Soil, Free Speech, Free Labor, and Free Men." With the victorious conclusion of the war against Mexico, Congress could no longer turn its back on a question now dividing the nation along sectional lines, breeding secessionist talk in many parts of the South.

The great Compromise of 1850 was designed to save the Union; it was engineered by Henry Clay in hopes of "concord, harmony and peace." This was an enormous challenge. In the North, abolitionists were depicting slavery as hateful and immoral, an institution incompatible with any form of democratic government. Although the majority still did not accept the militants' arguments, many northerners were increasingly impatient with any restrictions on economic opportunity. They became vocal opponents of slavery's expansion. In the South, abolitionist morality was answered by virulent, hysterical rhetoric and, at last, by a celebration of the slave system itself. Rhett, William Lowndes Yancey, and Edmund Ruffin spearheaded a new southern movement. Some have speculated on the vast burden of guilt that lay behind the angry response of these fire-eaters. Others have considered their perceived need to protect arrangements thought essential to the social and economic life of their families and their homeland. Whatever their motives, southern spokesmen insisted that any effort to drive them from the territories would lead to disunion. John C. Calhoun pointed to a growing disparity in the population and representation of the sections. If the South was not granted access to new land (he argued for free extension of slavery wherever a master took his slaves) there would be no alternative to secession.

With neither side yielding to the Missouri Compromise solution and the arguments of Wilmot and Calhoun unacceptable to one section or the other, the men of 1850 moved toward the proposals of Stephen A. Douglas and Lewis Cass for "popular sovereignty." The new territories of Utah and New Mexico were created with provision that either, or any part thereof, could be admitted to the Union "with or without slavery," depending on the persuasion of the settlers. The demarcation line of 1820 was wiped out. While California would enter as a "free" state and the slave trade would be abolished in the District of Columbia, southerners were offered protection in the passage of a more effective fugitive slave law. The Compromise of 1850 did avoid the civil war that seemed imminent in that critical year. It did not solve the problem.

The principle of popular or squatter sovereignty, when applied four years later to the Kansas and Nebraska territories, reactivated old hostilities. After a large proslavery force sacked a free-soil stronghold in Lawrence, Kansas, John Brown—ardent champion of freedom to some, murdering fanatic to others—led the historic raid on Pottawatomie in which southern sympathizers were indiscriminately massacred. Guerrilla war followed. "Bleeding Kansas" loomed in the background as the party system began to disintegrate. Shaped to serve a continent-sized nation with a variety of interests, avoiding ideological positions to appeal to a consensus of those interests, the parties failed the test of dealing with the most divisive American issue of all. With the breakup and disappearance of the Whig party, split and splintered by its "conscience" and "cotton" wings, the fear of disunion reappeared. The odious apparatus tied to enforcement of the fugitive slave law in the North—federal marshals, mandatory service in slave-catching posses, summary trials for suspected runaways—gave new meaning to the abolitionists' moral argument against slavery. Major Protestant denominations, like the political parties, divided on sectional lines. When had greater disorder threatened to destroy America?[3]

Later, historians would wonder whether the divisions of the 1850s inevitably pointed to those terrible consequences at Fredericksburg and Shiloh, Antietam and Gettysburg. But whether or not a different group of leaders, shrewder and more imaginative, could have managed the dramatic clashes of this unhappy decade and defused the issues that led to war, Americans had to live through a time of agonizing disorder, when every new development seemingly dragged them closer to the brink. If the image of the United States as an Edenic society, a nation unmatched in the world, was the source of special strength and support for many of its citizens, what could they feel as the specter of disunion loomed larger? One way sectional adversaries sought to heal their wounds was by uniting around a common cause and opposition to a common foe. In this way they could reaffirm their own unity by casting out the enemies, declaring them "un-American" by virtue of alien status and religion. These outsiders could be blamed not only for social disorder but also for the ominous collapse of faith in the future of the national community.[4]

The growing division between the sections suggested a disagreement about that very American way of life which was the source of nativist claims to national uniqueness. The descriptions of a slave-based, Athenian democracy emanating from the antebellum South exposed a difference in the idealized vision of the American dream from North to South. Against these dissonances, nativist rhetoric, with its appeal to traditional virtues, reasserted that there was one America after all. The movement flourished in both sections with a strikingly similar literature. Later, slavery and free soil deflected nativist energies, but in the early years of this crucial decade, the antialien movement gained strength from the sectional struggle. Americans in both regions found in nativism a crusade far less threatening than those offered by Robert Barnwell Rhett or John Brown.[5]

★★★

Urban and Industrial Upheaval

Americans needed nativism as a solution for other problems as well. These were years of accelerating industrial expansion, accompanied by a complex web of social problems. Those who profited from or were victimized by the change shared a common fate. They lived through a period of upheaval.

Nowhere was the upheaval felt more severely than in the communities affected by the massive railroad construction between 1849 and 1854. Michael Holt noted the dislocating impact of the building of these trunk lines. The work on the Erie, Baltimore and Ohio, Pennsylvania, and New York Central produced disruptive changes in the economic and social life of almost everyone in towns between the Atlantic Coast and the Midwest. Formerly isolated and homogeneous populations found armies of immigrant railroad workers in their midst. Prices rose, local labor faced increasing competition, and many lost their jobs when the railroads took trade from the teamsters and rivermen, forwarding and commission merchants who had controlled commerce in the past. In towns bypassed by the railroads the results sometimes were more traumatic, as entire communities were left behind to wither and die. The new railroads influenced changes in methods of manufacture, stimulating development of large-scale enterprises by successful businessmen who could now centralize operations. Many cities—Cincinnati and Pittsburgh, among others—eventually benefited from the resulting growth but not without wrenching structural changes in economies of scale. Skilled laborers, artisans, and others faced displacement. Immigrant workers became an obvious target for many of these dissatisfied natives.

The changes were not limited to railroads. Everywhere, the statistics of industrial development attested to the dramatic revolution transforming America's economy even in the pre–Civil War era. Water power had driven practically all mill machinery in early years, but now the vast coal reserves were being exploited, with output rising by some 3,000 percent to 14 million tons between 1820 and 1860. Industry was stimulated by new inventions appearing from every corner, and the number of patents registered increased fivefold in the 1850s. American manufactures were valued at almost $2 billion by 1860, four times the figure for 1840. This was a measure of the new importance of the nonagricultural sector in northern and western America that so concerned southerners. The number of workers in manufacturing establishments with an output valued at more than $500 rose to almost 1.5 million. Society remained predominantly agricultural, but more and more Americans were working to produce textiles, iron, flour, lumber, machinery, agricultural implements, cooperage, furniture, iron rails and locomotives, leather and cordage, lard, soap and candles, malt and distilled liquors.

Many of the workers recruited for these new factories were women and children; many were immigrants from Ireland and Germany. But the vast foreign population was not the only source of labor for the emerging industrial revolution. Not until the mid-1850s did newcomers constitute a majority of the mill workers in New England towns, and throughout the United States factory labor was initially recruited from among the natives. Abandoned farms pockmarked many counties of northeastern America as entire families left the country for city and town. Even when the farm was not deserted, sons and daughters often sought employment in new factories to help a struggling father with the mortgage, to send a brother to school, or to escape the constricting social life of the agricultural world and taste the excitement and diversions of the city. Throughout the period, native Americans played a central role in industrial development.[6]

For both the immigrants flooding into the urban areas from overseas and the natives moving in from the farms, mobility often did not end with arrival in the factory town. Stephan Thernstrom and other students of this period have suggested that many communities served only as way stations for men in motion, large numbers of new urbanites who did not sink deep roots. Studies of urban demography indicate that "long-distance or leapfrogging mobility seems to have been more common than short-distance movement in the antebellum period." The new urbanites were not permanently locked into an ethnic or economic ghetto. Their striking mobility is masked by the growth of the cities themselves: Boston almost tripled in size from 1830 to 1870 (61,000 to 178,000), and census schedules and city directories reveal that only 49 percent of heads of household persevered in one community for more than a decade in the period 1840–50, 39 percent from 1850 to 1860. Available figures read even lower if unmarried males are included in samples; in large cities a minority of men remained long enough to be counted by two successive census takers. In smaller towns, the outmigration rates were even higher.[7]

In the years following the influx of the Irish, immigrant mobility surpassed that of the natives. But native urbanites were also on the move. Those most likely to move in both groups were unskilled and semiskilled employees: day laborers, gardeners, blacksmiths, painters, carpenters. Professionals, property holders, and affluent merchants were obviously happier at home; they were the most stable part of the population.[8]

But did social mobility accompany physical mobility in the mid-nineteenth-century cities? Did the "rags to riches" myth become a reality for those leaving one urban center for another? Some analysts speculate that a "large majority of out-migrants . . . formed a class of permanent transients who continued to be buffeted about by the vicissitudes of the casual labor market." Others disagree, and even the pessimists conclude from one sample of Boston migrants to other Massachusetts communities that "for them, at least, American folklore about geographical mobility and success had some validity."[9]

Whether or not the transients were realizing the American dream, they suffered social and political consequences. Some argue that many were rendered "politically impotent and alienated from society" because of their lack of roots and unfulfilled aspirations. Heavy transiency was hard as well on those who stayed at home, whose communities lacked constancy and some measure of stability in an age of upheaval.

How would it be possible to reintegrate a social order shaken by unregulated growth and change? Americans have always been "joiners," and voluntary organizations, as Tocqueville noted, have been a peculiarly American phenomenon. Such associations have helped to create a sense of community in a large, often heterogeneous and mobile population. Traditionally, they provided a focus for social life as well as an instrument for exerting political pressure. In a larger sense they served to strengthen the role of an elusive democratic authority, putting the stamp of popular participation on formation of policies bidding for attention and implementation. In the United States at midcentury, many searched for order through associational activity. Such organizations could redefine the American community while exposing the threats to that community—the sinister adversary who could be defeated only through militant activity. At this critical time, the voluntary association would swell to the proportions of a social movement.[10]

★★★

The Sources of Nativism

In the literature of social science, there are many causal arguments concerning the emergence of social movements in periods of change and stress. Some writers have described "relative deprivation": the discontent emerging from an individual's perception of a widening gap between his or her legitimate expectations and the means for satisfying them. This discrepancy need have no relationship to real conditions. There need be only some reference against which to experience the relativity of deprivation. Although often this involves another social, economic, racial, or ethnic group, it might also be a past condition or an abstract ideal.[11]

Such discontent does not arise in a context of great despair or resignation. W. G. Runciman noted that "if people have no reason to expect or hope for more than they can achieve, they will be less discontented with what they have, or even grateful simply to be able to hold on to it." But despair and resignation were not a part of the American dream. In the 1850s, fears that change would bring transience without improvement and that the vagaries of urban-industrial life would not fulfill the bright prospects drawing more people into the cities contributed to feelings of acute unease. "Extremist movements," one theorist has suggested, are often "associated with a fall into marginal statuses."[12]

The theory of relative deprivation offers no complete answer to questions concerning the sources of nativism. Depressed or disordered conditions produce volatile political activity in some circumstances and political apathy in others. Anthony F. C. Wallace, considering the needs of a society under excessive stress—"a condition in which some part, or the whole, of the social organism is threatened with more or less serious damage"—introduced the concept of "revitalization." When the perceived primary environment in which a person lives is directly threatened, when the society ceases to be stable and recognizable, then individual life stresses can no longer be handled; peculiar and disruptive forms of stress demand new forms of resocialization and adaptation. "Revitalization movements" appear on the scene as efforts to revivify important beliefs and values. Frequently they focus on elimination of alien elements and influences.[13]

Michael Barkun, analyzing the impact of "disaster" in the creation of extremist movements, suggested that both deprivation and stress are tolerated by everyone in some form or other. But stress that involves a radical change in perception of the primary environment (that portion of the environment most significant to an individual) or deprivation that takes away the most valued part of the individual's world can produce the "psychological correlates of disaster." In such a setting, "anxiety and meaninglessness create the need for a new kind of movement."[14]

Barkun is concerned with the role of multiple disasters in the creation of social movements that offer immediate, collective, total salvation. In America at midcentury the vision of a homogeneous and unique society—the "perceived primary environment" for many —seemed directly threatened by multiple disasters. The sectional conflict was rupturing national institutions, and violence went beyond rhetoric in numerous clashes between abolitionists, free-soilers, and slaveholders. But Americans were facing this unique stress at the very time social disorder was occurring in an increasingly mobile culture. Vast immigration added a further disorienting dimension, creating the ideal setting for a dramatic social movement promising to help Americans handle terrible new problems and explain bewildering new predicaments.

Of course, some people were less caught up in the turmoils of the day than others. Recent migrants enjoyed temporary immunity from breakdowns in traditional social arrangements. Irish immigrants in American urban centers were unlikely to be affected by the political tremors of the slavery crisis or fears of disunion. Many still embraced the mores and values of the Old World and were supported by the religious faith they brought with them. This must have been galling to some natives: in a nation coming apart, it was hard to accept the clannishness of the Irish and the chauvinistic unity of Archbishop Hughes's church.[15]

Immigrants proved the perfect target for many Americans in these troubled times. They could associate their own loss of power or status with the emergence of a subversive group disrupting time-honored relationships. In a social order threatened by catastrophe, polarization between the forces of good and evil satisfied the desire for enemies on whom to pin the blame, whose defeat could restore the stability of the cherished past.

Nativism grew out of a search for America in an age of social upheaval, an age of deprivation, stress, and imminent disaster. It was, of course, a nonrational response to contemporary problems. The nation was not facing civil war because of immigration from Ireland and Germany. The dislocations of urban-industrial growth were not produced by the newcomers, more victims than villains in this story. Attacking the Irish would not resolve the dilemma of sectional strife. Striking out at the aliens would not bring an end to socioeconomic changes or even the illusion of stability. But in pursuing such "solutions," nativists were fugitives from that American way of life they celebrated; they were turning to the movement to escape the central problems of their time. Unwilling to accept the dark side of their American experience—the wages of slavery, the stresses of a competitive culture, the crisis of community—they struck out at the most vulnerable group within their midst.[16]

Nativists were fugitives as well as protectors, escaping from some new realities, responding to others. In many ways, their movement would bear a striking similarity to older and to contemporary millenarian movements. For like many millenarian uprisings, American nativism in the 1850s called for a dramatic return to conditions in the past. Like some millenarians, these Americanists constructed a polarized world in which the enemy was an alien intruder and they were the "chosen people." Like millenarianism, nativism in the United States was nurtured by deprivation and stress felt by millions in a threatened culture undergoing rapid change.

The parallels are particularly striking with millenarians in medieval and early modern Europe, who sought a regressive way of coping with fundamental tensions in their society. But there are important differences as well. Millenarian movements anticipate the "complete destruction of the existing social, political and economic order. . . . The old must be totally destroyed before a new and perfect society can be established in its place." The focus is on the future as the time when humanity will be liberated from the problems of the present. American nativists did not wish to destroy the contemporary world but to cleanse it. They were less concerned with dreaming of tomorrow than with changing conditions today. And they were less ambitious. Unlike many millenarians, they did not lay claim to a total, all-encompassing truth or enfold their members in a belief system that provided meaning and explanation for virtually all problems. Nor was there a dependence on charismatic leaders in possession of extensive and esoteric knowledge.[17]

The major nativist organizations of the last century were quasi-millenarian both in their rhetoric and their activities. Still, these Americanists can be only partially understood in transcultural terms. Their movement was created to defend a "unique" society and they were uniquely American. At the root of their problems lay the dilemma of community in the United States. They were all immigrants in a land of opportunity. How could order be created in an age of change, brotherhood in an increasingly heterogeneous population? Community seemed threatened everywhere: by newcomers who blurred the definition of "American," by urban-industrial growth that made a shambles of stability and offered mobility at the risk of personal failure, by the danger of disunion which imperiled the nation itself.

The search for America became a search for community. In a nation in which individualism was a cherished value, in which nativists were in the forefront defending the individualistic ethos, the rise of nativism became a monument to the desperate desire for community. If social upheaval was casting shadows across the future of the "chosen people," antialiens would find comfort in redefining America in their own image. It is not surprising that the American party found its origins in nativist fraternities, where exclusivity and camaraderie brought safe haven to troubled men.

CHAPTER 7

★ ★

THE EMERGENCE OF
THE KNOW NOTHINGS

ON A LATE DECEMBER EVENING in 1844, thirteen
men gathered in the home of printer Russell C. Root in New York
City. The group called itself the American Brotherhood, a name
that would be changed to the Order of United Americans (OUA) the
next month. One of these original "friends," Thomas R. Whitney,
recalled later that a "code of principles" clearly laid out their task
from the very start: "Our efforts must be to release our country
from the thralldom of foreign domination." A nativist fraternity
had been born.[1]

Various antialien groups flared briefly and then disappeared in
the 1840s. They were replaced by a number of these new fraternal
secret societies, which remained active after the political parties
bearing the name "Native American" disintegrated and continued
to meet after the periodic street demonstrations subsided. They carried the seed of the movement into the next decade and formed the
nucleus of a far larger nativist effort than ever before.

Such groups benefited from the fascination with fraternalism in
these years. Early in the century, anti-Masonry led to public suspicion of secret societies, but all that had changed by the 1830s and
1840s. The organization of the Odd Fellows and the Foresters, the
Good Fellows and the Druids, the Red Men and the Heptasops attracted men in eastern cities. The temperance movement added
still more orders—the Good Templars, the Sons of Temperance.
One writer suggested that this brotherhood of the lodge harked
back to communities the size and character of which men until
recently had always known, from prehistoric hunting party to medieval farming village; that the flamboyant ritual, exalted titles,
and claims to longevity for "ancient" societies were evidence of

men's need for permanence and stability in a world of change. In pursuing community, few demands were made on members of most lodges. They swore to practice an ethical code, to concern themselves with civic advancement. This was moral voluntarism.[2]

The nativist fraternities were different. When the Order of United American Mechanics (OUAM) was born in Philadelphia amid the antialien upheaval of 1845, its organizing committee pointed to the crisis in employment for "real" Americans. Its purpose was to provide mutual economic assistance: to patronize only businesses owned by natives, to assist one another in finding jobs, to contribute to relief funds for widows and orphans of deceased brothers. Calling for an end to "unequal foreign competition" and warning that cheap alien labor would reduce honest American workmen to "beggary," the OUAM prospered despite the decline of nativist political parties.[3]

It was not alone. The United Sons of America appeared in Philadelphia, and other "national" groups were organized in various eastern towns. One newspaper claimed that forty-eight thousand New Yorkers and forty-two thousand Pennsylvanians were involved in some form of nativist society by the late 1840s.[4]

★★★

The Order of United Americans

The most popular of all these new fraternities was the Order of United Americans. By 1848 there were twenty-one chapters in New York State alone. Within ten years, there were chapters in sixteen states and a total membership of at least fifty thousand. The thirteen founders organized themselves as Alpha Chapter and then recruited new units throughout the East. Most were named after national heroes: Oliver Hazard Perry, Ethan Allen, Stephen Decatur. These "patriot sires" had "bequeathed those glorious institutions now threatened with annihilation by events of a most alarming nature," said the preamble of Alpha Chapter's constitution. And Alpha's membership included a cross-section of mid-nineteenth-century Protestant urbanites who would respond to this call: masons and painters, machinists and seamen, butchers and grocers, shipsmiths and carpenters. But it also contained wealthier businessmen and professionals well placed in the society, and in fact it was from this group that the founders had come in 1844. Unlike the OUAM, the Order of United Americans was created by men on the margins of the establishment, not by "mechanics" seeking security for their families. The OUA would soon attract such members, but in the beginning it was led by Simeon Baldwin, prosperous real estate and insurance broker, brother of the governor of Connecticut, and son of a prominent judge; John Harper, successful publisher and brother of the mayor of New York; Thomas Whitney, a printer and prolific nativist publicist. They were not national figures, and they included no charismatic leaders. But they were the most affluent and influential of contemporary nativists, and they were good organizers.[5]

Like the other fraternities, the OUA had a complicated organization which created the illusion of antiquity and gave initiates and leaders mysterious titles and special perquisites. Central to its structure was the magical triad. There were three levels of authority (local chapter, state chancery, and national archchancery), three chancellors sent from chapter to chancery, three archchancellors sent on to national. But there was only one leader of the OUA (limited to a single year term) and in the language of the lodge vogue he was called the arch grand sachem. By 1850, he ruled over a truly national domain with groups in New York, Pennsylvania, Massachusetts, New Jersey, Connecticut, Missouri, and Ohio. Only white, native, Protestant males over twenty-one were eligible, although a women's auxiliary, United Daughters of America, was soon created, serving wives and friends of the nativist brotherhood.[6]

Meetings were advertised in the press, and chapters published directories of membership. But the OUA was nonetheless a secret society. Ritual and procedures were jealously guarded, not only to maintain the exclusivity that made the lodge a special community but to advance the political goals of nativism. Whitney explained that the "influences of Romanism are so subtle" that conspiratorial countermeasures were essential; the "machinery of the old parties is so complete and pervading" that "every open effort" to check the influence of the foreigner and his easily manipulated ballot was "strangled." Once again, antialiens attributed terrible power to the enemy. At the same time, they could experience "fascination on the brink of the precipice," as Georg Simmel described it; they could feel "the external danger of being discovered and the internal danger of self-discovery." Fantasies of surprise counterattacks on the papist juggernaut, of risking life and livelihood for the salvation of the American dream fit their romantic self-vision and brought drama and purpose to their lives. Shared secrets fostered group solidarity, the cumbersome apparatus of fraternity created brotherhood, and the assertion of risk-taking cemented the small communities of the OUA. The organization served a "common purpose," in Simmel's words, compensating for that isolation of the personality "which develops out of breaking away from the narrow confines of earlier circumstances."[7]

In its newspaper and magazine and in the addresses of leaders to chapter meetings and chancery conventions, the movement's rhetoric was vintage nativism: a potpourri of self-pity, anger, national chauvinism, and pride. While "the rich Irish brogue and heavy German accent supplants the American idiom," while every press is "muzzled . . . turned against the American and . . . every gathering of foreigners receives fulsome laudation," while the "aliens scorn our laws, customs, religion," the OUA "takes its stand before the altar of nationality instead of party." True patriots, striving together in fraternal brotherhood, its members organized to protect their utopian nation, with its vast agricultural and mining frontier, its burgeoning railroads, its unmatched waterways, the greatest country in the history of the world, "three times as large as the whole of Britain, France, Spain, Portugal, Prussia, Austria, Denmark, Belgium and Holland combined." The United Americans acknowledged that their great nation "owes much to people of many lands," but "it is unquestionable that the American family is essentially of the Anglo-Saxon branch of the Teutonic race."[8]

The OUA confronted the unsettling problem of intellectual and moral diversity in the United States. It insisted that the Protestant church and the Anglo-Saxon people were America. It demanded loyalty only to them and called that patriotism. Pure nativism was its motive force, but by the dawn of the 1850s, few ideologies were untouched by political opportunism and the order was to be reshaped by the imperatives of a party system in crisis.

Members of the OUA had been involved in New York politics from the very start. In the school board wars that pitted antialiens against William Seward and John Hughes, Baldwin played a vigorous role and later was elected to the Board of Education for Common Schools. In 1849, the fraternity used its growing influence in an unsuccessful effort to block Seward's election to the United States Senate. A number of prominent brothers appeared on the Whig ticket that year, and real muscle was shown in defeating a Democratic candidate for city comptroller who tried to turn contempt for the OUA into political capital. By 1850, the New York Chancery declared that all state members must vote for endorsed candidates on pain of expulsion.[9]

In 1850 the specter of disunion began to sever old alliances. Millard Fillmore, the conservative Whig politician from western New York, suddenly was thrust into the presidency in the midst of the desperate effort to patch over sectional hatreds through Clay's Great Compromise. Fillmore had played the traditionally passive role of vice-president to General Zachary Taylor until Taylor was fatally stricken with acute gastroenteritis in 1850. Now he was in the White House in time to sign Clay's bill. It was a momentous decision, bitterly opposed by Fillmore's hated old rival in New York, Senator Seward. Millard Fillmore might temporarily occupy 1600 Pennsylvania Avenue, but Seward had more support in Syracuse, where the Whig state convention met in 1850. The senator delivered an eloquent speech in Washington supporting the Wilmot Proviso and attacking the compromise: "Countless generations of the yet unborn are saying, 'the soil you hold in trust for us, give it to us free, free from the calamities and sorrows of human bondage.'" Many were deeply moved; Bishop Hughes had written that "you have revived the age of Burke." Now the majority at the state meeting passed a resolution praising Seward's course. Fillmore's chief supporter in the United States Senate earlier had called for Seward's expulsion. The President's conservative supporters in New York—who called themselves nationalists—now refused to accept the pro-Seward resolution. They attacked the "Conscience" Whigs (derisively characterized as Wooly Heads because they opposed slavery) and bolted the state convention. Francis Granger, courtly, silver-haired chairman of the meeting, led the walkout along with Daniel Ullmann. With their fellows, they would be known to contemporaries and history as the Silver Grays (after Granger's hair).

It was a rupture long in the making. The contending factions were at sword's point on the questions of slavery, expansion, and union. The conservatives were dismissed by their enemies as less concerned with principle than property—supposedly fearing that their personal commercial interests would be damaged by an angry

southern reaction to northern coercion. But the split was related
as well to the Whig fracture in the mid-1840s, when Seward and
Thurlow Weed had ruled out continued coalition with nativism after the debacle of 1844 and thrust the antialiens out of shared
power in New York City. Now, with the state Whig party in Seward's control and no American Republican alternative available,
some Silver Grays turned to fraternity for support and influence.
The Order of United Americans began to attract many conservative
Whigs whose nativist ideology conveniently intersected with political needs in a time of party disarray.[10]

★★★

Order of the Star Spangled Banner: From Fraternity to Party

The politicization of the OUA at first obscured the birth
of another nativist fraternity. The Order of the Star Spangled Banner (OSSB) was founded in the spring of 1850 in New York City by
Charles B. Allen, a thirty-four-year-old commercial agent born and
educated in Massachusetts. It was a local fellowship numbering no
more than three dozen men through the first year or two of its
history. Allen and his companions met in each other's homes in the
early months. There was little to distinguish their order from many
other "patriotic" groups, little reason for anyone to expect that it
would be the core of a major political party, the greatest achievement of nativism in America.[11]

In 1852, the Order of the Star Spangled Banner began to grow, and
the leaders of the Order of United Americans began to see it as a
fraternity devoted to political organizing in the interest of nativist
policies. OUA brothers conducted an "investigation" of the newer
order and many began to join; membership rose from under fifty
to a thousand in three months. Thomas Whitney earlier had advocated developing a "political party taking its cue from the doctrines set forth by the Order of United Americans." With the Bedini
and Gavazzi riots raising nativism to the level of national attention, displaced political leaders who before had sought entry to the
older fraternity were initiated in the new: Daniel Ullmann, Jacob
Broome, and James Barker (all members of Washington chapter
number 2 of the OUA) joined the OSSB. A network of local secret

councils emerged to receive the new recruits, although five black-balls could block anyone's initiation. The elaborate ritual that marked other nativist societies took new forms: grips, passwords, signs, phrases of recognition, hand signals for distress, anger, caution. The requirement, as with earlier groups, was that a man be twenty-one, a Protestant, and a believer in God, willing to obey without question the dictates of the order. (For those under twenty-one, the Order of the American Star was established; its members called themselves the "Wide Awakes.")[12]

Unlike its progenitors, the Order of the Star Spangled Banner became strictly political. Members had no benevolent responsibilities. There were no dues, no elaborate meeting rooms to hire. But as it shed its feeble early image of a parochial club, it borrowed many organizational forms from the OUA. By 1853 there were local councils organized by ward throughout New York (with subdivisions for individual election districts), state councils in areas where mass membership was being recruited, and a Grand Council for the United States. In the early years, there were two degrees of membership. The first degree was for all initiates, who pledged never to vote for a foreign-born or Catholic candidate. The second degree was for those who held office within the order, requiring an oath to work for the removal of aliens and Catholics from all positions of authority and to deny them jobs and profits in private business or public office.[13]

Above all, the order was devoted to secrecy. Some members feared reprisals from immigrants, who would boycott nativist businessmen if they knew they were in the organization. Some pamphleteers suggested that older political parties were so adept at "persuading the weak and overawing the timid" that they would "crush us at birth" if the OSSB did not have the protection of fraternal secrecy. The old parties were accused of being "secret" organizations filled with pernicious "wire pullers who were never open and public, never consulted the people," working their will through chicanery. "Secrecy is part of the American political system," said nativists Saunders and Thorpe, and if this did not mean that it was as American as cherry pie, it surely meant that secrecy was good or bad according to the uses made of it.[14]

The nativists insisted that they were protectors, spearheading a "lawful effort to stand up against public danger." If their goals involved not only secrecy but sanctions for aliens and Catholics, it was not nativism that deserted democracy but its enemies. "We value too highly the privileges of freedom to oppose it for anyone. Our only concern is attacking those who threaten our political liberty, our American principles."[15]

So it was that secrecy could be enlisted in the service of freedom. Instructed to tell outsiders that they "know nothing" of the society when inquiries were made, members of the Order of the Star Spangled Banner did not shrink from the term when it was applied to the entire movement. Horace Greeley, no friend of nativism, labeled them the Know Nothings in the *New York Tribune* in November 1853. The widespread use of the nickname marked the transition from fraternity to party. The fraternal order was about to become the American party, one of the two major political organizations of the mid-decade, the avowed instrument for converting nativist rhetoric finally into public policy.[16]

Only in extraordinary times could nativism shape the policies of and give its name to a major party. Such was the situation from 1852 to 1854. The Whig party, born of the Jacksonian opposition, led for years by one of the giants of American history, Henry Clay, suffered a crushing defeat in the 1852 presidential election. Its candidate was Winfield Scott, military hero of the Mexican War. He won the nomination with the help of Seward, who was more interested in denying the prize to incumbent Fillmore than in blocking the ambitions of the general, a man Greeley characterized as that "immeasurably conceited, aristocratic ass." William Seward and the Conscience Whigs were far from happy with Scott, who insisted on honoring a platform that endorsed the Compromise of 1850, with all its repugnant provisions on slavery. Southern Whigs and Silver Grays nonetheless were told that Seward and radicalism had backed Scott, and the candidate managed to carry but four states and forty-two electoral votes. The Democrats' choice, the dark horse from New Hampshire, Franklin K. Pierce, was president.[17]

No contemporaries could know that 1852 was the last national campaign for the Whigs. But by the end of the year, the factionalized southern wing of the party virtually ceased to exist. Members deserted to the Union parties appearing in Georgia, Alabama, and Mississippi, which offered loyalty to the United States and support for the compromise. In the North, leaders of the antislavery wing also were preparing to abandon the old organization. Senator Charles Sumner said that the time had come for a new party of freedom. Although William Seward was not ready to go that far, he wrote to Thurlow Weed: "The play is played out for this time and played out . . . for us perhaps forever." It would not be until 1854, after the passage of the Kansas-Nebraska Act, that a full political reorganization would take place and a massive antislavery party begin to emerge, but signs of the Whig disintegration were clear enough in the collapse of Scott's presidential race. For conservative northern Whigs in New York State—the Silver Grays—the nativist party became an increasingly attractive refuge.[18]

A new American party could appeal to many disparate groups in a political system in which one of the large old parties was unraveling and the other was suffering fissures in different states and sections. It might appeal to a frightened, angry, disoriented electorate, which soon would be facing a bewildering variety of party labels on election day: names like People's and Republican, Free Soil and Fusion, Anti-Nebraska, Temperance, Hard Shell Democrats and Soft Shell Democrats. In such a setting, a party organized around nativist themes, one that advanced "American" interests, one that could be called American and suggested stability and union, offered a way out of the conflict between northerner and southerner, abolitionist and slaveholder. A common crusade against the foreigner could cement broken institutions and warring people.

For the homeless politicians of the early 1850s, this party would offer an opportunity to rebuild shaken careers. Some who were attracted to nativism sought to use it as an instrument for combating the immigrant vote, which had thwarted their plans in the past. Others hoped to shape it into a tool for promoting reforms long overdue in American life, blocked by the machinations and distorted priorities of the old order. Still others, leaders who could not or would not turn away from the sectional crisis, wanted to tie even this new organization to the cause of freedom or the maintenance of slavery. In a time of political upheaval and realignment, nativism could serve as a means to a variety of ends.

In the summer of 1852, a tiny "national" convention of nativist politicians was held in Trenton, New Jersey. The thirty-one delegates nominated Daniel Webster for president and George C. Washington of Maryland (grandnephew of the Founding Father) for vice-president. This American Union party was doomed from the outset. Webster ignored its offer and the Order of United Americans gave it no help; a substitute ticket gathered but a handful of votes in two or three states. Still, the influence of the secret societies was being felt in a variety of local races that fall.

By the next year, OUA members, many of them sophisticated Whig politicians, had captured Know Nothing councils throughout New York State. James Barker, a dry goods merchant and a friend of many prominent Silver Grays, organized a rival "Wigwam," which threatened the control of Star Spangled Banner founder Charles Allen. The next spring, in May 1854, the two factions finally united into a Grand Council of New York, with each group taking a different geographical region in which to grant new charters. Barker won the presidency of the state organization and immediately sent letters to other state councils, calling a meeting in New York City in mid-June. This first national convention drew up a new constitution, formalized ritual, and established a federal table of organization. City or county councils, composed of representatives from the district chapters which chose and initiated members, selected local candidates to endorse or run for office. State grand councils would supervise political activities throughout their state, and the delegates they sent to the National Council would select officers and make major political decisions. The first president was Barker, serving with leaders chosen from different sections—Maryland, Ohio, and New Jersey. The Order of the Star Spangled Banner, the Know Nothing fraternity, had established the structure of a new political party.[19]

In New York, the conservative Whig refugees became the Know Nothing influentials. Within a year, Allen was shoved aside and Fillmore's supporters were in the seats of power. The former president did not join at once, but he counseled associates to move in and "give it proper direction." Daniel Ullmann (American party candidate in the New York gubernatorial race the next year), James and Erastus Brooks, and David P. Barnard helped Barker oust his rival and assume control. National developments gave new urgency to the Whig-nativist alliance: Democratic President Pierce had appointed a Roman Catholic postmaster general and several foreign-born Democrats to diplomatic posts. Fillmore spoke for disgruntled Whigs and committed antialiens in declaring that the foreign vote was "fast demoralizing the whole country; corrupting the ballot box—that great palladium of our liberty—into a mockery where the rights of native born citizens are voted away by those who blindly followed their mercenary and selfish leaders."[20]

In other areas, there were very different patterns of recruitment and leadership. In several New England states, the Know Nothings became a formidable force by appealing to the antislavery wing of the former Whig party. But throughout much of the South, displaced Whigs looked to nativism to protect their proslavery institutions. Passage of the Kansas-Nebraska Act accelerated the movement's growth; with talk of "bleeding Kansas" on every lip, converts flocked in at the rate of five thousand per week in 1854. Men with promising futures began to seek entry. In the South there were John Bell, to be presidential candidate of the Constitutional Union party in 1860, and John J. Crittenden, senior senator from Kentucky, author of the compromise plan to solve the sectional struggle in the months before the outbreak of war. Henry Winter Davis, powerful Whig from Baltimore, and Andrew Jackson Donelson became Know Nothings. In the North, Nathaniel P. Banks and Jerome C. Smith, who would ride the antialien tide to prominence, one as Speaker of the House of Representatives and the other as mayor of Boston, were initiated. Henry Wilson, vice-president of the United States two decades later, Edward Everett, a future secretary of state, and Edward Bates, Lincoln's attorney general, came to the new party. After considering the triumphant run of victories for the Know Nothings in the fall elections, even Millard Fillmore joined, taking the secret rites of the Star Spangled Banner in his own home in late winter.[21]

The election of 1854 was a stunning demonstration of the Know Nothings' magnetic appeal. Within months, nativism became a new American rage: Know Nothing candy, Know Nothing tea, and Know Nothing toothpicks were marketed, buses and stagecoaches received the charmed name, the clipper ship *Know Nothing* was launched in New York. The fraternity was now the American party, but those in the movement remained proud of the secret order at the heart of the political organization. Books appeared with "KN" on the cover, "Know Nothing" poems found easy publication, and the widely circulated *Know Nothing Almanac or True American's Manual* was issued. The *Almanac* had schedules for sunset and moon phases mixed with a potpourri of nativist polemics, including stories of Catholic machinations in Ireland, statistics of foreigners in the almshouses and charity hospitals, as well as warnings of every kind of alien conspiracy.[22]

Within a matter of months, nativism had found a vast following throughout the United States. There were councils of the order in thirty-three states and talk of controlling 1.5 million votes in elections to come. But even as the antialien crusade reached heights unimagined by earlier nativists, the politics of disunion threated its future prospects. Social upheaval had provided a rich soil for growth of the movement in a time of unparalleled immigration and concern about foreigners. But social upheaval was a volatile fuel for any movement, and in the months to follow, the party called American would struggle with the very forces that made its spectacular political success possible. In different parts of the nation, Know Nothings tried to hold on to nativism while conflicting passions within the movement sought expression over slavery.[23]

CHAPTER 8

★ ★

THE AMERICAN PARTY

IN THE NORTH

IN LATE FEBRUARY 1855, the native Americans buried Bill the Butcher Poole. One of the most remarkable funerals ever seen in New York, it attracted all the nativist notables in the nation's largest city. The arch grand sachem of the Order of the United Americans was there, along with Charles Allen, founder of the Know Nothings, and Thomas Whitney, the publicist for the new antialien party. Five thousand men rode in carriages or marched behind the hearse. Half a dozen brass bands played slowly as the procession moved down Broadway past sidewalks packed solidly with thousands of silent spectators. Everywhere the last words of the martyred hero were repeated, soon to be spoken in numerous melodramas hurriedly written for lower New York's cheap theaters: "Good-bye, boys; I die a true American!"[1]

Bill the Butcher was a hoodlum, but no ordinary hoodlum. He was leader of a feared West Side gang, a street fighter supreme, the most renowned of the tough men who fought pitched battles under the Know Nothing banner against the hated Irish gangsters who owed allegiance to Tammany Hall. In the bizarre underworld of mid-nineteenth-century New York, where street muggers, fistfighting champions, civic grafters, and political ideologists intermingled in the same neighborhood gangs, the tall, muscular Poole, former butcher and famed knife-thrower, was king of the nativist brawlers. His rivalry with John Morrissey, Irish pugilist, gambler, and politico was notorious; many awaited a showdown between the two. Instead, Poole was shot and killed by Lew Baker, a minor figure in Morrissey's circle. The murder led to renewed gang warfare and a lengthy legal struggle to catch the killer, but for many it symbolized the raison d'être for the Know Nothing party.[2]

In the 1850s New York was a madhouse of street violence. By 1855 it was estimated that thirty thousand men owed allegiance to gang leaders. The fate of Bill the Butcher suggested to many the need for a militant party dedicated to limiting the power of Irish Catholic immigrants and promoting the interests of native Protestants. The next year in the Dead Rabbit Riots, the infamous Irish gang from the Five Points won the election day street battle and terrorized voters, helping to reelect the hated enemy of both nativists and the urban reformers, Mayor Fernando Wood. As in Philadelphia and Boston in previous decades, street violence escalated hostility between groups long abuilding, particularly acute now in the years immediately after the great migration from the old country. Why lend support to the new party? Crime in the streets and corruption in public office were the answers. They were reasons that subsumed or gave immediate focus to more enduring concerns: the heritage of religious fear and hatred, revulsion bred by immigrant social disorder, fear of competition in the crowded marketplace of the growing city.[3]

But if there were abundant reasons why nativism should prosper in the urban North in these years, there were also at work forces that would shape the movement in ways unknown to traditional antialiens. In New York, shrewd conservatives fleeing the Whig party provided skilled political leadership that helped make Know Nothingism a national rage. But in struggling against old foes who still controlled the state Whig party, men who supported antislavery and stood for "conscience," these nativist leaders were forced repeatedly to confront the issue that threatened to break the American party as it had other institutions. In straddling the slavery question they bought time to build on the political successes of the past and to ride the nativist tide to new victories in 1855 and 1856. Yet slavery was an issue that had resisted compromise by men shrewder than the Silver Grays, and even at the height of its power, the New York party was confronted by the specter of its own dissolution.

The paradox of nativist success in the North was compounded by the lack of unity across state lines. The Know Nothings got their start in the New York nativist fraternities, and a New Yorker was the first president of the order's National Council. Nonetheless, the political party that emerged in 1853–54 had a very different complexion in different states. In Massachusetts, where nativism scored signal victories, there was no conservative straddling of the slave question as in the Empire State. Know Nothings supported the antialien program of the party—and did so in the name of reform—but they were virulently opposed to the expansion of slavery and to the fugitive slave law. In other parts of New England, antislavery also played an increasingly larger role in Know Nothing affairs. In the end, "Americans" would discover that the issues over which they differed were as important as the religious, ethnic, and political bonds that united them. In achieving spectacular early success, they had not found a way to handle the great divisive issue of the day. Still, it was that very success which made men both within the movement and without insist that they now must "take a stand." The road to defeat was paved with victory.

★★★

New York Know Nothings and the Paradox of Success

In 1854, these dilemmas lay over the horizon. That year, the New York nativists suddenly emerged as organizers of a formidable political party. In the previous year, Know Nothings had been content to endorse a major party candidate, but now being a pressure group was not good enough. Seward and Weed were sensitive to nativist concerns, and in choosing a nominee for governor on their Whig ticket they selected Myron Clark, a member of the order and a strong temperance advocate as well. But Barker, Ullmann, and the others now in control of the movement were old enemies of Seward, who hardly had credentials as a supporter of nativism. At a carefully orchestrated meeting of the state Grand Council, they expelled Clark and his local council followers, nominated Ullmann as an American party candidate for governor, and passed a disciplinary resolution requiring all members to vote for Know Nothing candidates on pain of sanctions from the movement. Thirty local councils, composed of nativists who supported Seward and his antislavery position, now bolted the meeting. Gathering in Utica, these defectionists (called Choctaws) wrote their own thoroughly nativist platform but pledged support to Clark. Ullmann pressed on with his candidacy, only to be attacked by Seward supporters and Choctaws, who cleverly selected the issue that would damage him most.

They circulated stories that he was an alien, that he was born in Calcutta, that his brothers were both German Jews. Ullmann's friends desperately urged him to respond: "If you were really born anywhere, for Heaven's sake say where." Ullmann managed to clear himself—he was a Delaware-born Episcopalian, a Yale-trained lawyer—but ever after many referred to his followers as "Hindoos." In the end, Ullmann ran a remarkably strong third in the election, winning 122,000 votes (winner Clark had some 30,000 more), and the Know Nothings shocked the old parties by electing 19 congressmen out of New York's delegation of 33, 8 of 13 state senators, 40 of 129 in the assembly.[4]

Now the Know Nothing managers organized to smash their longtime foe. Senator Seward faced reelection time in the New York State legislature, and with the new class of nativists and a handful of Democratic votes, the Silver Grays seemed to have their revenge in hand. Allies in the OUA even sent every member in Albany a copy of *Stanhope Burleigh: The Jesuits in Our Schools*, a novel that portrayed Seward as an agent of papal power.

They underestimated Thurlow Weed and William Seward. A combination of political pressure and political concession won over some nativists. To appease them, Weed offered to support the Act of Suppression of Intemperance, Pauperism and Crime. He promised not to oppose legislation mandating control of church property in the hands of the laity, out of Archbishop Hughes's control. Others, "conscience nativists," could not turn out the antislavery senator even in the name of nativist unity. Seward won a narrow reelection victory, and in a subsequent state meeting, angry Know Nothing leaders threatened reprisals against "cowardly defectors"; one legislator who did not vote as directed was physically attacked.[5]

The failure to destroy Seward did not slow the movement's growth. Violent unrest in gang-ridden New York City, resentment against the Irish in Erie Canal towns, and the attractions of secrecy in unstable communities across the state were drawing in new members. More than 1,700 delegates at a Grand Council in February 1855 were informed that statewide the order had grown from 60 councils in May the previous year to 960 councils with 142,000 members. Three months later, state leaders would claim 1,060 councils and 175,000 members.[6]

Now the enemies of nativism mobilized to meet the threat. One state assemblyman asked, "Which is the most proscriptive, intolerant, bigoted and slavish—the Jesuit oath or that of the Know Nothing, I mean of the Hindoo stripe." Another said of the title of Grand President Barker, "What a term to apply to an American citizen . . . he exercises a power today equal to that of a monarch in Europe, yet we know not of it, nor can those who have not been given access to the secret intricate machinery of the order . . . this grand iniquity, calling itself by the sacred name of American!" Still another referred to "the American inquisition . . . reporting to its supreme head, General Jesuit Barker." One legislator read into the record a statement of several Brooklyn constituents, accusing the Grand Council of an "anti-American, anti-Republican . . . abominable, dangerous assumption of despotic powers . . . equaled only by the Inquisition of Spain, worthy of imitation by the Grand Council of Cardinals in Rome."[7]

The effort to nail the movement to its own cross, to expose it as "un-American," gained currency across the country. William Seward rose in the Senate to accuse it of "breaking society into two classes" and denying basic rights to people who helped develop the country, citing the "alien labor" on the canal and sixteen thousand immigrants at work on the railroads. Congressman William H. Witte of Pennsylvania argued that any oath-bound, secret organization was "dangerous to the institutions of republicanism, hostile to the genius of this government . . . in direct violation of the spirit of the constitution." Louis Schade, author of one of dozens of anti-nativist books and pamphlets issued in these months, offered a "statistical and economic" study of immigration, concluding that if the Know Nothing theories had ruled in 1789, America in 1850 would have but one-eighth of the 20 million people who made the nation a power in the world; the "enormous increases in shipping, commerce, settlement of the west would be no more and our pride would be flattened." Two thirds of the Know Nothings themselves had parents who had arrived after 1790, he argued. What right did their descendants have to "degrade today's immigrant to the position of a Russian serf?" Henry Ward Beecher, the eloquent abolitionist, bitterly suggested that "the Know Nothings can't become the champions of liberty. . . . One might as well study optics in the subterranean tombs of Rome as liberty in secret conclaves controlled by hoary knaves versed in political intrigue; honest men in such places have the peculiar advantage that flies have in a spider's web—the privilege of losing their legs and being eaten up at leisure."[8]

Nativists responded to these attacks with their own familiar broadsides, colored now with the confidence born of success. They were no longer men on the margins of events but defenders of a cause whose time had come. Senator Stephen Adams of Missouri dismissed the charge that the movement was undemocratic. Unlike the immigrants of old, these "new foreigners are settling in bodies . . . retaining European tongues and habits," not assimilating as did "our ancestors." Adams was concerned about the German immigrants in his native St. Louis, but other newly elected legislators mentioned the Irish. Whitney, now a congressman from New York, spoke of the temporal power of Irish Catholic bishops, who controlled church property everywhere, hoping to become cardinals, "dreaming of being a second Pope." Jacob Broome of Pennsylvania told the House of Representatives that no American should tolerate "priestly interference in civil affairs." All the old antialien complaints were trotted out by nativists suddenly finding themselves members of Congress: the sinister effort to turn public funds to sectarian purposes in the parochial schools, the machinations of Jesuits, the evil influence of Catholic immigrants in the East Coast cities. If some of their adversaries tried to picture the American party as farcical in its pretensions to secrecy and conspiracy (Seward solemnly read the principles of the Know Nothings from a newspaper only to deny he addressed any members of the order—"I know nothing of the Know Nothings"), the men of the movement were not concerned. They knew that the nativist arguments were gaining wider currency daily, that in the ideological struggle they would more than hold their own.[9]

But could they handle the question of slavery? In New York, leaders of the order desperately tried to wish away the problem. At a national meeting in Cincinnati in November 1854, they had voted for the "third degree" of membership, that pledge to "maintain and preserve the union." Despite the antislavery forces which were stirring angrily within their own camp, these conservatives responded to the plea of the southern author of the "union" degree who had begged the New Yorkers to ignore slavery: "We do not ask you to say one word in its favor . . . all we ask you to say is that if this order is to be national, it must ignore questions that are sectional."

In a meeting the following spring, Barker characterized antislave Know Nothings as "betrayers" of the movement; a newly named congressman from Queens exclaimed, "Know Nothings of New York know no North, no South, no East, no West."[10]

It was a posture that could not be maintained. Within six months, more than a million members took the "oath of absolute fidelity to union . . . to discourage and denounce any attempt coming from any quarter to destroy or subject it," pledged to seek adjustment of all political differences threatening union, and promised to vote only for candidates who opposed disunion. But the issue would not go away. When the National Council of the American party gathered in Philadelphia in June 1855, everyone knew there would be bitter conflict over the same problem that was dividing the nation.[11]

The drafters of the Philadelphia Platform tried to restate the nativist themes of their organization. There was a plank advocating "a radical revision and modification of the laws regulating immigration and the settlement of immigrants," another asking for the "essential modification of the Naturalization Laws," another pleading "resistance to the aggressive policy and corrupt tendencies of the Roman Catholic Church." If the platform did not call for total exclusion of all foreigners, complete proscription of the Catholic church, or other radical sanctions that would give credence to charges that the party was undemocratic or unwisely seeking to weaken the nation by shutting off the influx of new labor, it was filled with antialien cant. No foreigner would be allowed to own land, no person to be nominated for office who recognized allegiance to a foreign prince (read pope) or power, and—a symbolic declaration—"America must be ruled by Americans."[12]

But nativist unity would not work in Philadelphia. Southerners came prepared to insist on an end to antislavery agitation. Barker was not reelected president, for no northerner would do, and the new national leader was E. B. Bartlett of Kentucky. Delegates from the two sections introduced proslavery and antislavery resolutions. In a wild debate punctuated by threats with loaded pistols against a leader from the North, the southerners prevailed. Their report read: "It is the sense of the National Council that Congress ought not to legislate on the subject of Slavery within the Territories." It was supported by New York's delegates, but most Know Nothings from the North would have no part of it. The entire delegation from

Massachusetts led a massive defection of northern state councils, which included men from Ohio, Indiana, Illinois, New Hampshire, Vermont, Maine, Iowa, Connecticut, Rhode Island, and Wisconsin. The southern plank was tucked into the Philadelphia Platform among the nativist proposals, pledges to maintain the Union, and promises to reform corrupt party methods and fight the spoils system. It was the same time bomb that had doomed so many other national organizations.[13]

After this meeting, a number of antislave nativists held their own session in Cleveland, issuing a three-part program opposing immigrant political power, commerce in alcohol, and "slave extremism." These "Know Somethings," as they called themselves, were natural allies of the growing Republican party, now emerging from the decay of Whig and Free Soil elements. In New York, Thurlow Weed and William Seward led their followers into fusion with the Republicans in September.[14]

The vast majority of Know Nothings in New York did not desert their party at this critical hour, but they did insist on changing its tone. Barker, Ullmann, and other leaders sought to stress only the Poole murder and other Catholic and immigrant issues, but moderates forced a modification of the State Council's position on slavery at its next meeting. The cleverly worded Binghamton Platform straddled the issue with an attack on the repeal of the Missouri Compromise, and a condemnation of the Kansas-Nebraska Act. The nativist party held together, and in the elections that fall swept to victory in statewide races, gathering twenty-five thousand more votes for the head of the ticket (the secretary of state) than the previous year. The Americans' nearest rival—Seward's coalition of Republicans and Know Somethings—trailed by twelve thousand.[15]

All across the nation the story was the same. The party may have been split by the events at Philadelphia and the Republicans might be mobilizing for the future, but everywhere the startling gains of 1854 were matched and eclipsed. State races in Rhode Island, New Hampshire, and Connecticut were carried by Know Nothings, and Massachusetts remained in the nativist column. Victory in Maryland and Kentucky revealed growing strength in the border states; Democrats carried Tennessee by only the narrowest of margins. Like New York, in elections in Pennsylvania and California state offices fell to Know Nothings. In Pennsylvania, they captured 40 percent of the vote. Even in the South, traditionally dominant

Democrats were almost upset in Virginia, Georgia, Alabama, Mississippi, and Louisiana. The *New York Herald* estimated that there were 1.3 million new nativist voters and glumly predicted a presidential victory the following year. Abraham Lincoln wrote Owen Lovejoy that he could not join another new party until the American party was in decline; only then would the Republicans have a chance.[16]

Much of this success was illusory. The Know Nothing party was now swollen by political fugitives and opportunists. To satisfy some of these converts it had to avoid divisive sectional issues. But because of the crazy-quilt pattern of its new membership—strikingly different in motives, values, and politics from section to section and in some places from town to town—pleasing part of this constituency meant alienating others. But few Know Nothings concerned themselves with the paradox of their success at the dawn of the election year of 1856. The presidency was heady wine, and almost overnight nativists could seriously consider winning the White House.

In fact it was the appeal of the White House which had led to New York's support of the southerners at Philadelphia. Two New Yorkers were the leading candidates for the Know Nothing nomination in 1856. Millard Fillmore, nativist favorite in 1852, newly initiated member of the order, was the front runner. He discreetly left for Europe in the months before the nominee would be named, but he obviously was seeking support, and in his home state, Daniel Ullmann was his particular champion. His major rival was "Live Oak" George Law, a self-made New York millionaire, known by many for his bribes of aldermen and legislators in pursuit of bigger profits for his streetcar line, railroads, shipping companies, and bank. Son of an immigrant from Protestant Ireland, a former Democrat, Law organized "Live Oak" clubs to spread his name and promote his political ambitions. He made an impact in New York City by sending his clipper in pursuit of the brig in which Lew Baker had escaped after shooting Bill the Butcher Poole; Law took credit for bringing the culprit to justice. Among his supporters were a number of southern Know Nothings and James Barker, the powerful leader of nativism in the Empire State.[17]

The split between Barker and Ullmann was in the making for months and had led Fillmore's friends to help block Barker's reelection as national president. In response, Barker had grasped control of the Order of the American Star (formerly the Wide Awakes, later known as the Templars), a young men's nativist organization that conducted violent forays against Irish gangs. He even tried to bring together leaders of this group, the OUA, and the main body of the Know Nothings in support of nativist unity under his personal direction. But Ullmann and the Fillmore forces outmaneuvered their rival. With the aid of Charles Allen, founder and erstwhile leader of the order, the anti-Barker group gained control. James Barker, salesman and real-estate broker, dedicated but nonfanatic nativist, was ousted at last from state leadership.[18]

At the National Council meeting in February 1856, Fillmorites were in control. Later, at the American party presidential nominating convention, they drove their man to victory over his rival from New York and the other candidate, Sam Houston of Texas fame.[19]

It proved to be a hollow victory. Despite attractions of national power, Know Nothings could not bridge the gap north to south. In Washington, they had been unable to agree on a single candidate for Speaker of the House in the long struggle to organize the Thirty-fourth Congress. New York nativists—as usual—were split on the issue. (Nathaniel Banks, a member of the order but backed by anti-slavery radicals, was the eventual winner; his victory helped to fracture the fragile ties that bound national "Americans" together.) This failure revealed again how many of the new party's spokesmen were not real nativists. At the National Council, angry northerners demanded elimination of the odious proslavery provisions established in Philadelphia the year before, and when New York's delegates again tried to compromise the issue, they were dismissed by southerners as having "repudiated" the South in the Binghamton Platform. A jerry-built compromise was offered by District of Columbia delegates, removing the offensive references to slavery, advocating perpetuation of union and "maintenance of the reserved rights of the several states on questions pertaining solely to states," and endorsing the concept of popular sovereignty in the territories. At the 1856 nominating convention that followed, the compromise was rejected. Antislavery northerners opposed the nomination of any candidate favoring the introduction of slavery north of the old Missouri Compromise line. When their resolution was tabled, another defection occurred, this time marking a permanent fissure. The Connecticut, Massachusetts, Rhode Island, and Ohio delegations walked out, joined by individual delegates from Indiana, Iowa,

Pennsylvania, and New Hampshire. Seventy-three delegates, 20 percent of the convention, left en masse.[20]

The ties that always had bound nativists together began to unravel at these meetings. Were "Americans" only to be found among the white, Protestant, native-born population? Now the New York Know Nothings offered a distinction between hated Irish Catholic foreigners and Protestant foreigners, influenced as they were by the growing numbers of Orangemen from Northern Ireland on the margins of their movement. In Louisiana, conversely, nonchurchgoing Creole Catholics, descendants of the French and solid proslavery advocates who also opposed the Irish and German immigrants, were considered by many to be excellent candidates for the movement. After some debate, the northern effort to seat Protestant foreigners failed, and the southern move to seat Catholic natives carried.[21]

Even as it was weakening the raison d'être for nativism, the National Council moved to eliminate the secret oaths and rituals that had given the order its appeal to so many. Of course, those advocating the move argued that secrecy repelled more men than it attracted, that if the movement asked prospective members merely to "accept its principles," those who opposed secret societies on ideological grounds might accept membership. They were tired of being objects of scorn. No more could Horace Greeley remark that "they ought to say and do nothing since they know nothing." There was no need for a special Know Nothing grip, for bizarre terms to describe local councils ("babelorium"), or for the three degrees ("mumsome," "mumore," "mummost"). They rejected the impossible gobbledygook that passed for code words, the ritual initiations featuring patriotic gestures that approached hysteria, the stone tables "cut from Plymouth Rock," the horseshoes of "revolutionary gems," the talk of foreign Vandals and Goths. In the end, local option on secrecy was established, but the national organization abolished it in further national proceedings and reporters were to be invited to its subsequent meetings.[22]

What was left of nativism? Fillmore would soon discover the answer. Many "North Americans," as they were now called, met in June, pushed along by a disappointed George Law and an angry group of antislavery men. They rejected Fillmore's candidacy and sought to pressure the Republican convention into nominating House Speaker Nathaniel Banks. But Banks already had agreed to

withdraw in favor of John C. Frémont, the California Pathfinder.
The nativists' hope that Governor William F. Johnson, their vice-
presidential choice, would be accepted was blasted when Republicans refused to alienate foreign voters. In the event, the "North
Americans" reluctantly backed Frémont and William Dayton of
New Jersey. Thus two different presidential candidates were endorsed by members of the old Know Nothing movement in 1856.
Fillmore, accepting his choice in a letter from Paris—"this unsolic-
ited unrequested nomination"—would return to face an impossible
task. Moderates who formerly considered themselves Whigs were
moving to the Republican camp. Southerners and wealthy northerners (New York merchants) who might be expected to back Fillmore were defecting to the Democratic nominee, James Buchanan,
because they feared that a thoroughly divided American party had
no chance. In such a setting, Fillmore stumbled toward defeat. Political nativism, in the moment of its triumph, suddenly found itself almost everywhere in disarray.[23]

In New York, articulate "North Americans"—antislavery men
who had been nativist notables in other states—toured city and
town speaking for Frémont. On election day, the debacle that had
become inevitable almost destroyed the American party, strangled
in its cradle by the forces of disunion. Fillmore received 124,000
votes to Frémont's 276,000 and Buchanan's total of just under 200,
000. The American party gubernatorial candidate, Erastus Brooks,
also was swept to defeat and one friend of William Seward's happily
wrote, "Know Nothingism is almost crushed out all over the northern states." In fact, this was not quite the end of the story in the
Empire State. New York's Know Nothings remained a party in being—although fatally weakened—into 1859. Many members strayed
to the Democrats or dropped out of politics; others would move
into the new Republican party by 1858, but only after the antislavery party overtly reached out to the nativists by offering them a
registry act that would hurt the "Irish rabble driven in swarms to
the polls." Still, 1856 was the crucial year. In the nation, Buchanan was chosen to occupy the presidency at a critical juncture in
American history, his vote total of 1,838,000 dwarfing Frémont's
1,347,000. The American party, which had such high hopes a year
earlier, ran a weak third. Fillmore received fewer than 875,000 votes,
some 22 percent of the total.[24]

The crushing defeat of 1856 was a blow to nativists in New York, but to the men who had led the Know Nothing movement in New England it was a fitting climax to a party that had fallen from grace. In Massachusetts, nativism won its greatest victories, yet it was there that the national order had found its angriest critics. In the tension-filled months in the mid-1850s, the appeal of the antialien cause had been washed away in the angry passion of antislavery rhetoric.

★★★

New England Nativists and the Politics of Reform

The leaders of the triumphant Massachusetts Know Nothings in 1854 were not really nativists, they were opportunists, politicians in search of a party. Henry Wilson, president of the Massachusetts Senate and named a United States senator in January 1855, was a Free Soiler, an antislavery man looking for a forum and a vehicle with which to achieve national influence. Henry J. Gardner, elected governor in the Know Nothing landslide with a thirty-three thousand-vote plurality, formerly had been an active Whig and president of the Boston Common Council. Gardner, at least, used the rhetoric of nativism, but like Wilson, he was there for personal reasons largely unconnected to the ideology of the old antialien crusade.[25]

It was a coalition of "Conscience" Whigs—who earlier had lost control of their state party to commercial forces sympathetic to the southern cotton trade—and angry anti–Nebraska Act Democrats who swelled the ranks of Massachusetts Know Nothings under the leadership of Wilson and Gardner, two men who rarely agreed on the issues. But many were reformers not only on the abolition and free-soil questions but on other matters as well. And they were given reason to channel their energy into nativist activity by the apparently reactionary role played by the Catholic church within their state.[26]

A state constitutional convention in 1853 had produced a document embraced by many reformers. But the proposed constitution was beaten in a ratification vote after the church mounted a furious campaign against it. The constitution had called for the elimination of property requirements for voting and reduced terms of office for judges. But the church's influential paper, the *Boston Pilot,* assailed it as a "monstrous" proposal because its adoption might result in withholding public money from sectarian schools, because it funneled "political power to non-Irish rural districts," and because it was "the work of Free Soilers."[27]

Was there a clear linkage between "Catholicism and Cotton" as some angry reformers now alleged? These "Irish," one noted, were backing fugitive slave proposals "only on the shallow pretext of upholding the law." Perhaps, as Theodore Parker charged, the Catholic clergy was "on the side of slavery." Nativism and antislavery shared the fear of powerful conspiracies threatening the republic; in one case it was the slavocracy, in the other, the church of Rome. One paper concluded that "these two malign powers have a natural affinity."[28]

Against such conservatism, the American party would become an instrument for reform. Some Catholics gave credence to this development by assailing it as "a product of French radicalism and German Socialism." With that opposition, nativism as liberalism seemed to make sense in Massachusetts. After all, the "Irish Democrats" were a negative force on many reform questions: temperance, feminism, and emancipation. The Know Nothing legislature that met in 1855 eliminated debt imprisonment, established the first insurance commission, strengthened women's rights, made smallpox vaccination compulsory, and, of course, endorsed antislavery laws. The assembly passing these bills was composed of political amateurs. There had been forty-six lawyers seated in 1854; the "Know Nothing Legislature" contained only eleven. These newcomers made a remarkable reform record.[29]

Still, it was a performance marked by anti-Catholic, antialien hostility. When Governor Gardner addressed the lawmakers, he cited the "frightening rise" in the population of the immigrants. After describing the crime, drunkenness, and poverty they brought to the state, he called for a "crackdown" on the "shipping of the poor to the United States," the exclusion of aliens from the military, and a constitutional amendment to prevent "these people" from gaining the franchise through rapid naturalization. The legislature that passed the agenda of reform now also sponsored a special committee to inspect nunneries and convents, a throwback to the hysteria of the Maria Monk scandal. The committee junketeers spent less time investigating Catholic institutions than at state-funded champagne dinners, but they reminded everyone that nativism remained part of the Know Nothing appeal even after the movement had become a receptacle for so many other ideas and passions. A party organ, the *Know Nothing and American Crusader*, gloried in the triumph of the legislature: "Old Massachusetts is thoroughly Americanized.... The Romish Harlot is on the defensive ... death to all foreign influences."[30]

But could it last? Could a party be both antislave and antialien, for freedom and for proscription? Lincoln wrote to abolitionist Owen Lovejoy in 1855 that "I do not perceive how anyone professing to be sensitive to the wrongs to the Negro can join in a league to degrade a class of White men." Emerson concluded that the Know Nothings represented an "abdication of reason ... an immense joke."[31]

In the end, the very divisiveness of the slavery issue eclipsed all other questions, including the philosophical problem raised by Lincoln. Henry Wilson, that senator who was elected as a Know Nothing but told audiences he had "no sympathy with the narrow, bigoted, intolerant spirit that would make war on a race of men because they happen to be born in other lands ... it is criminal fanaticism to oppress the Celt or the German," embodied the dilemma of nativism by 1855. Never a real nativist, he would abandon the American party if it did not reflect his exact views on slavery. Many rank-and-file Know Nothings in Massachusetts were in the party because of their fear of the Irish Catholic "menace," but their movement would founder if its leadership abandoned the cause. By 1855, Wilson was doing just that. He assailed the Cincinnati "Third Degree" as a plot by southerners with "the aid of dough-faces from New York" to endorse the "Slave Power." He was furious at the platform emerging from the Philadelphia convention—where he had been the man threatened by a revolver—and exclaimed that "I will support no man who stands upon it." By 1856, he said that "the transcendent issue of our age in America" was slavery, that any party which "represses the anti-slavery men ... surely shall begin to die and I will do what I can to make it die." At last, he rejected the American party as "broken and splintered to atoms by its failure on the question of abolition."[32]

For all its electoral and legislative success, the Massachusetts movement was doomed. Unlike New York, here nativism was the repository of reform, but in the end it made no difference. Once the movement was taken over by leaders largely concerned with another crusade, the antialien themes could serve as no enduring fraternal bond. Nativism always had been a refuge for some people escaping problems in American life, but never before had it been used in this way. After 1856, large numbers of those deserting the American party joined the new antislavery movement (although a significant minority voted Democratic) but many others did not. These true nativists, more concerned about the religious and ethnic enemy within their communities than the emancipation of black people far away, now refused to support Republicans or Democrats. They simply abandoned political participation. They were "Americanists," but their party was moribund. They had nowhere to go. In Massachusetts, nativist success had become illusion.[33]

So it was throughout the North. In Connecticut, the Know-Nothing triumphs were based on an influx of antislave politicians turning away from failed parties to any likely alternative to those national Democratic straddlers who embraced the Kansas-Nebraska compromise on slavery. In the case of the Whigs, they came from a party that never had stressed nativism; in 1854 that organization even courted the German vote. But now the Whig party was facing dissolution. The Temperance (Maine Law) alternative was not viable, and most members turned to the American party. In the 1855 election, nativism won a striking victory when the Know Nothings edged the Democrats and overwhelmed all other rivals, taking four congressional seats, the governor's race, and eighteen of twenty-one state senate seats.[34]

As in Massachusetts, a bloc of members had substantial ties to traditional nativism. In a state where Irish Catholic growth had been particularly rapid since 1850, with the number of churches tripling, the new government moved to limit the influence of the "papists" and foreigners. The legislature acted to circumscribe church control of property, to strengthen literacy tests for voting, and to eliminate Irish units in the militia. These newly elected Americans in the state assembly were from old-line families; one-half were farmers, most were Congregationalists, many could trace their ancestry to revolutionary days. Never friendly to the Irish or the "Jesuits," those who were recent Know Nothing recruits had rejected the Democratic party in part because it had pandered to the

Irish Catholic vote. Many of them, however, were even more concerned about slavery.[35]

Like their fellow new Know Nothings in New Jersey and Rhode Island—where handbills proclaimed "Americans to the Rescue" and the influential *Providence Journal*, in turning away from the Whigs to support the American party became increasingly anti-Catholic—these Connecticut nativists embraced the old themes of the movement. But most would not stay with the cause if it failed to deal with the great sectional question. As happened in Massachusetts, when the national party seemed to waver at Cincinnati and Philadelphia, most of the southern New England Americans lost their enthusiasm.[36]

At the National Council in 1856, Connecticut delegates walked out en masse. Soon after, the state party abandoned fraternal secrecy: "Every member shall be at liberty to make known the existence of the order and the fact that he himself is a member." Know Nothings no longer in form or principle, party members drifted away, many to the new Republican alternative. By 1857, most Connecticut State Council members wanted to dissolve their party, but only a handful cared enough to be present at a meeting to decide its fate. In a matter of months, the majority party of the state had disintegrated, its nativist program all but forgotten.[37]

What explains the sudden, spectacular rise of the Know Nothing party in the North and its equally sudden fragmentation and disintegration? A group of gifted historians who apply ethnocultural analysis to the study of political developments—including Michael Holt, Paul Kleppner, Joel H. Silbey, and Ronald P. Formisano, among others—have shed new light on this question. Clearly there were several forces at work. The enduring specter of the "Catholic menace" and the vast influx of Irish immigrants earlier in the decade created the setting for the political appeal of nativism. The breakdown of the old party system provided a vast new source of potential recruits, people suddenly without an allegiance. Moreover, many of these recruits, as some scholars have argued, were disgusted with politics as usual in America, with corrupt parties and crooked judges, with rigged legislative elections and a festering spoils system. A new party of new men might offer a fresh start, a way to deal with the danger of the Catholic foreigners who threatened stability, a way to unseat the old politicos who often schemed to stay in office by manipulating the votes of these dangerous but

credulous Irishmen. Particularly in New England, the curious linkage between nativism and reform seemed natural enough to these
new supporters.[38]

But could any major party ignore the issue of slavery and survive?
The traditional interpretation of the rise and fall of the American
party in the North attributed both its success and failure to the
question of abolition: it became a great party because it attracted
thousands seeking a way out of the Union-threatening dilemma,
and it collapsed when its new followers were forced to choose sides
on the issue. This view does not account for the rise of the party,
but it does help to explain its rapid demise. For if many nativists
simply dropped out of politics when the only party that spoke to
their real political interest dissolved in 1856, others did move toward the Republicans. (This was not true universally; the Know
Nothing voters were a varied group and a substantial minority
drifted to the Democrats.) But the shift of many former Americans
to the antislavery cause does not mean that the Know Nothing
party was merely a transitional stage in the recruitment of new
antislavery militants. It was the paradox of success that ruined the
nativist party in the North. Nativism's electoral and legislative triumphs were not keyed to the slave issue, but if there were enough
such victories, the party would be forced to take a stand on slavery.
No major American institution by the late 1850s could avoid this
choice, and once the American party became a major party—and
no longer a cohesive fraternal order—its fate was sealed. With
many opportunistic politicians using it for their own purposes—
some ideologues on slavery, some self-serving compromisers—it
could not avoid the question that would inevitably rip it apart.
Once its leaders made their choices, as with Fillmore in New York
and Wilson in Massachusetts, the party was doomed in the North.
The same outcome would occur in other sections as well.[39]

★ ★

CHAPTER 9

THE SEARCH FOR A
NATIVIST SOLUTION IN
THE WEST AND SOUTH

IN THE NORTHWEST, political nativism foundered for the same reasons as it did in the East. But its demise there stirred less interest because it was never as formidable as in New England and New York.

In the 1850s, the Know Nothing party west of Buffalo was based on hostility to foreigners who were German rather than Irish, "aliens" who were farmers in greater numbers than urbanites, newcomers economically more prosperous and socially more stable than immigrants in the East. Years later, Frederick Jackson Turner insisted that "western pioneer democracy" made this section infertile ground for nativism because "here all were accepted and intermingling components of a forming society, plastic and absorptive." It was a society, he insisted, in which "men learned to drop their old national animosities," in which America was taught "the lesson of national cross-fertilization instead of national enmities." Turner's vision, as always, was romantic. But there was no denying that in the West, facing so many obstacles, the Know Nothings were, at best, on the margins of power.[1]

Some Irish had moved west but not nearly as many as those emigrants from the German Empire. Between 1852 and 1854, German immigration reached a historic plateau, with more than one-half million arrivals in three years. By 1860, the German-born population in the United States climbed to 1.27 million from 587,000 a decade before. And most of these newcomers were heading to the Midwest.[2]

Some settled in the cities. Chicago's population became one-half foreign-born, the majority of them German; Cincinnati's 45 percent foreign, over two-thirds from the German Empire. But many of these new Americans found the resources to acquire farms in the great agricultural heartland. Helped by aid societies unavailable to the Irish back East, such as the National Society for German Emigration, these more fortunate settlers took advantage of the availability of relatively cheap land. They were heading for a familiar environment; they had been farmers at home, and they moved "from forest to forest," as one of their chroniclers reported.[3]

Of course, there was some resentment at these "aliens" taking fertile acreage which natives may have coveted, but such hostility did not last long. Unlike the festering ethnic slums of Boston, New York, and Philadelphia, the vast spaces of the western countryside limited abrasive contacts between groups. Nativism flourished more easily in the city, where social disorder could be linked to the coming of the immigrants. It flourished where the fraternal movement offered refuge to those having trouble adjusting to the perils of life in a changing urban society. Although the "beer-drinking foreigners" in Milwaukee and Cincinnati infuriated some of their Yankee-born neighbors, violating the sabbath with their "German Sunday," evoking comparisons with the "drunken and criminal Irish" in the great eastern cities, the urban strife in the West paled in comparison.[4]

★★★

The Fate of Nativism in the Midwest and West

But if political nativism lacked the setting for rapid growth in the West, it faced the same problems it encountered in the areas of its greatest success. In the West the party lacked ideological constancy from state to state and in different regions within states. In some places, it appealed to political reformers. In others, it was the temporary instrument of antislavery forces. In still others, its brand of nativism led to the acceptance of some immigrants into the movement in the hope of saving the Union through seeking compromise on its most divisive problem. From state to state, the party rose and fell for different reasons.

In Indiana, the party was particularly successful and grew rapidly after its birth in 1854. Within three months, national leaders claimed thirty thousand members; by September, Indiana was said to have eighty-seven thousand Know Nothings. Who were these nativists? One Terre Haute paper claimed that it was a "movement of faceless men" and wondered if "there is a K.N. wigwam among us?" To protect its secrecy, members were encouraged to meet in darkened rooms, to guard continuously against "snoopers," to gather in large numbers only in open cornfields. One state critic, a liberal politician named George Julian, attacked its subversive secrecy, its policy of "suppressing the freedom of speech."[5]

But the Know Nothings in Indiana were confronted from the very start by the question of abolition. When the Fusion or People's party was organized to advance the antislavery views of a polyglot collection of anti–Kansas-Nebraska Act Democrats, disgruntled "Conscience" Whigs, former Free Soilers, and assorted other Indiana abolitionists, the new Know Nothings were instructed at their secret lodge meetings to join this organization. They were to bore from within, to seek the nomination of nativists on Fusion tickets and the acceptance of antialien planks in its platform. Some Fusion leaders initially objected to the presence of nativism, arguing that it was a southern plot to keep the North from outstripping the South in the sectional struggle for national hegemony by limiting northern population growth. Other Fusionites feared that antialienism might eclipse antislavery as the major theme of their party. Still, the Know Nothings were successful in their infiltration. Nine of eleven Know Nothing–backed Fusion candidates won congressional and legislative races in fall 1854. This nativist victory would prove as Pyrrhic in Indiana as in Massachusetts.[6]

Know Nothings could no longer avoid the fatal divisiveness of the slavery question. Members recruited to the movement in the northern and central sections of the state had been abolitionists if they took a position on this issue. But some from the southern counties—émigrés from North Carolina in earlier decades—were not. They embraced the views of the national Know Nothing leaders who proposed the Cincinnati pledge of union, the avoidance of any abolitionist activity. Indiana's nativist organization now was pulled apart, as the majority of antislavery men rejected the Cincinnati straddle and joined many northeastern delegates and fellow midwesterners from Michigan and Ohio in walking out of the Philadelphia Know Nothing council in 1855 and the convention of their party in 1856. As in other states, Indiana's American party now split into "North" and "South" factions, with disappointed dissidents organizing "Know Something" groups on the margins. Finally, when the movement changed its policy on secrecy, reducing its fraternal appeal, eliminating its mystique, and removing the fear and dread it had inspired among some opponents, Know Nothings were finished in Indiana.[7]

In Wisconsin, political nativism also foundered in 1856, but its demise was less important because it had never made a significant impact. Here again, abolitionism was a central issue. The large German Catholic population in Milwaukee and its hinterland shunned slavery but was conservative on the issue of union. Immigrants who had risked so much to find a new home in a new land particularly feared the specter of civil war. They were steadfast Democrats, as were other midwestern German Catholics. The Know Nothings attempted to tie these "foreign mercenaries from the old world" to the slave conspiracy but made only modest gains by 1855. A nativist paper, the *Milwaukee Daily American*, announced that "the man who is a Roman cannot be an American" and claimed that the movement influenced twenty thousand nativists to vote for the Republican candidates that fall. The Know Nothings were not successful in fielding their own slate in Wisconsin, but their influence within the GOP also proved limited; the growing "foreign vote" seemed as attractive as the nativist vote to many of this new party. In addition, influential land speculators and railroad builders within the state who promoted development and wanted rapid population growth announced opposition to any nativist program restricting immigration. After the Philadelphia meeting of 1856, with the national party in tatters, the movement had no future in Wisconsin.[8]

In Illinois, nativism made a bigger impact at the polls but quickly was split on the slavery issue. As elsewhere, the Know Nothings emerged in 1854 out of the secret brotherhoods of the Order of the Star Spangled Banner. "The K.N.'s are suspected of being about, but no one knows anything of them or what they design," the *Illinois State Register* reported in late summer. Their "design" remained obscure even after congressional victories in two districts in the fall, for political nativism in this state failed to maintain cohesion from its very birth. Two factions—the Jonathans and the Sams—appeared within the movement, a reflection within the American party of the sectional crisis in America.[9]

The Sams, anti-Catholic and antiforeign, were truly nativistic in program and policy. But because they stressed traditional antialien themes and so avoided the slavery question, they attracted pro-Union interlopers from the Douglas wing of the Democratic party. These backers of the Kansas-Nebraska Act infiltrated Know Nothing lodges. Strikingly different, the Jonathans became antislavery people, whose "American Platform for Illinois" was a free-soil document with only a weak nod in the direction of nativism. Some German-Americans even joined the Jonathan group, a Know Nothing faction now nativist in name only. With such divisions, it surprised no one when the Illinois party disintegrated after 1856.[10]

Farther west, the course of interparty discord was different, but the result was the same. In California, political reform helped the Know Nothings at first but doomed them in the end. In 1854, the secret nativist councils throughout the state offered only a mild version of the antialien program of the eastern seaboard fraternities. They called for "judicious revision of naturalization laws" and "no union of church and state." They attracted new members in the sparsely settled region by offering a sense of community through the ritual and brotherhood of the secret society. What made the Know Nothings a force to be reckoned with here was not their nativist ideology but their appeal as the party of reform.[11]

In San Francisco, there had been calls for a "Citizen's Party" to clean up politics. The old system was breaking down, and the surviving Democratic organization had split into three factions, including a "Tammany Wing." The Democrats now were accused of being the party of vice and fraud, of manipulating elections and perpetrating wholesale corruption. The Know Nothings emerged to offer a "Citizen Reform Ticket," a crusade—as one paper called it—to "place new men in office." They achieved initial success in the fall and won major victories in Sacramento, Stockton, and other towns the next spring. They stuck to their reform agenda, shrewdly eluding the slavery question, opposing all "sectional" agitation.[12]

It was a promising beginning but it did not last. Despite their tepid nativist platform, Know Nothings soon were attacked by a "Freedom's Phalanx" of naturalized citizens, organized and encouraged by Democrats. In a state in which three out of eight people were foreign-born and Catholics had been the first settlers, nativism's proscriptive policies were unpopular. The Know Nothings had been careful not to offend the Spanish and Oriental-American populations, but even their modest slogan—"America for the Americans"—hurt them on the West Coast. So, too, did their political ineptitude and their image of political purity. These "new men" proved to be amateurs in office, lacking leadership and discipline, outmaneuvered in the legislature when they finally were seated. They also proved vulnerable to the attractions of the spoils system. Even their spokesman in the assembly soon asked: "Have some of us been willing to sink our honor and our sacred oaths to increase our own transitory fortunes?" Assailed for being as bad as the corrupters they had replaced, they were beaten soundly in 1856. In this year of national political crisis, they had backed Fillmore and voted for "non-interference with slavery" at their party's Philadelphia meeting, hoping to prevail at the polls in California on local issues. But by voting time, their local appeal was fast eroding and the slavery question only sealed their fate. With the breakup of the party in the East and the end of their secret fraternities, the California Know Nothings shared the fate of nativists everywhere by 1857.[13]

Nowhere did the western movement make the impact it did in the East. As one historian notes, it did serve to coalesce "pietistic discontent" against immigrant Catholics; it represented a response to cultural pluralism that would affect future political alignments. But it was a failure in the 1850s. In Michigan, Know Nothings were organized by summer of 1854; they opposed the Democrats and succeeded in influencing the emerging antislavery Fusionists in the state legislature of 1855. Nativists were rewarded for their support with a church property bill aimed at Catholics and were almost given a "nunneries" act, as in Massachusetts. But after the Philadelphia meeting, the Michigan delegates withdrew from the movement and as "Know Somethings," nativism in this state disappeared into the Republican organization. In some places it was even used by its enemies. In Iowa, Governor James Grimes was an antinativist but professed to like the Know Nothings because "they help to break down the old parties, to make the Republicans" the party of the future. In Minnesota, where Norwegian and Swedish-American papers had criticized German-Americans for drinking on Sunday and some Protestant Germans had been strongly anti-Catholic, the coming of the Know Nothings created bonds among formerly warring groups. Some people feared that nativism might succeed in the West—handbills were even distributed in Saxony in

1854 warning German émigrés of the hostile treatment they would face in the American West from the secret brotherhood—but the setting never existed for nativist success in this region. The population mix was wrong, ethnic strife was lacking, and the opportunists and ideologues from outside the movement manipulated nativism for their own purposes. But if the movement was weak in the west, it was a different story in the South.[14]

★★★

The Know Nothings in the South

At first glance, the rise of political nativism in the South in the 1850s seems inexplicable in its traditional terms. For where were the immigrants? With only a few notable exceptions, the South had been insulated from the great European migrations of 1847–54. If there were no aliens, why should there be a major antialien movement? Was the growth of the American party in this region unconnected to ethnic and religious hostility, merely a response to the sectional crisis that was reshaping the party system in these tumultuous years? But such a conclusion does not do full justice to a complicated story. As elsewhere, there were many elements to the search for a nativist solution in the South.

It was true that the South was the land of the native-born. In 1860, when over 21 percent of the population of Massachusetts and Rhode Island and 25 percent in New York was foreign-born, the states of the South Atlantic and South Central regions were almost unaffected by newcomers. In the West, 19 percent of the Illinois and Michigan populations were foreign, 35 percent in Wisconsin and Minnesota, 38 percent in California. But in the South, the numbers were minuscule: 1 or 2 percent or less of the populations of North and South Carolina, Georgia, Alabama, Tennessee, Florida, Mississippi, Arkansas, and Virginia. Only Texas, with 7 percent and Louisiana—including its cosmopolitan center of New Orleans—with 11 percent had large numbers of foreign-born. In the border states, significant numbers of immigrants had come to Baltimore and Louisville; Maryland's foreign population was over 11 percent in 1850 and Kentucky's over 5 percent, almost sixty thousand people.[15]

The lack of industry in the agrarian region, the presence of a vast population of slave laborers, and the absence of urban centers and ethnic communities in most areas discouraged immigration. But nativism made its mark for a variety of reasons, some linked to the same themes that appealed to "Americanists" in the North.

Many southerners viewed the immigrants of the Northeast and West as threatening to the southern "way of life." These new-comers were assumed to be opposed to slavery and in favor of free soil in the lands into which they hoped to move someday. They surely were ignorant of southern culture and irrationally resentful of the bourbon elite. They constituted a huge new voting constitu-ency that would unbalance the political scales in favor of a grow-ing North, if only because they represented an ignorant and pli-able mob to be manipulated by urban bosses, enemies of southern regional interests. For protectors of the southern version of the American dream in 1854, nativism seemed an answer.[16]

In addition, it represented an escape for those seeking refuge from the divisive struggle that threatened civil strife. Nativism offered a unifying theme in which all Americans—north and south—could work together against a common foe. It offered an alternative to the slavery question, a place where homeless politicians and anxious activists could find an answer to the racist fire-eaters who would bring the area to the brink of war. It was no surprise that prominent political figures in the South were attracted to the new American party.[17]

But if the Know-Nothing movement appealed to fugitives fleeing the slavery crisis of the 1850s, its national division on this issue offered an easy target to enemies in the South. If the nativists of Massachusetts and Connecticut, Wisconsin and Illinois were free-soilers and abolitionists, how could southerners in the Ameri-can party call for unified support of an antialien program? If some northern nativists assailed immigrants as tools of the slave power, how long before Know Nothing's enemies in the South would use this weapon against the party? By 1856, the political and emotional dynamite of the slavery issue was threatening to blow apart the dreams of a southern nativist solution. From state to state, the Americanists and their adversaries struggled with these questions.[18]

In Kentucky, a border state, the Know Nothings found a measure of success. Here, a growing population of German and Irish im-migrants provided the same setting of urban conflict and social disorder that stimulated nativist organization in the North. By 1856, the Catholic population of Louisville had almost doubled from the thirty thousand settled in 1845. The number of Catholic churches expanded to seventy-seven, and the presence of German immigrants was felt throughout the city.[19]

The secret Order of United Americans appeared in the state, pledging to check the expanding power of the "aliens." When the Know Nothing party was organized out of the fraternal lodges, it grew rapidly, its friends and adversaries alike claiming thirty-five thousand members by early 1855. Antinativist journalists attributed the growth—"almost bodily," the *Louisville Times* insisted— to the disintegration of the Whig party and the attraction of the new American organization for homeless politicians. But it was more than this. George Prentice, founder of the *Louisville Journal* (a nativist paper in its early years), announced that his study of the antidemocratic teachings of the Roman Catholic church had made him a believer in the new crusade: "an intolerant and persecuting church has thrived on the spoils of misery and ignorance." Germans and Irish, he insisted, must be checked in Kentucky.[20]

When Germans in Louisville reacted to the Know Nothing challenge by forming *Sag Nicht* or "Say Nothing" societies—secret orders intended to use the Know Nothings' tactics against them —tension between natives and their adversaries rose. Now came "Bloody Monday," a time of ugly violence in August, when the nativists won the street battle on election day, harassing voters without the Know Nothing "yellow ticket" and organizing mask-wearing mobs of men. According to German-American papers, these mobs threatened the cathedral and even menaced Protestants unfortunate enough to be discovered in the wrong neighborhoods.[21]

The mounting ethnic and religious hostility led to Know Nothing victories at the polls, with a governor, secretary of state, and six congressmen elected. The secretary would be named to the U.S. Senate. He was John J. Crittenden, an antiabolitionist dedicated to finding a Unionist solution, a major political figure, the most notable of the men who sought a new platform in the American party. In the Thirty-fourth Congress, Crittenden was also a believer in nativism; he said that he feared "foreign blocs," and he introduced legislation opposing the "facile access to citizenship" by immigrants. Other Kentuckians became prominent in the national party apparatus, and Major Edward B. Bartlett, named president of the national Order of United Americans, played a major role at the Philadelphia meetings of the party.[22]

But it was the sectional split over slavery at Philadelphia that ultimately doomed this state movement just as it would in New York, Massachusetts, and throughout the North and West. Representative L. M. Cox, a Kentucky Know Nothing, assailed the northern American delegates who walked out of the meeting as wanting an "Abolition Party": "I recognize no man as belonging to the American Party who bolts that platform. . . . I would rather vote for Archbishop Hughes for the Presidency than for any one of those who refused to acquiesce" to a compromise on the slavery issue. "One who supports the principle and purpose of abolition is un-Americanized, he should be thrown out of the party, not treated as a Know Nothing."[23]

In Kentucky, the American party endured to 1859 but only as a shell. Secrecy was abolished, the National Council abandoned, and election defeats inevitable in 1857 and 1858. The party had scored local successes earlier but failed to carry Kentucky for Fillmore in 1856, when Democrat Buchanan—and his Kentuckian running mate—was the winner by less than seventy thousand votes. Now it was moribund in this critical border region.

Nativism's failure in Kentucky was paralleled far to the south and west in Texas. Here antialienism was rooted in an enduring hostility to Catholic Mexico, against which the Texans had rebelled twenty years before the birth of the American party. In the 1830s, Stephen Austin had assailed "Rome . . . that mother of executions, assassins, robbers and tyrants who have desolated the civilized world." The preamble of the Declaration of Independence of the Republic of Texas had reviled that "most intolerable of all tyranny . . . the combined despotism of the sword and the priesthood." With the immigration of large numbers of Germans—attracted to a huge and empty land in need of new settlers in the early 1850s—the old nativist feeling in the state gained wider support. When the Know Nothings emerged out of the secret orders in 1854, the movement's paper attacked Germans and Mexicans as hostile to democracy and to the native-born. Now German voters flocked to the Democratic party, and Sam Houston appeared as a key nativist figure. Houston was a true believer. Secret societies, he argued, were the appropriate response to despotism and tyranny. He asked: "Have not Catholics cursed and threatened us? Are not their doctrines opposed to republican institutions?" Houston was a contender for the national leadership of the Know Nothings at Cincinnati in 1854, and Texas seemed a hotbed of American party activity. But in the end, the sectional division in the national party devastated its prospects in the state. The Americans were beaten two to one in the Texas vote for president in 1856, after the Philadelphia defections had split the nativist cause north and south. Further losses followed in the gubernatorial race in 1857. With the slavery issue looming larger, some Know Nothings tried to form a conservative popular front called the National Union party. But after John Brown's raid at Harpers Ferry, all efforts to avoid the sectional crisis collapsed and political nativism disintegrated in Texas.[24]

In Virginia, the story was similar. There was much nativist activity but few concrete results. Here, the movement made progress only after the unionist declarations at Cincinnati and Philadelphia, but even then it ran into problems. Shrewd opponents were able to use the Know Nothings' arguments against them, and the antialien alternative was short-lived in this major southern state.

In 1855, a Virginian, William M. Burwell, offered the majority report on slavery, sectional strife, and union, which angered northerners at Philadelphia. In the governor's race that year, Thomas S. Flournoy headed the American ticket, trying to link fear of immigration with the specter of sectional strife. He told his Virginia listeners that foreigners "shunned the south" because of the competition of slave labor, and in moving north "to make a majority against you," they "bred abolitionism" and put the South "at the mercy of fanaticism." Alabama Know Nothing leader S. F. Rice was quoted: "The Irish are by nature abolitionist, they hold fast to the abolitionist principles of Daniel O'Connell." But Flournoy was not an energetic campaigner, and for all his followers' talk of "Red Republicanism" and "immigrant paupers and criminals," he was overwhelmed at the polls. Democrat Henry A. Wise won eighty-three thousand votes to Flournoy's seventy-three thousand, with Americanists taking only 6 of 25 state senate races and 53 of 149 House seats.[25]

Wise proved a brilliant campaigner, the most effective antinativist candidate in the nation in the mid-1850s. He shrewdly manipulated both the symbols of democracy and the fear of abolitionists in his attack on the Know Nothings. "Truth," he said, "must be free to combat error," and the secrecy of the Know Nothings was "subversive of American principles and of the spirit of the Magna Carta." These skulking, secret intriguers must lack "pride and love of country," for they "seek to turn America against itself." Their nativism is nonsense, he insisted, for the only true natives are Indians, and it was a Catholic—Columbus—who discovered America for white men. The American Revolution was not fought for the antialien theory of exclusion; the Fathers created America as an "asylum for the oppressed of every land," and in so doing they were working in the tradition of the Protestant Reformation, "which also stood against bigotry, intolerance, proscription and persecution." Indeed, Wise deftly derided the Know Nothings' role as defenders of Protestantism, suggesting that if Catholics defer to priests in elections, it would be nonsense for Protestants to defer to nativist "priests," those who try to "out-Jesuit the Jesuits" by adopting "their Machiavellian Creed." If you dislike Catholics, Wise urged, "don't emulate their Jesuitical secret societies." Anyway, there was nothing wrong with these foreigners, argued this slaveholding southerner in his brief for civil liberties: the Irish had built roads and canals and made America a stronger nation. Still, Wise turned to slavery to make his most damning case against political nativism in the South. Great cheers greeted his statement that "the new party was formed especially for the sake of abolitionism," that it was led in the North by "the most notorious, most inveterate abolitionist leaders," that in standing against it he was "defending the cause of states' rights."[26]

The Virginia nativists had no persuasive answer to Henry Wise's polemics. They did try to tie nativism to the tradition of the Virginia giants of the days of the early republic, enlisting Madison as a supporter (he had taught that "Americans must rule America"), Jefferson (who had warned that "priest-ridden societies" never could embrace democracy), as well as George Washington. But few were listening. They warned that "if immigration continues . . . in thirteen years the foreign population will engulf the white population of fifteen slave states." But more important to most potential converts was the breakup of the national nativist movement, the warnings of Henry Wise made manifest in the defection of northern Know Nothings. After 1856, the party was finished in Virginia.[27]

In Louisiana, it would have better fortune. New Orleans had a long history of ethnic conflict. Latin Creoles, descendants of French and Spanish colonial settlers, had clashed for decades with Anglo-Americans, whose families had arrived after the 1803 Louisiana Purchase. A new element was introduced with the influx of Irish and German settlers during the great migrations of the 1840s and early 1850s. In the political struggles among these three contending blocs, the newcomers often held the balance of power. As early as 1850, one in five New Orleans residents was a native of Ireland; they were living in the South's largest city, the nation's third largest in the 1840 census. The alleged "clannishness" of these aliens in a densely populated urban environment and the even larger proportion of ill and handicapped foreigners in a community more permissive in accepting immigrants than New York or Boston created the familiar nativist reaction. The new settlers were seen by many as the source of crime and filth, of disease and poverty, of all the problems that plagued the city.[28]

But because New Orleans was a southern city and had a unique history of cultural divisiveness, nativism would flourish in ways different from in a northern metropolis. The breakdown of the Whig party left large numbers of Anglo-Americans in search of a political organization with which to confront the Democratic party, dominated by Creoles and Irish immigrants. As early as 1853, the *Daily Picayune* complained of "fraudulent immigrant voters marched to the polls," of "hand-picked Irish democratic election officials" manipulated by the Creoles. In such a setting, the Know Nothing cause would appeal to the politically homeless. It would seem to be an instrument with which to protect the community from the immigrant menace. But it could also be the party of reform, dedicated to cleaning up the Irish-Creole polling abuses. In fact, before becoming the American party, the Know Nothings were known as the Independent Reform Party. One spokesman explained that "ignorant tools can't be trusted with political power," that this new party offered a choice: "the vigorous vitality of the young eagle or the decrepitude of the Democratic Party." In this way, Know Nothings attracted Anglo-Americans. But they were opposed by most other groups, including non-Catholic Germans, offended by the antialien theme. Their passionate nativism contributed to the violent election day clashes in 1854, when Know Nothings met the "wild Irish." "Clear the polls you damned Dutch and Irish sons of bitches," shouted the Know Nothing gang leaders, and knife fights, street brawls, and killings soon followed. Nativists won major election victories in 1854, and by 1855 they were the most powerful political force in the city. Cloaked in fraternal secrecy, as elsewhere, they were now a mysterious but formidable movement. But they would remain strong only if they could straddle the slavery issue in this Deep South city. They maintained silence on the question, supported the Constitution, and sought to focus strong feelings on their antialien agenda.[29]

Of course, the bitter quarrel within the national party would threaten Louisiana Americans as all others. The New Orleans delegates to the national meetings played a peculiar role in these debates. A small number of Creoles had joined the movement, and one of them—Charles Gayarré—was a powerful spokesman in the Louisiana contingent, threatening his state party's disaffiliation from the national American movement if Catholics were not allowed admission to the nativist national hierarchy. An outspoken foe of "easy immigrant naturalization," a man who felt that his antialien credentials were in order but who made a distinction between "foreigners" and Catholics, Gayarré failed to win support and Louisiana temporarily withdrew from national party affairs. But the state organization did not dissolve as its Creole minority might have wished, and long after Gayarré's disappearance, the Know Nothings in New Orleans survived, outlasting their nativist colleagues in most other areas. They carried the city for Fillmore by a wide margin in 1856 (although losing the statewide race) and persevered in the city—if not in the rest of Louisiana—after the disintegration of the national party. Dismantling the secret orders and even appealing to Catholics after 1857, the Know Nothings in New Orleans now stayed alive only by retreating from nativism. They were active in supporting John Bell and the Constitutional Union ticket in 1860. After secession, they maintained a measure of cohesion, calling themselves the Southern American party, still the Anglo-American political alternative to the Creole-Irish majority. The slavery issue did not destroy political nativism in New Orleans as it had throughout the South and the nation, but it did turn it into a meaningless receptacle.[30]

In Maryland, the movement also survived longer than in most other areas, remaining active in 1860. But in this border state, the Know Nothings were more successful than in Louisiana or anywhere else in the South. Rooted in the traditional appeal of the antialien crusade, the party rose in Maryland in response to all the forces helping nativism across America.

Maryland might have been the original Catholic colony, but it was a center of nativist activity before the mid-nineteenth century. The American Republicans had been active in 1844, and anti-

Catholic messages long were spread by Protestant ministers and by proliferating secret societies, including the United Sons of America, the Junior Sons of America, United Daughters of America, and the more prominent lodges from which the Know Nothing organization would evolve in 1853. As the established social and economic arrangements were shaken by winds of change in the 1850s, many people sought an answer in the antialien crusade. The Whig party, dominant in Maryland politics for over a decade, was breaking up after 1852, and a Democrat carried the presidential election for the first time in sixteen years. The labor market in Baltimore was chaotic, with ironworkers, carpenters, and many other groups on strike. The spiraling immigration was changing the face of the city. In 1850 it was 20 percent foreign, with 12,009 aliens landing in that year (quadruple the figure for 1847). Baltimore was an ethnic center, with Hibernian societies and German associations making the native-born acutely aware of the dramatic shift in population. Meanwhile, in south Maryland counties, tobacco planters—facing increasing foreign competition and worried about exhausted land— had to watch the institution of slavery, to which they were committed, decline in the state. Maryland had the highest ratio of free Negroes to whites and the greatest population of fugitive and manumitted slaves in the United States.[31]

Along with social and economic developments creating doubt and fear for many long-term residents came a growing skepticism about conventional politics and politicians. Talk of corrupt practices, manipulation of lucrative job contracts, and personal fortunes made with public money created the setting for "antipartyism" in Maryland as elsewhere. Their world was in disarray and their governors would not help and could not even be trusted. The solution seemed to be to seek new men offering new ideas to deal with the new problems. When urban disorders between newcomers and native-born erupted in Baltimore, nativism as a political answer for the troubles of the times seemed to be that solution.[32]

Baltimore was a tough town. It had a small, weak police force and a reputation for mob violence. An observer noted: "One would as soon go out at night without his hat as without his revolver." Press gangs had been known to kidnap drunks and derelicts and vote them in squads at the polls. When Irish "aliens" joined in groups such as the New Market Fire Company, the nativist brawlers were ready for battle: the Rip Raps, Plug Uglies, and Wampanoogs were on the scene for the election struggles of mid-decade. Later, the Blood Tubs (known for the tubs of bloody water found outside polling booths into which beaten Irish and German would-be voters were shoved) made their mark on the nativist side. In one confrontation, eight were killed, fifty wounded.[33]

The Know Nothings conducted their first public meeting in Maryland in August 1853. By 1854 they fielded a complete municipal ticket in Baltimore, defeating the Democrats and electing the mayor. In 1855, they won four of six congressional races, elected fifty-four of seventy-five delegates, and took eight of eleven state senate seats. In 1856, they carried Maryland for Millard Fillmore —the only electoral votes he would win in the one national race the American party truly contested—and they refused to fold even when Know Nothings in other states were abandoning their movement. In 1857, they were still Maryland's majority party.[34]

With articulate spokesmen such as Congressman Henry Winter Davis, an orator with formidable talent and a careful student of classical rhetoric, the American party offered itself as a conservative reform organization. It promised to cleanse the state of political abuses while returning its leadership to the native-born and its ideology to the principles that had created the nation. Leaders proposed all the perennial nativist themes: immigration restriction, more rigorous naturalization laws, preservation of "our public schools," sanctions against the "Papists, whose church poured out money like water" and the "foreigners who used the money to arm themselves to the teeth." As everywhere, "America" was the Know Nothings' central symbol; they promised to bring back the old order and to preserve and protect the tradition of the Founders.[35]

Nativist leaders were wealthier in Maryland than in some other states. One writer observed that Marylanders "still preferred leadership by the gentry . . . it assured respectability and durability." But the men in control were not as wealthy as their Democratic rivals and not as likely to be slaveholders; they were farmers, lawyers, merchants, and proprietors. Their supporters in Baltimore were from the middle as well as the working class. Moreover, they appealed not only to former Whigs but to men of both parties. In the city, strong Democratic wards in the late 1840s became Know Nothing. Whereas in northern and western states and in the Deep South the Americanists' split over slavery ruptured allegiance to the new cause, in the border state of Maryland, the party's national compromise on the slave issue seemed appropriate. It captured the feeling of a people caught in the middle, hoping to wish away the divisive problem. It caused no immediate unrest, and with no Republican alternative available in the area, nativists were further insulated from the danger of defection.[36]

"Have you seen Sam" remained a central concern for opponents until 1860. The urban upheavals in 1857 and 1858 were the setting for more electoral triumphs that enemies of the party in Baltimore attributed to intimidation. The gangs representing the movement now were everywhere: Black Snakes, White Oaks, Thunderbolts, Rattlers. There were even rumors that Know Nothing toughs were imported from Washington to guarantee street dominance. It was too much. By 1859, many respectable people were put off by the violence, appalled at behavior so outrageous that it was featured in the *Illustrated London News*.[37]

Still, the Maryland Know Nothing party's success could not be attributed simply to thugs and gunmen. It produced state, judicial, and tax reforms applauded even by the opposition press. In Baltimore, it reorganized several city departments, created a paid fire service, and built new schools. Its nativist agenda was advanced in city and state assemblies, resulting, among other things, in the establishment of a public school system under a state superintendent.[38]

By 1860, the party was losing ground. Democrats took most statewide races that year and in the House of Delegates, the Baltimore contingent, consisting entirely of Know Nothings, was expelled, allegedly because representatives won their polling victories through street violence and brute force. The governor, Thomas Hicks, remained an American, but soon he and his associates would change affiliation and call themselves Unionists. The year before, Henry Winter Davis had declared the party dead. Now the jaws of the secession crisis finally closed around the Know Nothings in Maryland. John Bell's Constitutional Union party attracted the disbanding nativists in fall 1860. The American party could no longer offer an effective answer to those seeking to protect an old order or escape new problems.[39]

With the dissolution of the Maryland organization and the emasculation of the Louisiana party, the Know Nothings were finished in the South. In most Deep South states, nativism had won only transitory success. For example, the Know Nothings made an impact in Georgia in 1855, attracting former Whigs and dissident Democrats, but failed to find effective leadership. They secured the support of John MacPherson Berrien, an aging and distinguished former Whig senator, who seemed to embrace a moderate nativist program. But Berrien, like other converts with political reputations and ambitions, intended to use the party to promote unionism rather than nativism. The seventy-four-year-old Berrien's death, coming just after he assumed leadership of the Georgia Know Nothing convention in December 1855, was followed by the decline and demise of the party in that state. In North Carolina, the American party had sought to replace the shattered Whig party as home for those seeking a conservative national political organization, but failure had led to nativist collapse by 1857. In Alabama, Mississippi, and Tennessee, there was continued activity, with Know Nothing congressmen and their adversaries involved in a running battle on the virtues of nativism. Representative Smith of Alabama exhorted on the floor of the House: "Let Every Protestant . . . Be a Sentinel on the Watchtower of Liberty." But the party had not made real headway in many Deep South states and had not managed to channel the mounting sectional anxieties to the anti-immigrant, anti-Catholic crusade in those states in which it had found a constituency. As in the North and West, the Know Nothing solution seemed attractive but ceased to work in the heated months of secessionist hostility.[40]

★★★

The Demise of the Know Nothing Movement

Only in border state enclaves did the Know Nothings survive as a distinctive political force until 1860. Across America, the movement was all but over after 1856. The inability to reach reconciliation on the slavery issue doomed the American party and brought to an end the story of the nativist movement in the early history of the United States.

The last effort to bridge the gap between North and South within the party had failed at Philadelphia. The hybrid clause condemning repeal of the Missouri Compromise and demanding no interference with domestic and social affairs in the territories could not satisfy northern nativists. They insisted on opposing all candidates who would not endorse banning slavery north of 36° 30". When southern Know Nothings tabled their proposal, the northerners had walked out and the national party was fatally ruptured.

Millard Fillmore's candidacy now made little sense. Considered in the North a friend of the slavocracy, he was no nativist. He had joined a Know Nothing lodge in 1855 as a political maneuver; he never had been a foe of "foreigners" but had always counseled "tolerance of all creeds" in his speeches. He was friendly to Catholics, had contributed to Roman Catholic churches in his native Buffalo, and sent his daughter to Catholic schools. In 1856, he headed a party whose platform made only a mild gesture in the direction of traditional nativist themes. In the year of "bleeding Kansas" and "bleeding Sumner," thousands of confused and disaffected Know Nothings in the North and West deserted to the Republicans. In the South, many other nativists, fearing that Fillmore would split the vote with James Buchanan and give victory to the new antislave party, defected to the Democrats. The Know Nothings had emerged seemingly out of nowhere in 1854 to become the nation's second major party. By 1856, they were already in decline. Fillmore carried but one state, the American party candidate receiving only 874,534 of the over 4 million votes cast (394,652 in free states, 479,882 in slave states). In 1854, the Know Nothings had elected five senators and forty-three representatives (and many others were members of the order's lodges); after 1856, these numbers fell rapidly.[41]

In subsequent years, the remaining nativists were a group besieged. Their legislators were unable to turn the antialien agenda into law in Washington, where immigration restriction was voted down by the House Judiciary Committee and never came to a floor vote. Their representatives in the national capital and in state assemblies often were inexperienced and after 1855 increasingly were assailed as incompetent. They had to deal with mounting attacks on the un-American nature of their mysterious fraternal lodges and—worse—with ridicule about their secrecy: "owe nothing" and "do nothing" societies were invented by contemptuous critics. In 1857, the last National Council, meeting in Louisville, disbanded, *sine die.*

By 1860, where the movement still existed it could offer no viable national political alternative. Its very existence did help to shape the Republican presidential choice in this critical year, for Abraham Lincoln, no supporter of nativist ideology but a friend of

many Know Nothings, finally had joined the new GOP. His nomination was secured when supporters used rival William Seward's
antinativist past against the New Yorker. They persuasively argued
that Seward could never get the Know Nothing vote. In the election, many former Know Nothings did cast their ballots for Lincoln, many others supported Bell's Constitutional Union alternative, fewer split their votes between Douglas and John J. Breckinridge. The national American party was no more. Lincoln was
president, and the Civil War would bury what remained of the
Know Nothing movement.[42]

What had it all meant? The party's rapid demise following its
meteoric rise led to a simplistic dismissal of its significance. It soon
was seen as merely a political bridge from Whiggery to Republicanism in the North, a last desperate stand against secession in the
South. But, of course, it was more.

It represented a continuing expression of the nativist tradition
in America, a movement largely of modest, middle-class people
dealing with forces that threatened stability in almost every realm
of their lives. These Americans responded to nativism's appeal because it offered a way out of so many dilemmas: how to protect
their America from the disorder and urban strife accompanying
the great migrations, how to find community in a land undergoing widespread economic and social upheaval and—by the 1850s—
faced with the specter of civil war. The Know Nothings' passionate rhetoric, the fraternal communion of their lodge structure,
the promise of reform through the election of new men and the
rejection of corrupt old leaders, the movement's total identification
with the unifying idea of one America, gave comfort to the confused and disaffected. It offered extremist politics, of course, proscriptive and intolerant in many ways. But it was indigenously
American. This was no class revolution seeking to overturn institutional arrangements. It was no authoritarian strike for power to protect entrenched privilege. It reflected neither the Right nor Left as
understood in Europe. It was an American response—no matter
how ugly and unfair the implications of its program for millions
of Catholics and immigrants—to the questions troubling so many:
how to embrace the American dream with all its costs, how to
survive in difficult times in a nation in turmoil.[43]

But the movement was eclipsed at last by the greater drama of
the slavery crisis and the Civil War that followed. Once the sections

had organized their armies, once the blue and the gray exchanged gunfire, the theme of America for Americans was meaningless. The war unified North and South around issues more pressing and more tangible than found in any nativist broadside. When it was over, the older anti-Catholic, anti-immigrant impulse was arrested; too many Catholic boys and immigrant sons had fought and died for the cause of union; the ethnic and religious hostilities of the past were tempered by the war fires of recent memory. Never again would nativism be as formidable as in the days after the famine emigration and the coming of the Know Nothing movement.

But nativism did not disappear. It would reappear at the end of the nineteenth century and in the first half of the twentieth century. With waves of newcomers arriving in the United States in the 1880s and 1890s, with a vast new migration of Catholics and Jews from southern and eastern Europe coming to northern and western states undergoing the full impact of the industrial revolution, with America again beset by forces of historic change and flux, the movement returned in forms similar to the secret societies of the early 1850s. It took a somewhat different shape in the twentieth century, when the end of World War I led to both anxiety and prosperity, when fears of "un-American peoples" and "un-American ideas" in the 1920s provided a new setting for old concerns. Only in the 1930s and after, with the end of unlimited immigration, did traditional nativism fade away. But even then its passing would be accompanied by periodic episodes of political passion in which nativist themes reemerged in paradoxical new ways. The "aliens" were no more; the old antialien crusade could never be the same again.

PART II

★ ★

ANTIALIEN MOVEMENTS IN RECENT AMERICAN HISTORY

★ ★

CHAPTER 10

THE RETURN OF THE

NATIVIST FRATERNITIES

THE CIVIL WAR was the great watershed in the first century and a half of American national life. It reshaped political, economic, and social affairs throughout the country, and it had an enormous impact on nativism. After Appomattox, the antialien impulse seemed as arrested as after Sumter. The war not only united northerners—Protestants and Catholics, "natives" and Irish- and German-Americans—but it ushered in a new age of industrial expansion that brought with it renewed confidence in American destiny and American good fortune. The shooting war had been a bonding experience for all who supported the Union, and the peace that followed seemed at first to provide a community of pride in the transformation of the nation into an industrial powerhouse. But the absence of nativism would not be permanent; this was but an interregnum before its reappearance. The industrial revolution and the immigration it stimulated soon provided the setting for a return of nativist activity and a revival of the nativist fraternities.[1]

Industrial expansion was inevitable in the United States. With seemingly limitless raw materials available in the continent-spanning nation—timber stands, coal and iron deposits, cotton for textiles, vast pools of oil, waterpower sites, a dazzling mining frontier in the East and West—America was the prime candidate for industrial development on the planet. The tradition of technical innovation and "Yankee ingenuity" had been evident before the war, as had the talent for shrewd borrowing of industrial techniques developed in Europe. But the urban-industrial expansion of the 1840s and 1850s, which stimulated nativism's greatest growth in America, offered only an early vision of the revolution to come after Ulysses S. Grant's military victory. All that was needed was money, manpower, and political support—investment capital, immigration, and a friendly presence in Washington—to make the breakthrough. All three became available in the three and a half decades to 1900.

The Civil War destroyed the bourbon aristocracy and the southern congressional opposition to government support for industrial development. The emasculation of the presidency after Lincoln's death and Andrew Johnson's humiliation and impeachment gave the dominant party in the dominant section unchecked congressional control of political and economic affairs at this critical juncture. High tariffs now were provided to protect northern industries from competition; huge land grants led to spectacular railway development as well as unparalleled opportunities for corruption. And even as the politicians played their role, giving business everything it wanted and more than it needed, foreign investors provided capital for the boom, $3 billion worth by 1893. The nation was transformed. Value of manufactures increased 600 percent to $5.5 billion by 1900. Railroad mileage stretched to 190,000 from just 30,000 miles before the Civil War. Coal production increased tenfold, steel production many times more. The labor force, predominantly rural and agrarian in 1860, was overwhelmingly nonagricultural (18 million to 10 million) by the century's end. It was a revolution, but it took massive immigration to make it work.

★★★

New Immigrants and Anti-Asian Hostility

Between 1870 and 1880, more than 2.8 million newcomers arrived at the ports of debarkation. Between 1880 and 1890, there were 5.2 million more, a floodtide of immigrants, at the time the greatest influx in a decade in history. Almost 3.7 million more came in the 1890s, despite the economic panic and depression in those years.

At first, most of the aliens came from familiar locales; many were the very people nativists had feared and opposed in the past. Almost half the arrivals in the 1870s and early 1880s were Irish or from the German Empire. More Germans came at this time than in the earlier years of Know Nothing activism. In 1883, of 603,000 immigrants, 195,000 were German, 81,000 from Ireland, with only England and Scandinavia areas of origin of other groups of at least

50,000. But all that began to change later in the decade. By 1887, the "new immigration" had begun in earnest. By 1891 it was rapidly increasing; by 1900, these southeastern European émigrés were the dominant force in the huge wave of newcomers. In the first year of the new century, almost three-quarters of the 448,000 immigrants were from Italy, the Russian Empire, or Austria-Hungary, the Hapsburg monarchy. By 1907, of the record total of 1.2 million immigrants, 285,000 were from Italy, 258,000 from Russia, 338,000 from the Hapsburg monarchy, many of them South Slavs or Jews, subject peoples of the Hapsburgs. When the outbreak of the Great War in Europe finally arrested the process, more than 20 million had arrived between 1880 and 1915, the majority of them "new immigrants." They represented almost a quarter of the population of a nation that had doubled in size from 50 million to 100 million in those years.[2]

There were few restrictions to bar their access to America. Federal legislation in 1878, 1882, and 1891 did prohibit "the importation of women for prostitution" and "alien convicts." It imposed a fifty cent head tax on all immigrants and excluded "lunatics . . . idiots . . . persons likely to become a public charge" as well as people with "loathsome or dangerous contagious diseases." Still, nothing was done specifically to exclude groups by national origin, with the exception of a series of measures taken against Chinese and Japanese.[3]

It was a significant exception, even if the number of those affected and excluded was relatively small. The history of anti-Oriental activism in the West and anti-Chinese and Japanese action in Washington is another ugly monument to racist animus in America.

Chinese had come to California for the first time in 1849, during the gold strike. Racist violence was endemic in the mines, and by 1852 the governor told the state legislature that "measures must be adopted to check this tide of Asiatic immigration." Nonetheless, there were only 60,000 Chinese in the entire country by the end of the Civil War; little more than 300,000 had come by 1880 and two-thirds of them had returned to China. In the census of 1880, 105,465 of those counted, a minuscule .21 percent of the population, were Chinese.

But many had come in the critical decade of the 1870s. More than 80,000 arrived in California between 1870 and 1875, 23,000 in 1873 alone, the year of the great crash. Most had been brought to America by companies that had contracted to supply labor to mines, railways, and other enterprises needing unskilled help. To American workers, these people were "coolies," a horde of "mongol peons" willing to work for slave wages. When the economic disaster of 1873 intersected the news of the coming exhaustion of the richest silver mines in the Comstock Lode, economic turmoil ravaged the state. Thirty percent of California's work force was unemployed in the mid-1870s. But this was the very time when thousands of Chinese were paid off after working on the construction of the transcontinental railroads. Furthermore, this was the moment the Chinese were coming in record numbers.

Just beginning to organize, labor unions turned against this highly visible minority. These yellow men and women, speaking an alien language, eating strange food, crowding into unsanitary housing, wearing loose black cotton garments and skullcaps, seemed a breed apart. In the East, desperate labor leaders blamed their woes on Wall Street plutocrats; in California they blamed the Asiatics. The Democratic party responded, calling for an end to "cheap Chinese labor." Republicans would soon match the nativist hostility. Outbreaks of anti-Chinese violence, spreading to Seattle, Tacoma, Los Angeles, Denver, and throughout the Rocky Mountain mining frontier, further stimulated a sense of crisis. By 1882, Congress acknowledged the anti-Oriental mood with the Chinese Exclusion Act, a suspension of immigration from China for ten years. The renewal of the act and further nativist measures in 1892, 1893, and 1902 extended the racist legal assault on the Chinese. By the turn of the century, "not a Chinaman's chance" was synonymous with hopelessness in the American west.[4]

The Japanese in the West suffered a similar fate. The anti-Chinese campaign gave new impetus to protests against Japanese in California. The mayor of San Francisco announced that "the Chinese and Japanese are not bona fide citizens. They are not the stuff of which Americans . . . can be made." By 1905, newspaper headlines read "The Japanese Invasion," "Crime and Poverty Go Hand in Hand with Asiatic Labor," "The Yellow Peril—How Japanese Crowd Out the White Race." Again, prominent labor leaders played a key role in what became the Asiatic Exclusion League. When the Board of Education ordered all Japanese pupils out of "white" schools, President Theodore Roosevelt intervened with his "Gentlemen's Agreement" of 1907. Japan agreed not to issue passports for the United States to laborers who had never been in America in return for the end of school board discrimination.[5]

Asian immigration had been largely blocked. Yet the mass of "new immigrants" from southeastern Europe remained unaffected. Older nativist concerns were ignored in the immigration laws.

★★★

The European Immigrants and Racist Animus

But nativism was growing by the mid-1880s. A decade earlier, there had been only mild activity. In eastern cities, a few neo–Know Nothing councils operated, but with limited support. There were occasional disputes over Bible reading in schools, when Catholic spokesmen protested the use of Protestant texts. And although Chinese immigration did stimulate violent reaction, the first two decades of the postwar era offered but a faint echo of the anti-Catholic, antialien excitement of the pre–Civil War years. Then came the setting for change, what John Higham characterized as the "crisis of the eighties."[6]

In some ways, this setting was unconnected to the vast migration of newcomers from Italy and the Russian and Hapsburg empires. First, the closing of the frontier in the American West was announced officially in the census of 1890 but discussed widely in the press in years before. It created anxiety among those who tied American wealth and strength to the historic "safety valve" of free and unsettled land that Frederick Jackson Turner would celebrate in his famous paper of 1893. Coming at the same time was the economic downturn of mid-decade and a rising concern about labor strife in an unsettled industrial market. Added to this was the highly publicized radical activity of a handful of anarchists and socialists, notably anarchist involvement in the Haymarket Square killings in 1886. The bonds of community suddenly seemed strained, leading intellectuals now pointed to intractable racial differences as a reason to fear for the national future.

The focus shifted to the "new immigrants." Professor Woodrow Wilson, in his *History of the American People*, contrasted the "men of the sturdy stocks of the north of Europe" with "the more sordid and hopeless elements" which the "countries of the south of Europe were disburdening . . . men out of the ranks where there was neither skill nor energy nor quick intelligence." Professor John R. Commons made the same distinction between the "educated, thrifty" population and "a peasantry a single generation removed from serfdom." A few years later, another reform-minded academic, Professor Edward Alsworth Ross, sociologist at the University of Wisconsin, offered a similar grim assessment in *The Old World in the New*: "Thoughtful people whose work takes them into the slime at the bottom of our foreignized cities and industrial centers find decline actually upon us." Everywhere he saw evidence of "racial suicide." In natural ability, the new immigrants seemed markedly inferior. In "good looks," it was "unthinkable that so many persons with crooked faces, coarse mouths, bad noses, heavy jaws and low foreheads can mingle their heredity with ours without making personal beauty yet more rare among us than it actually is." But in "vitality," alas, the "Slavs are immune to certain kinds of dirt, they can stand what would kill a white man . . . [they] violate every sanitary law yet survive."[7]

The work of Reverend Josiah Strong and Professor John Burgess, the views of Henry Cabot Lodge and Theodore Roosevelt soon would reflect an even more forceful racist theory, part of an international conventional wisdom at the turn of the century. This was the time when skull sizes, cranial capacity, and other "scientific" tests were put in service of an ideology that could justify Anglo-Saxon and Teutonic superiority and British and German imperial expansion. Count Joseph Arthur de Gobineau's *The Inequality of Human Races*, that assault on "degraded savages" and other inferior people, which had found a small audience in America before the Civil War, was reprinted in English. It offered a pessimistic vision of the "mortal disease" of "degeneration" through "the mixture of racial elements" which haunted superior Aryan people. Houston Stewart Chamberlain, in *The Foundations of the Nineteenth Century*, presented a similar but contemporary treatise in which race was placed at the center of human history. Chamberlain endowed Aryans with superhuman qualities and warned of the absolutely un-Aryan spirit "of the Jews . . . this alien people." In the United States, these ideas appeared at a moment of uneasiness about the present and concern for the future. They provided an added impetus for the reappearance of nativist feeling.[8]

At the heart of the new concern was social upheaval brought about by the industrial revolution. Everywhere traditional relationships were being disrupted. Even more than in the 1840s and 1850s, eastern and midwestern cities experienced staggering growth and change. Huge new manufacturing establishments blackened skies and dominated urban landscapes. The influx of their workers transformed hundred of neighborhoods, exacerbated ethnic tensions, and strained facilities to breaking point. Sewers, lighting, and transport had to be provided for the new population, and the possibilities for graft and exploitation were limitless. But while this infrastructure was building, the stench, congestion, crime, and chaotic conditions seemed to some the palpable symbol of a nation imperiled. In the fetid slums where immigrant aliens were packed in shabby tenements, the old fears of nativist yesterdays could find new meaning. Were not these people responsible for the ugliness and disarray? Could they ever be assimilated into the national community? Urban reformers such as Jacob Riis and Richard Ely despaired of the conditions in the immigrant communities. E. A. Ross condemned "their pigsty mode of life, their brawls and criminal pleasures, their coarse, peasant philosophy of sex." Tom Watson, the Georgia Populist, would write in the 1890s: "The scum of creation has been dumped on us. Some of our principal cities are more foreign than American. The most dangerous and corrupting hordes of the Old World have invaded us. The vice and crime which they have planted in our midst is terrifying."[9]

In addition, these newcomers could be blamed for the economic anxieties haunting so many in an age when the capitalist cycle cruelly affected millions. The economic panic and depression of the mid-1870s and mid-1880s would be followed by the deadly downturn of the 1890s. People without any protection, with scant personal savings, with no government "safety net," faced an uncertain fate. Workingmen's associations opposed the importation of "cheap labor," which threatened jobs during the recession. Knights of Labor leaders asked Congress to stop owners from bringing in "ignorant and brutal foreign serfs" as strikebreakers. This demand came after some new immigrants were hired to replace striking coal miners, among whom were the Irish descendants of nativist victims of the past. In completing his assault on the newcomers, Watson had asked: "What brought these Goths and Vandals to our shores? The manufacturers and bankers are mainly to blame, they wanted cheap labor and did not care how much harm to our future might be a consequence of their heartless policy."[10]

But big businessmen were in fact ambivalent about the migration; some found the new immigrants untrustworthy laborers, and a few called for some restrictions. And organized labor's spokesmen, for all their occasionally passionate denunciations, never argued for an end to voluntary immigration at this time. The industrial revolution had not turned managers and unionists to nativism. What it had done was to create tension and indecision about the national future. It was at the center of that complex of disorienting developments that made this time reminiscent of the anxious years of the late 1840s and early 1850s.

Like that earlier period, the age of industrial expansion in the 1880s and 1890s saw fissures appear in the social structure of the nation and fears expressed about the survival of a cohesive, stable, and prosperous social order. Unspoken concerns surfaced about personal well-being in an age of change and flux. Some who would endorse American individualism, the way of life that offered the promise of upward mobility in a fluid culture—middle-class people in business and the professions, skilled workers in industry, farmers opening new lands or striving for greater profits in an agricultural marketplace—would find it hard to live with their dream in these perilous years. Some, like their nativist forebears, would blame alien peoples and alien religions for their problems. They would project their fear and anxiety on the outsiders.[11]

But the people who would join the new nativist movement were not only fugitives from the American values they may have embraced but which exacted such high costs in these years. They were also protectors of an America that seemed imperiled by the aliens. For like early nativists, they saw a nation suddenly transformed by immigration.

★★★

The Newcomers from Southern and Eastern Europe

Many of these newcomers had not wanted to emigrate. Like the Irish and Germans fleeing the potato famine, they had been forced out of their homelands. A decline in the death rate led to a population explosion and the fragmentation of landholding; the resulting tiny plots simply could not support all the children of poor, postfeudal agrarian families. In some areas, the flourishing new citrus crop sales from Florida and California depressed European markets; in other places, tariffs on local products (French barriers to Italian wine) further damaged fragile economies. For Jews in the "pale of settlement" in the Russian Empire, a series of pogroms forcefully uprooted people, pushed them off their land, and evicted them from their villages. Still, many of the émigrés hoped that their journey to the New World was only temporary. Of 604,000 Italian immigrants in the 1890s, only 484,000 were still in America in 1900; of 2.1 million coming in the next decade, fewer than 1.4 million remained in 1910. But most found no alternative to America. Over 70 percent of the new immigrants in the 1890s and the beginning of the twentieth century were men and boys aged fourteen to forty-five; after 1908, .women, children, and older men arrived in increasing numbers, giving "joining relatives" as a reason for their journey.[12]

They had been forced to come, and they brought with them the heavy baggage of their cultural heritage. Most were postfeudal peasants. More than three-quarters of the Italian newcomers were farm workers, the majority of them illiterate. Like the Irish a half-century before, these penniless folk had neither the capital nor the skills to venture west to the American agricultural heartland. When they did so it was at their peril; eleven Italians were lynched in one grotesque episode in 1891 in New Orleans. Like their immigrant forebears, they found community in the big cities of the East and Midwest—and in smaller industrial towns as well—and they found jobs.

They settled in neighborhoods that were ethnic not only by nationality but by region and even village. Among the Italians in Chicago and New York, there were Calabrian, Sicilian, and Neapolitan districts, and whole tenements would be inhabited by people of the same town. They had been despised and exploited at home by the "prominenti" of their land; they were the "contadini," the peasants, who had learned to trust no one save family members or, if necessary, fellow villagers. But with no urban skills, no knowledge of the language, no experience in a market economy, their fear of strangers led to manipulation by "padroni," countrymen in the employ of the bosses of the construction projects and industry. Hard to organize because of their hostility to outsiders, their need to send money home (and thus their reluctance to strike), their resistance to any action that could be considered radical or "un-American," the new immigrants were without friends or leadership in the New World. Some groups, particularly Italians and South Slavs, found few welfare agencies available to help them. The Italian-American *prominenti* were interested in erecting statues to Mazzini, Columbus, and Garibaldi but not in aiding the newcomers from south Italy. There was little mobility in this new land of opportunity. For some, particularly ethnic groups with a strong family-centered heritage in which there was no tradition of schooling, children in America were not encouraged to be ambitious. Personal accomplishments were deemed meaningless unless they directly gratified the family by maintaining closeness or advancing family interests through marriage. Business or professional achievement was not the highest value of parents long taught not to make "the child better than you." For these groups, the young were expected to drop out of school to find work and add to meager family incomes.[13]

They all needed work. Latest to arrive, they did the dirtiest jobs at the meanest pay. They built the subways and the water and sewer lines. (The Italians constituted three-fourths of all building labor in New York.) They worked in the hardest and most dangerous parts of the factories. On occasion, they could be used as scab labor in notorious strikes. Working at pitifully low wages—under $700 yearly for many families—they had no alternative to the congested tenement life of the ethnic ghettos. There they faced the same shocking contrast to the Old World village that had been the fate of the Irish in earlier years. They were packed together: in 1900 in New York, 1,231 Sicilians lived in 120 rooms. But loss of privacy did not necessarily bring community; the impersonality of the urban world was underscored for many because, for the first time in memory, breadwinners were away from the family on the job.

Everywhere they met hostility. They were the objects of vicious stereotyping. Italians were characterized as "volatile," "unstable," "undesirable . . . largely composed of the most vicious, ignorant, degraded and filthy paupers with an admixture of the criminal element." The intellectual John Fiske wrote: "The lowest Irish are far above the level of these creatures." Their dark appearance was compared to the "light complexions and blue eyes" of northern Europeans: "You don't call an Italian a white man . . . no sir, he is a Dago." Even their style of street fighting was a mark of inferiority. The Irish gangs had been derided as packs of fistfighting thugs in the old days, but "these people" had never even learned to brawl the right way: "The knife with which he eats he uses to lop off another dago's fingers or ears."[14]

The assault on the new immigrants came from many quarters. Intergroup violence at the borders of the Italian and Slavic neighborhoods involved Irish and German toughs. Jews, who brought urban skills to America, were also victimized by the children of that earlier generation of hated aliens. In New York's Lower East Side, Irishmen and Germans beat Jews in the streets and predominantly Irish police patrols were accused of harassment and brutality when called to intervene. Protective associations emerged in Jewish districts in major cities. Indeed, anti-Semitism rose in response to the evidence of increasing prosperity and social mobility in Jewish communities. At first assailed as dirty, bearded, lecherous foreign degenerates, they were soon seen as pushy, money-grubbing materialists. Although there was no organized anti-Semitic movement in this period, Jews—victimized by social discrimination—were convenient ethnic scapegoats for many, and they did not escape condemnation by some of the leading men of letters. Henry Adams, among others, was a virulent anti-Semite. He reviled "infernal Jewry," attacking "the Jew" as a central actor in the "irremedial, radical rottenness of our whole . . . system."[15]

★★★

The Revival of Nativism

But the most formidable opposition to the "aliens" did not come from elitist racist intellectuals or ethnic rivals in the precincts of poverty. It did not come from the Immigration Restriction League, an organization established in 1894 that sent letters to state governors asking if the immigrants were desired in their states and, if so, which "races." It emerged from the same quarter in America that had produced the Know Nothings and their nativist precursors fifty years before. In the late 1880s and 1890s, responding to economic problems and to the social disorder in the expanding nation, the nativist fraternities reappeared. Emotionally dead to the pain and confusion of immigrants who struggled in a hostile new world, nativist activists insisted that these outsiders threatened their way of life. They saw themselves as protectors of

America, and their movement echoed the themes of the nativist past.

Henry Baldwin, a New Yorker whose father had been a leader of the Order of United Americans in its years of influence, set up a clearinghouse for the proliferating nativist associations in the mid-1880s. He formed the National League for the Protection of American Institutions, and he organized conferences for "executive officers of the patriotic societies of the United States" at Morton House in New York City in 1889 and in Philadelphia the following year. The records of these meetings suggest the range of groups then assembling under the old banners of the antialien crusade. To Morton House came representatives of the Order of United Americans, the United American Mechanics, the Patriotic Order of the Sons of America, the Order of the American Union, the Daughters of Liberty, the Junior Order of United American Mechanics, the American Patriotic League, the American Protestant Association, the Loyal Orange Institute of the United States, the Templars of Liberty of America, the Red, White and Blue Organization ("Red to Protect Protestantism, White to Protect the Purity of the Ballot Box, Blue Against the Domination of Dictation by Foreign Citizens"), the Patriotic Daughters of America, United Sons of America, United Order of Native Americans, the Sons of Revolution, Loyal Women of America, the United Order of Pilgrim Fathers, the National Association of Loyal Men of American Liberty, and others.[16]

Some of the groups were little more than a handful of passionate activists with a fancy title. But many had growing memberships. Some, like the Junior Order of United American Mechanics, were revived organizations that had been moribund since the fraternal heyday of the late 1840s. Others owed only their inspiration to earlier groups. The Patriotic Order of the Sons of America claimed to be "descended" from the Junior Sons of America, organized in 1847. This fraternity boasted 112 chapters in Pennsylvania alone by 1888, with 406 other "camps" in Ohio, Illinois, Massachusetts, New Jersey, New York, and twelve additional states. Big or small, old or new, most of them called for concerted action to "crush the foreign elements" that had invaded the country. In the words of a Wisconsin leader of the United Americans, the new immigrants were "under the control of a political and religious system of foreigners antagonistic to the foundation of America." These newcomers, "unable to speak English, arrived in a low and vicious condition allied to serfdom," must not be allowed to overwhelm America. The new nativists called for an end to unrestricted immigration, to the "importation of the dregs of foreign populations."[17]

Some members of these new associations seemed frozen in time. One wrote Baldwin asking what was being done to "checkmate the work of the St. Leopold Foundation," the specter that had haunted Morse and the antialiens of the 1830s. Others wanted to emulate the Order of the Star Spangled Banner of the early 1850s and called for the creation of a nativist political party out of the many new groups, "a corporate organization in which to consolidate all American patriots." To this, Baldwin replied in the negative, citing the Know Nothing experience in which "outside elements" had invaded the nativist sanctum and perverted the movement to their own ends. Most leaders of the disparate "patriotic" groups agreed that they wanted no single political party. But most of them would make little progress in attracting a mass membership on their own. In fact, only one nativist fraternity became—if briefly—a truly mass movement in the 1890s, a possible heir to the Know Nothings of the past. That was the American Protective Association (APA).[18]

★★★

The Growth of the American Protective Association

Founded in 1887 in the small Iowa railroad and mill town of Clinton, the APA was the invention of Henry Bowers. A fifty-year-old widower whose father had been a German Lutheran immigrant, Bowers was a failed farmer but a modestly successful self-taught lawyer, a longtime member of the Masons who loved fraternal ritual. He remembered his adolescence in Maryland at the high tide of Know Nothing activity, and he bitterly recalled the closing of the public schools in those years—brought on by Catholic pressure on the state legislature—to which he attributed many of his later problems. He was friendly with Catholics in town but deeply antagonistic to "political Romanism"; he believed that Catholicism and Americanism were antithetical.[19]

The organization he created grew in an environment of mounting fear of Catholic influence. The church's Third Plenary Council in

1884 marked a rapid expansion of parish and parochial school construction in the United States, and efforts at public regulation of Catholic schools became a major political issue in Massachusetts, Ohio, Illinois, and Wisconsin. Even as the old fears found a new setting, anti-Catholic activists pointed to the rise to political power of Irish Catholics in many cities, noting with alarm that New York and Boston elected their first Irish mayors in these years. In 1884 the Reverend Samuel Burchard characterized the Democrats as the party of "Rum, Romanism and Rebellion." In 1887, the Reverend Justin D. Fulton, a Baptist minister in Boston and a virulent nativist who had been a Know Nothing in his youth, published *Race in America.*[20]

In the early 1890s, the stock market crash and the wrenching depression that immediately followed further stimulated mounting anti-Catholic, antialien activity. The American Protective Association, spreading across the Midwest with new councils in Wisconsin, Missouri, Illinois, Kansas, Ohio, and Michigan, had become a movement of seventy thousand members. When Roman Catholics celebrated the four hundredth anniversary of Columbus's discovery with parades and festivals in 1892, and when Archbishop Francis Satolli, visiting America as representative of the pope at the opening of the Chicago World's Fair, was named the apostolic delegate to the United States—"We looked upon Satolli as a representative of the Propaganda of Rome to direct and influence legislation in the country," Bowers would write—the APA won added converts. In Toledo, Cleveland, Columbus, and Cincinnati, in Peoria, Omaha, Milwaukee, and Louisville, in Detroit, Grand Rapids, Denver, and St. Louis, the movement opened new chapters. It was at this point, in 1893, at the organization's national meeting in Cleveland—with delegates from twenty-two states attending—that Bowers was pushed aside. He was replaced as supreme president by William J. H. Traynor, a forty-eight-year-old Detroit publisher. Traynor numbered among his newspapers the *Patriotic American*; he was an enthusiastic joiner of many fraternal orders, a committed nativist, the first president of the Michigan council of the APA. This ambitious promoter brought to the movement vigorous new leadership. The spreading depression and mounting national anxiety served as a powerful recruiting tool. The APA now accused Catholics of causing the crash by "running" on the banks. It pointed to Catholic immigrants as "job stealers" of positions "desperately needed by real Americans." The American Protective Association expanded to more than one-half million members. The period that Traynor had characterized as "guerilla warfare" was over; if only briefly, APA had become a mass movement. Between 1893 and 1895, it grew in New York, Pennsylvania, Massachusetts, Connecticut, and Rhode Island, in California, Washington, and Oregon (it was particularly strong on the Pacific Coast by 1894) and was penetrating parts of the South. Bowers later bitterly wrote to Henry Baldwin that Traynor was "unsettled," a "wild man," that he "had lost his balance." But the energetic new command seemed to be working.[21]

Under Traynor, strident attacks on Catholicism continued to be a central theme. The *A.P.A. Magazine* featured articles titled "The Society of Jesus: Will It Set the Next Pope in Washington?," "The Moral Code of the Jesuits," "Satolli and the Jesuits Must Go," and "Rome's Greed for Money." In a piece called "The Confession Box," old fears of Jesuitical manipulation found new expression: "Their festering immorality . . . is revealed in the filth of the Romish confessional." A nativist writer, offering an exposé titled *The Footprints of the Jesuits*, equated all Catholics with "foreigners" because Catholics were under the control of a political religion that "hates self-government" and was "inimical" to American democracy. The APA magazines and newspapers focused on this equation. The *Patriot* (Chicago) pointed to the "Black Pope" and his presence in all Catholic activity: the "foreign and evil Papacy is everywhere." The *Wisconsin Patriot* described "Papist Venom," which could not be blocked by weak-kneed Protestantism but required the antidote of "patriotic activism." Traynor, responding to charges that his movement was undemocratic because it was so hostile to Roman Catholicism, argued in the *North American Review* that "the Papal hierarchy declares its complete sovereignty over the state in utter disregard of the Constitution and the laws of the land." His organization printed forgeries of papal bulls and encyclicals in support of this contention, including documents in which the pope purportedly called for a massacre of Protestant heretics and absolved his followers in the United States of loyalty to their government.[22]

There was no limit to "Papist deviltry," according to movement publicists: "The Country Is in Danger," "The Society of Jesus Plans Conquest of the U.S.," and even "President Lincoln's Assassination Is Traced Directly to the Door of Rome." It was not simply Catholics but Irish Catholics who were the particular repositories of evil. "Pat's Grip on the Government" could be seen in the rise of Tammany Hall and the eastern Irish politicos, yet the "Pope's Irish in American Politics" threatened even those not living in "machine-ridden communities." The Irish could never be trusted; the *Wisconsin Patriot*, examining the role of the Irish in the war, alleged that 72 percent of all Irish enlisted men deserted during the Civil War. One *A.P.A. Magazine* contributor concluded: "Were two infamies ever created to fit each other, they are Roman Catholicism and the Irish race."[23]

But anti-Irish, anti-Catholic rhetoric was only a part of the American Protective Association's appeal to its constituency. These enduring nativist themes became a touchstone in this age of vast new immigration perhaps in part because they offered a familiar way of dealing with all aspects of the foreign peril. They also appealed to a disfranchised Protestant middle class experiencing status anxieties in an age of social upheaval, people who deeply resented the emergence of a visible Catholic middle class. They were essential, but they were not alone. Anti-immigrant tirades also were a staple of the nativist press.

Traynor told *A.P.A. Magazine* readers that he supported equal suffrage for women because "the grand women of America" were as worthy to cast a vote as "pauper and criminal riffraff of Europe . . . every ignorant Dago and Pole, Hun and Slav." These "brutalized scum" of papal Europe had prostituted our society and politics. The *American Patriot* ran a series titled "Our Italian Problem": "like a flood, the lower stratum of hand workers" had invaded our shores, less civilized and adaptable even than the sons of the Old Sod. Not only Catholics from southeastern Europe but also Jews must be feared, although the APA's anti-Semitism had its peculiar anti-Catholic slant. "The Jews have been brought in to wage war with Rome against America and Americans," one nativist reported, for this was part of the scheme of the papacy to "get the Jewish people on its side."[24]

In face of all this there was only one thing to do: "Shut the Gates," screamed the headline; immigration of these new hordes must be suspended at once. It was not enough that loathsome newcomers were degraded peasants and tools of Rome, poisoners of community and plotters against democracy. They were also taking American jobs. As in the days of the Know Nothings, protecting the nation meant keeping immigrants from replacing natives in the marketplace. The National Home Labor League of America called for effective restriction to preserve "home labor for the home market." Nativist papers in the Midwest attacked the bosses for importing these "Huns, Slavs and Dagos" at pitiful wages, another "scheme by the rich to grind labor in our country." Of course, status anxieties colored much of this inflammatory prose. The APA appealed to working class urbanites as well as members of the lower middle class. As in the 1850s, native Americans might not only be displaced at work but dragged down by association with these lower-class creatures.[25]

There were other ways as well in which the nativist fraternities of the 1890s echoed the anthems of their forebears. The nunnery books of earlier years suddenly appeared in new editions. Advertisements for reprints of Maria Monk's work were featured in many APA publications, as well as other old favorites: Edith O'Gorman's *Convent Life Unveiled*, Madam D.'s *Priest and Nun*, Leyden's *Secret Confessions to a Priest*, and Miss Cueak's *Life Inside the Church of Rome*. The *A.P.A. Magazine* featured new stories, such as W. J. Phillips's "Convent's Horror," which were filled with the old-time sadomasochism. In "A Priestly Liar," readers learned of the "libidinous rapist priest with lust in his heart," who "disgraced his victims . . . these trusting women." In the *Omaha American*, wild, sadistic fantasies of Romish violence were focused on the fate of women: "The priest swears that he will wage relentless war against the heretics . . . that he will burn, waste, boil, flog, strangle . . . rip up the stomachs of women and crush the heads of their infants."[26]

The new movement had its own convent heroine, a latter-day Maria Monk. Margaret Shepherd, author of *My Life in the Convent*, was on the lecture circuit for several patriotic societies, including the APA, in the 1890s. Shepherd's book related the strange tale of a girl whose first lover was a priest who had run off after fathering her child. The baby died but only after the broken-hearted young woman was imprisoned when she turned to petty crime to sustain herself. In desperation, Shepherd claimed, she entered a convent, only to be victimized by "licentious and lecherous priests . . . seeking to lure young and innocent girls into sin." Coerced into believing it "her duty to submit," the helpless female faced a "hell upon earth." She told of beautiful girls tortured in grotesque ceremonies, of orgies of sex and sadism in which girls were raped and brutalized.

Once again, through their nunnery literature, nativist fraternities were offering a vehicle for the displacement and projection of anger and anxiety in an age of change and uncertainty.[27]

By 1895, the APA seemed to be prospering, the reincarnation of the formidable nativist movement of four decades before. But it was only an illusion. The organization already was splitting apart, torn by squabbles over political influence, national party endorsements, and the personal ambitions of those who sought leadership roles.

The APA always had operated within the Republican party. In doing so it had won some modest victories in local school board elections in the early years. In fact, Democratic leaders in Wisconsin and Michigan used the nativists' support for Republicans against the GOP, appealing to Catholic and ethnic voters and to others who feared that a secret society threatened personal liberty. In this way, the APA had not always been helpful to the Republicans. But by late 1894, Traynor began to raise serious questions about the movement's commitment to the GOP. There had been little success in influencing major Republican policies. APA members claimed credit for helping Governor William McKinley win reelection in Ohio in 1893, but there was scant evidence that the McKinley campaign—sensitive to the Catholic vote—embraced this APA support. Similarly, the nativists who insisted that APA endorsement had elected opponents of Catholics and "Catholic sympathizers" in several states in 1894 discovered that "their" men in Washington and the state legislatures were unresponsive to their concerns. Now, looking to the 1896 presidential race, Traynor suggested an independent political role: "Patriotism will be the alchemy which will hold the APA together in politics." This proved a pathetic, failed hope. In fact, the national political issue became the instrument that finally split the movement and hastened its rapid decline into insignificance.[28]

The debate over the third-party role for the American Protective Association immediately became acrimonious. Some nativist editors accused Traynor of stupidity, some charged that he was on the Democratic payroll. Conversely, stories surfaced in the opposition press of financial ties between Republican candidates and APA advisers. The majority of nativists in the end rejected the creation of a separate party. The *A.P.A. Magazine* spoke for this majority in endorsing the role of a pressure group: "We must compel existing parties" to attend to the "patriotic agenda."[29]

Throughout 1895, when the movement seemed to be at the pinnacle of its influence, dissension continued within the ranks. The APA and its fellow nativist fraternities had been unsuccessful in achieving major legislative goals: immigration restriction, taxation of Catholic church property, the opening of monastic institutions to public inspection, and the refusal of diplomatic recognition to "representatives from any ecclesiastical body." Now, disputes over legislative and political policy combined with simmering personal quarrels to create a challenge to William Traynor's leadership. At the movement's national convention in Washington in May 1896, Traynor was removed as president, replaced by an obscure newcomer, John W. Echols of Georgia. The critical issue was APA endorsement of a presidential candidate. Traynor and his executive committee had issued a list of "acceptable" names, ignoring all leading contenders, most notably Governor William McKinley. Angry pro-McKinley delegates overrode the action of the committee, added McKinley's name, and abolished Traynor's advisory board before electing a new leader. But instead of beginning a renewed crusade with new blood, the APA was torn apart.

A bitter minority assailed McKinley throughout the campaign. "A cowardly tool of the Roman Catholic hierarchy," he "deliberately caters to the Catholic vote," wrote Traynor. The *A.P.A. Magazine* disagreed, announcing, "full and unequivocal support of the Governor." Other publications traded charges of "sellouts" by various nativist leaders, citing endorsements offered to different candidates. By election day, the organization had disintegrated, finished as a mass movement. It continued to function only as a shriveled rump group, with Henry Bowers returning as caretaker president, now an aging, slightly addled dreamer, a man out of touch with reality. The movement he founded had come full circle. It ended in pathos. The editor of *A.P.A. Magazine* was jailed for selling salacious literature—those convent exposés proved his undoing—and the Kansas state president was imprisoned for embezzlement.[30]

Why did the APA, the central organization in the new age of nativist fraternalism, fail and founder in the late 1890s? The movement was torn by internal dissension. Office-seekers used it, then ignored it. Its legislative agenda failed, and some state and national leaders proved to be self-interested hustlers who exploited the cause for personal gain. It was wracked by disagreements over its role as pressure group or party. But beyond these organizational difficulties, the APA met a fate reminiscent of the Know Nothings, for its nativist slogans in 1896 were lost in a political campaign in which larger concerns overshadowed everything else.[31]

This was the year of Populism's greatest influence, when William Jennings Bryan captured the Democratic Party and the agrarian debtors' crusade created dramatic new divisions within the land. In such a setting, the anti-Catholic, antialien crusade suddenly seemed much less significant. Of course, many Populist leaders harbored nativist passions and made major contributions to nativist literature. Ignatius Donnelly, a Populist editor and former Minnesota congressman, the author of much of the People's party platform in 1892, published *Caesar's Column*, in 1890. This was a grim futuristic novel foretelling the fate of America if Populism failed. Donnelly's tale was filled with anti-Semitic references to rapacious Jews whose control of the money supply and voracious business practices had helped turn farmers into brutalized serfs, "cruel and bloodthirsty peasants." Mary Ellen Lease, another agrarian publicist, the woman who urged Kansans to "raise less corn and more hell," offered a tract with the wonderful title *The Problem of Civilization Solved* in 1895. It was a celebration of the "Caucasian race" replete with derogatory references to "negroes" and "orientals" as inferior peoples and to "Jewish bankers" as sinister manipulators. In Gordon Clark's *Shylock: As Banker, Bondholder, Corruptionist, Conspirator* and William "Coin" Harvey's *Coin's Financial School*—featuring an evil and powerful English-Jewish banker named Baron Rothe, who sought to "bury the knife deep into the heart" of the United States—there was additional nativist cant. Still, Populism's major political and economic agenda was not concerned with nativism, and there were tolerant Populists as well as anti-Semites, anti-Catholics, and racist activists. Populism was a multifaceted phenomenon and the source of major excitement in 1896. Yet even if there had been no Populist upheaval to bury it, the APA movement had dug its own grave.[32]

Fixated like the nativists of the past on Romish plots and Catholic conspiracies, on the dangers of Irish papists and Irish politicians, the APA failed to exploit effectively that fear and loathing of the new immigrants found among large segments of the "native" population. It did assail southeastern European "aliens," but not with the consistency or clarity that would give it a viable raison d'être in eastern urban areas in the years when Catholic lay leaders and po-

litical figures were gaining respectability. The social upheavals that
could be linked to the new immigration and the new industrialism
were its greatest recruiting tools. Its leaders never used them to real
advantage.

Like its famous predecessor in the 1850s, the American Protective Association was a star that flared briefly, creating excitement
for its followers and anxiety for its adversaries, only to flicker and
die suddenly. But unlike the Know Nothing movement, the APA
had little real political success even in the short term. More significantly, when it disappeared, resurgent nativism did not take four
decades to return again.

★★★

Decline and Revival: Nativism, 1896–1915

For some time after the turn of the century, antialien
movements seemed to be eclipsed in the rush of new developments. Following the defeat of Bryan and the end of the depression
came the Spanish-American War. The quick victory over decrepit
Spanish imperial forces created a new surge of national confidence,
perhaps a new sense of community in a country now enjoying prosperity. If McKinley's assassination by an anarchist in 1901 brought a
brief shiver of fear of foreign radical conspirators, the ensuing presidency of Theodore Roosevelt featured a remarkable leader who effectively celebrated American power, pride, and destiny. The colorful presence of the most charismatic figure in national life in half a
century was only part of the excitement of the Progressive Era, an
age of optimistic activism, an age of belief in the ability of an alert
and rational citizenry to make a better tomorrow by reshaping institutions. So even as the new immigration reached its peak in the
years before 1910, the "patriotic societies" found relatively few
followers.

It was true that there was continuing concern about the great
immigration. Not only did T.R. respond to the racist fears of the
Californians who opposed Japanese newcomers, but the United
States Immigration Commission, headed by the restrictionist Senator William P. Dillingham of Vermont—and with a dedicated opponent of immigration, J. W. Jenks, as its technical director—issued
its forty-two-volume findings in 1911. The commission endorsed a

literacy test for immigrants and warned of economic peril if unskilled workers were allowed to displace natives in the labor force.
Its report was marked by ugly references to the "races from Southern and Eastern Europe." But the Dillingham Commission, for all
its influence in shaping policy in the next decade, did not influence
events at the time; Senator Dillingham offered an immigration restriction bill based on national origins quotas which failed in 1913.
And it did not go unanswered. Isaac Hourwich's *Immigration and
Labor: The Economic Aspects of European Immigration to the
United States* challenged the commission's assumptions and findings. Hourwich argued that there were few differences in the economic and social impact of the old immigration and the new. It was
indefensible, he wrote, for the commission to proceed "upon the
supposition that immigrant races represent separate zoological
species."[33]

The economy was booming, reform was in the air, the press and
the politicians seemed to favor immigration. Israel Zangwill's powerful play *The Melting Pot*, opening in New York in 1908, became
an anthem for faith in the soundness of a multiethnic society. The
setting for the displacement or projection of middle- and working-
class fears on the "alien" menace seemed only a thing of recent
memory.

The racist ideology that became fashionable among certain intellectuals and affluent elitists in these years had limited impact in
the larger nation. Of course, a small but influential group was discussing the work of Continental theorists. Perhaps they read Gustav Le Bon, who warned of the irrational nature of "the crowd,"
particularly in "nations without moral equipment," where there
were questions about "national character." Certainly, they knew of
the books by Gobineau and Chamberlain. And for such readers, the
academic dispute over the alleged natural inferiority of non-Teu-
tonic, non–Anglo-Saxon people would be most clearly delineated
by that wealthy sportsman, the founder of the New York Zoological Society, Madison Grant, who published *The Passing of the Great
Race: The Racial Basis of European History* in 1916. In it, Grant
offered the familiar theories concerning the superiority of the "blond
Nordic races" and the familiar grim prospects of "racial mixture."
He pointed to the obvious dangers posed by "Polish Jews," whose
"dwarf stature, peculiar mentality and ruthless concentration on
self interest" threatened the nation, as did the "Chinese coolies and

Japanese laborers," the "South Italians, breeding freely," and other inferior types. They were all part of the story of how "the American sold his birthright in a continent to solve a labor problem." But Grant and those other racist elitists in his audience created no major new nativist movement.

Still, by the middle of the second decade of the century there were signs of a modest nativist revival. The Junior Order of United American Mechanics, the nativist fraternity that first emerged in the days of the Know Nothings and linked antiradical activity to its anti-immigrant agenda in the 1880s and 1890s, had been losing its following in the first years of the new century; now it found a growing audience. Its membership increased to 224,000 by 1914. Much of it came in the South and West, where anti-Catholicism was supplemented by antiblack and anti-Asiatic arguments. Its leaders expressed fears that South European immigrants would intermarry with Negroes, as in Latin America.

In Georgia, there was another sign of nativist renewal. Here the former leader of southern Populism, Tom Watson, became increasingly fixated on the threat of "the Roman Catholic hierarchy, the deadliest menace to our liberties and our civilization." In 1911, together with aging veterans of the Civil and Indian wars, he helped organize the Guardians of Liberty, a miniature neo-APA group.

Watson was most concerned with the dangers of Catholicism, but he was also a rabid anti-Semite in these years. When Leo M. Frank, a young Jewish factory superintendent in Atlanta, was accused of sexually molesting and murdering a fourteen-year-old girl and convicted in a trial marked by mob coercion, in which the jury received messages threatening "Hang the Jew or we will hang you," Tom Watson added his voice to the racist assault. The evidence was overwhelmingly more incriminating against another suspect, but Frank was doomed. He was taken from jail by an armed mob and hanged. Watson had warned in his magazine: "The next Jew who does what Frank did, is going to get exactly the same thing that we give to negro rapists."

The newly emerging nativist impulse now surfaced in two seemingly very different forms: opposition to radical labor organizers of the Industrial Workers of the World and among the growing readership of *Watson's Magazine* and a new anti-Catholic newspaper, the *Menace*. This paper, issued first in 1911 by Wilbur Franklin Phelps, was published in a small Ozark community in Missouri, and its growth was remarkable; it had 1.5 million readers by 1915. Both publications were issued in rural areas and found a largely rural audience. Nativism had been centered in the big cities, which had attracted the bulk of the immigrants in the nineteenth century; the Know Nothings and their progenitors had started in New York, Boston, and Philadelphia. Even the APA found a following in the urban areas of the Northeast and Midwest in the 1890s. But now the ethnic millions seemed to dominate the urban environment, and the corporate power structure, hugely empowered with fortunes made in the industrial revolution, supported these newcomers as a pliant and useful labor force. It was increasingly difficult to build a nativist audience in such a setting; demographics and politics combined to create formidable opposition to urban antialien activism. But farmers and small townsmen, influenced by the political upheavals at the turn of the century, feeling displaced in this new America, and affected by an awakening Protestant fundamentalism, seemed more responsive to anti-Catholic and antiethnic arguments. Nativism soon would return to America.[34]

The world was sliding toward war. The American optimism of the Roosevelt years was to be sorely tested. The APA and the nativist fraternities had crumbled after the successes in the 1890s, but with the coming of war, a new setting of social unrest and social disorder would prove fertile ground for a revival of their mission. This time, however, the themes of the antialien crusade would first be reshaped by the international crisis and the postwar environment. The attack on un-American peoples, that staple of nineteenth-century nativism, would be subsumed into an assault on un-American ideologies. In the Red Scare, nativism would find new life and new direction.

CHAPTER 11

★ ★

THE RED SCARE,

1919-1920

THE CIVIL WAR arrested the growth of nativism in America. The Great War, 1914–18, stimulated it.

While the great powers of Europe sent their men to slaughter in the grotesque trench struggles of the western front, the United States had maintained an uneasy neutrality to spring 1917. But a war so vast and convulsive could not be ignored and was not contained; eventually the debate over American involvement and the passions evoked by this conflict eclipsed all else. The Progressive Era faded from view, another victim of World War I. Then the long tradition of American separation from the affairs of the world powers was violated, when Woodrow Wilson finally brought the United States into the war in April. In the emotional and divisive process leading to American entry, not only the age of reform and the age of isolation were at least temporarily ended. A period of relative quiet in the history of nativist activity also quickly dissolved as the debate over involvement in a war against foreign foes led some "real Americans" to seek out the enemy within, the link between the alien menace in the United States and the dangerous situation across the ocean. The Civil War had unified native-born and immigrants, Anglo-Saxon Protestants and Catholic ethnics, because the common enemy of all Unionists was the Confederacy. The Great War had the opposite effect. It provided a setting for new divisions between Americans in a world at war.

At first, the new nativism focused on once-familiar adversaries, German-Americans. Second only to the Irish as objects of Know Nothing hostility, German-Americans had been so successful in their journey to assimilation that few ugly words were directed at them by those fervid patriots from the nativist fraternities of the

1890s. But the war changed all that. Even in the years of neutrality, public opinion was solidly behind the British and French in their conflict with the German Empire. Shrewd manipulators of propaganda in the New World, the British had furthered the process, stimulating anger at "Hun atrocities" in Belgium and at the autocratic militarism of the kaiser's nation. Now German-Americans suddenly were seen as agents of an alien state. After demonstrations by German-American organizations favoring an embargo on the shipment of war supplies to Britain (Germany already was effectively cut off from U.S. ports by the British naval blockade) and meetings by group leaders in Washington, the *New York Times* accused these activists of being "completely subservient to foreign influence and a foreign power," of demonstrating "the un-American spirit." Theodore Roosevelt, out of power and anxious to test himself and his nation in military combat once again, not only beat the drums for war but assailed German-Americans, at least "those who spiritually remained foreigners in whole or in part." When the United States declared war on Germany, this nativist rhetoric was replaced by the politics of repression.[1]

The new anti-German nativism was unlike the old. This time the New World paradise was not threatened by Catholic immigrants, agents of a Jesuitical conspiracy. German-Americans were now seen as an arm of the official enemy. Their sin was not their religion but their nationality. In fact, anti-Catholicism quickly declined during the days of war fever. The *Menace*, that anti-Catholic newspaper which had experienced a brief celebrity, soon lost most of its subscribers and passed from view. In place of the old nativist fears were new ones: German-Americans poisoning food, spoiling medical supplies, undermining public support for the war effort. German-language training was dropped by many public schools, German names were changed, German dishes disappeared from restaurants. German shepherd dogs became Alsatian shepherds; Boy Scouts burned German-language newspapers in the streets of several cities; musical organizations purged Wagner, Schubert, and Beethoven. German-Americans were assaulted in a number of communities. In his pamphlet *The Tentacles of the German Octopus in America*, published by the National Security League, Earl E. Sperry declared that "overwhelming proof is afforded that large numbers of German-Americans are disloyal citizens." It was now a mark of patriotism to throw a rock through butcher Schultz's window. Violence spread from acts of individual hostility to the organized work of vigilantes like the Knights of Liberty. In Chicago, a group that would gain quasi-official status as an auxiliary to the Justice Department, the American Protective League (APL), emerged under the leadership of an advertising executive named A. M. Briggs. The APL (which claimed a quarter of a million members) sought out and tried to silence the proponents of un-American beliefs. But this new crusade was not limited to ethnic German-Americans. In the crucible of America's first major war in half a century, the enemy became not only the descendants of immigrants from the wrong fatherland but all opponents of the war effort. The Military Intelligence Division of the United States Army, working through field offices across the country, received reports on the activities of German-Americans and radical groups. Because radicals seemed most outspoken in their resistance, the stage was set for dramatic new nativist developments after the war.[2]

The Socialist party now was assailed as "dominated by men who are not American, but pro-German in sentiment," for "giving aid and comfort to the conscienceless enemies of mankind," for being "tools of the Hohenzollerans" "branded made in Germany." The National Security League, the patriotic propaganda organization, enlisted academics to make this case. Theodore Roosevelt joined the attack. "Russian exiles of the Bolshevist type," he exclaimed, these "Germanized Socialists" are "more mischievous than bubonic plague"; they would "lead our people into . . . subjugation to German autocracy." This bizarre effort to link "Reds" and "Huns" also informed the assault against the Industrial Workers of the World (IWW).[3]

The Wobblies, anarchosyndicalists who used the rhetoric of class warfare, had been objects of antiradical activity and victims of persecution in earlier years. The IWW was revolutionary: it called for the overturning of institutions. But its real crime, in the view of its enemies, was its insistence that the American way of life was a fraud, that millions of American workers never had a chance to experience social mobility but instead were manipulated and exploited by capitalist bosses, then cast shamelessly aside when they were old or sick or tried to change the system. Wobbly dissenters had been guilty of the unpardonable sin of questioning the American dream; now they could be prosecuted for un-American activities in wartime.

The instruments were the Espionage Act of June 1917, which outlawed statements "obstructing the war effort" or "aiding the enemy," and the even more draconian Sedition Act of 1918, which held that disloyal opinion and demeaning references to the flag or form of government could be punished by a twenty-year sentence. In addition, the Immigration Act of February 1917 contained provisions excluding people belonging to revolutionary organizations and allowing deportations to "their homeland" of aliens found expressing such views anytime after entry. Encouraged by this nativist legislation emerging from a Congress afire with war passion, vigilantes, sheriffs' posses, and federal agents descended on the IWW and other radicals. Wobbly strikers in the West were beaten, tarred and feathered, or packed into freight cars to be dumped on the desert. One Wobbly was kidnapped and lynched by masked gunmen in Montana as simultaneous government raids ordered from Washington ended with the arrest of hundreds of Wobbly and radical leaders in different parts of the nation. Included among those jailed in 1918 were William "Big Bill" Haywood, the most important Wobbly spokesman, and Socialist notable Eugene V. Debs. Victor Berger, a member of the national executive committee of the Socialist party, was sentenced to twenty years. Judge Kenesaw Mountain Landis said he would have preferred to have "Berger lined up against a wall and shot." (The Supreme Court later set Berger's verdict aside.) Some of the activists were held for deportation even though they were non-German aliens. Attorney General Thomas Watt Gregory was sure that Germany was bankrolling the IWW, and wartime hysteria made this mindless suspicion the raison d'être for persecution based on nativism, now the official policy of the American government.[4]

The United States had not been prepared for war. It suffered not only from the lack of arms production and the failure to recruit and train sufficient divisions but from the absence of political and emotional preconditioning. America was to be neutral "in thought as well as action," said Woodrow Wilson, a leader reelected on the slogan "he kept us out of war" as late as November 1916. How could public support be mobilized for a total war effort that began scant months later? It would be a moral crusade, the president explained, a war to end all wars, a war to make the world safe for democracy. Despite this idealistic rhetoric, the nation still would be asked to send its men to fight and die in a great power conflict for the first time in a hundred years with little warning that such a thing was possible. For many Americans, the need suddenly to justify this struggle meant making the enemy into a caricature of evil. They were encouraged in this direction by a vast campaign of government propaganda organized by George Creel's Committee on Public Education. It meant that all opponents of the war effort were sinister agents of an enemy conspiracy.

But even as war passions were heating up in 1918, it was over. The war had lasted barely twenty-one months, and significant numbers of U.S. troops had been in the front lines for only a few months. Unlike the British and French, allies who lost almost 2.5 million men dead during their four-year nightmare in the attrition battles of a conflict that began for them in 1914, Americans had to find a way to handle their new-found hatred of the Hun adversary. The allies, bitter at their foe but exhausted by their struggle, had fewer problems with postwar national hostility. In the United States, the German menace lingered in the public mind after German capitulation at Compiègne and the November Armistice. War fever could not easily be cured; postwar conditions would add to the problem.

★★★

The Setting for Antiradical Activity

After the war, the nation faced a difficult adjustment to a peacetime society. Population shifts stimulated by the war had brought large numbers of blacks from southern farms to northern cities, where factory jobs were available for all. Race riots ensued in several communities. Women were entering the urban labor force as well, their presence on the job a matter of patriotism as well as national policy. Traditional relationships would not easily be resumed in postwar America. There were also searing economic problems. With the dismantling of those powerful federal agencies which planned and controlled production, wages, and prices during the war, a spiraling inflation threatened to wipe away the gains made by so many during the conflict's boom years. In 1919, food prices were up over 80 percent, clothing over 125 percent, and the value of the dollar sank to less than half its worth in 1913. In the labor strife and social unrest to follow, Germanophobia was put to use in explaining the eruption of "radical" activity. The anti-German nativist groups at work during the war, the National Security League, American Defense Society, and American Protective League, endured, seeing the Teutonic hand behind strikers and labor organizers. Clayton R. Lusk, freshman state senator in New York, called radicals "paid agents of the German Junker class." It was only with some effort that Attorney General Gregory could persuade the APL to disband. But in time the anti-German themes would be fully replaced by antiradical ones, as the social upheavals brought on by war offered new reasons for people to seek the comforting community of a crusade against an alien enemy, seen as responsible for the postwar disorder.[5]

Everywhere there seemed evidence that America was coming apart. As in the earlier eras, social stress was the setting for nativism. In 1919, the Seattle general strike was called, to be crushed in the end by red-baiting Mayor Ole Hansen, who reveled in his heroic image as defender of democracy against revolution, outrageously exaggerating the specter of the Red menace and calling on "the people of Seattle to show their Americanism." When a bomb mailed to the mayor was intercepted by his staff and when other bombs exploded in Washington or were discovered before injuring the variety of prominent government and business figures to whom they were addressed (including John D. Rockefeller, J. P. Morgan, and Supreme Court Justice Oliver Wendell Holmes), the fear of revolutionary terrorism was felt across the land.

Labor discontent was spreading in 1919. The strike of overworked and underpaid Boston policemen was viewed widely as new proof of radical activity which threatened social chaos. The giant walkout of more than 350,000 steel workers, protesting average salaries of less than $1,500 yearly and average work weeks of sixty-nine hours, was attributed to "red agitators, catspaws of the Bolsheviks." The coal strike in the fall was called by a major newspaper the result of "men being soaked in the doctrines of Bolshevism." In Gary, center of the strike against big steel, where the U.S. Steel Company's autocratic chief executive, Judge Elbert Gary, had railed against the alien revolutionaries, vigilantes of the Loyal Legion reported that they maintained law and order by using blackjacks to break the hands and wrists of "these foreigners." In fact, those "foreigners"—many of them immigrants and their sons—were striking not only for higher wages in the midst of raging inflation but in response to their own growing confidence that their future was in the New World, not the Old. After all, they had provided the industrial muscle that won the Great War. But this spirit was missed by their enemies, who saw them only as aliens. Emerson Hough, admiring chronicler of the American Protective League, reported from Gary that Germans, Austrians, Italians, and "Chinamen" were all part of the problem. Aided by Russian Jews "with Americanized names," they were helping the "organization of the Red movement," and "like rats infested with plague, they should be exterminated or driven from the country."[6]

The drive to repress, jail, or deport what the president-general of the Daughters of the American Revolution characterized as "these foreign leeches" who will destroy "this free Republic if they are not cut and cast out," would proceed with little basis in objective reality. The bombs that had caused such fear were not the work of a powerful revolutionary cabal but of a handful of deranged anarchistic individuals. "Bolsheviks" in America also were less than formidable. They represented the majority of the seventy thousand people emerging from the left wing of the Socialist party in early 1919. These left-wingers responded to the cataclysmic events in the new Soviet Union, particularly the creation of the Comintern, the Third Communist International. They had formed two new political groups within the United States. One was the Communist party, claiming fifty-eight thousand members but probably much smaller, an organization with pretensions to becoming a militant cadre of revolution but in fact organized around foreign-language federations, a party many of whose members could not speak English, who sought community in the comradeship of other ethnic outsiders. The second was the American Communist Labor party, a much smaller group of ten thousand, led by men such as John Reed, advocates of a more opportunistic program tailored to American realities. Neither Communist sect threatened the nation in 1919. But all "Reds"—including Wobblies, socialists, and some foreigners who had nothing to do with any left group—now became fair game.[7]

Postwar nativism took a dramatic turn with the bombing of the home of the new attorney general, A. Mitchell Palmer. A poor boy from Pennsylvania, a Progressive legislator who had served as Wilson's alien property custodian, Palmer was not only an ambitious politician who dreamed of the presidential nomination but a man schooled in the antialien tradition. As a college student in the 1890s he had embraced nativism's hostile vision of southeastern European immigrants. Always responsive to the nativist passion, he now became the leader of the new Red Scare.[8]

Palmer replaced Gregory as head of the Department of Justice in March 1919. At first he seemed willing to reverse the repressive policies of his predecessor. He reaffirmed the decision to disband the APL, observing that "espionage conducted by private individuals and organizations is entirely at variance with our theories of government." He rejected remaining APL material dealing with German wartime propaganda as "gossip and hearsay," dismissed hundreds of suits pending under the Espionage Act, and granted clemency to many others convicted under the act. But after the May Day bombs were discovered at the New York Post Office—one of the thirty-six bombs was addressed to Palmer—and the May Day riots erupted in a number of cities, Mitchell Palmer lost interest in protecting civil liberties. The riots had rocked Detroit, Boston, Chicago, and New York City, when mobs broke up radicals' May Day parades and meetings as well as wrecking offices of socialist papers. In Cleveland, victory loan workers and army veterans stormed a socialist gathering, killing one person and injuring forty; 106 socialists were arrested but none of their assailants. The *New York Times* now called for "vigorous prosecution if the Bolshevist movement is to be held in check." Speakers at the first National Convention of the American Legion, meeting in St. Louis on 10 May, called for the "deportation of every one of those Bolsheviks." Soon afterward a bomb exploded at the attorney general's house, doing extensive damage. Palmer and his neighbor, Undersecretary of the Navy Franklin D. Roosevelt, found the mutilated remains of the terrorist and some anarchist pamphlets in the debris. A. Mitchell Palmer now announced plans "to run to earth the criminals who are behind this kind of outrage."[9]

★★★

The Palmer Raids

In early August, Palmer created the General Intelligence Division in the Justice Department, to collect information about radicals and coordinate efforts to meet the radical threat. Under the leadership of J. Edgar Hoover, this antiradical division reviewed newspapers and pamphlets published by radicals and "ultra-radicals" and issued lengthy "Weekly Bulletins on Radical Activities" sent to other federal agencies. Hoover and associates apparently were impressed by the strident but baseless posturing of that wide variety of warring anarchist and communist factions which had tiny constituencies and no real hope of influence. Hoover and Palmer moved to meet the sinister conspiracy. The attorney general had persuaded Congress to allocate $500,000 to investigate the enemy within. The labor strife of 1919 now was headline news, and he was being attacked by major newspapers in the fall for failing, as one editorialist put it, "to have these alien seditionaries, anarchists, plotters against the Government of the United States arrested, punished, deported." He later complained that "I was shouted at from every editorial sanctum from sea to sea; I was preached upon from every pulpit to do something and do it now." He responded with the Palmer Raids.[10]

On 7 November, the second anniversary of the Russian Revolution, agents of the Department of Justice raided meeting places of Russian workers in twelve cities. In New York, the Russian People's House was invaded, many were beaten, and 200 people inside were taken to jail. Some were members of the Union of Russian Workers, some were radicals, some were not. Throughout New York City, homes were searched without warrants and men arrested without stated cause. In all, 650 were incarcerated in New York. When the transport *Buford*, the "Soviet Ark," sailed in late December with almost 250 anarchist and socialist deportees bound for the Soviet Union (an inhospitable home for such non-Bolshevik radicals as Emma Goldman and Alexander Berkman), Palmer was widely praised in the press and saluted by the American Legion. Meantime, word was circulating of the ugly confrontation in Centralia, Washington, on 11 November between Wobblies and "patriots." Wobblies in Centralia had been beaten and driven from town in 1918 for opposing the war effort. When they reopened the IWW Hall in the fall of 1919, the members of the Citizens Patriotic League attacked them on Armistice Day. The Wobblies responded with gunfire, and three antiradicals were killed. The IWW Hall then was destroyed, Wobblies rounded up and jailed throughout the state, and one member, Wesley Everest, taken from jail to be mutilated and lynched. The nativist fever was building to a climax.[11]

The nation was without presidential leadership at this crucial juncture. Woodrow Wilson, exhausted from his arduous and often acrimonious negotiations with the French premier and British prime minister at the Versailles Conference, had returned from Paris to face mounting opposition to the peace treaty he had approved and to the League of Nations covenant, the instrument he hoped would justify his decision to lead America into the war. During the bitter struggle to win senatorial consent, he had suffered a stroke. Throughout the tumultuous events of the late fall, Wilson lay in a darkened White House, guarded by his doctor and wife, unable to control or even comprehend the full meaning of the Red Scare. And hysteria was spreading. In 1919, twenty state governments passed bills concerned with "criminal anarchy." In the House and Senate, bills were being debated providing draconian sanctions for those uttering "seditious" statements. Palmer, believing his own presidential ambitions might be fulfilled if he grasped the moment and responded to public clamor for antiradical action, now launched the expanded raids of 2 January 1920.

These were more sweeping than before, including dozens of cities. For days the operation continued, and smaller raids occurred in different parts of the country for the next six weeks. More than three thousand people were arrested and thousands more were taken into custody, held for hours or weeks without charges. In Chicago, hundreds of communist or IWW members—real or suspected—had been rounded up on New Year's Day by the district attorney, a Republican apparently attempting to upstage the Democratic attorney general. But Palmer could take credit for the wholesale assault on civil liberties. In thirty-three cities, Justice Department agents and local police broke into homes and meeting halls, indiscriminately arresting everyone in sight. In Detroit, 800 men were arrested and imprisoned for three to six days in a dark, windowless, narrow corridor circling the central areaway of the old Federal Building. Sleeping on bare stone floors, bullied by police, refused showers, given use of one drinking fountain and one toilet, deprived of food for almost twenty-four hours, denied communications with relatives or attorneys, their crime was that they had attended a dance or a class or had eaten at the House of the Masses, Detroit's Communist party headquarters. Almost half later conclusively demonstrated no interest in radicalism. In Boston, hundreds of Justice Department captives were shackled together and marched through the streets to be harassed by the taunts of "real" Americans. In Pittsburgh, 115 were seized although authorities had warrants for only 20. In Seattle, the victims were arbitrarily selected by police who went to pool halls and other places "where foreigners congregated" and then called for trucks to "take all of them away."[12]

Palmer's action at first was warmly received. One magazine called the "Fighting Quaker of the Cabinet" a hero, "Uncle Sam's Policeman, the Rooter Out of Reds," a man who showed a "quality of courage for practicing his ideas . . . we love him for the enemies he has made." Another monthly noted "the approval of all law abiding, government loving" Americans for their attorney general, the "scourge of the Bolsheviks." Palmer himself presented "the case against the Reds" in the *Forum*, explaining that "robbery is the ideal of Communism," that Reds are "obviously criminal aliens," that "the American Government had to act" because the nation was "in jeopardy." He now made the linkage between un-American ideas and un-American peoples: "My information showed that Communism in this country was an organization of thousands of aliens . . . direct allies of Trotsky, aliens of the same misshapen caste of mind and indecencies of character." In the *Annual Report of the Attorney General*, he stressed the point: "Fully 90 percent of Communist and anarchist agitation is traceable to aliens." Other writers had been developing this theme since 1919. A Colorado senator used a national magazine to argue that "the United States must restrict immigration and suppress all radical and anarchist groups in the name of law and order"; real Americans are not aliens or "descendants of aliens, the ark of Democracy's covenant was committed to Anglo-Saxon keeping long ago." In the *American Legion Weekly*, an article titled "Where Do the Reds Come From? Chiefly Imported, and So Are Their Red Theories" pointed more directly to the new immigrants from southeastern Europe: "In the 80's, the steerage space steamers" brought these aliens "who were not of our sort," who "could not speak English, were hostile to American institutions," people easily "recruited to the Red cause." A. Mitchell Palmer characterized the leadership of the movement as "disreputable aliens," particularly "a small clique of autocrats from the East Side of New York." He was referring to Jewish radicals; anti-Semitism was present in this Red Scare. The most frightening foreign enemy was no longer the papist conspirator.[13]

Nativism had taken a new turn. The setting was reminiscent of earlier episodes: social disorder that sent many in search of scapegoats, economic and political crises that divided instead of uniting Americans. The vision of the New World also remained the same for these nativists as in the past: America was the favored land, but it was a fragile paradise, susceptible to destruction from the enemy within. And alien people were the problem once again: foreigners, ethnics, non-Anglo-Saxons, folks "not of our sort." But in 1919–20, it was alien ideas that generated the brief pandemic of fear that energized the Palmer Raids, un-American ideas propagated by un-American peoples. The alien menace was partly old and partly new. This was a transitionary period to a different era of crusading against un-American activities. In the Red Scare, nativists were no longer anti-Catholic and not even anti-German but antiradical, yet they remained the scourge of dangerous immigrants and their untrustworthy descendants.

The raids of 1920 offered an early vision of the anticommunist probes of the 1950s, with the vital difference that in the first period foreigners were accused of embracing un-American ideas. There were other dissimilarities as well, notably that A. Mitchell Palmer, unlike Joseph R. McCarthy from 1950–54, barely had a year of national support for his efforts. During that time, some fellow activists throughout the country tried to share his spotlight. State Senator Lusk in New York headed the Joint Legislative Committee Against Seditious Activities. The Lusk Committee, conceived in the board rooms of the exclusive Union League Club in Manhattan, conducted raids on radical papers, investigated alleged radicals, and encouraged the expulsion of five duly elected Socialist party members of the state legislature. Lusk, like Palmer and others, attributed the "criminal anarchy rampant in the state" to the "shiftless and radical types" among the immigrant classes: "Less than five percent arrested in New York's raid on Communism are Americans." Radical hunters like Lusk saluted Palmer's plan for a final solution to the Red menace in America. Deportation seemed the appropriate measure for dealing with communism, an ideology inextricably connected by nativists to their fear of foreigners.[14]

The attorney general planned the deportation of more than 3,500 "red aliens." But in the spring of 1920 he was blocked by the acting secretary of labor, a forceful and reflective seventy-one-year-old independent thinker named Louis F. Post, who refused to authorize what he later characterized as "these illegal persecutions, symptoms of a popular frenzy." Post canceled deportation orders for 2,202 aliens. Despite the attorney general's angry rebuttal, the Red Scare now began to abate. The labor conflict of earlier months was ending, and it was ending in victory for management. Labor would be weakened for the rest of the decade by these events. But because of their success, business leaders in the spring of 1920 turned away from the attack on immigrant labor and grew disinterested in "equating aliens with radical unrest." As historians of these years have observed, the capitalist managers now would recall the value of the vast immigrant work force. Perhaps they also were free at last to recognize the irrational component in the Red Scare. Certainly many influentials seemed to turn against Palmer in the spring. The Inter-Racial Council, the American Constitutional Association, and the National Founders Association spoke out against the anti-alien movement. Twelve prominent legal figures, including Roscoe Pound, Zechariah Chafee, Jr., and Felix Frankfurter, produced a document titled *To the American People: Report Upon the Illegal Practices of the U.S. Department of Justice*, assailing the "continued violation of the Constitution and the breaking of laws by the Department of Justice of the United States Government," chronicling in detail "utterly illegal" techniques used by Palmer in pursuing his antiradical program. In courthouses in major cities, judges now found against the Justice Department. In Boston, Judge George W. Anderson exclaimed in dismissing the cases resulting from the raids: "Talk about Americanization! What we need is the Americanization of the people who carry out such proceedings as these."[15]

Palmer and the Red hunters were now facing heavy weather. The attorney general's call for a peacetime sedition act was rejected by the powerful American Newspaper Publishers Association. Publishers were opposed to a law that might expose citizens as well as aliens to prosecution for expressing proscribed ideas. When A. Mitchell Palmer announced in April that radicals would call a general strike on May Day and that revolutionaries were planning to explode a number of enormous bombs at the same time, this last desperate ploy marked the final chapter in the Red Scare.

Hoover's division issued bulletins about threatened assassinations and bombings for ten days before 1 May. Major cities ordered police to prepare for the emergency, state militias were called to service, and federal troops were on standby. Nothing happened.

Palmer was discredited. Already the target of a counterattack by civil libertarians, he now became almost a comic figure. He was caricatured in newspaper cartoons wearing a heavy overcoat on a fine spring day, a pathetic and foolish alarmist. In September, when a huge bomb did explode on Wall Street, damaging the headquarters of J. P. Morgan and the Stock Exchange and killing twenty-nine people, there was no rekindling of the Red Scare. The prospect of an economic upturn and the end of large-scale social disorder made the final difference. Palmer was finished, the "Fighting Quaker" now laughed aside as the Quaking Fighter, or the Faking Fighter, a man with no hope of winning his party's nomination for president in 1920. When the ensuing campaign resulted in victory for a conservative Republican, one of Warren Harding's first announcements was that "too much has been said about Bolshevism in America."[16]

The Red Scare was over. The debate about its effects would long continue. One result it had was to drive the infant Communist parties underground. Its purge of these "conspirators" temporarily created conspiratorial organizations. It also left a running scar across the decade; the Sacco-Vanzetti case, which began during the hysteria, ended only with the execution of the anarchists, accused of a payroll robbery-murder in Massachusetts, in 1927.[17]

But what was the ultimate meaning of the Red Scare? One analyst, borrowing from the work of a contemporary anthropologist, called it a "revitalization movement" and argued that like millenarian outbreaks in other cultures and other eras, it represented the response to unbearable social stress in America after the war. Traditional social "mazeways" had been disrupted by the upheavals caused by the war. The Red Scare offered some frightened and disoriented people a way of reconstituting their vision of a stable order.[18]

It is clear that this nativist phenomenon did emerge in a period reminiscent of the setting for the Know Nothings and the APA in the mid- and late nineteenth century. Postwar social and economic upheaval temporarily raised fears for many that their mobility would be blocked, that personal gains in the wartime economy would be lost; "relative deprivation" threatened those whose prospects now suddenly seemed less bright than before. As in earlier years, nativism projected these anxieties on the alien. The bombings, the strikes, the rumors of sinister plots also temporarily made many fear for the future of political institutions. For them, the psychological correlates of disaster would be there if something was not done.

But there were significant differences between the nativist movements of the past and the Red Scare. In 1919 and 1920, federal and state government officials became the leaders of the movement, national and state policies the instruments of repression. In addition, although there were no organizations with membership roles and initiation rituals this time, it was clear that many influential men in the circle of business and social elites endorsed and encouraged these developments, if only for a few months. The Know Nothings and the patriotic fraternities of the 1890s never won real government power and rarely had the support of society's wealthiest and most powerful people. Most significantly, these nativists in 1919 were fixated on the un-American nature of the aliens' ideas; not religion but ideology enraged them, another first. In the Red Scare, the changing nature of political extremism of the Right was on view. Before long, it would not be Catholic and Jewish immigrants but radicals who would be the sole object of the protector's wrath.

The legislation that would further this process and erode the structure of the old nativism was being put in place in these years. Senator William P. Dillingham, the man who had led the Immigration Commission when it issued its restrictionist and pessimistic report in 1911, drafted the bill that would limit immigration according to a national quota system. The Emergency Quota Acts and Immigration Acts from 1921 to 1924 represented the final flowering of nativists' dearest hopes. The "destructive and inferior" outsiders now would no longer be allowed entry to the promised land. Quotas would restrict immigration, and only a small percentage of southeastern European immigrants would be allowed in the country. This was particularly true after the last piece of legislation—the Johnson-Reed Act—tailored quotas to national groups on the basis of the population mix in the United States in 1890, before the new migration began.[19]

The raison d'être for nativism finally would be removed by the new acts. The problems of fresh new arrivals would no longer compound ethnic hatreds and national tensions. The old nativism—based on alien people and an alien religion—inevitably would wane. But before that happened, there would be one last dramatic outbreak of the old fervor. In the tumultuous 1920s, the setting was

right for traditional nativism's last stand. The vehicle was a fraternal organizaion, a secret society, a movement reminiscent in many
ways of the "patriotic" orders of the 1850s and 1890s. But it owed
its name and its liturgy to a very different heritage. It was the Ku
Klux Klan.

★ ★ ★ ★ ★ ★ ★ ★ ★ ★ ★ ★ ★ ★ ★ ★ ★ ★ ★ ★

CHAPTER 12

TRADITIONAL NATIVISM'S LAST STAND

THE KU KLUX KLAN

IN THE 1920S

ANTIALIEN MOVEMENTS in earlier years had emerged in times of economic instability and political disarray. Nativism's last stand in the 1920s flourished in the boom years of a decade marked by a conservative consensus. The modern Ku Klux Klan, unlike the Red Scare of 1919 or the APA in the 1890s, grew without a setting of runaway inflation and labor strife or panic and recession. Like a throwback to the 1830s, the Klan represented fear and hatred in an age of equality and opportunity.

Americans in the depression-ravaged 1930s would remember the previous decade as the golden era, that brief moment of glittering hope and growing affluence when the American dream seemed close enough for almost everyone to touch. This nostalgia for the "roaring twenties" was wrapped in myth and distorted in memory. But there was no doubt that it was a time of spectacular growth and infectious optimism.

The nation emerged from those postwar economic problems during which Palmer's raids were launched to enter a time of sustained expansion. In the nine years preceding the stock market crash at decade's end, real wages rose almost 25 percent. Most of the economic indicators pointed straight up. Gross national product and the index of industrial production almost doubled. Technological advances spurred a striking rise in productivity, which allowed the cost of living index to remain constant as salaries and profits spiraled upward and the average hourly work week was reduced.

America had emerged from the Great War as the only real economic winner. The creditor nation of the world, alone among the great powers undamaged by the struggle, the United States finally entered a period when its average citizens could share in the new prosperity. It was a startling development. The prewar industrial revolution had offered long hours and low pay to those émigrés from Europe and the American hinterland pouring into the factory towns, an economic fate attractive only by comparison with what was left behind. Now, the boom would at last put disposable income in the hands of millions. What followed was an unparalleled explosion in mass consumption, an emerging consumer society in which Americans spent their new money on the products that technology finally was pricing within the reach of many.

Automobiles led the way. By 1929, Americans owned 23 million passenger cars, one for every five or six people. Henry Ford was paying his assembly line workers enough to buy their own products, and automobile manufacture soon accounted for one-eighth of all industrial production. Like cars, electrical appliances were no longer playthings for the rich; the value of appliances sold in 1927 alone was over $1.5 billion. With an expanding advertising industry stimulating sales and installment buying an accepted part of a new and more confident way of life in which rising wages meant a willingness to accept debt to live the good life now, the boom moved forward. Some were so convinced, as John Kenneth Galbraith observed, that "God intended the American middle class to be rich" that they speculated wildly in the Florida real estate craze of 1925. (This was when hustlers marketed "suburban" lots in bogs, swamps, and scrublands fifty miles from any city.) Later, many more would join the buying frenzy that fueled the ill-fated stock market boom.[1]

New products and new industries seemingly were emerging from nowhere. Commercial radio did not exist at the beginning of the Red Scare in 1919. By 1920, the first station was on the air; by 1928 there was a listening audience of 50 million and radio sales approached $1 billion. The film industry experienced a similar decade of expansion; by 1929 there were twenty-two thousand movie theaters nationwide.

Many families remained at subsistence incomes throughout this period. The boom did not touch millions, and even for those blessed by the new prosperity, real wages grew much more slowly after 1923 than in the months before. But so many had been affected that the 1920s became a time of widespread confidence in the future and support for the leadership associated with this economic miracle, which offered the promise of more good years to come. This leadership was not composed of Progressive politicians calling for more equitable arrangements or intellectuals offering international crusades. Theodore Roosevelt and Woodrow Wilson were gone; in Washington, Warren Harding and Calvin Coolidge presided over a return to an earlier concept of federal power. Coolidge, who once remarked that "a man who builds a business builds a temple," celebrated the private sector and so did the majority of his constituents. The 1920s were years in which the "free enterpriser" was more than ever the American hero. Advertising man Bruce Barton's famous best seller of 1925–26, *The Man Nobody Knows*, deified the businessman: Jesus was not only the most popular dinner guest in Jerusalem—"he attended all the feasts, he loved to be in a crowd . . . no other public figure had a more interesting list of friends"—and "an outdoors man," but a great executive. Barton's portrayal suggested that Jesus picked up twelve men from the bottom ranks of business (the Disciples) and forged them into a selling organization that conquered the world, that in a sense Jesus Christ was the founder of modern business.[2]

A triumphant private culture in which capitalists were the models to emulate and the acquisition of material goods the only measure of success and personal fulfillment was rejected by an articulate minority. As in the nineteenth century, when the Transcendentalists revolted against the materialism of the post-Jacksonian boom years, intellectuals despaired at their society. Novelist John Dos Passos's stirring trilogy, *USA*, would describe how success was corrupting and failure corrosive in America. Fitzgerald's hero in *The Great Gatsby* was portrayed as putting all his energies into the quest for wealth, status, and power "in the service of a vast, vulgar and meritricious beauty." Sinclair Lewis skewered the Babbitts in the business community so effectively in the mid-1920s that a national business magazine defensively declared: "Dare to be a Babbit . . . what the world needs is more good Rotarians who live orderly lives, save money, send their children to school, go to church, and play golf." For many writers and artists, this was an increasingly insensitive culture, and they fled its degradations by retreating to Bohemian enclaves like Greenwich Village.[3]

But the intellectual nay-sayers did not speak for America. As in the past, people voted with their feet for the traditional American dream. Making it in the United States meant making more money, buying more things, improving one's social standing by getting promoted or a better job or achieving some other demonstrable mark of success. To make it in America often meant moving to the city, the heart of the urban-industrial marketplace. New York, Chicago, and other metropolitan centers became the magnet for millions, and the age of the skyscraper made the city of the 1920s a symbol of the triumph of this business order. But urban growth, as in the past, would take its toll. The way of life that flourished best in the big city created its own problems, and many caught in this compelling but cold, demanding, and impersonal environment found themselves searching desperately for community.

In place of broken ties to family and childhood friends—the fate of some newcomers to the city—many sought comfort in the proliferating fraternal groups of this joiners' decade. Service clubs like the Rotarians and social fraternities like the Knights of Pythias attracted new members. Older orders founded new lodges: Masons and Red Men, Elks and Odd Fellows, Eagles and Moose offered a place to go, a feeling of belonging, an intimacy in place of loneliness. The fading rural order, the world of small-town America, had provided stability and a sense of place, often at the cost of suffocating conformity. But even the values and traditional social arrangements of Middletown were changing in these years, as Robert and Helen Lynd revealed in their pioneering study of Muncie, Indiana. The private culture of the American 1920s, with its individualist ethos and promise of personal success, offered opportunity at a price. It sent many in search of something to share, some safe, communal relationship.

In this context, a celebrity culture emerged for the first time in modern U.S. history. It was necessary only to be an American to share with others the thrill of Charles Lindbergh's achievement in his lone flight across the Atlantic. Lindbergh, after all, was the quintessential hero for this age, not only a Minnesota farmboy who seemed the repository and embodiment of the pioneering heritage of the frontier but a bold young manipulator of the best products of the new technology. Lindbergh was the greatest celebrity, but there were many others: movie stars Charlie Chaplin, Douglas Fairbanks, Rudolf Valentino, and Clara Bow, famous criminals such as Al Capone, and sports heroes everywhere—Jack Dempsey and Bill Tilden, Gertrude Ederle and Babe Ruth, the Four Horsemen of Notre Dame and their legendary coach, Knute Rockne. One reason for the growing fascination with the athlete as hero was the disposable income that made spectator sports big business in these years. The crowds pouring into Dempsey's fights with Gene Tunney paid almost $4 million. Babe Ruth's salary approached $70,000 yearly to play in Yankee Stadium, the House that Ruth Built. Another reason was the media revolution, which put play-by-play reporting on the airwaves and made the sports pages among the most widely read parts of the daily press. But another factor was the sense of excitement and community that fandom offered so many. How else to explain the remarkable construction of huge stadia throughout the nation for college football teams. "Memorial Stadiums" dedicated to Great War veterans emerged in Champaign-Urbana, Illinois, Iowa City, Iowa, Ann Arbor, Michigan, Lawrence, Kansas, and dozens of other college towns. What were cavernous structures seating forty, sixty, and eighty thousand doing in small towns on the midwestern plains? They represented another way that Americans could find an innocent and acceptable brotherhood through allegiance to the home team. Everyone in Illinois could join in cheering Red Grange and the Fighting Illini. In a time when older community ties were strained, new ones had to be invented.[4]

But there would be no simple solution to the deeper problem of community. The German sociologist Ferdinand Tönnies's oft-quoted work *Gemeinschaft and Gesellschaft*, published in 1926, suggested the tension that would follow when rural or small-town social structures gave way to the new, "Gesellschaft" structure of the urban culture. The old order, homogeneous in ethnicity and religion, characterized by low mobility and traditional status arrangements—in which there was a measure of deference for the rich and powerful in town or village but a stable and secure place in the community for all—was being replaced by a secular order. This was a multiethnic, more mobile society in which religion lost its place of centrality and social and economic relations depended not on tradition and trust but on contract. The change was not occurring for the first time in the 1920s; it had provided part of the setting for nativist movements in earlier years. But the postwar boom had accelerated the pace of change, and for many Americans the certainties and sureties of the past were shaken by the growth of this dynamic, modern society.[5]

★★★

Resentment and Anger in an Age of Expansion

Some people reacted to the displacement of older values by the new not only with confusion and anxiety but resentment and anger, compounded by feelings of jealousy. Not everyone was prospering equally in the golden 1920s. Among those left behind were small-town folk in the South, West, and lower Midwest, outside the mainstream of economic growth. In the big cities, others could see how unequally rewards in the quest for the big money were dispersed, how failure—or relative failure—was the dark underbelly of this modern version of the American dream. More than money and status, however, the fabled world of the jazz age swingers offered sexual and social freedom condemned by the new outsiders, many of whom must have been furious at being denied access to these fascinating, forbidden delights. There were many losers in the boom years, and there were many who felt a terrible loss in the displacement of traditional values no matter what their personal economic or social situation. It was among these people that the search for community and the desire to protect older American ideals, compounded by feelings of bitterness at failure to share equally in the rewards of the new era, led to the rise of repressive movements. In an age of equality and opportunity, nativism beckoned once more to protectors and fugitives.

One repressive phenomenon was Prohibition. Enacted at last in 1919, the ban on the production, sale, and consumption of intoxicating beverages had roots deep in the nineteenth century and represented the crusading effort of prewar years. Yet it was in the 1920s that Prohibition filled its symbolic role. It reflected not only revulsion at drunkenness and contempt for the drinking immigrant masses, not only the power of the Women's Christian Temperance Union and its role in the emerging women's movement, but also an assault on the pleasures and amenities of city life. As one writer put it, this was "a measure passed by village America against urban America." Of course, it had its supporters among post-Progressive activists, who saw the state—in some perverse way—serving as an instrument of reform by protecting family and society from substance abuse, a kind of political utopianism. And it did not bother the urban elites, who knew Prohibition would not be enforced and could go to their favorite speakeasy with the added thrill of thumbing their noses at the constraints of legal convention. But it did appeal to many outsiders, who saw it as a way of punishing both the affluent urban winners and the ethnic urban millions, groups who together had made the new industrial world the economic centerpiece of modern America.[6]

Prominent among the urban winners and the ethnic millions were Jews, and anti-Semitism flourished in the postwar years. Henry Ford, that billionaire pioneer of mass production who had played the pivotal role in the auto revolution, was at the center of the attack on the "International Jew." He purchased the moribund *Dearborn Independent*, converting it into an anti-Semitic newspaper, published from 1920 to 1927. It reached a circulation of seven hundred thousand, largely in the Midwest. Excerpts from the *Independent* in 1920–21 were offered in book form, works titled *The International Jew: The World's Foremost Problem, Jewish Activities in the United States, Jewish Influence in American Life,* and *Aspects of Jewish Power in the United States.*

Here Jews were characterized not as victims but as "persecutors," subversive manipulators responsible for a bewildering variety of destructive activities. "Jewish gamblers corrupt American baseball," the *Independent* reported, and "every non-Jewish baseball manager lives in fear of the Jews." The "Yiddish controllers" of the American theater constituted a "Jewish theatrical trust," and a "Jewish song trust that makes you sing" had been responsible for "Jewish jazz becoming our national music." In the new media beginning to sweep the country, "Jewish supremacy in the motion picture world" had made films in America into "Jewish propaganda." But even more sinister than this Jewish influence on popular culture was its political and economic power. "Jewish organizations advance Bolshevism and revolution in the United States," Ford's paper insisted. "Swarming Russian and Polish Jews," these "dark, squat figures" with their "alien tongues" and their "sullen attitudes," a "strange Slavonic-Oriental admixture," influenced labor unions in service of their radical, un-American ideologies. Yet even as some Jews plotted to overturn the capitalist system, others were controlling it and reaping immense profits from their power in the financial world. But, of course, "the great Jewish banking houses of the United States are a foreign importation," and in "molding the Federal Reserve System," in moving to set up a central bank to serve their own interests, they demonstrated the ways in which the International Jew owed loyalty not to the United States but to the goal of Jewish world dominion. The *Independent* published lengthy excerpts from the "Twenty Four documents of the Protocols of the Learned Elders of Zion," seeking to prove "the terrible completeness of the Jewish World Plan."[7]

Ford's efforts to promote anti-Semitism were made in a setting of continuing fear and hostility. In 1922, a Chicago employment office reported that two-thirds of requests from employers specified that Jews were not wanted; in 1925, the majority of teacher agencies in the Midwest reported that most jobs were available for Protestants only. Even some academics seemed to share the mood. One sociologist, in a chapter on race attitudes in which anti-Semitism was assessed and deplored, observed that although "nearly every community of any size contains Jewish people as fine as members of any other race, there are enough of the low class Jews in business to keep the repulsive stereotypes before the public mind . . . 'money grubbing' . . . 'crude and loud mouthed' . . . the 'obtrusive, wealthy Jew' is often notorious."[8]

Still, if anti-Semitism was pervasive in these years, it did not constitute a major social movement. It was another example of one group of Americans being assailed for their ethnicity and their religion. But as this process continued, other developments in American religion provided an impetus for a different form of repressive activity.

The fundamentalist controversy emerged at this time. The Scopes trial in 1925 was a sensation because it featured famous adversaries—the aging Populist hero William Jennings Bryan and the noted "people's lawyer," Clarence Darrow—debating Darwin's theory of evolution. But it revealed again the anger at the values of the larger society displacing the verities of the old. In Dayton, Tennessee, schoolchildren must not be taught that the Bible was not the literal truth, must not be told that humans descended from lower orders and were not created by God in the first six days. When crowds of rural hill folk gathered to support Bryan in his pathetic defense of biblical truth, urban sage H. L. Mencken, famous journalist and spokesman for modernity against the values of Gemeinschaft community, had a field day. He contemptuously dismissed the spectators as "gaping primates," an "anthropoid rabble" cheering on an "inflammatory half wit."

In fact, fundamentalism was not merely a reaction to the social upheavals of the 1920s. It was the product of a religious controversy long in the making and had roots in nineteenth-century millenarianism, a movement that embraced biblical literalism, the belief in the inerrancy of the Scriptures. The clash between fundamentalists and Protestant liberals or modernists had taken a new direction with the end of the Great War, which not only left clerical progressives, the spokesmen for the Social Gospel, disillusioned and tired, but brought on what one scholar has characterized as "the rise of aggressive fundamentalism." The apocalyptic nature of World War I, ending as it did with a soured peace and no feelings of international brotherhood, stimulated a renewed belief that here might be the fateful prelude to the much greater trial before the Second Coming foretold by the premillennial reading of the Bible. It was in this setting that fundamentalism, attracting almost 15 million followers, emerged as a powerful force in America. Now efforts were made in a number of states, including Tennessee, to protect biblical truth from the assault of Darwinian teaching.

Nonetheless, the fundamentalist controversy which peaked in that heat-seared midsummer courtroom drama at Dayton was not simply a religious phenomenon. The one hundred journalists who crowded into the little village, issuing stories about people with "obvious mental irregularities of a religious tendency," as one of them put it, knew which side they were on. They reported on the appearance of T. T. Martin, the Blue Mountain, Mississippi, evangelist, author of *Hell in the High Schools: Christ or Evolution—Which*. They contributed to the circus atmosphere, and it was the fundamentalists who were portrayed as the clowns. The elites and intellectuals who applauded Darrow's dissection of Bryan, who gleefully read Mencken's dispatches in which the people of Rhea County were characterized as "hillbillies," "peasants," and "morons" who accepted the "degraded nonsense which country preachers are ramming and hammering into [their] yokel skulls," reviled these absurd protectors of a lost America, these simple folk who would not or could not comprehend modern society. But the objects of their scorn would not disappear. Although there was no inextricable ideological link between fundamentalism and nativism, many of the true believers in the 1920s were also attracted by the arguments of antialiens. Some would strike back at their detractors by joining an organization that appealed to their fears and their hostilities and spoke to their pride in an older vision of the nation. In some places, it is true, there would be modest rivalry between fundamentalist groups and the new organization, but in most areas the appeals of fundamentalism and nativism in the 1920s were compatible. For the fraternal order many now would join could provide community even as it offered a way of cleansing the country and checking destructive forces that threatened the nation, the moral order, and the life of white, Protestant America. This was the Ku Klux Klan.[9]

★★★

The Emergence of the Klan

Like Prohibition, the modern Klan was born before the 1920s. But it never prospered until the golden years, and it did not survive the decade. It was founded in 1915 in Atlanta, Georgia. Its creator was William J. Simmons, a fraternal organizer, a former circuit-riding minister, a veteran of the Spanish-American War. Simmons was a native of Alabama; he had been raised on the family farm. He recalled that his father, a doctor and mill owner, had been an officer in the post–Civil War Ku Klux Klan, when those hooded vigilantes emerged to repress black freedmen and restore "order" and native white supremacy in the South of Reconstruction. His own career had been a disappointment. Without the funds to study medicine like his father, denied an affluent ministry in the church, unable to survive on the meager stipend received for his revival meeting sermonizing, he had turned to what he called "fraternalism," joining several organizations and finally making money as a "colonel" in the Woodmen of the World.

Tall, thin-lipped, square-jawed, bespectacled, Simmons was blessed with a powerful voice. He became an effective stump speaker and was known as an ambitious, experienced local organizer. He long had dreamed of inventing his own fraternity, modeled on the Ku Klux Klan. In 1915, after copyrighting his idea, he led thirty-four "charter members"—recruited from other fraternities—to a symbolic cross-burning on Stone Mountain, the great granite outcropping a few miles from Atlanta. The date was 15 October, a week before D. W. Griffith's film adaptation of Thomas Dixon's novel about the early Klan, *The Birth of a Nation*, opened in Georgia. Griffith's film was a sensation, and its romantic, sympathetic vision of the old hooded fraternity served as an immediate organizing tool for the new movement. Simmons advertised for members wishing to join "The World's Greatest Secret, Social, Patriotic, Fraternal, Beneficiary Order." He had a measure of success.[10]

By 1920, the new Ku Klux Klan had several thousand followers and chapters in Atlanta, Mobile, Birmingham, and Montgomery. During World War I, Simmons had not been invited to work with the elitist, quasi-governmental American Protective League, but he had done his part in the struggle against the aliens and their dupes. He led his membership in forays against "disloyal" shipyard strikers, harassment of draft dodgers, and assaults on prostitutes loitering near army bases. He submitted reports on "untrustworthy" people to the Citizens Bureau of Investigation in Atlanta. During this secret war against the Huns, Simmons changed his organization from a relatively public order whose members sometimes wore lodge buttons to a true secret society. The allure of a closed, militant, patriotic fraternity did attract a following, but even after the war and the Red Scare, there were still fewer than six thousand Klansmen in Georgia and Alabama. Klan membership in Atlanta was smaller than the B'nai B'rith.[11]

Simmons had demonstrated that he was an ineffective organizer of a mass movement. In the summer of 1920, when A. Mitchell Palmer already had been discredited and the boom was soon to begin, he found himself financially strapped, searching for help. It was then that he came upon two talented publicists who would transform his regional order into a national phenomenon.

Edward Young Clarke, former journalist and fraternity organizer, a public relations man who had known only modest success, was promoting a Harvest Home Festival in Atlanta when he had met Elizabeth Tyler. This forceful and vivacious woman was handling publicity at the time for the "Better Babies" hygiene movement. The two formed a new business, the Southern Publicity Association, and found clients among the Anti-Saloon League, the Salvation Army, and the Red Cross. In June, a befuddled Simmons met with Clarke and Tyler. Their resulting contract called for the publicists to advertise the Ku Klux Klan and to recruit new members. They would receive $8 of every $10 "klecktoken" or initiation fee, dividing some of their profits with staff organizers. Clarke became imperial kleagle, head of the Propagation Department, and within a year, he and Tyler found success beyond their wildest dreams.

The two discovered that William J. Simmons's traditional appeal to join a mystical society dedicated to protecting southern "order," patriotism, and racial supremacy was tapping only a small part of an enormous potential market. Encouraging Imperial Wizard Simmons to attack what he soon was calling "the hordes of aliens who flock to the ballot box to outnumber you," arguing that the "foreign element is trying to get control of the government of the United States," the two helped turn the Ku Klux Klan into a traditional nativist crusade. They assailed Jews and Orientals as well as blacks but soon focused particularly on the evils of Catholicism and the inextricable ties between the church and the "foreigners." With their shrewdly structured sales department marketing the movement as never before under the amateurish Simmons, with the nation divided into provinces (regions within states), realms (states), and domains (groups of states) for the purpose of recruitment, with more than a thousand kleagles (salesmen) sent out to find new members in return for handsome commissions, the Clarke-Tyler team made over $200,000 in fifteen months. Simmons received $150,000 and a comfortable new house. An elaborate "Imperial Palace" was purchased as a headquarters in Atlanta. Total membership reached one hundred thousand, and the Klan was spreading across the South and Southwest, north to Ohio and the Midwest and Northwest. Soon its membership would pass 1 million. It had become a national organization.[12]

The Klan's growth was the result of high-pressure salesmanship, the attraction of mystical fraternalism, and the traditional appeals of nativism. It was a perfect movement for the 1920s. From field kleagles through king kleagles (regional managers) to grand goblins (district sales managers for domains), every organizer at every level got a cut of the initiation fee, with Clarke and Tyler receiving a minimum of $2.50, Simmons a fraction less. The motivation to market the movement was built into the free enterprise system, and Klan officials cleverly sought out fraternity joiners, clergymen, and area politicians as the first recruits in each locality. But "kluxing" (as Clarke called his recruiting system) was only one

profit center for this fraternity business. The initiates needed elaborate robes, hoods, and other paraphernalia; the Gate City Manufacturing Company of Atlanta became the sole producer of regalia.
The Searchlight Publishing Company was created to print the numerous Klan newspapers and magazines. Still, managerial acumen
would have been meaningless without the romance of the secret
society.

Initiates took the oath of obedience, secrecy, fidelity, and "klan-
ishness" before a blazing cross, circled by the white-robed, hooded
membership in the "klavern" or meeting place. The new "knights"
of the Ku Klux Klan repeated words similar to those spoken by
recruits to the Order of the Star Spangled Banner seventy years before: they promised to defend the Constitution, the American flag,
free public schools, Protestantism, free speech and press, liberty,
and separation of church and state. These newcomers learned an
elaborate ritual, were given the codes to a convoluted ceremonial
language, and were placed in a bizarre hierarchy in which exalted
cyclopes ruled over Klansmen, subservient in turn to grand titans
(in provinces), grand dragons (realms), and finally the imperial wizard (and his staff) of the Invisible Empire. The letter "k" was central: klokards were lecturers; kludds, chaplains; kligrapps, secre-
taries; the sacred white book of the order, the kloran; meetings,
klonvokations. The Klan offered structure, position, and brotherhood to many restive or disoriented men from small towns and big
cities in the America of the 1920s. It was a movement so remarkably suited to its time and place that its growth matched the boom
of the larger nation.[13]

But the Klan's explosive expansion bred opposition and internal problems. The *New York World* ran a series exposing it in fall
1921, citing the "revelations" of a few disgruntled former Klansmen about financial wrongdoings and immoral behavior by Klan
leaders. The *World* exposé, syndicated in eighteen newspapers nationwide, proved to be counterproductive. Other Klan critics soon
called it a "blunder" because it overestimated KKK strength and
gave the impression that the eastern establishment was aligned
against the Klan. In this way, it encouraged the credulous to join.
The editor of the *Imperial Night-Hawk* was delighted: "They over-
did it, this vicious advertisement gives us an impetus." The *World*
articles did draw some blood by including descriptions of allegedly
violent and coercive activities by Klansmen and Klan chapters:

whippings, tar and featherings, boycotts, harassment, even four murders. Simmons denied any wrongdoing. "The Knights of the Ku Klux Klan," he responded, "have been organized not to tear down but to strengthen the aim of the law in America and to clarify and preserve certain fundamental principles." Several congressmen successfully called for an investigation, but the ensuing hearings before the House Rules Committee did little damage to the organization. The attack from the press seemed contained. But the revelations of immorality had focused on Edward Clarke and Elizabeth Tyler. They would play a role in a change at the top of the movement.[14]

The *World* had reported that Clarke and Tyler were more than just colleagues and good friends; they were arrested for disorderly conduct in October 1919. They had been found partially clothed in a house of prostitution. Clarke's wife—who had called the police— subsequently sued him for divorce. These tales of sexual wrongdoing at the top of an organization dedicated to preserving family and protecting womanhood were bad enough but Clarke's iron control of finances made matters worse. When a few prominent Klan goblins called on Simmons to dismiss Clarke, only to be rebuked by the leader, the resulting quarrel led to national news coverage and lawsuits on both sides. Simmons prevailed over these dissidents, but the publicity was harmful. Tyler resigned from the order, and a weary, increasingly confused William J. Simmons faced a major insurrection. Clarke had recruited a number of forceful, able activists to the organization, and several of these new leaders now decided to remove both Simmons and Clarke. Hiram Wesley Evans, a heavyset, round-faced, outgoing dentist from Texas, an inveterate fraternity joiner and a skillful political infighter whom Clarke had brought to Atlanta to work at headquarters, was a key figure. He was aided by Fred Savage, former New York detective turned Klan chief of staff, and the grand dragons of Louisiana, Texas, Arkansas, and Indiana. Meeting with Simmons before the first national Imperial Klonvokation, they persuaded the founder to step aside "temporarily," to accept a $1,000-a-month salary and the title "emperor" while Evans was nominated new imperial wizard.[15]

Hiram Wesley Evans was in power only a short time before Simmons realized what had been done to him. Discovering that his new title carried no power, he first sought to organize a Klan affiliate for women, the Kamelia, which would give him complete control of at least some organization. Then he moved to reoccupy the

Imperial Palace and reestablish his authority in the larger movement, taking over when Evans was out of town. It was April 1923. Acrimonious charges and countercharges filled the pages of Klan papers, and the squabble became headline news in the national press. Lawsuits were filed once again on both sides. Because he still had many adherents in the order and held key copyrights to the Klan ritual and constitution, William Simmons was in a position to cause the new leadership real trouble.

Evans and his allies decided to buy Simmons out, offering a $1,000 monthly pension for life in return for the copyrights. Simmons accepted, but he would not stay bought. Convinced he had been cheated, he accused Evans of misappropriating Klan funds and encouraged a new round of harassing lawsuits through the summer and fall of 1923. Hiram Wesley Evans responded through his loyal Klan papers. Simmons was characterized as a "pirate," a "traitor to the cause," an "enemy of America doing all he can to ruin, exploit and disrupt the Ku Klux Klan," even as a "leader of Bolshevik Klansmen betraying the movement." The founder was unsuccessful with his new litigation, and Evans made a final effort to silence his rival. He expelled William J. Simmons from the Klan, but only after he succeeded in gaining agreement from Simmons to give up Kamelia, take a onetime payment of $146,500, and promise to cease all further contact with the order. The inept former imperial wizard, bilked by an associate of much of his final payment, retired in bitterness. He complained of a "fiendish frameup" by the new Klan leaders and tried vainly to organize rival fraternities—the Knights of the Flaming Sword and the White Bond—before disappearing into obscurity.[16]

Simmons was gone; Evans and associates were in complete control. They had solidified their hold by moving quickly to dismiss Edward Clarke. Evans announced that "Clarke no longer has any official position" with the Klan, "no longer receives one cent of revenue . . . I cancelled the contract for the good of the order." With his colleague Elizabeth Tyler not present to offer support and facing new criminal charges involving violation of the Mann Act (a year before he had been indicted for using the mails to defraud and for carrying whiskey in his suitcase), Clarke offered little resistance and received no payment when he was ousted. He did join Simmons in sniping attacks on the new leadership, complaining to President Calvin Coolidge about the "prostitution of the ideals of the Klan." In early 1926 he would reappear as a national figure, organizing a fundamentalist society called the Supreme Kingdom, dedicated to protesting modernism and the theory of evolution. He planned a crusade to censor "poisonous" books and to dismiss "unsound" teachers. But when newspapers revealed that he was pocketing two-thirds of the Kingdom's initiation fees, he was forced out, helping to discredit the fundamentalist movement as his last public act. But in 1923 Clarke had no influence and no following in the Klan. When he was gone, Evans dismantled his fund-raising apparatus, placing kleagles on salary rather than commission. He also moved to check lawless activity by Klan members, emphasizing once more the Klan's devotion to temperance, Protestantism, Americanism, and morality. A new leadership would take the order to new heights of popularity.[17]

★★★

Restating the Themes of Nativism

The Ku Klux Klan under Hiram Wesley Evans and associates offered a program reminiscent of its nativist progenitors, the Know Nothings and the APA. Klan papers and magazines, books and articles by Klan leaders, laid out the appeal of the new nativism.

One spokesman, Reverend E. H. Laugher, in *The Kall of the Klan in Kentucky*, explained that "the KKK is not a lodge or a society or a political party." Rather, it is a mass movement, "a crusade of American people who are beginning to realize that they have neglected their public and religious duty to stand up for Americanism." This meant remembering that America was discovered by Norsemen, colonized by Puritans, that the United States was "purely Anglo-Saxon and Nordic." It was essential to "preserve our racial purity," he insisted, to avoid "mongrelization." It was imperative to maintain separation of church and state because "the forces of Protestantism" were protectors of the "doctrine of Americanism." The Roman Catholic church, appealing to the polyglot peoples who threatened the good and pure society, must be blocked in its drive to dominate and destroy the great nation.[18]

In *The Fiery Cross, The Kourier, The American Standard, Dawn,*

The Imperial Night-Hawk, and other publications, Klan ideologists assaulted Catholics, Jews, and aliens. "Jesus was a Protestant," the faithful were told; he had "split with the priests" because he had truth and right on his side. The Roman Catholic church, laboring under "the growth of Popish despotism," was irreligious and un-American. In fact, the "Papacy's campaign against liberalism and freedom" made it a proper "ally of Mussolini's fascism," just as the church had been on the side of other autocracies since medieval times. In America, the "spirit of Bunker Hill and Valley Forge," that longing for democracy and individualism which informed the Revolution and the words of the Founding Fathers, was at odds with a "hierarchical Church, which, like an octopus, has stretched its tentacles into the very vitals of the body politic of the nation." The church's effort to undermine the public schools, to "reach out for the children of Protestantism," to "hit anywhere with any weapon" in an unscrupulous campaign to impose its will, meant that every Catholic in public life, from school board member to national politician, must be watched carefully. "Do you know," a Klan editorialist asked, "that eight states have Roman Catholic administrations, 600 public schools teach from the Roman Catholic catechism, sixty-two per-cent of all elected and appointed offices in the United States are now held by Catholics, who also are a majority of the teachers in many major city school systems?"[19]

The threat of the church was everywhere. The "Romanized press" tried to propagandize a gullible public. Catholics evaded taxes as a matter of course, refusing to share the burdens of government, preferring to subsidize sinister schemes hatched by their prelates. The church used Jesuits to engage in "occult mental manipulations" and tried to "subjugate the Negro race through spiritual domination." The pope favored child labor, and because "20,000 ordained priests in America are vassals to this Imperial Monarch in Rome," the same could be expected of church leaders in the United States. Indeed, Catholics were in no sense trustworthy Americans; during the Great War, "German sentiment was the fruit of carefully prepared and skillfully disseminated Roman propaganda." But it would be wrong to conclude that the Klan was anti-Catholic, leaders insisted, because its arguments were "wholly and solely concentrated on being one hundred per cent American." In fact, one writer suggested, the Klan is "no more aimed at Roman Catholics than it would be aimed at Buddhists, Confucianists or Mohammedans, or anybody else who owes allegiance to any foreign person and/or religion."[20]

Like the nineteenth-century nativists, Klan initiates were asked to protect America from the diabolical plans of Jesuits and other leaders of this un-American presence. From colonial days, anti-Catholicism had been a dominant theme in the history of these movements, a way of displacing fears and angers on alien intruders. In the 1920s, with Irish Catholics maintaining positions of prominence in urban and national politics, continuing to gain greater influence in a growing economy, Klan spokesmen returned to the old themes. The assault on the church was repeated in almost every Klan speech, article, and editorial. This modern Ku Klux Klan dressed its members in garb borrowed from the Reconstruction vigilante organization, but its real roots were in traditional nativism, stretching back much further in the American experience.

But to its attack on Catholicism, the modern Klan added an anti-Semitic element. The APA, emerging during the new immigration, had touched on this theme; Klan writers developed the argument. "Jews are everywhere a separate and distinct people, living apart from the great Gentile masses," said the author of *Klansmen: Guardians of Liberty*. But these people are not "home builders or tillers of the soil." Evans had made a similar argument in a speech at Dallas in December 1922: "The Jew produces nothing anywhere on the face of the earth. He does not till the soil. He does not create or manufacture anything for common use. He adds nothing to the sum of human welfare." Yet not only were Jews unproductive, Klan theoreticians insisted, they were un-American. They were not interested in integration: "No, not the Jew . . . he is different." These people, who "defied the melting pot for one thousand years," believed in their own superiority, in "Jewry Uber Alles." They hatched secret plans to advance their interests, to "cause wars and to subjugate America." Certain conspiratorial Jews must be "absolutely and eternally" opposed when they plotted their "crimes and wrongs." They were nothing more than money-grubbing and immoral vultures, "moral lepers who gloat over human tragedy, rejoice in the downfall of the guileless and inexperienced." The unethical practices of Jewish businessmen—often seen as winners in the economic competition of the boom years—and the radical schemes of Jewish Marxists were considered equally repugnant, dangerous to

America. But so, too, was the cultural depravity of strategically placed "Semites" in the media. "Jew Movies Urge Sex and Vice," the Klan headline shouted like an echo from Ford's *Dearborn Independent*; "Jewish corruption in jazz" was a result of "their monopoly over popular songs." In the big cities, "ninety five per cent of bootleggers are Jews."[21]

It was the Roaring Twenties, and as mores changed, as traditional social arrangements were overturned, as skirts went up and speakeasies flourished, as the movies and radio made their mark with Tin Pan Alley songs popularized by so many show business celebrities, the Klan found a way of identifying these disturbing developments in an antialien context, of standing up for America by assailing yet another band of un-Americans.

Still, the Jews were only one part of a larger alien problem in America. Again, like the Know Nothings and the patriotic fraternalists of the 1890s, these nativists were concerned with the threat they saw posed by all non-Anglo-Saxon immigrants and their descendants. Imperial Wizard Evans spoke of "the vast horde of immigrants who have reached our shores," these "Italian anarchists, Irish Catholic malcontents, Russian Jews, Finns, Letts, Lithuanians of the lowest class." Even after the Immigration Act of 1924, which Evans characterized as a "new era dawning for America" and took full credit for securing—"typifying the influence exerted by our organization"—he warned that undesirables "are still bootlegged into the nation," still try to "flaunt our immigration laws." This "polyglotism" was intolerable, for many of the most recent immigrants from southern and eastern Europe and from Asia still could not read and write English. They were unfamiliar with American history and tradition, "were unaware that America is fundamentally an Anglo-Saxon achievement." And because these alien peoples "congregate in our great centers, our cities are a menace to democracy," they are "modern Sodoms and Gomorrahs." Is "Petrograd in its ruin and desolation a picture of New York in the future"? There was only one possible response. "America for the Americans," Evans exhorted, for if "this state of affairs continues, the American race is doomed to cultural destruction." In words that might have been lifted from a Know Nothing broadside, he continued: "Illiteracy, disease, insanity, and mental deficiency are still pouring in among us."[22]

The "foreigners" were responsible for a host of social problems.

Evans lectured on "our alien crime-plague" and Klan papers reported on alien thugs, Italian mobsters and rum runners, even a "Newark alien hiding whiskey in U.S. flag." The aliens threatened female virtue: "Foreign women sell their bodies for gain." They threatened the safety of American womanhood: "Women Are Struck Down by Foreign Mob," screamed one headline, "Aliens Poison Hoosier Women," said another. Some aliens were radicals: "Russians Would Make America Red, Peril is a Very Real One." Others would destroy the nation through political sabotage: "Use the Ballot, the Italian Ambassador Recommends, to Advance the Interests of Italians' Native Land." And over all these perils loomed the threat of Irish Catholic party machine manipulators. Leaders of the church in America, most formidable of the foreign operatives, these "Irish Romanists in Tammany . . . lead the Jews, Poles, Italians, Germans, Czechs, Magyars"; it was a "vast army under command of the Irish Roman ward heelers." The only way to deal with the foreign devils, to safeguard our sacred institutions, was to re-Americanize the land. Evans announced: "Against us are all the forces of the mixed alliance composed of alienism, Romanism, hyphenism, Bolshevism and un-Americanism which aim to use this country as a dumping ground for the fermenting races of the Old World." But "we of the Klan are on the firing line . . . like the soldiers of the American Expeditionary Force in France, we stand up for America and take pride and joy in the wounds we receive . . . the Knights of the Ku Klux Klan have become the trustees under God for Protestant American nationalism."[23]

The cause of the Klan, in the phrases of its spokesmen, could not have been more noble, more dangerous, or more urgent. But among those many American values that Klansmen were sworn to protect, one had particular urgency. This was the protection of "womanhood." In pursuing this goal, the Klan invoked memories of that long line of femininity's defenders who marched under the banners of nativism, back to the days of Maria Monk.

A Texas Klansman, author of *Religious and Patriotic Ideals of the Ku Klux Klan*, reminded initiates that they had sworn to "promote good works and thus protect the chastity of womanhood, the virtue of girlhood, the sanctity of the home." Spokesmen repeatedly used the term "chivalry" in describing the movement's principles. The role of women in the literature of the Klan was explicitly traditional. They were the moral arbiters of society, for "even in the midst of all the pressing duties of maternal care and home making, women have found time to keep the spiritual fire of the nation burning on the altar . . . women have been the conscience keepers of the race." But the role was not so traditional that women would be repressed, for it was "Rome Which Opposes the Advancement of Womanhood," said the headline, the Jesuits who favor policies pushing women into "semi-oriental seclusion." The Klan would preserve and protect women so they might aid in the shaping of American destiny; "the fate of the nation is in the hands of women." As one Klan newswriter put it, they can be "not only help meets but help mates." After all, the "very mentioning of the word 'woman' always arrests the attention of every true man. Whatever else the human heart may forget in the rough experiences of life, it cannot forget its mother."[24]

The call to protect these fragile, sensitive, vulnerable women led to violence. Local Klans were accused of floggings, tar and featherings, and beatings in several states in the South, Southwest, and lower Midwest. The victims of the masked night riders often were alleged adulterers and wife-beaters, men said not to be supporting their families, men who had deserted their women. But the enemies of "pure womanhood" included sinners of both sexes. "Fallen women" were the targets in some rural bastions. Young women accused of prostitution or adultery were stripped naked, tarred, left half-conscious with their hair shorn. The sexual frustrations of these bands of white-robed small-townsmen, envious of the freedom exercised by millions of more liberated urbanites in the jazz age, finding perverse pleasure in this part of their crusade for morality, reveling in the projection of their anger and the displacement of their resentments on these symbolic villains, recalled the nunnery craze of the early nineteenth century.[25]

In fact, another generation of nativists meant another resurgence of convent tales. *Dawn* (a major Klan paper in Chicago) offered "Convent Cruelties: The True Story of Ex-Nun Helen Jackson," advertising offprints of this sadomasochistic piece for many months after initial publication. Other Klan journals featured, among several exposés, "Behind Convent Walls" and "Roman Priest Alienates Innocent Women's Love."[26]

Women who knew their role and understood their place were offered membership in affiliate groups open to "patriotic ladies." Simmons's Kamelia had been disbanded, but Hiram Evans introduced the Women of the Ku Klux Klan, an organization which absorbed such local groups as Ladies of the Invisible Empire in Louisiana and the Order of American Women in Texas. This new national organization established its own Imperial Palace, a pillared mansion in Little Rock, Arkansas. It sent its own kleagles into the field, calling on Klansmen to influence wives and sisters to join. By fall 1924, when the Ku Klux Klan said its membership numbered in the millions, the women's auxiliary claimed a following of two hundred thousand. The initiates were not, as one anti-Klan writer suggested, "nativist amazons." They were expected to perform customary housewifely chores; they prepared food for Klan outings, picnics, and klambakes. In fact, their order was little more than the instrument of one man's authority. James Comer, Evans's early ally and grand dragon of the Arkansas Klan, bankrolled the Women of the Ku Klux Klan and controlled its activities. He forced the resignation of its imperial commander to install Robbie Gill, an intimate friend who would soon be his wife, as new leader. It was Commander Gill who told the Second Imperial Klonvocation: "God gave Adam Woman to be his comrade and counselor . . . Eve's name meant life, society, company. Adam was lord and master." Like earlier nativists, Klansmen never questioned the assumption of male dominance. The American dream they sought to protect had no room for sexual equality. But the image of threatened womanhood was essential to their own search for masculine validation, even as it had been in the days of *The Awful Disclosures of Maria Monk.* That had been another age in which economic growth and status anxiety served as a setting for the resurgence of the antialien crusade.[27]

The attacks on Catholics and foreigners and the vows to protect imperiled American women tied the Ku Klux Klan to a long history of similar movements. It was traditional nativism's last stand. Its emergence in the 1920s raised questions to which contemporary journalists and academics offered a variety of answers.

Reporter Robert L. Duffus, author of a series of anti-Klan articles in the *World's Work,* argued that many recruits came from "the back counties of the south and lower midwest," where men carry guns, women are objects of deference but also of exploitation, and the disappointed seek causes outside themselves. Professor Frank Tannenbaum, writing in 1924, agreed in part, seeing Klansmen as seekers after "artificial thrills" as a way of dealing with the boredom of small-town life, people ready to use coercion in defense of social status, people "losing their grip" in a world of change. But Tannenbaum also looked to recent events as a source of this mood of restlessness. The Great War aroused human passions, he suggested, the "hope of a new and beatific world after the defeat of the German devil." The Klan offered an explanation of why the war brought no "dawning of Utopia." It was the Catholic, the radical, the foreigner who was in league with the devil.[28]

Later, scholars would embrace some of these views. Though not sharing pro-Klan journalist Stanley Frost's rosy vision of Klansmen as a knighthood of admirable reformers, they agreed that the Klan represented a response to the war, a zeal to cleanse and reform American society. The rise of fundamentalist fervor in the 1920s, which provided an additional setting for the Klan, was seen as another reaction to the war. Anti-Catholicism was in the air in many parts of the nation in these years. As with fundamentalism, the Klan's crusade for conformity to old values and old social arrangements was seen as a "characteristic response to a common disillusion."[29]

The Ku Klux Klan, like the Red Scare, was given new life by the souring of the international crusade. Almost all students of the Klan have made this point. But the reason why the Klan grew in the 1920s had more to do with social and economic strains in a society experiencing almost unprecedented growth.

Those who joined were not, as Duffus suggested, only losers in the boom years. Along with poor farmers, blue-collar workers, mechanics, and day laborers some bankers, lawyers, doctors, ministers, and prosperous businessmen were recruited in different regions. There were communities in which political careers and professional success depended on membership. But the Klan appealed more to those who were not members of any elite. Imperial Wizard and Emperor Evans observed: "We are a movement of the plain people, very weak in the matter of culture, intellectual support and trained leadership. . . . We demand a return of power into the hands of the everyday, not highly cultured, not overly intellectualized but entirely unspoiled and not de-Americanized average citizens of the old stock." The Klan everywhere appealed to those who believed that their older vision of America was at risk. In the struggle to preserve enduring American values, the movement offered a sense of common purpose in service of a cause greater than self. It offered an idealism that had a magnetic pull for many. Its shrewd managers, interested in money, power, and influence for themselves, knew how to package the movement. But the popularity of the Klan, once it began to spread across the land, did not depend on the Clarkes and Tylers or their successors as marketing specialists and sales-, men. Like the earlier nativist fraternities, it was rooted in a longing for order, in misty memories of some stable and happy past, in fears of what new perils modernity might bring, in the search for community in an age of flux.[30]

The movement provided community. Local Klans sponsored Sunday dinners and square dances, basketball tournaments and rodeos, carnivals and circuses, fireworks displays featuring "electric fiery crosses," social events of all kinds. It was comforting to be in the Klan, and it could be fun. Klansmen also took care of each other. Businessmen placed ads for Klan Klothes Kleaned or Krippled Kars Kured, expecting fraternal ties would result in new customers. Other activities offered bonding through unified action to clean up the community: boycotts of businesses run by "immoral men," committees to ferret out bootleggers and bars.[31]

The communal ties seemed at one with religious conviction. The movement that defended Protestantism won the tacit endorsement of many clergymen, some who joined the order. Most nationally prominent church leaders stayed away from the Klan, and some Methodist, Presbyterian, and Episcopalian notables and publications even attacked it, but these assaults from influential cosmopolitans only served to underscore Evans's claims that his movement was the instrument of the mass of common people. The Klan made inroads in many Protestant communities, particularly among Southern Baptists and others influenced by fundamentalist concerns. A major part of the Protestant press remained silent on the issue, but many local church papers endorsed the goals of an organization that appealed for support in the name of old-time values and that old-time religion.[32]

The Klan's growth was meteoric. In 1924, Stanley Frost reported that "some say it has six million members." Frost himself claimed only some 4.5 million in the movement. Robert Duffus put the number at 2.5 million in 1923. Other guesses ranged upward of 5 million. It was impossible to be certain; the Klan left only fragmentary local records and no national archives. But one modern scholar, using available data, estimated it had over 2 million recruits in 1924; another, in a careful review of conflicting claims, put it at over 2 million initiates across the years, with some 1.5 million at any one time. What is certain is that it had become a true mass movement, one of the major developments in the history of the 1920s, a great monument to the antialien impulse in America.[33]

★★★

The Klan across America

But it did not prosper equally in all sections of the country. In the Deep South, where the Klan was born, it exerted considerable influence in some states. Still, its membership never exceeded a quarter of a million.

In Atlanta, the home of Imperial Headquarters, the long struggle for control of the organization weakened the Klan. When Evans moved the national office to Washington in 1925 in search of a more visible role in national politics, it lost more ground. Only twenty thousand of the estimated sixty-five thousand Georgia Klansmen were Atlantans.

In other parts of the state, the Invisible Empire did make its mark. Although there were accusations of an epidemic of vigilante violence—police in Macon even set up an "antiflogging squad" of motorcycle officers in response—the order wielded formidable political influence. When Clifford Walker, former state attorney general, was elected governor with Klan support, he addressed the national Klonvocation in St. Louis. The subject was "Americanism Applied," and the new governor told Klansmen that they were an "aristocracy of service," the bulwark against the gang of Roman Catholic politicos who sought to manipulate voters "at behest of a foreign leader." The Klan's opposition to aliens was vital to the future of the nation, he exclaimed: "I would build a wall as high as Heaven against the admission of a single one of those South Europeans who never thought the thoughts or spoke the language of a democracy in their lives." The Klan's ties to Walker and to the chief justice of the state supreme court, Richard B. Russell, Sr., gave it influence beyond its numbers. As in other states, it did not focus on racial issues, emphasizing instead traditional nativist concerns. Its decline in 1926 followed national setbacks and attacks in the local press, but in the mid-1920s it was a force to be reckoned with in Georgia.[34]

In Alabama, it enjoyed similar success. There were sixty thousand members statewide, some fifteen thousand in Birmingham. The Robert E. Lee Klan No. 1, in the state's largest city, sponsored a huge rally in fall 1923 in which twenty thousand Klansmen in a crowd of sixty thousand witnessed the initiation of two thousand hooded knights. For some months, it seemed to be the wave of the future in this state. Hugo Black—later to be named to the U.S. Supreme Court—was only one of many ambitious young political climbers to join the ranks. But opposition to the KKK by Oscar W. Underwood, the distinguished senior senator, hurt the movement. Stories in Birmingham papers of an alleged Klan plot to kidnap and whip its opponents further weakened the order, as did the reports of Klan efforts to coerce and silence the press.

Developments in other southern states paralleled the Klan's history in Alabama. In Tennessee, it attracted almost forty thousand initiates, appealing most effectively to poorly paid white-collar workers or semiskilled blue-collar employees in Memphis and Knoxville. These men were fundamentalist in religion, believers in the old verities, responsive to anti-Catholic, anti-immigrant rhetoric. In Florida, Mississippi, and Virginia, the following was more rural, but the hundred thousand Klansmen in the three states also responded to traditional arguments. They joined an order that provided fraternity and social life but in the guise of militant patriotism. Though it declined throughout the region by 1926, the Klan made an impact in the Old South. Still, its notoriety was more striking in the Southwest, where its activities were shadowed by violence and rumors of violence.[35]

Louisiana was the scene of the most notorious episode of Klan terrorism in the 1920s, the Mer Rouge murders. When the Klan moved into Bastrop, a tough and shabby blue-collar town of wooden store fronts and meager frame houses, a place where most men worked in the pulp mill or carbon plant, it soon recruited almost all of the adult male population. These new hooded knights resolved to clean up the parish. Soon they were attacking any accused bootlegger or "immoral man" or woman in the region. The neighboring village of Mer Rouge was attractive and bucolic, with a very different lifestyle, and it proved resistant to Klan pressures. Hostility flared between the communities. When the exalted cyclops of the local Klan, an irritable and power-hungry old Civil War veteran in his seventies who had organized the flogging squads, was shot at during one of his night-riding adventures, his followers retaliated in a shocking act of brutality. Two young men from Mer Rouge were murdered, one of them the son of a wealthy planter. Their bodies were mutilated, dismembered, and dumped in a nearby lake. The case became a cause-célèbre for anti-Klan forces everywhere, a deepening embarrassment for the national movement. Governor John B. Parker, no friend of the Klan, declared the parish under martial law and sent in the state national guard. Federal agents entered the case, arresting local Klansmen. The resulting investigation was front-page news, and though the government could not prove its case, a number of Klansmen involved in the affair fled Louisiana. In the political campaign of 1924, the Klan became a central issue across the state, with leading candidates promising legislative action to curb the organization. The new governor pushed through bills proscribing secret societies and requiring the unmasking of all Klansmen. The order never recovered. When it failed to block the reelection of an anti-Prohibition Catholic to the United States Senate (Edwin Broussard) in 1926, it was on the road to dissolution.[36]

In Oklahoma, the Klan was stronger than in Louisiana. Almost one hundred thousand men joined the secret society. Near Tulsa in 1921, one thousand new knights were initiated in a gigantic day-long ceremony. The scene was a pasture near the city; a seventy-foot cross marked the site, and enormous congestion was created by ten thousand cars, two abreast for nine miles on the narrow country roads. A member observed: "It is the greatest traffic jam since the refugees fled the German invasion of France in 1914." The movement attracted a cross-section of rural and urban townsmen. They found friends in the secret society and wore their robes to funerals and weddings. They donated money to fundamentalist churches in the name of the Klan, supported "worthy widows," and practiced "active patriotism." But they lived in an area with a frontier heritage of violence and vigilantism. Some Klansmen, as in neighboring states, actively engaged in night riding. Flogging and coercion of accused bootleggers, wife-beaters, gamblers, and petty criminals were widely reported, and public officials in some towns welcomed the Klan as the most effective law enforcement agency available. KKK terrorism declined after Evans became imperial wizard and called for an end to violence. Yet it was at this point, in 1923, that the order ran afoul of the new governor, John C. Walton, former mayor of Oklahoma City.

Although Klan leaders had supported Walton's opponent in the election, the new chief executive subsequently had become—if briefly—a "Klansman at Large." But Jack Walton was a wildly erratic political operator. A man who had roused suspicions through his crude interference with the administration of both state universities, who had alienated both farm groups and political reformers, he irritated so many erstwhile supporters that he decided to seek a new following by assailing the Ku Klux Klan. Arguing that the Invisible Empire was encouraging "mob rule," that two governments "cannot exist in this state at the same time," he declared martial law in Tulsa, calling out the national guard. He banned all Klan parades statewide. Compared to George III by some publications, "King" Walton waged a war on the Klan that was news across the nation. But "King versus Klan," as one headline writer called it, ended in disaster for Walton, when the state legislature—with a substantial Klan membership—impeached the governor. Walton was convicted and removed from office. Still, it was a partially Pyrrhic victory because the legislature, pressured now by anti-Klan activists, felt compelled to enact antimasking statutes. The appeal of the secret society was eroded in Oklahoma, although Walton's humiliation allowed it to continue as an influential force in state politics for some months to come.[37]

In Texas, home of Hiram Wesley Evans, the Klan's membership approached two hundred thousand. Closely tied to several fundamentalist churches, large enough to encourage businessmen to join in search of new customers, the movement publicized its good works. In Dallas, it established an orphanage for homeless children, dedicating the building on "Klan Day" at the State Fair, when seventy-five thousand people assembled to hear the imperial wizard attack southern and eastern European immigrants. Later, a seven-day-long "Kolossal Klan Karnival" was sponsored to fund the orphan's home. The large Lone Star Klan at first wielded considerable political influence. But when it endorsed a losing candidate for governor, it was fatally wounded. This time, the new executive was not a loose cannon, like Oklahoma's Walton. It was Miriam "Ma" Ferguson, with her husband, the magnetic former Governor James "Pa" Ferguson, at her side. Ma was a dedicated fundamentalist. She had purged Darwin from high school biology texts. But when the nativist fraternity opposed her on election day, she became its enemy. Ma and Pa Ferguson fashioned a brilliant anti-Klan campaign. Pa tore into the "longhorn Texas KooKoos and their Grand Gizzard," his name for the state grand goblin. Instead of attacking the order in the name of liberalism, decrying its reputation for coercion and its nativist ideology, which certainly would have been out of character, he understood that the way to damage this movement in the Southwest was through ridicule. After their victory, the Fergusons sponsored legislation that unmasked the membership and called for the death penalty for hooded assault. The electric crosses on Klan buildings in Dallas and elsewhere were taken down by 1926 and the Klan was in decline throughout the state.[38]

In the West, the story was similar. In California, the order recruited well in Los Angeles and in parts of the adjacent San Fernando Valley, where Klansmen picketed Wobbly headquarters, lobbied for school Bible reading, and called for nativist legislation in the state assembly. Anti-Catholic, anti-Oriental, anti-black arguments were made by Klan spokesmen in these areas and elicited some response. By 1924, signs proclaiming AKIA (A Klansman I Am) and KIGY (Klansman, I Greet You) were seen in southern California service stations and hot dog stands. But Klan membership never grew beyond fifty thousand in the West's largest state. It was north, in Oregon, that the KKK had its greatest impact on the Pacific Coast.

There, the movement helped elect Governor Walter Pierce, rallying to the Democratic candidate when he announced support of legislation enforcing compulsory public school attendance. Although Catholics represented less than 8 percent of the population, antialien, anti-Catholic feeling ran high in the Northwest. Opposition to parochial education helped Klansmen influence political affairs in the state, and members were instrumental in naming the president of the state senate as well as the Speaker of the House, a man with the good fortune to have the magical initials: K. K. Kubli. Former Catholic nuns and anti-Catholic evangelists were hired to provide old-time nativist harangues at Klan gatherings. Soon membership in Portland alone approached twenty-five thousand. Klan leaders announced plans to build a ten-story "skyscraper headquarters," to replace the feeble Community Chest with a Klan Kommunity Kit, and to offer a Klan Komfort Insurance Fund. But bitter struggles within the state leadership, parochial disputes with other patriotic societies—notably the Loyal Orange Lodge—and squabbles over endorsements in state elections weakened the movement. Rumors of misuse of Klan funds by the grand dragon and of failure to donate promised dollars to a children's home and other charities added to damaging publicity. Portland papers attacked the order. Lem A. Dever, an editor and former Klansman, published a scathing exposé, *Masks Off! Confessions of an Imperial Klansman*, renouncing the Klan as anti-Christian. By late 1924, the movement was disintegrating in Oregon.[39]

In Colorado, the Invisible Empire also won major victories before coming on hard times. More than sixty thousand joined the Klan, its women's auxiliary, the Junior Klansmen, and another affiliated order, the Riders of the Red Robe. One of every ten residents of Denver, with a population of a quarter of a million, was in the order, and Mayor Ben Stapleton was elected with Klan support. The movement dominated his administration, Klansmen serving as manager of public safety and as city attorney. As in Oregon and elsewhere, former nuns told crowds of Catholic villainy in the inner sanctums of the convent, and anti-Semitic and antialien rhetoric filled the speeches of Klan leaders. But as elsewhere, the movement appealed most to those seeking community and finding fellowship behind the mask of nativism. Boxing and wrestling tournaments were sponsored before crowds of twenty-five thousand in the Klan's own stadium. A variety of special events kept members busy. The grand dragon, Dr. John Galen Locke, was a shrewd and able public relations man; he became one of the most powerful state leaders in the country and a major figure in Colorado life. But it was Locke's problems with the law—he was prosecuted by the Internal Revenue Service for tax evasion—and charges that he misused his office in making appointments that destroyed the Klan in Colorado. Scandal shook the state movement, and Evans was forced to intervene to sack Locke. The grand dragon at first refused to accept dismissal, and after his ouster, tried to organize a competing secret society, the Minutemen of America. By 1926, with an anti-Klan legislative majority acting in the state capital, the Klan was finished in this state.[40]

Moving east, the Klan found little support in New England but did better in the heavily populated middle Atlantic states. The movement was less successful in New York City—"the most un-

American city in the nation," Evans said, pointing to the small minority of white Anglo-Saxon Protestants—but it found a following in Nassau and Suffolk counties, both in the white bedroom suburbs and rural communities of Long Island. It also opened numerous klaverns in upstate cities and farm towns, with seven thousand members in Buffalo. Still, it met early opposition from powerful state politicians in New York, men responding to their large Catholic constituencies, acting in a liberal tradition of respect for the civil rights of all ethnic and religious groups. Antimasking laws were enacted by 1923.

In New Jersey, with 60,000 members, and in Pennsylvania, the movement was stronger than in the Empire State. Philadelphia, Pittsburgh, and their environs were Klan centers; there were over 150,000 initiates in Pennsylvania. Although some of these northeastern recruits were from privileged elites—chapters were established at Harvard, Princeton, and other private universities—most came from that same cross-section of farmers, industrial workers, modest middle-class shopkeepers, and small businessmen who responded to the Klan's appeal throughout America. And though there were scattered instances of violence and angry attacks by opponents on "hooded bigotry," the majority of members were not violent people. Unlike the hustlers and manipulators who led the state and local Klans, the men who joined these klaverns named for patriots and symbols of nationalism—the William Penn Klan, the Liberty Bell Klan, Old Glory Klan—sought solutions to problems created by a society undergoing rapid change, an economy that offered unprecedented access with the concomitant risk of failure. In the patriotic ritual of the fraternal order, in protecting public schools and threatened womanhood, in attacking Prohibition violators and celebrating Americanism at festivals and klonvokations, they found security, fraternity, and a way of making sense out of the dilemmas of the day.[41]

So it was in the Midwest, where the Ku Klux Klan had such striking success. In Kansas and Nebraska, one journalist reported, new recruits were policemen and insurance agents, printers and druggists, railroad workers, laundry truck drivers, bricklayers, and, of course, many farmers.

In Kansas, the Klan grew so rapidly that the famous editor of the *Emporia Gazette*, William Allen White, rose to challenge it. An author with a national readership, a friend of presidents and Washington influentials for many years, White was a lifelong Republican who viewed the Klan as a clear and present danger to civil liberties. He angrily printed the names of all members of the secret society he identified in Emporia. He was contemptuous of the Klansmen in his town, where the police department was dominated by the organization. At first, he argued that "the Ku Klux Klan have got to run their course . . . just lie themselves so full of absurd, malicious, incredible stories that their credulity being gorged will paralyze their suspicion." He insisted: "No arguments you may use, no facts you may present, no logic you may array will in the slightest affect these people. They have no capacity for receiving argument, no minds for retaining or sifting facts and no mental processes that will hold logic. If they had any of these they would not be Kluxers." But in 1924, convinced that the Klan was instrumental in securing the GOP gubernatorial nomination for Ben S. Paulen, White impetuously filed as an anti-Klan candidate for governor. It would be a campaign, as his biographer observed, that was "nation wide copy." White announced: "The issue in Kansas this year is the Ku Klux Klan . . . (it) is found in nearly every county . . . the Klan is subjecting [Catholics, Jews, Negroes] to economic boycott, social ostracism . . . every form of harassment. I want to offer Kansans afraid of the Klan and ashamed of that disgrace a candidate who shares their fear and shame." As an independent, William Allen White polled about 150,000 votes, but Paulen was easily elected with 323,000.[42]

In Michigan, there were seventy thousand Klansmen. Half of this state membership lived in the Detroit area, where a write-in candidate endorsed by the order made a remarkable race for mayor, losing by only a few thousand votes. Burning fiery crosses was a favorite tactic in Michigan, and opposition to the practice drew the wrath of the editors of the *Fiery Cross* (Michigan State Edition): "The Roman Catholics are behind this, the same people who would disrupt our public schools, they are filled with hatred for all things American." Similar arguments were made in Ohio, where the Klan rolls swelled to two hundred thousand, with many chapters in Dayton and Cincinnati, Akron, Youngstown, and Columbus. But the Klan had limited political success in Ohio, and it suffered from widespread reports of corruption in its leadership. Klan money was diverted to personal uses, promised charitable projects were abandoned, new Klan construction was canceled after funds mysteriously disappeared. As in other areas, a movement that was energized by the profit motive of its kleagle salesmen and attracted an entrepreneurial cadre dreaming of riches through managerial roles foundered in this state. Klansmen were betrayed by their leaders.[43]

In Illinois, the movement attracted fewer members but had a higher profile than in Ohio. Stories circulated about violence in "little Egypt," the southernmost region of the state around the town of Cairo. There, prominent figures in Williamson County were implicated in a Klan crusade against bootleggers, with the local Law and Order League subsumed into the Invisible Empire in preparation for the militant confrontation. The armed raiders of Herrin were accused of assault, kidnapping, conspiracy, and murder. The National Guard was called in on several occasions. "Bloody Williamson," as Paul Angle called it in his exposé, became the northern equivalent of the Louisiana Mer Rouge affair. But it was a relatively isolated event. Throughout the state, the Klan did not depend on gunfire, did not recruit by promising men roles in night-riding expeditions.

In Chicago, fifty thousand Klansmen answered the call in the metropolis of the Midwest, a city with a million Catholics and almost a million foreign-born immigrants, with a history of nativist activism dating to the days of the APA. *Dawn*, the local Klan paper, had a wide readership, and klaverns sprouted on the north, west, and south sides. Charitable work with friendly churches and a wide variety of patriotic gatherings advertised the Klan throughout the city. As in other urban areas, it drew in clerks, small store owners, and less successful white-collar and blue-collar workers. These were people most exposed, most anxious and resentful, in the urban expansion of the boom years of the 1920s. The movement's successful appeal to these Americans made it a powerful force throughout Chicago by 1923. But success bred opposition. An anti-Klan group, the American Unity League, emerged to publish *Tolerance*, a weekly that penetrated KKK secrecy and printed the names of area Klansmen. The league then sponsored boycotts of newly identified Klan businessmen and organized anti-Klan rallies to channel anger at the now unmasked knights. In a community whose City Council had passed anti-Klan resolutions, this campaign weakened the order at a critical juncture. Defeat of Klan-backed candidates in local elections, mounting opposition by the major city newspapers, and internal complaints about autocratic leadership marked the decline of the movement by 1924.[44]

The Klan lasted longer in Indiana, home of its most powerful, most successful organization in the United States. The man who was instrumental in recruiting a quarter of a million knights statewide—almost forty thousand in Indianapolis—was Grand Dragon David C. Stephenson. Only thirty years old in 1921, Stephenson had been one of the four key state leaders helping Evans oust Simmons before the first national meeting in Atlanta. Rewarded with the organizing rights for twenty-three states in the North, this charismatic figure, who liked to compare himself to Napoleon, already was a successful coal dealer when he joined the Invisible Empire. But in the Klan, he would make a fortune in recruitment fees and build a reputation as a mesmerizing orator, the super salesman of the national Klan.

In Indiana, his order sponsored parades and athletic contests, field days and picnics. It offered community and festivity, but always in the name of protecting Protestant America from its enemies. In "Middletown," the Lynds found it had become a working-class movement and "tales against the Catholics ran like wild fire" through Muncie. Local Klansmen vowed they would unmask only "when and not until the Catholics take the prison walls down from their convents and nunneries." Anti-Catholic, anti-Semitic, anti-black rhetoric filled Stephenson's colorful speeches: the Klan stood for temperance and patriotism, the aliens were threatening traditional American values. This appeal was so successful that store owners soon put TWK (Trade with a Klansman) in their windows; the secrecy of the order could be violated with little fear of retaliation in a state in which hundreds of thousands were flocking to join the most popular movement in memory. In fact, so many initiates paid their klecktoken to Stephenson that it was estimated he made between $2 and $5 million in eighteen months. The grand dragon acquired a ninety-eight-foot yacht, which he kept on Lake Huron, a fleet of automobiles, a palatial suburban home, and elaborate offices in downtown Indianapolis. There, the mayor opposed "Steve" and his order until a Klansman named Edward Jackson won the Republican primary for governor in 1923. Now the Klan took control of the county party machinery. Jackson's subsequent election gave Stephenson and his movement state power unmatched by any other Klan.[45]

A high point was reached with the fabled Konklave at Kokomo, when "200,000 men and women filled with love of country"—in the words of the *Fiery Cross* (Indiana State Edition)—gathered for the Klan's greatest single meeting. Tens of thousands of cars brought members from across Indiana and Ohio. Stephenson, attired in a sequined purple robe and escorted by his team of personal bodyguards, finally mounted the rostrum. He explained that he was late for the meeting because "the President of the United States kept me counselling upon matters of state." He proceeded to deliver a quintessentially nativist exhortation, filled with pleas for America and plans for vigilant opposition to the aliens. Always a riveting stump speaker, Stephenson was most respected for his organizational skills. But his Bonapartist complex and rumors of numerous sexual indiscretions and alcoholic binges soon led to conflicts with state and national Klan leaders. Evans turned against him, and he resigned as state grand dragon in September 1923. But D. C. Stephenson was not through. He marshaled support for a special state meeting the following May, in which his followers elected him once again their grand dragon, thus rejecting the authority of national headquarters. Stephenson continued to flout the hierarchical authority of the national Klan, staying in power during the election year of 1924, a time which marked the KKK's most significant impact in American politics. But by 1925, the Indiana chief was caught up in the scandal that ended in his prison sentence, a sordid affair that fatally wounded not only the Indiana Klan but the national movement as well.[46]

One major role of the Klan in the political struggle of 1924 was in opposition to Governor Alfred E. Smith of New York, a leading candidate for the Democratic nomination for president. Al Smith was everything the Klan abhorred: an Irish Catholic who had risen to power in the New York City political machine and a fierce enemy of Prohibition. He was both the embodiment of the alien menace and spokesman for the values of the jazz age, of Manhattan with its speakeasies and sexual freedom, of modernity and all its evils.

The Klan, with a predominantly Democratic membership in the South but appealing more to Republicans in the North and West, had little impact on the GOP convention or campaign. The party's platform carefully avoided the question of the Klan, and incumbent President Coolidge—understanding he had many supporters in the Invisible Empire—said almost nothing derogatory about the Klan or secret societies. (His running mate did deliver one anti-Klan address.) The opposition party was a different story.

At the Democratic convention in New York's Madison Square Garden, Klansmen in the delegations from several southern, southwestern, and midwestern states clashed with anti-Klan activists, particularly from New York and the Northeast. A long struggle over a platform plank "condemning political secret societies" was carried onto the floor, after a militant minority rejected a draft proposal in committee which had avoided mention of the Klan. In the acrimonious debate over the anti-Klan amendment, tempers flared and it was clear that the convention was almost evenly divided. In the event, the anti-Klan move lost, but by only one vote, 542 to 541. The ensuing race for the presidential nomination was dominated by the Klan and its implacable opposition to Al Smith.

Franklin D. Roosevelt, crippled by infantile paralysis, reemerged at this meeting to ask the party to choose the "Happy Warrior." But Klansmen looked to any viable alternative. Supporting Oscar Underwood, the conservative Alabaman, was out of the question; he was an outspoken Klan critic. William Gibbs McAdoo of California, Wilson's southern-born and bred secretary of the treasury, was the front runner, an able and articulate liberal, who not only had opposed "bigotry" in speeches but selected Jews and Catholics as important campaign aides and managers. Still, McAdoo had taken no position on the Klan. In this way he tacitly invited its endorsement. On the convention floor, Smith backers shouted, "Ku, Ku, McAdoo" at McAdoo's nominators, while the Californian supporters responded to Smith's spokesmen with "Booze, Booze, Booze." The Klansmen were making their presence felt. It was a stalemate. Neither man could gain the nomination. Klan opposition wrecked Smith's chances, and McAdoo was irreparably damaged by his association with E. L. Doheny, one of the two big oil operators involved in the infamous Teapot Dome affair. Harding's administration had been rocked by scandal, and Teapot Dome would color American political life long after Warren Harding's death in 1923. "Oil, oil, oil" was another favorite chant of the anti-McAdoo gallery, as corruption in the Republican administration reached out to the other party to deny candidacy to an attractive and viable figure. With Smith and McAdoo gone, the gray, bland John W. Davis became the Democratic candidate. Davis finally condemned the Klan, but he was such a pathetic campaigner that few noticed; the choice for president now seemed foreordained, and the Klan played little role in the inevitable Coolidge landslide. Klansmen did find their favorites winning in some states in 1924, but on the national scene the Klan's significant role was the attack on Al Smith in the struggle for the nomination.[47]

Although the Klan had suffered setbacks in Oklahoma, Texas, Colorado, Oregon, Illinois, and other states by early 1925, it still seemed a formidable national movement in the year after the election. Then came the Stephenson scandal in Indiana. The grand dragon was implicated in the death of a statehouse employee named Madge Oberholtzer. Although it was widely reported that he had known many attractive women in Indianapolis, D. C. Stephenson chose to lavish particular attention on Oberholtzer. She later testified that he compelled her to drink with him, finally forcing her at gunpoint to a train. In the private compartment he attacked and "sexually mutilated" her. Oberholtzer took a fatal overdose of drugs after this incident, but she lingered for weeks before her death; she had time to dictate the entire story to the prosecuting attorney, one of the few officials Stephenson could not control in Marion County. The revelations devastated the entire movement. The desperate grand dragon, on trial for murder, was abandoned by his former henchman, Governor Ed Jackson. Panicky Klan papers now assailed their leader. The *Indiana Kourier* headline declared: "D. C. Stephenson Not a Klansman," and called him an "enemy of the order," reporting that he had been "repudiated by all true Knights of the Empire." Stephenson responded by revealing the contents of his "little black box," which contained records implicating many highly placed, Klan-backed officials as corrupters, providing evidence of their malfeasance of office. The movement did not recover in Indiana. While Stephenson languished in jail (he would not be released until 1956), the Klan found its political influence evaporating, its membership deserting by the thousands. Hypocrisy, greed, and dishonesty by the leadership was bad enough, but Stephenson's violation of the symbolic crusade for purity, chastity, womanhood, and temperance was too much. As the greatest of the state Klans dissolved, the national empire of the Ku Klux Klan began to crumble everywhere.[48]

By late in the decade, the Klan was a shell of the powerful movement of 1923–24. Although thousands of hooded men marched in the last great parade down the boulevards of Washington in the summer of 1925, many more were abandoning the order. Al Smith's presidential candidacy in 1928 was the occasion for one final, convulsive anti-Catholic effort by the Invisible Empire, but Herbert Hoover's victory owed little to the Klan. In the 1930s, the shriveled movement receded from public view, and its remaining publicists turned away from Catholicism to communism when seeking the alien menace within. Hiram Wesley Evans, before he lost what had become the all but meaningless title of imperial wizard in 1939, even accepted the invitation of church leaders to attend the dedication of the Roman Catholic Cathedral, ironically built on the site of the old Imperial Headquarters in Atlanta. The old order was no more. By 1944, with the federal government pressing for the payment of back taxes on Klan profits from the prosperous 1920s, remaining national officers officially disbanded the Ku Klux Klan.[49]

Although small state and local organizations calling themselves Ku Klux Klan, using the terminology of the earlier movement, and dressing members in similar regalia would reemerge in the late 1940s to play occasional roles in antiblack and anti–civil rights violence up through the 1980s, the great Klan of the 1920s was long dead. It had faltered so quickly after the spectacular growth early in the decade for many reasons. It lacked a clear legislative agenda. It experienced heavy weather in the political struggles in several states, where adroit enemies could use its weaknesses to build support for their own interests. It was led, in many areas, by people who were the embodiment of precisely those qualities that Klan ideology asked initiates to oppose: heavy drinkers and swindlers, sexual exploiters and dishonest manipulators of the theme of patriotism. In the end, the movement that offered fraternity to men in tumultuous times, that provided a nativist response to the crisis of values troubling so many in the Roaring Twenties, could not endure the revelations of scandal, the lack of constancy, the confused policies of the leadership. Like its antialien progenitors, the Ku Klux Klan was a movement that symbolized a longing for order, a desire to displace anger and anxiety. With no programmatic reason for being, men would desert it if it ceased to fulfill its symbolic function. As major newspapers turned against it, as articulate figures in the ministry and education, as well as in public life, pointed to its hypocrisy and treated it with scathing contempt, the mass of members simply drifted away. As with the Red Scare, the patriotic activity of the 1890s, and the antialien excitement of the pre–Civil War years, nativism's last stand had a relatively short run.

This time, nativism would not return, at least not in its traditional guise. When the 1920s ended with the coming of the Great Depression, to be followed immediately by World War II, forces were at work which permanently reshaped the nature of antialienism in the multiethnic, multiracial, multireligious society. The immigration acts had arrested the flow of newcomers, and the old, anti-Catholic, antiethnic hostilities would not emerge as in the past. But political extremism of the Right did not die. The antialien activity of the 1930s and after would appear in new ways, some of them curiously inverted forms of the nativism of those days of old.

CHAPTER 13

★ ★

TO INVERTED NATIVISM
AND BEYOND, 1930–1945

THE GREAT CRASH OF 1929 marked the end of an era.
The Great Depression which immediately followed marked the beginning of modern American history. After 1930, many political,
economic, and social arrangements would be transformed throughout the land. Antialien activity in the United States would never be
the same again.

Large-scale immigration had been arrested for almost a decade
since the imposition of the national origins quotas. Without the
influx of millions of newcomers, with their strange languages and
attendant social problems, the source of much nativist hostility
was removed. But there were other factors at work as well. Unlike
the recession of the 1890s or 1919, the gigantic collapse of the early
1930s provided no setting for a major nativist movement. The scale
of this disaster was so vast, the effects so long-lasting, the victims
so numerous and spread across so many ethnic and religious groups,
that only a few sought to assess blame or seek scapegoats among
members of some "alien" population. In a nation where millions
shared the same fears and the same fate, economic strife was not
used to divide Americans along traditional nativist lines.

The dimensions of this depression eclipsed any economic crisis
of the past. The gross national product, over $87 billion in 1929, fell
to under $40 billion within three years. Unemployment grew at a
fearsome rate, rising from 4 million in 1930 to at least 12 million in
1932. Nearly one out of four workers was pushed out of the labor
force, with millions more on reduced wages or hours. In some cities, a writer observed, the toll of unemployed was like the British
casualty lists for the first day at the Somme in 1916: so awesome as
to numb the mind. In Chicago by 1932, 660,000 were out of work,

in Los Angeles, almost 200,000, in New York, a million. In the steel and auto towns of the Midwest, the devastation was staggering; 50 percent jobless in Cleveland, at least 60 percent in Akron and Toledo, even more in Detroit. Auto production was barely 40 percent of what it had reached in 1929, and it was not only assembly workers who were suffering but ministers, shopkeepers, lawyers, dentists, bank tellers, and their families. Communities had no resources to meet so great a crisis. Private charity or state and local welfare funds could not handle the task. Detroit and St. Louis simply dropped more than one-third of the families on relief. Other localities refused all new applicants no matter how grave their plight. The mayor of Chicago suggested that Washington send hundreds of millions of dollars now or federal troops later. A Community Council representative in Philadelphia, in a famous report, described the situation as one of "slow starvation and the progressive disintegration of family life."[1]

Thousands dug for rotten food in city dumps or stood outside back doors of restaurants to ask for edible leavings. With mortgages foreclosed or rent unpaid, people without homes found themselves sleeping in cemeteries, parks, even in inoperative city incinerators. Tarpaper, packing box shantytowns rose in many areas. These urban Hoovervilles, their names an ugly signature on the failure of the boom and its political leadership, a symbol of the blame cast by millions on the president for not alleviating this disaster, were matched by the grim conditions in the countryside. There, family farms—their owners in hopeless mortgage default—were auctioned off as crowds of angry, sullen men watched, often trying to intimidate the buyers of their friends and neighbors' acreage. Desperate farmers in Iowa in the summer of 1932 declared a holiday. They vowed to block roads into the cities to reduce supply and somehow force up prices, which had sunk so low as to make continued planting pointless. Across the plains, where a great drought would add to human misery, a blue haze darkened the sky as growers burned their wheat rather than have it further glut the market or sold for a pitiful return.

As banks failed—more than five thousand in 1932 alone—and businesses went bankrupt, as the suicide rate soared upward and the birth rate declined dramatically, there was widespread fear that the nation was coming apart. Tens of thousands of young Americans were set adrift from their families, wandering the land, riding the rails in the southern states, some bearing notes saying that there was no food to feed them at home. At least twenty-nine persons starved to death in New York City in the somber winter of 1932–33 and admissions to state hospitals for the mentally ill tripled. Anger born of desperation led to violence or to the fear of violence and to repression. In 1932 came the crushing of the Bonus Army, that band of World War I veterans who wanted the money voted them by a postwar Congress immediately and not in 1945, but whose presence in Washington led the panicky administration of President Herbert Hoover to act with a ruthless brutality that would not be easily forgotten. Later, there would be the forty-eight-mile-long "coal caravan" of ten thousand striking miners in southern Illinois, the seizure of the county-city building in Seattle, the raids on grocery stores by gangs of unemployed in Detroit, the mass refusal to pay streetcar fares in Des Moines, and assorted acts of defiance of law and theft of public and private property from coast to coast. From many quarters came a call to overturn an economic and social system that had failed, which some insisted had been the root cause of the abyss into which so many hopes and dreams had disappeared.[2]

Why had the system failed? What had happened to the economic triumph of the 1920s and the optimism it had fostered almost everywhere? At first, critics of the political and economic leadership of the old order pointed to the weaknesses they insisted should have been obvious all along. There had been a growing gap between the rich and the rest during the boom years, as income distribution—in an age of governments friendliest to the interests of the most affluent—put additional billions in the pockets of the wealthiest 5 percent. There was a shaky corporate structure, with many holding companies and investment trusts of dubious solidity. There was a national banking system with too many small and weak units, potential failures even in good times and economic basket cases in the early 1930s. There was the impact of a worldwide recession, which in turn had been partially stimulated by America's protectionist policy in the high-tariff days of the 1920s. There was bad economic advice by key economists, businessmen, and cabinet members. Later, as the Great Depression stimulated a more systematic scholarly inquiry, a variety of sophisticated explanations emerged. Still, the most influential could be placed in two camps: the monetarist and the structuralist. Milton Friedman, in his *Mon-*

etary History of the United States, argued that it was the "dramatic decline in the quantity of money during those years [1929–33] and the occurrence of a banking panic of unprecedented severity" which were at the heart of a crisis that need not have happened if the Federal Reserve System had managed the money supply in a more effective way. Many other economists, of course, have not been persuaded by this thesis. Some see decreases in spending—"a drop in autonomous expenditures, particularly in consumption"—as central to any explanation for the great contraction, and these decreases reflect some of those structural problems in the American economy that early Keynesian critics had subjected to such scathing analysis. The debate continues, and there is no consensus on why the system failed.[3]

But in the 1930s the quest for causes was vastly less important than the search for solutions. And in 1932, it was not only the melodramatic magazine writers calling for the appointment of a dictator or labor leaders warning darkly that "revolutions grow out of the depths of hunger." Numerous political activists believed that a critical choice was at hand: capitalism under the centralized authoritarian control of fascism, communism, or some socialist middle ground. The European revolutions were on many minds, and the alternatives seemed clear: the road to Berlin, the road to Moscow, or an American radical alternative which preserved democracy while abandoning capitalism.[4]

Of course, these believers in a radical alternative to America's traditional political and economic system were wildly mistaken. Even in the depths of despair in the depression's darkest hours, there was no setting for such a movement. American institutions retained their pervasive appeal, as the men and women of the Left discovered in the failure of the Communist party, the Socialist party, and a variety of other collectivist visions. The leaders of the Right would also discover it in different ways, but almost all the advocates of a radical break with the past would be affected by the enduring fear of alien, un-American ideas or the memories of the antialien crusades of yesterday.

★★★
Movements of the Left

The Communist party of the United States (CPUSA) seemed to have the perfect program in place when the Great Depression began. Through no initiative of its own but rather on the orders of the Communist International in Moscow, the American party had assumed a resolutely militant posture since 1928. Seemingly suicidal during the last year of the boom, this revolutionary "united front from below," which asked youth affiliates to study street fighting and barricade building in preparation for the final confrontation, called for the overthrow of the capitalist system in the years of capitalism's greatest crisis. But it had no success. Party membership rose only from a minuscule seventy-five hundred in 1929 to less than twenty-four thousand in 1934, in a nation of 130 million. The Communist presidential candidate polled barely one hundred thousand votes in 1932, despite the most extensive campaign ever conducted. And the party did not even keep the members it recruited. From 1930 to 1934, approximately fifty thousand new members were enrolled and the leaders wondered why "two out of every three recruited members have not been retained in the party."[5]

Later, during Franklin D. Roosevelt's New Deal, when the Comintern—in service of the Soviet Union's foreign policy objectives—ordered another change in the worldwide party line and American communists dropped their militant approach, the party at last found a measure of success. Embracing the Roosevelt administration in an effort to make a popular front against fascism, rejecting radical tactics and even radical objectives, the party announced that "Communism is twentieth century Americanism." Now it downplayed the influence of Moscow while emphasizing the movement's historic devotion to the American tradition. CPUSA membership finally rose to over one hundred thousand, and enrollment in fellow-traveler organizations swelled to many times that number. Only when the party became nonrevolutionary, when it rejected radical alternatives and sought to still criticism that it was an "alien," un-American movement, did it find even a small audience. And it found that audience in the years of a triumphantly successful reform administration in Washington. Earlier, even during the black days of 1932, the deviant nature of its program doomed it to total failure.[6]

The same was true of the Socialist party. In 1929, Socialist party membership hovered at only ninety-five hundred, but the Great Depression promised to bring vast new support. It did not. Membership in the organization which for three decades had called for an end to capitalism rose to less than seventeen thousand in the grimmest year of capitalism's failure. Norman Thomas, Socialist leader and presidential candidate in 1932, elicited little interest outside precincts that had voted for the party in earlier and less critical elections. Later, deeply divided after a series of bitter fratricidal quarrels, the party's appeal declined even further. There was, however, a small Red Scare in these years, and Congress launched investigations of un-American activities in 1930 and 1934. By 1938, the House established the special Committee on Un-American Activities. Still, this was not 1919; the economic crisis continued to eclipse everything else, and the organized attack on the radical vision as an alien force was mild by comparison. Nonetheless, it was clear that there was no hope for a Marxist new departure in America.[7]

There was also no hope for those seeking a nonsocialist, noncommunist cooperative commonwealth. The League for Independent Political Action, the Farmer Labor Political Federation, and all the other plans of radical insurgent intellectuals dreaming of a new industrial democracy based on government planning and "production for use" foundered, not only because of the appeal of Roosevelt's New Deal after 1933 but because of popular indifference to their ideas. The specter of radicalism, with its alien ideological implication even for these programs, could not be overcome. As Alfred Bingham, a leader in this effort, observed, Americans could not easily be recruited to a party offering to build an equitable, classless society because Americans believed they already were living in a classless society. Even the poor, the laborers, and the lower middle classes—propertyless, exploited, and desperate in 1933—could not be reached on this point. Americans identified not with the class to which they belonged, Bingham would say, but with the class in which they thought they belonged. That Americanist ethos, that middle-class mindset, could not be reshaped even by sensitive thinkers of the Left who rejected a rigid Marxist dialectic.[8]

★★★

The Quasi-Fascists

On the Right, the rejection of "un-American ideas" and the search for an "Americanist" solution to the depression also determined which self-proclaimed "leaders of the people" would fail and which would build a truly mass movement in the 1930s. Those who seemed to be offering quasi-fascist schemes imported from the European dictatorships made little headway. Among the men who bid for such support were Art J. Smith, founder of the Khaki Shirts of America, Gerald Winrod, and William Dudley Pelley, creator of the Silver Shirt Legion.

Smith, an army veteran who had been a soldier of fortune in Africa, Russia, and China, fancied the title "General" and wore a khaki shirt and riding breeches. He called his aides a "General Staff." He spouted anti-Semitic slogans and was reported to have threatened to "kill all the Jews in the United States." He proposed to lead a movement of veterans that would grasp power in America after a triumphal march on Washington in 1933, emulating the fascists' march on Rome: "The Khaki Shirts are going to kick every damn crook out of Washington." He vowed to set up a military government after he was seated in the White House. But Smith was no Mussolini and America was not Italy. After a violent encounter with radicals in New York in the summer of 1933, the Khaki Shirts retreated to their Philadelphia "headquarters." Police later reported that the "General" had fled with the movement's funds and dismissed Smith as a confidence man peddling shirts and boots to a handful of dimwitted followers. In short order, Art Smith found himself in jail on charges connected to the New York shootings. His effort to bring fascism to America disintegrated.[9]

Winrod, a fundamentalist preacher from Wichita, Kansas, had published the *Defender* magazine since 1926, assailing Catholics, communists, and other un-American enemies of true Protestantism. During the 1920s, he was a powerful spokesman for fundamentalism, and for a time he was a classic nativist. By 1934, his magazine's circulation was forty thousand; by 1936 it would reach one hundred thousand. Winrod, a tall, striking figure and an extraordinarily gifted circuit-riding orator, organized a movement, the Defenders of the Christian Faith, to advance his program. His following was limited, but those he reached were rural townsmen, many of the lower middle class, some former members of the Klan of the 1920s. But after a trip to Europe in 1934 to "study social, political, moral, economic and prophetic trends," he returned home smitten by Hitler and Nazism. Earlier, he had seen the führer as an agent of international communism and Mussolini as a candidate for the Antichrist, that "Beast" foretold in the premillennial literature of fundamentalism. After his visit he became an ardent pro-Nazi. He now embraced anti-Semitism with the passion of the newly converted believer. He sought an alliance with other crypto-fascists, including Harry Jung of the American Vigilante Intelligence Federation and one James True, the inventor of a billy club True had named the "Kike Killer." Winrod's personal strike for power came in 1938, when he ran for the U.S. Senate in Kansas on a platform that promised to "Keep Christian America Christian," to "Keep America Safe for Americans." He polled 53,149 votes, barely 20 percent of the total, despite an elaborately financed campaign. Winrod was a traditional nativist gone astray. A fervent enemy of "Papism" and "international Jewry" (his publication reprinted excerpts from the Protocols of the Elders of Zion), he even reached back 140 years to John Robison's work to link the Bavarian Illuminati with modern communism and an alien Jewish-Jesuit conspiracy. But in the late 1930s he drifted to an alien ideology himself. He continued his assaults on Jews into the war years, but the now infamous "Jayhawk Nazi" was indicted for sedition and his magazine named a vehicle for Hitlerite propaganda.[10]

Pelley was another would-be savior whose movement had the trappings of an elite corps modeled on the European dictatorships. The Silver Shirt Legion sounded like Hitler's SS, and Pelley, a Californian, a former screen writer, crime reporter, novelist, and magazine journalist—who had been a war correspondent in Russia for the *Saturday Evening Post*—said that he had been inspired to emulate "Adolph Hitler, a man of destiny." He talked of having his Silver Shirts "save America as Mussolini and his Black Shirts saved Italy, as Hitler and his Brown Shirts saved Germany." But William Dudley Pelley, a small man with a goatee who had a burning desire to change history, was dedicated to building a "native-born Protestant-Christian" organization, and his approach contained elements of the old nativism. Although Pelley was only mildly concerned with the Catholic menace, he was obsessed with the international communist and Jewish conspiracy. (He remembered with bitter resentment the power of Jews in the Hollywood film community.) He wrote of the evil designs of the "Dutch Jew, Franklin D. Rosenfelt," also known as "Mr. Rossocampo and his Jew Gang, head of the Great Kosher Administration," the "first Communist President of the United States." He referred to the New Deal's National Industrial Recovery Act (NIRA) as the National Israelite Recovery Act, and its symbolic flag as the "Soviet Blue Eagle." He warned that "the Jew's racial philosophy, flagellated by rabbinical instruction, is the exact antithesis of the American doctrine of freedom."[11]

Yet Pelley's movement owed as much to a bizarre religious messianism as to this admiration for foreign ideologists or to the American nativist tradition. His father had been an itinerant preacher, and he claimed to have had a "hypodimensional experience" in 1928, a journey to death and back, his "seven minutes in eternity," a vivid religious awakening which was "the turning point of my life." He published a piece titled "Why the Dead Are Alive," and as he began political organizing in subsequent years, referred continuously to his Silver Legion as the force that would lead surviving Americans to salvation after the Jewish-Soviet conspirators brought on Armaggedon. He stored provisions in his home against that day of reckoning, for only the Legionnaires would be prepared for the Second Coming, the millenarian resurrection.[12]

These Legionnaires were concentrated in the Los Angeles area and in smaller communities in the Midwest and the Pacific Coast. Like some other anti-Semitic movements, the Silver Shirts attracted people living in rural areas where there were few Jews. This was not a paradox. As with Ford's *Dearborn Independent* and the Klan's publications in the 1920s, the Silver Legion appealed to those who embraced a misty yeoman ideology in which Jews were the sinister, symbolic nonproducers: bankers, businessmen, and bond traders, parasites who grew nothing and made nothing except money. These anti-Semites personally knew very little about Jews or Jewish culture. It was the specter of unearned, unfair profits acquired by guile and deceit, the corruption of the traditional American dream of achievement through hard and productive work, which made an impact. The themes were powerful, but Pelley, with his weird personal references and overheated rhetoric, was a failure as a leader. His movement never numbered more than fifteen thousand members at its height; there were no more than five thousand Silver Shirts in 1938.

William Dudley Pelley kept trying across the years and was still on the political scene in 1942, to be convicted of sedition. He had called the national war effort a "fight for Mongolic Judiasts." He had the bad fortune to be defended by the attorney who had defended D. C. Stephenson of the Indiana Klan in his famous murder case. Pelley was called by a United States attorney a "traitor to your country, the arch-Quisling of America parading under a false flag of patriotism while you stabbed the U.S.A. in the back." He was another Americanist crusader in the depression decade done in by the antialien label.[13]

There were other small movements that seemed to have roots both in the American nativist past and in the fascist ideology imported from abroad. George E. Deatherage, a construction engineer from West Virginia, organized the Knights of the White Camellia in 1934, pressing home his ugly anti-Semitic, anticommunist, anti–New Deal arguments in a paranoid style reminiscent of Art Smith and Gerald Winrod. Deatherage knew Fritz Kuhn of the German-American Bund and established what he called a "casual liaison" with William Dudley Pelley. His followers were few in number, but the name and ritual of this tiny order was designed to appeal not only to crypto-Nazis but to former Klansmen in the years after the Klan's decline.

The same was true of the Black Legion, a more successful movement, which emerged in Ohio in 1931 when several hundred men violated the Klan rules and dyed their robes black, forming a separate organization. Its base of support shifted to Michigan, and it was in the industrial area around Detroit that the vast majority of its forty thousand members lived in 1936, the year of its greatest popularity. The legion appealed to unskilled and semiskilled workers migrating to the auto center from the South, small-town men stranded in the city at the center of the depression's worst economic devastation. The Black Legion modeled the Klan's ideology: it was virulently anti-Catholic as well as anti-Semitic, anticommunist, and anti-Negro. It was pervaded with religious mysticism; it promised a crusade to battle "degenerate morals," and it used intimidating tactics—including flogging—reminiscent of the Mer Rouge and Herrin marauders of the Klan's violent past. Its commander in chief was even accused of petty racketeering, taking money from monthly dues like some latter-day D. C. Stephenson. But it also displayed the characteristics of European fascists, offering its leaders military titles equivalent to army rank, declaring itself a "guerilla army" designed to fight the established parties. In the end, the Black Legion collapsed suddenly after legal action taken against fifty members implicated in terrorist activity.[14]

Owing little to American nativism but almost everything to the inspiration of Adolf Hitler's success in the Third Reich was the German-American Bund. By November 1935, the Bund was under the leadership of Fritz Julius Kuhn, a former chemist, a German army veteran of the Great War, a Nazi party member since the 1920s. At first the Bund served as a conduit for National Socialist propaganda sent from the Reich to the United States. It supplied a wide range of literature to pro-Nazi and anti-Semitic organizations. Pelley, Winrod, C. F. Fulliam (leader of a group he called the White Shirts), and Germanophile George Sylvester Viereck were among the beneficiaries. Kuhn, who wore black leather jack boots and a Sam Browne belt, who fancied the Nazilike title Bundesleiter and referred to himself as the American führer, argued that fascism and National Socialism were the American wave of the future. But this inept egocentric was a posturer and a crook. Despite his thick accent and unimpeachable Nazi credentials, he acted like a throwback to those hustlers attracted to the leadership of state and local Klans. He had a wife and two children but enjoyed visits to New York nightclubs with his various girl friends. In 1939, he would be on trial for the theft of Bund funds. With such leadership, the Bund had little hope of making any impact, despite the creation of seventy-one local chapters across the country. In fact, the spectacle of thousands of Bund followers singing the Nazi anthem, the *Horst Wessel Lied*, and *Deutschland Über Alles* in a Madison Square Garden rally only mobilized opposition to what appeared to be an obviously un-American activity.[15]

The proliferating sects on the extreme of the radical Right—by one count there were 120 American fascist organizations in the 1930s—never united in a larger cause. There were attempts in 1934, 1936, and 1937 to bring together some of the most notable leaders, with the German-American Bund working to coordinate them on one occasion. But jealousy among these self-styled führers made unity impossible. The fact was that there were no able, dynamic, intelligent men involved in these efforts, only charismatic thugs or fantastics. There was no integrated or effectively functioning party machinery. As traditional nativist concerns gave way to dreams of bringing Hitlerite authoritarianism to America, the many competing groups succumbed to that same popular revulsion at alien ideas which doomed so many other similar movements.[16]

Even the catastrophic collapse of the economy in the depression decade could not serve as a setting for organizations that threatened to overturn American institutions. None of these dreamers of an American revolution of the Right had the talent or persona to lead a mass movement, but they also had the wrong formula. Traditional nativism had lost its audience in the grim days of this crisis, for it was not enough to seek a way out of the abyss only by pointing to some un-American enemies. But fascism was obviously no answer; it exposed members to charges of un-American activities. If there was a way of mastering the problem of large-scale recruitment to a movement outside the traditional political system, it would have to take account of the devotion to Americanist themes while offering some satisfactory solution to the economic and social problems caused by the depression. Three leaders did emerge who created effective mass movements in the early 1930s. Two of them, Francis E. Townsend and Huey Long, seemed to operate outside the nativist tradition, neither overtly manipulating old antialien themes or falling victim to them. The other, Charles E. Coughlin and his National Union for Social Justice, was more significant, for the Coughlin movement represented a symbolic break in the long history of antialien activity in America.

★★★

The Townsend Plan

Dr. Francis E. Townsend was successful in leading an organization challenging the New Deal and the practitioners of conventional politics. The inventor of the Old Age Revolving Pension Plan, Dr. Townsend was an aging physician from Long Beach, California, who had devised a scheme for ending the depression by saving the old people of America, a population facing unparalleled privation in the 1930s. The Townsend Plan would provide a $200 monthly pension to every citizen aged sixty and over, providing the recipient agreed to spend the money within thirty days. If these "civil veterans of the republic," as he called his pensioners, poured their over $20 billion into the economy each year, people everywhere would prosper as factories reopened, unemployment shrank, and prosperity returned to the land. It was a hyperinflationary concept, and critics ridiculed the Townsendites' arguments and their turnover taxing program. One said that the doctor was trying to "teach people to believe in Santa Claus again." Another said that "what the Townsendites are really demanding is a revision of the science of arithmetic by law." The plan could not have saved the nation; in practice it would only have established a new privileged class—the elderly—with fiat money. Townsend called for spending more than half the gross national product in 1932 on pensions. One cynic suggested that everyone be given $200 every week; if the government could afford $24 billion it could afford $2,400 billion.[17]

But Dr. Townsend's program, despite its wild extravagance and obvious shortcomings, was not really radical, nor could it be characterized as "alien" in any way. It was not a Marxist concept; it was influenced by no fascist thinkers from abroad. Indeed, the old doctor embraced capitalism and celebrated the American way of life. One could be a Townsendite without being called a "Red," and as one member put it, "the Plan stands for everything a nice person ought to favor." Townsend, a sixty-seven-year-old country doctor with the smudge of a mustache over the high, stiff collars that he fancied, who had moved to California only after a lifetime of service as a family physician in a small Black Hills community in South Dakota, was the embodiment of the Protestant ethic, and individualism was central to his movement. These old folks, he argued, had "earned their vital role as circulators of money," and Townsend even declared that "the Plan will save America from radicalism." With such an appeal, the organization recruited 2.2 million members by late 1935; over 3.5 million were claimed by 1936 and there were more than seven thousand local Townsend clubs operating across America.[18]

These followers were mostly aging Americans, many of midwestern origin even in the hugely popular California clubs. The majority were traditionally conservative, registered Republicans. They were, an observer said, "just folks . . . just Methodist picnic people," retired farmers, small businessmen, clerks, or skilled independent workers. Although there was little evidence that many had been attracted to the Klan or other nativist sects in the past, they responded to the Americanist themes of this movement. Club meetings were opened with the salute to the flag and the singing of patriotic songs; the traditional American institutions were continuously celebrated by Townsend spokesmen, and it was expected that every speaker would emphasize how the Townsend Plan alone could "preserve the American Way of Life" in the depression. Like the nativist fraternity members, many Townsendites found community in the organization, and more than a few spouses complained of being "Townsend widows" or widowers. But most were attracted by the plan itself, which spoke to their fears and promised an end to their wrenching economic problems while underscoring pride in country and the belief in an ordered, religious life. Francis Townsend referred to his idea as "God-given" and said it was "ordained by the Lord." Religious songs became the anthems of the Townsend Plan; the banners on club walls proclaimed the movement "religion in action." Townsend and Townsendism prospered for awhile not by offering a turn to the Left or the Right but by promising prosperity in a quintessentially American context.[19]

★★★

Huey Long and the Share-Our-Wealth Movement

So, too, did Huey Long and his Share-Our-Wealth movement. The Kingfish of Louisiana insisted he was no socialist, no communist, no fascist. "Just say I'm sui generis and leave it at that." But Huey Long's ideas were not merely unique, they were uniquely American. When this remarkable man left the governorship of the state he had come to dominate personally and moved to the Senate, he was preparing for bigger things to come. He joked that he had rebuilt the governor's mansion to look like the White House, "so I'll be used to living in it," and many viewed his new national movement as a vehicle to take him to the presidency. He even published a book titled *My First Days in the White House.* The Share-Our-Wealth scheme owed much to the Populist tradition. Long embraced the ideal of private property and proposed to end poverty by providing every family a patrimony of "at least $5,000 debt free"—plus an adequate pension, home, automobile, radio, and college education for the kids—simply by taxing the rich. "Every Man a King," promised the Kingfish. But to produce this royalty, all savings would be seized above a certain figure, set at first at $10 million, lowered later to $1.7 million. His scheme, of course, was a wild dream. In computing the national wealth to be divided, he included latent resources, and only by some miracle could forests and mines, highways and schools, oil wells and factories be converted to a home and a bank account for each family. Many economists dismissed Share-Our-Wealth as a hoax, and one called it a "monstrous and tragic joke . . . based upon either demagogic hypocrisy or else ignorance so abysmal as to inspire awe." But the validity of Huey Long's panacea was no more important than Townsend's in gauging his appeal. Long spoke to the scared and angry people whose families were hungry, whose hopes were blasted in the depression. Their pain was real, and his was an eloquent voice calling for social justice and equality in a nation in which the concentration of wealth was a real problem. He believed he could gain the White House because "I can outpromise Roosevelt." His scheme was never intended to offer a radical alternative to the capitalist system. And though some contemporaries, like Raymond Gram Swing in his *Forerunners of American Fascism*, insisted that "the full menace of Huey Long" is that "the man is ruthless, ambitious and plausible enough to Hitlerize America," there was not the aura of the tinpot führer about this man. His appeal was unconnected to those quasi-fascist leaders of the Right or ideologues of the Left.[20]

Nor was it linked to the nativist past. Huey Long might have brilliantly manipulated Americanist themes, but he was no antialien crusader. Long fought the Klan, and when Hiram Wesley Evans denounced him as un-American, he declared that "that imperial bastard will never set foot in Louisiana." Historians and other scholars have conducted a vigorous debate about the allegedly nativist elements in the Populist tradition, but in Long's case, there was no evidence that he sought scapegoats among any ethnic or religious group. There were no anti-Catholic, anti-Semitic, or anti-immigrant arguments in his spellbinding speeches.[21]

His chief organizer for Share-Our-Wealth, the Reverend Gerald L. K. Smith, was a different story. Smith, a handsome, vigorous, charming, and powerful figure, was an extraordinary crossroads orator who bragged that "next to Huey, I'm the best stump speaker in America." This self-proclaimed "rabble rouser for the Right" was a minister turned political recruiter. After flirting with Pelley's Silver

Shirt League—to which he presented a lecture titled "Why I Left the Conventional Pulpit to Join the Christian Militia of the Silver Shirts"—he had been attracted to Huey Long. Gerald Smith was a demogogic schemer, promising that "when we have enough millions, we'll change things in this country." He helped to build the Share-Our-Wealth clubs throughout the South, telling one reporter that it might be possible soon to sweep the nation, "to duplicate the feat of Adolph Hitler in Germany."[22]

Whether or not there really were 7.6 million Share-Our-Wealth members by 1935 (or 3 million as claimed at another time that year), whether or not the "27,431 Share-Our-Wealth clubs in 8,000 communities" really functioned and the organization "voiced the demands of 12 million people," as Long's paper alleged, Huey Long's popularity and his movement's appeal were real enough. But after the Kingfish was assassinated by the son-in-law of a political enemy in September 1935, Gerald Smith was unable to grasp the leadership of the movement. He tried to survive the postassassination power struggle inside the Long machine, to retain his $600 weekly salary. Long's political heirs in Louisiana ultimately made a deal with the Roosevelt administration, which had been harassing archenemy Long and his Louisiana organization. This so-called "Second Louisiana Purchase" included the tacit agreement to end the Share-Our-Wealth effort. Denied the mailing lists of the organization, forced out of the state after being threatened with physical violence, Smith subsequently allied with the other mass leaders in 1936. Much later, he moved back to the poisonous anti-Semitic, quasi-Nazi activities of his days with the Silver Shirts. But this should not color the portrait of the mass movement of 1933–35. Neither the creator of Share-Our-Wealth, Huey Long, nor his aide Gerald Smith, was seeking a nativist or fascist audience at the time of the organization's greatest appeal.[23]

★★★

Father Coughlin's Crusade

Nativism was not a factor in the Townsend or Long crusades, two of the great movements of the 1930s. But the old anti-Catholic, antialien animus would have to be present in the case of the third, if only in the form of memories of former wrongs and shames. For the National Union for Social Justice was the creation of a Roman Catholic priest, Father Coughlin.

Coughlin's rise to national prominence was meteoric in the early 1930s. Canadian-born and educated, Charles E. Coughlin was raised in a lower-middle-class community in Hamilton, Ontario, and imbued with Irish-Catholic culture, attending church schools and St. Michael's College in Toronto. Trained for the ministry in the Basilian Seminary, he later became a secular priest and was assigned to the Detroit diocese. His work there brought him to the attention of Bishop Michael J. Gallagher in 1926, and he was given the task of building a new church in Royal Oak, a poor industrial suburb, a center of Ku Klux Klan activity. Only three dozen Catholic families lived in the town, and Coughlin soon found fiery crosses burning on the lawn of his tiny frame Shrine of the Little Flower. Desperate to increase congregation membership in the face of this nativist hostility, the thirty-five-year-old priest hit upon the idea of reading his sermons over the radio. The medium was still in its infancy when he went before the microphone for the first time in October, but by early 1927 he had to hire clerks to handle a flood of weekly mail which soon reached four thousand letters. By 1929, he was a fixture in the Detroit area, and when the Columbia Broadcasting System put his radio sermons on a sixteen-station network, he became an instant national celebrity. His voice, warmed by the touch of the Irish brogue, was musical. It was, a contemporary wrote, "without doubt one of the great voices of the twentieth century," a "voice made for promises." With a mesmerizing speaking style tailored perfectly to the new medium, this bland-looking, bespectacled prelate became the radio star of his age, with a weekly audience of millions for his Sunday sermons. Some analysts estimated that he had 30 million listeners by the mid-1930s. If the number was only 10 million, it still would have been by far the largest radio audience in the world.[24]

With the coming of the depression, his sermons turned to political and economic questions. Father Coughlin decided to challenge the men responsible for the crisis. He assailed the president as "the Holy Ghost of the Rich, the Protective Angel of Wall Street," titling one weekly address "Hoover Prosperity Breeds Another War." Attacking the millionaire secretary of the treasury, he likened Andrew Mellon to Judas and characterized Mellon's associates as "banksters." The response was a torrent of mail; the priest soon needed ninety-six clerks to deal with 80,000 letters a week. By 1931, his themes had become too controversial for CBS, which asked him to tone down his remarks. But when Coughlin fought back with an appeal for freedom of speech on his next program, the network was swamped with 350,000 angry letters. CBS subsequently dropped Father Coughlin and NBC would not touch him, but the radio priest was now more important than timid media managers. He assembled a private network of independent stations and by 1932 had more listeners than ever before. At the mere suggestion by the outlet in St. Paul that it was considering canceling Coughlin, 137,000 letters of protest poured in from a metropolitan area of a half a million. Charles E. Coughlin had become a political force to be reckoned with in America.[25]

By 1933, Father Coughlin's listeners were sending $5 million a year to his Radio League of the Little Flower. He opened a relief center for depression victims in Royal Oak. He built a huge 111-foot-high granite and marble Crucifixion Tower at his shrine and laid plans for a mammoth Shrine Church with a seating capacity of thirty-five hundred. In the basement of the tower were desks for a stenographic staff of 145 and facilities for handling mail equivalent to a post office of a middle-sized city. His own presses produced millions of copies of weekly sermons to fill mail requests. In an office at the top of the tower, Coughlin worked on larger political and economic concerns while several assistant priests cared for the congregation. And he felt the nation was heading in the right direction with the election of Franklin D. Roosevelt.

His attacks on Hoover had helped FDR in the 1932 campaign, and now he visited the White House on his frequent trips to Washington. He wrote adulatory notes to the president, whom he called "the Boss" or "the Chief," and prepared form letters which he dictated on the air, asking his followers to copy and send to Franklin Roosevelt: "I stand solidly behind you," "I appreciate what a terrific sacrifice you are personally making," even "I love you." But soon these words of praise would be forgotten. For Coughlin, who was proposing to defeat the depression through a program of cheap money, found that FDR was not a fellow inflationist on the scale he deemed necessary. Worse, the president soon was not responding to his advice. He had been convinced that the White House would do his bidding and had begun to fancy himself the Richelieu of the Roosevelt era. He had announced to his audience: "It is either Roosevelt or Ruin," FDR "is the new Lincoln, leading the fight against financial slavery," for "the New Deal is Christ's Deal." But when Coughlin found himself rebuffed by the president, he became as bitter in his denunciations as he had been expansive in his praise.[26]

Father Coughlin believed that the key to ending the depression and bringing social justice to America was the "money problem." Influenced by Pope Leo XIII's encyclical, _Rerum Novarum_, issued in 1891, which reminded employers that wealth was a stewardship and not a right, and Pope Pius XI's _Quadragiesmo Anno_ in 1931, in which Pius noted "immense power and despotic economic domination concentrated in the hands of a few," Coughlin's theories seemed to be grounded in good Catholic doctrine. But they owed even more to the Populist heritage in America. Speaking for the debtor community of the Middle Border and beyond, a number of Populist spokesmen in the 1890s had uncovered the "vast conspiracy against mankind" which led to "colossal fortunes for a few usurers." They had called for victory in "the struggle between the robbers and the robbed." The Populists argued for cheap money, among other things, for this would help debtors caught in a cruel and unjust system dominated by rich creditors. In the depths of the economic crisis of the 1930s, Coughlin had shaped his own inflationary program, first calling for the revaluation of gold, then for the remonetization of silver, and finally the issuance of large amounts of unbacked paper currency from a publicly owned central bank. The solutions changed, but the point remained the same: prosperity was denied only because certain men of great influence and great wealth made money and credit hard to obtain. The international bankers and businessmen were to blame along with their political tools. All that was needed was to manipulate the money supply through the government-owned national bank, to give the less affluent, the workers and small businessmen and other debtors, access to credit so as to "lift the crushing taxation from the slender resources of the laboring class."[27]

When it became clear that Roosevelt did not share these views and that the New Deal—which had revalued gold but had refused to remonetize silver—had no intention of following his central banking scheme, Coughlin turned to opposition. When personal relations chilled between the president and the radio priest, Coughlin announced the formation of his own social movement, the National Union for Social Justice (NUSJ). It was November 1934. Throughout the next year, Coughlin moved slowly toward opposition to the New Deal. Finally, he proclaimed to his huge audience: "Today, I humbly stand before the American public to admit I was in error. Despite all the promises, the money changer has not been driven from the temple. The slogan 'Roosevelt or Ruin' must now be altered to read 'Roosevelt and Ruin.' "[28]

The National Union for Social Justice was an immediate success. More than two hundred thousand people asked for membership applications within two weeks of the priest's declaration that "I am prepared to either stand or fall on this . . . God Wills It! Do you?" The famed Sixteen Principles of the NUSJ contained the blueprint for Coughlin's monetary panacea, but they called for no overturning of American institutions. Principle Five read: "I believe in upholding the right of private property yet controlling it for the public good." Like the Populists, Coughlin believed that America was so rich that no revolution was needed here; the wrong people were in control of the government and its currency and their replacement would bring a better tomorrow. "I am no Socialist, no Communist, no fascist and against . . . any un-Americanism," he exclaimed. "Capitalism is the best system of economics provided it does not run counter to the laws of morality." With such an Americanist program in place, by January 1936, Charles E. Coughlin could announce that the National Union had recruited "at least" 5,267,000 members and 8,500,000 had "expressed support" for the Sixteen Principles. (On another occasion, however, he referred to "1.6 million active and 6 million passive members.") Organized for maximum political influence, the NUSJ had units in 302 of 435 congressional districts, and Coughlin was prepared for action. Now his feud with the president would become famous. He called his former hero that "Great Betrayer and Liar . . . Franklin Double Crossing Roosevelt." In 1935–36, at the height of the New Deal's popularity, his huge audience would be asked to choose between the president and the priest.[29]

Who were Coughlin's followers at this time of decision? Students of his movement agree that his strongest appeal was to Irish and German Catholics of lower-middle-class origins. Other immigrant groups also responded to his appeal, particularly those in skilled positions. They were, as a recent scholar has noted, people with a "hard won status as part of a working class elite . . . carpenters, electricians, plumbers, postal workers, bricklayers, railroad workers," as well as clerks, small tradesmen, and some farmers. They were not rallying to Coughlin because the church endorsed him. The radio priest was no friend of the Catholic hierarchy and had been attacked by Boston's William Cardinal O'Connell, among others, as "this spectacularly talking man . . . popular in a false cause . . . making hysterical addresses." (Coughlin had responded in kind, questioning "the notorious silence of a certain cardinal on social justice . . . his opposition is natural if one will speak publicly the truth against great wealth.") Father John A. Ryan, an FDR supporter, and Father Wilfred Parsons, editor of the influential Catholic journal *America*, were other clergymen who challenged the radio priest, but his audience was unimpressed by the credentials of his Catholic opponents.[30]

What they found in Coughlin was a brilliantly articulate spokesman for their interests. Like the followers of Huey Long, Coughlin's supporters feared the "erosion of the individual's ability to control his own destiny" in a world of "large, faceless institutions" and "wealthy, insulated men." They were, as Alan Brinkley observed, imperiled members "in a world of modest middle class accomplishments," seeking "a system of decentralized power, limited ownership and small scale capitalism." Coughlin, no matter what the validity of his particular economic program, provided the right themes for people whose expectations of social and economic security or mobility had been shattered by the depression, whose own American dream, never more promising than in the 1920s, was now at risk. As did the Populists—and Huey Long—Coughlin appealed to those fearing loss of community and seeking to reestablish local control, hoping to wrench power from the remote plutocrats in the East. (Of course, the paradox was that relief was offered only in the form of enhanced federal authority.) His attacks on the "modern bands of exploiters devouring the homes of widows and children," on the men of great wealth, the "rulers of the world, dominating and controlling the economic and social life of this nation," touched a raw nerve. But many of these followers were also Catholic ethnics, and no matter what church leaders might say about him, Father Coughlin was a central symbol of their religious and national group.[31]

Most Coughlinites were heirs to the pain and suffering of America's nativist past. The Know Nothings, the APA, and the Ku Klux Klan had victimized them and their ancestors. They had been characterized as aliens in the land, as un-American, as an unassimilable horde of hated outsiders. Now, in the dark hour of depression, when economic privation exacerbated these memories of past humiliation and repression, Charles E. Coughlin offered not only succor but a measure of revenge. When Coughlin asked who were the real un-Americans, his answer was different than the one offered by that old nativist enemy. (The enemy was still there, however, with the Black Legion and Gerald Winrod attacking this "papist priest" throughout the period.) This time, it was "the Wall Street attorney," the "Congressman from New York City," the "erudition of Harvard and Yale, of Princeton and Columbia," the "bankers with their grouse hunting estates in Scotland who never traveled west of Buffalo." Later, his archvillains would be communists, Jews, and other left-wing ideologues, but now he was more concerned with the white Anglo-Saxon Protestant (WASP) eastern elites. It was the families of great wealth, the old-line upper-class Americans with impeccable social credentials, who were the real enemy. They were the cause of the suffering in the land. They were a gang of internationalists and exploiters; they had sold out America in the interest of their own greed. Many were international capitalists. Some, the intellectuals, were international communists, but all were something less than real Americans. And if that was true, then Father Coughlin's own followers—honest, hardworking, patriotic average citizens—were vindicated at last. In the Coughlin movement, traditional nativism was turned upside down. The rhetoric of the radio priest provided an inverted nativism that served both as a final ritual of assimilation for Catholic and ethnic followers and a way of striking back at ancient oppressors.[32]

Coughlin's ingenious manipulation of Americanist themes, his program of seemingly radical reforms which did not threaten revolutionary change and could not be characterized as "un-American," his call to organize against a sinister sect of subversives—the economic elites—who had grasped levers of power in the country, all provided a nativistlike appeal for the former victims of nativism. Most Catholics did not support Coughlin when he broke with the president, as the continuing rise of the Roosevelt coalition made clear. But many responded to his arguments, and though some may have done so only because his was a ringing "voice of protest" in a time of suffering, others may have found Coughlin's movement attractive in the same way many Protestants had turned to the nativist sects in earlier years. For Coughlinites, too, could be both protectors and fugitives. The priest's NUSJ would preserve and protect America from economic oppressors while punishing group enemies. But in the movement, members also could escape from the hard realities of American life in the depression decade.

Father Coughlin's crusade not only offered community, as did the Townsend and Long movements, but it provided the same charismatic authority. The "Father" could answer all questions; he could give structure and direction to the lives of his followers. At the national meeting of Coughlin's NUSJ in Cleveland in the summer of 1936, ten thousand people jammed the auditorium and the enthusiasm of the disciples put to shame the smaller, quieter gathering of the Republican party in the same hall that season. One delegate shouted: "Father Coughlin, test us, try us, LEAD us!" One woman announced, "For those of us who haven't a material father, he can be our Father and we won't need to feel lonesome." Some speakers compared him to Christ, and all delegates endorsed a resolution proclaiming him "the Greatest American of All Time." His followers cried, shrieked, and roared. They resolved, "We give thanks to the mother of the Reverend Charles E. Coughlin for bearing him." They stood as one to support an endorsement, "without any exceptions whatsoever, of all the acts of our President and great leader, Charles E. Coughlin . . . pledging our resources and our activities in his support . . . even as he has thrown into the battle every ounce of his energies." When hostile articles on Coughlin appeared in Catholic publications, one editor reported after reading his mail that "the motivation of Father Coughlin's followers is almost entirely one of hatred." To people who had found a savior, no criticism was acceptable. For some of his followers, the radio priest offered a solution to the central problems in their lives.[33]

But charismatic appeals would not be enough once Father Coughlin had decided to take on Franklin D. Roosevelt. The New Deal had not ended the depression, but the massive relief programs—the Federal Emergency Relief Administration, Civil Works Administration, Civilian Conservation Corps, Public Works Administration, and Works Progress Administration—the banking and securities legislation, the Wagner Act for labor, and other federal initiatives had brought back hope to millions. FDR, buoyant, tough, articulate, and optimistic, was enormously popular. But Coughlin, too, was now at the height of his power, and his 1936 NUSJ convention would serve as more than a national gathering of a social movement. It was also a political convention. In this election year, Coughlin made alliances with Dr. Townsend and with Gerald L. K. Smith, who had attached himself to the Townsend movement after his expulsion from Louisiana. Townsend was feeling oppressed by the administration after experiencing a grueling congressional confrontation with New Deal critics of his plan. This made him vulnerable to Smith's entreaties and responsive to Coughlin's proposal to join forces in support of a third-party candidate. William Lemke, congressman from North Dakota, a neo-Populist who had advanced his own inflationary solution for depression-ravaged farmers, became the candidate of Coughlin's new Union party.[34]

Unfortunately, the programs of these rival leaders of the masses did not easily fit together. When the Union party announced its platform for 1936, the fifteen planks were a potpourri of the sometimes complementary but often competing solutions which Coughlin, Townsend, Long, and Lemke had developed in earlier years. Coughlin, the creator and driving force behind the party, had never been completely happy with the Townsend Plan, which he considered simplistic, or with Share-Our-Wealth, which he suspected lacked an economic theory. Worse, Coughlin's new party had been created so late in the presidential season and on such short notice that it encountered severe filing difficulties. Despite the priest's prediction that "we will be on the ballots of all 48 states in spite of the election laws," the party would be denied a ballot line in fourteen states. They included California and New York, where Unionites missed requisite petition minimums in both places by a handful of signatures.[35]

In the campaign, the stodgy Lemke proved an earnest but uninspiring candidate, eliciting none of the excitement of the radio priest or the messiahs of the Townsend movement. Only in a handful of states—notably Massachusetts and Ohio, where Coughlin support was particularly strong in Catholic wards—did Democratic National Chairman James A. Farley have to worry about this new third party's presidential candidate. It fell to Coughlin to carry the campaign, and during his arduous days on the hustings, his arguments grew increasingly shriller. At the national convention of the Townsend Plan in the summer, he had joined Smith and Townsend in personal attacks on FDR, calling the president that "great betrayer and liar." Later, he turned to an uglier, neonativist rhetoric: "Well we all know whom we're voting for if we vote for Mr. Roosevelt ... [it's] the Communists, the Socialists, the Russian lovers, the Mexican lovers, the kick-me-downers." He now exposed "Commies" such as Rexford Guy Tugwell in the administration, even saying that "if FDR were elected" there would be "more bullet holes in the White House than you could count with an adding machine." In a Massachusetts speech, twelve thousand heard him vow: "So help me God, I will be instrumental in taking a Communist from the chair once occupied by Washington." Coughlin's inability to hold his temper—at one stop he had to be physically restrained from assaulting a critical reporter, vowing to "tear the man to pieces" as he was dragged away—or to temper his rhetoric took its toll. Calling Roosevelt "an anti-God and a radical" time and again led political analysts to write that the radio priest was "losing his grip" and his party was losing its early supporters.[36]

It was hopeless. Coughlin counted on some response in those areas where his movement was relatively weak but where the Townsend Plan and Share-Our-Wealth had been strong. Yet in the South and West, where Coughlin's radio network was thinnest and his Catholic and ethnic following smallest, the Union backing did not materialize. Smith's ties to Share-Our-Wealth were now rhetorical at best, and without his mailing lists, the old Long organization in the South was not even a paper tiger. The Townsendites refused to provide grass-roots help in many localities in the West, particularly after the priest's bitter speeches chilled whatever interest these patriotic, Protestant old folks might have had in Lemke. Reports to Lemke headquarters revealed a growing anti-Catholicism in this part of the Union coalition. With Democrats weaning away supporters with the traditional warning not to "throw away your vote" on a third party sure to lose, the Union effort came apart like a cheap toy.[37]

First Gerald L. K. Smith defected, declaring in October that he was forming a "nationalist organization aimed ultimately at seizing the government of the United States." Smith declared that "politics is prostitution ... the democratic method is a lot of baloney ... what I really want is an organization of 1,000 eloquent men to go up and down the country preaching true Americanism." His new "national front against Communism," the Committee of One Million, would be backed by wealthy businessmen, proclaimed this old scourge of the rich from the Share-Our-Wealth days. And he said: "I joined the Union Party only for a forum. What I am really interested in is forming this new force against Communism." Gerald Smith's erstwhile allies responded immediately. Townsend disavowed "any connection with fascism or un-American, dictatorlike politics," and cut his ties to Smith. Coughlin read him out of the Union party. Next, Townsend drifted away. Faced by internal opposition to the Union alliance within the leadership of his movement, he now discovered widespread refusal to back Lemke throughout the rank and file. He decided to withdraw from active participation in the new party and initiated a campaign to "support the lesser of the two evils"—Republican candidate Alfred E. Landon— in those areas where Lemke was not on the ballot.[38]

By election day, there was little left of the Union party. Its vote was minuscule—892,378—just 2 percent of the national total. FDR swept to a historic landslide victory with almost 28,000,000 votes to Landon's 16,679,000.[39]

After the disastrous defeat, Coughlin had to decide what to do with his career as a public leader. He had promised to "retire in obscurity if Lemke loses," but he could not stay away from his radio audience. Following a "retirement" of only six weeks, he was on the air again and *Social Justice*, his newspaper, still had a circulation of almost three-quarters of a million. Although he now faced problems within the church, complaining of censorship when the new archbishop of Detroit scolded him for his language—leading to the cancellation of his series of broadcasts in 1937—he soon was back to announce the formation of a new national movement. This time, Coughlin's Christian Front against Communism represented a dramatic turn to the extreme Right. His attacks on the "Red Menace" moved ever closer to the ideology of European fascists, and soon his speeches and writings were fixated on the "international Jewish conspiracy." Earlier, there had been only faint and isolated anti-Semitic remarks in his sermons, but after 1938, when he resumed his radio series, he became another American quasi-fascist. He spoke of the need to establish a "corporate state" in America, of a new system of government based on vocational representation. He praised the "social justice" dispensed in the Third Reich and reprinted speeches by Nazi propaganda minister Joseph Goebbels in his paper. He excused Hitler's "understandable effort to block the

Jewish-Communist plan for subjugating Germany." He became a popular speaker at German-American Bund meetings, and the Nazi newspaper *Der Stuermer* praised him as "one of the few men in the United States who has the courage to speak his conviction that National Socialism is right." By 1939, he was turning attention to "the problem of the American Jews," and young toughs in his Christian Front bragged of starting fights with teenage Jews and of attacking Jewish stores in Boston and New York.[40]

His audience, smaller than before, changed in these years. The radio priest could not tap the old anti-Semitic following of the Klan or the other nativist Protestant sects, but he seemed to appeal particularly to young, unemployed Irish-Americans in big eastern and midwestern cities. Angry and frustrated men of a different background now found satisfaction in assaults on a familiar scapegoat. The Protocols of the Elders of Zion were reprinted in *Social Justice*.

This anti-Semitic assault was mounted in an America where there was continuing suspicion and hostility toward Jews but in which the traditional stimulants for anti-Semitism were weakening. In the 1920s, despite the publications of Henry Ford and the work of the Ku Klux Klan, the very celebration of the business ethic and the emphasis on personal financial success had softened the image of the Jew as un-American "money-grubber," an "economic man." In the 1930s, Jews had not been held responsible for the crash; Coughlin himself had pointed to the great Wall Street banking houses dominated by the WASP elites as the real villains. During the depression, intellectuals, as John Higham has suggested, "identified themselves with all the underdogs," with the very groups gaining power in a New Deal administration that was sensitive to melting pot ethnic constituencies. These groups were seen by influential writers and academics as victims of the economic catastrophe. The liberal opinion leaders who embraced the new Roosevelt coalition of urbanites, labor, and ethnics not only included many Jews as a significant subculture, but they now saw anti-Semitism as a vile and discredited passion of old-order Protestants or demagogues such as Coughlin. Even earlier, in the report of the President's Research Council, *Recent Social Trends in the United States* (1929–32), there was none of the racist explanation of human behavior one could sense in the Dillingham Commission's studies of 1907–10.[41]

But if anti-Semitism was in retreat, it still had a residual appeal for many. As in the past, the issue was not the Jewish religion but alleged Jewish separatism and fears of Jewish power. Public opinion survey data from 1938 (the surveys were initiated only in 1937), reveal that 31 percent of a national sample answered "less" to the question, "Do you think Jews in the United States are as patriotic, more patriotic or less patriotic than other citizens"; 41 percent believed that "the Jews have too much power in the United States." In 1940, another survey found 17 percent of a sample naming Jews as that "nationality, religion or racial group" which is a "menace to America"; to the same question, 6 percent named Catholics; 2 percent, blacks; 14 percent, Germans; 6 percent, Japanese. Coughlin's prewar anti-Semitic appeals would find an audience, but given the stridency of his voice and his position as a Roman Catholic priest using arguments that traditionally had come from those of a fundamentalist and nativist persuasion—the very leaders and followers who also feared and reviled Catholicism—this audience would not be large.[42]

After World War II began, Coughlin retreated to an increasingly hyperbolic isolationism for America, but he rejoiced at the German invasion of the Soviet Union, "the first strike in the holy war on Communism." Even after Pearl Harbor, he continued to side with those who were now the enemy: the war had been caused by a British-Jewish-Roosevelt conspiracy against Germany and Italy, innocent "have not" nations who had dared to challenge the Antichrists. Roosevelt was "run by Jews," the United States was fighting only to save Britain and the communists.[43]

Coughlin had drifted to the extreme of the new alien Right; he had become a mouthpiece for the Nazis. He was now on the same level as Winrod, Pelley, and the other nativists turned quasi-fascists. And he was in an unspoken alliance once again with Gerald L. K. Smith, who also emerged as an anti-Semitic isolationist in these years. After the death of his short-lived Committee of One Million, Smith had turned to labor organizing, working with Henry Ford to check the growth of the United Auto Workers. He was attracted by Ford's anti-Semitic views, and he found a base in Detroit. There, he fashioned a Christian National party and then an America First party, receiving only 1,530 votes as a candidate for president in Michigan in 1944. He appealed to a tiny band of xenophobes, anti-Semites, and appeasers. For Coughlin, it was strange company for an Irish-Catholic priest who had risen to public attention with the National Union for Social Justice.[44]

It was also the end of Charles E. Coughlin's public career. *Social Justice* was charged in violation of the Espionage Act in 1942 and banned from the mails. Radio stations were now reluctant to deal with this apologist for the enemy. His most loyal followers were turning away from him when Archbishop Edward Mooney, to prevent a demoralizing sedition trial, forced the radio priest into silence. He now disconnected himself "from *Social Justice* and the movements it promoted" and retreated to permanent retirement. In the end, the man who offered the victims of earlier antialien crusades a program that pinned the alien, un-American label on the former oppressors, fell victim himself to the charge of alien, un-American activity.[45]

★★★

Antialien Activity in Wartime America

World War II marked this ironic end of the Coughlin phenomenon. It also brought a change in antialien activity in the nation. Like World War I, it provided a bonding experience for most Americans, and this time it proved a final nail in the coffin of the old nativism. But like the earlier Great War, it led to some infringements on civil liberties. Still, hostility to ethnic groups that could be linked to the enemy were milder in some ways in 1941–45 than in 1917–18.

German-American citizens were not the objects of attacks by vigilante "patriots" this time, as during the days of hatred of the Huns in the first war. Indeed, President Roosevelt went out of his way to praise them and directed that no action be taken against American citizens bearing Italian or German names. But German-American aliens were never offered accelerated naturalization as were Italian-Americans. Many Italian aliens, later comers to America than most Germans, had faced restrictive enemy-alien sanctions by the FBI and the Army and Navy departments. Many of these people were older immigrants who had lived with their families in the United States for more than twenty years; nonetheless they were confronted by a difficult plight. But on Columbus Day

1942, the enemy-alien designation was lifted, and simplified procedures for rapid naturalization for noncitizens were established. The episode even hastened the end of lingering Italian-American separatism. By the end of 1942, a liberal Italian-American intellectual concluded: "The war has given the final blow to the segregation of the Italian community in America."[46]

The fate of the Japanese-Americans, of course, was very different. The story of the 127,000 Japanese-Americans who endured years of privation and hostility is well known. They were but one-tenth of 1 percent of total population, but almost 90 percent of them lived on the West Coast. More than eighty thousand were Nisei, Japanese-Americans born in the United States and thus American citizens; forty-seven thousand were Issei, Japanese-born and ineligible for naturalization under the Immigration Act of 1924. But Nisei or Issei, they were all subject to forcible ejection from homes and communities in the days of rage, fear, and racial hatred after Pearl Harbor.

Spurious stories of Japanese conspiracies had been circulated throughout the West. Newspapers reported that saboteurs were infiltrating defense plants and oil refineries, that secret radio signals were being sent to imperial Japanese naval units from Japanese-American communities. The American Legion called for the evacuation and internment of all Japanese, both aliens and nationals. One Legion broadside in Oregon announced: "Jap and Alien War Sneaks Are Proving Thick in Our Coast Area . . . Help Us Remove the Danger." The Native Sons of the Golden West, a small California-based movement opposing Japanese presence on "biological grounds," responded with a similar racial assault in early 1942: "Had the warnings been heeded—had the federal and state authorities . . . rigidly enforced the Exclusion Law . . . had legislation been enacted denying citizenship to offspring of all aliens ineligible for citizenship, had the Japs been prohibited from colonizing in strategic locations . . . had the yellow-Jap been disposed of within the law . . . the treacherous Japs probably would not have attacked Pearl Harbor."[47]

Lieutenant General John L. DeWitt, officer in charge of the Western Defense Command, at first opposed mass arrests of Japanese-Americans. But with pressure groups calling for action, with Earl Warren, attorney general in California, pleading to "move the Japanese," DeWitt's own bigotry came into play. He would testify before a congressional committee in defense of the evacuation order: "A Jap's a Jap. They are a dangerous element. . . . There is no way to determine their loyalty. . . . It makes no difference whether he is an American citizen; theoretically he is still a Japanese and you can't change him. . . . You needn't worry about the Italian at all except in certain cases. Also the same for the German. . . . But we must worry about the Japanese all the time until he is wiped off the map. Sabotage and espionage will make problems for us as long as he is allowed in this area."[48]

The Japanese-American community in the West was dismantled by federal action. Franklin D. Roosevelt signed the order. More than fourteen thousand Nisei would volunteer for the army, most serving in Italy and with great distinction. They were awarded eighteen thousand decorations for bravery. Thousands more rendered invaluable service as military intelligence specialists attached to 130 different units throughout the Pacific theater. But in America their homes had been taken from their families. Accused of disloyalty, almost one hundred thousand of these innocents were forced into ten huge and grim internment camps called "relocation centers," set in remote areas of seven western states. There most of them remained until 1945. It was a shameful episode in American history.[49]

But for most other Americans, the war was free of that antialien animus which so often blighted the lives of so many. Of course, there was still anti-Semitism in the war years. Numerous pro-Axis anti-Semites persevered in distributing their publications, although many were named in indictments issued by a Washington federal grand jury in July 1942. They were accused of conspiring to "promote disloyalty and impair the morale of the military and naval forces of the United States." This was part of what Leo P. Ribuffo has characterized as the "Brown Scare," an exaggerated fear of the power of right-wing activists, which led to a campaign of legal repression, peaking with the indictments in *United States* v. *McWilliams*. Among the far rightists at work (and under suspicion) was Gerald Smith, publishing his paper the *Cross and the Flag*. FDR wanted something done about Smith, but Attorney General Francis Biddle reported that Justice and Treasury Department investigations had turned up no illegalities. Other leaders (and publications) active and under investigation were Carl H. Mote and his paper, *America Preferred* (from Indianapolis), David Gordon's *Catho-*

lic International (New York City), Court Asher's the *X-Ray* (Muncie, Indiana), Winrod's *Defender* (Winrod was sentenced to fifteen years in prison, but the sentence was reversed in 1947), Charles B. Hudson's *America in Danger* (Omaha), C. Leon de Aryan's *The Broom* (San Diego), Elizabeth Dilling's *Patriotic Research Bureau News Letter* (Chicago), as well as Pelley (who went to jail), George Deatherage, and Joseph E. McWilliams, leader of the Christian Mobilizers and a group he called the American Destiny party. Coughlin, save for one defeatist sermon at Royal Oak in March 1944, in which he declared "it matters not what military force wins this war," had been silenced. But an admirer and disciple from Brooklyn, Father Edward Lodge Curran, carried on in his name. Curran made numerous speeches praising the former radio priest and organized his own National Committee for the Preservation of Americanism. One of Curran's supporters called him "the successor to Father Coughlin, who was liquidated."[50]

In addition to the work of these racist activists, anti-Semitic utterances in the war years could be heard from John Rankin (D., Mississippi), a virulent Jew-baiter who referred to columnist Walter Winchell as "that little kike," and a handful of other legislators. They spoke in a context of occasional attacks against Jewish citizens and property. In New York City, more than thirty cases of violence and vandalism were recorded from 1942 to early 1944; the perpetrators were teenagers apparently influenced by anti-Semitic propaganda. In Boston, there were several occurrences in 1943, notably attacks on Jewish youngsters by gangs of teenagers, some of whom were connected to local cells of Coughlin's Christian Front.[51]

In the State Department, anti-Semitism was also an issue. Opposition to efforts to lower immigration barriers to enable those Jews able to flee the Holocaust (and other refugees from war-torn Europe) to enter the United States was led by Assistant Secretary of State Breckinridge Long, a supporter of FDR from back in 1932. Like those elitist antialiens in government and the academies at the turn of the century, Long was a nativist, clearly an anti-Semite. In 1941 he recorded in his diary agreement with the view that "large numbers [of Jews] from Russia and Poland [are] entirely unfit to become citizens of this country . . . they are lawless, scheming, defiant . . . just the same as the criminal Jews who crowd our police court dockets in New York"; this was true not of "the Russian and

Polish Jew alone but the lower level of all that Slav population of
Eastern Europe and Western Asia." Long also seemed fixated on the
specter of communists, radicals, and others with "subversive connections and intentions" within the Jewish community. In the
White House, where some of Franklin D. Roosevelt's advisers knew
that their administration had been characterized by racist opponents as the "Jew Deal," the president was preoccupied by major
wartime policy questions. He left the problem of shaping an American response to the Holocaust at first to the unsympathetic minis-
trations of Breckinridge Long and his subordinates and supporters
in Washington and the European embassies. With anti-immigration
forces on Capitol Hill opposing the acceptance of many refugees,
with the American Legion and the Veterans of Foreign Wars lobbying vigorously for massive restrictions, with public opinion polls
showing continuing opposition to an open door for escapees from
the war zone, with some influential American Jews at first fearing
an adverse response to changing policy, and with syndicated columnists such as Westbrook Pegler attacking FDR on the point, American efforts to help some of the relatively few surviving European
Jews were less than effective.[52]

Anti-Semitism did endure during the years of the American war
against Hitler and Hitlerism. But it was not well organized; many
leaders of movements harassing Jewish Americans would soon be
facing jail or fighting sedition charges. And if fears of Jewish immigration had heartbreaking implications during those months of unspeakable genocide in the nightmare world of Nazi Europe, the basic public support for restriction—as opposed to the attitudes of
Secretary Long and company—was less a case of hatred of Jews than
of concern about unlimited access in a land that had endorsed immigration barriers for a generation and in which memories of de-
pression-bred unemployment remained widespread. Refugees were
viewed as a threat to American jobs. In fact, anti-Semitism seemed
to decline as VE Day approached. Surveys in 1945 found only 4
percent of a national sample saying Jews had too much power in
America; 6 percent thought it was the government that had too
much power. Like the "Zoot Suit" outbreaks in Los Angeles in
1943, when mobs of soldiers and sailors attacked groups of Mexi-
can-American teenagers—some attired in bizarre garb—who had
been accused of juvenile delinquency and assaults on servicemen,

the episodes of anti-Jewish activities reflected intergroup tensions in an age of wartime anxiety and war-bred economic, social, and psychological dislocations.[53]

Certainly, there were other painful examples of such tensions. There was racial hostility aplenty, as blacks moved north to the booming factories and were met by sullen resentment in some places, by violence and repression—as during the Detroit race riot of June 1943—in others. But this was not a traditional antialien reaction; it was a historic American tragedy of a different kind.[54]

Most of the older forms of nativist and countersubversive activity were in abeyance from 1941 to 1945. The nation became unified in a gigantic national effort to smash the Axis, and America was allied with communism's heartland, the Soviet Union, in history's greatest military conflict. This was no simple moral crusade, as in 1917. It was a struggle at the perfect intersection of realism and idealism. The Nazis, the fascists, the imperial Japanese warlords were textbook villains; Hitler, as Winston Churchill said, was "that repository and embodiment of a thousand forms of soul destroying hatred." Against such foes, the great multiethnic, multiracial, and religious community could be unified. In a prodigy of concentrated energy, the full resources of the world's largest industrial plant would be mobilized to arm the nation and the Allies. Between 1939 and 1945, the United States produced 297,000 aircraft, 71,000 vessels, and 83,000 tanks. Deficit financing, John Maynard Keynes's prescription for ending the depression, was the unchallenged answer to the Axis. This meant spending over $320 billion, ten times the amount for World War I, more than the government had spent in the entire history of the United States.

America outproduced the world. It accounted for 45 percent of the total arms of all belligerents and, by 1944, 50 percent more than the combined output of Germany and Japan. Full employment was one by-product of the process, and it reshaped the destinies of millions of families. With real wages rising and overtime available, with consumer goods disappearing and thus personal savings mounting in war bond sales and bank accounts, the prosperous years after VE and VJ day were assured. Victory over the Axis would bring victory as well over the depression. It would end the years of want and revivify the American dream. The war not only bound Americans together in an exquisite community of crisis—the source of much nostalgia in later decades—it provided the setting for the postwar boom. But two famous episodes of antialien activity had marked the last postwar period, 1919–27. This time, there would be no nativist movement like the Ku Klux Klan. But there would be a new Red Scare, although in a different form and with a very different kind of leadership.

CHAPTER 14

★ ★

THE NEW RED SCARE
AND AFTER, 1946–1968

IN THE MONTHS that followed VJ day, American veterans occasionally asked new acquaintances if they "had a good war."
In a larger sense, relative to all other major combatants, the United
States itself had a very good war. Of course, sorrow had come to
many homes, families had been uprooted, and personal relationships ruptured throughout the years of struggle. But as the war
ended, it was clear that the United States was not only triumphant
on all the fields of battle but was also the real economic winner of
World War II.

The United States emerged from the war with half the gross national product of the planet as measured in the first year of peace.
Of all the great powers, only America had escaped occupation or
siege. Alone physically untouched, the nation was the giant of the
New World, which had increased its enormous wealth through an
epic period of war-stimulated construction. At the time, it seemed
to many a final fulfillment of that old arrogant assertion that
America was specially blessed, truly "God's American Israel."

With its massive, newly built military establishment, no nation
had ever been stronger. With pent-up consumer demand waiting the
return of a peacetime economy, its citizens prepared for a period of
sustained expansion. Why should there be concern in such happy
circumstance? Where was the setting for a new "age of anxiety," a
fear of alien, un-American enemies within?

In so many ways, conditions seemed different than during that
last postwar year, 1919, which was the setting for the first Red
Scare. This time, there were more savings in more pockets and
even brighter prospects for postwar prosperity. This time, there
were fewer of those hostile wartime passions that had not been

273

discharged because the last conflict had ended so soon. This war, unlike the first one, had stretched over three and a half years of brutal worldwide battles. The lingering hatred of the enemy that colored the months after the Armistice in 1918 had no real analogue in 1946. And the peace that followed this war left no soured idealism in its place. World War II had not been an innocent crusade to "make the world safe for democracy" as many had believed of the first war; there was no Versailles Treaty to stimulate feelings of disillusion and betrayal.

But if the economic boom—after a brief period of inflation and capital reconversion to peaceful production—was assured, it might bring with it some of the same tensions that had accompanied the last great postwar boom in the 1920s. And if the result of this war was a new "realism" about foreign and military affairs, it would provide other reasons for fear and anxiety in a time of national strength and international primacy. The setting for the new Red Scare was built into that climate of confidence in American power and belief in America's destiny to dominate the world which Time-Life founder Henry Luce had characterized in 1941 as the "American Century."

Central to the new anxiety was the seeming paradox of unmatched American strength and unprecedented American vulnerability. Even after the demobilization of millions of GI's in the months following the Axis surrenders, the vast power of the new American air force and navy, both by far the largest in the world, the huge stock of mechanized weapons in the arsenals of the army, and the secret of the atomic bomb should have ensured security as never before. But this war had brought a technological revolution that wiped away the basis for the old confidence. Even before Pearl Harbor, Franklin Roosevelt had warned his countrymen that "our ocean-girthed" land was no longer immune from attack. The oil-fueled navies of the early twentieth century had reduced the "invulnerability" of a nation surrounded by weak and friendly neighbors and the two great oceans. Now the aircraft carrier and the long-range bomber ended the age of isolationism as surely as any treaty. The United States had carried the war to its enemies across thousands of miles with these new weapons. If the Japanese carrier force was insufficiently strong to threaten America from the West, and if the Luftwaffe's four-engined "New York" bomber had been canceled in development before appearing in the skies over the eastern United States, it was obvious that in the future there would be no safety in distance. The atomic bomb added to the peril. Secretary of War Henry Stimson, counseled by the scientists, had made it clear from the outset that there could be no permanent monopoly on the mysteries of the city-killing device. At war's end, the country never had been stronger but never was it more exposed to danger in international conflict.

Even if some leaders had wanted to retreat to isolation—in spite of the new military realities—political developments suggested otherwise. Most leaders of the nation with unmatched power now believed it had commensurate responsibilities. The American empire had been created by World War II. The failure of Hitler's bid for European mastery and the Japanese effort to dominate East Asia had left the United States with vastly expanded influence and authority. There had been no master plan to place the nation in this role. The breakdown of the prewar international balance had projected the United States into the war, and the concerted military effort left America at the center of the world. In Europe, the "balance of power" was finished. The great powers of previous decades were not only in disarray but now were dwarfed in every way. The peace of the future could not depend on the preparedness of Continental armies or the maneuverings of European diplomats. The fall of France in 1940 had exploded that myth; the division into occupation zones of a ravaged Germany not only eliminated the aggressor but made it unlikely that any great power could reemerge from the Old World of western and central Europe. In the rubble of war, two continent-sized superpowers now appeared as the decisive forces.

The Soviet Union, its casualty lists beyond comprehension, faced a monumental task of reconstruction. But it emerged from the war with a new empire in eastern and central Europe and boasted a huge and victorious army. The communist motherland of that Bolshevik menace of America's Red Scare past loomed once more as the source of danger, this time vastly more formidable than after World War I.

The wartime alliance with the USSR was eroding even before VJ day. Events from 1945 to 1950 would create an ever-deepening rift, a new cold war, which provided the setting for the new Red Scare.

Renewed American hostility to the Soviet Union began in 1945, with bitter complaints that the Russians were violating agreements made at the Yalta Conference of the previous February. After FDR's death in April, President Harry S. Truman assailed the USSR for imposing its will in areas where the Red Army had moved, blocking free elections throughout the liberated lands of eastern Europe, expressly refusing freedom of choice in Poland, and "breaking its word" in Asia.

By 1948, the Cold War was the predominant theme in international affairs, and a growing consensus had developed concerning relations with the Red adversary. A few people did respond to arguments from the Left by former Vice-President Henry Wallace, who accused a "Truman-led, Wall Street-dominated, military-backed group" of "supporting Kings, fascists and reactionaries" in an ugly effort to surround the USSR with a ring of steel. And some others endorsed the call by rightist academics (many of them eastern European émigrés) and rightist politicians to reject the Truman "policy of weakness," to roll back the communist sphere of influence by practicing a "forward strategy" aimed at removing Soviet power from its new client states. But most rejected these alternative visions. The new containment policy won converts from among a wide cross-section of influentials in government and out, including important former isolationists in the opposition party.

Containment, the need to confront the Russians "with unalterable counter-force at every point where they show signs of encroaching upon the interests of a peaceful and stable world"—as George F. Kennan put it in his famous "long telegram" from America's Moscow embassy—became the foreign policy of the United States, the major concern of the administrations in the postwar years. In 1947, the Truman Doctrine directed hundreds of millions of dollars to Greece and Turkey to support governments threatened by communist revolutionaries or by Soviet intimidation. In 1948, the Marshall Plan would allocate billions for economic support of war-torn economies in western Europe. Churchill had called the area a "charnel house, a rubble heap, a breeding ground of pestilence and hate," a breeding ground of communist revolution. He characterized the Marshall Plan, like Lend Lease, as one of the most "unsordid acts" in history; Arthur Vandenberg of Michigan, an erstwhile isolationist, on the other hand, told the Senate that "American self-interest, national economy and international security are inseparably linked to these objectives." In 1949 came the North Atlantic Treaty Organization, the military bulwark against the spread of Soviet power.[1]

As the containment edifice was erected, critics complained that America was misreading Soviet actions and intentions, inferring a kind of "Red Fascism" to Russian policy, which actually was only a defensive response to the lessons of World War II: a desire for a buffer zone, a sphere of influence, a guarantee that the eastern European "highway" through which Russia had been invaded and almost conquered twice in the past thirty years would never again be in unfriendly hands. They wrote of gratuitous American hostility, of the canceling of Lend Lease and denial of German reparations to the nation that had borne by far the heaviest burden in the wartime alliance. They pointed to the initial Soviet discouragement of Greek revolutionary activity in 1944, Soviet withdrawal from Finland and parts of Austria, the acceptance of elections in Czechoslovakia and Hungary just after the war, and even the dismantling of the Polish railroads (without which military movement was inhibited) as evidence that Russia planned no sweep to the West.

Though entertaining no illusions about the benevolence of Soviet occupation forces, some of the critics of containment—soon to include formulator George Kennan along with Walter Lippmann, Hans Morgenthau, and a few other major figures in the academic and journalistic world—argued that political realism dictated an acceptance of Russian dominance in its new sphere of influence. They warned against the Truman administration's commitment to confront the USSR anywhere and everywhere, to risk war by shaping alliances with chaotic, disorganized, and repressive governments, to stretch American influence to those parts of the world in which the United States would have trouble projecting power and maintaining control.

But advocates of containment focused on how the USSR had spurned cooperation in Germany, subsumed the Baltic states, parts of Romania, East Prussia, and eastern Poland into Soviet territory, then strangled democracy in Czechoslovakia and throughout eastern Europe by 1948. They saw the Iron Curtain as a Soviet instrument to imprison millions of innocents and the Berlin blockade of 1948 as an effort, just short of war, to deny freedom to millions more. With the attack across the thirty-eighth parallel in June 1950 by North Korean forces, containment theorists found new evidence that their policy was the right response to these new imperialists, who seemed willing to use force to impose their will, even as Hitler had in the prewar years. They insisted that there was no alternative to America assuming the role of defender of the "free world." American troops must now be sent to fight to preserve the peace in what was seen as a long twilight struggle with a sinister and powerful foe. The realists raised disturbing questions, but containment was embraced by the key policy makers and by the public.

As the Cold War developed, marked by some apparent successes for the Soviet enemy, many Americans struggled with its implications. How could this have happened? After the spectacular victories of 1945, with unquestioned wealth and power, how could the United States suddenly be on the defensive in a new worldwide conflict? A population that had grown up in an age of isolation but had sacrificed much and taken pride in the triumphs of World War II now wondered why it should be immediately confronted with this new dilemma. Was it possible that more was at work here than the inevitable change in the balance of power following the war, centrifugal forces at work in a new bipolar world? Had we won the war only to lose the peace? If so, perhaps it was not only because of the communist adversary abroad but also that old communist enemy within. The search for answers to the origins of the Cold War provided the setting for a new search for un-American activists who had stabbed the nation in the back. The question of loyalty became a major domestic issue in the postwar years.

It was an issue with deep roots in American history. The fear of un-American ideas could be traced to colonial days and had energized antialien movements across two centuries. But in the past, the alien ideologists had been castigated as alien peoples: Catholics, immigrants, those bearing some alien mark of deviance from the white, Anglo-Saxon, Protestant norm. Even in the first Red Scare, people accused of Bolshevism and anarchism, the "radical agitators" of Palmer's purges, were seen as foreigners, and many victims were ruthlessly deported. This time, the new anticommunist crusade would not focus on the old alien menace. The nativist tradition had passed into history.

★★★

The Decline of Nativism

But why had nativism all but disappeared in post–World War II America? After periodic eruptions of massive hostility toward "un-American" peoples, after generations had experienced the antialien anger surfacing in major movements from the Know Nothings to the modern Ku Klux Klan, after waves of newcomers— Irish and German, southeastern European and Asian, Catholics and Jews—had been the objects of the nativist assault, it now seemed unacceptable to attack groups of Americans because of their religion or ethnicity. Of course, Gerald Smith and a few survivors of those crypto-fascist sects in the 1930s still sought an audience for the old hatreds. But they were even less successful in the 1950s and 1960s than in their failed crusades in the depression decade. Traditional nativism had lost its appeal. Why?

There is no single explanation that serves as a satisfactory answer to this central question. Instead, there were a series of interrelated developments—occurring over a period of a generation—which together helped to end this perennial and peculiarly American phenomenon. After World War II, nativism seemed to have suddenly disappeared. In fact, forces were at work for years that would bury it.

The most important factor, of course, was the end of unlimited immigration. Since the series of measures culminating in the national quota acts of 1924, over a generation had passed in which the golden door had been closed. The millions of newcomers arriving yearly—with their poverty, language problems, and strange ways— were no more. Earlier arrivals were settled in; many were beginning to achieve a measure of mobility, the realization of their own American success story. The second and third generations had no language difficulties and, in some cases, were moving out of the old communities. As they moved into the middle class, they would no longer exhibit the "alien" ways of their immigrant ancestors. The rallying cry of many nativists in the past had been to do something about the "aliens" flooding over the dikes and into a fragile America. But both the political cause of immigration restriction and the social disorder of the newcomers were now part of history. As assimilation proceeded in its inevitable way, the reasons for antialien movements would wither away.

Yet even as immigration restriction in the 1920s began to soften hostility to ethnics by removing what nativists had seen as the running sore of social problems accompanying new arrivals, other factors were contributing to a similar feeling.

The nativists' last stand in the 1920s had been part of that "mas-

sive power of non-metropolitan America," that dominance of rural, small-town, "village" values in the national public life, which
Loren Baritz and others have pointed to in describing the rise of
fundamentalism and Prohibition as well as the Klan in the years
after World War I. The attack on ethnic and religious pluralism was
part of this narrow provincial mentality. It was another desperate
response to the growth of the new urban-industrial culture with its
"alien" masses that threatened an older rural order and its mores.
But it could not last. The new technologies of the emerging consumer society contrived to erode the traditional values of provincial
America. The automobile, which gave young people sexual freedom
as never before, brought mobility to millions. Radio, film, and pho-
nographs contributed to an assault on rural separatism and the circulation of urban ideas and imagery. The "roaring twenties" were
the setting for nativists' resistance to modernity and its pluralism,
but it was also the time of the rise of the skyscraper city, the years
in which the "village" finally would lose its struggle to stave off the
inevitable triumph of an urban culture marked by a polyglot, multiethnic, multireligious population. Nativism had not been centered
in rural America in the nineteenth century, but with ethnic millions now dominating the big cities of the East and Midwest, it was
strongest there in the 1920s. With the decline of an embattled pro-
vincialism would come the decline of nativism. (Of course, the
preservation of "traditional family values" would appear again as
the rallying cry of a different right-wing movement in the 1980s,
but this effort to resurrect yet another lost vision of America has
not been exclusively rural nor has it focused on nativism.) In the
1920s, the shaping of the new urban society was the prelude to the
end of the old antialienism.[2]

In the 1930s, the process continued. The age of the Great Depression marked another major watershed in this long episode in
American history. Not only did the depression provide the setting
for Coughlin's inverted nativism, not only did it erode the raison
d'être for anti-Semitism and was so unkind to so many would-be
leaders of antialien causes, but it had at least two other major
consequences.

It was in the 1930s that the New Deal came to power. It was the
"Roosevelt Coalition," embracing Catholics, Jews, and a variety of
former immigrant subcultures, which not only newly empowered
ethnic political constituencies and "minority" religious groups but

celebrated again the glories of the melting pot. So powerful was FDR's leadership, so overwhelming his mastery of electoral contests, so indelible the signature the New Deal would place on American politics and society, that traditional nativism, like many other traditional arrangements, was transformed. In this age of reform, unlike the Progressive Era at the turn of the century, there was no residue of elitist antialienism among the leadership. This "Roosevelt revolution" might have been led by an East Coast patrician, but its shrewdly orchestrated symbolism and its overt political appeal were to the former victims of the antialiens. Now these groups would not only dominate the politics of many large urban centers—as did the Irish in the Northeast and some midwestern cities—but would play a larger role on the national scene. After the New Deal, it would be much more difficult to assail any group of citizens as "un-American."

But even more than its political policies, the Roosevelt administration's economic and social programs helped to bury the old nativism. Responding to the vast immigration from Ireland in the 1840s and from southern and eastern Europe in the 1890s, responding to the anxieties and dislocations accompanying ages of expansion in the 1830s and 1920s, nativist movements had emerged proposing solutions for the problems of millions caught up in times of change and flux. These movements offered the "aliens"—poor, diseased, and disorderly newcomers pouring into the port cities, Catholics or Jews who threatened natives' jobs or subscribed to practices that seemed threatening—as villains, the groups that must be repressed if order and happiness were to return to the land.

These religious and ethnic outsiders, these symbolic scapegoats for the complex problems of difficult times of crisis, served not only as the rallying points for nativist movements but as lightning rods during periods of heavy weather for the American dream. The individualist ethos had exacted its toll again and again. Americans were expected to make it in their land of opportunity, but if they were less than successful, economic and social failure carried such somber meaning that some found it necessary to blame evil others for all their problems. For who else could be blamed in the country of the self-made man? If it was not some sinister, un-American presence, the reason for one's failure—or fear of failure—must be oneself.

The New Deal changed all that. In earlier ages of economic distress and depression, "rugged individualism" retained its authority. The government was not viewed as the employer of last resort, the "system" was not widely seen as the central source of failure. In the Great Depression, there were similar feelings in the early and mid-1930s. As Studs Terkel and Warren Susman both have observed, "an overwhelming sense of shame engulfed many middle class Americans." One psychiatrist noted that "in those days everybody accepted his . . . responsibility for his own fate . . . blamed himself for his delinquency . . . or bad luck . . . it was your own fault, your own indolence, your own lack of ability." Such fear, shame, and guilt, paralyzing for millions, could lead some to movements offering a way of displacing these feelings on traditional ethnic scapegoats. Yet this would not happen in the years of FDR. His administration, despite its economic inconsistencies, insisted that people had not failed; the system had failed. The government had a responsibility to step in where the private sector had ceased to function, for average men and women could not be expected to survive a crisis not of their making without massive help from Washington. No need to blame Catholics or Jews, Irish or South Slavs, European ethnics or Asians for this crisis. The economic and social programs of the New Deal permanently enhanced the power and responsibility of the federal government but they also served to weaken the appeal of nativism. In giving those people who embraced their American way of life a way of dealing with the fear of failure without the need to project their anger or anxiety on some "un-American" elements, an important part of the historic source of nativism was eliminated.[3]

The social and political upheavals of the 1920s and 1930s, along with the end of unlimited immigration, played major roles in the erosion of the nativist impulse in the two decades preceding Pearl Harbor. But so, too, did the emergence of a more complex business and professional culture during that same period and after. In what Robert Wiebe, in a brilliant essay, called America's "segmented society," significant changes were at work in finance, marketing, law, medicine, advertising, and other specialized fields. Large corporations increasingly would be directed not by the risk-taking entrepreneurs who had given them their birth but by a new class of managers trained and certified to handle the complex problems of a new age. In the professions, a person's occupational credentials became the central variable in judging acceptability; "skills, not culture, supplied the natural standard for admission to a secure elite segment." The toleration of ethnic diversity widened as strict professional rules took hold. This process was further stimulated in the crucible of the war effort, when performance, not caste or class, was the critical issue. Making it in America more and more would become not a matter of who you were but of how skilled (and well educated) you appeared to be. It was a matter of how well you could do the job. Catholics, Jews, and ethnics would have more freedom to move up in this new age of access and opportunity. Barriers to their entry into elite colleges and professional schools disappeared. In such a society, with opinion leaders turning to pluralism in service of their new definition of what it took to achieve success, ethnic differences soon seemed to be disappearing everywhere. In clothing and food, in language and even in religion, distinctions were blurred and the old animus seemed out of place, even un-American.[4]

In fact, nativist attitudes had become disreputable in every way. Not only were they at odds with the emerging criteria for hiring, promoting, and evaluating managers, professionals, and others, but by the 1950s they were seen as intellectually indefensible in any educated circle.

During the first decades of the century, of course, it had been a different story. Influenced by the work of Count Joseph Arthur de Gobineau, Gustave Le Bon, Houston Stewart Chamberlain, and other European racist theoreticians, major political figures such as Henry Cabot Lodge had unblushingly defended Anglo-Saxonism, the superiority of the "original" American stock. The eugenics movement flourished in these years. Theodore Roosevelt and Woodrow Wilson embraced racist theories; Henry Adams, Henry James, the president of Harvard, and other cultural heavyweights did the same. Many key members of the new generation of social scientists, including E. A. Ross and John R. Commons, doubted the intellectual capacity of racial and ethnic minorities. These pioneers in sociology and economics provided additional authority to nativists' arguments. As late as the early 1920s, when the prominent social psychologist William McDougall proposed a racist interpretation of history based on the results of intelligence tests, when Madison Grant's *The Passing of the Great Race* and Lothrop Stoddard's *The Rising Tide of Color* found a wide audience of college-trained readers for their racist theories, the "genetic case" for nativism remained a position that could be defended in rational discourse. That was no longer true after World War II.

The assault on the intellectual apologia for antialienism had been under way for years. Even as racist theorists received a respected hearing among educated men and women, the counterarguments were being shaped by popular writers and by scholars.

Horace M. Kallen, in articles and books published during and after World War I, celebrated the "deep-lying cultural diversities of ethnic groups" as the "reservoir of individuality, the springs of differences on which freedom and creative imagination depend." Against the image of the melting pot he offered the prospect of cultural pluralism. Against the insistent cries for Americanization of immigrants, he called for a recognition that the nation was strengthened by the influx of newcomers bringing their own diverse communal institutions and talents. These people were not inferior; they were different. The United States was a better place for their having chosen to come here.

But had not the racists "scientifically" proven their inferiority? Franz Boas, the immensely influential anthropologist, disputed these claims in a growing body of work across the first decades of the century. He rejected the assertion that race determined ability and performance. Physical attributes such as skull capacity and head form, he noted, might be influenced by social or cultural conditions; indeed, "American-born descendants of immigrants differ in type from their foreign-born parents." Environment not heredity was the key to Boas's scientific antiracism. His research led to the assertion that "a great diversity of racial traits occurs in every race and they are inherited not racially but in family lines," that "environmental influence acts upon different individuals in the same direction," that the "general experience of ethnology indicates . . . whatever differences there may be between the great races are insignificant when considered in their effect upon cultural life."[5]

Boas's students, including A. L. Kroeber, Paul Radin, Melville Herskovits, Edward Sapir, and Ruth Benedict, continued to test the assumption that certain people were destined to be inferior. They were joined by other anthropologists and by a growing number of sociologists and psychologists—based at Chicago, Columbia, Berkeley, and Yale—whose works strengthened the case for a relativistic approach to race. They concluded that there was no basis for the belief that culture was determined by biology, there were no racial "cultures" or racial "moralities," there was no persuasive evidence that some races were intellectually superior to others. Ruth Benedict, in *Races and Racism*, published in 1942, dissected the physical, psychological, and historical arguments for racism and concluded that it "had been a travesty of scientific knowledge and has served consistently as special pleading for any group to which the pleader himself belonged." The scientific debate was now one-sided. In a series of resolutions passed by the American Association of University Professors, the American Anthropological Association, the American Psychological Association, and biologists meeting at the International Genetic Congress in 1938 and 1939, racist arguments were not only rejected but were reviled by a vast cross-section of scientific professionals. The setting here was the resistance to Hitler's racism before the outbreak of Hitler's war, but the effect in America was a final destruction of any credible intellectual defense of "scientific" antialienism. When the noted Chicago sociologist Robert E. Park considered "racial ideologies" in the midst of America's war effort in 1943, he concluded that the ability of the United Nations "to win the peace will depend . . . on a revolutionary change in their attitude toward alien . . . peoples." This message would be seen in the sociology, anthropology, and social psychology texts published in the early postwar years. "Racism," "prejudice," and "nativism" now were assessed as irrational, destructive, even pathological phenomena.[6]

By war's end, nativism was all but finished. Stripped of its intellectual respectability, increasingly irrelevant in the modern world of commerce and professions, irreparably damaged by the transforming experience of the years of the 1920s and the depression, lacking the focal point of massive new immigration and its social problems, the old antialienism was over.

Finally, there had been the impact of World War II itself. Not only was the war a bonding experience for most, not only did it provide the setting for a postwar prosperity that would remove some of the economic anxieties in which the old antialienism had taken root, but it left America alone at the pinnacle of Western power. The Cold War had its origins in the emerging international conflicts of the postwar years, and these conflicts were not centered on tensions involving ethnic or religious enemies but on ideological enemies. Disloyal Americans now were identified not by religion or ethnicity but only by their dangerous, un-American views.

★★★

Postwar: The Emergence of a New Red Scare

In 1946 came the revelations of a Canadian Royal Commission, reporting on a communist spy ring that had penetrated high-ranking government circles in Ottawa during the war. Earlier, investigators for the Office of Strategic Services (OSS) and the Federal Bureau of Investigation had discovered hundreds of documents classified secret and top secret by the OSS and the Departments of State, War, and Navy in the New York offices of *Amerasia*, a leftist journal concerned with Far Eastern affairs. Were subversives also at work in the American federal bureaucracy?

Now Congressional critics sounded the alarm at "subversionists high up in the government" who were "boring from within." The words were used by new Speaker of the House Joseph Martin after assuming office following Republican victories in the midterm election in November. Control of the Eightieth Congress had passed to the GOP opposition. Faced with this challenge, Harry Truman sought to defuse the loyalty issue by grasping executive leadership in an effort to purge radicals from high places. He faced a further problem with the House Un-American Activities Committee (HUAC). Organized in the early 1930s to investigate Nazi activities in the United States as well as other forms of subversive behavior, the committee had been converted from Representative Samuel Dickstein's antifascist vehicle into the instrument of Chairman Martin Dies and his supporters: anticommunist, antiunion, and anti–New Deal. HUAC had almost expired in 1945, but after a close vote, it had won new life as a standing committee; now it had a passionately anticommunist chairman seeking headlines, J. Parnell Thomas. Truman moved to "take the ball away from Parnell Thomas," as he told one aide. He signed Executive Order 9835, the "Employee Loyalty Program in the Executive Branch of the Government."[7]

In the next five years, the Loyalty Review Board supervised investigations of 4 million government employees. In the end, charges were brought against some 9,000 individuals, with only 379 dismissed as security risks, not as spies. But though some writers supported the program as a necessary evil, many others attacked it as a dangerous, unwarranted invasion of civil liberties. The president had feared "gestapo tactics" by the FBI before the probe, but he misread the greater danger done to the careers of thousands of innocents by the faceless bureaucratic procedures of the review board. In retrospect, Truman's critics would accuse him of being a central actor in the making of the new Red Scare in part because of this executive initiative. Even the president's friendly biographers would characterize it as the "misguided loyalty program."[8]

Harry S. Truman had acted in part because of political pressures by self-proclaimed anticommunists within and without the government. Chairman Thomas of HUAC insisted that "the Communist menace in America is no myth . . . this Moscow-directed fifth column . . . this foreign directed conspiracy . . . must cease." Many congressional figures who embraced vigorous action against "Reds" responded to such arguments and were needed by the president as supporters for his foreign and domestic programs. But not only political expediency was at work here. In the private sector, the U.S. Chamber of Commerce announced a "campaign to oust Reds in U.S. posts" and issued a report titled "Communist Infiltration in the United States." In 1946, one chamber leader—in words that might have been lifted from the Red Scare of 1919—even had declared that "we will have to set up some firing squads in every good sized city . . . and liquidate Reds and Pink Benedict Arnolds." The new anxiety about alien ideologists at work inside America was finding a wider constituency.[9]

Leaders of the Catholic church were important spokesmen for the new anticommunist crusade. Francis Cardinal Spellman of New York warned of communists "digging deep inroads into our nation"; he called for redoubled efforts to "protect America against aggressions by enemies within our borders." He delivered sermons from the pulpit of St. Patrick's Cathedral in Manhattan on the imminent danger of "Communist conquest and annihilation." He authored an article in the Catholic press entitled "Communism is Un-American," insisting that "it can happen here . . . in America, Communism is growing . . . their subtle sinister schemings sway and mislead . . . those pseudo-Americans would rob Americans of [their] heritage . . . no citizen can dare to compromise . . . with Communism, this insidious enemy of Americanism." And Spellman was not alone. Bishop Fulton J. Sheen, one of the church's most prolific writers and speakers, was the philosopher of Catholic anticommunism during these years. He assailed the "alien ideology" in a torrent of books, articles, lectures, and sermons, notably in one volume called *Communism and the Conscience of the West*. With other Catholic priests carrying the word to their congregations across the country, with the Catholic War Veterans and the Knights of Columbus organizing mass protests in support of the cause, the church was well represented in the new struggle against the Red menace.[10]

In one sense, the Catholic assault was the product of long-standing views held by churchmen such as Spellman and Sheen. Communism was atheistic, they argued; it was the sworn enemy of Roman Catholicism. It was the system that had been imposed on eastern Europe after the war, and cardinals, clergymen, and parishioners throughout that region had suffered; many were imprisoned. But why church leaders turned their fervid rhetoric to the specter of un-American activities by radicals within the United States is less clear. Whatever the reason, the very presence of church notables in the forefront of the anticommunist crusade demonstrated once more that the old antialien tradition was finished. The un-Americans of yesterday, the former victims of attacks on the alien enemy, were leaders of the new attack on the internal enemies of America. In the depression decade, the Coughlin movement and its inverted nativism had signaled the end of nativist politics as it had been traditionally practiced in the United States. Now, the very spokesmen for that hated Irish-Catholic clergy of the antialien past were spearheading a new Americanist drive to root out the enemy within.

Of course, the original impetus for the new Red Scare was centered not only in political agitation, business and church activism, and the grudging response of the administration in the loyalty program. It was linked inextricably to the Cold War. The more the president warned against the spread of monolithic Soviet power, the more the world was seen as divided into spheres of light and dark, with the United States defending the free world against the evil empire, the greater the response to those who called for an anticommunist program at home to match the anticommunist program abroad.

The loyalty program would not satisfy the growing numbers of converts to the new cause by the late 1940s. With his own attorney-general, J. Howard McGrath, warning that "there are today many Communists in America . . . they are everywhere . . . in factories, offices, butcher shops, street corners, in private businesses," Harry

Truman had responsibility for the new anxiety. It was, after all, his Justice Department which pressed for the conviction and imprisonment of eleven Communist party leaders on the grounds that they secretly conspired to advocate the violent overthrow of the United States government. The Smith Act, passed in 1940, had made it a felony to "willfully advocate . . . or teach the duty . . . of overthrowing or destroying any government in the United States by force or violence," to "print, publish, edit, issue, circulate, sell, distribute or publicly display any written or printed matter" that advocated armed uprising, "to organize or help to organize any society for that purpose." In the *Dennis* case, the Supreme Court upheld the verdict, citing the "clear and present danger" doctrine. The White House was clearly involved in the making of the new Red Scare. But when the president and his aides sought to oppose it, they found themselves victimized by it.[11]

In the months following the end of the war, former communists Louis Budenz, Elizabeth Bentley, and Whittaker Chambers had made a series of sensational charges concerning the activities of Soviet spies. The image of a federal government infested by Red agents had threatened the Truman administration and the loyalty program was designed, in part, to limit the damage. In August 1948, new developments in the Bentley-Chambers affair raised the question anew. This time, it was before the House Un-American Activities Committee that Whittaker Chambers accused Alger Hiss, a well-known member of the foreign policy establishment and a former officer in the State Department, of secretly being a member of the Communist party from 1934 to 1938. An outraged Hiss denied the charge and challenged his accuser to "make those same statements" outside the privileged sanctuary of the committee, where he could be sued for libel. The lawsuit that followed seemed to end the matter, particularly after Harry Truman's spectacular reelection victory in November. With Democrats now in control of the House and of HUAC (and with Parnell Thomas soon to be under indictment in a payroll-padding scandal), President Truman's contemptuous dismissal of the Hiss probe as a "red herring," a political fishing expedition in which unscrupulous communist-hunters seeking headlines for themselves were "slandering a lot of people who don't deserve it," took on new meaning. But then came Chambers's new charges: Hiss was not only a communist but part of an espionage ring in the 1930s, a conduit of secret documents to the USSR. Whit-

taker Chambers, the brilliant but troubled *Time* editor, was working with a young congressman, Richard Nixon of California, who
was seeking a national reputation as the scourge of communists
and their sympathizers. Chambers took the committee to his Maryland farm, revealing the microfilm of classified State Department
documents which Hiss allegedly provided the conspirators. The
Hiss case now became a national sensation.[12]

The Hiss-Chambers story continued across 1949. Following the
microfilm episode a grand jury indicted Hiss for perjury. The first
trial ended with no decision; the second found against Hiss, but not
until January 1950. The long public agony of Alger Hiss revealed
once more the new face of the "alien menace" in this new age. For
Hiss was the quintessential establishmentarian, a graduate of Harvard College, a former member of an elite law firm, a man listed
in the Washington Social Register. He was tall, handsome, well-
groomed, and upper class, a white Anglo-Saxon Protestant of impeccable credentials. Now he was on trial in the larger courtroom of
public opinion as an un-American. His defenders were damaged by
their association with him, and many seemed to share his class and
background. The most significant former associate, Dean Acheson,
now secretary of state, announced that "I do not intend to turn my
back on this man." Acheson, a graduate of Groton, Yale, and Harvard Law School, "born to the Social Register," as one writer observed, would soon be accused of complicity. The new Red Scare
had changed the terms of the antialien crusade. Those "skulking,
disreputable Bolsheviks" of eastern European ancestry in the headlines of 1919 were no more. The enemy within in 1949 was a new
breed.[13]

By 1950, the anticommunist agitation reached new heights. In
September, the Internal Security Bill was passed by Congress, and
President Truman's veto was easily overridden in both Houses.
This McCarran Act required all communist organizations, including front groups, to register with the attorney general and to fur-
nish him with lists of their members. It denied communists passports for travel and blocked aliens belonging to communist organizations, or advocates of "other forms of totalitarianism," from admittance to the country. Harry Truman's veto message insisted that
these provisions, "instead of striking blows at Communism, would
strike blows at our own liberties . . . we need not fear the expression
of ideas, we do need to fear their suppression." The president now

became the defender of civil liberties against a rising tide of fear of foreign intrigue. But in a nation in which communities were soon celebrating "I Am an American Day" and "Loyalty Day," in which the American Heritage Foundation summoned delegates from forty-eight states to draft a "Re-Declaration of Faith in the American Dream," this counterattack attracted few recruits. For in the months before the final passage of the McCarran Act, the communist menace had become an even more frightening presence.[14]

The victory of the Chinese Communist armies in August 1949, despite almost $3 billion in total U.S. aid to the Chinese Nationalist opposition, was featured in news reports and congressional debates as a catastrophic setback. The vast Eurasian land mass now appeared on school maps colored in red, and Truman was accused of "losing a quarter of the world's population" to communism. Then came the report of the USSR's explosion of an atomic bomb in September 1949. Some U.S. scientists had predicted a Soviet success within five years of Hiroshima, but public opinion was not ready for the news. There was hysteria in some communities: dog tags were issued to schoolchildren so their bodies could be identified after an attack, ads were placed in papers offering homes or farms "out beyond the atomic blast," editorialists called for preventive war "before it is too late." Who had sold out China? How had Russia gotten the bomb? In February 1950, Klaus Fuchs, a British physicist on trial in London, who had been involved in the Manhattan Project during the war, seemed to provide one answer. He confessed to passing atomic secrets to the Soviet Union between 1943 and 1947. His testimony led to the arrest of a number of alleged coconspirators in the United States by July. It was only days after the North Korean attack. Included among those apprehended in this new "crime of the century" was Julius Rosenberg, operator of a small machine shop, and his wife.

Two of the Americans implicated in the conspiracy, chemist Harry Gold and machinist David Greenglass, pleaded guilty. Identified by Greenglass, his brother-in-law, Rosenberg and his wife insisted they were innocent. Their story made headlines throughout 1950. The trial in March 1951 ended with a guilty verdict. Alone among those accused, the Rosenbergs were sentenced to death. Amid mild protest in the United States but angrier demonstrations against this "legal lynching"—as Jean-Paul Sartre called it—in Europe, the Rosenbergs were executed in June 1953.

Like the Hiss case, the atomic spy trial has been the subject of a passionate historical dispute. Like the Hiss case, the most persuasive works have concluded that the accused were guilty, that the two were leaders of a Soviet espionage ring. But did they deserve the death penalty? Judge Irving Kauffman, in passing sentence, told them that their spying had "already caused . . . the Communist aggression in Korea, with the resultant casualties exceeding 50,000 and who knows but that millions more . . . must pay the price of your treason. . . . By your betrayal you undoubtedly have altered the course of history to the disadvantage of your country." The judge had a long and distinguished career ahead of him in 1951, but this statement was preposterous. The crude sketch of the implosion device to detonate the plutonium weapon (used at Nagasaki and earlier at the Trinity test in July 1945), which Greenglass passed to the Russians, could not have "altered history"; the Soviet bomb project was not dependent on this shabby information. The causes of the Korean War are still a matter of historical controversy and should have had no role in any intelligent jurist's decision. But the Cold War was distorting the judgment of many Americans in these years. The Red Scare claimed another temporary convert in Irving Kauffman when he sent the Rosenbergs to the electric chair on the basis of that reasoning.[15]

The accused in the spy trials—Gold, Greenglass, the Rosenbergs, and Morton Sobell—were not WASP influentials like Alger Hiss. They were Jews; so was Judge Kauffman. But there was no attendant outburst of anti-Semitism during the affair. Julius Rosenberg, noting support for his cause from some elements of the Jewish press, assailed other "self-appointed leaders of Jewish organizations" for taking on "the role of an American Judenrat," identifying with the aggressors to head off anti-Semitism. Indeed, Rabbi S. Andhil Fineberg, director of community service of the American Jewish Committee, published a remarkably bitter polemic in 1953. "The hurt to their nation was incalculable," he wrote, "the evil they did is endless." He endorsed the death sentence. But whatever the motives of Fineberg and others, this new un-American crusade did not revive the antialien animus of earlier years."[16]

Ethnic and religious outsiders of yesterday were not the victims this time. In fact, many were part of the movement. In 1950, the major actor in the entire history of this new Red Scare emerged for the first time. He was a senator, a midwesterner, a man of Irish-Catholic descent. He was Joseph R. McCarthy, Jr., of Wisconsin.

★★★
McCarthy and "McCarthyism"

It was in the unlikely setting of a Republican women's club dinner gathering in Wheeling, West Virginia, in early February that McCarthy delivered the speech which would catapult him to national celebrity and power:

> Today we are engaged in a final, all-out battle between Communistic atheism and Christianity. The modern champions of Communism have selected this as the time. . . . The war is on. . . .
>
> Six years ago . . . there was within the Soviet orbit 180,000,000 people. Lined up on the anti-totalitarian side there were . . . roughly 1,625,000,000 people. Today, only six years later, there are 800,000,000 people under the absolute domination of Soviet Russia. . . . On our side, the figure has shrunk to around 500,000,000 . . . in less than six years the odds have changed from nine to one in our favor to eight to five against us. This indicates the tempo of Communism's victories and American defeats in the Cold War. As one of our outstanding historical figures once said, "When a great democracy is destroyed, it will not be because of enemies from without, but rather because of enemies within." . . .
>
> The reason why we find ourselves in a position of impotency is not because our only powerful potential enemy has sent men to invade our shores, but rather because of the traitorous actions of those who have been treated so well by this Nation. It has not been the less fortunate or members of minority groups who have been selling this Nation out, but rather those who have had all the benefits that the wealthiest nation on earth has to offer—the finest homes, the finest college education, the finest jobs in Government we can give.
>
> This is glaringly true in the State Department. There the young men who were born with silver spoons in their mouths are the ones who have been the worst.[17]

Senator McCarthy had laid out the major indictment. But his charges would not have captured headlines without specific names and numbers: "I have in my hand 205 cases of individuals who would appear to be either card carrying members or certainly loyal to the Communist Party, but who nevertheless are still helping to shape our foreign policy." The "disloyalty, the treason in high Government positions must stop."[18]

Joseph R. McCarthy was on a cross-country speaking tour when he delivered the Wheeling address. The next day, he was in Salt Lake City, and he substituted "57 card-carrying members of the Communist Party" for the larger number. Neither figure, of course, referred to "communists" in government, and the senator had no list. They were the result of subtracting the raw number of federal employees discharged from their positions by 1948 from the number of employees about whom some damaging information had been uncovered in preliminary security screenings in 1946 or 1948. This information could have referred to political views from the Left or Right (one "suspect" was described as "a bit leftist"), sexual deviance as defined by the probers, alcoholism, gambling, even, in one case, the "entertainment of Negroes and whites, men and women, in her apartment." McCarthy was no expert on the "Red menace," and he was reading a speech drafted by a Washington newsman hired to provide a text on "Communist subversion." But the senator knew anticommunism was the critical issue of the hour and had used it on occasion earlier in attacking enemies in Wisconsin. Now, the incendiary nature of his specific charges made headlines from coast to coast.[19]

McCarthy was forty-one, a first-term senator, his name hardly a household word, when he delivered the speech. Born on the family farm near Appleton, Wisconsin, he was the fifth of seven children raised in very modest circumstances. His grandfather had been one of the relatively few Irish-Catholic émigrés during the potato famine to move west in search of his own land, coming to Wisconsin in 1855 after serving as a farmhand for seven years in Livingston County, New York, while raising money to bring his family to the New World. Joe McCarthy's family was close and linked to a community of neighboring farms in the small "Irish settlement." Still, Irish Catholics were a distinct minority in the region, treated as outsiders by many of the leading families. But when Joe quit school, as had his brothers, it was not because of status anxieties tied to low self-esteem. It was the dream of making money such as his family had never known by taking a chance in the chicken business. McCarthy failed in this venture and, after managing a grocery store for some time, decided, at age nineteen, to return to school. It was 1929. He completed high school under a special program in one year before entering Marquette University. Working at odd jobs to pay his way, earning some notoriety as a poker player and class politician, he had his law degree by 1935.[20]

The young McCarthy cultivated the image of a tough guy. With rugged features, thick arms and wrists, thinning hair, and heavy beard—acquaintances said he almost always looked as though he needed a shave—he was a formidable figure. Later, when he had become king of the anticommunists, he maintained this persona: rumpled, muscular, crude but unafraid, the perfect champion of every man against the polished elitists who were betraying America from their positions of privilege. Schoolmates remembered his political tactics in running for class office as unethical, but life had been hard on that meager farm at home, and growing up meant testing himself continuously against brothers and neighbors. He thought survival required such tactics. He began his career as a small-town lawyer in Wisconsin with a reputation as an ambitious, sometimes ruthless, occasionally unscrupulous, but curiously likable fellow.

By 1934 he was running for circuit judge, accusing the sixty-six year-old incumbent of being seven years older than his real age and inferring that the man had made huge sums of money while in office. There was no basis for his allegations, but Joe McCarthy saw politics as a no-holds-barred struggle, and he emerged a winner, at thirty, one of the youngest such judges in the land.

His life on the bench featured long hours, five- to ten-minute divorce proceedings, and an extraordinary effort to reduce a huge case backlog. His informality and occasionally self-deprecating humor endeared him to some observers. Others were angered by his judicial shortcuts, and ultimately he was censured by the chief justice of the Wisconsin Supreme Court for one case in which his actions "constituted an abuse of judicial authority." But by that time, Joe McCarthy was already planning his senatorial campaign.

His race had to be postponed awhile when the attack on Pearl Harbor propelled America into the war. But McCarthy never forgot his goal during his years in the Marine Corps, affixing placards on jeeps announcing: "Headquarters, McCarthy for U.S. Senate." He rose to be a captain, an intelligence officer for a dive-bomber squadron in the South Pacific. He did take part in eleven strike missions but was hardly the "tail-gunner Joe" trumpeted in his subsequent campaign literature. Back in Milwaukee by spring 1944, he bragged about his war deeds and made ready for his race. He failed in his first try but was better prepared in 1946, when Judge McCarthy grasped the Republican nomination and won a narrow victory over Robert M. La Follette, Jr. It was the year of the Republican congressional success and the beginning of the Cold War. In the campaign, he accused La Follette of "playing into the hands of the Communists" and of "paving the way for what the Communists have done in Poland and the rest of eastern Europe." When he arrived in Washington, his credentials as an enemy of "un-American betrayers" already were in order.[21]

In the Senate, his career failed to blossom. He had come to the Capitol with an impressive record: only thirty-eight, a farm boy who had made good through hard work and dedication, the man who had beaten the son of the legendary Progressive leader, Robert M. La Follette, Sr. But he had not become an important figure, a rising senatorial star. By 1950, facing reelection in two years, he was known in Washington as an uncouth outsider without personal or legislative polish. Stories circulated about his drinking, his loans to support gambling, his vulgar sexual liaisons at Capitol parties. He earned the nickname "Pepsi-Cola Kid" for his service to the soft-drink and sugar lobby, calling for decontrol of sugar prices. He was known as a spokesman for real estate interests and for earning handsome fees speaking at real estate meetings. He ingratiated himself with few colleagues, and Republican as well as Democratic senators helped strip him of choice committee assignments by 1949.

His political fortunes were already low when he made a brief stir by accusing the U.S. Army of a coverup in its investigation of allegedly ruthless treatment of captured German SS troops implicated in the murder of Americans at Malmédy during the Battle of the Bulge in 1944. Critics in Wisconsin now were attacking McCarthy as an embarrassment to the state, and Joe McCarthy responded by impugning the loyalty of the city editor of the *Madison Capitol-Times*, his most outspoken antagonist. At the time of the Wheeling speech, the senator's career needed a new direction. In the days after he returned from his speaking tour, he would face angry political adversaries, furious at his charges. But now he could demonstrate to the nation that talent for accusation and innuendo which would make him famous. He became the leading spokesman for the new Red Scare.[22]

On 20 February, he went before the Senate to restate his accusations about security risks in the administration. He had torn through
"Truman's iron curtain of secrecy," he said, but he could not identify the "81 cases" of "Communists in the State Department." In a
bizarre, hours-long exchange with Majority Leader Scott Lucas, he
was mercilessly grilled about the different numbers he had used—
205, 57, 81—in making the charges. He responded in an angry, ad-
hominem style that breached Senate decorum but earned him headlines. Democrats in the Senate, sure they could unmask this crude
posturer, called for an investigation into McCarthy's allegations by
a subcommittee of the Foreign Relations Committee, chaired by
Millard E. Tydings of Maryland.[23]

Now Joe McCarthy called for help. Journalist friends, right-wing
industrialists, former communists, and conservative politicians responded. One key figure was Alfred Kohlberg, a wealthy importer of
Chinese goods and a friend of Chiang Kai-shek. Kohlberg, the publisher of an anticommunist newsletter, was a leader of the China
lobby and was convinced that American opponents of the Nationalists in China were traitors. Louis Budenz, the convert to communism turned born-again Catholic after his meeting with Bishop Fulton Sheen, was another important influence in McCarthy's camp.
So was J. B. Matthews, former staff director of HUAC. Among the
politicians, Richard Nixon made available part of his files. When
the Tydings Committee gathered, McCarthy was ready with new
charges. What Richard Rovere called the technique of "multiple
untruth" now was introduced to the national audience.[24]

Sparring with the Democratic majority, McCarthy would provide
no hard evidence to support his allegations, referring only to State
Department files. But he "named names," implicating several members of the department—old "China hands"—as responsible for
the communist victory in Asia. They were men with "a mission
to Communize the world," he charged, "consorting with admitted
espionage agents." Among the accused was Professor Owen Lattimore, director of the Page School of International Relations at Johns
Hopkins University. An Asia scholar and a prolific writer, Lattimore had been editor of *Pacific Affairs*, a publication of the Institute of Pacific Relations. He had been a fellow traveler in the past, a
defender of Stalin's purges in the 1930s. Certainly he was sympathetic to the communist cause in China and long had been convinced Chiang would fail. But in McCarthy's treatment, Lattimore

suddenly became "one of the principal architects of our Far Eastern Policy," "the top Soviet spy," a "member of the Communist Party." Freda Utley, a former communist, was brought in to condemn Lattimore as a "Judas cow . . . his function has been to lead us unknowingly to destruction." Now Owen Lattimore, who was not even a State Department employee, emerged as a Red mastermind, controlling the secretary, using ambassadors as "stooges." "I am willing to stand or fall on this one," Joe McCarthy told the press, for he was about to reveal the name of "the top Russian espionage agent in America." Rovere, covering the developing McCarthy story in Washington, said that he was convinced that McCarthy had not the slightest notion which unfortunate's name on the list he "would pick out for this distinction." Lattimore was elected, and the senator's case was so weak that his foes could counterattack with a vengeance.[25]

The committee proceedings were marked by extraordinarily bitter exchanges between McCarthy and his senatorial adversaries. In its majority report (three Democrats concurring, two Republicans refusing to sign), the Tydings Committee said, "We have seen the character of private citizens and of Government employees virtually destroyed by public condemnation on the basis of gossip, distortion, hearsay and deliberate untruths." The majority concluded that McCarthy's "complaint concerning disloyalty in the State Department . . . is false," that the "methods employed to give [these charges] validity are a fraud and a hoax perpetrated on the Senate of the United States and the American people." In subsequent weeks, seven Republican senators signed a Declaration of Conscience repudiating "the selfish political exploitation of fear, bigotry, ignorance and intolerance" and exclaiming that "it is high time . . . we all stopped being tools and victims of totalitarian techniques . . . [that] if continued here unchecked, will surely end . . . the American way of life."[26]

It appeared for a brief period that McCarthy had overreached himself, that his anticommunist attack might founder. In fact, Joe McCarthy would dominate the headlines. "Tydings Report Whitewash," shouted papers sympathetic to his cause. The report is "a green light to the Red Fifth Column in the United States," he announced. Robert A. Taft, the influential conservative senator from Ohio, "Mr. Republican," now publicly encouraged McCarthy. In

March 1950 he advised him to "keep talking, if one case doesn't work, proceed with another." McCarthy's wholesale assault on communist "subversion," his style of moving from one allegation to another, was making its impact.[27]

He was getting support from people across the land. Affluent Americans who had financed other anticommunist activities sent him money, but so, too, did average folk, many in small denominations. They were encouraged by radio commentator Fulton Lewis, Jr., a devoted supporter, labor columnist Victor Riesel, and editorial writers in many communities. But most heard about him first in the news columns of their daily papers and on radio news broadcasts. This was perfect for Joe McCarthy, who had an intuitive genius for using the press, shaping its stories, and writing its headlines.

The canons of "objectivity" in journalism meant, in McCarthy's case, reporting charges without assessing their truth or falsity. The author of a work titled *Joe McCarthy and the Press* quotes a former wire service reporter: "All the wire services were so goddam objective that McCarthy got away with . . . murder, reporting it like he said it, not doing the kind of critical analysis we'd do today." And because the wire services supplied the radio stations with virtually all their news, as well as over 80 percent of the national news published in daily or weekly papers, McCarthy's domination of the wire reports meant domination of the national news output. Some major papers opposed him and responded with analytic reporting (notably the *Washington Post*), but the Associated Press (AP) and United Press (UP) provided coverage for papers without large Washington bureaus. "I felt trapped," a UP correspondent recalled of those years, "the feeling of powerlessness was terrible." The stories were "objective" and the headlines told America what that meant: "McCarthy Has New Evidence" (*Baltimore Sun*), "Knows Names of 57 Reds" (*Kansas City Star*), "Senator Asks Ouster of Reds in State Department" (*Dallas News*). Even the response by McCarthy's senatorial critics was grist for this news mill: "Senate Votes Probe of Reds in State Department" (*Chicago Tribune*), "Senate to Hunt State Department Spies" (*Cleveland Pain Dealer*), "State Department Spy Hunt Ordered" (*Los Angeles Times*). McCarthy was always a step ahead with another allegation, another "objective" report, another headline. And he could always count on a headline for that most potent part of the technique he was perfecting: accusing his political adversaries of being themselves soft on communism.[28]

A midterm election was slated for 1950, providing an opportunity for the Republicans to regain congressional control, to punish the embattled Truman administration, now struggling on two fronts: the Korean War and the assault on its "coddling of communists" at home. Joe McCarthy had become a celebrity, in demand by candidates in many areas, and he spoke for GOP hopefuls in several states. He virtually took over the campaign of John Marshall Butler, an obscure Baltimore attorney challenging Millard Tydings. With McCarthy's staff support and money he helped raise, this hated foe was beaten, but only after a squalid, gutter campaign, a "disgraceful, backstreet" effort, as an elections subcommittee characterized it. Joe McCarthy called Tydings a "Commiecrat," a man "protecting Communists for political reasons." The junior senator from Wisconsin received the credit for the reversal of political form, and he was willing to claim credit for other Democratic defeats. These included another old enemy, Scott Lucas of Illinois, as well as Frank Graham in North Carolina and Claude Pepper in Florida. Analysts challenged McCarthy's impact in the southern races, but the impression spread that he was now a man of charismatic authority—to cross him was to risk defeat. Herblock, the *Washington Post's* syndicated cartoonist, had published his famous rendition of the tar bucket titled "McCarthyism" during the Tydings hearings. It was a powerful image and offered in derogation by an influential liberal, but McCarthy could embrace it. He published a book called *McCarthyism: The Fight for America.* Joe McCarthy now seemed bigger than life, more than just a senator. His picture would soon be on the covers of *Time* and *Newsweek.* He had become the embodiment of what many were calling a movement.[29]

The specter of the enemy within, an evil but shadowy presence threatening to destroy the American dream, became part of popular culture in the early 1950s. Hollywood offered two films that embodied the message of McCarthyism: *Red Nightmare*, in which communists somehow indoctrinate the wives and children of average American businessmen, and the science fiction thriller *Invasion of the Body Snatchers.* In this setting, important figures in the movie industry were brought to Washington to help HUAC ferret out "subversives" in the business; the "Hollywood Ten" were victims of the ugly affair. The anxiety was spreading. On some college campuses, controversial speakers were censured and appointments of alleged radicals avoided by nervous administrators. Earlier, at the University of Washington, the president and regents dismissed three professors for being members of the American Communist party. What Senator Margaret Chase Smith called the "Four Horsemen of Calumny: Fear, Ignorance, Bigotry, and Smear" were taking their effect.

In winter and spring 1950–51, with the Korean War going badly, many people sought to confront the Red menace anywhere it could be identified. The Chinese had entered the war in November, and Americans, preparing for victory over North Korea by Christmas, now were told of new defeats by U.S. forces confronting more than three hundred thousand Chinese "volunteers." "Who lost China" became more than a political exercise; U.S. boys were fighting and dying in Asia. Harry Truman, who had engaged in bruising rhetorical exchanges through the press with McCarthy, bore the brunt of public disappointment with the war news. His decision to fire the legendary Douglas MacArthur in the spring led to a historic outpouring of emotion. The war front had been stabilized when American troops cleared the enemy out of South Korea and reached the Thirty-eighth parallel once again. But General MacArthur's insistence that there was "no substitute for victory," that the United States must carry the war to "Red China," "unleash" Chiang's forces in Taiwan, and this time complete the liberation of North Korea was rejected by Truman after consultation with Generals of the Army George Marshall and Omar Bradley, two other heroes of World War II. MacArthur's plan could widen the war, placing U.S. and allied interests at risk in other parts of the world. MacArthur had to go. But many Americans, frustrated by a pathbreaking decision not to end a shooting war through victory, made their feelings known. On 14 June 1951, at this moment of mounting frenzy and anger, Joseph McCarthy addressed the Senate. After Wheeling, it would be his most important performance, a landmark speech in the history of the new Red Scare.

It is almost certain that he did not write the sixty-thousand-word address. He did not present most of it. Perhaps one-third was delivered on the floor, the rest inserted in the *Congressional Record*. But this remarkable polemic echoes across the years. In it, McCarthy referred to many of the old targets. Yet it was the celebrated George

Marshall, chief of staff and most important military leader in the West in World War II, a former secretary of state, who emerged as the real devil. Marshall was accused of serving Soviet interests throughout his career, from his plan for a cross-channel assault in 1943 to the Marshall Plan, which emerged from an "almost complete blueprint supplied in 1945 by Communist leader Earl Browder." Marshall and Acheson were portrayed as instrumental in communist conquests in Europe after the war, a product of "the path of appeasement." But it was in the "sellout" of China that "the complete, sinister, treacherous, traitorous picture" was most damning. It was "criminal folly," for now the United States was at war with China in Korea. America, under Marshall, had become a "nation that cringes in fear." And "how can we account for our present situation unless we believe that men high in this Government are concerting to deliver us to disaster. This must be a product of a great conspiracy, a conspiracy on a scale so immense as to dwarf any previous such venture in the history of man." Who constitutes "the highest circles in this conspiracy"? Dean Acheson is "high on the roster." The president "is the captive," the servant of "his master," Acheson, only "dimly aware of what is going on." But it is Marshall, "this grim and solitary man," who is the pivotal figure in this "strategy of defeat."[30]

The speech infuriated Truman, who considered Marshall the greatest man he had known. It poisoned the last years of Marshall's career. But it brought new notoriety to McCarthy. He was becoming more reckless now, assailing almost anyone from the other party. Throughout 1951 and 1952, he attacked the administration with abandon and played a role in the presidential race in 1952. Dwight D. Eisenhower, who owed so much to Marshall, who had brought him to the chief of staff's office and named him supreme commander of the Allied Expeditionary Forces in Europe, was the GOP nominee. This leader "above party" had taken the prize from the conservative Taft after a bitter convention struggle, but he was not prepared to engage in a partisan campaign. When speaking in Wisconsin, Eisenhower found McCarthy at his side in Milwaukee. Ike had prepared a speech with one passage strongly defending his friend George Marshall. Now he dropped the passage and did not mention the general or McCarthy's allegations. Harry Truman and Mrs. Marshall never forgave Eisenhower.[31]

Across the election year, the fear of alien ideologists continued to grow. In the spring, Congress passed the McCarran-Walter Immigration and Nationality Act. Codifying existing legislation and restating the 1924 quota system based on national origins—although providing this time a tiny quota for Asiatics—the act also established a convoluted procedure for barring "subversives" and other undesirables. It empowered the attorney general to deport any immigrants who had a "Communist affiliation" even after they had received citizenship. President Truman vetoed the bill in late June. "The basis of this quota system was false and unworthy in 1924," he wrote, "it is even worse now." But in addition, "the reenactment of highly objectionable provisions now contained in the Internal Security Act of 1950" made the new measure completely unacceptable to the president. "These provisions are worse than the infamous Alien Act of 1798, passed in a time of irrational fear and distrust of foreigners . . . [they] are inconsistent with our democratic ideals." Harry Truman's message was powerful, passionate, and unpersuasive in the midst of this new Red Scare. Congress overrode his veto.[32]

Throughout the campaign, Eisenhower kept a distance from McCarthy, and relations between the two were never very cordial. But the senator was the darling of his party's right wing, invited to a dozen states to campaign for congressional candidates. He also proved useful to the GOP national committee by questioning the loyalty of Democratic nominee Adlai Stevenson of Illinois. In a nationally televised address on 27 October, he declared that "the Democratic candidate endorsed and could continue the suicidal Kremlin-directed policies of this nation"; Stevenson was "part and parcel of the Hiss-Lattimore group"; he had "given aid to the Communist cause"; he was "unfit to be President." McCarthy, referring repeatedly to "Alger—I mean Adlai" Stevenson, was not alone in this effort. Vice-presidential candidate Richard Nixon, traveling the "low road" for a ticket featuring Eisenhower's bland appeals, called the Democrats the "party of Communism, Korea and Corruption," and their candidate, "Adlai the appeaser," who "carries a Ph.D. from Dean Acheson's Cowardly College of Communist Containment." Nixon and McCarthy were now old allies, and the Californian referred to "my good friend Joe McCarthy" in endorsing the senator's own reelection drive in Wisconsin.[33]

McCarthy won easily, with 54 percent of the total and a 140,000 vote plurality. But he profited from the Eisenhower landslide. Analysts later called his victory less than impressive, pointing out that he carried no major city in the state. They insisted he had not influenced the outcomes of other campaigns; Democrats had been beaten less by McCarthyism than by the long coattails of an enormously popular Republican presidential candidate. But at the time, the defeats of Senator William Benton in Connecticut, Senate Majority Leader Ernest McFarland in Arizona, and others against whom McCarthy had spoken seemed added examples of the magnetic appeal of his anticommunist rhetoric.[34]

In office, Dwight Eisenhower recognized that McCarthy's insatiable appetite for celebrity would make trouble even for a newly elected Republican administration. He wrote in his diary on 1 April 1953: "Senator McCarthy, of course, is so anxious for the headlines that he is prepared to go to any extreme. . . . I really believe that nothing will be so effective in combating his particular kind of troublemaking as to ignore him. This he cannot stand." The man who said that he would "not get down in the gutter with that guy" wrote a corporate executive friend that he would not confront McCarthy: "Nothing would probably please him more than to get the publicity that would be generated by a public repudiation by the President."[35]

In Congress, where McCarthy was now insisting that "we've only scratched the surface on Communism," even conservative Republicans were wary of him. Robert Taft told Richard Rovere in January that the party leadership had decided to "direct" McCarthy's "attention to other matters." Once again in the majority, the GOP managers thought they were giving the anticommunist issue to William Jenner of Indiana, the new chairman of the Senate Internal Security Committee, and in the House to Harold Velde of Illinois, chair of HUAC. But neither man had McCarthy's personal force or his genius for dramatizing events. They were routine mediocrities and no match for McCarthy, whose attention could not be redirected by being pigeonholed in the chairmanship of the innocuous Committee on Government Operations. He refused to supervise "motor pools and office furniture." Instead, he created a permanent subcommittee, made himself its chair, and used it as the instrument for maintaining and expanding his leadership of the anticommunist campaign in Washington.[36]

He hired Roy Cohn, brilliantly precocious twenty-five-year-old son of a prominent New York judge, as chief counsel for his subcommittee. Cohn's passionate commitment to anticommunism had attracted the support of influential right-wing commentators in press and government. Now he helped Joe McCarthy prepare for new crusades against the internal enemy. The senator made mischief within the administration throughout 1953. He meddled in foreign affairs and attacked the Voice of America on the "loyalty issue." He then allowed Cohn and G. David Schine, the wealthy young heir to a hotel fortune serving as an unpaid subcommittee "consultant," to make their notorious tour of Europe, seeking to uncover and remove "subversive" books and articles in the International Information Administration's overseas libraries. These "junketeering gumshoes" made front-page news and intimidated some panicky librarians into burning works by "questionable" authors. Meanwhile, McCarthy kept up a steady stream of highly publicized hearings at home, assailing such liberals as James A. Wechsler, editor of the *New York Post*, who heard his paper characterized as "next to and about paralleling the *Daily Worker*." McCarthy also referred to the new president of Harvard as a "rabid anti-anti Communist," a man hiding "behind a cloak of phony, hypocritical liberalism."[37]

By the fall of 1953, the junior senator from Wisconsin seemed to be at the height of his powers. Newsmagazines were speculating on a 1956 presidential bid. Yet now came a reversal of fortune. Joseph McCarthy was a demagogic politician with a formidable talent for dominating the headlines. But he operated on instinct, and he was never a calculating schemer capable of building a career aimed at the White House. His instincts began to betray him.

First, he appointed J. B. Matthews, that former Marxist turned ultraist Red hunter, as executive director of his subcommittee. A magazine article by Matthews, accusing Protestant clergymen of being the "largest single group supporting the Communist apparatus in the United States," led to a revolt by subcommittee Democrats, who walked out in anger. A firestorm of protest by leading southern conservatives finally forced McCarthy to abandon Matthews, but he retaliated with a threat to probe the CIA. Joe McCarthy was losing his bearings, turning his accusatory rhetoric on institutions—the churches and security agencies—which were above suspicion even in this Red Scare and could not be subjected to the politics of McCarthyite innuendo. He was now drinking heavily, perhaps an added reason why he blundered into the imbroglio that effectively ended his career and marked the final major chapter in the anticommunist hysteria of the 1950s. He decided to take on the United States Army.[38]

At the center of this sordid affair was Schine, who was drafted in the summer of 1952. Cohn and McCarthy pressured the Department of the Army to grant their man a commission or at least special privileges. But as those efforts continued, McCarthy's subcommittee opened an investigation of communist infiltration of the army. He charged that clerks from the Quartermaster Corps in New York had communist ties and that a spy ring was present at Fort Monmouth in New Jersey. In the midst of these attacks, he went on the air with a speech lashing former President Truman but also implying that communists remained in government even in the Eisenhower administration: "Communism is an issue and will be an issue in 1954." Now he had become too reckless. But he could not stop. In January and February 1954 he brought an army dentist, Irving Peress, before his committee, a man who earlier had been the subject of Defense Department and FBI security probes for refusing to answer questions about involvement in organizations declared subversive by the attorney general. When Major Peress took the Fifth Amendment before his committee, McCarthy responded with a vicious ad hominem assault. When the army announced Peress's honorable discharge, McCarthy called Brigadier General Ralph Zwicker, commander of Fort Kilmer, New Jersey, where Peress had been stationed. Zwicker earlier had cooperated with the subcommittee, but now he became just another object of Joe McCarthy's wrath. Disregarding the witness's distinguished military career, McCarthy told the general: "You are ignorant . . . you're shielding Communist conspirators . . . you should be removed from any command . . . you are not fit to wear that uniform." When the text of this remarkable tirade was made public, even McCarthy's allies in Congress and the conservative press were appalled. The *Chicago Tribune* finally turned away from the senator: "We do not believe [his] behavior was justified . . . it has injured his cause." NBC radio commentator H. V. Kaltenborn, an erstwhile admirer, went even further. He decided that "McCarthy has too often hit below the belt . . . he has become completely egotistical, arrogant, arbitrary, narrow-minded, reckless and irresponsible. Power has corrupted him."[39]

In Washington, Zwicker was defended by Chief of Staff Matthew B. Ridgway, who called for support from Secretary of the Army Robert Stevens. But when Stevens issued a "memorandum of understanding" between the army and McCarthy's subcommittee, it appeared even to neutral observers as an unconditional surrender. While McCarthy gloated over this "abject capitulation," the president encouraged Stevens to modify his politically damaging posture, to issue a statement refusing to "accede to [Army personnel] being browbeaten or humiliated." Ike finally seemed ready to confront Joe McCarthy directly. But Eisenhower's subsequent press conference provided only a mild rebuke, earning the contempt of columnist Joseph Alsop, who shouted out, "the yellow sonofabitch," and causing Adlai Stevenson to call the Republican party, "Half Eisenhower, Half McCarthy." Nevertheless, McCarthy responded to the tepid statement with a personal assault on the president, implying that Eisenhower was aiding "extreme left wing elements" in a "mudslinging attack" on his committee. Six days later, on 9 March, Ralph Flanders, seventy-two-year-old Republican from Vermont, told the Senate that McCarthy was "doing his best to shatter the Republican Party," for he represented "a one man party called McCarthyism, a title which he has proudly accepted." The next morning, the president congratulated Flanders for his "public service." McCarthy was cutting his last ties with his party, and now he was vulnerable as never before.[40]

The night of the Flanders speech, Edward R. Murrow, the "father of broadcast journalism," the most important figure in the history of the electronic news media, aired his famous "See It Now" television episode on McCarthyism for a prime-time audience on CBS. Using film footage of the senator's speeches and his treatment of committee witnesses, Murrow concluded: "The line between investigation and persecution is a very fine one, and the junior Senator from Wisconsin has stepped over it repeatedly. . . . This is not the time for men who oppose Senator McCarthy's methods to keep silent." Murrow said that McCarthy's actions "have caused alarm and dismay, but whose fault is that?" Pointing to the origins of the Red Scare, he observed: "Not really his; he didn't create this situation of fear, he merely exploited it and rather successfully. Cassius was right, 'The fault, dear Brutus, is not in our stars but in ourselves.' "[41]

McCarthy was on the defensive. But long before he could respond with his own CBS presentation, he faced an even more serious cri-

sis. On 12 March, the army issued a report charging him and Roy
Cohn with threatening army leaders to obtain preferred treatment
for G. David Schine. Clearly, the administration had decided to act
at last, and the liberal press applauded. The senator's response was
vintage McCarthyism, a claim that the army was trying to "black-
mail" him into dropping his investigation of subversive activities
in the service. The army-McCarthy affair now became Washington's cause célèbre. Sides had to be taken, and even Richard Nixon
turned on the senator, referring to "men who have in the past done
effective work exposing Communists . . . [who] by reckless talk and
questionable methods have made themselves the issue." McCarthy
had to agree that his own subcommittee conduct a full, public inquiry, with Karl Mundt of South Dakota, second-ranking Republican, in the chair.[42]

The army-McCarthy hearings became a national television spectacular, carried live by ABC with news coverage by the other networks. The subcommittee appointed its own special counsel and
the army hired Joseph Welch, senior partner in the prestigious Boston law firm of Hale and Dorr, who agreed to serve without com-
pensation. He brought with him two junior associates but asked
one of them, Frederick G. Fisher, Jr., to return to Boston, after
learning that Fisher had briefly been a member of the National
Lawyers Guild, a target of an earlier probe by HUAC. The hearings
began on 22 April, and they proved to be the undoing of Joseph R.
McCarthy.[43]

The story is well known. McCarthy's bullying, menacing style,
his discourtesy to senatorial colleagues, his repeated interruptions,
punctuated by the monotonal "point of order, Mr. Chairman," were
on display throughout the televised event. In this setting, McCarthy could not use the media to manipulate the news. He was the
news. Between 1951 and 1954, television sales had skyrocketed everywhere. Price cuts, program development, and community pressure made ownership of a set almost mandatory, and by the year
of the hearing, more than three-quarters of American homes were
part of the television community. Across the nation, people had a
chance to see this angry man with the heavy beard at work for the
first time. They responded adversely.

In the end, it was the absent Fred Fisher who became the unlikely
victim and hero of McCarthy's final significant attack. Frustrated
by the clever Welch, Joseph McCarthy—acting as he had in so many

other cases—sought to impugn the loyalty of his adversary. Welch could not be personally touched, but Fisher became the issue: "He has in his law firm a young man . . . who has been for a number of years, a member of an organization which was named, oh years and years ago, as the legal bulwark of the Communist Party." This provided the opportunity for Joseph Welch, who may have planned the masterful trap, to reveal McCarthy's brutal and bullying persona. "Little did I dream, Senator, that you could be so reckless and so cruel as to do an injury to that lad," he responded. "I fear he shall always bear a scar needlessly inflicted by you." When McCarthy persevered, in the hushed silence of the Senate Caucus Room, Welch responded in words that became part of modern political history. "Let us not assassinate this lad further, Senator. You have done enough. Have you no sense of decency sir, at long last? Have you left no sense of decency?" It was a dramatic moment. It revealed once more the character of the new assault on alien ideology and the character of McCarthy. Fisher was a member of the WASP elite, like many others accused by the new movement. Of course, he would bear the "scars" well and was to have a prosperous career at Hale and Dorr; in 1973 he became president of the Massachusetts Bar Association. But the leader of the antialien crusade of the 1950s was undone. Welch told McCarthy that "if there is a God in heaven it will do neither you nor your cause any good." The room exploded with applause, even members of the press standing to cheer. In the courtroom of national public opinion, the television audience agreed. The hearings continued, but this exchange was the symbolic conclusion.[44]

Editorialists across the land turned on the senator from Wisconsin. His ratings in the Gallup Polls declined from 50 percent favorable in January to less than 35 percent in July. His enemies in the Senate finally were emboldened to act. It was Ralph Flanders who called on the Senate to censure McCarthy in what became a nonpartisan effort. McCarthy's supporters launched a campaign to defend their man, and demonstrators on Capitol Hill wore badges declaring, "I Like McCarthy, I Like His Methods." Petitions with a million signatures flooded congressional offices. But after lengthy hearings, the vote was 67 to 22 to "condemn" McCarthy for contempt and abuse of Senate committees. Joe McCarthy was only forty-six, but he was finished. Isolated on the Hill, ignored by former enemies and even former friends, he increasingly turned to drink. Soon his alcoholism was so bad he had to be hospitalized for detoxification. By May 1957, he was dead of cirrhosis of the liver. One diehard right-wing publisher announced that "McCarthy was murdered by the Communists because he was exposing them." But there were too few passionate antialiens left to respond to the old rhetoric. McCarthyism had been dead for almost three years before the death of the man who provided its name.[45]

★★★

The Debate over the Meaning of McCarthyism

What had it meant? Supporters insisted that it had helped the nation. William F. Buckley, Jr., and L. Brent Bozell argued in *McCarthy and His Enemies* in 1954: "America's back has stiffened," for "we are at war" with communism. "McCarthyism is a weapon in the American arsenal. . . . As long as [it] fixes its goal with its present precision, it is a movement around which men of good will and stern morality can close ranks." But there was scant evidence of a powerful subversive communist presence in America or even a substantial communist constituency, despite the investigatory zeal of McCarthy, HUAC, and others. The Communist party of the United States had been losing ground ever since its mild revival during the war years. Under hard-line leadership responsive only to Moscow's direction since 1945, its membership had declined. If communists or fellow travelers had dominated a few important unions after VJ day, they had been expelled from the CIO by 1947. If communists had played a key role in organizing Henry Wallace's Progressive party presidential candidacy in 1948, these efforts resulted only in a crushing defeat. By 1953, membership had plummeted from fifty-four thousand to twenty-four thousand within four years, and a significant percentage of this tiny group of card-carrying communists were double agents, representatives of intelligence services. The Communist party was moribund, and the specter of subversion was an illusion. There had been Soviet espionage agents in the United States in the past, and security procedures in the State Department and other federal agencies were lax in the 1940s. But communism in America represented no real enemy within during the postwar era.[46]

Then why had McCarthy proved so effective? In 1955, a group of prominent social scientists offered one provocative set of answers. Rejecting as simplistic the thesis that Joe McCarthy was merely a gifted demagogue playing on old fears of alien conspiracies, the authors of *The New American Right* argued that McCarthyism represented the status anxieties of the upwardly mobile in an age of opportunity. This "pseudo-conservative revolt," as Richard Hofstadter called it, "a product of the rootlessness and heterogeneity of American life," appealed to many people, but particularly to ethnic Catholics, happy to have "as the objects of their hatred the Anglo-Saxon, Eastern, Ivy League, intellectual gentlemen." A neo-Populist element was seen in this "revolt against the elites" during the years of expansion after World War II—the postwar boom time, the age of a new private culture—and it was suggested that McCarthyism represented an ugly and dangerous form of mass politics. Status concerns, as opposed to real economic interests, distorted realities and led followers to subsume their fears and hatreds into allegiance to McCarthy, the practitioner of an irrational politics of resentment.[47]

The "status politics" explanation was initially influential. It was presented during the emergence of a paradigm shift in American historical writing, the rise of "consensus historiography." This was a vision of an American people who shared a common set of values, and one corollary held that "status anxieties" were an endemic but dangerous by-product of the consensus. In a land in which real ideological disputes were absent and Americans traditionally worked out their differences in a variety of pluralistic interest groups, "mass politics" could represent only a politics of unreason, the displacement of real anxieties on some victim group. McCarthyism was seen as a by-product of social pathology, the dark underbelly of the consensus.

This interpretation was soon under attack. Three political scientists led the way. Nelson Polsby, in a 1960 essay titled "Toward an Explanation of McCarthyism," pointed to the role of party—not status—in the McCarthy phenomenon; most followers of the senator, he argued, were Republicans. Earl Latham concluded his 1966 study *The Communist Controversy in Washington* with a development of this thesis: "Eager for office, disappointed by frustration, the Republican Party with help of conservative Democrats . . . found a storm leader in McCarthy." Republicans "managed to achieve in 1952 the victory they had been denied for two decades. . . . McCarthyism was the agent of a fundamentalist conservatism" that had been kept from national power since FDR's election in 1932 and used the "Communist issue" only as the "cutting edge for the attack." In 1967, Michael Paul Rogin, forcefully rejecting the linkage between Populism and McCarthyism made by the "pluralists" who had authored *The New American Right*, pointed to "the traditional right wing of the midwestern Republican Party" and said McCarthy appealed less to rank-and-file voters (the "masses" in the mass politics argument were not really present) than to militant activists and elites. Rogin also pointed to the setting of the Cold War and the role of anticommunist politics in the preceding years. The same analysis was underscored a few years later by the editors of a book titled *The Specter: Original Essays on the Cold War and the Origins of McCarthyism.*[48]

The debate over the meaning of McCarthyism reflected, in one sense, the larger debate over the direction of American history. The "consensus" historians were under attack in the late 1960s and early 1970s; a "New Left" revisionism emerged in the context of the social upheavals of the decade and the protest against the Vietnam War. The consensus writers now were assailed for their "fear" of radicalism. They were attacked for characterizing "mass politics" as irrational in a decade in which mass politics was seen as liberating, for linking McCarthy to the Populist revolt against privilege and injustice. The revisionist critics of the "pluralists," writing during and after the years of "The Movement" (1968 to 1970), insisted that McCarthyism was not really a movement at all but merely a handy instrument of conservative power seekers. In an age when no one was writing any more of "the end of ideology," the passions of the hour gave this debate its initial intensity.

With the passage of time, it seems clear that both sides contributed to an understanding of the issue. If the connection to Populism was dramatically overdrawn by some authors of *The New American Right*, it is hard to accept the conclusion that there was no real mass support for McCarthy. Granting that Americans were not "trembling lest they find a Red under the bed," as one analyst of public opinion observed in 1954, there still was a high level of support for the senator and his cause. This was demonstrated in public opinion polls taken across four years until the critical spring of 1954. It was not only some shrewd political operatives on the Republican Right and a relative handful of fanatic anticommunists who made McCarthy and McCarthyism. The senator, a brilliant manipulator of popular fears as well as the popular press, had tapped into the traditional fear of alien ideas and alien ideologists which had a long history in America.[49]

But who were the McCarthyites? If Irish, Italian, and many German Catholics were among the most pro-McCarthy groups, as several scholars (on different sides of the controversy) have concluded from studies of poll data assembled by the Gallup and Roper organizations, the Survey Research Center, and the International Research Associates, did this suggest that McCarthyism was only another episode in inverted nativism? Were the former victims of the anti-aliens having their day as victimizers of the old elites? The list of Joe McCarthy's targets—from Dean Acheson to the president of Harvard—suggested as much. But many Catholics also opposed McCarthy, and large numbers of fundamentalist Protestants and other right-wingers endorsed him. (For his supporters of all groups, poll data indicate that "lower classes and rural populations" gave him his most fervent following, although there was some correlation between higher socioeconomic status within these lower educational or occupational groups and McCarthyism. The status anxieties of the upward bound were present.) It seems clear that the new Red Scare contained echoes of the old nativist antagonisms. Yet it offered a politics of resentment which appealed to a number of groups—Catholic ethnics and their former enemies—during the postwar boom. These were people who may have found even more satisfaction in McCarthy's methods—intimidating and humiliating the "Ivy Leaguers born with a silver spoon in their mouths"—than in his struggle to save the land from communism.[50]

But this Red Scare was a complex phenomenon and more than just a replay of earlier conflicts. It could not have endured across most of a decade without the emergence of international tensions and the impetus of the Cold War. Like the first Red Scare, this crusade against the alien within was inextricably connected to crises in military and foreign affairs abroad.

Following the triumphs of 1945, it was the unprecedented political and financial burden of international leadership, the growing concern about vulnerability in an atomic age, and the widespread fear of Soviet expansion in Europe and Asia that fueled the Cold War and shaped the policies of two administrations. This Red Scare did not begin with Joe McCarthy and would not have begun at all without the crusade to contain communism abroad. Confronted by seeming setbacks in the international conflict and with the stalemated war raging in Korea, McCarthy effectively manipulated the issue of internal communism in a land initially unprepared for the world crises in the postwar era.

The Americans who affirmatively responded to his attacks were grappling with a world turned upside down. They sought an answer to the damning and disorienting question of their moment in history: how had America, apparently at the height of its powers, come to appear everywhere to be on the defensive? McCarthy's response was part of an ancient tradition of comforting hostility, a way of explaining the intolerable by pointing to an enemy within.

The "predilection toward conspiracies," Robert Wiebe observed, "has been extremely useful in the cause of cohesion" in America. In a nation where power was located in so many different centers, in a democracy where "people controlled their government and established their own values and goals, what other than a conspiracy, could explain a general change for the worse?" In the 1950s, this "normal American predisposition" focused on alien ideologies. The very homogenization of modern postwar society stimulated this process. A growing private consumer culture, a more mobile social order, and an awareness of the emergence of a nationwide marketplace in which new occupational elites played central roles helped to erode hostility toward religious and ethnic subcultures, those older enemies within. But these developments also spurred a new celebration of American capitalism and its role in a life-or-death struggle against alien ideologies. The "defeats" overseas by communists made it imperative that America be defended at home from such ideologies.[51]

Expunging alien "ideas" and "subversive activities" long had been the rallying cry of political opportunists in America. The Cold War provided the perfect setting for Joe McCarthy to build on the fears of communism already rife by 1950. McCarthyism had roots in the domestic tensions of the time, as the pluralists observed. But it had deeper roots in the international crisis and in the rhetoric of the Cold War struggle against communism.

It could not endure. With the fall of Joe McCarthy, the new Red Scare was fatally weakened. It was 1954. Eisenhower, a Republican, was president. The Korean War finally was brought to an end. The tensions between the United States and USSR continued, but even there changes were under way. Joseph Stalin was dead in 1952, and by 1956, Nikita S. Khrushchev would tell the Soviet people and the world that Stalin had been a mass murderer. The "Red menace" was under very different leadership. Although the Cold War did not end, the initial shock of world crisis and America's loss of security was over. The new Red Scare was built in part on disturbed expectations following World War II. That era was past, and with it the critical element in the making of the anticommunist crusade was removed. There would be anticommunist activists and anticommunist movements across the next decade and a half, but they would have only limited appeal. The next group concerned with combating this "alien" ideology would find an audience only among true believers.

★★★

The John Birch Society

The John Birch Society (JBS) became the most prominent organization on what liberal critics began calling the "radical right" in the late 1950s and early 1960s. Founded in December 1958 by Robert H. W. Welch, Jr., a wealthy, fifty-nine-year-old former candy manufacturer from Massachusetts, the John Birch Society was organized to "alert the nation" to the menace of communist subversion at home and communist victories abroad. "Our enemy," Welch wrote, "is the Communist—nobody else." Named for an army captain and Baptist missionary killed during a confrontation with Chinese Communists shortly after the end of World War II, the John Birch Society, under Robert Welch's dominant leadership, grew to membership of forty thousand by 1963, organized in more than three hundred chapters. The founder had explained to the eleven "influential and very busy men" he had invited to the organizational meeting in Indianapolis that "so-called democratic processes" could play no part in JBS affairs. "Communist infiltrators" were everywhere; it was necessary to "operate under authoritative control at all levels." The local chapters (ten to twenty members) would have chapter leaders, reporting to section leaders (for four to eight chapters), and in turn to coordinators, major coordinators, district governors, and the National Council, all under the command of the founder and president. The society became a hierarchical body reflecting the anticommunist passion of its originator.[52]

Welch published his manifesto, presented in a two-day session with those first recruits in 1958, as *The Blue Book of the John Birch Society*. In it, he appealed to political conservatives, lamenting the growth of the "cancer of collectivism" threatening the free enterprise system in the West. He praised Barry Goldwater and a handful of other "patriot" politicians who embraced "Americanist principles." But this was no traditionally conservative document. Welch returned again and again to the danger of "Communist conspirators" within the United States, "deliberately helping to spread the virus for their own purposes." He eulogized Joseph McCarthy as the victim of "smears by his enemies," the man "the Communists just had to get rid of," and repeated McCarthy's attacks on George Marshall and the "Acheson-infected State Department." Facing the "imminent and horrible . . . danger of the physical enslavement of the whole world, including ourselves," Welch told his first followers that he could be "the 'man on the white horse' on our side in this war." With "the aid, counsel, organizing ability and executive know-how offered by the ablest men in America among the staunch anti-Communists," he was convinced that he could meet the sinister challenge of the alien enemy. The John Birch Society program was presented; implementation would follow.[53]

The movement attempted to shape public opinion by establishing hundreds of reading rooms across the nation, American Opinion Libraries, filled with books and articles exposing the communist enemy. Welch announced support for a number of periodicals, notably his own *American Opinion*, to combat the "metropolitan press and big circulation general magazines which consciously or blindly promote the Communist line." Anticommunist radio commentators were endorsed through contributions and through pressure exerted on station owners. Organized letter-writing campaigns to political and corporate leaders were mounted in pursuit of John Birch Society goals. Some of these efforts seemed almost pathetically irrelevant to all but the initiates, as when Birchers flooded the offices of United Airlines with their letters, insisting that the United Nations insignia be taken off United planes.

In addition to these "educational" efforts, Welch wanted to "shock the American people" by exposing particular communists in positions of influence by name. These were people "too slippery to put your finger on in the ordinary way," people who could be damaged by "bombshells" printed about them in Birch journals. More important, Welch had his Birch Society emulate the "successful tactics of the Communist enemy." Front groups were organized or aided: the Committee of One Million, devoted to "keeping Red China out of the United Nations," the Committee for Withdrawal of Recognition (from the Soviet Union), the Committee for the Impeachment of Earl Warren, the Committee to Investigate Communist Influences at Vassar College, et al. Like the Know Nothings of old, the Birchers were so convinced of the conspiratorial genius of their foes that they had to operate in part through secrecy.[54]

Welch's work contained other echoes of old antialien themes. In 1964, for example, he returned to John Robison's "exposé" of the Bavarian Illuminati, linking the Illuminati's alleged role in the making of the French Revolution to the contemporary communist conspiracy, suggesting that only the John Birch Society could prevent "collectivists . . . perpetrating repetitions of [this] tragic history." But Welch did not share the ethnic or religious prejudice of other antialiens in history. The nativist animus was absent in his writing. As with McCarthy, all were welcome to the anticommunist crusade, regardless of race, religion, or ethnicity. Approximately one-quarter of the national membership was Catholic, and two Catholic priests served on Welch's council. So did Clarence Manion, former dean of the University of Notre Dame Law School and a self-proclaimed "unreconstructed McCarthyite," the radio voice of the anticommunist "Manion Forum." The role of Jews in the organization was a different story; Welch was forced to deny charges of anti-Semitism on several occasions. If the founder had once characterized Jewish leaders of the early years of the Communist party as "traitors to their race," he personally avoided religious slurs, yet anti-Semitic passages by other contributors did appear in many Birch publications.[55]

The John Birch Society attacked the alien enemy on many fronts. It "exposed" liberal writers, academics, and film and media celebrities as dupes or agents of communism. Eric Sevareid was implicated, as was J. Robert Oppenheimer. Fredric March ("one of the most notorious Comsymps in the whole Hollywood menage"), Mark Van Doren ("an unbroken record of coming to the support of Communists and Communist fronts"), and Carl Sandburg ("the great patron of Stalin's American contingent in the Spanish Civil War") were also objects of attack by the Birch Society. It spearheaded drives to "Support Your Local Police," circulating bumper stickers with the slogan as a response to "Comsymp efforts to undermine security forces." It attacked the civil rights movement as an instrument of subversion, and Welch berated Martin Luther King, Jr., exclaiming that Birchers must "show the Communist hands behind [him]." Welch was particularly vitriolic about Earl Warren, leader of the "Warren Gang" in the Supreme Court, author of the *Brown* decision outlawing segregation in public schools, defender of the "lawlessness paraded as civil rights." The Warren impeachment affair was as important as the campaign to "take the U.S. out of the U.N.," another Birch perennial.[56]

These efforts, for all their passion, angered some liberals but only amused many others, who were indifferent to Welch and his movement. They had little impact on national affairs and elicited limited comment outside the circle of the faithful. But Robert Welch found a different response to his other "major work," a companion to the *Blue Book* known as the "black book" because of its binding. This was a volume so controversial he had to say repeatedly that neither the John Birch Society nor its members had ever been connected with *The Politician*.

The first version of this study of the public career of Dwight D. Eisenhower, "the Pro Communist," appeared as an "unfinished manuscript" in 1958. So hostile was the reception to it that an amended version was published in 1963. Some of the most incendiary passages were removed, including statements that the president was "a dedicated, conscious agent of the Communist conspiracy" and "the chances are very strong that Milton Eisenhower is actually Dwight Eisenhower's superior and boss within the Communist party." In the expurgated version, Welch still repeatedly accused Eisenhower, as general and as president, of serving the interests of his "Communist bosses." In the White House, he offered a "continuation and expansion of the activities begun under the Communist-directed Truman Administration." He named as secretary of state John Foster Dulles, and Welch explained that "for many reasons and after a lot of study, I personally believe Dulles to be a Communist agent." In his foreign and domestic policies, Eisenhower received and "abided by Communist orders." Although Welch equivocated in the revised version, suggesting that Ike might be "only the tool of the Communists, a politician entirely without principles," he returned once more to his original premise in the conclusion. "The word is treason," he wrote, for Eisenhower "is a Communist assigned the specific job of being a political front man."[57]

Welch's overheated conspiracy theories, the bizarre world he constructed in which famous conservatives were secret enemy agents, was too much even for those who had championed the anticommunist activities of McCarthy and others. He went too far in accusing Eisenhower of being a Red. He compounded his problems by asserting that the CIA "is on the Communist side" and by alleging, in 1962, that the United States is "50–70 per cent under Communist control" and the "government of the United States is under operational control of the Communist Party." Conservative editors, columnists, and politicians now began calling for Welch's resignation from the presidency of the John Birch Society. But the founder would not go. His movement continued to grow, reaching a membership of eighty thousand in 1967 and numbering four hundred chapters in states from coast to coast, with the largest and most active following in southern California, Florida, and Texas. The headquarters in Belmont, Massachusetts, was expanded and the Society had a staff of 220, including 75 coordinators in the field. It was spending over $5 million a year. Still, there was no sense of momentum. The Birch Society was losing influence. Members had to defend themselves from charges that they had become part of the "kook right." The circulation for *American Opinion* stalled at an unimpressive forty-three thousand, and Welch's promise of "getting a million members truly dedicated to the things in which we believe" became a forlorn hope.[58]

In 1961, when the movement was less than three years old and Welch's bête noire, Dwight Eisenhower, was retired, a youthful and articulate President John F. Kennedy gave new life to the old Cold War rhetoric by declaring that "this generation" is by "necessity rather than choice" the "watchmen on the walls of world freedom."[59]

Kennedy, of course, was an Irish Catholic. He was the first Catholic elected to the presidency, and his success in grasping the Democratic nomination and then defeating Vice-President Richard Nixon to reach the White House marked yet another way in which the old nativism had lost its appeal.

As recently as 1948, in response to a Gallup Poll question asking if people would vote for a "well-qualified person" who "happened to be Catholic" if nominated for president, 34 percent of Protestants had said "no." Some Democratic insiders, including Jim Farley, had dismissed Kennedy as a candidate in the late 1950s because "America is not ready for a Catholic." Acutely aware of the problem, John F. Kennedy had made it clear when he began his race in 1958 that "I believe . . . that separation of church and state is fundamental to our American . . . heritage." As public awareness of JFK's religion increased during his preconvention campaigning, the ancient fears and hatreds did seem to affect his standing in the public opinion surveys. But he handled the problem adroitly throughout the primaries. He told students at one fundamentalist institution that if he received a political directive from his archbishop, "I simply would not obey it." He told a television audience during the West Virginia primary that he "would not take orders from any Pope, Cardinal, Bishop or priest." He said that a president who did not uphold his oath to support separation of church and state not only "committed a crime against the constitution" but "committed a sin against God." He carried 61 percent of the vote in West Virginia.[60]

Once Kennedy was nominated, the religious question did not disappear. Throughout his campaign he had to respond to the old charges that Roman Catholicism was guilty of bigotry and a threat to democracy. A Minnesota Baptist convention declared Catholicism "as serious a threat to America as atheistic Communism." But the most influential opponents of this Catholic candidate were different from those nativist and fundamentalist adversaries confronting Al Smith in 1928. The old antialien animus was now but a weakened remnant from the past; the critics of John Kennedy were establishment Protestants. An organization of prominent clergymen, the National Council of Citizens for Religious Freedom, a group that included Norman Vincent Peale and editors of major Protestant publications, insisted that no Catholic could be free of the Church hierarchy's "determined efforts . . . to break the wall of separation of church and state." Peale, who argued that it was "inconceivable" that a Roman Catholic president would not be "under extreme pressure from the hierarchy of his church," went farther than such Protestant notables as Eugene Carson Blake of the United Presbyterians or Bishop G. Bromley Oxnam of the Methodists. But all of them, and members of a group titled Protestants and Other Americans United on Separation of Church and State, admitted to "being uneasy" about a Catholic in the White House. These were not responses by traditional nativists, yet they raised the old questions.[61]

It was only when Kennedy addressed the Ministerial Association of Greater Houston on 12 September 1960 that he finally overcame the religious problem. "I am wholly opposed to the state being used by any religious groups," he said, "I am not a Catholic candidate for President, I am the Democratic Party's candidate . . . who happens also to be a Catholic. I do not speak for my Church on public matters, and the Church does not speak for me."[62]

On election day, Kennedy profited from support by Catholics, even as he had in the primaries, when Wisconsin Catholics crossed over from the Republican camp to engage in what one columnist characterized as religious "bloc-voting." In the presidential race, he carried 80 percent of the Catholic vote (which was some 20 percent of the total) although this included only 50 percent of the German Catholic subcommunity. He did appear to lose a substantial number of Protestant Democratic votes; by one estimate—George Gallup's—he carried only 38 percent of the Protestant constituency; in the view of another analyst, it was 46 percent. But his level of support among Jews and blacks was higher than among Catholics, whom he had helped to bring back to the Democratic party in large numbers after they had defected to the GOP in the Eisenhower years. It was also significant that many more Protestants voted for Kennedy than Catholics and Jews combined. The young, eloquent, affluent war hero from New England, of course, was a very different figure than Al Smith, that earlier Catholic aspirant for the presidency. But John Kennedy's successful race was also a monument to how far the nation had come from the nativist passions of yesterday.[63]

Kennedy had triumphed over Richard Nixon in a land in which assaults on "alien" religious and ethnic groups were disappearing. But he played a major role in leading the fight against ideological enemies abroad. Still, JFK's militant anticommunist foreign policy did not help the Birch Society's crusade against un-American ideologists at home.

Under Kennedy, the thaw in relations between the United States and USSR, much celebrated when Nikita Khrushchev paid his lengthy and cordial visit to America in 1958, was over. Fidel Castro's victory in Cuba, Viet Cong successes in Vietnam against an American-backed regime, and the building of the Berlin Wall added impetus to JFK's insistence on building American military strength —"paying any price, bearing any burden"—to check what he considered the spread of communism. The Cuban missile crisis of 1962 brought the United States and the Soviet Union to the brink of nuclear war. But even then, Robert Welch's brand of frantic anticommunism had little impact. Public opinion might support a foreign policy aimed at the external enemy, but there was no longer a setting for an attack on the alien enemy within. Welch and his spokesmen thrashed about for an issue to energize their fading crusade throughout the decade. The effort to indict the triumphant civil rights movement as communist-inspired had few takers in 1964. The attack on opponents of the Vietnam War, after U.S. intervention on the ground in 1965, was lost in a larger national debate over the nature of the war and the tactics of its critics. The Birch Society was becoming irrelevant even in an age of political and social turmoil. The antialien slogans of the countersubversive activists no longer had a major audience in America.

For a time, the John Birch Society had made a modest impact among that relatively small number of people responding to the themes of the postwar Red Scare and persevering after the death of McCarthyism. But there were differences between Birchers and the McCarthyite majority. Although Welch had used McCarthy-like rhetoric in exposing "the leaders of Communism [who] come from . . . the wealthy and best educated classes" and had referred to "Harvard accents in Communist circles in America," survey data on the social base of the radical Right suggest that his members were well-educated and had higher incomes and occupational status than most Americans. The McCarthyite majority was a different breed. The self-made millionaires that Welch initially recruited to the cause may not have come from the old elites, but they remained at the center of the movement. In 1967, the National Council of twenty-four included fourteen company presidents, three physicians, and a banker.

With this affluent constituency, the society had made some political gains in a few regions, notably when activist John H. Rousselot of California was elected to Congress and addressed the House of Representatives on the beliefs and principles of the John Birch

Society. Living in areas of rapid growth and social disorganization, Birchers had found comfort in Robert Welch's answers to their questions. They wondered how America could have won the world war but lost the peace, how spokesmen for "foreign" ideas and proponents of social disorder could have gained so much authority in government, the media, and academia. Robert Welch at first had provided a vehicle for their anger and fear. But Welch's conspiratorial fantasies turned away many of these people by the late 1960s.

The society continued to function through the 1970s, and American Opinion Libraries remained fully staffed in many communities in the mid-1980s. Yet the promise of a new national crusade against the alien ideologists foundered. Some former members of the John Birch Society or its front groups did emerge as part of the "New Right" in the early 1980s, attacking the "collectivists" once again and supporting a military and foreign policy that would "stand tall" against the "evil empire" of communism. But they were no longer trafficking in antialien rhetoric, no longer accusing enemies of being "Comsymps," agents of subversion. In the end, the Birch Society could not revive the Red Scare; that had ended with McCarthy. It proved to be only the most publicized of many anticommunist efforts in the 1960s, perhaps the last convulsive gasps of this form of antialien extremism in American history.[64]

Some of the other efforts were literary. These included John H. Stormer's book *None Dare Call It Treason*, featured in JBS reading rooms as "the carefully documented story of America's retreat from victory." It sold over 3 million copies in 1964 alone. There was also Ezra Taft Benson's *An Enemy Hath Done This*, which portrayed civil rights as a "tool of communist deception," and E. Merrill Root's two volumes, *Collectivism on the Campus* and *Brainwashing in the High Schools*. Other anticommunists used the electronic media. There were the Life Line radio broadcasts, sponsored on five hundred stations by oil billionaire H. L. Hunt. There were the radio reports of Major Edgar C. Bundy's Church League of America and the radio and televised "Dan Smoot Report," offered by a former FBI agent and former Hunt employee. But there were also efforts in the 1950s and 1960s to build movements beyond the Birch Society, groups reminiscent of some earlier organizations. They proved either receptacles for crazies or pale shadows of yesterday's antialien successes.[65]

★★★

Neo-Nazis and Other Extremists

The most aberrant "movements" recalled the quasi-fascist schemes of the would-be dictators of the 1930s. The National Renaissance party (NRP) was a self-proclaimed neo-Nazi organization. Its "elite guard" wore dark caps and trousers and brassards with lightning bolts on them. Its *Bulletin* advertised itself in the 1950s as "the only Fascist publication in America" and exclaimed: "What Hitler accomplished in Europe, the National Renaissance Party shall yet accomplish in America." Its founder, James H. Madole, warned of the "colored hordes in Africa and Asia" and of the sinister machinations of "the Jewish Race, a completely Alien race . . . the motivating financial and intellectual force behind Communism." His "program" was devoted to "the preservation and advancement of the culturally dominant White Aryan Race," which, for Madole, included "Celts, Latin and Slavic peoples." He advocated the suppression of Jews (who would be deprived of American citizenship), the deportation of blacks, Asiatics, and Puerto Ricans, and the "alliance of American technology with German scientific and military genius" to stop communism. Several NRP members had been associated with Coughlin's Christian Front before World War II, but the total membership remained minuscule. The Renaissance Guard was led by Matt Koehl, Jr., who became head of the American Nazi party in the late 1960s.[66]

The Nazi organization was founded in 1958 by George Lincoln Rockwell, a former navy flyer and a sometime artist. Rockwell totally dominated his group until he was shot to death by a party member in 1967. Influenced, he said, by Joseph McCarthy and Gerald L. K. Smith as well as Hitler, he believed that a Jewish-communist conspiracy was attempting to subvert America through racial integration and miscegenation. "I don't hate niggers any more than I hate monkeys," he wrote. "But they don't belong out here on the streets with our women." He declared that "about ninety per cent of all Jews are traitors" and should be gassed. These "Jewish Bolsheviks" were aiding "the niggers rampaging in the streets" (who were led by "Martin Luther Coon"), the "queers," the anarchist students, and other enemies of "Decent White Christian America." But there was no point in looking to the John Birch Society for relief. Rockwell loathed "Rabbit Welch" as much as he did the other aliens, and he variously equated "Birchers and Communists" and "Birchers and the Little League Kosher Conservatives" in his harangues. The American Nazi party never attracted more than a few hundred members, but George Rockwell's flamboyant personality and his clever if venomous stunts often produced headlines. Besides producing and distributing leaflets and his newspaper, he drove a "hate bus" through the South (to counter integrationist Freedom Riders), and he tried to picket the movie *Exodus* in eastern cities. Even in death he was controversial; his followers attempted to bury him in a U.S. military cemetery clothed in his Nazi uniform.[67]

These modern disciples of Adolf Hitler were no more influential than the William Dudley Pelleys and Art J. Smiths of the early 1930s. Nor was Robert Bolivar DePugh, the Missouri businessman who founded the Minutemen in 1960. This was a "patriotic," paramilitary secret society dedicated to protecting America from communist invasion from abroad and communist subversion at home. If somewhat larger than the other tiny sects, the Minutemen never attracted more than five to six thousand followers, although DePugh claimed five times that number. Like some paramilitary groups of the 1970s and 1980s, members trained with rifles and other weapons, studied guerrilla tactics, and secreted arms in remote areas to be used when the Reds invaded. They endorsed the work of the National Rifle Association, embracing as a keystone of their program resistance to "the passage of laws which regulate the private ownership of firearms or which detract from the individual's ability to defend his family and personal property."[68]

Unlike some survivalists (groups of gun-toting loners in the West and Southwest) of the next decade, the Minutemen's ideology was overtly antialien. Members were called on to "resist and expose the spread of Communist influence within our national leadership," investigate "by means of our secret members" any "infiltration of Communist sympathizers into any American organization," and detect and "expose disloyalty in the American defense effort." Pamphlets asked: "What do you really know about the Congressman, State Senator or State Representative from your district? Could these men have been indoctrinated in Communist ideology?" If the Minutemen occasionally cooperated with anti-Semitic activists, their major enemies were communists. But these old fears of foreign conspirators did not work for the Minutemen any better than for the other would-be mass organizations of the

1960s. The group drew in only a handful of white Protestant men, most of them blue-collar workers, along with a number of self-interested gunshop owners. After its leaders were sentenced for violating the Federal Firearms Act, the Minutemen gradually disappeared from the national scene.[69]

The quasi-fascistic movements were only part of a proliferation of right-wing organizations appearing for a time in the 1960s. One study listed almost three hundred such groups. Some seemed to be echoes of the nativist past, emerging again in the context of the civil rights crusade and the rise of black power, the new feminism, the student rebellions, and the emergence of gay rights. In a time when racial relations and sexual relations were undergoing dramatic changes, when the "youth culture" offered traumatic new challenges to traditional arrangements, antialien movements reminiscent of forebears in the nineteenth century and the 1920s could be expected. Yet despite the social upheavals of these years, the new movements had little attraction. The various neo–Ku Klux Klan groups made news when members were pictured in hoods and involved in violent resistance to integration, but their total following never exceeded sixty thousand by decade's end. Many more poor white southerners may have endorsed some of their activities during the civil rights revolution, but relatively few committed themselves to the cause. Of course, this collective version of the Klan was not a nativist movement like the great Klan of the 1920s. It focused almost exclusively on the crisis in racial relations and served as just another instrument in the rear-guard actions of defeated poor white segregationists. Anti-Catholic and anti-immigrant anthems had lost their audience long before, and if anti-Semitic slogans were still used by some extremists, there was no chance of a nativist revival even in the years of historic disarray. In fact, antiblack rhetoric and attitudes may have played a double role for some contemporary racists, serving as well as a way of discharging nativist xenophobia now deemed inappropriate in a land where white ethnic "aliens" were part of mainstream culture. When a new Know Nothing Society was formed in the summer of 1965, this secret order—unlike its namesake—was designed as an anticommunist movement, hopeful of infiltrating left-wing organizations and checkmating Red conspirators. It never recruited more than a handful of members. The old nativistic antialienism was buried; the newer anticommunist version was on its deathbed.[70]

Among the last notable practitioners of anticommunist remedies were religio-political spokesmen appealing to those who feared Marxism as the work of the devil, the enemy of Christian faith. There was a long tradition of such appeals in America, and some of the older ministerial anticommunists, particularly Gerald L. K. Smith, still found a following through the 1960s.

Nearing age sixty-six in 1964, Smith had lived in style, reputedly maintaining homes in Tulsa and Los Angeles before purchasing 167 acres of land in the little mountain town of Eureka Springs, Arkansas. There he would build an elaborate house, although keeping a residence in California for the winter. He lived lavishly in Eureka Springs, even acquiring a chauffeur-driven Lincoln limousine. He focused his energies on the construction of an enormous, seven-story, ivory-white statue called *The Christ of the Ozarks*. He also produced annual performances of what he called "The Great Passion Play." This was a remarkable show involving hundreds of actors and actresses and dozens of animals on a set the length of a football field; the play described Jews as the killers of Christ.

Retaining the magnetism, confidence, and vitality of his youth, he continued to publish the *Cross and the Flag*, which was replete with his usual anti-Semitic attacks as well as racist slurs against blacks. Gerald Smith never wavered from the malevolent fantasy world he had constructed in his earlier years concerning sinister Jewish conspiracies. The Jews had destroyed McCarthy, he argued. They were behind the assassination of John F. Kennedy. In one issue, his paper reported, "even Communist Poland is fed up with Jewish control." On another occasion, it referred to "Negroes as fundamentally an inferior race"; without whites they "would never have got past the loin cloth or the G-String." No Christian southerner, Smith wrote, "hates the Negro. He recognizes in the Negro a child race, fresh from the jungle, not sufficiently matured to take responsibility for running communities."[71]

Smith was still at work throughout the decade, but other leaders appeared on the scene in these years. The growth of radio and television gave such men additional opportunities for celebrity and profit.

In the past, Protestant fundamentalist preachers had infused their antialien work with anti-Catholic and anti-Semitic slogans. This was still true of the aging Reverend Carl McIntire, a radio preacher who had organized the right-wing American Council of Christian

Churches in 1941 to combat "religious modernism" and "expose Communist infiltration of the Church." An ultrafundamentalist whose extremist rhetoric and dubious personal qualities had alienated even rightist fund-raisers—one called him a "scoundrel and a crook"—McIntire still had a network of almost six hundred stations for his "Twentieth Century Reformation Hour" broadcasts offering "a religious indictment of the Communist conspiracy." McIntire was the exception, a remnant of a fading past. The new crusaders avoided alienating any Christians in their audience. Like Robert Welch, their sole enemy was "the Communist."[72]

★★★

The Christian Right in the 1960s

The best known of these newcomers on the Christian Right were Dr. Fred Schwarz and the Reverend Billy James Hargis. Schwarz was an Australian physician, the son of a Pentecostal preacher, a Christian evangelist who maintained a home in Sydney but came to America to organize the Christian Anti-Communist Crusade in 1952. An impressive platform speaker, Schwarz was also an effective polemicist; his *You Can Trust the Communists (To Be Communists)* went through ten hard-cover printings in 1960, selling over 1 million copies. Dr. Schwarz insisted that the only way to check the spread of communism was to organize study groups, "schools" of anticommunism. "Communism should be taught," he wrote, "but it should be taught with a moral directive . . . as a system of tyranny. The object of the teaching should be to protect the students against the deceptive subtleties of the Communist dialectic." Schwarz found a following among upper-status business and professional people, particularly in California and the Southwest. Almost 80 percent of the "students" interviewed at one of his schools in the San Francisco Bay area were college graduates. The vast majority were white Protestants. They obviously were not involved because of economic woes or status resentments, motivating factors in antialien movements across history, present as well in McCarthyism. Instead, they represented a very conservative constituency in regions undergoing sudden expansion. They were men and women exposed to "strains produced by institutional instability that comes with rapid economic growth," as a group of

Stanford researchers who studied the crusade were to put it. Comfortable but fearful, like the Birchers they equated their good fortune with a virtuous commitment to the American dream. They looked with anxiety at the change around them in their communities and in the nation. As did Robert Welch for his followers, Schwarz offered an explanation for their anxieties. They shared his fear of internal subversion. They responded to his argument about "the Communist orientation of intellectuals found in the ivy cloisters of the colleges and universities." They heard him repeat his assault on "thousands" of Protestant ministers included "in the Communist apparatus." By the end of the 1960s, Schwarz's crusade had collected almost $3 million, with donors including banks, corporations, even Rotary Clubs.[73]

More passionate and more famous than Fred Schwarz was Billy James Hargis. "Dr." Hargis, as he was referred to by aides and in his publications, was ordained a minister in the Disciples of Christ church in 1943 at age eighteen after attending Ozark Bible College in Arkansas for a year. He received honorary doctorates from the Defender Seminary in Puerto Rico and Bob Jones University. In 1950 he left his pastorate to devote all his energies to building "a force for God and against Communism: I consider it my Christian responsibility to fight Godless, atheistic Communism because I want to save this nation." Incorporating his organization in Oklahoma as a "religious, non-profit making body," he built a large audience as a radio preacher. The Christian Crusade, which he developed to spread his political gospel, proved the most lucrative fundraising venture on the radical Right of the 1960s. By 1961, he was taking in almost a million dollars a year. He lived in a comfortable "parsonage," traveled in a luxuriously reconditioned Greyhound bus, and purchased a resort hotel in Colorado as site of the Christian Crusade's Summer Youth Anti-Communist University. He marketed Hargis pamphlets, films, records, songs, and sayings. He instituted Hargis Anti-Communist Leadership Schools.

With headquarters in Tulsa, Billy James Hargis circulated a weekly newspaper and authored a book, *Communist America—Must It Be?* which echoed his radio themes. He attacked the United Nations, "that traitorous outfit in New York City," and raised questions about civil rights, a "crisis bred in the pits of Communist debauchery and conspiracy . . . for segregation is a law of God." He assaulted political leadership: "America is being sold out by treasonous leaders," he wrote, "America is being surrendered to the enemy by a deceived people." Nazi George Lincoln Rockwell had been "a front, a stooge for liberals"; John F. Kennedy had been a tool of "Harvard radical eggheads." The only "salvation from satanistic Communism," he insisted, is "an immediate return to the faith of our Fathers in Jesus Christ, Son of God." This Protestant fundamentalist creed informed all his work; he attacked the National Council of Churches as "Treason against God and Country" and continuously reminded listeners that "America is and always has been a Christian nation." It was a compelling message to his audience of white, working-class Protestants, people with less education than most, a different following than those who responded to Welch or Schwarz, a group whose parents might have joined the Klan of the 1920s.[74]

Hargis acknowledged his debt to earlier right-wing extremists such as Gerald Winrod. He praised the work of Robert Welch, "a Great American," and other contemporary anticommunists in the 1960s. In his assaults on "left-wing liberals" and "the Liberal Establishment," in his shrewd manipulation of Christian rhetoric in the service of an ultraconservative ideology, and in his brilliant use of the media to mobilize funds and followers for his cause, he offered a model for future evangelical preachers who would reach millions with their television ministries in the next decades and make an impact on larger political affairs. But the Protestant fundamentalist media masters of the 1970s and 1980s, for all their warnings about collectivist threats at home and Soviet expansion abroad, would not stress the danger of a subversive communist presence inside America as did Hargis. It is a subtle difference but of central importance in the history of right-wing, antialien activities in America. By the late 1960s, the fear of alien and un-American conspirators was losing its appeal even for the most fervent antialiens of earlier years.

At first glance, it seems curious that this should be so. By 1968, the United States had experienced a stunning sequence of social and political shocks in the preceding three years. There were the chain of "civil disturbances" in inner-city communities, which set whole neighborhoods ablaze and caused the mobilization of National Guard and elite paratroop divisions in major metropolitan areas. There were the succession of dramatic confrontations on college campuses across the land, a staple of evening television news.

There was the growing protest against the war in Vietnam, which recruited hundreds of thousands to demonstrations in Washington, New York, and other cities and led to widespread civil disobedience. There was the virtual resignation of President Lyndon Johnson on the war issue in March and then the epic public tragedies of April and June: the assassinations of Martin Luther King, Jr., and Senator Robert Kennedy. If ever the social fabric of America seemed to be unraveling it was in 1968. In the past, such a period of upheaval might have served as a setting for new forms of anti-alienism. This time, the crisis produced very different political responses. The most powerful right-wing movements that eventually emerged from that time of troubles—and the unhappy years that would follow—were outside the tradition of the old movements. Antialien activities as they had been known in America were coming to an end. They would be replaced by a new crusade against a different set of enemies offered by a New Right.

CHAPTER 15

★ ★

THE DECLINE OF
ANTIALIENISM, THE RISE
OF A NEW RIGHT,
1968–1986

THE DECLINE OF the antialien impulse was revealed in that year of unparalleled trauma and tragedy, 1968. It would mark a major change in the history of right-wing movements in America.

In the theater of national television in April, Americans witnessed the most convulsive and violent of all campus confrontations, the strike at Columbia University. The fiery leader of the Students for a Democratic Society (SDS) "action faction" had proposed the "radicalization of students . . . showing them how our lives are unfree in this country." Five buildings were occupied on the Columbia campus, and for eight days the siege continued. It became a fixture on national news. Red flags flew from the barricaded structures; famous journalists, poets, scholars, and writers were pictured being hauled up onto ledges to meet with the rebels. It was a bizarre spectacle, capped by a police assault in which one hundred students were injured and five hundred arrested, leading in turn to a strike enveloping the entire institution.

Later that month, in the days following the assassination of Martin Luther King, urban disorders exploded in black central city communities across America. Plumes of smoke from the fires in the Washington ghetto darkened the sky over the congressional buildings. The Capitol itself was surrounded by troops, standing in front of a protective wall of sandbags.

Throughout the spring, the climate of confrontation and the

threat of violence permeated the nation. These were days when millions still grappled with the shock of the Tet offensive in Vietnam and received the somber daily casualty dispatches from Southeast Asia, mounting toward sixteen thousand more dead by year's end.

Yet it was a presidential election year. By January the Coalition for a Democratic Alternative had offered Eugene McCarthy as an antiwar candidate challenging President Lyndon Johnson in the primaries. The collegians responding to this new "McCarthy Movement" offered a different public picture of activist youth than in the campus sit-ins. But though many of them bitterly resented Senator Robert Kennedy's late-blooming antiwar candidacy when it was announced in March, for it soon eclipsed their campaign and led to a chain of primary victories for the dead president's brother, it was clear after RFK's assassination in California two months before the Democratic convention that Eugene McCarthy could not be a viable candidate for president. With Johnson having faced the inevitable and taken himself out of the race, it was Vice-President Hubert Humphrey who would carry the administration's war policy to the chaotic nominating meeting in Chicago in August. There he would be the inevitable choice of his party. Throughout the summer, many resistors laid plans to meet "the establishment" in a Chicago showdown on the war.

The convention was catastrophic for the party and a bitter microcosm of the confusion, hostility, generational mistrust, and ideological divisions that had been growing for half a decade. As demonstrators shouted, "the whole world is watching," the police riot in front of the Conrad Hilton Hotel provided a grisly spectacle on the major networks: the forces of "law and order" unleashed against the opponents of the war, water cannon and billy clubs smashing the young critics of American society and its values. The protestors in Grant Park that week were a cross-section of antiwar activists and other dissidents, but the media had featured the most passionate or the most flamboyant figures. The "Yippies," a tiny sect of self-advertisers who represented the nihilistic extreme of "the movement," a group who reveled in gestures of contempt for the system and nominated a pig as their presidential candidate, knew how to attract the cameras. Yippie Jerry Rubin, whose *Do It!* was published in 1970 with the injunction "read this book stoned," and featured chapters with such titles as "Fuck God" and "Sirhan

Sirhan is a Yippie," noted that "every revolutionary needs a color TV . . . Walter Cronkite is the radicals' best organizer." With such "leaders" seemingly prominent, it was not surprising that much of "the whole world" that was watching the Chicago confrontation sided against the demonstrators. McCarthy voters in the primaries told interviewers that they had been right: the army must be brought home from Vietnam to put down destructive mobs like the ones at the Democratic convention. For many, the police attack appeared at first a satisfactory ritual spanking of those "kids" who denounced their government, rejected their parents, and reviled the American way.

★★★

George Wallace and the American Independent Party

Who would defend "America" and its traditional values? Who would take on those angry activists scrawling "Amerikkka" on college classroom walls? Hubert Humphrey's voice was muffled by the divisions in his party and his own ambivalence about the war. Richard Nixon, emerging once more to seize the Republican nomination in a year when the GOP seemed destined to win because of conflicts in the camp of its opponent, now tried to mask his reputation as an anticommunist and a political gut fighter. The "Old Nixon" had made many enemies; the "New Nixon" would use the rhetoric of moderation. It remained for a third-party candidate to emerge as the scourge of the new radicals. Governor George Wallace of Alabama and his American Independent party promised a return to discipline and a celebration of the old virtues while providing scathing denunciations of the dissidents who rejected patriotism and the American way of life.

Was Wallace leading a new nativist movement? Some scholars insisted that he was not only a "preservatist" but a racist appealing to bigots, a right-wing extremist trafficking in antidemocratic, repressive rhetoric, a practitioner of the "new nativism" conjuring up new conspiracy theories to explain America's social disorder. But if George Wallace outraged intellectuals and alarmed students of extremism and anti-Semitism at the time, it seems clear that he cannot be placed in the tradition of antialien leaders in American history. He did speak to the fears, jealousies, and hostility of an audience whose ancestors might have been protectors and fugitives in an earlier age, embracing the nativist fraternities of the nineteenth century, the great Klan of the 1920s, or even the Coughlin movement of the 1930s. He brilliantly shaped his inflammatory speeches around attacks on urban elites and their angry radical children as might such spokesmen of the past. Still, he avoided the overt antialien appeals of nativists, inverted nativists, and anticommunists.[1]

Wallace's followers were enraged by the spectacle of an apparently affluent youth who seemed to reject an America that made their life so easy. They were incensed that a war against a tiny nation apparently could not be won, that a reform agenda in race relations asked them for sacrifices which others might avoid. They responded to the New Left's bitter critique of American values as they did the Viet Cong flags at antiwar rallies: with an outpouring of angry invective and paeans to patriotism. George Wallace was one of them, a working-class leader for a working-class constituency, who knew which themes to use in his role as defender of the forgotten "real" Americans. But he knew that their passions need not and could not be turned against the old victims of antialienism.

He used no anti-Catholic or antiethnic arguments. Indeed, part of his audience was found in those blue-collar precincts where descendents of Irish Catholic and southeastern European immigrants lived and worked. These were people proud of their heritage and now both confident enough in their American role and angry enough at their lack of influence that they would become part of that "rise of the unmeltable ethnics" Michael Novak described in 1971. They put their ethnic pride on their bumper stickers, and Wallace spoke to their dreams and their resentments. He also used no overt or covert anti-Semitic slogans. He did not even use racist appeals, although he had emerged on the national political scene in the early 1960s as one who promised to "make race the basis of politics" in Alabama, as the author of the ugly vow "never to be outniggered again," as he claimed to have been in his first campaign in 1958. He did assail "forced busing" to achieve integration in big city northern schools. But this was a shrewd Populist plea, a response to the frustrated rage of those who felt they were expected to pay a price for the end of racial injustice that "limousine liberals"—safely ensconced in comfortable white suburbs—would not have to pay.

He did attack welfare mothers "breeding children as a cash crop." But this was part of his appeal to groups who felt left behind or left out, neither fully profiting from the new affluence of the Kennedy-Johnson economic boom that had raised real incomes in the mid-1960s nor receiving the full benefits of the social programs put in place during Johnson's Great Society.[2]

George Wallace said he was speaking for "my cab drivers, barbers, beauticians," for "the policeman on the beat, the man in the textile mill, the steel worker, the rubber worker, the little businessman," for "the average man on the street." Buffeted by so many unexpected, disorienting, and threatening developments since the early 1960s, these "average folk" found a champion in Wallace. He won 43 percent of the Democratic vote in the Maryland primary and 34 percent in Wisconsin before forming his new party. He had the support of 21 percent of the entire electorate in national polls by September. He told his listeners that it was their sons who had been sent to fight and die in Vietnam; America needed such patriots, but the children of affluence had refused to defend their country yet were now praised in the press for burning their draft cards and defiling the flag. He told his followers that they were the heart and soul of the great nation; they worked hard, paid their taxes, took care of their families. But now they were being ignored and pushed around by the agents of big government and big business, people who were coddling welfare bums when they were not busy protecting their radical children or their own predatory special interests. The "pointy headed bureaucrats with their briefcases," he told his rallies, should be "thrown into the Potomac." His words were met with tumultuous cheers.[3]

Wallace won the support of millions. Some may have been Birchers, disciples of Hargis, members of or sympathizers with the contemporary Klan, right-wingers of other persuasions. They embraced his calls for "law and order" as code words for violence and the repression of their enemies. They shouted with approval when he promised that if demonstrators "lay down in front of my car, it will be the last car they ever lay down in front of." But these groups remained a small fragment of the population. Their endorsement could not explain his success.

The majority in George Wallace's movement responded to his visceral appeal to the plight of the virtuous underdogs in a world turned upside down. They were the good folk who still believed in the American dream but who felt they lived now in a land where elites and opinion leaders had abandoned the old faith and where a bloated government used its power to impose its will on them while lacking the conviction to pursue the war in Asia to a successful conclusion. Wallace and the Wallace movement cannot be explained as just another episode in the history of bigotry. The leader would return to the Alabama governorship in less than a decade and a half with the support of blacks; many of his followers at the time told pollsters that their second choice after Wallace had been Robert Kennedy. The Wallace majority need not and would not accept the old antialien appeals. The communists were the enemy in Vietnam, but neither the "bureaucrats" not those "long hairs and pot smokers breaking the law in the colleges" were called Comsymps by Wallace. Neither the ancient religious and ethnic animus nor the more recent assault on alien ideologists within had a part in his meteoric rise in the summer of 1968. In earlier years, social upheaval might have elicited a different response by such a leader, but the attack on "un-American activities" now seemed part of the past.

Nowhere could this be seen more clearly than when the Yippies were called before the House Un-American Activities Committee for the second time in the fall of 1968. Earlier, Rubin had "testified" wearing an American revolutionary war costume and a tricornered hat. He claimed to have arrived on Capitol Hill "stoned" and had been prevented from distributing his statement, which turned out to be copies of the Declaration of Independence that he had found in a San Francisco American Opinion Bookstore of the John Birch Society. He said that when "one member of the Communist Party" had told his group that "HUAC had destroyed reputations overnight and forced people to lose their jobs," the response was: "Reputations? We have no reputations to lose. Jobs? We have no jobs. How could HUAC hurt us? What names could they call us? Communists? Anarchists? Traitors? . . . The worse the better." Now he appeared at the House Office Building in new garb: the beret of the quasi-military Black Panthers, a bandolier with live bullets around his chest, headband, beads, cowbells, and black Viet Cong pajamas with a toy M-16 rifle on his shoulder. His cohort, Abbie Hoffman, was even more provocative. He wore a shirt made out of the American flag. When the befuddled HUAC probers tried to link this strange tribe to the Communist party, the "witnesses" laughed and shouted obscenities. These radicals, who had written that "ideology is a brain disease," who dismissed the communists as they did the committee, who insisted that because Santa Claus gives everything away free he must be "a stoned Commie . . . Santa represents the Red Peril," were the self-conscious wild men of the Left. But they demonstrated why the larger, serious movement could not be subjected to the politics of innuendo by those last remnants of the Red Scare interrogators.[4]

★★★

The Upheavals of the 1960s, the Defeats of the 1970s

The New Left was nonideological; it was an indigenous American radical movement that did not owe its origins to any "alien" inspiration. Although "red diaper babies" from the Communist party's W. E. B. DuBois Clubs, Trotskyists from the Socialist Workers party youth affiliate, the Young Socialist Alliance, and Maoists from the Progressive Labor party's Workers-Student Alliance did operate on the margins of events, the main thrust of the New Left had little to do with these sects. When the ideologists were allowed into the Students for a Democratic Society, their sectarian struggles helped to rip this organization to shreds by 1969, but the larger "movement" hardly noticed that SDS was gone.

Marxists might believe that the end justifies the means, but most new American radicals insisted that the means would create the ends. It was existential politics in which action against a despised old order would itself create new conditions. The *U.S. News and World Report* issued a book titled *Communism and the New Left: What They're Up to Now* in 1969, but this was a strained and pointless linkage. Even if there had been some life left in the McCarthyite Right, it could have found little leverage in an attack on these activists of the Left. Some of them might fly the flag of the Viet Cong enemy and rip up the stars and stripes, reject the individualist ethos as soul-destroying and alienating, revile the nuclear family and celebrate communal lifestyles, scorn careerism and upward mobility, but they were not "alien" ideologists. Despite the occasional cries of "America—Love It or Leave It," they would not be assailed as "Reds" or "Commies." Their activities might be remembered with anger by Americans turning back to "traditional values" and old-time patriotism a decade later, but they could not be accused of being "un-American" at the time.

In any case, there were too many of them; hundreds of thousands had been involved in demonstrations on campuses from coast to coast. Although some were intolerant, engaging in a kind of McCarthyism of the Left during intimidating college confrontations, practicing a politics of morality in which only their side had the truth and could impose it on others, the "movement" was much more than its most hostile and passionate spokesmen. It involved a wide spectrum of people calling for changes in America. Many were full-blown critics of the values of the culture, but others were involved only because of opposition to the war or were initially attracted by civil rights or the crusades for campus reform. George Wallace used the "protestors" to help energize his campaign. They were convenient scapegoats to be manipulated in a dozen televised confrontations during his cunning speaking tours of the colleges. His followers included a large percentage of young people; "they're going to find out," he had exclaimed, "that there are a lot of rednecks in this country." They embraced his simplistic explanation for the emergence of the protest, but in fact it was a complex phenomenon. For though some of the celebrities of the activist era would prove to be only self-interested posturers—Jerry Rubin reappearing the next decade as a "venture capitalist" marketing singles parties at which upwardly mobile young affluents could make social and business contacts—the mainstream leaders of the movement did consider, if only briefly, a serious agenda. They called for commitment in service of causes greater than self. They challenged the arrangements in contemporary America, but they were impervious to attacks as "un-American." Anticommunism could not explain the social upheavals of the 1960s.[5]

Richard Nixon, erstwhile ally of Joe McCarthy, understood this when he won his hair-thin victory in November. If his attorney-general designate, John Mitchell, warned his countrymen to "watch what we do," not listen to "what we say," the new president himself told the inaugural audience that "we must stop shouting at one another." Like his predecessor, Nixon might believe that foreign enemies were behind some of the demonstrations in the streets, but he avoided making a major public issue out of the old alien fears, for that would be a road to nowhere in 1969. His purpose, he said, was to heal the wounds in the society, to heed the plea on the sign he had seen during the campaign, to "bring us together."

The Nixon years, of course, were hardly free of passionate protest. In the spring of 1970, after the "Cambodian incursion" elicited widespread fears that the administration was seeking to widen the war, upheavals rocked more than two hundred campuses. The student deaths during confrontations at Kent State and Jackson State heightened the sense of national crisis. At many universities, barricades blocked roads, the president was hung in effigy, classes were canceled. At Syracuse, a two-story sign on the student government building showed a clenched fist and the injunction "By Any Means Necessary." But in Washington, where thousands of protestors had gathered, a shaken Richard Nixon—visiting student activists at the Lincoln Memorial in a strange foray at five in the morning—could relate to Syracusans there only by inquiring about the prospects for the Orange football team. The Nixon administration could not understand the protest. It arrested many dissidents that week. But it continued to steer clear of the overt red-baiting of yesterday, and already it had set into motion policies that would help to end the campus disorder while confounding critics on the Right.[6]

The president's "secret plan" to end the war in Vietnam, which he refused to reveal during the 1968 campaign, turned out to be American disengagement. It was a recognition that the war could not be won by any prudent means. "Vietnamization" would put the combat burden on the twice-defeated Army of the Republic of Vietnam (ARVN), which had been whipped while fighting alongside the French in the 1950s; its defeat at the hands of communist guerrillas by 1965 had been the reason for American involvement on the ground. Now, in creating the fiction of an ARVN capable of defending itself, the Nixon team was accepting the inevitable, although it vigorously denied that it would tolerate the defeat of America's clients in Vietnam. Through the staged withdrawal of U.S. troops and by a combination of military and diplomatic initiatives, it sought some way out of the dilemma that had devoured its predecessors. The last troops were scheduled to leave in time for Nixon's reelection campaign. The draft calls no longer threatened college students; the protests declined. The political, military, and moral crisis that had become the war, a running sore that was poisoning the body politic, was ending.

But it would be a difficult time for many on the Right. Those who had shuddered when Harry Truman rejected the tradition of "no substitute for victory" would squirm about the so-called "Vietnam bug-out," this time the fatal prelude to defeat and not to the status quo antebellum as in Korea. Militants who had endorsed Richard Nixon's anticommunist rhetoric in the past would have an even harder time accepting his other major foreign policy initiatives: the "opening to China" and detente with the Soviet Union. When the old China lobby spokesman visited Peking, when the foe of atheistic communism spoke of an end to the Cold War with the USSR, his former adversaries were confused, his right-wing supporters befuddled. It worked because it was moral judo; only the famous anticommunist could reach out to the communists. But in communities where the "movement" had taken root, the seeming paradox of these new policies emerging from such an unlikely source was yet another reason why more activists turned away from the politics of confrontation. In communities where trafficking with the Reds had been the reason to mobilize old antialien slogans, the pictures of Richard Nixon toasting Mao Tse-tung and Chou En-lai on the front pages now made the un-American activities arguments seem absurd and irrelevant.

The sources of antialienism were disappearing, but the troubles of the 1970s were just beginning. In the last year of his first term, the president had wrestled with economic difficulties that had begun with the overheating of the economy in the late 1960s. This was when the soaring costs of the war intersected the economic boom, first stimulating a growing rate of inflation. Yet even in this difficult hour for national and family budgets, social critics pointed to dramatic changes in society resulting in part from the affluence of the earlier years. What some were calling the "sexual revolution," a sweeping transformation in mores accompanying the period of prosperity and protest, was featured on newsmagazine covers and television documentaries. The sophisticates of the over-thirty generation seemed to be emulating the young activists who proclaimed sexual liberation. The human potential movement got a similar play. From Encounter to Gestalt to EST, the search for self might be dismissed as the self-absorbed, narcissistic world of the "me generation" by analysts, but it, too, was celebrated as liberating by many opinion leaders of the 1970s. Meanwhile, the growing divorce rate became a national issue, with the family besieged seen as a problem rooted in the social upheavals of those years. The war was ending, the protest in campus and community disappearing, but here were new anxieties for old. No repressive political movements emerged in the early 1970s, but in response to this perceived crisis in family values and traditional social arrangements came the rise of new evangelists. They offered the search for meaning in another realm, a way of bringing order to the land and stability to those reeling from contemporary events.

Even as these issues were taking shape, the Watergate scandal engulfed the nation, dominating political life and media interest until mid-decade. The crisis of presidential government further undermined the confidence of many in their institutions, already shaken by years of conflicts in the streets, defeats abroad, assassinations at home. And as Richard Nixon struggled to survive, the Yom Kippur War of 1973 unleashed the oil boycott. With the Nixon presidency paralyzed, Americans faced not only long lines for gasoline but a shocking new awareness that the land of limitless wealth was now at the limits of its resources. The boycott occurred when the oil-producing states of the Middle East reacted to the decline in U.S. reserves; for the first time, Americans had to deal with a problem of resource insufficiency. The "people of plenty" now could be intimidated even by the sheiks and the shah. It was unthinkable, a historic event. The resulting energy crisis intensified the inflation, weakened Western economies, and further shook the confidence of Americans. In addition, the desperate search for answers to the problem of energy self-sufficiency led many to argue that the efforts to meet the environmental crisis would have to be shelved. This recognition in the late 1960s that the nation might be choking in the effluvia of its affluence, polluting its waters, poisoning its air, threatening the ecosystem, had led to policies aimed at protecting the environment. But now the oil emergency suggested that the nation might not be able to meet both crises successfully. God's American Israel never seemed less secure.

The social upheavals of the 1960s had been followed by the defeats of the 1970s. In 1975, the spectacle of the last desperate people extricated by helicopter from the roof of the American embassy before the fall of Saigon and the final collapse in Vietnam was a signature not only on a policy of failure but a period of growing awareness of the limits of American power. The angry rebels on the steps of the Pentagon in 1967 and in the streets of Chicago in 1968 were stilled. They had attacked their government, insisting that America was the source of most of the problems on the planet. But implicit in their passionate protests was the assumption that the United States was at the center of the world. If they had control of the levers of power, there would be vast possibilities for creative change. In a new age in which the nation now appeared everywhere on the defensive, such anger and arrogance seemed inappropriate, even pathetic. It was another reason why the "movement" evaporated. And as Americans celebrated the bicentennial in an outpouring of national fervor in 1976, a search for a bonding experience touched by new strains of self-doubt, it was clear that the bad news was not over.[7]

In the troubled year of 1969, the influential British journal, the *Economist*, had featured the United States economy as its cover story. America was the "Neurotic Trillionaire," the editors announced, for despite the social turmoil in the great nation, the most significant "news story in history" was the economic genius of the Americans and the unmatched power of their industrial plant. Whether they be managers, factory assemblers, or professionals, housewives or farmers, Americans were simply harder working and more productive than any other people. The economies of scale in the continent-sized nation, it was argued, could account for only a fraction of the "residual" that gave the United States its huge comparative advantage in the struggle to dominate the world marketplace. The larger part of the "American advantage" came from those imponderables that made up the individualist ethos, the old American dream.

But times were changing. It took only six years for the *Economist* to rethink its argument. In 1975 the cover featured a rising sun, and this time the story announced the end of the "American Century," 1875 to 1975; Japan's economic miracle would own the future. The growing perception that the United States was being whipped in the markets of the world, that American automakers and steelworkers could not even hold their own home markets without import quotas, convinced the fickle editors that the communal ethos in Japanese industrial life and the central planning of product development and marketing—those alternative forms of economic organization found among America's competitors—were too much for the Americans. The United States was suddenly seen as over-

matched in many areas, no longer the pioneer land of Yankee ingenuity but a nation in relative economic decline. The decade of defeats had taken a new turn.[8]

Many younger Americans soon recognized the peril. Children of
the postwar baby boom, they now discovered they were part of a
crowded age cohort, some facing the professional school crunch,
many confronting other employment disappointments of the 1970s.
It was a final reason why the old activism was over, for the New
Left was replaced by the workaday anxieties of a less optimistic if
less passionate era. Jimmy Carter, the moralist and outsider who
had won the White House in 1976 with an attack on the "imperial
presidency," grappled with these new realities. He told his countrymen in 1978 that they were suffering from a crisis of confidence. It
was true, but it was not a substitute for leadership. The gloomy
atmosphere darkened further with the Iranian revolution, when a
new oil crisis added to the spiraling rate of inflation, touching 20
percent by 1980. Economic heavy weather threatened millions. It
had been over a decade since many people had known a rise in real
wages, and the hard times exacerbated memories of recent international defeats and ugly domestic conflicts. The hostage affair (involving American diplomatic personnel imprisoned in their embassy, guarded by armed youths) only underscored perceptions of
U.S. weakness; the burning helicopters of the rescue force left at
Desert One in 1980 were a final agonizing reminder of the shocking
reversal of fortunes of the past decade and a half.

In such a time of disappointment and national humiliation, the
old antialien response might have been expected to surface again in
new forms. Who was responsible for this series of setbacks? Were
there enemies within who could be blamed for the unhappy developments that affected so many? But it did not happen that way. The
events that stretched back to the mid- to late 1960s did serve as
the setting for the rise of a New Right. This movement, however,
would contain only a few elements of the antialien activities of the
past. Neither nativism nor anticommunism could explain the defeats of the 1970s.

Ronald Reagan was elected president in 1980 with a call for a
return to the world of the past. He promised an end to "fifty years
of failed federal programs." He offered to reconstruct an older order
in which the "bureaucratic cadres"—also reviled by New Leftists
and Wallaceites alike—would be checked, in which the "individual-

ist genius of American free enterprise" would be allowed once more to bring prosperity back to the land. It was the rhetoric he had used for twenty years as a conservative politician and a spokesman for the General Electric Company. But in 1980 it had particular appeal. He championed a return to "family values" and assailed the social and sexual practices of activist youth and urban elites. Somehow stability would be brought back to homes, order to school classrooms. He spoke glowingly of his own faith and the role of religion in traditional American life. He declared that America would "stand tall" in the world once more; after Vietnam and Iran, massive defense spending would allow the nation to face down the Russians and deal severely with all who threatened American interests. It was a turn to the Right, a program ridiculed by critics and a dramatic contrast to the presidential direction of any Republican or Democratic predecessor for half a century.

But it had force. The reaction to the defeats and dislocations of the previous years made the new agenda seem attractive to many. The social upheavals and the passionate rejection of traditional values during those years—brought forcefully into the homes of Americans living in a world of television—made the agenda seem essential to many others. The president's domestic, military, and foreign policies won wide support in opinion polls and on Capitol Hill in 1981. The severe recession of 1982 temporarily dampened public and congressional enthusiasm, but the economic recovery of mid-1983 stimulated renewed discussion of an emerging conservative majority. Millions of Americans now yearned to put the troubles of the recent past behind them. They wanted to celebrate America and its "way of life." The patriotic outburst at the 1984 summer Olympics in Los Angeles featured chants of "USA, USA." The stars and stripes bedecked halls of both national political conventions later in the summer, and some of the same passion was expressed at the conventions. The magnetic appeal of many of the new conservative themes was on display at the Republican gathering in Dallas: national chauvinism, "family" values, optimism about American destiny, contempt for "whiners," critics, and pessimists. Party leaders, counseled by their media consultants, would shape their campaign around the "new patriotism." "I Love America" emerged on bumper stickers; it became the subject of cover stories assessing the pervasive mood of the land. But this was a nation in which Americanist fervor had been accompanied in the past by attacks on internal, "un-American" enemies. This time, however, the old antialienism was far weaker than in the 1950s or before.

★★★

Antialien Fringe Groups in the 1980s

Of course, nativist and anticommunist conspiracy theorists still remained active in the mid-1980s, working on the frayed edges of a lunatic fringe. In California, publisher Jack Chick offered a series of books and "adult comic books" telling the story of Alberto Rivera, who claimed to be an apostate Jesuit priest and bishop. Allegedly a Spaniard, trained in Costa Rica before coming to America, Rivera "uncovered" a sinister planetary conspiracy in which the Catholic church joined forces with the communists, the Zionists, the Illuminati, and the Mormons to crush Protestantism and take over the world. The pope was an agent of Satan, Rivera reported, and Jim Jones, the maker of the Jonestown massacre, was "a powerful warlock and a well-trained Jesuit." Rivera claimed to be the victim of vicious mental and physical coercion by diabolical Jesuits, and his illustrated volumes not only describe his own torture but the continuing tradition of Catholic repressive violence. They include drawings of the tunnels between nunneries and Jesuit houses where the bodies of babies were buried and of the wooden racks on which innocent girls and women were beaten and brutalized. Maria Monk returned in 1984.[9]

The old-time nativism still had its practitioners, as did the tradition of American fascism. The National States Rights party, with its lightning bolt logo taken from Hitler's Waffen SS, mixed racism with anti-Semitism after its formation in 1958 by two Georgia anti-Semites, Jesse Stoner and Edward Fields. Stoner, who earlier had created something he called the Stoner Anti-Jewish party, offered himself as a candidate for the United States Senate in the early 1970s. He proposed to make Judaism a crime punishable by death and in one television interview called the mayor of Atlanta a "Jew gangster" and a "Christ Killer." He had only a handful of supporters in the mid-1980s, but his followers were involved in joint paramilitary training with scattered elements of the Nazi party and the contemporary Klans.

The Nazis, by one federal estimate in 1983, had "probably less than 500 members." (One observer suggested that they were one-third "nuts," one-third queer people "who enjoy dressing up in uniforms," and one-third agents of "the police or the ADL.") They barely functioned following Rockwell's death, although briefly making headlines in 1977 when Holocaust survivors and others moved to block a parade permit for Chicago National Socialists, who proposed to march down the streets of Skokie, Illinois, a suburb with an estimated population of thirty thousand Jews in a total of seventy thousand.[10]

The Ku Klux Klan also failed to prosper following its very limited revival during the civil rights movement. In 1977, the FBI estimated a maximum membership of twenty-two thousand in the various Klans and Klan-style front groups. The "movement" never coalesced, remaining an aggregation of competing sects under jealous and inept "leaders." There have been a dozen rivalrous factions. Robert Shelton, imperial wizard of the United Klans of America, based in Alabama, demanded a meeting with President Jimmy Carter in the late 1970s, calling for federal protection after his Klansmen were attacked by a group of blacks during a Columbus, Ohio, rally. But Shelton was not the only man calling himself by the title that meant something in the days of Hiram Wesley Evans. Bill Wilkinson was imperial wizard of the Invisible Empire, Knights of the Ku Klux Klan, based in Louisiana, and David Dukes, another Louisianan, imperial wizard, Knights of the Ku Klux Klan. A younger man who enjoyed some success on the television circuit, Dukes appeared on more than one hundred talk shows, creating an illusion of the Klan as a formidable force. Other Klan leaders include the aging James Venable, imperial wizard, National Knights of the Ku Klux Klan, based in Georgia, Bill Chaney and his Independent Northern and South Klans of Indiana, Dale Reusch and his Ohio-based Knights of the Ku Klux Klan, Robert Scoggin, grand dragon of South Carolina, among several others.

These various Klans and associated groups, with names like the White Knights of Mississippi and the White Patriot party (which successfully recruited a small number of marines and soldiers stationed at Camp LeJeune and Fort Bragg in North Carolina in 1985), struggled to maintain even their shrinking following in the mid-1980s. By most estimates, hard-core Klansmen numbered fewer than twelve thousand as the Klans lost more ground in 1986. But in one sense, the various Klan cells gained a new direction. In the 1980s, many turned to a more vitriolic anti-Semitism than they had practiced in the days of the antiblack struggles in the 1950s and 1960s. Some Klansmen even established tenuous links to a new, more vigorous, and more violent branch of the contemporary neo-Nazi movement.[11]

The most violent of those groups that suddenly emerged in mid-decade was a small but murderous sect known as the Order. (There were a variety of other names, including the Bruder Schweigen—the Silent Brotherhood—and the White American Bastion.) It was only when a man named Thomas Martinez was arrested for distributing counterfeit money in 1984 that the federal authorities became aware of the existence of the Order. Martinez agreed to become a federal informer after telling the FBI a bizarre tale of a spree of violent crimes conducted by a tiny Nazilike "brotherhood" that was modeling its strike for power on the fictional blueprint for a racist revolution offered in a fantasy novel, *The Turner Diaries*. Authored by neo-Nazi William Pierce under the pseudonym Andrew McDonald, the novel described the murder of prominent American Jews and the financing of a revolution (ending with an American nuclear strike against Israel) through counterfeiting and armored car robberies. Under the leadership of its founder, Robert Jay Mathews, the Order produced more than $500,000 in counterfeit bills in 1983 and 1984. More than $4 million was stolen in armored car robberies in Seattle and Ukiah, California, in April and July 1984. At Ukiah, a dozen men dressed in camouflage military garb and carrying heavy automatic weapons escaped with $3.6 million. On 19 July 1984, Denver talk show host Alan Berg, a frequent and scathing commentator on racist activities, was killed by submachinegun fire outside his home. Later, a suspected informer was bludgeoned with a hammer and shot to death in Idaho. There were discussions of plans for the assassination of a member of the French branch of the Rothschild family (visiting Seattle), as well as the killing of Henry Kissinger, David Rockefeller, the heads of the three national television networks, and several well-known American Jews. The Order was preparing its revolution.

Law enforcement agencies responded. The FBI made its war on the Silent Brotherhood a priority in late 1984. With the aid of informers, federal agents ferreted out Mathews, who died after a shootout with two dozen federal and state officers in a hideout on

Whidbey Island in Puget Sound. The Order now used a computer bulletin board, the Aryan Liberty Network, to call for the execution of "traitors" in the ranks, but a federal roundup of those involved in the crimes was successful. At a lengthy trial in Seattle in late 1985, twenty-three members were charged, ten negotiated guilty pleas and testified against the Order, one committed suicide, and five were sentenced to long prison terms. One man, Bruce Caroll Pierce, thirty-one, of Hayden Lake, Idaho, was convicted of shooting Alan Berg "because he was a Jew" and sentenced to one hundred years; prosecutors said they could not recall "a more frightening danger to society." Gary Lee Yarborough, thirty, another Idahoan, told the judge: "I am just a common man, worldly dumb but spiritually wise." The movement, he said, would continue: "Blood will flow."[12]

The Order was effectively silenced by the trial, but the larger neo-Nazi phenomenon of the 1980s endured. In prison, members might continue their work, for the "Aryan Brotherhood" already had been recruiting in the nation's jails, distributing copies of *Mein Kampf* and other fascistic tracts, eliciting signed "oaths of allegiance." In fact, the Order was but a splinter group of another organization, the Aryan Nations church, headquartered in Hayden Lake. When Mathews and Pierce referred to the United States government as ZOG (the Zionist Occupation Government), when they preached that Jews and blacks were the evil other, when they exclaimed that "the Aryan yeomanry is awakening . . . do you hear the approaching thunder . . . war is upon the land," they were describing the world as seen by the Reverend Richard Girnt Butler.[13]

An engineer who leads the Church of Jesus Christ Christian (founded by Wesley Swift), the "religious" heart of Aryan Nations, Butler, born in 1920, is a theoretician of racism. At his twenty-acre compound in the remote hills of northern Idaho, with "Whites only" signs posted and patrolled by armed men in blue uniforms modeled on Hitler's SA, Butler preaches white, Christian supremacy. Jews are the offspring of Satan in "the line of Cain"; like blacks, they are the descendants of the devil. These "hook-nosed anti-Christs" control the press and the courts; it is the "Jews-media" and the "Jewdiciary." America must be purged of "Jewish villainy and government treachery"; the "Aryan Warriors" will lead the way.[14]

Members of the Order apparently split from Aryan Nations because the parent group provided too much talk and not enough action. Other defectors included Kenneth Gilbert, founder of the Restored Church of Jesus Christ in Post Falls, Idaho, who insisted that *Mein Kampf* should be considered a book of the Bible and suggested that Butler was not sufficiently committed to Nazism. Together, there are at most several hundred or a few thousand such true believers. (Butler claimed a mailing list of five thousand.) In July 1986, Butler played host once again to an Aryan Nations Congress in Hayden Lake. (In April 1987 he would be part of a group of neo-Nazis indicted on charges of conspiracy to overthrow the government of the United States.) On the agenda of his congress were plans for "declaring a territorial sanctuary" in the Northwest and "forming a provisional government" in Oregon, Washington, Idaho, and Montana. Among those invited to attend the "Congress" were representatives of the National States Rights party, a former Klansman who had organized a California group called White American Resistance, and Klan activists from Arkansas and North Carolina. They were all part of a still larger group of sects with a common allegiance to the doctrine of "Christian Identity" theology.

Reportedly created in 1946 by Swift, a former Klansman, and Bertram Comparet, a California racist activist, Identity teaches that Jesus Christ was an Aryan, not a Jew; the lost tribes of Israel were Anglo-Saxons and other Aryan peoples. (It opposes the New Right fundamentalists because Jerry Falwell and others consider "Israelites" God's chosen people.) The United States may be the promised land but only if Jews are eliminated and non-Christian Aryans subjugated by the true "white races." The belief that the U.S. government is a vast conspiracy, the tool of the racial enemy, and that true patriots must engage in military training for the terrible day of reckoning to come, is the bonding tie that connects the Order, the Aryan Nations Church, and several other small paramilitary groups. Prominent among them are the Christian Patriots Defense League and two associations with striking names: the Covenant, the Sword and the Arm of the Lord (CSA) and the Posse Comitatus.[15]

The Christian Patriots Defense League (CPDL), founded and led by a Southern Illinois millionaire, John Harrell, is as concerned with communism as racism. Linking both strands of America's right-wing antialien tradition, CPDL prepares against a communist invasion of Christian America from Mexico or Canada. It called for survivalists to train at its summer encampment in a 232-acre "Mo-Ark Survival Base," preparing to ensure a "Mid-America Survival Zone" in which white Christians could prevail in tomorrow's Armageddon. The emphasis on guerrilla warfare, the location in the Ozarks, and sessions conducted on tax rebellion connect Harrell's small following to those other groups that received national attention because of the violent confrontations associated with them. In fact, federal officials in 1985 believed they had established some links between sects related to Identity, particularly the most militant.

The Covenant, the Sword and the Arm of the Lord was brought to the attention of law enforcement officials when they sought to arrest a fugitive member of the Order accused of killing a state trooper. Like other Order activists, the man was from the Northwest (Athol, Idaho). But he had fled to the Ozarks. In this wooded, mountainous region on the Arkansas-Missouri border, where other survivalists had emerged or relocated, hundreds of officers in battle dress surrounded a 224-acre compound on Bull Shoals Lake, where James D. Ellison had founded what one agent described as a cult of "fanatical racists." Forcing Ellison to surrender after a four-day siege in April 1985, lawmen uncovered a huge cache of heavy weapons, including an armored car under construction. They also discovered four members of the Order hiding in the compound, working with their new allies in paramilitary training. At the ensuing trial, the CSA founder was sentenced to prison under the same statute evoked in the Seattle trial and previously used against organized crime: the Racketeering Influenced and Corrupt Organization Act.

The CSA was a minuscule "movement." Federal officials estimated its membership at 150, with 55 in the compound during the days of siege. They included women and small children, some born at the headquarters and living in shelters without electricity or water. The men, most of them bearded, were affectionate to their families and punctuated their speech with exclamations of "Praise the Lord." But this was a male-dominant culture, and Kerry Noble, second in command, explained that women must be subservient: "This nation was founded on racism and sexism." Certainly racism was at the center of CSA "theology," which was part of Identity, in this case called the Church of Zarepath-Horeb. As elsewhere, Jews were seen as the offspring of Satan. CSA leaders were accused of planning to bomb a Jewish community center and linked to other acts of violence. Officials noted that part of their terrain was known as "silhouette city," where members practiced urban street fighting. CSA spokesmen had warned that chaos was coming: "Communists will kill white Christians and mutilate them, satanic Jews will offer people up for sacrifice, Blacks will rape white women, homosexuals will sodomize whomever they can." The conviction of founder Ellison apparently dismantled the Covenant, the Sword and the Arm of the Lord, which Noble explained had taken its title from scripture (Matt. 10:34): "Think not that I come to send peace on earth. I come not to send peace, but a sword." Still, other groups retained their momentum.[16]

Posse Comitatus is larger than the Order, CSA, or other Identity sects. Thought to be founded by a retired machinist (and, by one account, a former Silver Shirt) named H. L. "Mike" Beach in Portland, Oregon, in 1969, Posse Comitatus had no charismatic leader, no headquarters, no publicity arm producing literature. It was built on local groups of friends and acquaintances. Active in the late 1970s in towns in Oregon, northern California, and Idaho (where Richard Butler served as its Kootenai County "marshal"), the Posse found its largest following in the upper Midwest, particularly Wisconsin. It had an impact in Iowa, Nebraska, Kansas, and the Dakotas during the agricultural crisis of the mid-1980s. Estimates of its central membership ranged from three to ten thousand.

The name comes from the Latin approximation of "Power of the County." Adherents argue that federal and state law is meaningless, the highest authority is county law, and the county sheriff is the most authoritative official. But the sheriff is not considered all-powerful; if he does not follow the will of the "people," the people's Posse has an obligation to hang him at high noon in the center of town. The emblem of the Posse Comitatus is a golden hangman's noose.

Members of the Posse were involved in several armed confrontations with law enforcement officers and with Internal Revenue Service agents in the late 1970s and early 1980s. Denying the power of the federal and state government, they resist paying taxes as well as applying for driver's and hunting licenses. One member, Gordon W. Kahl, a sixty-three-year-old retired farmer and fugitive tax protestor, a gun fancier with a large private collection, shot and killed two federal marshals at a roadblock in Medina, North Dakota, in February 1983. Fleeing to the Ozarks as would the Order fugitives, he was located hiding on the farm of another tax resistor. The owner had built his farmhouse of concrete, in bunker style, because "the end of time is coming, the Bible is being fulfilled, but Russia is going to take over this country first." Kahl held out in this redoubt for hours after killing a sheriff; in the end his charred body could be identified only by dental plates.[17]

The Kahl episode alerted lawmen to the potential danger of a membership which some earlier had believed used only "wild rhetoric, not wild violence." At Tigerton Dells, in the hardwood forests of the northern part of Wisconsin, the largest Posse center had been posted with signs: "Federal Agents Keep out; Survivors will be Prosecuted." Neighbors heard gunfire and saw camouflaged figures practicing with automatic weapons and rocket-propelled grenades. But Posse leaders claimed they were acting in the tradition of Jackson and Jefferson because they would "obey no unconstitutional statutes." Still, they set up a "Constitutional Township of Tigerton Dells" on their fourteen hundred acres and appointed their own judges and foreign ambassadors.[18]

The Posse Comitatus at first appeared to be only a quasi-anarchist group of angry, isolated loners, "psychotics who have lost touch with reality," as one federal official called them. The search for Gordon Kahl suggested new links to the other heavily armed right-wing groups. The ties, FBI spokesmen suggested, were not organizational but ideological and theological. The self-proclaimed "national director of counterinsurgency" for the Posse, James P. Wickstrom, gave new life to this theory when he teamed with the Reverend William Potter Gale, founder of the Ministry of Christ church, a part of Identity, in offering succor to desperate farmers in the Midwest.[19]

Gale had served on General Douglas MacArthur's staff in World War II, helping supervise guerrilla operations in the Philippines. He now offered paramilitary training ("killer teams in hand to hand combat, murder by ambush") in several midwestern states. In joint appearances with Wickstrom in Kansas, Iowa, and Nebraska, Gale exclaimed: "We're gonna cleanse our land with a sword. You're damn right I'm teaching violence. You better start making dossiers ... on every damn Jew rabbi in the land." The group gained access to a small radio station in Dodge City, Kansas, and its recorded messages assailed Jews, Catholics, blacks, the courts, the banks, and the Internal Revenue Service. Jews, in particular, "the children of Satan," were the objects of attack. The solution was self-defense: "garroting people" in their sleep, "cleansing the earth of the black beasts." Senator Robert Dole and the state attorney general condemned the use of public airways for these statements.[20]

But as the farm crisis deepened, Posse Comitatus found an audience for its messages. In 1984 and 1985, some desperate farmers, facing loss of their land, turned to violence. There were murders of bankers in Minnesota and Iowa; there were ugly confrontations, suicides, and other family tragedies throughout a troubled region. Groups with names such as the Populist party, the Committee to Restore the Constitution, the Anti-Lawyer party, the Christian Nationalist Crusade (a remnant of Gerald L. K. Smith's organization), NAPA (the National Agricultural Press Association, which had nothing to do with the press) emerged to offer "answers" to the heartbreaking questions of the hour.

How could an agricultural region experiencing unprecedented prosperity as late as 1979, with family farmers "millionaires on paper" because of the spectacular increase in land values, suddenly sink into the abyss of the worst crisis since the depression? In a land with some of the richest soil on the planet, where independent farmers had been living a legendary part of the American dream for more than a century, thousands faced ruin seemingly overnight. In the 1970s bankers, government experts, and agricultural specialists had encouraged them to expand, to take advantage of the new golden age. Family farmers had borrowed money for new equipment and new acreage. But the boom had turned to bust. Inflation pushed up interest rates; the international market for midwestern produce was weakened by fluctuations in the world money markets; the value of the land plummeted by a third. Farmers could not meet their loans, and bankers foreclosed. By one estimate in fall 1985, 30 percent of 113,000 Iowa farmers faced loss of their land. In many cases the farms had been in the family, regulating the rhythm of life, for generations.

The Posse and similar groups offered an explanation for the plight of despondent people facing ruin. Before being shot to death by a Nebraska Special Weapons Action Team in a confrontation on his farm near Grand Island, one heavily armed older man who owed $300,000 exclaimed: "They destroyed everything I ever worked for." Who were "they"? His response was the "filthy lying lawyers," the

"Luciferized bank directors," and the "Goddam Jews." It was not the state police he confronted but "the Mossad" (agents of Israeli Intelligence.) "I know who I'm facing, they are worse than the NKVD." He had read an article titled "How the Jewish Question Touches the Farm." Wickstrom and other Posse leaders had been explaining throughout the region why the "stinking Jew insurance companies," the World Bank under control of the Jews, the Rothschilds, Lehman Brothers, and other "Jew bankers" were responsible for the destruction of white Christian American family farmers. As in the teachings of Pelley and Gerald Smith in the depression-ravaged 1930s, of some Klansmen in the 1920s, and of certain Populists in the agricultural crisis of the 1890s, anti-Semitism once again offered a simplistic explanation for the plight of the farmer. Once again, there were relatively few Jews in the region; it is easier to hate the unknown and unseen enemy. Once again, the specter of people who allegedly grow and make nothing, who exploit others and reap great profits through manipulation, satisfied those who could not understand or accept the grim circumstances of their economic crisis.[21]

There is something particularly poignant about the search for scapegoats by desperate family farmers in the mid-1980s. The same newspapers that announce the bankruptcies, foreclosures, and premature deaths of their neighbors carry stories of investment bankers and arbitrageurs, many of them young professionals, earning millions arranging or speculating on mergers and acquisitions, hostile takeovers, and "greenmail" back East. There are headlines about illegal insider trading and other unethical behavior in a Wall Street world marked by a frenzy of "deal doing." Never has the unearned increment seemed so fashionable, celebrated, or lucrative. Little wonder that some men and women, choked with rage, guilt, and frustration at the loss of their land, homes, and way of life, were willing to listen—if only briefly—to the spokesmen of a sinister ideology.

The Posse Comitatus is not a major movement. Even taken together with all the other groups aligned with the Identity phenomenon and with the Ku Klux Klan, total membership remains only a fraction of the following of some state Klans in the 1920s, a fragment of the Coughlinite millions of the 1930s. Like other neofascist sects in the American past, the Posse and the others made noise and received press attention. But they did not represent a rebirth of powerful right-wing antialienism in contemporary America. They appeared in a nation still recovering from the setbacks of the 1970s, a country in which memories of Vietnam endure and fears of nuclear war are rife, in which survivalist magazines proliferate and a few lonely figures stockpile food and weapons and prepare for the collapse of civilization. They emerged in an age of conservative dominance, with its patriotic celebrations, military "rearmament," and militant rhetoric about "standing tall" in a world of communist enemies. Although the Identity sects reviled the hated government, their brand of right-wing extremism appeared in the Reagan years even as left-wing extremists (the Weatherman underground and its "days of rage" and bomb factories, the Black Panthers and their verbal pyrotechnics) appeared as a minor feature in an era of liberal dominance—with its emphasis on social justice and racial equality—in the late 1960s.

But no real movement arose on the neo-Nazi Right, merely the fantasies and frustrations of a poorly educated group of outsiders, some with criminal records. They lived in areas far removed from the urban centers of power, angry loners from the mountainous Northwest, the Ozarks, and the upper Midwest. These racist sects provided a way of dealing with their anger and their fears. It is an old tradition in America, if now a stunted one.

But are there leaders and organizations that do not appeal only to such isolated outsiders which have made a significant mark? Here, too, the answer seems to be no. Neither Willis Carto's Liberty Lobby nor Lyndon La Rouche's multifaceted organization represented an emerging mass movement.

Carto created his Liberty Lobby, based in Washington, in the 1950s. In the 1970s, this right-wing assemblage turned to overt anti-Semitism, mixing it with traditionally hyperbolic anticommunism. It began supporting Nordic-racist books and newsletters. It lobbied against the appointment of Henry Kissinger as secretary of state: "As a Jew, Kissinger cannot help but feel a personal stake in the fortunes of Israel." It referred to Israel as a "bastard state." Through the Institute of Historical Review, the lobby supported "revisionist" writers who argued that the Holocaust was a myth. (In the early 1980s, the institute announced a $50,000 prize to the person who could prove the existence of gas chambers and death camps. It withdrew the offer after an Auschwitz survivor moved to collect the "reward" and brought suit against the institute.) The

Liberty Lobby claimed a membership of 25,000 and a mailing list of 200,000 in the mid-1970s; its publication *Spotlight* claimed a readership of 145,000 in 1985. It raised millions of dollars after 1970 but still has received virtually no national visibility. Trying to appeal to a far more educated and sophisticated audience than those small violence-prone groups of racists in the West and South, it made almost no impact in America.[22]

Unlike Carto, Lyndon La Rouche was not ignored by the press. Particularly after two La Rouche followers stunned Democrats in Illinois in April 1986 by winning primary contests to gain party nomination for lieutenant governor and secretary of state, the "La Rouchians" became the focus of widespread media attention. Now many Americans for the first time began to learn something about a man who had been trying to influence public policy for a generation.

La Rouche had been on national television several times as an independent candidate for president in 1984. There were relatively few viewers, but those watching heard him accuse Walter Mondale, Gary Hart, and other Democrats of being "agents of Soviet influence." He named many other "houseservants of the wealthy, liberal families" who decided to "turn over large areas of the world to Moscow for a few decades." The Harrimans, the Rockefellers, and others "employ stooges like Kissinger," who act under orders while Izvestia supports them from the sidelines. A key issue is the nuclear freeze effort in which Democrats, said La Rouche, "serve as the catspaw of the KGB." In this characterization of the un-American activities of WASP elites and conservative as well as liberal political leaders, antialienism returned in yet another form.[23]

The man who made this argument announced in 1986 that "I'm the best economist in the world today"; by a "large margin of advantage I am the leading economist of the twentieth century." But this world's best economist was also a man at risk. He told interviewers that a variety of forces were plotting to kill him. His enemies included the KGB, Colombian drug dealers, the British Secret Service, and Henry Kissinger, who had "run operations against me and these have . . . involved assassination potentialities." Other foes, named on other occasions, included the FBI, the CIA, the Anti-Defamation League, Israeli intelligence, and Murder, Inc.[24]

Lyndon La Rouche's extraordinary view of his own intellectual eminence and political importance makes him a figure not easily categorized in the chronicles of political extremism in American history. Indeed, this balding, graying, bespectacled man, born in Rochester, New Hampshire, of "evangelical Quaker" parents in 1922, had a unique journey to the leadership of a right-wing organization in the United States.

La Rouche first made a reputation as a left-wing political activist. Known then as Lyn Marcus or L. Marcus, he was a Marxist theoretician active in the Socialist Workers party, a Trotskyist organization, from 1948 to 1963. Building a reputation as a formidable debater in leftist circles, a Greenwich Village lecturer who could integrate the works of political philosophers, economists, poets, classical composers, and physicists into his discourse, he attracted a following. In the late 1960s he organized the National Caucus of Labor Committee (NCLC), and some of his young followers were briefly, if marginally, involved in the clashes at Columbia University. Investigative reporters, interviewing defectors from the La Rouche camp, painted a picture of a small number of "upper middle class" collegians who were the core of his following of perhaps a thousand by 1972. Then a striking change took place in what had been a leftist sect. Some writers have suggested that it was after he was left by one of his disciples (a woman with whom he had been living), who went to England with another young defector, that he suddenly became more remote, autocratic, abusive, and insulting, intolerant of any dissent within his circle and persuaded that he needed armed bodyguards because he was being stalked by assassins.

It was at this time that La Rouchians moved dramatically to the Right. The leader ordered "Operation Mop Up," an attack on Communist party and other left-wing groups, in 1973. Bands of his followers brandishing clubs and wearing motorcycle helmets assailed these new enemies. "Brainwashing sessions" were held, according to some defectors; members who had resisted militant activity were accused of being infantile, impotent, and sexually deviant.

La Rouche now appeared to be creating a new political cult. One defector called it "the great freak-out of '74," with the leader "deprogramming" recalcitrant followers. A former member, in the group for a decade, described the result: "If you don't apply the word cult to La Rouche, it has no meaning. The people in it are totally dominated by the whims of one man. They break up their marriages at his suggestion or they come back together." Another

dropout characterized it as "total immersion . . . he demands syco-
phantic obedience . . . he repeatedly tells [us] he is in total control
. . . it is pure psychological terror." Why do many stay? It is suggested that for some members who have abandoned friends and
family, who have dropped out of school or have no other careers,
leaving La Rouche would be leaving the only community they have
known. The movement gives meaning to their lives. Lyndon La
Rouche's response to this view is that it is all "garbage . . . I don't
have any control." There is "no such thing as a La Rouche organization." Members of his group also deny the very concept of a La
Rouchian cult.[25]

In any event, the movement did not decline after its turn to the
Right. In 1976, La Rouche made his first race for president. By 1979,
he retained some one thousand members with thirty-seven offices
in North America and in 1980, he raised over $2 million for his
campaign. In 1984 he raised $6.1 million, received almost $500,000
in matching federal funds, and attracted seventy-eight thousand
votes on election day. During these years, the La Rouche establishment was reshaped and new elements added to it. Under the um-
brella of the NCLC, the National Democratic Policy Committee
(NDPC) was created to contest primary elections within the
Democratic party. The Fusion Energy Foundation was organized to
promote La Rouche's growing interest in nuclear power and his
endorsement of President Reagan's Strategic Defense Initiative
(SDI), which he claimed partial credit for conceiving. Newspapers,
magazines, and the *Executive Intelligence Review* were established.
Through the *Review* and the New Solidarity International Press
Service, La Rouche supplied "intelligence" reports on political, economic, and military matters to subscribers and clients, apparently
including a few foreign governments.

Clearly, La Rouche had attracted at least a small number of disciplined and well-educated followers. Unlike the neo-Nazi cults of
the West, this right-wing movement appeals to people with a taste
for high culture. Lyndon La Rouche sponsors poetry readings and
classical concerts at his Schiller Institute. He describes his philosophy as "neo-Platonic Humanism" and continues to impress followers with his ability to manipulate concepts from disparate disci-
plines. A few leading aides even won access to members of the
National Security Council and to certain key players in cabinet

departments early in the Reagan years; some of these presidential appointees praised the La Rouchians for their mastery of the details of military and political questions.

Although there had been complaints about allegedly unethical fund-raising practices (including the illegal use of credit cards), the La Rouche groups were able to raise over $30 million yearly by the mid-1980s. As the leader embraced various mainstream conservative causes including SDI, the anticommunist effort in Central America, and a "war on drug pushers," some critics feared that he was achieving a limited measure of influence in policy-making circles. But the aura of hostility, the rhetoric of violence, and the armed guards that are all part of the La Rouchian style have linked his movement to an uglier brand of right-wing militancy, making it impossible for his organization to gain real respectability.

In the late 1970s, his followers received paramilitary guerrilla training under the guidance of Mitchell Wer Bell III, formerly of the OSS. After he moved his headquarters to an elaborate $2.3 million estate near Leesburg, Virginia, in 1983, neighbors complained about excessive security arrangements, and one who had criticized La Rouche told reporters that she had been subsequently harassed and threatened. La Rouchian defectors and investigative writers also have had problems. Dropouts said they were called thieves, liars, psychotics, and KGB pawns. Reporters, columnists, and television producers who had written critical accounts about La Rouche told tales of late-night threatening phone calls, dead cats on porches, and leaflets inviting neighbors to their "gay coming out party." La Rouche denied such charges, but his newspaper called one critical journalist a "noted drug lobbyist" and said that the "*Wall Street Journal* joins drug lobby attack on La Rouche." He sued many detractors, including NBC. His $150 million suit was dismissed and his organization was fined $200,000 in a countersuit brought by the network. He explained that the verdict was "rigged," that "they somehow got to the judge." When he refused to pay NBC in September 1986, claiming that he had no money or income, federal magistrates further fined him $200 a day until he told the court who paid for his estate and other heavy personal expenses. La Rouche's followers, on station at major airports where much of his printed material is sold, have been involved in violent confrontations with celebrities, including television star Phil Donahue and former Secretary of State Kissinger. Other La Rouchians have disrupted news conferences and speeches of those officials Lyndon La Rouche dislikes. Richard Burt, then an assistant secretary of state, was interrupted with shouts that "you're a Soviet agent . . . an enemy agent . . . a traitor to the United States."[26]

These activities and La Rouche's left-wing history made him anathema in conservative circles. He was characterized by the Heritage Foundation as a possible "asset . . . for the KGB disinformation effort." He was dismissed by Richard A. Viguerie as "no conservative," indeed as an enemy of the New Right. Viguerie quoted him as attacking evangelist Marion G. "Pat" Robertson as "a peddler of snake oil for the KGB." Of course, he was much harder on liberals: headlines in *New Solidarity* announced, "Liberals Plot Crises to Hand Russia World Power," "Gary Hart's New Yalta Policy Selling Out to Soviets."[27]

La Rouche, assailed by liberals and conservatives when they took him seriously enough to comment, also was accused of anti-Semitism. Critics quoted him as having once referred to Judaism as a "cult founded by Babylonians," of implying that the Holocaust was largely a myth. In response, he pointed to several of his Jewish aides and insisted he was "anti-Zionist" not anti-Semitic. But there is no question that he sees conspirators almost everywhere. He called the queen of England the figure at the "head of the world drug lobby." He characterized the International Monetary Fund as "engaged in mass murder on a larger scale than the Nazis" and as having created the AIDS epidemic. For years, back to his leftist era, he railed against the Trilateral Commission as a Rockefeller-led cabal out to deindustrialize the West: "The Trilateral Commission functions as part of 'the Trust,' the East-West joint stock company that put the Bolsheviks and Nazis into power earlier in this century, and which now seeks to co-manage a new fascistic world order with Soviet Russia." His aides called the State Department a "hot bed of treason," and he "jokingly" suggested a "necktie party" for Secretary of State George Schultz. Views such as these led many analysts to conclude that the publicity following La Rouchian victories in the Illinois primary in 1986 would hurt not help his cause; as more people became aware of the world according to La Rouche, there would be virtually no support left.[28]

Students of Illinois politics attributed La Rouche's success not to his program but to Democratic organizational overconfidence, mischievous Republican crossover voting, and the ignorance of many voters who may have pulled levers for the anglicized names of the unknown La Rouchians because they rejected the ethnic names of the regular candidates. But in addition to this mildly nativistic re-action, it was clear that La Rouchians shrewdly exploited some of the themes being used by the Posse Comitatus: in agricultural downstate areas they pointed to the villainy of bankers, the need to protect family farms, the dangers of drug traffic in big cities. The results would not be easily replicated. In primaries later that spring and in the general election in November, La Rouchians were swamped by alerted party machines; their legislative initiative in California calling for the quarantining of AIDS patients was over-whelmingly rejected. Lyndon La Rouche had enjoyed his moment in the spotlight, insisting after Illinois that he represented the "for-gotten majority," and that like "the Wallace phenomenon some years ago," voters "want me to stick it to Washington," to confront "the sneering face of the eastern liberal establishment." But his political organization, despite recruiting many candidates (some of whom were unaware of his history or program), did not represent the cutting edge of a mass movement. Although he claimed almost thirty thousand members of his NDPC in more than forty states, observers argued that his hard-core following in the mid-1980s re-mained very small, numbering at most a few thousand. By October 1986, his movement was under growing pressure, the subject of a sweeping federal fraud investigation. A 117-count indictment named ten La Rouche subordinates and five of his affiliated campaign com-mittees and corporations with unauthorized use of credit cards, a plot to defraud a thousand people out of $1 million during his 1984 presidential campaign. La Rouche was not indicted (in April 1987, assets of his organization would be seized by federal marshals), but he warned that "any attempt to arrest me would be an attempt to kill me," and he did not "preclude" use of violence against law enforcement officials.[29]

Lyndon La Rouche was a charismatic leader for a coterie of the devoted. He built a small political cult of personality, attracting and retaining a following that apparently included sad and dependent people who could respond to his peculiar vision of his own historic importance and accept his self-inflating tales of murderous ene-mies. It is a different form of antialienism, as befits a man who made the long leap from the radical Left. But like Robert Welch in the days of his assault on Dwight Eisenhower, La Rouche's right-wing vision of an America led by traitors, of famous Democrats and Republicans who are "agents of Soviet influence," has no chance of finding a real following.

The activities of La Rouche and Carto, of Rivera and the neo-Nazi sects, of the Klans and their front groups, remind us only that the far reaches of the antialien tradition will endure, no matter how small the movements, how counterproductive their attempts to publicize their views or to impose their will on others.

But what of more substantial efforts to organize against religious, ethnic, or ideological enemies within?

★★★

Immigration Reform and the Fear of a Neo-Nativist Revival

In August 1984, a riot exploded through a ten-square-block area of Lawrence, Massachusetts. The community was torn by racial strife in a blue-collar neighborhood housing Hispanics and whites. Reminiscent of intergroup violence in other Massachusetts towns 150 years before, when Catholics were met by convent raiders and fire companies representing "natives" and Irish fought pitched battles in the streets, did the Lawrence strife suggest a neonativist upheaval in process? With the Simpson-Mazzoli bill before Congress, some Americans saw the emergence of a new assault on ethnic outsiders, this time an effort to restrict access by Hispanics—particularly Mexicans—who had come north to America to build a better life. Henry B. Gonzalez (D.-Texas), a leading member of the Hispanic caucus in the House of Representatives, reached back to the past to condemn the proposed legislation: "Simpson-Mazzoli is, sadly, the latest in a long history of immigration laws that springs from the heart of the Know Nothings, those who feared and loathed all foreigners."[30]

But was it? Did the emerging concern with a new alien influx represent a return to the un-American crusades of yesterday?

Immigration had been rising since major changes in the laws from 1965 to 1980. In 1965, the national origins quota system finally was abolished. It could not survive in a new age of egalitarianism, the years of the Great Society and the passage of the great Civil Rights Acts. There would be no more overt discrimination against Asian immigrants, and the historic preference for western Europeans would disappear. Still, fear of a vast migration of newcomers from Latin America led at first to a ceiling on Western Hemisphere immigration (170,000) as well as those coming from the Eastern Hemisphere (120,000) and to a cap on the total number of newcomers admitted each year. With further amendments to immigration laws in 1976, 1978, and 1980, the annual total was reduced to 270,000, with a limit of 20,000 visas to emigrants from any one country, without regard to its geographic location. But in the event, there would be many more legal immigrants than that coming each year. The preference system for new arrivals, established at first in 1965, was based on family ties with American citizens as well as on needed occupational skills applicants might bring to the United States. But because spouses, minor children, and parents of adult U.S. citizens are not subject to national ceilings, immigration from Mexico and other lands was much higher than the official national quotas. Almost as important, generous provisions for refugees from Vietnam and for others seeking political asylum, notably from Cuba, led to further increases in legal immigration. In 1978, there were 601,442 legal immigrants; in 1981, 596,600; in 1985, 570,009. More such newcomers were expected in the 1980s than in any decade in American history except for 1901–10.[31]

Yet legal immigration, despite the dramatic increases of recent years, was not the major cause of concern. It was the far greater number of illegal aliens, of "undocumented immigrants," that raised questions that some insist echo the themes of the historic nativists.

In April 1986, the chief patrol agent, San Diego Sector, of the U.S. Border Patrol reported that with sixty-six miles of border responsibility, his unit had arrested 270,000 illegal entrants in the previous six months. Most were from Mexico, but 6,500 represented fifty-five other countries. In April, 71,000 arrests would be made. "We're encountering an average of one illegal every thirty-five seconds here in San Diego County," the agent wrote. "I look at thousands of people massed along just twelve miles of border each night, waiting for darkness to conceal their northward trek."[32]

The illegals referred to by the chief patrol agent were the surreptitious entrants, people who walk, drive, swim, row, or climb across a part of the nation's borders. Some come alone, but most come in groups, guided or transported by smugglers for a fee. In the Southwest these smugglers are called "coyotes," and they are in a lucrative business; their estimated profits in 1985 were between $200,000 and $500,000 a month. Most of the EWIs (entered without inspection), as the Immigration and Naturalization Service (INS) calls them, come from Mexico and Latin America. Others, "visa abusers," are people who come from all parts of the world, entering the United States through an established port of entry, either unlawfully posing as American citizens or presenting authentic documents but subsequently violating their terms of entry. But how many illegal aliens come each year and how many take up permanent residence in the United States is a matter of controversy. Yearly Border Patrol apprehensions, only 79,610 in 1966, rose from 696,029 in 1976 to 1,262,435 in 1985, with a projected 1,800,000 for 1986. Some of those arrested, of course, were repeat offenders. But many more hundreds of thousands avoided arrest. (In one study, about 70 percent of all illegal immigrants interviewed at work in Los Angeles said they had never been apprehended.) Moreover, most of the arrested were EWIs, 90 percent of them Mexicans; visa abusers generally escaped detection. How many illegals are there? As early as 1974, the commissioner of the INS estimated the number of those "illegally in the United States" at 6 to 8 million but added, "It is probably as great as ten to twelve million." All careful students of the question agree that there is a glaring inadequacy of critical data. With national estimates of illegals ranging from 2 to 12 million by the mid-1980s (many experts agreeing on a range of 4 to 8 million), but with estimates of illegal aliens in Los Angeles County alone at 2 million and New York City at 1 million, it was clear that the numbers were large and the problem was growing. Many analysts shared the view of INS agents: the United States was losing control of its borders.[33]

The mushrooming nature of the problem of illegal entrants led to the creation of the Select Commission on Immigration and Refugee Policy (SCRIP) in 1978. Chaired by the Reverend Theodore Hesburgh, president of the University of Notre Dame and former chairman of the Civil Rights Commission, SCRIP gained increased public attention with the influx of 125,000 Cuban and 10,000 Haitian "boat people" by 1980. The Cubans, embarked on the so-called "freedom flotilla" of boats departing Mariel Bay, had been allowed to leave by Fidel Castro. (More than 2,000 of them had been released from prisons or mental hospitals for this voyage; they were Castro's special gift to America. The Marielito criminals would account for significant increases in the rates of violent crimes in Miami, Las Vegas, and other cities in subsequent months.) In its report, the commission called for deterring illegal immigration through better border enforcement and for civil and possibly criminal penalties for employers who knowingly hired unauthorized immigrants. This was a critical issue, for it was previously no crime to employ those who violate the law through their "entry without inspection." SCRIP also recommended, among other things, amnesty for those illegally resident in the United States before 1980.[34]

Important proposals from the Select Commission would become part of the major congressional effort to amend the Immigration and Nationality Act in the 1980s. Earlier, Representative Peter Rodino (D.-New Jersey) had introduced legislation against hiring illegal aliens. These "employer sanctions" passed the House but failed in the Senate in the 1970s. Now, under the leadership of Senator Alan Simpson (R.-Wyoming), a member of SCRIP, and Representative Romano L. Mazzoli (D.-Kentucky), chairman of the House Subcommittee on Immigration, Refugees and International Law, a new legislative assault was mounted. Employer sanctions and legalization (amnesty) were at the heart of the Simpson-Mazzoli bill. But it also provided for an "expanded" and "streamlined" version of the existing H-2 program (so called because it was section H-2 of the 1952 act), which allowed for the admittance of aliens for temporary jobs "if unemployed persons capable of performing such service or labor cannot be found in this country."

The bill was supported by the *New York Times*, which declared that it was "not nativist, not racist, not mean," but "a rare piece of legislation, a responsible immigration bill" at once "tough, fair, and humane." The *Times* cited the "astonishingly liberal idea of amnesty in this era of conservatism." (The *Times* editorial writer on this issue would receive a Pulitzer Prize.) With the great recession of 1982 pushing unemployment figures past 10 percent, others rallied to Simpson-Mazzoli. But there was widespread opposition. Hispanic political groups attacked it as discriminatory. Organized labor turned against the House bill because the temporary worker program was seen as threatening Americans' jobs. Many conservatives rejected it because it meant the legalization of large numbers of people who would swell the population and burden expensive social service programs. Others, agricultural and industrial employers of illegals, including many who had actively solicited border crossers, bitterly rejected the concept of sanctions directed against them. Nonetheless, the growing concern about illegal immigration allowed Simpson-Mazzoli to pass the Senate easily (80 to 19) in the Ninety-seventh Congress in 1982. But with members of the Hispanic caucus working against it, with lobbyists for growers and manufacturers who employed illegals particularly active, numerous amendments weakened the resolve of the bill's supporters in the House, and it was dropped after days of debate.[35]

Reintroduced in the Ninety-eighth Congress, Simpson-Mazzoli became enmeshed in the politics of the election year. The Senate again voted affirmatively, 76 to 18, but a slightly different variation passed the House. Numerous disputes over a joint version led to the demise of the bill in conference committee; the *Times* headline declared "the death of a humane idea." Throughout the process, leading Democratic presidential candidates Walter Mondale, Gary Hart, and Jesse Jackson opposed important provisions. President Ronald Reagan, also fearing reaction by Hispanic voters, refused to embrace the bill fully. (SIN, the national Spanish-language television network, called the legislation "the most blatantly anti-Hispanic bill ever.") Other Washington influentials, notably Speaker of the House Thomas "Tip" O'Neill, turned away from it. Earlier, Senator Edward Kennedy, fearing a "vehicle for discriminatory action against Hispanic Americans and other minority groups," had rejected employer sanctions as "offensive and repugnant to the concept of individual dignity and liberty" because Americans would have to prove their citizenship to "establish their legal right to work." Senator Peter Domenici of New Mexico had returned to the theme of nativism in discussing his Italian immigrant parents, saying his mother had been "an illegal alien for a long time" and remembering when INS agents "visited my home . . . one of the most frightening memories of my childhood." Senator S. I. Hayakawa evoked the specter of roundups, "the way we did to the Japanese in World War Two." Columnist Carl Rowan might complain about "a barrage of demagoguery . . . shamefully misleading statements . . . distortions and blatant misrepresentations," but Simpson-Mazzoli was beaten. Still, a Simpson-Rodino bill would emerge in the next Congress. This issue would not die.[36]

The nature of the debate over the bills revealed the curious coalitions of liberals and conservatives on each side of the question. It is also reminiscent of the disputes involving nativists and their opponents over the vast immigration from Ireland and Germany in the 1840s and 1850s and from southern and eastern Europe in the 1890s and 1900s. But most significantly, the debate illuminated the differences between many of the new antialien concerns and those in the past, the reasons why nativism has not returned in some new guise in the 1980s, why the image of a "neo–Know Nothingism" is inappropriate in this context.

Surely the sides taken in this controversy did not fall neatly into traditional ideological divisions. Both conservatives and liberals have opposed restrictive legislation such as Simpson-Mazzoli.

These theorists argue that illegal aliens take only those jobs that American citizens reject or, at worst, they compete with "secondary workers" such as "youth and housewives." Indeed, these analysts insist that illegals serve to expand employment, not contract it. "They make jobs, not take jobs," because their purchases, in the words of one economist, "increase the demand for labor, leading to new hires." Similarly, it is argued that illegals cost less than they contribute to federal and state revenues. These immigrants, in America temporarily and fearing apprehension, use few public welfare services but through their taxes provide a "substantial surplus to natives." In the end, their champions assert, immigrants—including illegals—are the key to national prosperity, for they boost productivity in the 1980s even as did immigrants in the years when nativists were assailing the European migrants. The illegal entrants should not be victims of "repression"; that would be unfaithful to our heritage, unwise for our economy, and unnecessary for the health and well-being of the country.[37]

But these arguments are unpersuasive to the proponents of immigration reform. There is no such thing as a free lunch, say those who want vigorous action to stem illegal immigration. They point to studies which demonstrate that illegals do make use of a wide range of social programs—food stamps, Aid to Dependent Children, unemployment insurance, medical and welfare benefits—and strain these resources in a time when many call for cutbacks that would adversely affect the American poor. More important, the critics insist that native Americans, particularly the most vulnerable, are losing jobs to the illegals.

Of course, unemployed Americans are willing to take hard, dirty jobs; the implication that low-skilled native workers are lazy or indifferent, it is argued, is not only absurd but tinged with racism. One survey of employers of illegals in Chicago revealed that when asked to develop their initial response that no native Americans were available for these jobs, the employers observed: "I don't think black people want to work in Chicago," "Blacks are the most unreliable help you can get," and the like. Locked out of many restaurant, cleaning, and supermarket jobs, refused basic agricultural employment in some cases because "undocumented immigrants" are available, these American poor—many of them blacks and Chicanos—suffer because of their nation's failure to control its borders. But it is not only the "secondary" labor market that is affected. In the "primary" market—jobs in construction and manufacturing— illegal aliens also cause significant displacement. In Los Angeles, San Antonio, Miami, and other cities, these illegals are often regarded as "preferred hires" because they are less likely to join unions or to complain about sex discrimination, safety problems, or the denial of equal employment opportunities. In Houston, according to one 1982 study, foremen preferred illegals because they could extract large kickbacks from them. Indeed, a substantial minority of illegals may be engaged in so-called "black work" in service and light manufacturing industries, with these desperate would-be employees willing to work below minimum wage and to accept violations of overtime and child labor standards. It was not surprising, said proponents of immigration reform, that in the first major survey of Hispanic and black attitudes toward immigration policy, conducted in summer 1983, substantial majorities of both Hispanic and black Americans favored proposals to curb illegal immigration through penalties and fines for employers. Majorities of both groups believed that American jobs were being lost and that tougher immigration laws were essential. Despite the activities of Hispanic political leaders, many Hispanic as well as black Americans appeared to be calling for reform.[38]

The survey was sponsored by the Federation for American Immigration Reform (FAIR), a national organization founded in 1979. Though recognizing and, in some cases, echoing the concerns of what Otis L. Graham, Jr., has characterized as the voices of "conservative restrictionism"—issues of border control and social welfare costs—FAIR leaders focus as well on the case for "liberal restrictionism." They point to the problem of a population "time bomb" threatening the resources and the environment of the United States. They argue that concerns for racial justice, social equality, and job displacement in America also point to the need for immigration reform.[39]

The population of Latin America had exploded to over 350 million by the mid-1980s. Mexico, its population doubling within a generation from a birth rate approaching an astounding 3.5 percent in the 1970s (although declining somewhat in subsequent years), represented a particular problem. With a per capita income just over 20 percent that of the United States, it is as if, one writer suggested, "Algeria were to border directly upon the South of France or West Germany upon Zaire." With its economy in shambles as a result of economic mismanagement and the oil price slump of the 1980s, Mexico faced skyrocketing inflation and massive unemployment. It could not support its huge new population, swollen by an immense baby boom that resulted in 49 percent of all its citizens being under age seventeen. In fact, the population explosion, "far from being the root of the problem," as one analyst insisted, was itself the result of the "desperate need in poor rural households" for wage earners. But where to go to earn a wage?[40]

The United States has been the magnet. Its affluence beckons to those in despair even as it served to provide jobs in an earlier age for temporary agricultural workers in the contract-labor Bracero Program from 1942 to 1964 and for hungry illegals—*los mojados*, "the wetbacks"—from the 1940s to the 1970s. Now, with Mexico's population soaring past 70 million (it had been below 30 million in the 1950s), with border towns swelling at unprecedented rates (Tijuana, 65,000 in 1950, 754,000 in 1980), there are millions close enough to learn of employment prospects to the north and to be guided there for a price. Some Americans might counsel against restriction because of foreign policy concerns, particularly the fear that Mexico, denied a safety valve for its "domestic discontent," will slide into political chaos and threaten the stability of the entire hemisphere. But advocates of immigration reform look to a larger danger. Most of these illegal newcomers, they argue, will not be temporary workers this time. Many of them are young men, and like migrants of the past and in other lands, they will bring their families northward or build new families here. They will have an enormous impact on the American future.[41]

If not checked now, analysts cited by FAIR argue, the population increase in the United States from Mexico and other parts of the Third World could change the nature of America within a century. Post-1980 immigrants and their descendants would account for more than 40 percent of elementary school students and of the labor force if population and demographic patterns of 1985 continue unchecked. In California, two-thirds of the population would consist of these newcomers and their progeny. Although these concerns sound familiar to students of nativist fears during the immigration influx in the nineteenth century, there are vital differences today. Reformers argue that America has changed and so has the population pressure on the planet since the golden door was closed in 1921. The United States, its economy buffeted by the wrenching defeats of the 1970s, simply cannot absorb these illegal aliens as it did the millions in an earlier century, when the underpopulated continent-sized New World was undergoing its industrial revolution. Moreover, the revolutionary growth of global population from the present 5 billion to 6.2 billion by 2000, and perhaps 10 or 12 billion in the next century, according to some analysts, makes any "open borders" policy untenable even for most optimists about the resilient, absorbent quality of the American economy. In addition, huge population increases would surely affect the ecology of the nation, voraciously depleting its land and water resources.[42]

There are other concerns beyond population. Social justice for poor Americans and equal treatment for all minorities will not be promoted, it is argued, by a wave of illegal immigration that not only eliminates many job opportunities for natives but leads to exploitation of the newcomers. This is a prescription for the creation of a growing American underclass. Not only is it unfair that many enter illegally through porous borders while many others wait patiently for a place in a legal quota, but the wave of illegals helps promote an ominously more segmented society, ever more ethnically and racially divided by economic and social station. Worse, as the conflict in Lawrence demonstrated and as other episodes of intergroup violence in Miami, Denver, and Los Angeles have suggested, working class and poor, Hispanic and black, Asian and Anglo in America have been set against one another. This is particularly tragic when, as Graham has noted, "the enemy ought to be the exploiter," not these "ragged volunteer laborers worse off even than our own unemployed."[43]

Although the clashes between aliens and citizens seem to mirror

events in an earlier age of upheaval and anxiety, social and economic changes in this century suggest a different conclusion. Nineteenth-century nativists' fears were rooted in part in a rational
appraisal of the massive impact of immigrants on their urban environment. But their antialien animus was marked by both an un-
realistic appraisal of economic opportunity in their age and an irrational projection of fears and hatreds on foreigners because of ethnicity and religion. The new concern about illegal aliens emerges
from a very different analysis of the problem and does not come
from the purveyors of racial hate and religious intolerance. A few
members of those tiny sects of right-wing neofascists and fragments of the Klan might attack the new immigration, making it
appear to some that there is a "bizarre coalition" emerging on this
issue, but there is, in fact, no major right-wing antialien effort calling for action in the name of old nativism. Indeed, there is no
"movement" at all. There is FAIR, an educational lobby. There are
the political activities of some members of Congress of very different ideological persuasions. There are the efforts of some labor
leaders and their union rank and file. These "antialiens" all call for
an end to massive illegal immigration but with provision for the
humane treatment of those illegal entrants and refugees already in
the country and concern for protection of the civil liberties and
rights of citizens and immigrants alike.

They insist that massive immigration must be checked for a variety of reasons, but it is the illegal entrants who are seen as the
major concern. And though the reformers believe that America
cannot absorb all of those in the world who desire admittance,
their fear is not that there are at present "unassimilable hordes"
within the land, as nativists argued in the past. Indeed, they argue
that the assimilation of many newcomers is itself put at risk by the
insistence of Hispanic groups on a policy of bilingualism. This can
make it difficult, it is asserted, for many immigrants, living in ethnic enclaves served by Spanish-language radio and television stations, to master English and follow in the footsteps of ethnic millions who came before. It is also discomforting to many natives in
Miami and elsewhere who already complain that they feel strangers
in their own land. There are people who believe they are at a disadvantage in local job markets because they speak English, who fear
that America is building a "Quebec" to the south, places perma-

nently removed from the American mainstream because of language.

There are many major issues involved in the new debate about immigration. But the advocates of immigration reform are hardly operating in a spirit "that springs from the heart of the Know Nothings." They represent but one side of a vigorous dialogue involving quarreling academics, social critics, journalists, citizen activists, and politicians. They do not represent a "movement." They certainly do not represent a return to the nativist traditions of the past.

On 17 October 1986, the Simpson-Rodino bill, declared "dead" by Representative Peter W. Rodino only a few days earlier, won final approval in Congress. A last-minute compromise, deemed "miraculous" by Rodino, was engineered by Representative Charles E. Schumer of New York. It involved special amnesty for illegal aliens serving as agricultural workers and guaranteed the "supply of seasonal farm labor" through 1993; this provision satisfied powerful growers and their congressional friends. With members of the Hispanic caucus no longer presenting a unified front of opposition to reform— for some of these representatives were now reporting the endorsement of the measure by large numbers of their own constituents— the bill cleared its final obstacle with a 63 to 24 vote in the Senate.

The provisions were similar to the SCRIP–Simpson-Mazzoli agenda for reform: employer sanctions (ranging to $10,000 per illegal alien for a third offense, up to six months in prison for "a pattern or practice of violation"), amnesty for illegals entering the United States before 1982, strengthened border security, and efforts at identification of all job applicants along with provisions to protect Hispanic citizens. Although critics warned of threats to the civil liberties of Hispanic-Americans, the probability of a surge in bogus documents for recent and future illegals, and new strains with Mexico, others saluted the bill as a landmark measure. By early December, preliminary returns from the INS indicated that arrests along the Mexican border had dropped nearly 30 percent in comparison with the year before. Nonetheless, most knowledgeable people predicted that massive numbers of those "entering without inspection" would continue to cross the American frontiers and that the agonizing questions concerning this new immigration would continue to generate concern and stimulate debate.

But it would not be a debate conducted in the rhetoric of nativism.[44]

The old forms of right-wing antialienism, for all the headlines involving the tiny racist sects and the fulminations of a Lyndon La Rouche, are in decline. So, too, are other forms of truly nativist animus. Even the fear that anti-Semitism might be emerging from the splenetic fantasies of the minuscule Identity groups into the larger nation seems groundless, despite the flurry of concern during the 1984 Democratic primaries. This was when the Reverend Jesse Jackson characterized Jews as "Hymies" and was quoted as referring to "Jewish control" of labor unions and the media, when Jackson supporter and Black Muslim leader Louis Farrakhan was alleged to have referred to Judaism as a "gutter religion." But there was no real issue here, and candidate Jackson, damaged by the episode, apologized.[45]

Just as traditional nativism is no longer a force in America, neither is the assault on domestic communism. Of course, in 1986, the John Birch Society still functioned. In fall 1984, the widow of Georgia Congressman and Birch Society notable Larry McDonald—killed en route to a JBS conference in Seoul, South Korea, when his airliner was shot down over Soviet territory—toured the country for the Crusade to Stop Funding Communism. Birchers alleged that the Red Air Force attacked the Korea Air Lines flight in September 1983 as part of an assassination plot against a key member of the society. McDonald's wife called for renewed efforts to halt trade with the barbaric Soviet Union and its clients. Meanwhile, the John Birch Society was busy during the political campaign. JBS "national spokesman" John F. McManus denounced the Democratic candidate for the Senate in Massachusetts, John Kerry, for "near treasonous activities" as a leader of the Vietnam Veterans Against the War in the early 1970s. Accused of being a "Communist sympathizer," Kerry, a highly decorated Vietnam war hero, responded by observing that "all decent Americans" reject the positions of the Birch Society. His opponent, a millionaire businessman named Roy Shamie, had been briefly affiliated with the JBS in 1974. Now, fearing that any linkage with what he quickly characterized as an "extreme" organization would damage his chances, Shamie disavowed any connection with the Birchers. The society remained a disreputable fragment on the fringe, as much an embarrassment to its friends as in the days of Welch's overheated fantasies. In 1986, staggering under a $9 million deficit, it made a desperate appeal for funds in order to stay alive. The antialien crusade is not good politics even for the most conservative candidate. For despite Ronald Reagan's remarkably bitter rhetoric about the Soviet Union, the shadow of the Red Scare has faded. Even as the Cold War reached a new nadir by 1983–84, with relations between the superpowers more strained than any time since 1948 or 1961, there was no neo-McCarthyism on the horizon.[46]

★★★
The Rise of the New Religious Right

But what of the New Right? The elements supporting Ronald Reagan included groups well to the right of many in his administration. Does the "religious Right" and what some characterize as the "hard Right" embrace the old tradition? Through the New Right, will right-wing antialienism emerge once more as an important force in years to come?

Many believe it will. In fall 1984, a national interfaith group formed in 1965 to protest U.S. policy in Southeast Asia, the Clergy and Laity Concerned (CALC), called for "people of all faiths" to speak out against the religious Right. In a direct mail appeal, CALC leaders described a land in which people who advocate a freeze on nuclear weapons are "characterized as un-American," in which those who "oppose arms buildups, work to improve the plight of poverty-stricken women," and show concern "about human rights and hunger" are "characterized as un-American." Meanwhile, on television screens throughout the nation, the media celebrities of the new religious Right preached the sermons used by their adversaries as evidence of the return of the antialien appeal.

Jimmy Swaggart, perhaps the most effective and surely the most histrionic of these television preachers, often uses the old themes in his spectacular performances. Based in Baton Rouge, Louisiana, but traveling the world to deliver the word, he has staged his crusades before large crowds and ever-present cameras in Brazil, Italy, Argentina, Central America, and the Philippines, as well as across the United States, particularly in Sunbelt cities. By the mid-1980s, surveys indicated that he was drawing the largest personal audience of all ministers in what had quickly become known as the elec-

tronic church. He was reaching some 2.6 million households in the
United States (he was also being seen in eighty foreign countries)
for a weekly show aired on more than two hundred stations. An
Assemblies of God minister, a believer in the healing gifts of the
Holy Spirit (charisms), Swaggart had built a $30 million World Min-
istry Center complex in Baton Rouge, featuring a luxurious car-
peted seven-thousand-seat amphitheater, a huge printing plant, the
elaborate Vance Teleproduction Center, and the campus of Jimmy
Swaggart Bible College. He was raising $140 million yearly, mostly
from direct on-the-air appeals but also through the marketing of his
music, sermons, T-shirts, and Bibles. He was directing efforts to
feed starving children in Africa and Asia, but this did not interfere
with his own upscale lifestyle. He had constructed two large homes
for his family costing over $1.1 million; the five-acre estate was
across the road from the Country Club of Louisiana. "You're not
looking at an evangelist who is fresh from the golf course," he told
his viewers, "you're not looking at an evangelist who is dabbling in
real estate."[47]

Jimmy Swaggart is a brilliant platform performer, capable of speaking for hours without notes while walking back and forth across
the stage, shouting, whispering, laughing, or crying into the microphone. "People are tired of hearing dead preachers preaching dead
sermons to dead congregations," he proclaims. Since finding God at
age nine, "forty two years ago, I have never cooled down and I never
will!" Because "Jesus is alive!" he shouts. "Mohammed is dead but
Jesus is alive! Buddha is dead but Jesus is alive! Marx, Lenin, Stalin
are dead but Jesus is alive! Glory." Occasionally he sits at the piano,
evoking memories of his first cousin and boyhood companion, the
troubled rock star Jerry Lee Lewis. Swaggart has sold 13 million
copies of his gospel albums, including "Jimmy Swaggart's Greatest
Hits." His show is most popular in the South, but the largest single
television market is New York, and as early as 1982 he had a standing room crowd at Madison Square Garden, with five thousand people turned away. A school dropout with sparse formal training in
theology, this tall, striking blonde man with glasses is contemptuous of mainline Protestant clergymen, referring to them as a "litur-
gical, religious mandarinate." He turned to full-time "preaching" in
1958 and began his television career in 1973.[48]

In his American sermons, he reviles those old enemies "socialism, communism, materialism." Sometimes he sounds like a nativ-

ist publicist from the 1850s: "The United States has had more light than any country on this planet. . . . God has placed His hand upon America." Sometimes he sounds like an unreconstructed McCarthyite from the 1950s: "Fellow traveling Communist liberals spit on the flag of America and praise Russia . . . why don't they go back to Russia if they like it so much." Sometimes he evokes memories of Robert Welch: "Communists have penetrated the schools, gotten control of television and the media, manipulated public art and have infiltrated the churches." He quotes old Red Scare warriors such as W. Cleon Skousen, author of *The Naked Communist*, and calls for the United States to get out of the United Nations and "get the U.N. out of the U.S." He argues that the United States misunderstood the USSR in the 1930s, "modernized the Soviet Union in the 1970s at the cost of the American economic crisis of the eighties," and now we "should break off diplomatic relations with those thugs and gangsters" and stop selling to "atheistic, God-hating, U.S.-hating governments." In Swaggart, the line from the Know Nothings to the New Right often seems straight and true. But in this case, selective quotation obscures more than it clarifies. The religious Right is not just the reemergence of yesterday's movement.[49]

In most of his sermons, Swaggart seems much more concerned with the social agenda than the political, with the perils of modernity than the need to combat communism. Like evangelists of the nineteenth century, he attacks the Satanic presence tempting people into sin. Like fundamentalist preachers at the Scopes trial in the 1920s, he assails the "benighted lies" of "evolutionism," which has "no place for God in its story of how man came from monkeys." He is concerned with the sexual revolution, characterizing masturbation, oral sex, and homosexuality as "the filth of hell running rampant over this nation," assailing sex education as a program to teach children "how to enjoy fornication without having to feel guilty." He says he is "sick of the Equal Rights Amendment and the ACLU," those counselors of change. He says it is his mission to expose that "slimy snail crawling out from under a rock" which is the "liberalistic press," peddling "filth, moral sewage and demonic dehumanism." He characterizes the real enemies within not as American communists or socialists, not as Catholics, Jews, or un-American ethnics, but as secular humanists, the people who "have come within a hairbreadth of destroying this nation."[50]

"Secular humanism" is the real adversary for much of the new religious Right. According to movement theoretician Tim LaHaye, author of the basic text for those of this persuasion, *The Battle for the Mind*, the foundations for modern humanism were laid by Thomas Aquinas in the thirteenth century. The effort to "raise human wisdom" to a level "equal with biblical revelation" flourished with the work of Voltaire and Rousseau, "the French skeptics." In the United States, John Dewey, "atheist and board member of the American Humanist Association," played the key role in a humanist takeover of the American educational system in the twentieth century. American humanists have become the leading advocates of "amorality, evolution and atheism." They constitute a religious faith, but unlike the Catholic enemies of earlier nativism, these believers are not born into their sect but simply accept its malevolent ideas. They are part of those "pagan religions" which also number "Confucianism, Buddhism, Mohammedanism" (as opposed to "biblical religions": Christianity and Judaism). "Humanist obsessions," LaHaye writes, include "sex, pornography, marijuana, self-indulgence, rights without responsibilities and disillusionment with America." They lead the young to rebellion against "God, parents and authority," as well as to a "tragic lack in skills . . . self-worth, purpose and happiness." LaHaye sees an enormous conspiracy, involving the "humanist controllers of the American Civil Liberties Union," the Ford, Rockefeller, and Carnegie foundations, the National Organization for Women, the National Education Association, the "unions," the courts, and academics. Together, they have gained control over the public schools, book distributorships, the press and television, the movie industry, some mainline Protestant churches, and "to a large degree, the government." Although there are only 275,000 such humanists in America, they are the agents of "depravity." They had achieved almost total control despite the presence of "60 million religious pro-moralists" and "60 million born again Christians," people concerned with "decency." Secular humanism's satanic influence is present everywhere and has brought gambling, prostitution, drug abuse, homosexuality, and abortions on demand in its train. It is the atheistic enemy of "America as a Christian nation."[51]

Whether or not the media celebrities of the new electronic church accept LaHaye's assessment of secular humanism's conspiratorial origins, they do share a resolve to confront this enemy from their television pulpits. Several such preachers bid for attention in 1986. Swaggart might be the most dynamic, but the others also are relatively young, articulate, and confident before the cameras, with the striking good looks of the leading men of network serials or anchor men of network news.

In fact, Pat Robertson, the emerging star in a firmament of televangelists by 1986, made his mark as an anchorman and host of a syndicated TV talk show. The "700 Club" is the programming heart of the Christian Broadcasting Network (CBN), founded and directed by Robertson. It is named for the seven hundred people the minister tried to recruit to donate $10 a month to keep alive a tiny UHV station he had purchased in 1962.

Pat Robertson is the son of A. Willis Robertson, formerly a powerful United States senator from Virginia. He was a marine captain in Korea and graduated from Washington and Lee University and Yale Law School. But he never practiced law; he failed the New York bar examination, explaining that his heart was not in it. He soon left a business career to enter a theological seminary in New York City in which the Charismatic or Neopentecostal fellowship spoke in tongues and practiced faith healing. Later, after renouncing worldly goods and serving as a church worker in a religious commune in a Brooklyn slum, he emerged to "claim for Jesus" the defunct station in Virginia Beach, Virginia. He was the pioneer among the new generation of television preachers. He had no money, but through appeals to his viewers he first saved WYAH and then built a media empire.

By 1986, Robertson had become a TV entrepreneur unmatched even by the most successful of his fundamentalist colleagues. First to create a religious television station, first to solicit commercial sponsors, he capitalized on the cable revolution to make CBN, the first religious network, not only the largest Christian network but the fourth largest of any kind. (With over 30 million subscribers in 1986 it trailed closely behind the leader, Entertainment Sports Programming Network [ESPN], with 36.9 million.) By 1982, he already had built a $33 million broadcasting campus on 347 acres in Virginia Beach, where CBN, with thirteen hundred employees, was on the air twenty-four hours a day and had thousands of volunteers answering millions of "prayer calls." Four years later, his enterprise was flourishing. It owned three commercial television outlets and the CBN University graduate school. It was preparing to open a law school, and the minister-director met a nationwide schedule of appearances with his own large jet transport. His fund solicitations were extraordinarily successful; called a "marketing genius" by one publication, he was raising $233 million a year.

But the "700 Club" remained the key to the empire. It was here that Pat Robertson, at the age of fifty-five in 1986, made his greatest impact on events. Unlike Swaggart or many other famous preachers, this pleasant, soft-spoken man with a nonthreatening persona does not shout or cry. He tries not to frighten or anger his audience. Indeed, he seems not to be the "star" of the show at all, but simply a genial co-host (with his colleague Ben Kinchlow), sitting in a comfortable living room—a set created in front of an audience in a vast studio—and chatting with his guests. These guests have included President Ronald Reagan and his two predecessors, cabinet members, visiting foreign dignitaries, and other celebrities. In these exchanges, Robertson speaks with considerable mastery of a variety of complex questions involving the national economy and domestic, international, and military affairs. "There is nothing churchy at CBN," he has said. But his own views about society and government set the tone for the "700 Club" and the network. Like the other leaders of the new religious Right, he assaults the humanist enemy. But he does so in a subtle and peculiarly effective way, emanating from his own modest and appealing personality. His earlier observation that "we have enough votes to run this country" took on new meaning in 1986.[52]

Pat Robertson not only was the fundamentalist media pioneer but he was responsible for the emergence of some other national figures of the genre. Jim Bakker, who said that "my spiritual gift, my specific calling from God, is to be a television talk-show host," got his start with Robertson in the early years of the "700 Club." After leaving CBN, he joined Paul Crouch, who had followed Robertson's lead and established the Trinity Broadcasting Network (TBN). For Crouch, Jim Bakker introduced a show called "Praise the Lord," but he left TBN after a personal disagreement with its chief. He moved to Charlotte, North Carolina, and borrowing from his mentors, organized the PTL network (for Praise the Lord or People That Love). PTL soon became the second-ranked Christian network, available in 13 million homes for twenty-four hours of daily religious programs.[53]

The son of a Muskegon, Michigan, machinist, a Bible college

dropout who was later ordained in a Pentecostal order, another practitioner of faith healing and glossolalia (speaking in tongues), Bakker became another entrepreneurial minister. By 1985, he was raising $100 million a year. He had opened an immense Disneyland-like theme park at Fort Mill, South Carolina, Heritage USA, along with a shopping mall, a luxury hotel, Heritage University, the Heritage School of Evangelism and Communications, and his own Assemblies of God church. He offered the message that Christ and the gospel will bring not only happiness but a higher standard of living to believers. Born into poverty, he preached a sunny materialism: "If you pray for a camper, be sure to tell God what color." His sermons, Jeffrey Hadden observed, argued that Christianity "is not just a religious experience but a life-style success." In this regard, Bakker, at forty-six a man with an exceptionally boyish appearance who shared the leadership of his network with his wife, Tammy, was very different from some of the other media preachers. For example, James Robison, the powerful Fort Worth fundamentalist, described by Frances FitzGerald as looking like a cross between James Dean and Burt Lancaster, is also a fervent enemy of secular humanism. But his sermons were much closer to Swaggart's than to Bakker's. His program, called "James Robison, Man with a Message," was syndicated on more than sixty stations by the early 1980s. It offered a sterner, more confrontational message, and he stirred controversy in an early crusade by characterizing homosexuality as perversion. "Wake Up America," his television special in 1980, was titled "We're all Hostages." The American government had been captured by the ungodly. Secular humanism was the enemy once again.[54]

Different from those older television preachers—Billy Graham, Oral Roberts, Rex Humbard—who celebrated patriotism and occasionally attached themselves to presidents (notably Graham and Richard Nixon), these newcomers tie their sermons to "social issues." They call for political action against the secular humanists who are corrupting America and threatening "family values" and national stability. In fact, the new fundamentalists reject many aspects of the broader evangelical movement, particularly its preference for "penetration" as opposed to "strong confrontation" as a means of social change. Many evangelicals are criticized for a willingness to cooperate with traditional denominations and for avoiding "ecclesiastical separatist activity" and biblical polemics. The

New Evangelicalism's "toleration of error," its "accommodation" and "cooperation" with error, has led to "contamination by error" and "capitulation" to error. "There is very little doctrinal difference between Fundamentalism and Evangelicalism," Jerry Falwell and colleagues have observed, but the "approach to others" is all-important. The New Right fundamentalists are particularly critical of Graham, "an ecumenical evangelist," whose inclusive crusade sponsorship they see as a concession to apostasy. Billy Graham, Falwell and colleagues have noted, has preached at a Roman Catholic institution, to a World Council of Churches conference, and to meetings sponsored by those who "propagated liberal ideas regarding the creation." This is intolerable.[55]

Although some older fundamentalists, characterized by Falwell as "hyper fundamentalists," notably the leaders of Bob Jones University, have rejected the new media stars because of their insistence on becoming involved in secular political matters and not sticking strictly to spiritual concerns, the celebrities of the new Christian Right captured the leadership of the fundamentalist movement in the 1980s. They have their differences. Some, notably Jerry Falwell, have implied that faith healing is theologically unsound; others, including Robertson and Bakker, have been practitioners. The Pentecostal and Neopentecostal Charismatic followers who respond affirmatively to such practices and to the more emotional style of their ministries have often been less enthusiastic about the stern, more austere message of the Independent Baptist fundamentalist Falwell. But their theological differences pale before their common purposes.[56]

They are the militants of the religious Right, and they took advantage of Federal Communications Commission rulings in the 1960s and 1970s which allowed paid religious broadcasts to satisfy the mandated public service time required of all local stations. Because these fundamentalists immediately proved to be brilliant fund-raisers, willing to use their ministerial authority in direct, passionate appeals for dollar contributions from their unseen audiences, they soon pushed conventional, local religious leaders off the air. By 1980, 90 percent of all religious programming on television was commercial; local stations could satisfy the FCC and make money at the same time. By 1984, dozens of religious-oriented TV stations, five networks, and more than fourteen hundred religious radio stations were also on the air. Satellite transmissions and cable channels enabled them to reach millions of homes. A Nielsen study in 1985, commissioned by CBN, reported that 21 percent of the 85 million American households with television sets tuned in to religious programming for six minutes or more during one week. Another study in 1984 estimated that 13.3 million people (or 6.2 percent of the television audience) were regular religious viewers.

But the road to media success was not uniformly smooth. Bakker's PTL Club faced a continuing series of financial crises from its establishment in 1974 until the scandals that rocked the ministry in 1987. CBN was experiencing severe financial heavy weather in 1981 until Pat Robertson decided to reduce the network's religious content to only one-quarter of its air time. Certainly the New Right televangelists have always exaggerated their audience. Jerry Falwell has used the phrase "ministerially speaking" in joking reference to his estimates, and national newspapers and magazines have printed grossly distorted numbers. With some ideological enemies of the Christian Right anxious to inflate the size of the adversary for their own purposes—a liberal fund-raiser admitted that "you always need a devil to succeed in the direct mail business"—the religious Right media stars sometimes have seemed bigger than life. Still, the rapid growth of their enterprises and their following was startling in the mid-1980s. Their annual revenues exceeded one-half billion tax-free dollars in 1985. Their audiences were in the millions, and there was good reason for Robertson and Falwell to appear on different occasions as newsmagazine cover subjects. Like some latter-day version of Father Coughlin or Gerald L. K. Smith, when they had radio listeners in the millions, the new religious Right had found its forum—a huge electronic camp meeting—from which to confront its enemies.[57]

Those enemies were the "secular humanists" and their allies, seen as dominating the major institutions and influencing government policies, particularly social policies that undermined "traditional" arrangements and "family values." The reaction to the social upheavals of the 1960s and the setbacks of the 1970s now intersected with an emerging fundamentalist passion, blossoming in the 1980s as it had sixty years earlier in another age of conservative consensus. But should religious figures involve themselves in such secular affairs? The media fundamentalists insisted from the start that their faith mandated involvement; the way to serve God and ensure a Christian future was to mobilize believers against the sinful policies of a manipulated state and to encourage others to join the ranks of the saved and the militant. Yet there was another reason why preachers could now "meddle in politics." The precedent established by the Reverend Martin Luther King, Jr., and his fellow ministers in the Southern Christian Leadership Conference (SCLC), as well as the religious figures involved in the antiwar movements of the 1960s, suggested that clergymen could play a major role in shaping public policy. Critics might argue that the televangelists of the religious Right play a somewhat different role than did the ministers of civil rights and the peace marches. Now the preachers insist that they are not only passionately committed to a cause but are the very instruments of the Almighty in their crusades for particular policies, but this distinction is obscured by the parallels. Jerry Falwell had criticized King and the others in 1965: "We need to get off the streets and into the pulpits and prayer rooms." Twenty years later, he had changed his view.[58]

Indeed, of all the leaders of this new movement, Falwell, the minister of the Thomas Road Baptist Church in Lynchburg, Virginia, emerged as the most famous and most influential figure in the early 1980s. "The Old Time Gospel Hour," his television vehicle, was established as the videotaped sermons Falwell delivers in Lynchburg at eleven every Sunday morning. By 1980, he had 2.5 million people on his mailing list and an audience of almost 1.3 million for a show appearing on 180 stations. By 1986, he had established his own National Christian Network. Slightly older than some of his contemporaries, Falwell was born in 1933 in Lynchburg. After graduating as valedictorian of his high school class, he turned to the church, finishing his education at Baptist Bible College in Springfield, Missouri. Falwell started the Thomas Road Church with thirty-five parishioners meeting in a bleak, used factory building that had housed a Donald Duck bottling plant in 1956. Thirty years later he had twenty-one thousand members and an elaborate complex of buildings with a "supermarket-sized" parking lot for the famed Sunday sermons.

Funded by local members and aided by the huge revenues brought in by the national broadcast appeals—$115 million in the period 1977–80, $100 million per year by 1985—Falwell built a Christian Academy (kindergarten through grade twelve), a correspondence school with fifteen hundred students, a Bible institute, a seminary, a home for alcoholics, a summer camp, and the expanding campus of Liberty University, an institution with seven thousand students and plans for fifty thousand students plus a Division IA football team in fifteen years. Through the International Bible Center he offered computerized Bible programs and a video-Bible teaching series. In this way he hopes to establish "5000 new churches by the end of the century." He has proved an extraordinary promoter and has taken advantage of new technologies and marketing tools, employing advertising agencies and computer consulting firms. If he is less flamboyant than some other media preachers—a heavyset man in a sober three-piece black suit facing the weekly cameras and rarely resorting to verbal pyrotechnics—he became the central figure in the new religious Right.[59]

Jerry Falwell once described himself as a "separatist, premillennialist, pre-tribulationist sort of fellow." Falwell and the other modern fundamentalists, like their precursors in the nineteenth and early twentieth centuries, embrace the doctrine of biblical inerrancy, holding that every word of the Bible is literally the Word of God. Thus they attack the "evolutionists," those tools of secular humanism, with the fervor of William Jennings Bryan half a century ago. They lobby vigorously for "creation science" as an alternative to Darwin in the public school curriculum, for the Bible teaches that creation was carried out in exactly six days some six to twenty thousand years ago.

In *McLean* v. *Arkansas Board of Education*, a federal district court ruled against "creationism," striking down a law barring the teaching of evolution in Arkansas classrooms. The presiding judge concluded that "creation science" was not a science at all but a religion. The state did not appeal this verdict in 1982, but four years later the Supreme Court accepted an appeal of a similar verdict involving a Louisiana law. The fundamentalists have insisted that not only is the received truth of God on their side—despite the opinion of the overwhelming majority of scientists—but to expose their children to "evolutionism" was to undermine their faith and thus weaken the free exercise of their religion.[60]

But even more dramatic than the creationist controversy has been the way the new fundamentalists wrestle with the problem of Armageddon. Their literal reading of the Bible suggests that there is a terrible tribulation to come, after the Antichrist strikes for power and before Christ returns to bring his millennial reign of peace and justice. Hal Lindsey's *The Late Great Planet Earth*, "the number one bestseller of the decade," with 10 million copies in print since publication in 1970, has been an important work in this regard. This book and subsequent volumes tell the story of a vast conflict involving an invasion of Israel by huge armies from the Soviet Union and an alliance of Arab and African states. They are met on a field of battle of unparalleled scale by the combined forces of the "revived Roman Empire," a new United States of Europe. (In this scenario, America is no longer the leader of the West.) Emerging from the struggle is the "Future Führer," the Roman dictator, the Antichrist. But as the Soviet and Arab armies are destroyed with nuclear weapons, an "incredible Oriental army of 200 million soldiers" emerges "under the leadership of the Red Chinese war machine." The ensuing conflict ends with a murderous nuclear exchange, obliterating the major cities of the world, including New York, Los Angeles, and Chicago. Yet as this final battle of Armageddon—World War III—reaches its awful climax with missile-borne devastation, radiation poisoning, and nuclear winter, "in this very moment" Jesus Christ will return and save man from self-extinction. Just before the awesome and terrible military engagements, "pretribulationist" theorists of Armageddon offer salvation to true believers. Fundamentalist Christians will be lifted up to meet Christ in the air in the Rapture; while others are doomed, the Saved are literally saved.[61]

In these prophecies of unimaginable destruction to come, the fundamentalists imply that not only is the biblical blueprint for the future "inerrantly" true but nonbelievers are going to get what is coming to them for their failure to heed the word. Believers should not worry; Jerry Falwell has said that he does not own a cemetery plot, he does not need one. They even look with excited anticipation to the event: "The countdown to Armageddon," according to Tim LaHaye, "has begun." Certainly this is a very different world view than is held by those fervent survivalists of the Christian Identity sects. Those people believe they will have to fight their way through the time of catastrophic tribulation against a variety of alien enemies. The fundamentalist premillenarians, on the other hand, are sure of survival and of enjoying the thousand years of peace and bliss to follow.

As Timothy Weber has noted, "The atomic age and apocalypticism are made for each other." The planet may be a terrifying place in the nuclear age, but the religious word is offered to calm the fears of those living in a world seemingly headed for disaster. It may be true that these New Right Armageddon theorists were only part of a wider climate of pessimistic opinion when they began propounding these arguments in the 1970s. This was the decade of the Club of Rome's dire vision of world economic disaster in *The Limits of Growth*, of the predictions of resource exhaustion, inflation-bred collapse, and a nuclear "fate of the earth." But the arguments of the premillenarians have had a powerful impact on listeners.[62]

Of course, this view led to a brief flurry of concern in the 1984 presidential campaign, when a coalition of Christian and Jewish leaders condemned "the ideology of nuclear Armageddon," arguing that fundamentalist theology made nuclear war appear to be the fulfillment of the prophecies. They attacked President Reagan for his statement during an appearance on the PTL television network with Jim Bakker that "we may be the generation that sees Armageddon." They condemned his observation in a 1983 interview that "there has never been a time in which so many of the ancient prophecies seem to be coming together . . . people thought the end of the world was coming before, but never has there been anything like this." The president and Reverend Jerry Falwell immediately denied that they believed a nuclear holocaust was imminent. In fact, Falwell insisted that if the United States remained militarily powerful and continued to reject the arguments of the "peaceniks and freezeniks," no war need occur. But the controversy focused on the president's characterization of the Soviet Union as an "evil empire." Critics argued that this image could be embraced by fundamentalists, seeing the communist state as that satanic instrument foretold in the Bible which would bring on the great and bloody trial before the Second Coming.[63]

Several of the media ministers—advocates of massive defense spending and an aggressive foreign policy of confrontation with the USSR—have suggested on occasion that the final chapter in the holy war might come "in our time." But this does not mean that these Armageddon literalists are agents of a new antialienism, offering to conduct a new Red Scare against the communist enemy. Their vision of the communist beast is of the enemy without, not the enemy within. Those internal enemies who can weaken the United States and make it vulnerable in the titanic struggle to come are not the Reds but the secular humanists and other evil mischief makers of modernity. For this new party of fear, the focus is on the fear of a new adversary. In Swaggart's words, they are the ones "working to make America rot from within." These are the men and women who have advocated sex education, intrusion by social workers in family affairs, "freedom of the press for pornographers," the divisiveness of feminism, rampant homosexuality, et al. These immoralists, not "alien" ideologists advocating Marxism, represent the real internal peril. They are corrupting and destructive, but they are not un-American. In this way, the very literalism of the fundamentalist Right militates against significant involvement with the antialienism of the past. It is true that in the mid-1970s, Falwell did once talk of "a return to McCarthyism," of "registration of all Communists . . . stamping it on their foreheads and sending them back to Russia." But as he gained national attention, he moderated these views. Now Falwell and most other leaders of the new religious Right turn away from the old Red Scare and focus their attacks on more accessible and more important enemies.

These leaders have also avoided the old nativist crusades which their fundamentalist forebears helped along in the days of the Know Nothings, the APA of the 1890s, and the Klan of the 1920s. Of course, these fundamentalist preachers know the truth, and they cannot always mask their contempt for those who continue to live in darkness and worship false gods. The Reverend Bailey Smith, elected president of the Southern Baptist Convention in a significant victory for the new religious Right in 1982, has said that "God Almighty Does Not Hear the Prayers of the Jews." The Reverend James Robison, who opened the GOP convention in 1984, once observed that an "anti-Semite is someone who hates Jews more than he's supposed to." The Reverend W. A. Criswell, a spectacularly successful Texas minister presiding over a $200 million complex of church buildings in downtown Dallas, the man who gave the final benediction at the Republican convention, once referred to the Catholic church as a "political tyranny." He opposed John Kennedy's presidential candidacy on religious grounds, authoring a pamphlet in the 1960s asking, "Can a man be a loyal Roman Catholic and a good president of the United States?" Jimmy Swaggart has evoked angry comments with allegedly anti-Semitic and anti-Catholic remarks. "Don't ever bargain with Jesus," he once advised an audience. "He's a Jew." In 1983, he told an Anti-Defamation League representative that "a person who does not accept Jesus Christ . . .

takes himself away from God's protection and places himself under Satan's domain." The same year, three television stations canceled his show after he told a crusade audience that Mother Teresa of Calcutta, winner of the Nobel Peace Prize, would go to hell unless she had a born-again experience. (He explained that this was merely the Protestant opposition to the doctrine of works; good deeds will not get one into heaven.) But he did nothing to change his image with a "Letter to my Catholic Friends," referring to those "poor, pitiful individuals who think they have enriched themselves spiritually by kissing the Pope's ring." Even Falwell has used the old stereotypes, speaking of "full-blooded Jewish men" and telling congregants that "I know why you don't like the Jew. . . . He can make more money accidentally than you can on purpose."[64]

But these are not the nativists of old. The ancient tradition of fundamentalist anti-Catholicism, with its three centuries of poisonous references to the "whore of Rome," its fixation on the imaginary sexual underground within the church, its politicoreligious alignment against Irish-Catholic immigrants, is not a factor in the appeal of the new religious Right. In fact, in the mobilization of the "right to life" movement, the fundamentalist television stars have made a curious alliance with such Catholic prelates as the archbishop of New York, who sits in John Hughes's seat. The days of the Catholic-Protestant clashes of the 1840s, when Bishop Hughes fortified St. Patrick's Cathedral against nativist mobs stirred to violence by fundamentalist preachers, are long forgotten. Jerry Falwell has said, "John Paul . . . is the best hope we Baptists ever had."[65]

This curious new accord between historic adversaries is a final testament both to the decline of American nativism and to the forceful appeal of the new crusade against secular humanists and other enemies of "traditional values." The irony of the emerging ecumenical coalition on the Right is not lost on critics of the televangelists, but they seem unaffected by charges of inconsistency with the teachings of their fundamentalist forebears. Of course, they argue, Catholics are following the wrong path if they truly seek personal salvation. But if Catholics do share the social and political agenda of the enlightened, they can be welcomed as allies in the struggle to save the nation. Catholicism is no longer the enemy. Nativist hatred passed into history in the decades preceding 1950. The new villains are not identified by their un-American religious or ethnic roots, not marked by their un-American Marxist ideologies, but by their dangerous and destructive attitudes toward social practices and political solutions. Against such foes, even those ministers who know they have seen the light and become the chosen messengers of the truth are willing to make common cause with misguided believers and former opponents. Anti-Catholicism is no longer a factor.

Nor is anti-Semitism a real issue with the new fundamentalists. Indeed, Falwell, with his literal reading of the Bible, continuously refers to Jews as "the Chosen of God," who will return in safety to Israel. He even raised money for Israel and visited there, preaching, planting trees, shaking hands with Prime Minister Menachem Begin. He has met Jewish leaders in New York and exclaimed, "To stand against Israel is to stand against God." Jews, he has said, "have a God-Given Right to the Land." In fact, "God has raised up America in these last days for the cause of the world evangelization and for the protection of his people, the Jews. I don't think America has any other right or reason for existence other than those two purposes."[66]

Even as the leaders of the religious Right turned away from the overtly racist views of their youth, when the civil rights revolution changed the South in which they were raised, most of them turned away from nativism. They have abandoned the segregationist themes so effectively that some have recruited black viewers. Their message is not linked to the racial tensions of the region in which they got their start. Although they sometimes traffic in the code words which elicit knowing looks from their larger audience— attacking "welfare chiselers" and "urban rioters"—they have no need for the divisive rhetoric of the old days of southern white supremacy just as they have rejected the discredited anthems of nativism. They do not appeal to the hatred of some designated "un-American" peoples. But they do provide an explanation for the defeats, disappointments, and social disorders of the recent past. They do offer a way of bringing back stability and community to their legion of disciples.[67]

Television's older evangelists long have found an audience among single women over the age of forty-five, people seeking a measure of otherworldly comfort to help them deal with difficult personal circumstances. Falwell's audience also contains isolated outsiders, as well as other troubled folk, men and women from "damaged or difficult childhoods" in which violence, crime, or alcoholism ravaged original nuclear families. But in the church in Lynchburg and across America, many of his listeners, and those of his fundamentalist colleagues, seem to come from normal upwardly mobile family groups. Particularly in their areas of greatest popularity—the New South and Southwest—the media preachers have found a following among clerical workers, technicians, small businessmen, and skilled and semiskilled workers. As one analyst of his appeal notes, these Falwell followers have come off the farms and out of Appalachia to the expanding cities. Like others, they are seduced by the consumer culture; they will not give up their cars or television sets. But they seek explanations for the disorienting developments of modernity and the shocks of recent history.[68]

Fundamentalism, of course, is not an exclusively American phenomenon in the 1970s and 1980s. Fundamentalist movements have swept across Iran and other very different lands experiencing the upheavals accompanying an age of change. But Falwell's followers have responded to a peculiarly American environment. When he asks them if they oppose the Equal Rights Amendment, women in combat, homosexual teachers, and the rising divorce rate, they shout with the enthusiasm of the angry and betrayed. They endorse his attacks on Gloria Steinem, Hugh Hefner, and Jane Fonda, a curious triumvirate to most but not to these people. They respond when he tells them that secular humanists dominate academia and will throw their children "into confusion" if they are sent to anything but Bible colleges. They find comfort in the Word, in the assurance that God will protect and support the truest believers no matter how distressing the messages in the daily headlines. They can cut through the complexities of contemporary social, economic, and international developments by holding onto the Bible as literal truth and listening to their celebrity ministers as its trusted explicators. If school prayer is allowed once more, juvenile delinquency and adolescent immorality can be checked. If gospel singing or religious rock replaces the odious sexuality of hard rock music, drug usage, deviance, and teenage suicide may decline. If America "stands tall" in the arms race, the communist Satan will be kept at bay. This may not be an antialien movement, but it is antiurban and antielitist and is suffused with the simplistic slogans of yesterday. It emerges from a world of change reminiscent of the setting for nativist upheavals in the 1890s and 1920s, only this time compounded by the fear and anxiety resulting from the American defeats of the last decade. Thus, Falwell and the other electronic fundamentalists were speaking to the longing of millions for a return to a safer and simpler order when they came on the scene in the mid-1970s.

Most of their listeners, as Ben Wattenberg has suggested, are "the unyoung, the unpoor and the unblack." Of course, there are many teenagers and some minorities present as the cameras sweep across the audiences, and this is true particularly at the Swaggart crusades. But most do appear to be "middle age, middle income, middle minded." Their very television dials have suggested the ways in which an older vision of America has been shaken by recent developments. They seek out their televangelists from a welter of cable channels featuring programs on good sex, rock video, how to get rich in real estate, the lifestyles of the rich and famous, as well as a variety of major network shows focusing on murder, drug dealing, sexual infidelity, and family disaster.

In a sense, it was inevitable that the new generation of media ministers would find an audience. What Robert Bellah has called the "quasi-therapeutic blandness" afflicting much of mainline Protestant religion did not answer the questions raised in an increasingly bewildering world. In Falwell and his colleagues, the followers could have it all. They were offered certainty about the present and future in an age beset by uncertainty, rapid change and bizarre social practices. They found the surety of religious moorings without the need to renounce the compelling attraction of material ambition, the creation of a community of the saved in place of personal relationships put at risk in a mobile, competitive, and intensely individualistic culture. Thus, even the economic success that some people would find in the mid-1980s, following the troubled 1970s, could provide additional reasons to embrace the themes of the fundamentalist celebrities.[69]

★★★

The Emergence of the Political New Right

Their success attracted emulators but also fascinated a group of ambitious young political operatives. It soon became clear to these men that the new religious Right could be enlisted in a larger political campaign being planned around social as well as economic issues. These operatives were the makers of what Kevin Phillips called, in 1974, the New Right.[70]

At the center of this group was Richard Viguerie. Born—like Falwell—in 1933, he is a Catholic, a Texan, whose parents were Louisianans, a law school dropout, a former oil field clerk who worked for conservative politicians and conservative organizations in the early 1960s. He became involved in direct mail appeals as a fund-raiser for the Young Americans for Freedom. Soon he established his own firm, the Richard A. Viguerie Company (RAVCO), which he would build into a business grossing over $15 million a year by 1982. He made his mark by compiling a master list of conservatives across America, combining the names of those interested in supporting each of his expanding roster of right-wing clients. He accepted a contract from George Wallace in the early 1970s, raising millions, adding to his computer tapes of potential contributors until the list reached 5 million names. Watergate helped his business. A few private investors had contributed huge sums to Richard Nixon's campaign. After the scandal erupted, new laws were passed prohibiting individual contributions of more than $1,000. The direct mail business boomed. But now Viguerie learned from Wallace how "social issues" might be mobilized in service of political objectives, how "populism" could be fused to more traditional conservatism.

Although his clients were Republicans, Viguerie had always rejected the eastern, "liberal" establishment in the GOP. In 1974, after Gerald Ford picked Nelson Rockefeller, the quintessential liberal, as his vice-president in the difficult days after Watergate, Viguerie turned to a circle of like-minded associates who were neither politicians nor important bureaucrats. Together, they decided to form a new conservative movement outside the mainstream of the Republican party. The New Right was born.[71]

One key member of Viguerie's group was Paul Weyrich, a Catholic from Wisconsin, the short, chubby son of blue-collar workers from Racine, who had secured the help of millionaire beer maker Joseph Coors to organize the rightist Heritage Foundation as well as the Committee for the Survival of a Free Congress. (Falwell would later observe: "Paul Weyrich is a wonderful man but you have to realize he is pretty far out. He is the Ralph Nader of our side.") Another was Howard Phillips, a Boston Jew in his early thirties like

Weyrich, a Harvard graduate and a founder of Young Americans for Freedom (YAF). Phillips had worked for the Nixon administration but had left after being frustrated in his efforts to dismantle the Office of Economic Opportunity, the Great Society war-on-poverty program of which he had been named acting director. He joined Viguerie in forming the Conservatives For the Resignation of the President before Richard Nixon's final hours. Later, in 1974, he organized the Conservative Caucus. This rightist lobby claimed three hundred thousand members by 1981. Finally, there was Terry Dolan. Twenty-three in 1974, Dolan was a YAF lawyer who would form the National Conservative Political Action Committee (NCPAC), using Viguerie's computerized lists to become a powerful fund-raising force (the nation's richest PAC by 1981) for rightist candidates and causes. Dolan, a Georgetown graduate, who once called the Civil Rights Act "irrelevant" and the Voting Rights Act "absolutely silly," would characterize himself as a "born-again Catholic." By 1978, these four men turned to the fundamentalist movement and its famous media ministers. They were searching for new allies in the struggle to save the nation from the liberals of the Democratic and Republican parties.[72]

Two men brought them into contact with the churchmen. One was Edward McAteer, a former sales manager with Colgate-Palmolive and the national director of the Christian Freedom Foundation (financed by J. Howard Pew of the Sun Oil Company), which had been organized to elect "real Christians" to public office. He was joined by Robert Billings, former president of a fundamentalist college in Indiana and a Christian school lobbyist from the National Christian Action Coalition. Through these men—and with Paul Weyrich playing a central role—Viguerie and his colleagues met Robertson, Robison, Bakker, and Falwell. In 1979, this alliance of the New Right and the New Christian Right produced the Moral Majority. The title was coined by Phillips and used by Weyrich in a presentation to Jerry Falwell. (Weyrich claims credit for the achievement: "The alliance between religion and politics didn't just happen. I've been dreaming and working on this for years.") The Moral Majority would be led by Falwell, with Billings as the initial national director, before he left to join the Reagan administration.[73]

The Moral Majority, Jerry Falwell explained, would provide a vehicle for religious groups that had clashed in the past but now put doctrinal conflict aside to combat the common enemy. Paul Weyrich asserted that "Catholics in this country do not differ with the views of the moral majority . . . Pope John is on our side and the people are on our side." Jerry Falwell declared: "Evangelicals, fundamentalists, conservative Catholics and Mormons are all working together now." Later, he would add orthodox Jews to the list. It was another farewell to the old nativism, and Falwell exclaimed, in this new spirit of right-wing ecumenism, "We are fighting a Holy War, and this time we are going to win."

In addition to the Moral Majority, those "millions of fundamentalists in America who were a political army waiting to be mobilized," as a Viguerie follower put it, were offered a companion group. This was the Religious Roundtable, led by McAteer, who was serving as well as field director of the Conservative Caucus by 1979. They found additional allies in the California-based Christian Voice, with its "biblical scorecards" rating candidates and legislators on "Christian issues." (The legislative director of the Christian Voice was Gary Jarmin, who had spent more than six years in Reverend Sun Myung Moon's Unification church, not exactly a Christian enterprise.) They cooperated with the nonsectarian Eagle Forum, led by antifeminist Phyllis Schlafly, and with Family America, a new group cochaired by Tim and Bev LaHaye. Working with conservative Republican politicians such as Gordon Humphrey and Jesse Helms, two of Viguerie's clients, they found a particularly unifying theme in the antiabortion effort. The New Right and the religious Right could join in this crusade. They were shaping what Weyrich called a "pro-family coalition."[74]

Falwell was too busy organizing the Moral Majority to participate in a vast Washington for Jesus prayer meeting during two days in late April 1980. But Robison, Bakker, Crouch, and others were present, with Robertson as chairman. The leaders claimed that almost four hundred thousand people gathered on the Mall; the National Park Service estimated two hundred thousand. The media paid little heed to the vast assemblage, but the message of the political power of the New Christian Right was not lost in Washington. Meanwhile, calling for America not to separate "God from Government," Falwell entered the political arena with the Moral Majority Political Action Committee, Moral Report Cards on Congressmen, and the endorsement of candidates' stands on social issues. During the fall campaign, Falwell claimed 2 to 3 million members for the new group. He purchased time on 215 stations for a June television special entitled "America, You're Too Young To Die." When candidate Ronald Reagan—who described himself as a creationist—met the leaders of the religious Right in 1980 to announce that "you can't endorse me but I endorse you," he apparently misunderstood how quickly the religiopolitical ties were coalescing on the New Right. He understood this well enough by 1982, but in that year conservative forces suffered numerous defeats in the midterm election, conducted in the teeth of the most severe recession since the Great Depression. Falwell's Moral Majority, Dolan's NCPAC, Weyrich's Free Congress Foundation, and Viguerie's computerized appeals failed to deliver victory for conservatives. Many right-wing regulars—including John Rousselot, the John Birch Society leader of the 1960s—were beaten. But this was also the time when New Right leaders were wavering in their devotion to Ronald Reagan, who had picked moderate George Bush for the vice-presidency and allowed an agent of the liberal wing of the GOP, James A. Baker III, to gain White House influence as chief of staff. Weyrich observed that "Reagan is not the answer; he is not a man of strong character." Phillips wondered if this "72 year old Leopard who can't change his spots," a man who "talks like Winston Churchill and acts like Neville Chamberlain," could lead the movement in its struggle against the enemy.[75]

But what of this enemy and its policies? How were they best combated? The new alliance on the New Right spoke in the patriotic rhetoric gaining fashion again in the early 1980s. Long before the "USA, USA" chants of 1984, Falwell had addressed I Love America rallies and established I Love America Clubs, so it was natural that the new movement would wrap itself in the American flag. It even influenced its adversaries to do the same, as when television producer Norman Lear organized the People for the American Way, to argue, as the bumper stickers put it, that "The Moral Majority is Neither." But if the New Right was emulating the "patriotic" fraternities and Red Scare spokesmen of the past in its chauvinistic style, was it also turning back to the theme of un-American activities used by the old antialiens?

At the Republican National Convention in 1984, when Phillips and Weyrich conducted a well-advertised press conference on the subject "Are Liberals Soft on Communism," it seemed that this might be the case. But calling adversaries "Comsymps" lost its utility for those seeking real power more than a generation ago, and this effort seemed destined to die in gestation. One example of someone "who has been softened up by Communists" offered at the conference was Senator John Warner, the conservative Republican from Virginia. Not only liberal Democrats but Gerald Ford, Henry Kissinger, Senator Robert Dole, and even Barry Goldwater were not above suspicion. This was not the older conservatism, concerned with fiscal prudence and skeptical of big government, it was what Bill Moyers and others began calling the "Hard Right." By the standards of the Phillips-Weyrich press conference, most of Congress would be on the enemies list, and so would most Americans. This is the very route that led McCarthy to disaster in 1954 and made Welch a laughingstock ten years later. It is not likely to be the direction a serious New Right can take. If it goes down that road, it is doomed to early rejection as just another group of "crazies that the party would love to dismiss as a minor irritant," as Viguerie defiantly but fearfully observed at the time of the convention. The obvious alternative for the movement is to focus on the broader themes that brought it initial success and to turn away from antialienism. These themes are the attack on "immorality" and "Godless" policies, that panoply of social issues which make up its appeal to "traditional family values" in which the ministers play a key role. They are also the economic and international concerns that are vital for Viguerie and his associates.[76]

The New Right seems to have a clear agenda on defense and the economy. It is for massive military spending and confrontation with the communist adversary on the frontiers of the "free world." It is for reduced taxes and rejects social programs that undermine "American individualism" and the "entrepreneurial genius" of the capitalist system. This position brought it into league with the big monied interests of the Sunbelt states and back to Ronald Reagan during the 1984 campaign. NCPAC, as part of its Heroes for Reagan Project, held a fund-raising Texas Gala during the GOP convention on the ranch of oil billionaire Nelson Bunker Hunt, an heir to H. L. Hunt's fortune and the man who tried to corner the silver market and make a fortune in soybean speculation. Falwell and other notables on the New Right were there. Hunt distributed his "statement of principles," in which he observed that "aid should be forthcoming to the truly troubled, by a body most likely to know him by name."[77]

Attacking the Great Society and the work of liberal reformers, with their insistence that government has a responsibility to provide opportunities to move up for those at the bottom and a measure of social security for all, is a major theme of the New Right and attracts the new rich to its cause. But the social agenda remains at the center of its efforts. The American Coalition for Traditional Values (ACTV) was organized by Tim LaHaye and Paul Weyrich to promote this agenda. The ACTV hoped to place a "quota" of born-again Christians in political and civil service jobs. Jerry Falwell played an important role in its voter registration drive in 1984. Touring the nation for the coalition—and claiming that "six million Americans consider themselves members of the Moral Majority" throughout this tour—Falwell focused on the need for Supreme Court reversal on the abortion issue. But the coalition also concerns itself with the other social questions. Spokesman Colonel V. Doner observed in a national television appearance that "God would oppose pornography, homosexuality and favor school prayer." He argued for a return to the moral order of the past, when prayer was encouraged in schools, sexually explicit materials outlawed in bookstores and newsstands, and legal sanctions taken against homosexuals. In calling for legislation to repeal the sinister, immoral developments of recent years, Doner explained that the coalition wanted to "check the liberal initiatives taken by an elite group."[78]

"Elitism" is a repetitive theme in New Right rhetoric. In summer 1984, Richard Viguerie was predicting a revolution against the "elite establishment" and prophesying a new "populist" party. Organizing yet another new group he titled the Populist Conservative Tax Coalition, Viguerie—then the editor of the *Conservative Digest*—spoke for a larger movement that rejects traditional conservatives as being "as elitist as the liberal intellectuals." It is a movement supported by new-money millionaires in the South and Southwest but profoundly suspicious of the "effete gentlemen of the northeastern establishment," who run the big law firms and the big corporations, which are "as bad as big government; they're in bed together." In assailing the "northeastern old right," Weyrich says: "Look at our backgrounds. We're not the product of third generation wealth."[79]

In a book entitled *The Establishment vs. The People: Is a New Populist Revolt on the Way?* Viguerie defined the "establishment" as a "class of persons with unusual access to the political process gained through economic power or social status or old-boy networks." These establishment elites are responsible for the very programs the New Right rejects: antipoverty, school busing, and consumer protection. They are "part of the upper crust," like those limousine liberals of George Wallace's imagery, measured by "how many university degrees they have." The Ivy League is a particular problem, for "after years of government controlled by the best and brightest from Ivy League Schools," what "we have to show for it" is stalemate in Korea, defeat in Vietnam, a $1.6 billion debt, inflation, an epidemic of violence, and a federal budget out of control. Viguerie's elites are related to the New Christian Right's secular humanists. He approvingly quotes Jerry Falwell that "the populist movement speaks for the very soul of this country" and notes that Pat Robertson has said that "a small elite has frustrated the majority of the American people, will the populist revolt be necessary?"

But Viguerie has doubts about Ronald Reagan. In 1983, it was obvious that "there is little difference between Reagan's foreign policy and Carter's foreign policy." There was no excuse for Reagan supplying money for the National Endowment for the Arts and Humanities and the Corporation for Public Broadcasting, to "provide entertainment for a well-to-do audience." Indeed, the "failure to bring about a significant realignment of political loyalties is one of the great tragedies of history." It was clear that "we can't depend on either of the major parties." The ethnics, southerners, traditional Christians, Orthodox Jews, and blue-collar workers, repeatedly "put down" by the political, corporate, legal, and academic elites, must shape a new populist movement. It will evolve from a new coalition including religious conservatives, outdoor sportsmen and gun owners, ethnic anticommunists and right-to-life activists, "gold bugs" and middle-class landowners "standing up to the environmental lobby," private school advocates and "sagebrush rebels."[80]

To save America, to promote their moral and nationalist agenda, the New Right returns once more to the antielitist language of the past. Populism is a historical cause with enormous symbolic power, and it has served to energize movements of both the Right and Left in the twentieth century. In the 1890s, the original Populist party called for federal intervention to check the power of the rich and provide support for the weak and the vulnerable. But even then, Populism spoke in part to those who felt left behind or left out in the emerging urban-industrial society, people who desperately wanted to defend older customs and mores, to maintain a sense of community and local authority. This was the element of Populism that reappeared in the appeals of Coughlin and Long in the 1930s and in the rhetoric of Wallace in the late 1960s. For the call to protect the nation—along with one's own subculture—by checking the power of the privileged and well-positioned is an ancient theme, and it has attracted Americans of different religious and ethnic origins across the years. The new element is the New Right's shrewd manipulation of the fear and hatred of "big government" in the wake of the upheavals of the 1960s and the defeats and disappointments of the 1970s. Now, in the 1980s, Populism emerges as an anthem of those who reject not only the welfare state but the wealthy old conservatives who oppose the welfare state. It is used by those who promote a return to traditional values with the knowledge that the managerial and professional elites of both the Democratic and Republican establishments are contemptuous of their arguments, unsympathetic with their proposals, opposed to their vision of a moral community in America.

The New Right is led by passionate and angry men who might believe that the Populist "masses" can be recruited to their banners but who know they are taking on the entrenched elite leadership of the nation. In fact, their enemies are so numerous, so well placed in the media, the bureaucracy, academia, and the professions—present in all sectors of American life—that they cannot dismiss them as un-American, alien ideologists. So although there is an ugly, repressive tone to their language, reminiscent of the rightist extremists of the past, calling for sanctions against wimps and weaklings who want an accommodation with the evil Soviet Satan, softhearts and spendthrifts who advocate giveaways to welfare bums and other losers, agents of moral corruption who foster sinful social practices in the name of liberalism's "freedom," they cannot deal in the old-time antialienism.[81]

Like the nativists, inverted nativists, and anticommunist activists of history—the Know Nothings, the APA, the Ku Klux Klan, the Coughlin movement, and McCarthyism—the New Right offers not only an explanation for the social and political upheavals of the age but an enemies list against which to organize. Yet this time it is different.

With the end of immigration and with other developments from the 1920s through the 1940s, the sources of nativist hostility were removed. The very religious and ethnic profile of New Right political leadership reminds us that that nativism is dead. With the end of America's isolationist innocence in the mid-1950s, the sources of the Red Scare were removed. Anticommunism remains a powerful theme in the New Right but not as a crusade against the enemy within. Viguerie, Weyrich, and others on the Hard Right may be tempted by the old politics of innuendo—calling foes "soft on Communism"—and Falwell may revert to characterizing programs he rejects as "socialism." But the feeble state of the Birch Society reminds us that the old Marxist witch-hunting days are over. The New Right will steer clear if it is to remain a serious movement. In fact, by 1986 there was evidence that leaders of the movement were trying to avoid extremist rhetoric as they faced wrenching economic problems, enticing political opportunities, and new strains in their alliance.

Jerry Falwell was moving even closer to the conservative Republican establishment. Already on record as saying that Ronald Reagan is "the greatest President since Lincoln," he endorsed Vice-President George Bush as Reagan's successor. Bush appeared at a meeting of Falwell followers, telling the minister, "America is in crying need of the moral vision you have brought to our political life." But Falwell had little opportunity to enjoy the compliment. He was feeling the effects of repeated attacks on his positions and his programs. He acknowledged that his "enemies" had placed his organization on the defensive.

His support of an autocratic Marcos government in the Philippines about to fall from power had been followed by an impassioned defense of "our strategic ally, South Africa," just before growing repression in that country would further tarnish his reputation as an international statesman. The minister was now reported to be experiencing severe budgetary problems, laying off two hundred employees at his Lynchburg headquarters and making a dramatic televised appeal for funds, saying that "we have been under vicious attack . . . we have been accused of being bigots and evil." He accused the "American Atheist Society," the National Education Association, National Organization for Women, "militant homosexuals" and the People for the American Way (PAW) of harassing him. PAW clearly was making its mark. Chaired by John Buchanan, a Southern Baptist minister and former congressman from Alabama, it had attracted two hundred thousand members. Along with other groups, its scathing assaults on the term "Moral Majority" forced Falwell to retreat. "It sounded right at the time, but looking back I would say it was wrong because it presumes everyone who does not agree with us to be immoral, which was not the intent." He said that "the press for six years has bloodied and beaten the name 'Moral Majority.' . . . There are a lot of people who dare not stand with us on particular policies for fear of getting tarred, hurt." Jerry Falwell now changed the name to the Liberty Federation. Indeed, "Liberty" became the Falwell universal term, not only for his Liberty University but even for "Liberty Mountain" outside of Lynchburg. The year of the centennial of the Statue of Liberty seemed a good time for this move, but as one writer observed, "liberty" was a clear loser as a rightist title. From the sorry legacy of the Liberty League of 1936 through a succession of unsuccessful right-wing groups in the post–World War II era, notably Carto's Liberty Lobby, it has been a signature on failure.[82]

But Falwell had to retreat. He admitted that he had been forced to drop his toll-free telephone line to Lynchburg; it had cost "two million dollars in 15 months" because hostile mischief makers had flooded the phones with abusive messages and "one ACLU fellow" linked "his computer to a telephone and made 500,000 calls." Don't allow "the gays, the Norman Lears," and other "enemies of Christ," he implored, to injure the enterprise. Jerry Falwell's star was no longer in the ascendancy. He acknowledged that his television image was seen by some as stridently partisan: "Pat Robertson is at least as political as I am, maybe more. But he is more subtle." One Republican pollster, noting that the minister's support had become a very mixed blessing and that Democrats were tempted to "push the Falwell button in their campaign," observed that "Jerry Falwell has the highest negative rating of anybody except Khomeini" in public opinion polls. By the fall, the minister announced that he had decided to pull back sharply from the political battle: "I am not going to get involved in campaigns . . . as I have in the past. . . . I'm going to take a more balanced approach."[83]

Falwell was not the only luminary on the New Right having trouble in 1986. Richard A. Viguerie had faced a series of lawsuits from suppliers claiming that RAVCO was not paying its bills. The rightist direct-mail business was suffering from oversaturation of a limited market. It was clear that too many television ministers were competing in the same market. While the traditional, nonpolitical evangelicals were having particular problems, with revivalist Rex Humbard forced off the air and faith healer Oral Roberts facing a dire crisis, the New Right was also undergoing a shakeup. But one apparent winner was Robertson. Like Falwell, he was trying to speak less as the intrepid adversary of a national conspiracy of secular humanists and more as a traditional political operative. But unlike Falwell or some other friendly rivals for the attention of religious televiewers, he was not on the defensive. Indeed, he was testing the waters for his own presidential race in 1988. Although he did not have the backing of Jerry Falwell, at least one major New Right figure thought he would be a formidable candidate. Paul Weyrich characterized Robertson as having a Reaganesque appeal. Like the "teflon President," here was "a nonthreatening figure" capable of "deflecting animosity."[84]

Robertson organized the Freedom Council, a tax-exempt foundation with a staff of fifty and a budget of $5.5 million to prepare for a possible race. In June 1986, his supporters recruited more district delegate candidates in Michigan (the first step in a complex state system for choosing 1988 GOP convention delegates) than any other major candidate save George Bush. Celebrating his success, he announced: "The Christians have won . . . what a breakthrough for the Kingdom." While supporters of other Republican aspirants grumbled at the implication that the Almighty had endorsed their rival, Robertson moved closer to active candidacy. In a massive closed-circuit television appeal to thousands of supporters gathered in 220 rented meeting halls across the nation, the CBN founder pledged that "if by September 17, 1987 [a year from the date of his address], three million registered voters have signed petitions telling me that they will pray . . . work . . . give toward my election," he would seek the Republican nomination. In his prepared remarks, he repeated favored themes, particularly attacks on humanists, evolutionists, and communists. "We have taken the Holy Bible from our young and replaced it with the thoughts of John Dewey, Charles Darwin, Sigmund Freud and Karl Marx." He promised a "new vision" of "drug-free public schools" and an "efficient, decentralized government."[85]

In the days preceding the televised event, he had solicited the support of hundreds of Pentecostal, Charismatic, and independent Baptist preachers as well as some of the leading media evangelists of the new religious Right. Jimmy Swaggart suddenly announced his endorsement in a passionate public exclamation: "When he said he felt led of God to do it, I had no alternative but to support him." Swaggart predicted that "he will get just about all the Pentecostal and Charismatic vote . . . 20 or 30 million people." Jim Bakker gave only a mild response, saying, "Our viewers would welcome his candidacy . . . I would have no problem standing with him," and even Jerry Falwell admitted that "he will have the poll position going out." Oral Roberts and Rex Humbard also were persuaded to join the Robertson evangelical bandwagon.

But such support would come at the cost of intensified scrutiny by the press and political rivals. Questions emerged in late fall concerning the minister's luxurious but rent-free lifestyle in the Georgian mansion owned by CBN, with its stables and pool. The Internal Revenue Service was reported to be examining charges that several of his tax-exempt organizations—including CBN, Inc.—had filed false or incomplete information. And two Democratic politicians, former Representative Paul N. McCloskey, Jr., of California and Representative Andrew Jacobs, Jr., of Indiana, were sued by Robertson for $70 million after Jacobs asked McCloskey to put his recollections of Robertson's military service into a widely circulated letter. McCloskey, a rifle platoon leader in Korea and a shipmate of the future minister on a troop transport, remembered that Robertson's father, the Virginia senator, "had pulled strings in Washington" to keep his son out of combat duty in Korea. Other veterans endorsed McCloskey's account. Robertson denied the charge and insisted he had to sue: "If I am elected President, how could I as Commander in Chief ever order a young American into combat if the record is not absolutely clear that I never shirked military duty."[86]

On another front, Pat Robertson was busy denying he was an extremist or a "right-winger." Responding to a fund-raising letter signed by the Democratic party national chairman declaring him a "radical right leader," Robertson accused his critic of "virulent, anti-Christian bigotry." He declared: "I'm hardly a right-wing ideologue."[87]

But other opponents of the New Right insisted that Robertson could never be just another mainstream politician. They quoted a 1984 CBN broadcast in which the minister had said, "The Constitution of the United States is a marvelous document for self government by Christian people . . . non-Christian and atheist people can use it to destroy the very foundation of our society and that is what's been happening." They noted an uncharacteristically intemperate letter to Norman Lear, in which Robertson wrote: "You are trying to silence a prophet of God. . . . Your arms are too short to box with God. . . . God himself will fight for me against you and He will win." Interviewed for a *Time* magazine cover story keyed to his presidential ambitions, the minister presented a political agenda similar to priorities of the Reagan administration, but he also observed that "one day the Soviets or their satellites will invade Israel," as in biblical prophecy. He responded to the "fear that an evangelist Christian would use the power of government to force people to accept certain political values" by saying, "I have no intention of doing that." But he had to add that "our schools shall have moral values based either on Judeo-Christian values, humanism or Communism." In the end, Pat Robertson could not avoid the confrontation with the humanist enemy which has informed the work of all the major actors on the New Right. The fervent fundamentalists can hardly deny that they believe their cause is totally right, that in many ways they and their cobelievers are the exclusive keepers of the truth.[88]

The New Right, for all its efforts to move closer to mainstream political positions, rejects pluralism and has difficulty meeting the accusation that it represents a politics of extremism. But at least it has resisted manipulating the antialien themes of its right-wing predecessors. In this regard, it marks a new departure in American history.

But whether this multifaceted religious and political movement could be sustained and expanded through the campaign of 1988 and beyond was put into question by the spectacular PTL scandal in the spring of 1987. The unfolding story of Jim Bakker's sexual and financial improprieties—receiving headline coverage in newspapers, cover story treatments in the newsmagazines, and nightly features on national television—proved immensely embarrassing for the televangelists and their political allies, deeply divisive within the leadership community of the religious Right, and added to the growing cash flow problems of many of the ministries. More important, it made a central theme of the New Right, the endorsement of traditional family values, a laughing matter even in those regions where the cause had won its widest support.

Bakker's initial admission that he had committed adultery with a comely church secretary in 1980 and had paid her $265,000 to remain silent and not to press charges was only the beginning of a chain of widely publicized revelations. Bakker soon would be accused of homosexual activity, wife-swapping, and habitual involvement with prostitutes; he denied all of these charges. He was assailed for siphoning millions of dollars from his ministry through huge salaries and secret slush funds to subsidize the purchase of Rolls Royce autos, lavish homes, wardrobes, and other items of personal consumption. This was something more than "Christianity as lifestyle success" that he had preached about in the past. His accusers included fellow media celebrities of the religious Right. In fact, Bakker's aides initially insisted that Jimmy Swaggart was involved in the attack on his character and was plotting a "hostile takeover" of the PTL empire. Swaggart denied such plans, but he characterized Bakker as "a cancer that needs to be exorcised from the body of Christ." Jerry Falwell insisted he was asked by Bakker to assume temporary leadership of PTL; but when he moved to take the permanent directorship of the $129 million organization, including its theme park, hotels, and television network, the founder of PTL turned on Falwell. In a bitter exchange between the two, Falwell announced that he had no alternative but to displace the disgraced Bakker (now dismissed as an Assemblies of God minister) and that PTL was $70 million in debt as a result of Jim and Tammy Bakker's "greed and avarice." He noted that he had heard "taped testimony" of witnesses to Bakker's "deviant sexual" encounters.[89]

The scandal badly damaged all of the famous television ministries. Already facing financial problems, their contributions declined dramatically. "We are getting our hands slapped," Falwell observed, "national credibility for the cause of Christ is at an all time low." Swaggart agreed: "I'm ashamed, I'm embarrassed. The Gospel of Jesus Christ has never sunk to such a level as it has today." Editorial writers, columnists, and cartoonists skillfully attacked the leaders of the new religious Right. In the heart of the southern Bible Belt, a dozen country and western songs emerged lampooning the movement, including "The PTL Has Gone to Hell So Where Do I Send the Money" and "Would Jesus Wear a Rolex on His Television Show." How could they ever again preach of moral decay and moral corruption, it was asked; how could they dare to offer to lead America to a better tomorrow, when key figures had been revealed as cheats, hypocrites, blasphemers? The image of probity, decency, and virtue they had nurtured was badly tarnished. So was the sense of common purpose among the several leaders of this legion of self-styled defenders of America. "We may be seeing the dissolution of the unholy marriage between television and religion," one critic predicted. Not only Pat Robertson's presidential aspirations but the larger effort of all the ministries to impose their evangelical political agenda on national social policies might be affected by the widening scandal.[90]

Nonetheless, the new religious Right and its allies on the political "hard Right" marched into the late 1980s still insisting that there was momentum in their assault on those they called the enemies of America. For like most right-wing movements in the American past, they had not appealed to an aristocracy of the privileged. As with the Klan and McCarthyism, the American party and the Coughlinites, they insisted from the start that they spoke for the average citizen in their crusade to save the nation from the destructive designs of secular humanists and other elitists. Because antiestablishmentarian Populist rhetoric had become fashionable even in mainstream Republican and Democratic politics by 1986, the New Right leaders would remain optimistic; despite the scandals and the setbacks, in having grasped this quasi-Populist theme, the momentum built in the previous decade might be maintained.[91]

But though the defiantly Populistic tone of their crusade tied them to many earlier right-wing groups, the differences between this new movement and its predecessors on the Right remain even more important. This movement grew by capitalizing on the time of troubles in the recent past, the social upheavals of the 1960s and the economic and political setbacks of the 1970s. Yet these developments created the final setting for the removal of that energizing theme of the earlier movements. Antialienism was inextricably linked to the vision of the United States as God's special creation, the American Israel impervious to foreign challenge but vulnerable only to sinister internal enemies and so in need of vigilant protectors combating un-American activities. Now the very failures of the recent past—the new awareness that for all of America's greatness, it is but one nation in a world beset by troubles—have changed the nature of right-wing extremism in the present.

Like the Wallace movement of 1968, the New Right deals in a politics of resentment, an attack on elites who are responsible for the problems that have plagued the nation and disrupted the lives of the followers, elites who have let America down. In different ways, the two movements have appealed to protectors and fugitives, people wishing both to identify the enemy and to explain away the defeats and disappointments of recent history, to find comfort and community once more within a cause claiming to be the real America, defiantly patriotic and wrapped in the red, white, and blue.

But the old antialien themes are no longer part of that appeal. By the end of World War II, the demise of nativism—that assault on alien people—had eliminated one part of this ancient right-wing tradition. Robbed of its intellectual underpinnings, weakened by the political, economic, demographic, and social changes of the interwar years, nativism was no longer viable by 1950. And anticommunism, the assault on an alien ideology, endured for only a generation longer as a truly effective organizing theme for right-wing movements. The events of the 1960s and 1970s fatally undermined its appeal. The New Right would have to look to other sinister and conspiratorial elements as the enemy against which to mobilize America. It was no longer necessary or possible in the 1980s to organize a powerful movement around attacks on un-Americans.

In the 1990s, recovering from a series of shattering setbacks, there would be new opportunities for activists of the New Right. Changing their tactics and reshaping their agenda, they would succeed in influencing mainstream politics in America in striking new ways. And there would be new developments, as well, on the farther shores of the far Right. While some of the antialien fringe groups of the previous decade would disappear, new organizations would emerge and some older ones would gain renewed strength; with new means of electronic communication, these disparate extremist movements would recruit members and explore ways of linking together.

Finally, there would emerge for the first time another surprising and distinctive party of fear: the militia movement. Most of the paramilitary groups suddenly organizing in states across America made a point of overtly rejecting the old antialien themes; for this new party of fear in the nineties, the central fear was of "the federal government."

CHAPTER 16

★ ★

TO THE RESHAPING OF THE
NEW RIGHT AND THE RISE
OF THE MILITIA MOVEMENT,
1987–1995

THE SUDDEN, shocking end of the Cold War and the subsequent collapse of the Soviet Union unhinged the plans of foreign ministers and military planners across the world. But it also had a profound effect on domestic politics and on the themes and concerns of movements on the far Right in the United States.

In the extraordinary years 1989 to 1991, the long glacial period of Cold War history suddenly ended, not with conflict but with the disintegration of the communist empire. America's fierce and formidable adversary was no more.

For many mainstream politicians and pundits in Washington, anticommunism could no longer be the familiar posture, framing their approach to almost all public questions. Some would drift back to isolationism, others would find new themes around which to build new coalitions. For many who would lead or join extremist movements, fear of communists at home and abroad no longer made any sense.

Now the process under way in the previous decade could continue and the New Right found renewed life in the nineties by focusing on those domestic adversaries—not alien peoples or alien ideologies—it had first identified in the eighties.

But another party of fear, the militia movement, also would emerge in the nineties, and it discovered an enemy at home even more frightening and formidable than the government of the Soviet Union: the federal government of the United States. With the "evil empire" gone, new foes loomed to threaten those who had focused their fear and anger on the Red Menace.

Even the efforts of the White House to deal with a new international arena—suddenly lacking the perilous but stabilizing fact of continuing bipolar confrontation between the thermonuclear superpowers—proved a source of anxiety for right-wing activists. Of course, the Gulf War was merely a delayed response to one particular threat and—as the Bush administration's handling of the Bosnian and Somalian crises would reveal—it was hardly a new blueprint for foreign policy, as was the containment doctrine of the forties or fifties. When President George Bush used the term "New World Order" in trying to explain America's goals in the Gulf War in 1991, he could not know how those words would affect people on the far Right.

International upheavals were only part of the setting for changes on the far Right in the nineties. Continuing concern over America's economic prospects and growing anxieties about the job market in an age of global competition and corporate downsizing did more than shape the nature of debate in Congress and throughout the country over domestic policies. Such tension and uncertainty led some citizens to deal with fears about their future—and the nation's—as many had in the past: by seeking to identify enemies responsible for their problems.

The last years of the Reagan administration had been shadowed not only by the wide-ranging Iran Contra scandal, with its sorry spectacle of corruption of executive power and the portrait of incompetence and/or cupidity at the very top of the government, but also by growing concerns about the massive and mounting national debt. The President who had run against the government and its profligate ways, who had insisted in 1980 that the debt of over $700 billion was indefensible and insupportable, would leave office with the figure having swollen to over $2.2 trillion. Ronald Reagan promised to "get the government off our backs and out of our pockets" and his message of hostility to federal spending and taxation not only would color the views of mainstream conservatives, it would influence activists of the far Right in subsequent years.

But on his watch, while federal income taxes for the affluent were dramatically reduced, government spending for defense rose by almost $1.5 trillion. The result was not only a widening gap between the real annual incomes and total wealth of the rich and of the rest of the nation (pushing the United States, by 1995, to the bottom of the list of modern industrial powers in studies of relative equality), but a growing mountain of debt that would affect the plans and policies of his successors.[1]

George Bush was elected President in 1988 in an ugly campaign featuring covert appeals to the discredited themes of America's nativist and anticommunist past, as well as to veiled racial fears. His opponent was assailed for being "a card-carrying member of the American Civil Liberties Union" (an unsubtle reprise of McCarthyite rhetoric), an unpatriotic figure who refused to insist on the pledge of allegiance to the flag in schools (with candidate Bush even visiting a flag factory to demonstrate his patriotism), a state governor who pardoned murderous convicted felons (with a black male pictured emerging from behind bars in a notorious television advertisement). But once elected, President Bush promised "a kinder, gentler America." Still, the debt burden loomed large and the new president sadly noted that "our will is strong, but our wallets are thin."

Attacked for lacking what he once characterized as "the vision thing" in domestic affairs, George Bush would have to confront a severe recession near the end of his term. Never a favorite of the conservative wing of his party—people who doubted his commitment to advancing their economic and social agenda—he would be beaten in 1992 by Bill Clinton, whose campaign manager had placed the famous phrase, "It's the Economy, Stupid," on his headquarters wall.

But now it would be President Bill Clinton who faced the dilemma of spiraling yearly deficits and the need to stimulate economic growth. His budgetary initiative in 1993, calling for a decrease in debt growth achieved in part through increases on the tax rates of those with the highest incomes, was a major victory. But it was not viewed that way by the press, with reporters more interested in how narrowly it was passed over the unanimous opposition of Congressional Republicans. Efforts by the Clinton administration to increase federal spending for job creation and infrastructure development met fierce resistance. His health care proposals to provide universal coverage while slowing the massive rise in medical spending failed after a lengthy struggle on Capitol Hill. The Clinton team's efforts to "downsize" the government went unnoticed by press or public, but the President's success in winning approval of two significant (if modest) gun control measures, his use of executive initiative to support abortion rights, and his muddled effort to protect gay rights in the military enraged a growing number of Americans. Some of these people would take their passionate anger (and personal animus at Bill Clinton) into movements on the far Right.

Unlike other activist leaders (Franklin D. Roosevelt, Lyndon Johnson) in the White House, President Clinton, with no "working majority" for his program in Congress and with the debt question looming so large, could provide few social programs to ameliorate the pain many felt in an age of economic peril.

In the post-Vietnam, post-Watergate era, the federal government had become an object of suspicion and contempt for millions of citizens. The painful economic crisis of the seventies had not been addressed by any successful government initiative; in the Reagan years, the antigovernment rhetoric of the very people running the government further eroded faith in Washington's ability to do almost anything right, and the debt crisis added to the problem.

For some Americans, the government now became the enemy. It was in this context that they would respond to new groups organizing in 1994, because of "fear of the federal government." The vast majority rejected such extremism, but for Bill Clinton and others who would call for federal initiatives to deal with a wide range of issues facing America, conditions long in gestation had created a skeptical public, a media which was indifferent when it was not adversarial and, most significant, implacable hostility in Congress.

It was in such a setting that the Republican Congressional leadership offered its Contract For America and won a startling victory in both houses in the midterm election of 1994. By 1995, a major effort to repeal much of the activist agenda of the twentieth century was under way. Regulatory agencies dating back to the Progressive Era and the New Deal; urban and welfare programs shaped in the thirties, sixties, and seventies; environmental policies thirty years in the making; and health initiatives from the Great Society were all under review and under attack. Balancing the budget was the rallying cry, but shrinking the size, scope, and power of the federal government was the major theme.

Yet this upheaval in the midnineties was focusing not only on economic and political issues. There was a strong "social agenda" at work, as well. Powerful forces instrumental in electing this new Congressional majority now insisted that they would be satisfied with nothing less than a major assault on those policies, programs, and attitudes viewed as threatening "traditional family values" in America.

The New Right had made a remarkable comeback.

★★★

From Defeat to Triumph: The Reemergence of the New Right

After a series of shattering setbacks in the last years of the eighties, which seemed to bury the New Right and its religious media stars, few would have predicted in 1990 that the New Right would reemerge within half a decade as a critical player in American politics and a growing force in American life.

In the two years following the scandal that destroyed the career of Jim Bakker and sent him to prison, three even more famous and formidable televangelists of the Christian Right faced personal humiliation, devastating political defeat, or wrenching economic woes.

First to fall was Jimmy Swaggart. Within a year of the revelation of the Bakker sex scandal, Swaggart was brought down in a similar affair. In February 1988, he was suddenly called before a special board convened by his denomination, the Assemblies of God, to explain charges of misconduct lodged against him by another religious figure, Marvin Gorman. Gorman, a defrocked minister whom Swaggart had denounced as a philanderer to denominational leaders only two years before (when Gorman was beginning his own television ministry), had incriminating photographs. In the event, it was revealed that Swaggart had been involved in a lengthy relationship with a prostitute in New Orleans, who had been paid by the famous evangelist for posing nude for him in a seedy motel.

Newspapers and newsmagazines reported the story with glaring headlines. The scourge of Jim Bakker—reporters invariably recalled Swaggart's scathing remark that Bakker was "a cancer on the body of Christ"—was now revealed not only as a hypocrite but as a "dirty old man." The story stayed alive for days and some reports suggested that Swaggart had been addicted to pornography for many years. A tearful Jimmy Swaggart—in one of his more memorable performances— asked his television audience for forgiveness. But irreparable damage had been done. The national Assemblies of God leadership, rejecting the three-month ministerial suspension that Swaggart had accepted from the denomination's Louisiana council, imposed sterner measures: a total ban for one year from the pulpit of his television ministry. The televangelist refused to accept this decision, and he was defrocked by his church.[2]

Jimmy Swaggart continued to receive standing ovations before his flock, but his television audience—and its contributions—melted away. In early 1991, the Arbitron rating service reported that he had lost eighty percent of his 2.2 million viewers.[3]

Swaggart's fall, just three days after the New Hampshire presidential primary, came at the worst possible moment for Pat Robertson, whose campaign for the Republican nomination had begun to falter and would be further damaged by yet another sex scandal involving a celebrity of the Christian Right.

Robertson had surprised political experts when he had outpolled Vice President George Bush and nearly upset favored Senator Robert Dole of Kansas in the Iowa caucus. "The Lord brought me to New Hampshire," he remarked during this first critical primary campaign. But then he proceeded to fall victim to a series of self-inflicted wounds.

During a nationally televised debate with candidates Bush and Dole, Pat Robertson insisted that he had information indicating that the Soviet Union was in violation of the Khrushchev-Kennedy agreement and that twenty-five nuclear-armed SS-4 and SS-5 missiles had been placed in Cuba. When subsequently pressed to supply evidence in support of this charge, he failed to do so.

It was not his only miscue. Reporters asked him to defend a story he had told about a woman who contracted AIDS from kissing her impotent husband; he was asked about his tale that a second grader had learned to read at seventh grade level in less than a month through a reading program he had sponsored; he was queried about his claims that he had "rebuked" Hurricane Gloria when it was menacing the coast of Virginia, that one-fourth of all automobile workers used illegal drugs, that Planned Parenthood had a plan to sterilize blacks, Jews, mental defectives, and fundamentalist Christians, and that his Christian Broadcasting Network knew the specific locations of American hostages in Lebanon. A defensive Pat Robertson, struggling to explain such statements, grew testy with the press corps. His subsequent assertion that the Bush organization might have been behind the downfall of Jimmy Swaggart only added to the damage the candidate's "slippery lips and misstatements"—as he characterized them—were causing his campaign.[4]

The result was disaster at the polls. After a crushing defeat in New Hampshire, he pinned his hopes on the upcoming Southern primaries. But in early March, he finished a distant third in South Carolina, with barely one-third the votes of leader George Bush. On "Super Tuesday," with sixteen state primaries (fourteen in the South), he was humiliated, managing to win but twelve delegates out of 707. He persevered for a time, appearing before dwindling crowds and a shrinking press corps, but his campaign was finished. In mid-May, after a meeting with Vice President Bush, he quit the race, promising support for the GOP candidate in the fall.[5]

What was the cause of this political debacle for the shining star of the religious wing of the New Right? Many analysts insisted that it was not only that he had undermined his credibility with dubious assertions and had been hurt by the Swaggart scandal, that Jerry Falwell had broken ranks with the evangelical movement by endorsing George Bush, or even that the Robertson campaign had amateurish management. They concluded that Pat Robertson had failed because his movement had limited appeal.

"The Christian Right was always smaller than many commentators noticed," argued one writer; another suggested that the "recent decline of the Christian Right" was caused in part because Robertson was "never able to move beyond his narrow base of support among Charismatic Christians." One contributor to a scholarly journal concluded that only a minority of Americans accept the "values and attitudes of the Christian Right." A different author stated that "the failure of the Christian Right" was caused by "overarching historical trends," for "the born-again movement had been tied to the particular wave of nostalgic politics embodied in Ronald Reagan's . . . terms in office," and that it "could never have had the influence it enjoyed" without Ronald Reagan's "vociferous support." Even the titles of books told the tale: *The Rise and Fall of the Christian Right, Fall from Grace: The Failed Crusade of the Christian Right.*[6]

If 1988 represented a new low point for the religious leaders of the New Right, the months that followed brought only more bad news. In August 1989, Jerry Falwell officially dissolved the organization he had originally named The Moral Majority. He announced that he was closing it down after ten years because it "had accomplished its goals," but few found this explanation convincing. Former supporters were turning away from all the televangelists. In 1985, the top twenty syndicated religious programs had more than eleven million viewers, but by November 1990 the total was down to 7.7 million.

Swaggart's ratings collapse forced the sale of property adjacent to his estate and three radio stations; he made frantic pleas for larger contributions from the remaining faithful in order to stay on the air on even a few cable stations. Falwell decided that television was too costly and canceled "The Old Time Gospel Hour" on most of his outlets, nearly 200 stations. In subsequent months, he struggled to save his Liberty University, auctioning off part of the campus and fighting the foreclosure of loans. He announced in 1992 that "only now" was "the worst year of my life behind me." Twelve months earlier, Pat Robertson told interviewers that, for his enterprise, as well, "it was a couple of very difficult years."[7]

"What Happened to the Religious Right?" asked the headline in a prominent religious publication. Journalists speculated that many viewers who abandoned the electronic church became active in local congregations, especially the growing number of "super churches" with memberships of 5,000 to 20,000, offering special programs addressing parishioners' personal needs. Sociologists were quoted on "the rise and fall of the New Right," on its loss of momentum, its less visible national role. Such rumors of impending death proved not merely premature, but remarkably ill-informed. In fact, learning from the crisis of the late eighties, the movement would reshape itself. It was to become more formidable than even its strongest supporters or most fearful enemies had believed possible.[8]

The key element in this new rise of the New Right was the birth of the Christian Coalition, a movement created by Pat Robertson in the grim months after his failed presidential race. Robertson, perhaps recognizing that his name now had heavy negative connotations— and burdened by challenges to other parts of his extensive holdings— asked a young political operative named Ralph Reed to serve as executive director of the organization. But Robertson remained "the guiding spirit," in the words of a newsmagazine writer, of the organization which he had founded.[9]

Reed, only twenty-nine when he joined the Christian Coalition, presented a persona very different from other leaders of Christian Right. A Ph.D. in history from Emory (with special interest in the American South), his deeply conservative credentials were in order:

he had been a director of the National College Republicans and worked on the campaigns of Representative Newt Gingrich and Senator Jesse Helms. But this extraordinarily youthful figure, a fresh new face with a choirboy appearance, not only looked different from the aging television ministers who had worn out their welcome in many households, he also understood how important it was to move quickly in the direction of Pat Robertson's new vision for the New Right. For what Robertson argued in 1990 was that the new effort must avoid what had just failed for him: a quixotic national campaign organized around the personal leadership of some celebrity minister. Instead, the Christian Coalition must go to the grass roots. With a mailing list of 1.8 million names from the Robertson presidential effort, there was a good start.[10]

In this new effort to work at the state and local level, it was important not to appear to be a Christian entity. Evangelical Protestants would be the object of the organizing effort, but other voters might be antagonized if it appeared that such forces were being mobilized in their area. It must be "stealth politics."

The Christian Coalition, focusing on elections for school boards, city councils, and state legislatures, would not announce its presence. It would recruit candidates, train its workers, and keep its name out of the races. Ralph Reed, who had observed that the Robertson campaign had given activists "an advanced degree in hardball politics," told one interviewer, "we tried to change Washington when we should have been focusing on the states." He told another writer: "I want to be invisible. I do guerrilla warfare. I paint my face and travel at night. You don't know its over until you are in a body bag. You don't know until election night."[11]

The first great success of the new tactic was in San Diego, in 1990. Prior to the election, many local office holders were completely unaware that they faced any serious opposition. The Coalition mobilized its voters through church newsletters, leaflets, "in pew" registration. The result was that sixty of eighty-eight candidates were elected. It became known in the circles of the religious Right as the "San Diego Model." Reed told *The Los Angeles Times:* "But that's just good strategy . . . if you reveal your location, all it does is allow your opponent to improve his artillery bearings."[12]

The Coalition prepared organizing manuals for those it was recruiting to operate this stealth enterprise and it established leadership training schools. Soon it would have "rapid response networks" connected by phone, fax, and modem in hundreds of counties; information would be updated monthly via satellite downlinks.

But "keep your profile low" was the message. The grand design might be there but most voters should be told only about the local issues. Reed was quoted in the Religious News Service in the spring of 1990: "What Christians have got to do is to take back this country, one precinct at a time, one neighborhood at a time and one state at a time. . . . I honestly believe that in my lifetime we will see a country once again governed by Christians . . . and Christian values." But saying such things to the larger public only would frighten the majority, who might find this an extremist vision in a pluralistic society.

"You should never mention the name Christian Coalition in Republican circles," the Coalition's Pennsylvania manual instructed. Guy Rodgers, Coalition national field director, advised one leadership school gathering to "stop using redemptive language . . . [if] we want to Christianize when talking to an audience that doesn't understand Christianize . . . we end up sending a message we don't want to send . . . the public policy arena is not intended to save souls."[13]

This became the new conventional wisdom of the New Right. And it was clear that New Right activists outside the religious world were involved from the very first in shaping this strategy. A fall 1990 "Road to Victory" conference for the Christian Right had been held under the auspices of the Heritage Foundation. Thomas C. Atwood, managing editor of the Heritage journal *Policy Review*, argued that the religious leaders had "often come across as authoritarian, intolerant and boastful." He warned against "messianic rhetoric" and counseled that "the best thing that could happen to the movement is for it to be less identifiable as a movement."[14]

But such was the success of the Coalition that it would be impossible for very long to "fly below the radar," in Reed's words. The Coalition grew steadily throughout 1991 and 1992; membership climbed from 57,000 to 250,000 and telemarketing techniques were swelling the voter data bank. By 1993, journalists reported that it had 350,000 members, 750 local chapters, and a full-time staff in fifteen states operating with an annual budget of some $10 million. By 1994, Ralph Reed would claim that the Christian Coalition had 1.2 million supporters. By 1995, the number was 1.6 million and the annual budget was at $25 million.[15]

The Coalition—tax exempt and supposedly nonpartisan—grew so

quickly that its supporters had seized control of entire Republican party organizations. In Virginia, Texas, Minnesota, and Iowa it captured the GOP state committees. A survey by one magazine concerned with campaigns and elections reported that by 1994 the Christian Right exercised "considerable control of Republican parties in thirteen states and completely dominated eighteen others." In some states the new power was used to advance a strident agenda opponents saw as extremist. In Iowa there was an effort to adopt a state GOP platform calling for a ban on all abortions, the institution of Bible reading, and the teaching of creationism. But such efforts went against the new policy of moderation. If the powerful presence of the Coalition could no longer be denied, such power must be used in the least alarming manner. Stealth rhetoric would replace stealth politics.[16]

By 1994, Ralph Reed could no longer talk of wanting to be "invisible." The Christian Coalition had become very visible and Reed now said, "I don't think it's the American way to oppose people with religious faith getting involved." A contemporary conservative had complained that those who criticized religious activists were guilty of "the last respectable bigotry"; Reed now embraced this argument. His widely advertised new book carried the words "Mainstream Values Are No Longer" before the title, *Politically Incorrect: The Emerging Faith Factor in American Politics*. In this work, Reed's central themes were that religion in politics is the American way and that the Coalition's way is a moderate one in keeping with the values of the "populist" majority.

"People of faith want to exercise their rights of citizenship and serve their fellow Americans just like anyone else in public life," he argued. "The conventional wisdom that religious conservatives seek to legislate a radical agenda is not borne out by the facts . . . in fact," he suggested, "the agenda of religious conservatives seems quite minimalist and mainstream." Reed even invoked Marxist theorist Antonio Gramsci's academically fashionable concept of "cultural hegemony" in service of his thesis: "the cultural hegemony of the institutions controlled by the elites in the United States" will be challenged by "people of faith" who can find support for their efforts across the nation, notably among those who had backed "Ross Perot and the Populist Revolt" of 1992.[17]

However moderate and "minimalist" the Coalition's agenda truly had become, its leaders were trying to avoid involvement in controversial issues. One newspaper reported that Pat Robertson was steering clear of discussions of abortion and homosexuality, as the Christian Coalition attempted to "soften its image" and "tone down" rhetoric that had "sunk George Bush." The reference was to the tough, passionate, extremist speeches given by New Right supporters for a national television audience during the 1992 Republican Convention in Houston.[18]

But so successful was the Coalition in turning out the vote for Republican candidates during the critical Congressional campaign of 1994, when the GOP reversed four decades of Democratic dominance in a momentous victory, that even if its agenda was much more than "minimalist," the Coalition would wield immense influence on Capitol Hill.

One exit poll survey had revealed that over twenty percent of voters in the 1994 election identified themselves as evangelicals or born-again Christians and three out of four of these voters supported Republican candidates. With a total turnout of less than thirty-eight percent, the impact of voters energized by efforts of the Christian Right was extraordinary. It constituted the largest single voting bloc among Republicans, just about a third of the entire GOP vote. Coalition supporters remained a small fraction of the total electorate, but they voted and most people did not. They could turn defeat into victory.

Over sixty percent of the 600 candidates endorsed by the religious Right won in November 1994. They included Rick Santorum, who returned to "stealth campaign" tactics in mobilizing Coalition activists in his Pennsylvania senatorial race, while downplaying his extreme views. It is "increasingly difficult to tell the Republican party and the Christian Coalition apart," one reporter wrote in the late spring of 1995.

When the forces of the Religious Right were in Washington in May to offer their own Contract With The American Family, Speaker Gingrich, surrounded by other GOP luminaries, warmly received the document and promised quick legislative action. The party leadership was unanimous in its fulsome praise; prominent Republicans offered no words of criticism for the Coalition or its allies. The lengthy contract included guarantees for prayer in schools, vouchers for parents to send their children to parochial schools, limits on abortion and "access" to pornography, abolition of the Department of Education, the eventual end of all federal welfare programs (turned over to private charity), and other proposals. Senator Robert Dole, welcoming the contract, remarked that "it may not be fashionable inside the Beltway, but I believe that we must restore religious expression to its rightful place . . . in our public life."[19]

Coalition leaders were discovering by mid-1995 that "toning down" their rhetoric was not necessary for political success and was not acceptable to the growing number of activists they had recruited to their cause. Ralph Reed found that his members were not happy with his agreement not to press for a school-prayer amendment earlier in 1995. In response he gave his so-called "litmus-test" speech, in which potential GOP presidential candidates were warned that those who did not oppose abortions would not be acceptable to conservative Christians in 1996.

In fact, there were reasons to doubt that the Christian Right had become just another "mainstream" conservative political organization (with a "minimalist" agenda) by 1995. The views, policies and programs of both its founders (discussed in Chapter 15) and of contemporary movement activists suggest a very different conclusion. For all their rhetoric of moderation following the period of "stealth politics," the shapers of the Christian Right, as Ralph Reed himself argued with his reference to "Christians . . . taking back this country," see the real America as Christian America.

Does this mean that the Christian Right can be seen as practicing a kind of "religious nativism"? No, the movement, as noted in the preceding chapter, has made efforts to celebrate its own brand of right-wing ecumenical policy-making.

But it does mean that its peculiar vision of the moral superiority of "Christian values" and "Christian morality," its constant concern with the threat to Christian America it sees posed by "liberal elites" and others supporting abortion rights, gay rights, "pornography," and similar developments, keep it a part of the party of fear. Despite its striking success in mobilizing a voting constituency, despite its striking influence in the Republican party—where economic conservatives committed to slashing federal taxes and weakening the power of the federal government will embrace its "social agenda" in return for support in their areas of interest—it remains what it was in the eighties, a movement on the far shore of American politics. For while the Christian Right no longer refers to "secular humanists" as the evil other, it continues to picture a fearful climate in which Christian America is threatened by powerful enemies.

The state chairman of the Oklahoma Coalition told a training session: "Only we can restore this nation. . . . Only Christian believers doing the work . . . in the thick of the battle." A Coalition recruiting brochure in Chicago asked: "Can You Spare 12 Hours to Save Christians From Destruction?" Lou Sheldon, chairman of the Traditional Values Coalition, stated in the fall of 1993: "We were here first. You don't take our shared common values and say they are biased and bigoted. . . . We are the keepers of what is right and what is wrong." And Pat Robertson, the founding father and key player in the Coalition crusade, has angrily observed: "They have kept us in submission because they have talked about separation of church and state. There is no such thing in the Constitution. It's a lie of the Left, and we're not going to take it anymore."[20]

Indeed, both Robertson and Jerry Falwell, the televangelist founders of the movement and still the best known names on the Christian Right, were trafficking in conspiracy theories in the nineties and sounding more like extremists than back in the eighties, when their media stars were rising.

By 1995, Pat Robertson had overcome any temporary financial setbacks to build a vast enterprise larger than any created by a religious broadcaster. Despite a decline in contributions to CBN, Robertson's world was expanding. His leveraged buyout of the Family Channel, the 10th largest in America, led to a vast profit (estimated at $90 million) after that company went public in 1992. His International Family Entertainment includes a famous national ice show and television production companies. He had the resources to try to purchase United Press International and added more radio and television stations, along with a Hollywood animation company. His graduate school, now called Regent University, seemed to flourish, as did the Christian legal and civil rights group he organized, the American Center for Law and Justice. With the Christian Coalition a spectacular success, the Robertson empire seemed without a care. But then came the controversy over his latest book.[21]

Pat Robertson has written seven books, but it was his 1991 work, *The New World Order*, a "New York Times bestseller" with over half a million copies in print, that rekindled discussion about extremist leadership at the helm of the Christian Right. In this work, Robertson offers a complex and bizarre theory of history. Readers of earlier chapters will find some of it familiar, for Pat Robertson seems to borrow from several extremist theorists and right-wing activists of the American past. But in creating his vision of a "grand design" in which sinister forces of high finance manipulate power, control politicians, create depressions, and shape military affairs to serve their predatory interests, the founder of the Christian Coalition is also working the same ground as extremist activists on the very fringe of contemporary American society. Indeed, some of the "Christian Patriot" and even Christian Identity disciples to be discussed in the next section, in addition to many members of the new militia movement, might find much to agree with in *The New World Order.*

Robertson pictures a vast conspiracy dating back to the Bavarian Illuminati in the eighteenth century. Like some latter day Jedidiah Morse (see Chapter 1), Robertson sees the Illuminati as a demonic and powerful force, which used Freemasonry as an instrument and served as the intellectual seedbed of world communism. The Illuminati eventually grew into an immense financial power center. This center was controlled at first by European bankers (particularly the Rothschilds) but soon became dominant in America, as well.

"The European bankers and money lords of America" have been the constant, shadowy and almost all-powerful force behind much of American history. Through the instruments of their self-serving schemes in the twentieth century—men who created the Federal Reserve System, the Council on Foreign Relations, the Trilateral Commission—they have been the shapers of policy and the enemies of the people. When confronted with brave opposition, they have acted ruthlessly: "It is my belief that John Wilkes Booth, the man who assassinated Lincoln, was in the employ of the European bankers who wanted to nip this American populist experiment in the bud."

There are numerous figures who appear as agents or dupes of the financial masterminds. Woodrow Wilson gave us the Federal Reserve System and, with Colonel Edward House, called for "a new world order" in 1917. They also gave us the League of Nations, "one small part of House's grand design" for "a one-world government, a one-world army, a one-world economy under the Anglo-Saxon financial oligarchy, and a world dictator served by a council of twelve faithful men." The United Nations was the latter-day creation of the same group.

It is "relatively easy," Robertson writes, to "trace the continuity and purpose of our policy elites." There is an "invisible cord" connecting "Wilson . . . to the J. P. Morgan bank, to the Rockefellers and the Council on Foreign Relations . . . to the powerful Carnegie, Rockefeller and Ford Foundations, to the United Nations, to Henry Kissinger (appointed by Richard Nixon, and for whom Nelson Rockefeller had been 'employer, benefactor and landlord'), to the Trilateral Commission, to Jimmy Carter, to George Bush."

These policy elites served the interests of the financial powers, who profited by the wars of the twentieth century and even the Cold War. Some of the wars (Korea, Vietnam) had been unwinnable, but only because civilian authorities "were actually prohibiting our troops from winning" by conceiving "incredible rules of engagement." The reason: "Their plan for this country was not victory over communism but ultimate union with the Soviet Union in a world government." The Cold War led to immense profits for the power brokers and also to the huge U.S. debt. And the Gulf War: "could it be" that it was an unnecessary conflict in which Saddam Hussein was intentionally sent "the wrong signals" because "powerful people wanted a situation that was so obviously dangerous to the entire world that all nations would join together" and President George Bush could proclaim "the new world order."[22]

There is much more to this remarkable book, including the dark meaning of Masonic imagery on the Great Seal of the United States, the role of New Age religions, the ways in which "the Left" is linked to the money power. It concludes with a consideration of "the battle ahead" and "the Christian agenda." But its general tone and themes evoke memories of Ku Klux Klan broadsides about "Jew bankers" in the twenties, of William Dudley Pelley's Silver Shirt Legion publications and Father Coughlin's sermons on those "banksters . . . rulers of the world, dominating and controlling the economic life of this nation" in the thirties, of Robert Welch's conspiracy fantasies in the fifties and Lyndon La Rouche's assault on the Trilateral Commission in the eighties. Can there be a stronger argument for placing Reverend Pat Robertson, leader of the Christian Right, as a leader of a party of fear?

His allies understood the problem presented by *The New World Order*. When *The New York Review of Books*—in February 1995— printed a lengthy, devastating review of the book, which was subsequently cited by *New York Times* columnist Frank Rich, not only was Robertson forced to send a statement to the *Times* but conservative columnists rallied to his defense.[23]

One approach was to portray him as a harmless eccentric with monetary obsessions. Another response was to dismiss any anti-Semitic overtones in the book (which delved into the role of Jewish bankers in Europe and America and cited some notoriously anti-Semitic sources) by pointing to Robertson's support for Israel. In an earlier effort to defend Robertson from charges of intolerance, one conservative writer even attacked the attackers: "Pat Robertson is a target" because "those in the liberal Left are determined to delegitimize any challenge to the power they have long enjoyed over the basic institutions of American life and culture."[24]

Not only were these responses unpersuasive, they did not deal with the major question raised by the publication of the book. Pat Robertson might begin his defensive statement by insisting that "my book does not embrace a conspiracy theory of history," but a reading of the book leads to the opposite conclusion. Could there be no connection between the approach of the Christian Coalition and the conspiratorial, extremist views of its founder and leader?

Moreover, Robertson was not the only religious leader of the New Right dealing with conspiracy. Jerry Falwell, recovering from his financial crisis, reappeared in the spring of 1993, preaching strident sermons criticizing the separation of church and state. He talked of reviving the Moral Majority in service of the new crusade, but some observers now remarked that the religious Right had outgrown him. Perhaps in response to this feeling of marginalization, he turned his attention to lurid attacks on President Clinton.[25]

He offered his *Old Time Gospel Hour* viewers a videotape, "Bill Clinton's Circle of Friends," in which the President was accused of being a liar, thief, cocaine addict, drug-money launderer and murderer, and a man who had arranged mob-style assassinations.

Of course, the New Right includes a variety of organizations and activists; the televangelists and the Christian Coalition are its best known products, but there are several other notable groups at work to protect "traditional family values" in Christian America. Two such organizations, the Traditional Values Coalition and Focus On The Family, are particularly significant. Extremist rhetoric is also present in the language of the leaders of these groups.

The Traditional Values Coalition (TVC), founded in 1983 and led by the Reverend Louis P. Sheldon, claims active chapters in twenty states and affiliation with 31,000 churches, 6,000 in California, where it maintains headquarters in Anaheim. Homosexuality is a particular object of TVC concern. Sheldon has called it "the most pernicious evil today. We must stop it before it spreads throughout the nation like cancer." One fundraising letter, "They Want Your Children," described gays and lesbians living "perverted, twisted lives that feed upon the unsuspecting and the innocent." According to some publications, the movement leader suggested that victims of AIDS should be segregated in "cities of refuge" for the good of society. TVC has been active in supporting anti–gay-rights initiatives in several states.[26]

Focus On The Family (FOF), is among the wealthiest and most successful evangelical organizations concerned with reshaping public policy in America. Founded and led (since 1977) by Dr. James C. Dobson, a Ph.D. in child development whom Jerry Falwell once predicted would emerge as the religious Right's leading figure in the nineties, FOF's annual budget was $101 million in 1995. The money is used to produce its ten radio programs, and to publish eleven magazines, as well as its vastly popular family advice books, films and videotapes. Dobson's syndicated daily half-hour radio program is broadcast on 1,600 radio stations (and hundreds of stations in other countries). His book on child rearing, *Dare to Discipline*, sold more than two million copies.

Dobson told the Religious Broadcasters Convention: "We are engaged at this time in an enormous civil war of values" in which "the Judeo-Christian, biblical prescriptions we trust" battle "the humanistic, avant-garde point of view that there are no absolutes." To take this struggle into the national political arena, his FOF bought the Family Research Council, which would grow into a leading religious Right lobbying enterprise under its leader, Gary L. Bauer. "We will be legally separate, but spiritually one," Dobson said of the two groups.

The FOF organization, moving its headquarters from Southern California to Colorado Springs, formed numerous affiliated political groups in thirty-five states, which hosted church-based political training sessions, known as "Community Impact Seminars." The FOF training handbook for these seminars, the "Community Impact Curriculum," warned against "moral decay in our society," and an early version argued that "this really was a Christian nation . . . and . . . to try separating Christianity from government is virtually impossible and would result in unthinkable damage."

Dobson, who has likened abortion to the Holocaust, has hosted Randall Terry on his radio program. Terry is the founder and former leader of Operation Rescue, whose "direct action" effort includes abortion clinic blockades, as well as the stalking and harassing of doctors and clinic staffs. Dobson has endorsed the youth training program of

Summit Ministries, established in the sixties by Billy James Hargis; Summit has been directed since the 1970s by David A. Noebel, a former Hargis associate and longtime activist in the John Birch Society, who focuses particular attention on the perils of homosexuality.

Still, Dobson seems less threatening than the televangelists of the eighties, when they took on the dangers of secular humanism. One observer noted that "he has such a rapport with average people that he doesn't scare them." Instead, he offers a "safe haven" in a world of change and flux, a message that endorses the biblical lessons of his listeners' youth.

His vast audience is intensely loyal; a supporter insists that "he commands armies of people . . . he is a heavy hitter in the conservative Christian movement." Which made it political news when, in the spring of 1995, Dobson cautioned Republican leaders against a "big tent" strategy that avoids embracing a conservative social agenda: "I think you should warn Republican presidential hopefuls that it would be impossible to skirt the moral issues in 1996."[27]

It is unlikely that the GOP would attempt to skirt such issues, for the New Right has risen from defeat to become an enormous force in American public life. It is a practitioner of the politics of "moralism" and sees Christian America locked in a life-and-death struggle with destructive forces. Not only its religious leaders cast the issue this way. Paul Weyrich, the political organizer who was present at the creation of the movement, stated: "This is really the most significant battle of the age-old conflict between good and evil, between the forces of God and the forces against God, that we have seen in our country."[28]

It was no small achievement to mobilize the mass following which became the shock troops of the Christian Right in the nineties. As Weyrich and Richard Viguerie had argued in the previous decade, the key theme to use in creating a successful political force was "populism." The New Right has spoken to the fear, confusion and anxiety found during an age of cultural and social change by offering to recapture America for "the people." It has offered to purge "destructive forces"—emerging with the social upheavals of the sixties—which, it argued, had gained the approval of "liberal elites" who controlled the media, the universities, the judiciary and the Democratic party. Christian America was at risk, and the Christian Right and its political allies would return the land to traditional values, Christian values.

A major reason for its success is the way its agenda has been meshed with the interests, policies and programs of those allies, the mainstream conservatives. Of course, "populism" also has been the rallying cry of Republican economic conservatives ever since the Reagan years. In the nineties, riding the tide of antigovernment feeling, these major political figures—whose interest is tax cuts, the elimination of regulatory agencies and entitlement programs, as well as massive "privatization"—spoke of an "opportunity society" in which American individualism would be celebrated and "the people" would be encouraged to "stop whining" and care for themselves without the interference of corrupt and incompetent federal bureaucrats. "Welfare cheats" and others would "get out of the wagon and push" for a change. Pat Robertson and others on the Christian Right had no objection to this approach.

As one writer noted, these were the "contemporary Calvinists." While their social agenda was central to their activism, they also embraced laissez faire capitalism (and certainly the leaders of their movement were doing very well for themselves), reviled the evils of economic equality—no "class politics" for them—and endorsed the need to revive "personal responsibility."[29]

The end of the Cold War had fractured many bonds in American politics, and Ralph Reed observed that "the old dichotomies of liberal-conservative, internationalist-isolationist, hawks-doves are breaking apart . . . postwar eras are periods of realignment." Now was an opportunity for a new alignment of the New Right believers who sought to reimpose the values of Christian America and for the conservative believers who sought to re-create the economic environment of pre–New Deal America.[30]

In reviving the New Right in the nineties, its key leaders and organizations have achieved historic success. Only the American party of the 1850s or the McCarthy-era anticommunist crusade of the 1950s can be compared with it for the impact made by a movement on the far Right.

The same cannot be said for leaders and movements farther out on the political spectrum. For while there has been considerable ferment on the racist fringe of the far Right, with some groups effectively using the rhetoric of contemporary antigovernment animus (as well as modern electronic communications) to create an image of growing strength, their overtly antialien themes have kept them confined to a small population of true believers.

★★★

Ferment on the Fringe: from Klan, Skinheads and Christian Identity to Christian Patriots

The enormous bomb which destroyed the Alfred P. Murrah Federal Building in Oklahoma City on April 19, 1995, killing 168 people and shattering the lives of hundreds more, focused national attention on right-wing extremism in the United States.

When law enforcement officers arrested Timothy J. McVeigh as the prime suspect in the most destructive act of domestic terrorism in United States history, the investigation revealed his involvement in a strange culture of antialien fringe groups. This culture had been present for many years in America, but it had become a shifting mixture of survivalist loners and self-styled constitutional experts preaching against federal tyranny, of neo-Nazi theorists and Christian Identity ministers, of young white supremacist toughs and their adult mentors, of fragmentary Klan chapters and fierce tax resisters, of angry travelers on the gun-show circuit and manipulators of the far-Right radio, video and internet world. Whether or not Timothy McVeigh— or anyone involved in the bombing—was a member of one of these small movements on the fringe, the horror of Oklahoma City and press reports linking him to this culture raised new questions about the size and scope of these most extremist forces on the American Right.[31]

Some of the radical right-wing organizations that had made a brief impact in previous decades were still in operation, but barely alive. These included such disparate groups as the La Rouche cult, the Liberty Lobby and the dwindling chapters of the Ku Klux Klan. Other phenomena of the fringe—like the skinhead gangs—had emerged only in the late eighties but were already in decline. There were, however, new movements surfacing in the nineties, using the now familiar fear of federal power and the urgent new fear of gun control, who were more successful in finding a following: These were the "Constitutionalists," Christian Patriots, and others with vague links to the militia movement. And, of course, there was that most powerful force of all on the antialien Right—Christian Identity—which was undergoing its own crisis but finding new allies in its struggle to save the nation from the Zionist Occupation Government and the race-mixing enemies of Aryan America.

Lyndon H. La Rouche reappeared on the scene in January 1994, paroled after five years of a fifteen-year sentence for defrauding elderly persons of their life savings. Many of his brightest and most talented disciples had abandoned his organization, and though La Rouche returned to his Virginia estate to take up control of his group, there was little life left in it. The extensive fund-raising entities, policy institutes, news services, magazines and journals were all damaged by his trial and imprisonment. However, La Rouche watchers would find it interesting that the cult was able to open an office in Moscow.[32]

Willis Carto's Liberty Lobby endured into the mid-nineties, continuing to publish *The Spotlight* (which Timothy McVeigh used in 1993 to advertise the sale of a military-style antitank launcher), and continuing to offer anti-Semitic materials. He even acquired several radio outlets and a satellite broadcasting network. Carto had founded the Populist party in 1984. After being expelled from his own party in a raucous internal struggle in 1986, he was forced to establish another faction (under the same name) and it was this Populist party which nominated David Duke for President in 1988. Carto's publications were still seen across the far Right spectrum into 1995; attempting to keep the group current, he featured virulent attacks on President Clinton and offered various conspiracy theories involving the federal government. But Willis Carto is sixty-nine and appeals to an aging population. He remains just a minor figure on the fringe.[33]

Even the John Birch Society stayed alive into the mid-nineties. For a movement committed to the struggle against the internal communist enemy, this was quite a trick in the post–Cold War era, when there was no Soviet Union to control its dupes or agents in America—people like Dwight Eisenhower. The Birch Society shifted to attacks on big government, the welfare state, "humanism" and the "absence of morality." Of course, one earlier theme found new life in this age of anxiety about the new world order; Birchers had been among the first on the far Right to intone "Get the U.S. out of the U.N. and the U.N. out of the U.S." The John Birch Society still offered the old literature, dating back to the fifties (although it was forced to close many of its bookstores). But it had the money to produce a handsome magazine and also went modern with a web page on the internet: "The John Birch Society: Less Government, More Responsibility, And With God's Help, A Better World."

It had lost most of its audience long before, although it had continued to make some impact in a few scattered and remote regions, notably Idaho. It was in Idaho, in the fall of 1994, that Republican Helen Chenoweth, close to the Birch Society for years and a featured speaker on tours sponsored by Birch chapters, won election to Congress. Birch leaders claimed that their support was "one of the many ingredients" in her victory. However, on the national scene, the John Birch Society remained a tiny cell lost on the fringe.[34]

In a different sense, the same was true of the Ku Klux Klan. As noted in Chapter 15, the Klan was beset in the eighties by fratricidal struggles between rival leaders and factions. It was menaced by successful lawsuits brought against it by civil rights groups, and some of its members were attracted to the Christian Identity movement. In the nineties, the process continued, and Klan rolls shrank until by mid-decade the estimates of its total size ranged from 4,000 to 5,500.

At the start of 1987 there were dozens of local Klans, but the three that competed for national attention were the United Klans of America, the Invisible Empire, and the Knights of the Ku Klux Klan (once led by David Duke). The United Klans, led by Robert Shelton, collapsed that year after being ordered to share in the payment of $7 million to the family of a young black man in Alabama who was murdered by several of its members earlier in the decade.

It was the Southern Poverty Law Center that brought that lawsuit and which also brought the lawsuit that doomed the Invisible Empire. This case involved a 1987 Klan-mob attack on civil rights marchers in Georgia; in 1993, the court ordered the IE to dissolve. For some Southern traditionalists in the movement, that might have seemed only proper, for the Invisible Empire's Grand Wizard, taking power in 1986, was James W. Farrands, a car mechanic and a Roman Catholic. (It must be noted that Farrands' more charismatic predecessor, Bill Wilkinson, had been exposed as an informant for the FBI.) When the leader tried to revive the organization as the Unified KKK, he was ordered by a federal judge to disband it.

There remained two large Klan groups, but both were floundering by 1995. They were the Knights of the Ku Klux Klan and its clone, the Federation of Klans. Imperial Wizard Thom Robb, leader of the Knights, had quarreled with his state leader from Illinois, Ed Novak, who then invented the Federation. The quarrel was reported to be over money and ideology. Novak, a militant figure who had been attracted to neo-Nazi activism, might have rejected Robb's efforts to offer a more moderate approach, counseling members to avoid harsh, racist rhetoric and saying: "The KKK does not preach against Negroes.

We believe everyone has a right to love their heritage and race." Of course, Robb is a pastor in Christian Identity and moderation is a relative thing. He has stated: "I hate Jews. . . . We've let antichrist Jews into our country and we've been cursed with abortion, inflation, homosexuality."

In any event, while the number of groups—most of them local cells—still totaled ninety-eight in 1994, students of the Klan expected continued decline of a movement long on the downward slope.[35]

Several Klan alumni, however, had made their individual marks in the late eighties and into the nineties. Two notable figures were David Duke and Tom Metzger.

Duke became the best known of all antialien fringe leaders when he entered the political arena with surprising success. The former Imperial Wizard of the Knights had left the Klan after clashing with Bill Wilkinson, one of several important right-wing personalities first recruited by him. The telegenic Duke had gone on to create the National Association for the Advancement of White People. He had been running for state senate without success for years, but received some attention when polling over 47,000 votes as the Populist presidential candidate in 1988. Then came his remarkable breakthrough that captured national press coverage: election in 1989 to the Louisiana Legislature as a Republican.

The next year, he sought the U.S. Senate seat. He was "ready to say publicly what the crowd was talking about privately," and he assailed "welfare systems that encourage illegitimate births," and "set asides that promote the incompetent." This would become standard conservative Republican rhetoric, but Duke was a former Klansman with a long record of racist activism; he had sold Nazi literature from his office in the Legislature. Still, he forced a runoff with incumbent Democrat J. Bennett Johnston and won 43.5 percent of the total vote.

When he edged out the incumbent Buddy Roemer in a nonpartisan three-way primary for governor in 1991, national GOP leaders were distressed, and Duke suddenly was seen as a serious if menacing presence on the political landscape. On election day, while receiving almost 700,000 votes—and the majority of white votes—he ran well behind Governor Edwin W. Edwards (who had been twice indicted for corruption). David Duke's political career already had peaked. But the press corps was in attendance when he mounted a campaign for the Republican nomination for President in 1992. This time, his effort foundered from the start. He received humiliating single digit votes throughout the primary campaign until quitting the race in April. Duke's moment on the national stage was over.[36]

Tom Metzger, former Grand Dragon in Duke's Klan, followed a different path to national notoriety. It was Metzger who would become the most influential mentor of the new skinhead movement.

Born in a small Indiana town in 1939, Metzger, a California TV repair service owner, is a veteran of many movements on the extremist fringe. In the sixties he joined the Birch Society but soon left, when "I found out you could not criticize the Jews." He had a brief stay in the Minutemen, but, finding that group old and stodgy, moved on to other passions. He was a campaign worker for George Wallace in 1968, before turning to the Klan. Joining David Duke's highly anti-Semitic Knights faction in 1975, he split with Duke—whose first campaign he managed—after becoming Grand Dragon for California. By this time he, too, had been ordained a "minister" in an Identity church and some reports suggest he now found Duke "too soft" on racist issues.

But like David Duke, Metzger tried running for office: "You don't make change burning fiery crosses out in cow pastures, you make change by invading the halls of the Statehouse and the Congress." He failed badly in several county and state races but then surprised many by winning a Congressional primary in 1980 before suffering a crushing defeat in the general election. Now he changed the name of his California Klan, first to the White American Political Association and then to White Aryan Resistance (WAR). This was not a membership organization. One writer noted that he fancied himself a "Leninist," working with "a minority of dedicated people to create a fanatical inner structure." He began producing videotapes for television ("Race and Reason"—featuring interviews with various hate group activists), publishing *WAR*, the "revolutionary newspaper of working class whites" and promoting neo-Nazi literature, as well as instructional handbooks on terrorism and guerrilla warfare.

Metzger, the defender of the "white working person," has celebrated the careers of Father Coughlin, Dr. Townsend and Huey Long, depression decade "American heroes" more citizens should know about. But it was in the late eighties that he was to make his greatest impact, by reaching out to a new, diffuse, anti-Semitic, white supremacist phenomenon imported from overseas. This was the skinhead movement.[37]

Skinheads first appeared in America in the mid-eighties. Like the originals who had emerged from the working-class youth culture of Britain, not all skins were antialiens, but many were virulent racists. Their shaved heads, tattooed arms, neo-Nazi insignia, and "Doc" Marten steel-tipped boots made them a distinctive new presence on the extremist scene. They responded to racist rock music (London-based Skrewdriver, playing Oi—the Cockney phrase for "hey"—music was the first and foremost band). They had rock concerts, not national conventions or national meetings, although they occasionally marched with Klan members and other racists at rallies. At first they had no national leadership and there is little organizational structure. They operate as youth gangs. They attack gays, blacks, "immigrants" and Jews.

A high school dropout from a Chicago suburb, Clark Martell, has been credited with creating the first neo-Nazi gang, Romantic Violence. This group published leaflets like "Skrewdriver News," calling on "White Youth" to "escape from our nightmare world of multira-cialism, unemployment and degradation."

Violence played a central role in the subculture of these skinhead gangs from the start. Instead of the turf struggles or drug wars which lead to murderous confrontations in the inner city, these gangs seemed to use violence only to intimidate those they dislike, to promote the racist goal of a pure white, Aryan, heterosexual society.

For the most part suburban or small town groups, the neo-Nazi skins do share with other gangs certain characteristics: most members come from broken or dysfunctional families in which there has been physical and/or sexual abuse. Growing up in a blue-collar culture in which economic opportunity is declining, often facing joblessness and poverty, burdened by educational failure, their hostility is channeled to the enemies of the group. Like other youth gangs, they find community in the collective, and conformity to its norms determines their action.[38]

With names such as Eastern Hammer Skins, the National Socialist Skinheads, the Confederate Hammer Skins, American Front, Skaters, New Nation, Nordic Thunder, First Strike, Legion of Aryan Warriors, Aryan Nation Skinheads, and Hail Victory Skinheads, these gangs emerged across the nation. Klanwatch, one of the organizations studying such groups, printed a yearly map with skinhead cells in states in every region of America. The Anti-Defamation League described twenty-eight "skinhead-related homicides" through mid-1993.[39]

Tom Metzger reached out to these groups by creating a neo-Nazi skinhead confederation. His instrument was the Aryan Youth Movement, and his son John emerged as its new president in 1987. Following his father's advice, John counseled a less threatening style and did not shave his head, wear the obligatory boots, red suspenders, bomber jacket or "white power" T-shirt. Like his father, John was a media-wise leader. (In 1991, one publication characterized Tom Metzger as "the producer of the greatest number of hate programs shown on public access channels.") John Metzger took advantage of television's desire for the aberrant and the confrontational by getting on the talk show circuit with his skinhead disciples. In one remarkable TV moment, a skinhead struggled with and broke the nose of host Geraldo Rivera. It was a good recruiting device.

But Tom Metzger was serving as mentor to these racist youths and helping to shape the activities of skins on the West Coast, and there were many violent incidents involving skinhead gangs in California and the Northwest. One of these incidents led to the trial which weakened the entire movement. It was the SPLC and the ADL that filed a $10 million lawsuit on behalf of the estate of an Ethiopian, Mulugeta Seraw, killed after a confrontation with skinheads in Portland, Oregon. Three skinheads pleaded guilty and received long sentences, but Tom and John Metzger were named as principals in the civil suit filed in the name of the dead man's estate. The issue was vicarious liability; Morris Dees, the attorney for the SPLC, persuasively argued that the Metzgers shared major responsibility for the killing, by virtue of their instructions to Portland skinhead leaders. The jury assessed even higher damages than Dees asked, including $3 million from WAR and $5 million from Metzger. The WAR leader already faced a jail sentence for involvement in a cross-burning in Los Angeles, but this was a devastating verdict, which he would lose on appeal in 1993.[40]

Tom Metzger and his White Aryan Resistance remained active on the antialien scene. But skinhead membership, which peaked in 1991 with 144 groups, dropped to eighty-seven in 1993, with an estimated 3,500 members active in forty states. Although there were now internet links to skinhead groups in Germany and Europe, and there were continuing reports of violent incidents nationwide, the American movement was losing headway. Despite some notorious episodes in 1994—notably two Pennsylvania skinhead brothers charged with the brutal murders of their parents and younger brother—the gangs were melting away. Klanwatch reported that the total number had plummeted by sixty percent to thirty-four active gangs in 1994.[41]

But even as their strength was ebbing, the skinhead bands were being courted by another, more powerful movement on the anti-Semitic, neo-Nazi fringe. This was Christian Identity. Aryan Nations, the political wing of the Church of Jesus Christ Christian and the strongest force in Identity, was reaching out to the young racists with its Aryan Youth Assembly, bringing them to its Idaho compound. Skinhead recruitment was part of a wider effort to make Aryan Nations the center of a grand alliance of racist orders. Already, various Klan fragments had been enlisted in the common cause. Other groups would follow.

In fact, there are a number of minuscule neo-Nazi cells across America, with such titles as SS Action Group, National Socialist White American Party, National Socialist Vanguard, Aryan Revolutionary Party, and SS of America. But one tiny organization had more to offer to those seeking a coalition of racist groups.

This was Gary "Gerhard" Lauck's NSDAP-AO (founded in 1972). The title stands for the German language name of Hitler's party, with the term "Foreign Organization" added at the end. Lauck, who has said "I was a born Nazi" and "I think Adolf Hitler was the greatest man who ever lived," began distributing homemade Nazi propaganda while still a teenager in the sixties. He is not German—he has lived in Lincoln, Nebraska, since age eleven—but has taken a German first name, speaks with a German accent and faults Hitler only for being "too humane": "We National Socialists declare total war on World Jewry and shall not rest until you have disappeared from the earth."

Although he has few followers and little influence in the United States, he has made a major impact on Europe. This "Farm Belt Fuhrer," as one news report called him, has become the world's largest distributor of Nazi literature, publishing in ten languages and sending materials to thirty countries. He boasts that "tons" of his work has saturated Germany, and German police authorities—dealing with a smuggling operation—agree that he is a problem for them. The German government banned him from the country; it is against the law to distribute Nazi material in Germany. In addition to books and pamphlets, he sends videos (including SS films in which Jews are likened to rats), flags, armbands and other memorabilia.

Lauck's links to German and European Nazis, his international contacts via the world internet, make him a valuable ally of Aryan Nations, the heart of the Identity movement. In 1994, Lauck's lieutenant, Mike Storm, attended the Aryan World Congress as NSDAP-AO ambassador. The movement was finding new allies.[42]

Aryan Nations, with its headquarters in Idaho but with almost twenty chapters in states across the nation, also was making contact with another notable anti-Semite by mid-decade: Dr. William L. Pierce, leader of the National Alliance. Pierce, of course, is best known as author of that venomous, anti-Semitic, white supremacist novel *The Turner Diaries* (185,000 copies in print), which served as the inspiration for the terrorist activities of the Identity group called "The Order" in 1983–84. (After federal agents killed its leader in a shootout, Pierce praised The Order and wrote: "How will the Jews cope with the man who does not fear them and is willing to give his life in order to hurt them? What will they do when a hundred good men rise to take Robert Mathews' place?")

Attention was focused once more on William Pierce after the Oklahoma City bombing. Timothy McVeigh, it seemed, was a passionate fan. "He carried that book all the time" said a gun collector, "he sold it at the shows. He'd have a few copies in the pocket of his cammies . . . it was like he was looking for converts." The bomb—made of a mixture of fuel oil and ammonium nitrate fertilizer—at Oklahoma City was a virtual twin in type and size of the bomb that a racist terrorist "hero" detonated at the FBI headquarters building in Washington (at the same hour in the morning) in Pierce's novel.

Pierce, who said of Oklahoma City that he was "shocked" but not surprised, for "when people . . . believe that they have nothing left to lose . . . they will resort to terrorism," had been a long-time fixture on the neo-Nazi scene. A leader of the American Nazi Party in the sixties, his small National Alliance had been distributing books, publishing periodicals and sponsoring his shortwave radio programs for years. Although there are chapters in other communities, in 1985 he moved his headquarters to a farm in West Virginia, where he leads a tiny "Cosmotheist Community." Rejecting traditional religions, Cosmotheism extols the advancement and ennobling of the white race. And Pierce, a scholarly, soft-spoken figure who writes lengthy articles on the "New World Order and the Deindustrialization of America," a Ph.D. in physics who taught briefly at Oregon State, does not resemble the violent and murderous loners who are heroes of his novels.

In his second novel, *Hunter* (35,000 copies sold), another tale of a killer who assassinates Jews in order to cleanse America and save the white race, he characterizes Christian Identity as a collection of unsophisticated "rural folk" completely absorbed with the idea that Jews are the agents of Satan; one character observes that "they can't recruit anyone but hicks ... their doctrine is crazy." Pierce has referred to Identity theology as "lowbrow." Thus it is not an easy fit to create ties between National Alliance and Aryan Nations. But a closer relationship between many elements on the racist Right was being shaped by 1995.[43]

And more was known by the mid-nineties about the nature of the strange religious movement that even Pierce has found difficult to embrace. As noted in Chapter 15, Identity evolved from the mildly philo-Semitic posture of British-Israelism, that curious late-nineteenth-century social movement whose eccentric adherents argued that the British—not the Jews—were the lineal descendants of the ancient Israelites. But in America these ideas underwent a radical transformation. Early figures reshaping them in the twenties were Howard Rand, an attorney and prolific organizer, and William J. Cameron, a key aide to Henry Ford in the days of the anti-Semitic *Dearborn Independent.*

During the forties and fifties, it was Gerald L. K. Smith, that most famous of all American anti-Semites, who served as mentor for Bertram Comparet and Wesley Swift. These two, as noted earlier, along with William Potter Gale, completed the conversion of the old movement and fashioned Christian Identity. The name of Swift's church, Jesus Christ Christian (because Jesus was not a Jew), would be used by Richard Girnt Butler as his pulpit, and Aryan Nations was invented as the political arm of what was the founding church of the movement. The fully-formed Identity theology—followers should rejoice in the rediscovery of their historically suppressed "Identity" as the "Children of Israel"—saw Jews not only as the evil financial and political manipulators described in the work of earlier anti-Semites and as not the heirs of the Israelites, but as the literal biological offspring of Satan. Thus, as one writer notes, Identity theology "casts Jews in the role of God's adversaries on earth."

What has emerged is a world in which Identity adherents see Jews as even more than an immensely strong and satanic force. They are at the center of a conspiracy of power so all-encompassing that it is impossible to trust anyone not sharing Identity's vision of them. It is a closed system of thought: Identity believers will reject any arguments of prestigious academic, church or government officials because these authoritative individuals must be either part of the conspiracy or dupes of the Jews. This circular system of reasoning, in which all who have a different view are dismissed as fools or enemies, is seen, as well, among Christian Patriots and militia members.[44]

Christian Identity churches have appeared in many parts of the nation, but particularly in the West. They have names like Christian Israel Covenant Church, American Christian Ministries, America's Promise Ministries, and Judah's Praise Ministries. Total membership probably is not more than a few thousand, but those involved often appear as ordinary people at their Sunday place of worship—singing hymns, eating potluck lunches, hearing announcements of upcoming church socials and then listening to an Identity sermon. "Judeo-Christianity is a lie from the pit of Babylonian Hell . . . Judaism is the pinnacle of filth and everything evil. You are either a Christian following Christ or a Jew following the satanic religion."[45]

But like other movements on the radical Right across American history, Identity—and its related anti-Semitic, white supremacist religious orders—has been affected by tensions caused by the jealousies and conflicting schemes of various strong personalities who would be "leader." Containing such rivalries is a great challenge.

Tom Metzger has been in and out of Identity. Thom Robb has been a minister even as he leads his Klan. Ben Klassen's virulently anti-Semitic Church of the Creator was never part of Identity but he shared many beliefs with them. This wealthy figure, who committed suicide in August 1993 at his compound in North Carolina, an author of books advocating racial and religious violence, had sought recruits among skinheads and prisoners in federal penitentiaries. But other Identity ministers have stayed in the organization, although not necessarily deferring to Aryan Nations as headquarters of the movement.[46]

Peter J. "Pete" Peters of the Church of Christ (LaPorte, Colorado) has emerged as a major figure. While his congregation numbers only a few dozen regulars, this forceful speaker has made shrewd use of cable television, appearing on more than twenty stations in a dozen states. Embracing the Jewish-menace view which is at the heart of Identity teaching—as well Identity's doctrine of the inferiority of "mud people" and most other non-Aryans—Peters adds a particular fixation on the threat of homosexuality. In one of his publications, he promotes the idea that the Bible demands the execution of gay men and lesbians.[47]

A much less incendiary brand of Identity is found in Muldrow, Oklahoma, where Robert G. Millar presides over the religious community he calls Elholm City (a partial Hebrew name for City of God). Mr. Millar has led his community, which resembles a small village, for twenty-two years. Cautious in discussing his church's racial outlook with visitors, he does not speak of violent confrontations. But he served as "spiritual advisor" to James D. Ellison when the leader of the CSA was persuaded to surrender after the 1985 siege at his Arkansas compound.

Millar also served as "spiritual adviser" for Richard Wayne Snell, white supremacist and murderer, who was put to death in Arkansas the very day of the Oklahoma City bombing, muttering as he was about to be executed, "look over your shoulder, justice is coming." In fact, James Ellison had told federal attorneys in 1988 that white supremacists had hatched a plot to bomb the federal building in Oklahoma City, although nothing had come of this plan. (There was no evidence linking the 1995 attack with this scheme.)

Ellison's testimony was at a trial of white supremacists held in Fort Smith, Arkansas. Fourteen people in the movement were accused, but Federal attorneys were particularly interested in prosecuting three major Identity figures: Robert Miles, pastor of the Mountain Church in Michigan (now deceased), whose farm had been the site of many racist gatherings, Richard Girnt Butler, and Louis Beam, an ex-Klansman. Ellison, seeking to shorten his prison term imposed after the CSA confrontation, offered evidence of conspiracies by the accused to foster civil unrest through a series of terrorist acts. Despite extensive testimony by Ellison and other turncoats (Ellison would win release and enter the witness protection program), the jury acquitted all defendants. It was a significant victory for extremists of the Right.[48]

Louis Beam, one of the targets at the sedition trial, would grow in stature as an Identity leader in the nineties. A Vietnam veteran who had served for eighteen months as a helicopter door gunner, he had left the Klan to become Aryan Nations ambassador-at-large. He established the Aryan Nations Liberty Net, a computer network, and became known as one of Identity's most powerful public speakers.

In 1992, at a meeting in Colorado called by Pete Peters, Beam introduced the concept of leaderless resistance, which would become so influential in Identity, patriot and militia circles. He called for a "fundamental departure" in the theory of military organization; instead of the "pyramid" structure with the mass at the bottom and the officer-leader on top, the only way "to defeat state tyranny" is the "cell system." In leaderless resistance, patriots must emulate "the communists" and operate in independent cells, isolated from each other and impervious to penetration by agencies of the hated federal government.[49]

In 1995, Beam's impressive persona was noted by those who study Identity and consider the future leadership of Aryan Nations, home of the annual Aryan World Congress. Richard Girnt Butler, at seventy-six, would need a successor. Carl Franklin, Butler's chief of staff and, by some accounts, his heir apparent, had proved an uninspiring figure; he resigned in 1993 and set up his own Identity church in Montana. Franklin was criticized for a dictatorial style and, even in Identity circles, "oddball racist theories." (Franklin's aide and security chief Wayne Jones allegedly taught that pigs are the offspring of Jews, and that aliens from outer space populated the earth with blacks and other "mud people.") It remained unclear whether Franklin would some day return to the Hayden Lake compound as leader, Louis Beam—now living in Idaho—might be interested in the post, or another activist, such as Tim Bishop, who succeeded Franklin as staff director and second-in-command, would emerge to play this critical role in Identity.[50]

But it was clear that of all the elements on the extreme antialien fringe, Christian Identity remained the most important organization. Still, Identity in the nineties remained a relatively insignificant group in total membership. Because of the acts of violence that had been connected with it and because of the extraordinary nature of its fearful racist ideology offered inside a pluralistic democratic state, it was no longer a shadowy phenomenon. By effectively using the information highway to carry its message across the internet, cable TV, shortwave radio, video and fax, it had reached a larger audience. Yet the question remained, what could the future be for this movement?

Despite the millenarian fantasies and apocalyptic rhetoric of some of its spokesmen, who have talked of preparing for "the final battle," Identity believers cannot succeed through direct, violent confrontation. All efforts in this direction have met disaster. There was the quick destruction of The Order. There was the rapid arrests of members of the local Idaho group calling itself Bruder Schweigen Strike Force II (Order II), after that band engaged in murder, counterfeiting and pipe bomb assaults in 1986. While Gordon Kahl has become a cult martyr for many believers, the Posse Comitatus was dissolved, its "township" near Tigerton, Wisconsin, emptied, the owners and leaders imprisoned.[51]

There can be no agreement on the total number of followers of Identity and related white supremacist, neo-Nazi sects, including Klan and skinhead groups. Danny Welch of Klanwatch has observed that "you can't put a number on it, nobody really knows." Still, it is unlikely there are many more than 100,000 people—probably less— in the 250 to 300 groups operating at any one time. This little party of fear cannot grasp power in America and expel or expunge its racist enemies. Antialienism now has limited appeal, and this peculiar agenda of hate cannot find real support beyond the small circle of true believers. (The only scenario in which a strike for power offers any promise is an apocalyptic situation similar to the one in Pierce's novel: if nuclear proliferation affords terrorists access to such weapons, then a nuclear Oklahoma City or World Trade Center attack could unhinge the nation, and armed bands of marauding and murderous racists might pose a threat to the future of the democracy.)

If triumph in race war against the hated enemy is no alternative, what are the other options? There is a survivalist retreat from the larger society, with its Zionist Occupation Government. This would mean the creation of more "cultic communities," such as Ellison's CSA or Millar's Elholm City. There is the territorial sanctuary idea, which also surfaced in the eighties, now being refined into a "Northwest Imperative." Group members from across America might migrate to the Pacific Northwest and adjoining mountain states, creating a critical mass of like-minded residents. But given the rapid population growth in this area, with large numbers of "ordinary people" who don't share the views of the racist Right moving in from California and other states, there is no chance of creating such an Aryan homeland.

Neither alternative seems a promising prospect for the angry, noisy, confrontational, but still tiny groups of America's most overtly white supremacist activists. But if their political goals and cultural beliefs could be meshed with others who also proclaim disgust at contemporary developments, fear of the government, hostility to the "elites" dominating national institutions (and their own racial and religious bias), then the racists from Identity might find new influence inside a larger movement.

One shrewd observer of these fringe groups says that what is "scary" is the way Identity followers and like-minded extremists might be finding links with other bands of angry Americans: It is the "blurring" of such distinctions which might create new possibilities on the edge of the radical Right; it is the possible ties of the racist Right to the evolving Christian Patriot, Christian Constitutionalist and militia phenomenon.[52]

"Christian Patriot" is an amorphous movement, a potpourri of tax protestors, constitutional literalists, survivalists and others who embrace a conspiratorial view of American life. But the title tells the tale; these groups like to see themselves as patriots—the new incarnation of the Pilgrims or the Revolutionary Minutemen—struggling to protect Christian America.

For Christian Patriots, America is a white Christian nation menaced by corrupting alien forces. Seeming to sense that nativism can no longer be a source for mass movements on the American far Right, group leaders often mask their white supremacist views. While not saying they embrace the bizarre racial theology of Identity or the stridently neo-Nazi rhetoric of National Alliance, WAR, or other fringe cells, the patriots fold their racist views into discussions of constitutional rights. They glorify American individualism, the "freeman" living in virtuous community with his family, freed of government taxes and regulations, subject only to the laws of God. But there is a subtext of bigotry in much of what they say and do.

For opposing their idealized world of sovereign American citizens is the familiar conspiracy of anti-Christian power. The Jews, who dominate the notorious legion of international bankers, the Federal Reserve system, the Rockefellers and, of course, the United Nations, are among those aligned against the true patriots. But democracy is not at stake, for in a quaint return to John Birch rhetoric of the fifties, this party of fear insists America is a "republic," not a democracy or "mobocracy." (One Oregon-based patriot group even was named "Republic v. Democracy Redress.")

Their concept of the American republic is not the conventional view. While many patriots make frequent references to the Constitution, there are parts of the great document they don't support. Several make a distinction between "state citizens" (white Americans deriving their rights from God) and "Fourteenth Amendment citizens," because these African American citizens derive their rights from the government. It is the post–Civil War Fourteenth Amendment, holding that "no state shall make or enforce any law which shall abridge the privileges or immunities of citizens of the United

States," which particularly disturbs Christian Patriot states-rights defenders.[53]

Being self-styled experts on the Constitution, some also reject the Sixteenth Amendment ("Congress shall have power to lay and collect taxes on incomes") but, of course, are great believers in the Tenth Amendment: "powers not delegated to the United States by the Constitution, nor prohibited by it to the States, are reserved to the States . . . or to the people." It is the treatment of the Sixteenth and Tenth Amendments that will link patriots to other "constitutionalists": tax resisters, protestors against environmental regulation, and gun control opponents, many of whom will have close ties to the militia movement.

The patriots have their greatest presence in the West. The Christian Patriot Association in Oregon runs a bookstore and mail-order catalogue, and publishes a newsletter. It markets many favorite works of Identity supporters; its newsletter carries the motto: "Unless the American Patriot is Christian, Liberty Cannot be Restored." The Pilot Connection in northern California is led by Philip Marsh, author of *The Complete Patriot*, in which the "Protocols of the Elders of Zion" are described as a set of rules followed by communists in their quest for world domination.

In Montana, Martin J. "Red" Beckman, a leading tax protestor who has been close to Identity, is prominent in patriot circles. He has written that "our government, banks, major media and legal professions are dominated by men who are believers in the Anti-Christ religion." He also has been a leader of the Fully Informed Jury Association, which argues that jury members have the right to rule not only on the case in question but on the merits of the law. Such "jury nullification" doctrine has attracted activists of many kinds across the nation.[54]

Best known of all Christian Patriots is Lieutenant Colonel (Retired) James "Bo" Gritz, the leader of the "Christian Covenant Community" in Kamiah, Idaho. A legendary figure in the army from his days as a Green Beret commander in Vietnam, the "real life Rambo" who looks the part, Gritz was on the Populist ticket with David Duke (as vice presidential candidate) but dropped out of the race. He was the Populist presidential candidate in 1992 and was also a regular speaker at Pastor Pete Peters' annual Family Bible Camp. Later, he would disavow links to Duke, Willis Carto, and Peters, saying "anyone who is a racist, anyone who is a bigot . . . I don't want their support."

Gritz is acknowledged in patriot circles for his intervention in the siege involving the family of Identity survivalist Randall Weaver on a mountain top at Ruby Ridge, Idaho, in August 1992. The killings at Ruby Ridge and the subsequent trial would become (with the Branch Davidian affair) one of the two critical recruiting issues for militia and Christian Patriot members. Revered by patriots, Gritz created his community, offering lots for sale in what he christened Almost Heaven. But in addition to this separatist retreat from the intrusive world of government regulators, he offers his SPIKE (Specially Prepared Individuals for Key Events) training program. SPIKE training sessions, some writers note, seem to be paramilitary training. Bo Gritz apparently can admire the well-executed assault in any context; he said of Oklahoma City that "it was a Rembrandt." Of his training program, Gritz advertises: "Our classes will include instinctive combat and special purpose marksmanship."[55]

Military training for confronting the menacing agents of a tyrannical government is a specialty for this most famous of the Christian Patriots. But it is also the avowed reason for the creation of that other new development on the far Right, the militia movements. Yet there are many other links between the new militias and these groups of patriots.

Most Christian Patriots, like so many in the new Christian Right, seem to be part of an alternative culture. Their books, magazines, newsletters, videos, and internet links are not seen in academia, not read by the professional or managerial classes, not part of the life of most Americans outside the circle of the believers. Their commitment to what most other citizens would consider a strange conspiratorial world view is a product of their religious beliefs, the passionate feelings of family and friends, the persuasive power of some movement leaders. But strains, tensions and upheavals in recent history play a critical role. This is true for the patriots and it is true for that potentially more formidable party of fear, the militia movement.

★★★

The Emergence of a New Party of Fear:
The Militia Movement of the 1990s

It was only in the days after the Oklahoma City bombing that most Americans became aware, for the first time, of the presence of a strange new movement in their midst. The revelation that the bomb had been detonated by home-grown terrorists, not some band of sinister foreigners, led to news stories about groups of heavily armed people in camouflage uniform, often meeting in secret, practicing military maneuvers in the countryside near their towns.

As more became known about the militia movement, many noted that not all the groups were secretive, not all militia members clad themselves in camouflage, not every small unit even called itself a "militia." But early impressions were formed by such scenes as the *Nightline* television town meeting in Decker, Michigan, where host Ted Koppel brought together the uniformed leaders of the Michigan Militia Corps and many of their neighbors, some of who were unaware of the existence of the militia and expressed discomfort at the discovery. It was the report that two bombing suspects had attended meetings of the Michigan group which brought the national cameras to Decker, but it was the portrait of the militia leadership which would prove most memorable.

In the weeks following the Oklahoma City bombing, newspapers and newsmagazines discovered a new party of fear inside America. "Paranoia" was the headline in the *Washington Post*. "Inside the World of the Paranoid" announced *The New York Times*. "How Dangerous Are They" asked the cover of *Time*, for an issue with a story titled "Calling All Paranoids."

The articles portrayed a group of Americans who found conspiracy almost everywhere. It was not terrorists who had set off the bomb in Oklahoma City, it was agents of the federal government, planning to use the tragedy as an excuse to crack down on the militias and other patriots. Timothy J. McVeigh was a "fall guy," a federal agent, just like Lee Harvey Oswald. The Environmental Protection Agency has a remote-control vehicle-tracking system to hunt down and arrest citizens trying to defend their property from federal autocrats. The government has secretly installed electronic devices in car ignitions to stall the autos of patriots at the moment the new world order takes over. The global secret government is organizing a strike force of 300,000 shock troops, including fearsome Nepalese Gurkhas, urban street gangs like the Los Angeles Crips and Bloods, and Hong Kong police to seek out and arrest gun owners.

There was more. The financial masters of the United Nations have mobilized invading armies with Russian and German tanks—imported across the Canadian border on long trains—to crush resistance in America and impose the new world order. Hillary Clinton belongs to a coven of witches. Yellowstone National Park has been taken over by the United Nations. Salt mines beneath Detroit have been prepared to hold thousands of Russian troops. Black helicopters flown by mercenaries of the new world order are harassing patriotic citizens preparing to defend their families. House to house searches and seizures are being conducted without warrants across the country. Surveillance cameras are in place atop tall light posts; 130 detention centers, "concentration camps . . . mostly located on former military bases," are being constructed already; bright colored reflective stickers—troop marker indicators—are in place on the backs of road signs to direct U.N. forces; "four large crematoriums . . . located in Minneapolis, Indianapolis, Kansas City and Oklahoma City . . . containing guillotines . . . capable of processing 3000 people daily" are in place; the country has been divided into martial law regions.[56]

What was all this about? Who believed such stories? Where had these militias come from? How many of them were there? What links did they have with other extremist groups? Why did Americans join such a movement in 1995? Who were these earnest, troubled "patriots" talking to reporters; these angry, intense leaders addressing militia audiences; these frantic folk sending fevered messages out across the internet? "Let's assume that there ARE raids this weekend and some people are forced to kill federal agents. They need places to hide and get medical care. They need our support."

The militias seemed a new development in the annals of the far Right but there were groups in recent history serving as antecedents. The Minutemen operated as a paramilitary secret society in the sixties. In the same decade, a racist paramilitary organization known as the California Rangers was founded by William Potter Gale. This small group, which soon disbanded, was called "a threat to the peace and security of our state" by the state attorney general, who had recommended outlawing such armed bands. Of course, Gale, present at the creation of Christian Identity, would go on to become the key actor in the founding of Posse Comitatus, whose adherents engaged— as noted earlier—in paramilitary exercises in the eighties. In 1982, Posse Comitatus ran a "survival school," with instruction in the demolition of roadways, dams and bridges.

During the eighties, the Christian Patriot Defense League was running its own paramilitary camps, training 1,000 people in 1981. Gordon "Jack" Mohr, U.S. Army Colonel (Retired), served as "National Director of Defense Coordinators" for CPDL, which he described as "made up primarily of Christians and/or Patriots, who see what is happening in our government and are preparing for difficult times we believe are ahead." The Texas Klan, then headed by Louis Beam, ran paramilitary camps for white supremacists the same year.

The eighties also saw the emergence of an anti-Semitic group of tax protestors known as the Arizona Patriots, led for a time by former television actor Ty Hardin, who had been involved in a dispute with the IRS and who subsequently edited *The Arizona Patriot*. This journal printed antigovernment articles and called for "Christian Patriots" to band together. An FBI probe would uncover a plot to finance a paramilitary base through robbery, as well as plans to bomb the offices of human rights organizations. Three movement leaders (Hardin was not involved) were sentenced to prison, where one of them wrote a lengthy manuscript calling for an "all-out, do or die, last man civil war" against the federal government.

In the late eighties, two older fixtures on the racist fringe scene were involved in militia-style preparations. Glenn Miller's White Patriot Party followers marched in camouflage in 1986 and used paramilitary training. In 1988, James Wickstrom, subsequently charged for conspiring to pass counterfeit money, was allegedly planning to set up a paramilitary camp in Pennsylvania.[57]

It was in the early nineties that proponents of paramilitary activities to "protect citizens" from "the government" would find vastly increased interest in their schemes. Two critical incidents involving federal law enforcement agencies served as recruiting themes for what became a movement.

The first was the Randy Weaver siege in Idaho. Weaver allegedly had been selling illegal guns to an informer for the Bureau of Alcohol, Tobacco and Firearms. Failing to appear in court, he was hiding with his family and a young associate in a cabin in the remote northern Idaho mountains. When authorities came to arrest him, an armed confrontation resulted in gunfire killing a decorated federal deputy marshal and Weaver's wife and son were killed. This was followed by an eleven-day siege. Weaver and his co-defendant would be acquitted in a jury trial after being charged with the killing of the marshal. No one was indicted in the deaths of the Weaver's wife and son.

The second incident was the April 1993 FBI attack on the Branch Davidian compound near Waco, Texas. This came at the end of a fifty-one-day siege, which was the result of the shooting deaths of four ATF agents in late February. These federal law enforcement officers had attempted to enter the compound in order to arrest David Koresh, the sect's leader, accused of stockpiling a huge cache of illegal weapons. Eighty Davidians, including eighteen children, died in the FBI action, when a massive fire erupted, which federal authorities insist was started by the Davidians themselves in a mass suicide scheme.

FBI Director Louis J. Freeh reprimanded a dozen federal employees after the botched and bloody standoff in Idaho. In a subsequent action, Freeh suspended Larry Potts, the former head of the criminal division who had recently been named deputy director of the agency, for his involvement in the affair. There had been a failure to follow agency rules-of-engagement procedures. The specially trained Hostage Rescue Team departed from the Bureau's standing lethal force policy, which permits agents to shoot only in self-defense, acting instead on orders, issued after the marshal was killed, improperly allowing agents to shoot virtually on sight.

The BATF was criticized for failing to arrest Koresh, the self-styled "lamb of God" who grasped leadership of his cult in an earlier shoot-out, when he was off the compound grounds. Some journalists, students of religion and others would also raise questions about FBI tactics during the siege, speculating on a different result if federal authorities had tried to "wait out" Koresh.

But a federal agent was killed attempting to enforce the law at the Weaver cabin at Ruby Ridge. The ATF raid at Waco, no matter how poorly timed or mounted, resulted in the death of four agents and the inevitability of federal prosecution of Koresh and other Davidian gunmen.

Nonetheless, Randy Weaver and Waco would become key symbols of murderous federal power menacing the freedom of innocent American citizens. Militia activists continually have used these incidents as examples of government tyranny. Some even use them in offering their own interpretation of the Oklahoma City bombing: "I believe the tragedy in Oklahoma is a cover-up to divert attention away from Waco," said the chairman of Citizens of Liberty, a militia-style group in Washington state.[58]

Building on the paramilitary activism of the previous decade, manipulating the theme of government coercive violence supposedly demonstrated at the two sieges, using the fear of gun control stimulated by the passage of the Brady Bill and the assault rifle ban, responding to other pressures within the nation in the mid-nineties, militia organizers were at work recruiting members and founding small new groups across America by the spring of 1995. The Oklahoma City tragedy suddenly pushed this new movement into the national media spotlight. How many militias were there in America? Analysts studying this phenomenon estimated in June that at least 224 militias and their support groups were active in thirty-nine states.[59]

The *Klanwatch* staff, which made this assessment, listed thirty militias and support groups in Michigan, twenty-two in California, twenty in Alabama and Colorado, fourteen in Missouri and Texas, thirteen in Florida. There appear to be obvious links to the neo-Nazi and racist Right in a number of these small organizations—the estimate was forty-five groups with ties to such white supremacist elements—but many other militias seemed to offer more moderate agendas with what the analysts considered more "law-abiding goals."[60]

The linkage between the racist Right and the militia movement was growing in 1995, with groups having such ties present in twenty-two states, up from nine states in 1994. The best known of these militias and among the first paramilitary bands to emerge as part of the new movement of the nineties is the Militia of Montana (MOM).

MOM was founded in January 1994 by John Trochman (a retired maker of snowmobile parts who came to Noxon, Montana, in 1987) and his brother David. John Trochman's wife and David Trochman's son also play important leadership roles, along with Bob Fletcher. The Trochmans met Fletcher at a patriot meeting, where both men were speakers. A former manager of a toy manufacturing business, which he claims to have lost when a CIA operative "raped . . . and stole my company," Fletcher has told a journalist that he has been the object of assassination plots by a shadowy government conspiracy.

The Trochmans have ties to Christian Identity. They have held Bible studies with long-time Identity followers. Their association with

Aryan Nations spreads over a number of years. In 1990, John Troch-man was at the Aryan Nations World Congress as a featured speaker and while he has attempted to minimize his ties to the racist Right since creating his militia, Richard Girnt Butler has been quoted as saying that Trochman traveled to the Hayden Lake compound "quite often . . . [he] even helped us write out a set of rules for our code of conduct on church grounds."[61]

Members of the Militia of Montana have been involved in armed encounters with local police officers. Judges and district attorneys in the state have been threatened for enforcing even routine traffic laws. But MOM is better known for its public rhetoric of violence. It sponsors speaking tours by militia activists; Fletcher told a Colorado audience: "You better damn well learn how to use a gun if you don't know how to use one now; if you don't have bullets now, you better flat get them. . . . How did our government reach a point where they are backstabbing the American people?" Even more notable is the extensive catalogue of videotapes, audiotapes and literature which it markets. The 200-page, $75 *M.O.D. Training Manual*, apparently intended to serve as a home guide for preparing guerrilla warfare specialists and terrorists, was at the center of these offerings.

The *M.O.D. Manual* provides instruction in sabotage "to cripple the economy of the country," noting that "public offices, centers of government services" are "easy targets." It counsels the destruction of "firms and properties of people that are not Americans," conducting a "war of nerves" through false rumors and disinformation campaigns, raiding of armories, kidnapping of personalities "who are known artists, sports figures or outstanding in some other field," executing of spies, government officials and "those who go to the police." When asked about this document, David Trochman told an interviewer that he had not read it, did not know its contents, adding that "this manual has not been checked out thoroughly . . . we didn't realize this kind of stuff was in there. This one slipped by."[62]

What does not "slip by" are similar materials, including another bomb-making and guerrilla warfare manual, *The Road Back*, produced by an affiliate of the anti-Semitic Liberty Lobby. The M.O.M. description of this offering: "a plan for the restoration of freedom when our country has been taken over by its enemies." Particularly popular in militia circles is the video *Invasion and Betrayal,* in which the Montana group provides other paramilitary activists with a quick review of many new world order conspiracy scenarios making the rounds in their circles: massive holding facilities being constructed for prisoners, modern American weapons being pushed over cliffs into the sea while Russian tanks sit on railroad cars in Montana, thousands of Russian guns and biological, chemical and radiological warfare materials amassed in guarded compounds, motor pools of Russian mechanized weapons just across the Mexican border.[63]

The believers in conspiracy who lead the Militia of Montana had captured widespread attention by mid-1995. Journalists for national newspapers and magazines journeyed to Noxon to interview them. And while the size of their MOM following remained relatively small, the influence of their group inside the militia movement grew larger due to their catalogue marketing skills and their willingness to speak out—as opposed to the secretiveness which shrouded some other paramilitary groups. In making their voices heard, MOM leaders often endorsed the work of others on the fringe shaping complementary organizations concerned with advancing similar agendas. These were "constitutionalists" of a variety of connected interests, people who operated on the edge of the militia movement and of the related Christian Patriot phenomenon.

Included among these constitutionalists were groups opposing environmental regulation, the collection of income taxes, the convening of constitutional conventions and state legislative meetings, as well as a variety of jury empowerment organizations.

They appeal to those who find comfort in literal interpretations. Like biblical literalists, "constitutionalists" seem to revel in their knowledge of "the written word," the seemingly simple and obvious meaning of documents. As one writer noted, they "tend to quote selectively and read literally . . . they are Constitutional fundamentalists." When so many other citizens are unaware of the very number or nature of different constitutional amendments, these self-appointed authorities appear to know what they are talking about and insist that they have penetrated the mysteries of law and history. The average person has been blinded by ignorance; the constitutionalist has studied the documents and can unmask the federal tyrants, the intrusive bureaucrats, the conspirators of power who have twisted the law and would deny Americans their rights. Their papers, bulletins, leaflets, and videos have been widely distributed in militia and Christian Patriot communities.

The people who produce this material and many of those who receive it and pass it along to fellow movement members are not analysts who understand subtlety, complexity, or the meaning of clashing interpretations of history, law, and the Constitution. Like biblical literalists of the Christian Right or the racist extremists of Christian Identity, many have seen the word and that is all they need: it shapes their understanding of the world. It is another closed system of thought. Confronted by different interpretations offered by jurists, members of the executive or legislative branch of government, Constitutional lawyers, or academic authorities on Constitutional law, political history or political science, the reaction is amused or outraged contempt. These "experts," these scholarly priests, are manipulated dupes or agents of the oppressive power. Most "constitutionalists," like those who propagate and embrace the stories of invading U.N. armies and menacing black helicopters, are not people who engage in rational discourse as it is usually found in the larger community.

Of course, many of the antienvironmental organizations have vested interests in the outcome of their effort. It is a clear and—for them— very rational agenda. The "Wise Use" groups in the West are lavishly funded by resource extraction industries. It is obviously in the financial interest of large mining, timber and ranching corporations to rid themselves of environmental regulations. Thus they fund "populist" entities like the Grassroots Endangered Species Act Coalition. Among other such Wise Use groups is the National Federal Lands Conference, which publishes *Federal Lands Update*, featuring lead stories on "why there is a need for the militia in America," and warning against federal martial law, "the mode by which Hitler, Stalin, Mussolini and Mao came to power."

In addition, there are a number of county groups that have been established, including one in Washington state calling itself the Snohomish County Property Rights Alliance (PRA). One environmental association officer, after speaking at a public hearing in favor of wildlife and wetland protection, was accused by members of this group of "taxpayer rape." This PRA had attacked environmentalists in newsletters as "eco-Nazis"; after her council meeting appearance, the environmentalist was confronted by a man in the audience who pulled out a noose and said, "this is a message for you." Another whispered, "If we can't beat you at the ballot box, we'll beat you with a bullet."

Similar organizations, such as the Coalition for Land Use Education, have emerged in several areas. Journalists interviewing members of some groups have noted links with militias and other movements on the far Right.

One notable episode among antienvironmentalists was the action of a Nye County, Nevada, local commissioner named Dick Carver, who has led the fight against the federal government's management—and even ownership—of national parks. He also denies that there is federal power to regulate grazing, mining and logging. Reviving the vision of Posse Comitatus, Carver insists that counties are the highest level of government. The federal government has no authority; his county adopted a resolution to that effect. Supported by militias in his own state and elsewhere, he has built a following. In the summer of 1994, he drove a bulldozer and reopened a long-closed road in a national forest in Nevada. It was a direct challenge to federal authority to which the Clinton administration responded with a suit filed against the county.[64]

The antitax forces also question federal authority. Distressed about the Sixteenth Amendment, they offer a variety of defenses against paying taxes. Some argue that "historical research" demonstrates that this amendment was never properly ratified and is not part of the Constitution. Others insist that "the income tax amendment is plainly without an enforcement clause!" Still others focus on what is constitutionally allowable as income, concluding after "studying" the document that average Americans with no interest or dividend income, people who merely work for wages, are not required to file a tax return.

Such tax-protest material finds favor in the antifederal ambience of the militia movement. So, too, do the offerings of groups opposing the nation's banking system, such as one titled "We The People," whose leaders described elaborate conspiracies inside the American military and political elites. Also of interest were marketing schemes to show citizens how to evade unfair and "illegal" taxes; one group apparently took in $4 million selling a kit called the Untax package. Some antitax activists even advocate frustrating federal officials by filing nuisance liens and civil rights lawsuits against them, forcing government investigators and prosecutors to go to court to reclaim full title to their own homes.[65]

Of course, Constitutionalists must be on guard against sinister efforts to repeal or replace the great document itself. Militia members circulated material from the Liberty Lobby assailing discussions by some academics in 1964 and 1970 about possible revisions: "Is our Constitution doomed, to be replaced by this document which will signal the death of our Free Republic?" They rally against the dreaded

"Con-Con," plans for a Constitutional Convention, which would result in the destruction of the Constitution. Many feared this convention was being promoted "under the guise of establishing a Balanced Budget Amendment."

In a related effort, which also found "Constitutionalists" and militia activists aligning against conservative politicians, far Right forces rallied their members to flood the offices of state legislators with messages of protest, which scuttled plans for the Conference of the States, a meeting scheduled for October 1995. It was designed to find ways of increasing state power at the expense of the federal government; it was supported by conservatives. But the "Tenth Amendment" activists saw a darker motive. For them, it was a thinly disguised ruse to amend and dismantle the Constitution. Some of the same far Right state politicians opposing this meeting have played a role in resolutions passed by several state legislatures endorsing the conspiracy theories so prevalent in the militia movement. The Oklahoma Legislature resolved: "The United States Congress is hereby memorialized to cease any support for the establishment of a 'new world order,' or any form of global government." State Senator Charles Duke of Colorado (Colorado Springs) became a national figure as a major force in this "Tenth Amendment movement," attacking "tyrants" and "puppets" in Washington and making frequent references to the "New World Order."[66]

For the militia activists and related bands of Christian Patriots, "Second Amendment Groups," of course, offer a natural outlet for fear of gun control. And those who join such movements also have responded to a number of jury empowerment efforts, similar to the Fully Informed Jury Association, with a widely circulated "Jury Handbook" (produced in Arizona) telling readers: "the Juror has more power than the President, the Congress and all of the judges combined!" If all other efforts to check the federal tyrants fail, twelve likeminded patriots can repeal unjust laws.[67]

The militia movement is inextricably linked to these varied "Constitutionalist" endeavors. Through them, paramilitarists discover new information concerning dangers menacing their land; they find some of the most persuasive arguments supporting their commitment to the cause.

And as the militias spread across America in 1995, two organizations made a particular impact. One was the Militia of Montana. The other was the Michigan Militia Corps.

The Michigan Militia was organized by Norman Olson, a Baptist minister and gun shop owner, and Ray Southwell, a real estate agent and a deacon in Olson's church in a small eastern Michigan town. Opposition to gun control was a key factor in recruiting for "God's army," but they pointed, as well, to other specific concerns: abortion, environmental regulation, "socialistic values" being taught in local schools. Beyond this were larger anxieties. "The lesson," Southwell exclaimed, "is that you are not in control of your life, your children, your home. The Government is in control. . . .We are preparing to defend our freedom." Washington was the enemy: "We have to let the tyrants, the politicians and the bureaucrats know that we're taking a stand. . . .When martial law is declared I'm gonna have my neighbor there helping me." Olson, the leader of the Corps—calling himself "Commander"—shared this vision: "It's not a Government by the people anymore. . . . We are ceasing to be a Republic." The people's "fear is a response. When people sense danger, they will come together to defend themselves."[68]

Olson said that "when we started the militia, I thought it might get big very fast." So it did. Within six months of its founding in the spring of 1994, organizers claimed that "brigades" had formed in sixty-three of the state's eighty-three counties. Meetings were drawing fifty to one hundred people. Within a year, leaders claimed ten to twelve thousand members, a number which could not be independently verified. Unlike many secrecy-obsessed militia organizers across the nation, Olson publicly appealed for members and welcomed reporters to group training sessions. There they found "Commander" Olson leading his followers—clad in camouflage and heavily armed—in "maneuvers" on an eighty-acre tract of pine and meadow, prepared with obstacle courses and bunkers. The members were mostly middle-aged white family men but there were a number of women in the group. Olson's image, with camouflage cap worn above his bemedaled uniform, appeared in several newspapers; after April 19, 1995, he was seen in color in the national newsmagazines.

It was the bombing in Oklahoma City that focused particular attention on the Michigan Militia Corps, when word spread that suspects in the bombing may have attended meetings of the group. Olson and Southwell were on national television and their rhetoric became a problem. Olson exclaimed: "Within two years, I expect to see the Constitution suspended. We will be prepared to defend it." Then the Commander sent faxes to the news media blaming the bombing on the Japanese government; a newsmagazine reporter at his home later that day was asked, "Why are you bothering me? Can't you see I'm trying to stop World War III?" Olson, who had left his ministerial position earlier, now resigned under pressure from the militia. (But he would continue to wear his "Commander" uniform when testifying at the Senate hearings on the militia later in the year.)[69]

Under Olson or his successors, the Michigan Militia was accused of numerous hostile and threatening actions. Members of the group shouted "traitor" at the Mayor of Lansing during a U.N. Day celebration, when the United Nations flag was raised at City Hall; police reserves were called in to hold back an angry crowd. Senator Carl Levin (D.-Michigan) presented the complaints of law enforcement officers in five Michigan cities who said they had been threatened and stalked by Michigan Militia members. Militiamen were seen at airports writing down license numbers of cars driven by federal agents. According to a former member who alerted federal authorities, other militiamen—concerned about rumors of Russian tanks being transported to Camp Grayling National Guard base—hatched a plot to attack the camp. One brigade leader allegedly said: "Let's blow up those tanks and kill those bastards who put them there."[70]

The membership manuals for the Michigan Militia (and some similar groups in the state) assert that the organization will be "non-denominational, non-political, non-racial." It appears to be a modest agenda. But the literature that is widely circulated through the group represents the complete range of extremist passions found across the far Right. Glossy magazines from the John Birch Society telling of plans to build a "New World Army" to make the U.N. "the supreme world power" are found alongside *Flashpoint*, a newsletter ministry warning of the "Monstrous Masonic Plot Against America." Magazines detailing the dangers of "technotronic surveillance" by the government, including the much-feared implantable biochip transponder, "poised and ready for application in humans," accompany lengthy descriptions of "Concentration Camp Plans for U.S. Citizens." And, of course, there is a detailed study demonstrating that the Oklahoma City federal building was not destroyed by a fertilizer bomb, but an "A-Neutronic bomb," part of a government plot. The Michigan Militia is deeply committed to its conspiratorial vision.[71]

The most articulate exponent of such conspiracy theories is one of most celebrated Michigan Militia personalities, Mark Koernke, better known to his lecture audiences and shortwave radio listeners (over

World Wide Christian Radio) as "Mark from Michigan." A janitor at the University of Michigan, Koernke sees the threatening hand of the government everywhere. The Federal Emergency Management Agency (FEMA) is not really concerned with disaster recovery, most of its 3,600 employees are "there to manage the system after they take over." The General Agreement on Tariffs and Trade is part of a plot to eliminate national sovereignty, allowing Americans to be put on trial in other nations. His two-hour video—*America in Peril: A Call to Arms*—marketed through the militia network, offered a bewildering variety of conspiracy tales which then spread across the paramilitary world.

Koernke was a featured speaker at the Palm Springs "Taking Our Country Back" Convention in the spring of 1995. But he had run into problems with his shortwave radio outlets after his bizarre broadcast following the Oklahoma City bombing, in which he denied militia involvement but pointed to a government conspiracy and suggested that U.N. observers were somehow involved in the disaster. Koernke, who everywhere paints a picture of coming armed conflict between patriots and agents of government tyranny, has armed associates working with him. In one incident, three men identifying themselves as his bodyguards were arrested in a car packed with assault rifles, semiautomatic pistols, night goggles and other military equipment. The accused failed to appear for their arraignment, but a score of uniformed militia members in camouflage appeared to taunt the police.[72]

One of Koernke's competitors in the conspiracy video business is Linda Thompson, the self-described Acting Adjutant General of the Unorganized Militias of the United States. Thompson claims to have contacts with militias across America. It was her expertly-edited video series on the Branch Davidian affair ("Waco: The Big Lie Volume I—Battle of Ideas" and "Waco: The Big Lie Volume II"), picturing a peaceful religious community violently assaulted by brutal federal agents, who murdered innocent people, which appeared frequently on public access cable television and made her a celebrity on the extremist talk show circuit. This led to a career as a lecturer to large audiences in the South and Midwest.

Linda Thompson is an attorney who served in the army in the mid-seventies, describing her role then as "Assistant to the U.S. Army Commanding General NATO" with a "Cosmic Top Secret/Atomal Security Clearance." She lives in Indianapolis, where she chairs the American Justice Federation, which markets the videos. She has been active on the internet through her Associated Electronic Network computer bulletin board, which has focused on government tyranny and the menace of the New World Order. But it was her next major video production, *America Under Siege*, which made Thompson a more influential force in the paramilitary culture.

Thompson begins the film by announcing that "this is a beautiful country" but it has been "taken over by murderers, liars and thieves. Our biggest problem is the people who are running the government." Along with the videos from MOM and Mark Koernke, it is her tales of "black, unmarked helicopters" harassing patriots (including following the Thompson family through the streets of Washington) and her descriptions of extensive preparations for the imposition of the New World Order which supply many of the conspiracy scenarios making the militia rounds.[73]

The "Acting Adjutant General" called for a march on Washington by armed and uniformed militiamen in September 1994. Their mission: "arrest Congressmen who have failed to uphold their oaths of office," who will then be "tried for treason by citizens' courts." Finding little enthusiasm for this adventure, she turned to other interests. She was arrested in Indianapolis for trying to block the motorcade for President Clinton; agents found several weapons in her car. After the Oklahoma City bombing, she observed: "Who does it benefit most? It benefits the killers of Waco." But her incendiary style—"most of the people with balls in this country lately seem to be women"—did not endear her to other leaders on the far Right, some of whom she referred to as "traitors" and "government agents." Journalists reported that she had made hostile comments about Mark Koernke, "Bo" Gritz and other figures. One observer concluded, "She has caused more divisiveness and disruption in the patriot movement than anyone else."[74]

There are scores of paramilitary units, organized in every corner of America in 1994 and 1995, which are part of that militia movement. While none have the national exposure of MOM or the Michigan Militia, several have made a regional impact.

In Ohio, an officer of the Ohio Unorganized Militia was killed after an encounter with a local police official on a rural highway in May 1995. The militia man, who was serving as the "chief justice" of a court the militia had established "based on Scripture and the Constitution," was stopped because he had refused to equip his car with regulation state license plates. The state could not control his "right to travel." The police officer claimed he was defending himself; the militia member had a handgun. In the days following the incident, rumors swept through the area and the newspaper headline was: "Ohio town lives in fear of militia revenge." While denying that violent reprisal against the officer was planned, Ken Adams, Executive Director of the National Confederation of Citizen Militias, an Ohioan who testified at the Senate militia hearings, exclaimed: "If it continues to happen, then it is going to get dangerous out there. A militia person when he stops is going to defend himself."[75]

In Idaho, Samuel Sherwood, the director of the United States Militia Association, made news when he told the state's lieutenant governor in March 1995 that he was being "duped by those who are quietly plotting to throw out the U.S. Constitution." A computer salesman from Blackfoot, Idaho—reputedly involved in militia organizing in four states in addition to his own—Sherwood claimed that his USMA had branches in fourteen of Idaho's forty-four counties. He had gained attention earlier by charging that "Bill Clinton is bringing up to 100,000 Hong Kong Chinese to America to be his federal police . . . Clinton is planning to seize every gun in America." In confronting the state political leadership, he was focusing on the fears by miners and loggers that they might lose their jobs and homes. Sherwood told them that joining the militia was the way to defend themselves against the "green Gestapo" of the environmental movement which was threatening to use the courts to "close down" the Idaho national forests. The militia director had warned that if the federal district judge acted, "blood would flow in the streets."[76]

In Arizona, a racist band of militiamen—heirs to the Arizona Patriots of the eighties—emerged in Kingman, also using the name Arizona Patriots. But the state is the home of other movement notables. The best known is Gerald "Jack" McLamb, a former Phoenix policeman who leads an organization he calls Police Against the New World Order. The recruiting manual for this group, *Operation Vampire Killer 2000*, "a step-by-step plan to re-educate our fellow law enforcers to the plans of the global elite" (with their schemes to eliminate 2.5 billion people by the year 2000), became another militia favorite. Pictured in his police uniform with the caption "Officer Jack McLamb (Ret.)," he argues that while "the Traitors and Thieves in government leadership" and "those treacherous demonic Elitists who own the Federal Reserve" are the "real enemies," it is the local police officers who do the actual deed of dispossessing Americans of their "land, homes, businesses, cars." The solution: "If officers don't enforce treason, it won't get enforced." This is the theme of his journal, the *Aid & Abet Police Newsletter*, calling for the "infiltration" of police departments by "informed patriots." A key player in Christian Patriot circles, where he has worked with James "Bo" Gritz, McLamb's publications have become a standard part of militia literature.[77]

Colorado, home of state senator Charles Duke, has been another center of militia activity. Several groups calling themselves patriots emerged in communities in different parts of the state in 1995, offering standard conspiracy views but also encouraging members to read anti-Semitic literature. A better known militia enterprise is Guardians of American Liberties (GOAL) in Boulder, a multistate organization with chapters in Texas, Nevada, and California. Stewart Webb, GOAL's leader, another right-wing talk show regular, also has a history of anti-Semitism. A third group, the Colorado Free Militia in Johnstown, has sent off newsletter and training materials, hoping to build a statewide network. But there are underground militia members in Colorado who consider such organizers as bumbling amateurs, people who would be nothing more than "cannon fodder" in the coming battle with the federal government. Secret, tight-knit cells whose members shun contact with reporters, these underground units had found a small following in a few Western states in 1995.[78]

In Florida, where numerous Klan chapters have been active, there is another cluster of militias, several with racist ties. Perhaps the most significant group is the Florida State Militia led by Robert Pummer, an ex-convict who has been widely quoted exclaiming: "we have had enough drugs and crime, violence and bloodshed, enough Waco." His militia materials instruct: "Buy ammo now. You will not be able to get it later!" This Florida State Militia handbook recommends a "patriot list" of readings, replete with anti-Semitic and antiblack hate literature. Florida militias, like those in New Hampshire, Michigan, Pennsylvania and elsewhere, are active participants on the gun show circuit and help sponsor such events as the "Information Fair and Campout," the "U.S. Constitution Rally" and other gatherings of the angry and the fearful.

In Texas, there are similar militia developments. The Texas Constitutional Militia claimed 1,500 members in thirty county units in early 1995. Organized in 1994, this militia held a large Alamo Rally in San Antonio, and advertised in anti-Semitic publications; racist literature, including materials produced by Liberty Lobby and the

National Alliance, was distributed at the rally. Some militia members have told reporters that they are simply law-abiding, tax-paying citizens fearful of the new world order and opposed to gun control. But militias in Texas have conducted elaborate paramilitary and survival exercises, proudly advertising them as conducted by "former Rangers, Seals, Green Berets and Martial Arts Experts."[79]

In North Carolina, a small group called Citizens for the Reinstatement of Constitutional Government made news when leader Albert Espositio counseled amassing caches of "the Four B's: Bibles, Bullets, Beans and Bandages." With many members owning semiautomatic weapons, the overheated rhetoric took on new meaning. The goals of this "Citizens" unit: "to make the Holy Bible and the United States Constitution the law of the land" and, of course, to "resist the coming New World Order." How to accomplish the goal: "Remove treasonous politicians and corrupt judges from positions of authority."

In Virginia, the modestly named Blue Ridge Hunt Club may be a tiny cell, but it captured the attention of federal law enforcement officials when James Roy Mullins, its founding member, set out to arm and train confederates, in the words of the BATF, "for conflict with government authorities." Searches of members' homes found numerous guns, homemade silencers, explosives, hand grenades, explosive material. Mullins, who had written that "hit and run tactics will be our method of fighting . . . human targets will be engaged," pled guilty to federal firearms offenses in February 1995 and was sentenced to a five-year prison term.[80]

The themes, practices and literature of the many small militias emerging in 1995 are similar, although some activists—as in Virginia—have moved beyond the rhetoric of anger and paramilitary posturing, stockpiling illegal firearms and intimidating federal judges or marshals. But how to explain the presence of such parties of fear in the mid-nineties?

Is it because they reflect a growing feeling across America that the government represents a menacing power? No. A major national news poll conducted in mid-May revealed, as one columnist put it, that "the anger isn't out there." Only six percent of the large sample said the government was their enemy; only nine percent think it is ever justified for citizens to take violent action against the federal government. The overwhelming majority did not think the government threatened their personal rights and freedoms but half were fearful of private militia groups. Three quarters believed that "people in this country are too quick to criticize the federal government."[81]

The amateur soldiers and amateur lawyers of the militia and "patriot" movements—those weekend warriors on maneuvers in camouflage, those "information junkies" scouring newspapers for obscure factoids, those "constitutionalists" trying to tease out of the *Federalist Papers* support for their arguments—are certain that Washington autocrats and U.N. armies are a clear and present danger. But not only do most Americans reject their fears, there seems to be no substance to their bizarre conspiracy scenarios.

Of course there are black helicopters, and the National Guard may have even operated a few over Idaho. Of course there are Russian tanks seen at U.S. bases; they were brought back for testing after the Warsaw Pact collapsed and the Iraqi armies were crushed. But no investigator has uncovered the Russian divisions hiding in salt mines under U.S. cities, the extermination centers awaiting victims of the coming federal holocaust, the masses of Hong Kong police and Gurkha units en route to impose the new world order. The very notion of U.N. forces, a pathetic failure in Somalia and Bosnia, as the instrument to crush American democracy is comical.

Are these people paranoid? That was the word found in the headlines of newspapers and newsmagazines when the militia and patriot movements emerged as national stories in the weeks following the bombing in Oklahoma City. Can so many members of different groups across the land be dismissed by simple placement in such a category? Some militia members have exclaimed to reporters: "I'm not paranoid," or "Am I a nut, a fruitcake? We're out here embittered, angered and disillusioned, and we want to have our guns to shoot the bastards if we have to." It does not help us understand this phenomenon by just calling the members of the movement "sick."[82]

Of course, some people will believe almost anything. There may be Americans who are sure there is a secret project which has mastered time travel and that a door to the past is located on Long Island; there may be Americans who are sure that mysterious German submarines have bases in Antarctica. There is a literature for such readers and an underground publishing world serves them. But political conspiracy is a special case. It has attracted believers throughout the history of this country, as is clear from recalling earlier movements considered in this work.

Today, with the internet and desktop publishing, formerly isolated loners who believe in conspiratorial machinations can communicate their concerns and find companions in fear. They even find strong support in the work of celebrity conspiracy theorists outside the militia movement; Pat Robertson's "new world order" fits in perfectly with the militia model.

But why have scores of militia and patriot groups appeared in these years? Why this intense "fear of the federal government" as an organizing theme for a substantial movement in the nineties? Why have so many Americans who call themselves "ordinary people" responded to the leadership of the angry militia leaders? "Paranoia" is not a satisfactory answer. The dismissive "people like that have always been around," will not do.

There are various responses that have been offered for these questions: It is hate talk in the media which has stimulated hostile feelings in an impressionable and vulnerable minority. It is just about guns— fear that "they" will take away "our" firearms is at the heart of the burning personal anger felt by the new paramilitarists. It is the calculated manipulation of fear by mainstream politicians, most of them opportunists, but some who actually seem to embrace the conspiratorial fantasies of the militias, which has given credence to the new groups. It is the shadow of Vietnam, America's lost battle, which produced its Rambo myths and "warrior dreams," that has been the critical setting for ordinary Americans wanting to play soldier.

There are ways in which all of these "answers" help to explain the recruiting of some militia members. But much more important reasons for the new movement are to be found in the end of the Cold War and the social as well as economic upheavals which are affecting all Americans.

Right-wing "talk radio" has been a forum for those wanting to stimulate hostility and even incite to violence. G. Gordon Liddy, the Watergate felon named "talk show host of the year in 1995," shouted "kill the sons of bitches" in reference to BATF agents, but added, "they've got a vest on . . . head shots, head shots." (He later revised this advice: "You shoot twice to the body, center of mass . . . then to the groin area . . . you'll probably get a femoral artery.") Liddy, purveying such wisdom over more than two hundred outlets, supports militias; he also told his audience he uses drawings of the President and Mrs. Clinton for target practice. And Liddy is not alone. In San Francisco, a hate radio host advised "lynching a few liberals" and "shooting illegal immigrants" for reward money; in Colorado Springs another radio personality advocated armed revolution against the U.S. government. Even Rush Limbaugh moved beyond his usual talk of "environmental wackos" and "femi-Nazis"—standard fare for his audience—to something closer to militia country. Speaking of property rights, he said that the "second violent American revolution is just about—I got my fingers about a quarter of an inch apart—is just about that far away. Because these people are sick and tired of a bunch of bureaucrats in Washington driving into town and telling them what they can and can't do with their land."[83]

But talk radio is just talk. Gun control is a more serious proposition. There are over 200 million guns in circulation in America and tens of millions of gun owners. Most of them—sixty-five percent according to a national poll in 1995—have an "unfavorable impression of militia groups." (Only eleven percent had a favorable impression.) Most of them favor stricter gun control laws, and almost seventy percent of these gun owners opposed repealing the ban on assault rifles passed by Congress in 1994. But among the militia faithful and their fellows there is a very different view.

At "Gunstock '95," a gun rights rally held in Michigan in the spring, the bumper sticker read, "where is Lee Harvey Oswald when his country needs him." A T-shirt called President Clinton a "Socialist-Marxist Commu-Nazi." A Republican state representative, speaking to the crowd, repeated the slogan seen in much extremist literature: "Adolf Hitler was the first one who supported gun registration."

The fury of these gun lovers is the result of two very modest federal actions taken on Bill Clinton's watch—passage of the Brady Bill (calling for checking handgun purchasers for criminal records) and the ban on several types of assault rifles. While people in other nations look on in wonderment at the level of gun violence and the size of gun ownership in the U.S., while most Americans and most American gun owners support the administration's actions, a passionate few have screamed with rage and many of them have joined the militias. Their argument is that they are only defending the second amendment, that they are the modern-day Minutemen—like revolutionary heroes of old—protecting threatened individual and local rights from the tyranny of Washington autocrats, that an armed citizenry is the last defense of democracy. But the tone and temper of their response suggests even deeper anxieties.

Playing on fear that "the federal government wants to take away your guns" is the National Rifle Association. Claiming 3.5 million members, the NRA is led by a militant faction committed to confronting any politicians favoring any form of gun control. Walter LaPierre, the group's executive vice president and top paid staff member, the man who made headlines with a fundraising letter calling federal agents "jackbooted government thugs," has been characterized as a relative moderate compared to the real power in the NRA: Neal Knox, the second vice president, who controls the NRA board. In December 1994, Knox wrote a gun magazine column theorizing that the assassinations of President John F. Kennedy and the Rev. Martin Luther King, Jr., as well as mass killings by gunmen in schoolyards, were committed by antigunners pressing the gun control cause. Such "theories" put the NRA leadership right at home with the most imaginative conspiratorialists in the militia movement.

The NRA, belligerently insisting it was helped, not injured, by the "jackbooted" appeal, which cost it the membership of former President Bush, soon acknowledged it was facing big deficits and big trouble. It spent the spring of 1995 trying to distance itself from the militias. LaPierre announced, "we condemn hate groups, terrorist groups . . . we have never had anything to do with any of these paramilitary-type groups you see on television. That's not the National Rifle Association." But while that may be true for a majority of the NRA's membership, it has not been the message of its leadership. Militia fears have been fed by NRA prose.[84]

Mainstream politicians, fearing the NRA and courting the gun vote, have also fed these fears. In 1995, two years after the event, the Republican majority in the House scheduled extensive hearings on the Waco incident and Democrats accused GOP staff members of using a consultant for the NRA—which has called for the disbanding of the BATF—as an "investigator" (an allegation that the GOP members of the committee have denied). Meanwhile, Speaker Newt Gingrich blocked efforts by Representative Charles E. Schumer (D.-New York) to organize hearings on the militia movement. Speaker Gingrich, one critic insisted, apparently feared that the Republican party, proud of its "law and order" posture and long accustomed to accusing its opponent of being soft on crime and coddlers of a deviant counterculture, would become identified with "a new gun-crazy counterculture of its own." Some far Left extremists had talked of "offing the pigs" in the sixties; now some armed "patriots" talked of shooting the "jackbooted government thugs." Better not to have such hearings.

But the Senate did have a brief day of hearings on the militias. Senator Arlen Specter (R.-Pennsylvania) was responsible for this session. (It was this senator who also called for 1995 hearings on the Randy Weaver affair.) At the militia hearing, senators listened to John Trochman of MOM lecture them on "billions of dollars" sent to bail out banking elites, foreign armies training on "our soil" and the "twisted, slanted media" blocking understanding of these matters. They heard Norman Olson of Michigan, seated in uniform, explain how "the primary defense of the state rests in citizen militias" and how the bombing in Oklahoma City "may be a conspiracy at higher levels." Bob Fletcher of Montana raised questions about civilian inmate labor camps inside U.S. military bases, flatcars carrying foreign military equipment across America, and weather-tampering techniques to establish the new world order. While Representative Schumer had organized informal hearings in which witnesses described intimidation and violence by members of militias and associated fringe groups, the formal Senate hearings had a different tone and served as a useful recruiting device for the movement.[85]

Of course, a number of GOP legislators had found strong support in militia circles. They served these constituents by making inquiries to the Justice Department on their behalf. Two Senators—Larry Craig (R.-Idaho) and Lauch Faircloth (R.-North Carolina)—asked about rumors that federal police officers were training in Fort Bliss, Texas. Representative Steve Stockman (R.-Texas), after receiving word from militias that agents of the new world order were preparing to attack them, had written Attorney General Janet Reno warning that a "paramilitary-style attack against Americans" could lead to a "bloody fiasco like Waco." Representative Stockman, a first-year congressman who defeated veteran Jack Brooks with vigorous NRA support, later would struggle to explain the mysterious faxed message he received about the bombing the morning of Oklahoma City, which his office had then sent along to the NRA.

The Washington legislator most popular among militia and associated groups is the representative so admired by the John Birch Society, Helen Chenoweth (R.-Idaho). Representative Chenoweth, another GOP freshman in 1995, appeared in the MOM catalogue with a video of her speech described as "explaining" how more than fifty percent of the United States is now under "the control of the New World Order." This member of Congress, elected with strong support of the Christian Right and the Wise Use movement—whom she once

addressed on the need for "spiritual war" with environmentalists—
had been endorsed by Sam Sherwood of the United States Militia
Association. He claimed that "a thousand volunteers" had been put
to work on her campaign. While insisting to an interviewer that she
"hardly knew who militia members are," Representative Chenoweth
could not have disappointed such invisible supporters when she introduced a bill requiring armed agents or police officers with the federal government to get permission from local sheriffs before entering
the state. The Posse Comitatus seemed to be alive and well in this
proposal.[86]

Congressional supporters, NRA and other gun-lobby activists, and
talk-radio extremists may all have offered some comfort to those who
might consider joining the militia movement. But has such paramilitary recruiting in America been made easier because of memories
of Vietnam? In *Warrior Dreams; Paramilitary Culture in Post-Vietnam
America*, James William Gibson argues that "America's failure to win
that war was a truly profound blow. The nation's long, proud tradition
of military victories . . . had finally come to an end."

No militia movement emerged in America in the years following
World War I, World War II or the Korean War. No private armies or
paramilitary groups proliferated in Britain or France after the Great
War. But in the Germany of the Weimar Republic, the "front line
generation" of 1914–18, with its "blood and steel" literature, did
produce recruits for the street-fighting forces of extremist political
parties, most notably the Nazi Storm Troopers. It took the defeat of
a great army, which had a proud tradition of victory and no expectation
that it could lose a war, to produce such a response. Victorious armies,
even in exhausted nations barely able to claim "victory," are not the
seedbeds of a romantic, paramilitary culture. Could this be the case
in America?

There are decorated Vietnam veterans who have played important
roles in far Right movements. Some may be present among the camouflaged folk on "maneuvers" during militia weekends. But there is
no evidence that many such veterans are in these groups, and it is
over a generation since significant numbers of U.S. troops were in
ground combat in Southeast Asia. Still, it is not necessary to have
fought to share the anger at defeat, the belief—as both Pat Robertson
and Sylvester Stallone's Rambo have suggested—that "they" would
not let "us" win the war. The anger at the government for having
betrayed its brave warriors, perhaps because Washington elitists were

in thrall to shadowy forces unwilling to allow American victory, could serve as another reason to believe in conspiracy today.

It was the liberals, the war protesters, the feminists, the "gutless wonders" who stabbed America in the back; they are in control of the government and they may be at it again in 1995. The readers of *Soldier of Fortune*, the widely circulated magazine founded in 1975 by a former Green Beret commander in Vietnam, are offered stories of the "new low in Gun Gestapo Terror Tactics" by the BATF and other federal agents. Putting on a uniform can be an empowering act for a few, a way of joining a community of patriotic risk-takers, a way of bringing drama into bland lives and reenacting dreams of revenge, even for an unacceptable and unjustifiable defeat twenty years in the past.[87]

There are many factors to consider in assessing the sources of this new movement. But as with so many other developments in American life in the nineties, the emergence of the militias may be best understood as another byproduct of the end of the Cold War and the social and economic upheavals of the time.

The collapse of communism, the breakup of the Soviet Union, the end of the Cold War suddenly eliminated the enemy whose menacing presence had shaped American military and diplomatic planning and deeply influenced all aspects of public life for two generations. One important consequence of this extraordinary occurrence was the need—or the opportunity—for some politicians and activists to identify new enemies around which to organize their energies and, perhaps, to create new movements. As noted earlier, this was a critical element in the rebirth of the New Right and its Christian Coalition leadership.

But the end of the Cold War did more than provide the setting for the rise of new enemies for old. It raised questions in the minds of those who may have been always suspicious of central power—but who had accepted Washington's enhanced role as a necessity given the threat emanating from Moscow—concerning the need for a "swollen" federal government. If there was no more Red Menace, why was there a huge national establishment? Of course, the militia members have not turned their wrath on the armed forces as much as on "federal agencies" such as ATF, FBI, FEMA and the environmental bureaus. They can still support the Americans in the real camouflage uniforms. But those attracted to far Right activism are now free of the fear of communist autocracy, Soviet military might and even left-wing enemies within the United States. They now can see links between the American government and a larger international organization—seemingly harmless enough in the days of confrontation across the Iron Curtain—which may have captured control of Washington due to the traitorous attitudes of the liberal elitists. This, of course, would be the United Nations, spearpoint of the new world order.

Perhaps even more significant, the end of the Cold War has taken the lid off regional and local hostilities in many parts of the world. The rise of ethnic nationalism, the enhanced freedom of leaders (and followers) living in former theaters of the Cold War to reinvent clan, tribal, religious and ethnic conflict, is a somber story seen daily on television news and in the headlines of the world. In Russia, the former Yugoslavia, Somalia, Afghanistan, and other lands, there is a rise of what Michael Barkun has called "radical localism." Ever smaller groups of people demand authority in the name of their own distinctive culture or interests. So, too, in America. And the militia movement, aligned as it is with the so-called "county movement"—with those Posse Comitatus protectors and "constitutionalist" defenders from the antienvironmental and tax resister ranks—represents another part of the new localism. Armed bands of paramilitarists will defend their homes and their little regions from the federal invaders. It is their property. It is their land if it is in their county (even if it is a national park). It is only law if they—the locals—think it should be enforced as law. They say they are devoted to the Constitution; they really are devoted to the Articles of Confederation. These are people freed by the end of the Cold War to question the very meaning of national community.[88]

Still, developments inside America were at least as important as the changing international balance of power in the rise of the paramilitary movement and related fringe groups. The social upheavals beginning in the sixties, imperiling what were seen as "traditional family values," shaped the rhetoric and programs of the New Right of the eighties. In the nineties, there appeared even more reason for those fearful of the forces of modernity to try to stem the tide of change. They had to protect and preserve their America, which seemed very much at risk. The renewed strength of the New Right—with its Christian Coalition activists in the lead—is a result of the passions engaged by what many see as a "cultural" war for the soul of the nation.

Because of the newness of the movement and the secretiveness of many of its component groups, there is only anecdotal evidence suggesting that some members of the militias also support positions taken by the Christian Coalition, the Traditional Values Coalition and other major organizations on the Christian Right. In the speeches of militia leaders there is anger at liberal elitists controlling the educational system; for some, the home schooling movement is the only alternative. Militias have not welcomed the gay community, and overt homophobia is a central theme not only in the Christian Patriot world but in those militia units tied to that part of the far Right. Antiabortion sentiment is also strong in many of these small-town and suburban groups.

Despite the confrontational tone of many militia spokesmen, despite the rhetoric of violence that these posturing paramilitary commanders use on so many occasions, there are many "ordinary Americans" in the general membership of the mushrooming militia groups in Missouri, New York, Kansas, Illinois, California, Pennsylvania, and across the nation. For these people, the same concerns as those animating the Christian Right seem to be present. The vision of stable family life seems threatened by sexual promiscuity on television, in the movies and in rock radio. There is the appalling rise of out-of-wedlock birth rates and the fearful presence of violent crime in the cities. Social chaos is loose in the land; black gangs—the Crips and Bloods—loom large in the imaginations of their conspiracy theorists, threatening to invade the communities of the faithful.

Who did this to America? It must be the elitists in Washington. The "liberal" President, the same one trying to disarm them and make them more vulnerable to the invaders, is a friend of Hollywood celebrities and is married to a feminist. The venom directed at the President and his wife in these circles is extraordinary. The weak and complicit judges, lawyers, academics, media members are all part of the problem, encouraging (or excusing) the very developments which can destroy the nation. Like the Klan members of the twenties, who also garbed themselves in uniforms and joined community groups linked to a movement dedicated to saving traditional America from forces of corruption and depravity, militia recruits take up arms to save their land and their families.

Beyond these social concerns are even more menacing economic woes. Among the legacies of the eighties is the immense national debt and trade deficit, as well as the growing gap in income and wealth between the rich and the rest of the population. These conditions have created the terms of the political debate of the nineties. The solution offered by mainstream politicians of the Right and their allies, the new Calvinists of the Christian Right, is to deregulate the economy, cut taxes (particularly for the most affluent), make dramatic reductions in middle class entitlements such as Medicare and educational loans, and discipline the welfare constituency through massive cuts in benefits. Linking these initiatives to the social agenda of the Christian Coalition makes the alliance work. But for those who might be attracted to the militia movement, the response is less clear. Here there seems to be an acceptance of downsizing the hated federal government—anything making Washington smaller receives a warm response—but continuing hostility to all politicians, Right and Left, conservative and liberal. Bill Clinton may be next to Satan but Newt Gingrich and Phil Graham are not heroes in the world of the militias.

Are these people cut off from the consequences of the economic crisis? These are "ordinary Americans," as they like to describe themselves. These displaced factory workers, small business owners and small farmers, real estate brokers, appliance dealers, gun shop salespeople face the same uncertain future as most other citizens. They are, for the most part, not part of the "verbalistic elites." They don't have the skills, the educational credentials, or the inherited wealth to insulate themselves from the grim economic realities of their time.

In the nineties, politicians and academics, journalists and social critics report that Americans are less secure than ever before. Wages of white male college graduates have begun to decline, yet the gulf between the incomes for those with college degrees and high school graduates continues to widen. The "downsizing" of corporations leaves hundreds of thousands of members of the managerial class facing hazy prospects for the future even as the industrial labor force continues to shrink, with displaced members of the blue collar class still vainly seeking good jobs with good wages. Increasingly, large companies are releasing permanent employees and hiring temporary workers at reduced salaries, with little or no health or pension benefits, and no guarantee of full-time employment or longevity with the firm. As the salaries, benefits and perquisites of corporate CEOs continue a spectacular rise (their median income was forty times the average worker's in 1972, this number ballooned to 140 in 1995), there are new questions about the meaning of the "American Dream" for many who once believed that their future prospects would be at least as good as their parents' in the land of opportunity. For those who could ignore (or revile) the poor people stranded in hopelessness in the inner cities, the new market realities now allow no personal escape.[89]

Who speaks to the anxieties of this moment in history? The Clinton administration, of course, will get no hearing in militia circles. But the politicians of the mainstream Right, while more acceptable, seem to have little impact. Yes, say the militia members, their major concern is "the problem of the federal government." But like extremist movements throughout history, focusing on the object of their fear appears to be only the way of channeling anger at circumstances beyond their control.

Those "conspirators" so hated by nativists and anticommunists in the past were not responsible for the deeper social and economic problems of their time, but they were convenient scapegoats for the anxieties of millions.

In the years of the Know Nothings, western expansion, massive immigration, early industrial development and urban growth—in which many communities became mere way stations for itinerant workers—created the setting for a movement attracting those who searched for order through associational activity. In the nativist secret societies the recruits found groups which would redefine the American community while identifying the sinister adversary responsible for their distress. They could displace their anxieties about an America in upheaval onto the alien enemy.

In the years before the turn of the century, an even larger wave of immigration accompanied the advent of the industrial revolution (and a series of devastating recessions) which transformed America. As a result, new patriotic societies (those on the far Right are always "patriots") and renewed nativist fervor appeared; there must be some reason for the disorder which threatened so many, some group responsible for the forces destabilizing the land, they concluded.

In the "roaring" twenties, when the Klan chapters were proliferating, there was a similar setting. The economic boom did not penetrate all parts of the nation and even among the winners in this new age there was great unease about the breakdown of social values. Dressing not in camouflage but in hoods and robes, the members of the Klan gathered in fraternal brotherhood in an atmosphere of secrecy. It gave this new generation of self-described patriots a way of dealing with the anxieties of their time.

What of this time? The Washington conservatives' call to downsize

the federal government does not seem to appease the militia movement, this new party of fear. Perhaps that is because "the government"
is not responsible for the problems confronting so many Americans.
But for some frustrated people, there may be nowhere else to turn.
And so the militia members, who seem unimpressed by the economic
nostrums of the Contract for America, turn in fear and anger on the
evil agents of federal power serving as the cat's-paws of the new world
order. Government spending and many government economic programs don't seem to interest them, they are concerned about government as superadversary, the enemy of their freedom.

The CEOs, calling for "meaner and leaner" organizations with a
reduced work force in order for their international corporations to
compete in an integrated global market, seem too remote to attack.
So, too, do the acquisition and merger makers whose maneuvers often
determine the fate of industries, communities and employees. In a
sense, the militia recruits, like so many others, have accepted the
arguments of these economic winners and the inevitability of their
own loss of security. But they cannot live with it. Somebody must be
responsible for this new uneasy age and the tarnished promise of the
American Way of Life. Maybe that "global marketplace" that
"coerces" the innocent CEOs to make their harsh choices is the real
villain. Maybe there is a global conspiracy at work, with immensely
powerful financial manipulators (the Federal Reserve? The Trilateral
Commission? The Rothschilds?) organizing a new world order in
which free democratic citizens of America will be crushed by the
tanks and black helicopters of those invading U.N. armies of the forces
of international capital. That sounds like Pat Robertson. It also sounds
like MOM, Koernke and Thompson.

The assault on "the government" may appear to be a pathetic response to threatening anxieties and—even for some militia recruits—
a counterproductive one. After all, not all these middle-aged figures
in camouflage crawling through the brush on weekend exercises are
such rugged individualists that they don't need Social Security and
even Medicare in their future or Medicaid to care for their aging parents. Moreover, the "government" and its law enforcement agencies
would seem a peculiar object of hatred by those who are concerned
with crime, drugs, gang violence and urban disorder. But the old stand-
bys of the far Right are no longer available. Unless you are a fringe
group disciple of an Identity order, assailing ethnic or religious minorities, as in the nativist days of old, is a road to nowhere. Com-

munism is dead and so is the Red Menace inside America. What is left? "I Love My Country But I Fear My Government." The new patriots have discovered the available enemy.

How large will the militia movement grow beyond 1995? No one can say. After the Oklahoma City bombing brought national attention to their groups, paramilitary recruiters grandly predicted rapidly expanding enrollments. But the image of deviance connected with the militias in the early news reports almost certainly had a chilling effect on growth. Joining a paramilitary force, a kind of private army, is a serious undertaking. If the militia movement becomes associated only with the most bizarre of the conspiratorial fantasies of its self-aggrandizing leaders, it is likely to be marginalized and to remain a small phenomenon of the fringe. But if the militia movement truly has tapped into the deep subsoil of discontent created by the social and economic dilemmas of the age, it could draw numbers approaching the membership of those significant extremist groups in earlier America. By using videotapes, audiotapes, radio shows and computer networks, it can reach out to potential recruits like movements of the past never could using newspapers and pamphlets. In this way, it could become a new party of fear for a new age of anxiety in America.

NOTES

★ ★

PROLOGUE

1. M. W. Cluskey, ed., *The Political Text Book or Encyclopedia* (Philadelphia: James B. Smith, 1859), pp. 57–68.

2. Carroll John Noonan, *Nativism in Connecticut, 1829–1860* (Washington, D.C.: Catholic University of America Press, 1938), pp. 199–200.

3. An American [Frederick R. Anspach], *The Sons of the Sires* (Philadelphia: Lippincott, Grambe, 1855), pp. 18–20; Frederick Saunders and T. B. Thorpe, *A Voice to America* (New York: Edward Walker, 1855), pp. 207–10; Anna Ella Carroll, *The Great American Battle* (New York: Miller, Orton and Mulligan, 1856), pp. iii–iv.

4. For descriptions of some different forms of nativism, see Ralph Linton, "Nativistic Movements," *American Anthropologist* 45 (1943): 230–40.

5. For more extensive efforts to define "extremism" and the nature of an American "Right" see Seymour Martin Lipset and Earl Raab, *The Politics of Unreason: Right-Wing Extremism in America, 1790–1970* (New York: Harper & Row, 1970), pp. 3–31; and Daniel Bell, ed., *The Radical Right: The New American Right; Expanded and Updated* (New York: Anchor Books, 1964), pp. 1–73.

6. On the immigrants' ordeal see Oscar Handlin, *The Uprooted* (Boston: Little, Brown, 1951); and Marcus Lee Hansen, *The Atlantic Migration* (Cambridge, Mass.: Harvard University Press, 1940).

7. Frederick R. Barkley, "Jailing Radicals in Detroit," *Nation* 110 (31 Jan. 1920): 136–37.

8. Gustavus Myers, *History of Bigotry in the United States* (New York: Capricorn Books, 1960); Benjamin R. Epstein and Arnold Forster, *The Radical Right* (New York: Simon and Schuster, 1955); Reinhard H. Luthin, *American Demagogues* (Boston: Beacon Press, 1954).

9. See John Higham, *Strangers in the Land: Patterns of American Nativism, 1860–1925* (1955; 2d ed. New York: Atheneum, 1963), pp. 46–48, 61–63, 68–73.

10. H. R. Trevor-Roper, *The European Witch-Craze of the Sixteenth and Seventeenth Centuries and Other Essays* (New York: Harper Torchbooks, 1969), p. 165.

11. Richard Hofstadter, *The Paranoid Style in American Politics* (New York: Knopf, 1965), pp. 4, 29, 37, 87; Daniel Bell, "The Dispossessed," p. 42, Talcott Parsons, "Social Strains in America," p. 217, and essays by Richard Hofstadter, David Riesman, Nathan Glazer, and Seymour Martin Lipset in Bell, ed., *Radical Right*. See also Lipset and Raab, *Politics of Unreason*;

and Robert A. Schoenberger, ed., *The American Right Wing* (New York: Holt, Rinehart and Winston, 1969).

12. Murray Kempton, *Part of Our Time* (New York: Simon and Schuster, 1955), p. 1.

13. R. W. B. Lewis, *The American Adam* (Chicago: University of Chicago Press, 1955), p. 1. The statement of John Locke is cited in Leo Marx, *The Machine in the Garden* (New York: Oxford University Press, 1964), p. 120. On the question of myth and the Edenic vision in the American past, see ibid.; Charles L. Sanford, *The Quest for Paradise* (Urbana: University of Illinois Press, 1961), pp. 24–35; and Edmund Leach, "Lévi-Strauss in the Garden of Eden: An Examination of Some Recent Developments in the Analysis of Myth," *Transactions of the New York Academy of Sciences* 23 (1961): 386–96.

14. The classic statement on America as a unique civilization, of course, is found in Alexis de Tocqueville, *Democracy in America* (London: Oxford University Press, 1953). Among the gifted historians who have described an American experience dramatically different from the European are Daniel J. Boorstin, *The Americans: The Colonial Experience* (New York: Random House, 1958); Louis Hartz, *The Liberal Tradition in America* (New York: Harcourt, Brace, 1955); and David M. Potter, *People of Plenty* (Chicago: University of Chicago Press, 1954).

15. Daniel J. Boorstin, *The Genius of American Politics* (Chicago: University of Chicago Press, 1953).

16. Robert K. Merton, *Social Theory and Social Structure* (Glencoe, Ill.: Free Press, 1957), pp. 166–67.

17. Tocqueville, *Democracy in America*, pp. 406–9.

18. David Brion Davis, "Some Ideological Functions of Prejudice in Ante-Bellum America," *American Quarterly* 15 (Summer 1963): 118–21.

19. Arthur M. Schlesinger, Sr., *Paths to the Present* (New York: Macmillan, 1949), p. 13. See also George W. Pierson, "Mobility," in C. Vann Woodward, ed., *The Comparative Approach to American History* (New York: Basic Books, 1968), pp. 106–20; and Rowland Berthoff, "The American Social Order: A Conservative Hypothesis," *American Historical Review* 65 (April 1960): 500–506.

20. Carl N. Degler, "The Sociologist as Historian: Riesman's *The Lonely Crowd*," *American Quarterly* 15 (Winter 1963): 484–93.

CHAPTER I

1. Extract from J. Hector St. John de Crèvecoeur's *Letters from an American Farmer* (London, 1782) reprinted in Edith Abbott, ed., *Historical Aspects of the Immigration Problem: Select Documents* (Chicago: University of Chicago Press, 1926), pp. 16–17.

2. John Tracy Ellis, *Catholics in Colonial America* (Baltimore: Helicon Press, 1965), pp. 27, 30, 49, 317–24; and H. R. Trevor-Roper, *The European*

Witch Craze of the Sixteenth and Seventeenth Centuries and Other Essays (New York: Harper Torchbooks, 1969), p. 165.

3. James Hennesey, S.J., *American Catholics* (New York: Oxford University Press, 1981), pp. 36–37; Thomas More Brown, "The Image of the Beast: Anti-Papal Rhetoric in Colonial America," in Richard O. Curry and Thomas M. Brown, eds., *Conspiracy: Fear of Subversion in American History* (New York: Holt, Rinehart and Winston, 1972), pp. 7–8.

4. Curry and Brown, eds., *Conspiracy*, pp. 7–8; Ellis, *Catholics*, pp. 337–41, 373; Ray Allen Billington, *The Protestant Crusade, 1800–1860* (Chicago: Quadrangle Books, 1964), pp. 5–9; Hennesey, *American Catholics*, pp. 35-43.

5. Sister May Augustina Ray, *American Opinion of Roman Catholicism in the Eighteenth Century* (New York: Columbia University Press, 1936), pp. 101, 112–13.

6. Ibid., p. 82; John Tracy Ellis, *Perspectives in American Catholicism* (Baltimore: Helicon Press, 1963), p. 43; and Elisha Williams, "The Essential Rights and Liberties of Protestants," in Alan Heimert and Perry Miller, eds., *The Great Awakening* (Indianapolis: Bobbs-Merrill, 1967), pp. 323–25.

7. Ray, *American Opinion of Roman Catholicism*, pp. 122, 130, 225, 250–58.

8. Thomas T. McAvoy, *A History of the Catholic Church in the United States* (Notre Dame: University of Notre Dame Press, 1969), p. 41; Hennesey, *American Catholics*, pp. 59–60, 63, 68, 117.

9. Ray, *American Opinion of Roman Catholicism*, pp. 316–17, 327–35.

10. Jonathan Mayhew, *Discourse Concerning Unlimited Submission*, in Bernard Bailyn, ed., *Pamphlets of the American Revolution*, vol. 1, *1750–1776* (Cambridge, Mass.: Harvard University Press, 1965), pp. 204–10, 213, 239–45; and McAvoy, *History of the Catholic Church*, p. 59.

11. Ray, *American Opinion of Roman Catholicism*, pp. 345–50; and Lyman H. Butterfield et al., eds., *The Adams Papers*, ser. 1, vol. 1, *Diary and Autobiography of John Adams, 1755–1770* (Cambridge, Mass.: Belknap Press of Harvard University Press, 1961), pp. 199–255.

12. Billington, *Protestant Crusade*, pp. 24–34; and Marshall Smelser, "The Federalist Era as an Age of Passion," *American Quarterly* 10 (Winter 1958): 301–19.

13. Vernon Stauffer, *New England and the Bavarian Illuminati* (New York: Columbia University Press, 1918), pp. 142–228; and John Robison, *Proofs of a Conspiracy Against All Religions and Governments of Europe Carried on in the Secret Meetings of Free Masons, Illuminati and Reading Societies* (Philadelphia: T. Dobson, 1798), p. 203.

14. Stauffer, *New England and the Illuminati*, pp. 64–68, 102–41.

15. Ibid., pp. 229–35; and "A Citizen of the United States," *A Discovery of a Clan of Conspirators Against All the Religions and Governments in the Whole World* (Baltimore: J. Hayes, 1799), pp. 50–52.

16. Stauffer, *New England and the Illuminati*, pp. 268–320.

17. Edward A. Shils, *The Torment of Secrecy* (Glencoe, Ill.: Free Press,

1956), pp. 34–35; Hofstadter, *Paranoid Style*, pp. 10–14, 31–32; and Robert Welch, *The New Americanism* (Belmont, Mass.: Western Islands Publishers, 1966), pp. 125–26, 137.

CHAPTER 2

1. Robert H. Lord, John E. Sexton, and Edward T. Harrington, *History of the Archdiocese of Boston*, 3 vols. (New York: Sheed & Ward, 1944), 2: 206–22; and "Burning of Ursuline Convent," in Richard Hofstadter and Michael Wallace, eds., *American Violence: A Documentary History* (New York: Vintage Books, 1971), pp. 298–301.

2. "Anti-Catholic Movements in the United States," *Catholic World* 22 (March 1876): 810–11.

3. Marcus Lee Hansen, *The Atlantic Migration* (Cambridge, Mass.: Harvard University Press, 1940), pp. 102–4, 107–18.

4. Ibid., pp. 120–22, 132–35; extract from "Poor Laws—Ireland," three reports by George Nicholls (English poor law commissioner), 1836–37, in Edith Abbott, ed., *Historical Aspects of the Immigration Problem: Select Documents* (Chicago: University of Chicago Press, 1926), pp. 85–90.

5. Eric Strauss, *Irish Nationalism and British Democracy* (New York: Columbia University Press, 1951), pp. 80, 104; *The Statistical History of the United States* (Stamford, Conn.: Fairfield Publishers, 1865), ser. C88-114, p. 57; William J. Bromwell, *History of Immigration to the United States* (New York: Redfield, 1856), pp. 21–123; and Ray Allen Billington, *The Protestant Crusade, 1800–1860* (Chicago: Quadrangle Books, 1964), pp. 37–41.

6. Marvin Fisher, *Workshops in the Wilderness* (New York: Oxford University Press, 1967), pp. 11–13; Glyndon G. Van Deusen, *The Jacksonian Era, 1828–1848* (New York: Harper & Row, 1959), pp. 3–8; George R. Taylor, *The Transportation Revolution* (New York, 1951), p. 79; Douglas T. Miller, ed., *The Nature of Jacksonian America* (New York: Wiley, 1972), p. 7.

7. Calvin Colton, *Manual for Emigrants to America* (1832; rpt. New York: Arno Press and the New York Times, 1969), p. 128; Fisher, *Workshops in the Wilderness*, pp. 45, 65.

8. Fisher, *Workshops in the Wilderness*, pp. 30–45, 112; Charles L. Sanford, *The Quest for Paradise* (Urbana: University of Illinois Press, 1961), pp. 157–58, 162–67; Leo Marx, *The Machine in the Garden* (New York: Oxford University Press, 1964), pp. 73–144; and Daniel J. Boorstin, *The Americans: The National Experience* (New York: Random House, 1965), p. 1. A striking statement of American optimism as well as the celebration of new commercial and industrial development is found in Edward Everett's famous Fourth of July address at Lowell in 1830 (rpt. in Miller, ed., *Nature of Jacksonian America*, pp. 21–30). Everett exclaimed that but "ten years only ago . . . these favored precincts, now resounding with all the voices of successful industry . . . lay hushed in the deep silence of nature,

broken only by the unprofitable murmur of those streams which practical science and wisely applied capital have converted into the sources of its growth . . . we can scarcely believe that we do not witness a great Arabian tale of real life; that beneficent genius has not touched the soil with his wand, and caused a city to spring from its bosom."

9. Frederick Jackson Turner, *United States, 1838–1850* (New York: Holt, Rinehart and Winston, 1935), pp. 18–28; Arthur M. Schlesinger, Jr., *The Age of Jackson* (Boston: Little, Brown, 1946); Richard Hofstadter, *The American Political Tradition* (New York: Vintage Books, 1954), pp. 45–67; Bray Hammond, *Banks and Politics in America* (Princeton: Princeton University Press, 1957), pp. 326–61; Lee Benson, *The Concept of Jacksonian Democracy* (Princeton: Princeton University Press, 1970), pp. 329–38.

10. On the central role of Jackson in the Bank War, see Frank Otto Gatell, "Sober Second Thoughts on Van Buren, the Albany Regency, and the Wall Street Conspiracy," *Journal of American History* 53 (June 1966): 19–40; on Jackson's appeal for "declining farmers," see Michael A. Lebowitz, "The Jacksonians: Paradox Lost?" in Barton J. Bernstein, ed., *Towards a New Past: Dissenting Essays in American History* (New York: Random House, 1968), pp. 72–73. See also Robert V. Remini, *The Revolutionary Age of Andrew Jackson* (New York: Harper & Row, 1976), pp. 137, 144–45.

11. See excerpt from William M. Gouge, "Short History of Paper Money and Banking in the United States" (1833), and Andrew Jackson, "Veto Message," in Edwin C. Rozwenc, ed., *Ideology and Power in the Age of Jackson* (Garden City, N.Y.: Anchor Books, 1964), pp. 111–12, 198.

12. Alexis de Tocqueville, *Democracy in America* (London: Oxford University Press, 1953), p. 49; Talcott Parsons and Winston White, "The Link between Character and Society," in Seymour Martin Lipset and Leo Lowenthal, eds., *Culture and Social Character: The Work of David Riesman Reviewed* (Glencoe, Ill.: Free Press, 1961), pp. 103–6. James Roger Sharp, *The Jacksonians versus the Banks* (New York: Columbia University Press, 1970), pp. 3–24, 327–29, analyzes politics in the particular states after Jackson's retirement and after the Panic of 1837, concluding that the "hard-money" Jacksonians represented a powerful egalitarian and democratic thrust in a predominantly agrarian society, a movement to check power and privilege, which would be revived years later in the Greenback and Populist uprisings. See also Richard B. Latner, *The Presidency of Andrew Jackson* (Athens: University of Georgia Press, 1979), pp. 122–23.

13. Thomas Jefferson, *Notes on the State of Virginia*, ed. William Peden (Chapel Hill: University of North Carolina Press, 1955), p. 165; Henry David Thoreau, "Life without Principle" (1863), in Carl Bode, ed., *The Portable Thoreau* (New York: Viking Press, 1976), p. 633; Ralph Waldo Emerson, "The Transcendentalist," in Emerson, *Nature: Addresses and Lectures* (Boston: Houghton, Mifflin, 1903), pp. 340–41.

14. Marvin Meyers, *The Jacksonian Persuasion* (Stanford: Stanford University Press, 1960), p. 12; John William Ward, *Andrew Jackson: Symbol for an Age* (New York: Oxford University Press, 1962), pp. 44–46, 208–13. See also Latner, *Presidency of Andrew Jackson*, pp. 209–10.

15. On social mobility and the "ideology of egalitarianism" in America, see Seymour Martin Lipset and Reinhart Bendix, *Social Mobility in Industrial Society* (Berkeley and Los Angeles: University of California Press, 1960), pp. 76–83; on social mobility and the egalitarian ethos in Jacksonian times, see Lee Benson, *Toward the Scientific Study of History* (New York: J. B. Lippincott, 1972), pp. 218–23.

16. William G. McLoughlin, "Introduction to Charles G. Finney, Lecture on Revivals of Religion," in Frank Otto Gatell, ed., *Essays on Jacksonian America* (New York: Holt, Rinehart and Winston, 1970), pp. 241–46; and Bernard Weisberger, *They Gathered at the River* (Boston: Little, Brown, 1948), pp. 128–35, 155–56.

17. Martin E. Marty, *Righteous Empire: The Protestant Experience in America* (New York: Dial Press, 1970), p. 130; Billington, *Protestant Crusade*, 54–60.

18. Billington, *Protestant Crusade*, pp. 61–76, 85–90; Thomas T. McAvoy, *A History of the Catholic Church in the United States* (Notre Dame: University of Notre Dame Press, 1969), p. 134; Alice Felt Tyler, *Freedom's Ferment* (New York: Harper & Bros., 1944), pp. 368–69.

19. Richard Maxwell Brown, "Historical Patterns of Violence in America," in Hugh David Graham and Ted Robert Gurr, eds., *Violence in America* (New York: New American Library, 1969), pp. 49–50, 74; Paul O. Weinbaum, *Mobs and Demagogues* (New York: UMI Research Press, 1979), pp. 5–6, 55–57; "Flour Riot in New York, 1837," and "Anti-Mormon Riot, 1838," in Hofstadter and Wallace, eds., *American Violence*, 126–29, 301–4; Richard Maxwell Brown, *Strain of Violence* (New York: Oxford University Press, 1975), pp. 29–30; David Grimsted, "Rioting in Its Jacksonian Setting," *American Historical Review* 77 (1972): 361–97; "Spring Election Riots of 1834," in J. T. Headley, *Pen and Pencil Sketches of the Great Riots* (New York: E. B. Treat, 1882), pp. 66–78; Oscar Handlin, *Boston's Immigrants, 1790–1865* (Cambridge, Mass.: Harvard University Press, 1941), pp. 161–62, 193–95; Herbert Asbury, *The Gangs of New York* (New York: Capricorn Books, 1970), pp. 28–42; *New York Journal of Commerce*, 16 July 1834; Charles Tilly, Louise Tilly, and Richard Tilly, *The Rebellious Century, 1830–1930* (Cambridge, Mass.: Harvard University Press, 1975); Louise A. Tilly and Charles A. Tilly, eds., *Class Conflict and Collective Action* (Beverly Hills: Sage, 1981), pp. 13–15.

20. William C. Brownlee, *Popery as an Enemy to Civil and Religious Liberty* (New York: John S. Gaylor, 1836), pp. 13–14; *American Protestant Vindicator and the Defender of Civil and Religious Liberty against the Inroads of Popery* (New York), o.s., 14 Sept. 1836.

21. Billington, *Protestant Crusade*, pp. 93–96.

22. Samuel F. B. Morse, *Imminent Dangers to the Free Institutions of the United States* (New York: E. B. Clayton, 1853), pp. 1–32.

23. Ibid., pp. i–iv, 1–6; Jefferson, *Notes on the State of Virginia*, pp. 84–85.

24. Samuel F. B. Morse, *Foreign Conspiracy against the Liberties of the*

United States (New York: American Protestant Society, 1844–46 ed.), pp. 59–73, 105–6, 164; Morse, *Imminent Dangers*, pp. 13–28.

25. Morse, *Imminent Dangers*, pp. 8–10; Morse, *Foreign Conspiracy*, pp. 13, 33–51, 117–22, 159.

26. Weisberger, *They Gathered at the River*, pp. 128–35; Lyman Beecher, *Plea for the West* (Cincinnati: Truman S. Smith, 1835), pp. 1–19; Marty, *Righteous Empire*, pp. 128–29; Robert T. Handy, *A Christian America* (New York: Oxford University Press, 1984), pp. 50–51; Henry Nash Smith, *Virgin Land* (New York: Vintage Books, 1950); James Hennesey, S.J., *American Catholics* (New York: Oxford University Press, 1981), pp. 118–21.

27. Allen Churchill, "The Awful Disclosures of Maria Monk," *American Mercury* 27 (Jan. 1936): 94–98; Reuben Maury, *The Wars of the Godly* (New York: Robert T. McBride, 1928), p. 64.

28. Maria Monk, *The Awful Disclosures of Maria Monk as Exhibited in a Narrative of Her Sufferings during a Residence of Five Years as a Novice and Two Years as a Black Nun in the Hotel Dieu Nunnery at Montreal* (New York: Howe & Bates, 1836), pp. 19–22; Churchill, "Awful Disclosures," pp. 96–98; Billington, *Protestant Crusade*, pp. 99–102; Theodore Dwight, *Open Convents: Or Nunneries and Popish Seminaries Dangerous to the Morals, and Degrading to the Character of a Republican Community* (New York: Van Nostrand and Dwight, 1836), pp. 38–39, 99–114.

29. Rebecca Theresa Reed, *Six Months in a Convent* (Boston: Russel, Odiorne & Metcalfe, 1835), pp. 76–180, 186.

30. Monk, *Awful Disclosures*, pp. 56–58, 62–73, 90, 167–75; and Rosamond Culbertson, *Rosamond: A Narrative of Captivity and Sufferings of an American Female under the Popish Priests in the Island of Cuba* (New York: Leavitt, Lord, 1836), pp. 6–7, 15–32, 133.

31. Culbertson, *Rosamond*, pp. 101–2, 197–217; Monk, *Awful Disclosures*, pp. 14, 111–20, 186, 196–210; *American Protestant Vindicator*, 10 May, 16 Aug. 1837.

32. Dwight, *Open Convents*, pp. 73–89; Billington, *Protestant Crusade*, p. 67.

33. Billington, *Protestant Crusade*, pp. 104–7, 114–17; Dwight, *Open Convents*. Maria Monk's story was attacked from many quarters; particularly damaging was a report by Colonel William L. Stone, a Protestant and editor of the New York *Commercial Advertiser*, who investigated the convent at Montreal (Billington, *Protestant Crusade*, pp. 104–7).

34. Kai T. Erikson, *Wayward Puritans: A Study in the Sociology of Deviance* (New York: Wiley, 1966), pp. 4–19. On the function of the "criminal act" as integrator and unifier of societies, see Emile Durkheim, *The Division of Labor in Society* (Glencoe, Ill.: Free Press, 1947), p. 102, and Lewis Coser, *The Functions of Social Conflict* (Glencoe, Ill.: Free Press, 1964), p. 127.

35. David Brion Davis, "Some Ideological Functions of Prejudice in Ante-Bellum America," *American Quarterly* 15 (Summer 1963): 119; David Brion Davis, "Some Themes of Counter Subversion: An Analysis of

Anti-Masonic, Anti-Catholic, and Anti-Mormon Literature," *Mississippi Valley Historical Review* 47 (Sept. 1960): 219; William R. Taylor, *Cavalier and Yankee* (Garden City, N.Y.: Anchor Books, 1957), pp. 144–51; Tyler, *Freedom's Ferment*, pp. 428, 444–46; Sarah M. Grimké, *Letters on the Equality of the Sexes and the Condition of Woman* (New York: Burt Franklin, 1837), pp. 1–128; Dwight, *Open Convents*, p. 168.

36. Tyler, *Freedom's Ferment*, pp. 318–19; Weisberger, *They Gathered at the River*, pp. 155–56; Steven Marcus, *The Other Victorians* (New York: Bantam Books, 1967), pp. 265–66; David M. Reese, *Humbugs of New York* (New York: John S. Taylor, 1838), pp. 211–25.

37. See, for example, Paul Friedman, "Sexual Deviations," in Silvano Arieti, ed., *American Handbook of Psychiatry*, 3 vols. (New York: Basic Books, 1959), 1:603.

CHAPTER 3

1. John Hancock Lee, *The Origin and Progress of the American Party in Politics* (Philadelphia: Elliott and Gihon, 1855), pp. 136–59; *Important Testimony Connected with Native American Principles* (Philadelphia: Native American Party National Convention, 1845), pp. 1–13.

2. Charles McCarthy, *The Antimasonic Party: A Study of Political Antimasonry in the United States, 1827–1840*, in American Historical Association, *Annual Report for 1902*, 2 vols. (Washington, D.C.: U.S. Government Printing Office, 1903), 1: 367–83; John Bach McMaster, *A History of the People of the United States*, 8 vols. (New York: D. Appleton and Co., 1896–1913), 5: 109–19; Frederick W. Seward, ed., *Autobiography of William H. Seward, 1801–1834, with a Memoir of His Life and Selections from His Letters, 1831–1846* (New York: D. Appleton and Co., 1877), pp. 71–72, 77–80.

3. Whitney R. Cross, *The Burned-Over District* (Ithaca: Cornell University Press, 1950), pp. 116–18; Sister M. Felicity O'Driscoll, "Political Nativism in Buffalo, 1830–60," *Records of the American Catholic Historical Society of Philadelphia* 48 (Sept. 1937): 279–84; *Tuscarawas* (Ohio) *Chronicle*, 16 Apr. 1829, and *Greensburg* (Pa.) *Gazette*, 30 Apr. 1830, quoted in McCarthy, *Antimasonic Party*, p. 544; Report of the New York State Senate Select Committee quoted in Marvin Meyers, *The Jacksonian Persuasion* (Stanford: Stanford University Press, 1960), pp. 76–77; Lee Benson, *The Concept of Jacksonian Democracy* (Princeton: Princeton University Press, 1970), pp. 19–21. Benson cites the Anti-Masonic party as evidence that the "age of egalitarianism" was not exclusively Jacksonian, that the demand for equality came from vigorous anti-Jacksonian elements such as the anti-Masons. Charles McCarthy suggested that many anti-Masons reviled Jackson because he had supported and praised Masonry, even called the Masonic order "calculated to benefit mankind," and in the midst of the anti-Masons' attack had said of Masonry that "I trust it will continue to prosper" (*Antimasonic Party*, p. 532).

4. Louis Dow Scisco, *Political Nativism in New York State* (New York: Columbia University Press, 1901), pp. 25–31; Billington, *Protestant Crusade*, pp. 130–135; Lee, *Origin of the American Party*, pp. 15–16; Sean Wilentz, *Chants Democratic* (New York: Oxford University Press, 1984), pp. 266–71.

5. Sister M. St. Henry, "Nativism in Pennsylvania with Particular Regard to Its Effect on Politics and Education, 1840–60," *Records of the American Catholic Historical Society of Philadelphia* 47 (Mar. 1936): 9.

6. Harry J. Carman and Reinhard H. Luthin, "Some Aspects of the Know-Nothing Movement Reconsidered," *South Atlantic Quarterly* 39 (Apr. 1940): 214; John Tracy Ellis, *American Catholicism* (Chicago: University of Chicago Press, 1956), pp. 71–73; Benson, *Concept of Jacksonian Democracy*, pp. 118–19, 188–91; Seward, ed., *Autobiography of William H. Seward*, pp. 535–36; *New York Tribune*, 27 Jan. 1844; Billington, *Protestant Crusade*, pp. 142–58; Diane Ravitch, *The Great School Wars* (New York: Basic Books, 1974), pp. 33–76.

7. Billington, *Protestant Crusade*, pp. 166–85; *American Protestant* (New York), 7 Aug., 2 Oct. 1844, 1 Jan. 1845; *Protestant Vindicator*, n.s., 22 Sept. 1843, 24 Jan. 1844.

8. Lyman Beecher, *Six Sermons on the Nature, Occasion, Signs, Evils and Remedy of Intemperance* (Boston: Marvin and Co., 1829); *Permanent Temperance Documents of the American Temperance Society* (Boston: Seth Bliss, 1835), 1: 3–226; Joseph R. Gusfield, *Symbolic Crusade: Status Politics and the American Temperance Movement* (Urbana: University of Illinois Press, 1966), pp. 46–57; Tyler, *Freedom's Ferment*, pp. 322–50. Earlier, temperance was tied to anti-Masonry through the rumor that Masons used "ardent spirits" in initiation ceremonies; see Cross, *Burned-Over District*, pp. 116–18.

9. John Bach McMaster, *With the Fathers* (New York: D. Appleton and Co., 1899), pp. 92–95; Carroll John Noonan, *Nativism in Connecticut, 1829–1860* (Washington, D.C.: Catholic University of America Press, 1938), pp. 116–18; *Native American* (Philadelphia), 17 May, 19 July 1844; Wilentz, *Chants Democratic*, pp. 315–38.

10. Lee, *Origin of the American Party*, p. 27; *Native American*, 19 July 1844.

11. Scisco, *Political Nativism*, pp. 44–52; Wilentz, *Chants Democratic*, pp. 318–20; Ira M. Leonard, "The Rise and Fall of the American Republican Party in New York City, 1843–1845," *New York Historical Society Quarterly* 1 (Apr. 1966): 151–67.

12. Leonard, "Rise and Fall of the American Republican Party," pp. 160–67; "Principles of National Convention of Native American Party, 1845," in Lee, *Origin of the American Party*, pp. 233–49; Benson, *Concept of Jacksonian Democracy*, pp. 114–22; *Senate Document 173*, 28th Cong., 2d sess., 3 Mar. 1845; Seward, ed., *Autobiography of William H. Seward*, pp. 697–98.

13. *Brooklyn Daily Eagle*, 6 Nov. 1843.

14. *Native American*, 27 Aug. 1844; Billington, *Protestant Crusade*,

pp. 197–98; "Political Nativism in Brooklyn," *Journal of the American Irish Historical Society* 32 (1941): 29–34; "Irish Laborers Charged with Violence and Crime," in Edith Abbott, ed., *Historical Aspects of the Immigration Problem: Select Documents* (Chicago: University of Chicago Press, 1926), pp. 569–72.

15. "Philadelphia Nativist Riots, 1844," in Richard Hofstadter and Michael Wallace, eds., *American Violence: A Documentary History* (New York: Vintage Books, 1971), pp. 304–9; James Hennesey, S.J., *American Catholics* (New York: Oxford University Press, 1981), pp. 122–23.

16. Reuben Maury, *The Wars of the Godly* (New York: Robert T. McBride, 1928), pp. 83–89; Michael Feldberg, *The Philadelphia Riots of 1844* (Westport, Conn.: Greenwood Press, 1975), p. 60; Humphrey J. Desmond, *The Know-Nothing Party* (Washington, D.C.: New Century Press, 1904), pp. 4–45; Billington, *Protestant Crusade*, pp. 224–34; Lee, *Origin of the American Party*, pp. 30–110, 162–94; Michael Feldberg, *The Turbulent Era* (New York: Oxford University Press, 1980), pp. 9–27; St. Henry, "Nativism in Pennsylvania," pp. 19–20; *Native American*, 6, 7 May 1844; Robert T. Handy, *A History of the Churches in the United States and Canada* (New York: Oxford University Press, 1977), pp. 217–18.

17. Hofstadter and Wallace, eds., *American Violence*, pp. 304–9; Billington, *Protestant Crusade*, pp. 224–34; Feldberg, *Turbulent Era*, pp. 27–32; Benson, *Concept of Jacksonian Democracy*, pp. 167–68. On the allusion to Belfast, Benson quotes *Freeman's Journal*'s argument that Irish Orangemen were the "most active although not most prominent" members of nativist mobs, "innoculating our young native Americans . . . with antisocial views" (ibid.).

18. *Important Testimony Connected with Native American Principles*, pp. 8–13; St. Henry, "Nativism in Pennsylvania," p. 29.

19. *American Republican* (New York), 9 May 1844; Billington, *Protestant Crusade*, pp. 231–37.

20. Billington, *Protestant Crusade*, pp. 231–37; Benson, *Concept of Jacksonian Democracy*, pp. 214–15; Robert Ernst, "Economic Nativism in New York City during the 1840's," *New York History* 39 (Apr. 1948): 170–86. .

21. Scisco, *Political Nativism*, p. 42; Billington, *Protestant Crusade*, pp. 200–202; Benson, *Concept of Jacksonian Democracy*, pp. 121–22, 140–50, 156–64, 171–73, 187–93, 213–15; *New York Tribune*, 20 Apr. 1844; Leonard, "Rise and Fall of the American Republican Party," pp. 190–92.

22. *Important Testimony Connected with Native American Principles*, pp. 1–4; Scisco, *Political Nativism*, pp. 51–61.

CHAPTER 4

1. Charles Gavan Duffy, *Four Years of Irish History, 1845–1849* (London: Cassell, Petter, Galpin & Co., 1883), pp. 430–33, 527–32.

2. Cecil Woodham-Smith, *The Great Hunger: Ireland, 1845–1849* (New

York: Harper & Row, 1962), pp. 163–64; Marcus Lee Hansen, *The Atlantic Migration* (Cambridge, Mass.: Harvard University Press, 1940), pp. 247–48.

3. Hansen, *Atlantic Migration*, pp. 10–11; *The Statistical History of the United States* (Stamford, Conn.: Fairfield Publishers, 1865), ser. C88-114, p. 57; Arnold Schrier, *Ireland and the American Emigration, 1850–1900* (Minneapolis: University of Minnesota Press, 1958), p. 151; Stephen Byrne, *Irish Emigration to the United States* (New York: Arno Press, 1969), pp. 17–21; U.S. Congress, Senate, *Reports of the Immigration Commission* 9 vols. 61st Cong. 3d sess., Document 747 (1911), 1:58–59, 74–77; J. D. B. DeBow, *Statistical View of the United States: Compendium of the Seventh Census* (Washington, D.C.: Senate Printer, 1854), p. 119.

4. Hansen, *Atlantic Migration*, pp. 197–225; Woodham-Smith, *Great Hunger*, pp. 75–77.

5. Oliver MacDonagh, "Irish Emigration to the United States of America and the British Colonies during the Famine," in R. Dudley Edwards and T. Desmond Williams, eds., *The Great Famine: Studies in Irish History, 1845–52* (Dublin: Brown and Nolan, 1956), p. 319; Woodham-Smith, *Great Hunger*, pp. 94–102; Oscar Handlin, *Immigration as a Factor in American History* (Englewood Cliffs, N.J.: Prentice-Hall, 1959), pp. 21–24; Michael Kraus, *Immigration, The American Mosaic* (Princeton: D. Van Nostrand, 1966), pp. 44–46; Barbara Kaye Greenleaf, *American Fever* (New York: New American Library, 1970), pp. 34–38; Duffy, *Four Years of Irish History*, pp. 430–33.

6. MacDonagh, "Irish Emigration," pp. 321–27; Hansen, *Atlantic Migration*, pp. 245–51; "Irish Emigration Assisted by Irish Landlords," in Edith Abbott, ed., *Historical Aspects of the Immigration Problem: Select Documents* (Chicago: University of Chicago Press, 1926), pp. 120–26; George Potter, *To the Golden Door* (Boston: Little, Brown, 1960), pp. 126–28, 145; John A. Hawgood, *The Tragedy of German-America* (New York: G. P. Putnam's Sons, 1940), p. 55; Woodham-Smith, *Great Hunger*, pp. 226–77. The famine eroded the social base of "Whiteboy" movements, those peasant organizations resisting landlords. See Michael Beames, *Peasants and Power* (Sussex: Harvester Press, 1983), pp. 211–14.

7. Hansen, *Atlantic Migration*, pp. 266–76; Kraus, *Immigration*, pp. 47–51; Woodham-Smith, *Great Hunger*, pp. 227–28; and "General Causes of German Emigration," in Abbott, ed., *Historical Aspects of the Immigration Problem*, pp. 95–97. Three out of five of the emigrants in this period were men, with 62.2 percent of new arrivals male in 1850. See U.S. Senate, *Reports of the Immigration Commission*, 1: 58–59.

8. William Forbes Adams, *Irish and Irish Emigration to the New World* (New Haven: Yale University Press, 1932), p. 340; Carl Wittke, *The Irish in America* (Baton Rouge: Louisiana State University Press, 1956); Philip Taylor, *The Distant Magnet: European Emigration to the U.S.A.* (New York: Harper & Row, 1971), pp. 66–76; Hansen, *Atlantic Migration*, pp. 248, 276–83, 288; Schrier, *Ireland and the American Emigration*, pp. 11–26, 42; "What Does North America Offer to the German Emigrant," in Abbott,

ed., *Historical Aspects of the Immigration Problem*, pp. 36–47; D. V. Glass and P. A. M. Taylor, *Population and Emigration* (Dublin: Irish University Press, 1976), pp. 60–62.

9. Marcus Lee Hansen, "The Second Colonization of New England," *New England Quarterly* 2 (Oct. 1929): 543; Adams, *Irish and Irish Emigration*, p. 407; MacDonagh, "Irish Emigration," pp. 364–65; and Harry Pratt Fairchild, *Immigration* (New York: Macmillan, 1925), p. 90. Steamships cut the length of passage by over half, but almost 95 percent of all emigrants embarked on sailing ships as late as 1856.

10. Friedrich Kapp, *Immigration and the Commissioners of Emigration* (New York: Nation Press, 1870), p. 26. See also John Francis Maguire, *The Irish in America* (London: Longmans Green, 1868), pp. 134–83.

11. "American Cholera Epidemics and Emigrant Ships," in Edith Abbott, ed., *Immigration: Select Documents and Case Records* (Chicago: University of Chicago Press, 1924), p. 47; Kapp, *Immigration*, p. 23; Hansen, *Atlantic Migration*, pp. 255–56; MacDonagh, "Irish Emigration," pp. 366–70; Edwin C. Guillet, *The Great Migration: The Atlantic Crossing by Sailing-ship* (Toronto: Thomas Nelson, 1937), pp. 89–98.

12. Marcus Lee Hansen, *The Immigrant in American History* (Cambridge, Mass.: Harvard University Press, 1940), pp. 30–52; Kapp, *Immigration*, pp. 34–37; Terry Coleman, *Going to America* (New York: Pantheon Books, 1972), pp. 100–127; Guillet, *Great Migration*, pp. 81–88.

13. Lawrence Guy Brown, *Immigration: Cultural Conflicts and Social Adjustments* (1933; rpt. New York: Arno Press and the New York Times, 1969), pp. 87–91; Coleman, *Going to America*, pp. 128–54; MacDonagh, "Irish Emigration," pp. 378–79; Hansen, *Atlantic Migration*, pp. 237–58, 379; and Kapp, *Immigration*, pp. 51–60, 105–41.

14. Quoted in Brown, *Immigration*, p. 90.

15. Kapp, *Immigration*, pp. 61–67, 83–84; *Report of the Select Committee to Investigate Fraud upon Emigrant Passengers*, New York Assembly Document 46 (1848), pp. 4–8; Coleman, *Going to America*, pp. 169–88.

16. Wittke, *Irish in America*, pp. 63–64; Hansen, "Second Colonization," p. 551; MacDonagh, "Irish Emigration," pp. 383–84; Adams, *Irish and Irish Emigration*, pp. 341–42; *Citizen* (New York) 1 (18 Feb. 1854); *Citizen* 2 (3 Feb. 1855).

17. Schrier, *Irish and the American Emigration*, p. 6; MacDonagh, "Irish Emigration," pp. 383–85.

18. MacDonagh, "Irish Emigration," pp. 384–85; Kapp, *Immigration*, pp. 69–82; Schrier, *Ireland and the American Emigration*, pp. 4–6; Adams, *Irish and Irish Emigration*, pp. 207–8; Hansen, "Second Colonization," p. 554.

19. Hansen, "Second Colonization," pp. 544–46; Hawgood, *Tragedy of German-America*, p. 238; Hansen, *Atlantic Migration*, p. 288; MacDonagh, "Irish Emigration," pp. 384–85; Jeremiah O'Donovan, *Irish Immigration in the United States: Immigrant Interviews* (New York: Arno Press and the New York Times, 1969).

20. Earl F. Niehaus, *The Irish in New Orleans* (Baton Rouge: Louisiana

State University Press, 1965), pp. 134, 167; Adams, *Irish and Irish Emigration*, p. 360; Woodham-Smith, *Great Hunger*, pp. 248–50; Oscar Handlin, *Boston's Immigrants, 1790–1865* (Cambridge, Mass.: Harvard University Press, 1941), pp. 16–116; Fairchild, *Immigration*, p. 84; Robert H. Lord, John E. Sexton, and Edward T. Harrington, *History of the Archdiocese of Boston*, 3 vols. (New York: Sheed and Ward, 1944), 2: 453–54.

21. De Bow, *Statistical View*, p. 123.

22. "Paupers in the Poor House," June 1850, ibid., pp. 163–64; Woodham-Smith, *Great Hunger*, pp. 246–47; Benjamin J. Klebaner, "The Myth of Foreign Pauper Dumping in the United States," *Social Service Review* 25 (Sept. 1961): 307; U.S. Congress, House of Representatives, *Foreign Criminals and Paupers: Report from the Committee on Foreign Affairs* 34th Cong., 1st sess., Document 359 (1856), pp. 6–10; David J. Rothman, *The Discovery of the Asylum* (Boston: Little, Brown, 1971), pp. 193–94, 290.

23. *Pilot* (Boston), 12 May 1849; Harry J. Carman and Reinhard H. Luthin, "Some Aspects of the Know-Nothing Movement Reconsidered," *South Atlantic Quarterly* 39 (Apr. 1940): 172; U.S. House of Representatives, *Foreign Criminals and Paupers*, pp. 16–17; Handlin, *Boston's Immigrants*, pp. 124–25; Speech of Sen. James Cooper, *Congressional Globe*, 34th Cong., 2d sess., 25 Jan. 1855, pp. 389–91; Rothman, *Discovery of the Asylum*, p. 262. "Pauper dumping" by European governments was a common theme in nativist literature in the 1850s, but only some thirteen thousand paupers from Great Britain were sent to North America in the period 1834–60 (a tiny percentage of total emigration), and German states (but not the central government) sent a few thousand more. There was no "European plot" and Edward Everett ironically observed that support of needy immigrants equaled the sum of the interest on foreign-owned debt repudiated by certain American states. See Klebaner, "Myth of Foreign Pauper Dumping," pp. 302–9.

24. Massachusetts Commission on Lunacy, *Report on Insanity and Idiocy in Massachusetts* (Boston, 1855), pp. 57–68; Rothman, *Discovery of the Asylum*, pp. 254–55, 273.

25. Rothman, *Discovery of the Asylum*, p. 283; Massachusetts Commission on Lunacy, *Report on Insanity*, p. 5; U.S. House of Representatives, *Foreign Criminals and Paupers*, pp. 6–10; extract from "Report of Joint Committee of Massachusetts Legislature on . . . Amending Laws Relating to Alien Passengers," in Abbott, ed., *Historical Aspects of the Immigration Problem*, p. 591.

26. New York State Assembly, *Report of the Select Committee to Examine . . . Trusts under the Charge of the Commissioners of Emigration*, Document 34 (1852), pp. 218–19; U.S. House of Representatives, *Foreign Criminals and Paupers*, p. 10; extract from Boston Committee on Internal Health, "Report on Asiatic Cholera," in Abbott, ed., *Historical Aspects of the Immigration Problem*, pp. 593–96.

27. Extract from Massachusetts Sanitary Commission, "Report of a General Plan for Promotion of Health, April 25, 1850," in Abbott, ed., *Historical Aspects of the Immigration Problem*, pp. 596–600.

28. Ibid., p. 597; De Bow, *Statistical View*, p. 152; Leonard Wibberley, *The Coming of the Green* (New York: Henry Holt, 1958), pp. 24–26; Niehaus, *Irish in New Orleans*, p. 93; Handlin, *Boston's Immigrants*, p. 121; William V. Shannon, *The American Irish* (New York: Macmillan, 1966), pp. 40–41.

29. Lord, Sexton, and Harrington, *History of the Archdiocese of Boston*, 1: 365, 373; Lee Benson, *The Concept of Jacksonian Democracy* (Princeton: Princeton University Press, 1970), pp. 187, 321–22; Adams, *Irish and Irish Emigration*, pp. 365, 373.

30. Adams, *Irish and Irish Emigration*, p. 382; *New Haven Journal*, 5 Mar. 1847; Handlin, *Boston's Immigrants*, p. 193; Wittke, *Irish in America*, p. 116.

31. *Citizen* (New York) 2 (10 Mar., 25 Aug. 1855 and 9 Feb. 1856); Florence E. Gibson, *The Attitudes of the New York Irish toward State and National Affairs, 1848–92* (New York: Columbia University Press, 1951), pp. 60–62. Irish clannishness led to attacks on fellow immigrants as well as natives, as in Dr. John McElheranon's celebration of the Irish "divine spark" and his denigration of Germans and "Anglo-Saxons," in *Pilot*, 5 Apr. and 12 July 1856.

32. *Citizen* (New York) 2 (25 Aug. 1855). The Irish Emigrant Aid Society figured prominently in the Cincinnati trial of Samuel Lumsden and eleven others in 1856, when it was contended that the accused "threaten to interrupt our peaceable relations with Great Britain" and hinder the "vigilant enforcement of the neutrality laws of the United States." See Brown, *Immigration*, pp. 107–8. German organizations were also accused of destructive chauvinism, with the additional charge of socialism directed against émigré groups fleeing from the revolutionary upheaval of 1848. In many cities, German Social Democratic associations were formed, and nativist writers accused them of planning "abolition of the presidency . . . all powers vested exclusively in the masses, and the constitution must give way to the caprices of the people." See Samuel C. Busey, *Immigration: Its Evils and Consequences* (1856; rpt. New York: Arno Press, 1969), p. 21.

33. Robert Ernst, "Economic Nativism in New York City during the 1840's," *New York History* 9 (Apr. 1948): 174–77; Klebaner, "Myth of Foreign Pauper Dumping," p. 304; Handlin, *Boston's Immigrants*, pp. 60–63.

34. An American [Frederick R. Anspach], *The Sons of the Sires* (Philadelphia: Lippincott, Grambe, 1855), pp. 65–72.

CHAPTER 5

1. E. H. Chapin in William H. Ryder, ed., *Our Country or the American Parlor Keepsake* (Boston: J. M. Usher, 1854), pp. 215–16.

2. Thomas R. Whitney, *A Defense of the American Policy* (New York: DeWitt and Davenport, 1856), pp. 16–17; Alfred B. Ely, *American Liberty: Its Sources, Its Dangers and the Means of Its Preservation* (New York: V.

Seaman & Dunham, 1850), p. 15; Frederick Saunders and T. B. Thorpe, *A Voice to America* (New York: Edward Walker, 1855), pp. 361–62.

3. Saunders and Thorpe, *Voice to America*, pp. 361–62; and An American [Frederick R. Anspach], *The Sons of the Sires* (Philadelphia: Lippincott, Grambe, 1855), pp. 109–10.

4. Ernest Lee Tuveson, *Redeemer Nation: The Idea of America's Millennial Role* (Chicago: University of Chicago Press, 1968), pp. 1–175; Ely, *American Liberty*, pp. 20–21.

5. J. Wayne Laurens, *The Crisis, or the Enemies of America Unmasked* (Philadelphia: G. D. Miller, 1855), pp. 44–45.

6. U.S. Congress, House of Representatives, *Foreign Criminals and Paupers: Report from the Committee on Foreign Affairs*, 34th Cong., 1st sess., Document 359 (1856), pp. 49–66; Samuel C. Busey, *Immigration: Its Evils and Consequences* (1856; rpt. New York: Arno Press, 1969), pp. 107–26.

7. W. S. Tisdale, *Know Nothing Almanac for 1856 or True American's Manual* (New York: DeWitt and Davenport, 1855), p. 40; Busey, *Immigration*, p. 131.

8. Ely, *American Liberty*, p. 26; Laurens, *Crisis*, p. 45; Busey, *Immigration*, pp. 78–81, 83–89; [Anspach], *Sons of the Sires*, pp. 200–223; Whitney, *Defense*, pp. 149–65; Louis Schade, *The Immigration into the United States* (Boston: A. O. P. Nicholson, 1854).

9. Laurens, *Crisis*, pp. 47, 68–124, 298–301; Ely, *American Liberty*, p. 27; Carl Wittke, *The Irish in America* (Baton Rouge: Louisiana State University Press, 1956), p. 116.

10. [Anspach], *Sons of the Sires*, pp. 16–17, 205–9; Theodore Dwight, *The Roman Republic of 1849* (New York: R. Van Dien, 1851), p. 34; Anna Ella Carroll, *The Great American Battle* (New York: Miller, Orton and Mulligan, 1856), pp. 108–10. Despite nativist fears, illegal immigrant voting was not widespread. See the analysis of William E. Gienapp, "Politics Seem to Enter into Everything," in William E. Gienapp et al., eds., *Essays on American Antebellum Politics, 1840–1860* (College Station: Texas A & M University Press, 1982), pp. 27–31.

11. Busey, *Immigration*, p. 43, 139–51; [Anspach], *Sons of the Sires*, pp. 115–18, 173; *The Wide-Awake Gift: A Know Nothing Token for 1855* (New York, 1855), pp. 40–41.

12. Saunders and Thorpe, *Voice to America*, pp. 288, 336; Busey, *Immigration*, pp. 9, 62, 151–53.

13. Andrew A. Lipscomb, *Our Country: Its Danger and Duty* (New York: American and Foreign Christian Union, 1854), p. 9.

14. Ibid., pp. 79–87; Saunders and Thorpe, *Voice to America*, p. 147; Theodore Dwight, *Open Convents or Nunneries and Popish Seminaries Dangerous to the Morals, and Degrading to the Character of a Republican Community* (New York: Van Nostrand and Dwight, 1836), pp. 224–28; E. Hutchinson, *Startling Facts for Native Americans Called 'Know Nothings'* (New York: American Family Publication, 1855), pp. 5, 9–65, 96–110.

15. Kirwan [Nicholas Murray], *Romanism at Home* (New York: Harper &

Brothers, 1852), pp. 179–81; Lipscomb, *Our Country,* pp. 87–95; Whitney, *Defense,* pp. 66–72; and Thomas T. McAvoy, *A History of the Catholic Church in the United States* (Notre Dame: University of Notre Dame Press, 1969), pp. 177–78. Nativists called the Catholic press a papal mechanism for keeping the immigrants in chains. But Roman Catholic newspapers did not proliferate in these years. Some papers were more Irish than Catholic, such as the *Pilot* (Boston) or the *American Celt* (Buffalo). Others clearly expressed the Catholic viewpoint: the *Freeman's Journal,* the *Catholic Herald* (Philadelphia), the *Catholic Mirror* (Baltimore), and the *Pittsburgh Catholic.* German-language Catholic newspapers were published in Cincinnati, St. Louis, New York, and Baltimore.

16. [Anspach], *Sons of the Sires,* pp. 57–59; Hutchinson, *Startling Facts,* pp. 66–67, 100; Saunders and Thorpe, *Voice to America,* p. 249; Whitney, *Defense,* pp. 105–6; Carroll, *Great American Battle,* pp. 72–74.

17. Whitney, *Defense,* p. 116; [Anspach], *Sons of the Sires,* p. 190; Carroll, *Great American Battle,* p. 40. Some nativists allowed a shaft of optimism. Nicholas Murray believed that "the son of an Irishman will not wear his father's breeches nor brogue nor will he kneel to his priest." This tone of relative moderation was the exception (*Romanism at Home,* pp. 248–49).

18. John Hughes, *The Decline of Protestantism and Its Causes* (New York: Edward Dunigan & Brother, 1850), pp. 26, 28.

19. Ibid., pp. 1–28; John Tracy Ellis, *Perspectives in American Catholicism* (Baltimore: Helicon Press, 1963), pp. 100–104. The veteran nativist Reverend Nicholas Murray soon countered Hughes with an address at Broadway Tabernacle in January, published as *The Decline of Popery and Its Causes* (New York, 1851).

20. John Bach McMaster, *With the Fathers* (New York: D. Appleton and Co., 1899), p. 98; James Hennesey, S.J., *American Catholics* (New York: Oxford University Press, 1981), pp. 124–25; Harry J. Carman and Reinhard H. Luthin, "Some Aspects of the Know-Nothing Movement Reconsidered," *South Atlantic Quarterly* 39 (Apr. 1940): 215; Ray Allen Billington, *The Protestant Crusade, 1800–1860* (Chicago: Quadrangle Books, 1964), pp. 263–71; McAvoy, *History of the Catholic Church,* p. 171; *American and Foreign Christian Union, Fifth Annual Report* (New York, 1854), p. 47; Alfred G. Stritch, "Political Nativism in Cincinnati, 1830–1860," *Records of the American Catholic Historical Society of Philadelphia* 48 (Sept. 1937): 256–70; Sister M. Felicity O'Driscoll, "Political Nativism in Buffalo, 1830–60," *Records of the American Catholic Historical Society of Philadelphia* 48 (Sept. 1937): 300.

21. Allessandro Gavazzi, *Father Gavazzi's Lectures in New York* (New York: DeWitt and Davenport, 1853), pp. 139–55, 188–89; Billington, *Protestant Crusade,* pp. 305–14; McMaster, *With the Fathers,* p. 98; Robert H. Lord, John E. Sexton, and Edward T. Harrington, *History of the Archdiocese of Boston,* 3 vols. (New York: Sheed and Sheed, 1944), 2: 669–72; "Political Nativism in Brooklyn," *Journal of the American Irish Historical*

Society 32 (1941): 34–36.

22. See David Brion Davis, "Some Ideological Functions of Prejudice in Ante-Bellum America," *American Quarterly* 15 (Summer 1963): 124.

23. Josephine M. Bunkley, *The Testimony of an Escaped Novice* (New York: Harper & Brothers, 1855), pp. 37, 41–42, 59, 91, 136–43, 225, 252–62, 312.

24. Hutchinson, *Startling Facts*, pp. 75–78; Charles W. Frothingham, *The Convent's Doom* (Boston: Graves & Weston, 1854), pp. 1, 21–32; Lord, Sexton, and Harrington, *History of the Archdiocese of Boston*, 2:656–60; William Hogan, *Auricular Confession and Popish Nunneries*, 2 vols. (Hartford: Silas, Andrus, 1850), 2:212; and *Pilot* (Boston), 9, 16 Apr. 1853.

25. Billington, *Protestant Crusade*, pp. 311–14; John Gilmary Shea, *History of the Catholic Church in the United States*, 4 vols. (New York: J. G. Shea, 1886–92, 4: 510, 543, 617–18; *Pilot*, (Boston), 18 June 1853, 15, 22, 29 July, 28 Oct. 1854, and 2 June 1855.

26. Orestes A. Brownson, editorials, *Brownson's Quarterly Review*, ser. 3, vols. 2 and 3 (1854 and 1855). See vol. 2, no. 3, 328–54; vol. 3, no. 4, 49–50, 461–73; vol. 3, no. 1, 123–25; vol. 3, no. 2, 250–53; and vol. 3, no. 4, 473–82. McAvoy, *History of the Catholic Church*, p. 180, calls Brownson "the intellectual giant of American Catholicism."

27. Thomas Low Nichols, *Forty Years of American Life, 1821–61* (New York: Stackpole Sons, 1937), pp. 257–65; Saunders and Thorpe, *Voice to America*, pp. 271, 283; U.S. House of Representatives, *Foreign Criminals and Paupers*, pp. 19–26; Chapin in Ryder, ed., *Our Country*, pp. 56–57; Carroll, *Great American Battle*, pp. 156–57, 191–210, 316, 321. Antinativist writers took many different approaches to the "problem" of immigration and Catholicism. Edward Everett Hale, *Letters on Irish Emigration* (Boston, 1852), pp. 47–58, acknowledged that "Celts from Ireland in pure blood are inefficient compared with the Saxons and Germanic races which receive them." But Hale rejected nativism because "in any community there must be manual labor and by every spade blow that foreigners have driven . . . our country is richer for their coming." Others simply rejected antialienism as incompatible with the American ethos. Reverend W. H. Lord, *A Tract for the Times: National Hospitality* (Montpelier, Vt., 1855), pp. 5–44, argued that "it is for our highest interest to extend the most generous and indiscriminatory hospitality to these foreign races." A. Woodbury, in "The Moral of Statistics" in 1855 (reprinted in Edith Abbott, ed., *Historical Aspects of the Immigration Problem: Select Documents* [Chicago: University of Chicago Press, 1926], p. 810), insisted that "we should welcome them and give them on our soil a free and happy home" for there are not, after all, "a very formidable array of them" compared with natives. *The Report of Select Committee on Allowing Resident Aliens to Hold Real Estate*, New York Assembly Document 168 (1848), pp. 1–5, expressed another liberal view of Catholic immigrants: "All experience and observation has shown that there are no truer American citizens than the children of those who come among us as aliens."

CHAPTER 6

1. Quoted in Avery Craven, *The Coming of the Civil War* (Chicago: University of Chicago Press, 1957), pp. 275–76.

2. F. Scott Fitzgerald, *Tender Is the Night* (New York: Charles Scribner, 1934), p. 61. See also Louis Hartz, *The Liberal Tradition in America*, (New York: Harcourt, Brace, 1955), and Daniel J. Boorstin, *The Americans: The National Experience* (New York: Random House, 1965).

3. On the setting for sectional crisis, see, for example, Craven, *Coming of the Civil War*; Allan Nevins, *Ordeal of the Union*, 2 vols. (New York: Charles Scribner, 1950); David Potter, *The South and the Sectional Conflict* (Baton Rouge: Louisiana State University Press, 1968); and Eric Foner, *Free Soil, Free Labor, Free Men* (New York: Oxford University Press, 1970). Also see John P. McGivin, *The War against Proslavery Religion* (Ithaca: Cornell University Press, 1984), pp. 84–92.

4. On the question of causation, see, for example, Thomas J. Pressly, *Americans Interpret Their Civil War* (Princeton: Princeton University Press, 1954); Thomas N. Bonner, "Civil War Historians and the 'Needless War' Doctrine," *Journal of the History of Ideas* 17 (Apr. 1956): 193–216; and John S. Rosenberg, "Toward a New Civil War Revisionism," *American Scholar* 38 (Spring 1969): 250–72.

5. Rowland Berthoff, *An Unsettled People: Social Order and Disorder in American History* (New York: Harper & Row, 1971), pp. 284–88.

6. Michael F. Holt, "The Politics of Impatience: The Origins of Know Nothingism," *Journal of American History* 60 (Sept. 1973): 325–29. On the growth of industry, see Harry J. Carman, *Social and Economic History of the United States: The Rise of Industrialism, 1820-1875* (New York: D. C. Heath, 1934).

7. Stephan Thernstrom and Peter R. Knights, "Men in Motion: Some Data and Speculations about Urban Population Mobility in Nineteenth-Century America," *Journal of Interdisciplinary History* 1 (Autumn 1970): 7–35; Stephan Thernstrom, *Poverty and Progress* (Cambridge, Mass.: Harvard University Press, 1964), pp. 96–97; and Peter R. Knights, "Population Turnover, Persistence, and Residential Mobility in Boston, 1830–1860," in Stephan Thernstrom and Richard Sennett, eds., *Nineteenth-Century Cities: Essays in the New Urban History* (New Haven: Yale University Press, 1969), pp. 258–74.

8. Knights, "Population Turnover," pp. 269–72; and Thernstrom and Knights, "Men in Motion," pp. 24–26, 29–30.

9. Thernstrom and Knights, "Men in Motion," pp. 30–33; Stephan Thernstrom, "Working Class Social Mobility in Industrial America," in Melvin Richter, ed., *Essays in Theory and History* (Cambridge, Mass.: Harvard University Press, 1970); Clyde Griffen, "Workers Divided: The Effect of Craft and Ethnic Differences in Poughkeepsie, New York, 1850–1880," Herbert G. Gutman, "The Reality of the Rags-to-Riches 'Myth': The Case of Paterson, New Jersey Locomotive, Iron and Machinery Manufacturers, 1830–1880," Stuart Blumin, "Mobility and Change in Ante-Bellum Phila-

delphia," in Thernstrom and Sennett, eds., *Nineteenth Century Cities*, pp. 48–97, 98–124, 165–208.

10. A major inquiry into the history of social disorder and its consequences in America is Rowland Berthoff's incisive *An Unsettled People*. See also Arthur M. Schlesinger, Sr., *Paths to the Present* (New York: Macmillan, 1949), pp. 23, 38–39.

11. Ted Robert Gurr, *Why Men Rebel* (Princeton: Princeton University Press, 1970), pp. 24–26.

12. W. G. Runciman, *Relative Deprivation and Social Justice* (Berkeley and Los Angeles: University of California Press, 1966), p. 9; Gurr, *Why Men Rebel*, pp. 46–56. Relative deprivation takes different forms, according to the curves of expectation and capability of the people involved. "Decremental deprivation" occurs when a group's expectations concerning its well-being remain unchanged but it believes that they will not be fulfilled; "progressive deprivation," when expectations and aspirations rise but perceptions of fulfillment decline or remain constant. In one case, the group believes it will be worse off in the future than in the past or present, in the other, that its justified expectations of improvement will be denied.

13. Michael Barkun, *Disaster and the Millennium* (New Haven: Yale University Press, 1974), pp. 35–39; Anthony F. C. Wallace, "Revitalization Movements," *American Anthropologist* 58 (Feb. 1956): 264–81. For the contributions of theorists who offer other categories of social movements —transformative, reformative, redemptive, value-oriented, norm-oriented, and so on—see David F. Aberle, *The Peyote Religion among the Navaho* (New York: Wenner-Gren Foundation, 1966); Neil J. Smelser, *Theory of Collective Behavior* (New York: Free Press, 1962), pp. 270–81; and Bernard J. Siegel, "Defensive Cultural Adaptation," in Hugh Davis Graham and Ted Robert Gurr, eds., *Violence in America* (New York: Signet, 1969), pp. 743–54.

14. Barkun, *Disaster*, pp. 55–56.

15. Charles Tilly, "Collective Violence in European Perspective," in Graham and Gurr, eds., *Violence in America*, p. 11.

16. On the problem of clearly separating so-called rational and irrational movements, see Barkun, *Disaster*, pp. 131–33.

17. Ibid., pp. 11–33; Norman Cohn, *The Pursuit of the Millennium*, 2d ed. (New York: Harper Torchbooks, 1961), pp. xii, xvi; Yonina Talmon, "Pursuit of the Millennium: The Relation between Religion and Social Change," in William A. Lessa and Evon Z. Vogt, eds., *Reader in Comparative Religion: An Anthropological Approach* (New York: Harper & Row, 1965), pp. 526–40; E. J. Hobsbawm, *Primitive Rebels: Studies in Archaic Forms of Social Movement in the 19th and 20th Centuries* (New York: Frederick A. Praeger, 1959), pp. 57–65; and David Brion Davis, "Some Ideological Functions of Prejudice in Ante-Bellum America," *American Quarterly* 15 (Summer 1963): 124–25.

CHAPTER 7

1. *O.U.A.* (New York), 18 Nov. 1848; Thomas R. Whitney, *A Defense of the American Policy* (New York: DeWitt and Davenport, 1856), pp. 257–66.

2. Rowland Berthoff, *An Unsettled People: Social Order and Disorder in America* (New York: Harper & Row, 1971), pp. 272–74; Louis Dow Scisco, *Political Nativism in New York State* (New York: Columbia University Press, 1901), pp. 62–65.

3. *Constitution and By Laws, Fredonia Council, No. 52, Order of the United American Mechanics of Pennsylvania* (Philadelphia: J. C. Klonegar, 1853), pp. 1–5; Whitney, *Defense*, pp. 308–14.

4. Whitney, *Defense*, p. 314; Humphrey J. Desmond, *The Know-Nothing Party* (Washington, D.C.: New Century Press, 1904), pp. 45–46.

5. *Directory, Alpha Chapter No. 1, OUA, August 1848* (New York: R. C. Root & Anthony, 1848); *Constitution and By Laws, OUA Alpha Chapter No. 1* (New York: Narine & Co., 1849), pp. 1–2; *Rules and Regulations for the Government of Chancery, OUA, State of New York* (New York: Wm. B. Weiss, 1852), pp. 4–8; Thomas J. Curran, "Know Nothings of New York State" (Ph.D. dissertation, Columbia University, 1963), pp. 70–71; Scisco, *Political Nativism*, pp. 62–65.

6. Whitney, *Defense*, pp. 257–70; *O.U.A.* (New York), 10 November 1848.

7. Curran, "Know Nothings of New York State," p. 73; *Directory, Alpha Chapter No. 1, OUA*; Whitney, *Defense*, p. 303; Georg Simmel, "The Sociology of Secrecy and of Secret Societies," *American Journal of Sociology* 11 (Jan. 1906): 462, 465–66; Georg Simmel, *Conflict and the Web of Group-Affiliations* (New York: Free Press, 1956), pp. 19, 65, 163.

8. Thomas R. Whitney, *An Address Delivered on the Occasion of the Seventh Anniversary of Alpha Chapter, Order of United Americans* (New York: John A. Gray, 1851), pp. 2, 5–6; Daniel Ullmann, *Oration at the Convention of the Order of United Americans, February 1856* (New York: OUA, 1856), pp. 19–20; Whitney, *Defense*, pp. 268–70.

9. Scisco, *Political Nativism*, p. 80; Curran, "Know Nothings of New York State," pp. 71–76.

10. Curran, "Know Nothings of New York State," pp. 41–44; Glyndon G. Van Deusen, *William Henry Seward* (New York: Oxford University Press, 1967), pp. 121–34. On the nativist sentiments of conservative Whiggery and the hatred of "foreign desperadoes and Irish politicians," see Sam C. Crane, *Facts and Figures for Native Born Americans* (Ithaca, N.Y.: A. E. Barnahy, 1856), p. 3.

11. Curran, "Know Nothings of New York State," pp. 86–87; Reuben Maury, *The Wars of the Godly* (New York: Robert T. McBride, 1928), p. 110; Scisco, *Political Nativism*, p. 65; Desmond, *Know-Nothing Party*, pp. 49–57; Ray Allen Billington, *The Protestant Crusade, 1800–1860* (Chicago, Quadrangle Books, 1964), pp. 380–81.

12. Whitney, *Defense*, pp. 280–82; Anna Ella Carroll, *The Great American Battle* (New York: Miller, Orton and Mulligan, 1856), p. 67; Curran,

"Know Nothings of New York State," pp. 81, 89–93, 107; Scisco, *Political Nativism*, pp. 65, 94.

13. Scisco, *Political Nativism*, pp. 100–101, 135–37; Robert D. Parmet, "The Know Nothings in Connecticut" (Ph.D. dissertation, Columbia University, 1966), pp. 68–71.

14. *Principles and Objects of the American Party* (New York: American Party, 1855), p. 1; John Hancock Lee, *The Origin and Progress of the American Party in Politics* (Philadelphia: Elliott and Gihon, 1855), pp. 200–201; Frederick Saunders and T. B. Thorpe, *A Voice to America* (New York: Edward Walker, 1855), p. 369; Whitney, *Address*, p. 6.

15. *Principles and Objects of the American Party*, pp. 19–21.

16. *New York Tribune*, 16 Nov. 1853; Scisco, *Political Nativism*, p. 88; Max Berger, "The Irish Emigrant and American Nativism as Seen by British Visitors, 1836-1860," *Pennsylvania Magazine of History and Biography* 70 (Apr. 1946): 159. The name "Know Nothing" has also been attributed to E. Z. C. Judson, radical nativist and prolific author of western stories under the pseudonym "Ned Buntline."

17. Glyndon G. Van Deusen, *The Jacksonian Era, 1828–1848* (New York: Harper & Row, 1959), pp. 141–42.

18. Ibid.; Eric Foner, *Free Soil, Free Labor, Free Men* (New York: Oxford University Press, 1970), pp. 125–26.

19. Carroll, *Great American Battle*, pp. 267, 271; Curran, "Know Nothings of New York State," pp. 77–84, 107–10; M. W. Cluskey, ed., *The Political Text Book or Encyclopedia* (Philadelphia: James B. Smith, 1859), pp. 57–60; Charles O. Paullin, "The National Ticket of Broom and Coates, 1852," *American Historical Review* 25 (June 1920): 689–90. The replacement candidates of the American Union party were Jacob Broome of Philadelphia and Dr. Reynell Coates of New Jersey. Their best showing was in Pennsylvania, where they received 1,670 votes.

20. Desmond, *Know-Nothing Party*, p. 148; Theodore C. Smith, *Parties and Slavery, 1850–1859* (New York: Harper & Brothers, 1906), p. 116; Robert J. Rayback, *Millard Fillmore* (Buffalo: Buffalo Historical Society, 1959), pp. 381–92; Scisco, *Political Nativism*, pp. 96–98; Billington, *Protestant Crusade*, p. 328; *New York Herald*, 30 Oct. 1854.

21. Rayback, *Millard Fillmore*, pp. 392–93; Desmond, *Know-Nothing Party*, pp. 142–48; John Bach McMaster, *With the Fathers* (New York: D. Appleton and Co., 1899), pp. 101–5.

22. *Congressional Globe*, 34th Cong., 1st sess., Pt. 1, 5–7 Jan. 1856, pp. 156–58, 168; W. S. Tisdale, *Know Nothing Almanac for 1856 or True American's Manual* (New York: DeWitt and Davenport, 1855), pp. 1–15, 26–29, 33–46; Billington, *Protestant Crusade*, pp. 387–88.

23. Whitney, *Defense*, pp. 280–81.

CHAPTER 8

1. Herbert Asbury, *The Gangs of New York* (New York: Knopf, 1928), pp. 93–100.

2. Ibid., pp. 100–117; Carleton Beals, *Brass-Knuckle Crusade* (New York: Hastings House, 1960), pp. 18–24; William Knapp, *I Died A True American: Life of William Poole, with a Full Account of the Terrible Affair in Which He Received His Death Wound* (New York: DeWitt and Davenport, 1855), pp. 5–7.

3. Asbury, *Gangs of New York*, pp. 105–17; *New York Tribune*, 15 June 1854; Thomas J. Curran, "Know Nothings of New York State" (Ph.D. dissertation, Columbia University, 1963), pp. 97–102; "Spring Election Riots of 1834," in J. T. Headley, *Pen and Pencil Sketches of the Great Riots* (New York: E. B. Treat, 1882), pp. 131–34; Florence E. Gibson, *The Attitudes of the New York Irish toward State and National Affairs, 1848–1892* (New York: Columbia University Press, 1951), p. 81; John Denig, *The Know Nothing Manual or Book for America* (Harrisburg, 1855), p. 17.

4. Louis Dow Scisco, *Political Nativism in New York State* (New York: Columbia University Press, 1901), pp. 120–27; Curran, "Know Nothings of New York State," pp. 117, 128–39; Harry J. Carman and Reinhard H. Luthin, "Some Aspects of the Know-Nothing Movement Reconsidered," *South Atlantic Quarterly* 39 (Apr. 1940): 217–18.

5. Carman and Luthin, "Some Aspects of the Know-Nothing Movement," p. 219; Curran, "Know Nothings of New York State," pp. 148–64; Scisco, *Political Nativism*, pp. 128–29.

6. *New York Times*, 8 Mar. 1855; Scisco, *Political Nativism*, pp. 140–42.

7. *United States Senatorial Question: Speeches Delivered in the Assembly of New York State on the Oaths, Obligations and Ritual of the Know Nothings* (Albany: Week & Parsons, 1855), pp. 10–62.

8. Louis Schade, *The Immigration into the United States of America* (Washington, D.C., 1856), pp. 1–15; *Congressional Globe*, 33rd Cong. 1st sess., 13 July 1854, pp. 1708–9; *Independent*, 18 Jan. 1855; *Congressional Globe*, 34th Cong., 1st sess., 5 Jan. 1856, pp. 156, 158, 168; Richard H. Sewell, *Bullets for Freedom* (New York: Oxford University Press, 1976), pp. 268–69.

Seward, of course, was a longtime enemy of nativism on political and ideological grounds. Not only did he believe that the anti-immigrant animus had weakened his Whig party and that conservative Whigs had become his enemies in part because of his association with Catholics, but he saw the nativist question in larger terms. As a passionate enemy of slavery and an advocate of free soil, he found nativism's threat to the expansion of the labor force through immigration unacceptable. He was a believer in the assimilationist vision of the melting pot; nativism was incompatible with this view of democracy. He wanted free soil and free labor; the settlement of immigrants in the West would be a strong obstacle to the extension of slavery. See Eric Foner, *Free Soil, Free Labor, Free Men* (New York: Oxford University Press, 1970), pp. 234–37; Glyndon G. Van Deusen, *The Jackso-*

nian Era, 1828–1848 (New York: Harper & Row, 1959), pp. 205–6; George E. Baker, ed., *The Works of William H. Seward*, 3 vols. (Boston: Houghton Mifflin, 1889), 1: 198–99, 2: 480, 489–90.

9. Orvilla S. Belisle, *The ArchBishop: or, Romanism in the United States* (Philadelphia: William White Smith, 1855), pp. 359–60; John Bach McMaster, *With the Fathers* (New York: D. Appleton and Co., 1899), pp. 102–5; [A Know Something], *An Exposé of the Secret Order of Know Nothings* (New York: Stearns & Co., 1854), pp. 2–3; Curran, "Know Nothings of New York State," pp. 110–12; Van Deusen, *Jacksonian Era*, pp. 157–58; Thomas J. Curran, "Seward and the Know-Nothings," *New York Historical Society Quarterly* 51 (Apr. 1967): 141–59; *Congressional Globe*, 34th Cong., 1st sess., 16 June 1856, pp. 1409–14, Appendix pp. 967–69, 1083–87.

10. *Syracuse Journal*, 28 Oct. 1854; *New York Tribune*, 4 June 1855; Curran, "Know Nothings of New York State," pp. 174–77, 224–25.

11. Curran, "Know Nothings of New York State," pp. 178–80; Scisco, *Political Nativism*, p. 144; Theodore Smith, *Parties and Slavery, 1850–1859* (New York: Harper and Brothers, 1906), pp. 136–37.

12. *New York Times*, 15 June 1855; Curran, "Know Nothings of New York State," pp. 178–80; M. W. Cluskey, ed., *The Political Text Book or Encyclopedia* (Philadelphia: James B. Smith, 1859), pp. 55–56; *The Philadelphia Platform: Adopted Universally by the South and Part of the North at a Regular Meeting of the National Council of the American Party, June 9, 1855* (Philadelphia, 1855), pp. 1–5.

13. Scisco, *Political Nativism*, pp. 144–47; *New York Times*, 15 June 1855; Thomas R. Whitney, *A Defense of the American Policy* (New York: DeWitt and Davenport, 1856), pp. 294–96.

14. Curran, "Know Nothings of New York State," pp. 158–59, 172–80; Foner, *Free Soil*, p. 243; Scisco, *Political Nativism*, pp. 158–59.

15. *New York Tribune*, 29 Aug. 1855; *New York Times*, 24 Aug 1855; Curran, "Know Nothings of New York State," pp. 185–90; Scisco, *Political Nativism*, pp. 148–52; Mark L. Berger, *The Revolution in the New York Party Systems, 1840–1860* (Port Washington, N.Y.: Kennikat Press, 1973), pp. 70–77.

16. Scisco, *Political Nativism*, pp. 161–67; Humphrey J. Desmond, *The Know-Nothing Party* (Washington, D.C.: New Century Press, 1904), pp. 66–67; David M. Potter, *The Impending Crisis, 1848–1861* (New York: Harper & Row, 1976), p. 250.

17. Curran, "Know Nothings of New York State," pp. 206–12; Scisco, *Political Nativism*, pp. 172–179; Robert J. Rayback, *Millard Fillmore* (Buffalo: Buffalo Historical Society, 1959), pp. 155–56, 384–93.

18. Scisco, *Political Nativism*, pp. 142, 169–74; Curran, "Know Nothings of New York State," pp. 210–15; *New York Times*, 14 Dec. 1855.

19. Curran, "Know Nothings of New York State," p. 232; Scisco, *Political Nativism*, pp. 174–75, 210–18. Law did receive twenty of New York's thirty-eight votes on the first ballot.

20. *New York Times*, 19, 20, 21, 23, 24, 25 Feb. 1856; Curran, "Know Nothings of New York State," pp. 222–32; Potter, *Impending Crisis*,

p. 256; Whitney, *Defense*, pp. 367–69; Foner, *Free Soil*, pp. 247–48; Fred H. Harrington, "The First Northern Victory," *Journal of Southern History* 5 (May 1939): 186–205; Berger, *Revolution*, pp. 109–120.

21. *New York Times*, 20, 24, 25 Feb. 1856; Curran, "Know Nothings of New York State," pp. 221–22, 231–32.

22. Curran, "Know Nothings of New York State," pp. 235–40; [A Know Something], *Exposé*, pp. 7–16, 19–30; *A Few Words to the Thinking and Judicious Voters of Pennsylvania* (Harrisburg, 1855), pp. 19, 38–39.

23. Curran, "Know Nothings of New York State," pp. 236–63; Scisco, *Political Nativism*, pp. 180–85; *New York Tribune*, 27 Feb. 1856; Fred H. Harrington, "Fremont and the North Americans," *American Historical Review* 44 (July 1939): 842–48.

24. *New York Times*, 18 Sept. 1856; Curran, "Know Nothings of New York State," pp. 246–62; Joel H. Silbey, *The Partisan Imperative* (New York: Oxford University Press, 1985), pp. 151–65.

25. John Raymond Mulkern, "The Know Nothing Party in Massachusetts" (Ph.D. dissertation, Boston University, 1963), pp. 81, 162–95; George H. Haynes, "The Causes of Know-Nothing Success in Massachusetts," *American Historical Review* 3 (Oct. 1897): 68–70.

26. William G. Bean, "Puritan versus Celt, 1850–1860," *New England Quarterly* 7 (Mar. 1934): 72–74; Mulkern, "Know Nothing Party," pp. 170–95.

27. Robert H. Lord, John E. Sexton, and Edward T. Harrington, *History of the Archdiocese of Boston*, 3 vols. (New York: Sheed and Ward, 1944), 2: 582–86; *Pilot* (Boston), 5 Mar., 25 June, 1, 8 Oct., 5, 12 Nov. 1853; Bean, "Puritan versus Celt," pp. 75–81; Mulkern, "Know Nothing Party," pp. 78–80.

28. William G. Bean, "An Aspect of Know Nothingism: The Immigrant and Slavery," *South Atlantic Quarterly* 23 (Oct. 1924): 321–22; Bean, "Puritan versus Celt," pp. 78–81; Potter, *Impending Crisis*, p. 252; *Pilot*, 12 May 1855.

29. Oscar Handlin, *Boston's Immigrants, 1790–1865* (Cambridge, Mass.: Harvard University Press, 1941), pp. 201–6; George H. Haynes, "A Chapter from the Local History of Knownothingism," *New England Magazine* 15 (Sept. 1896): 87–96; Dale Baum, "Know-Nothingism and the Republican Majority in Massachusetts: The Political Realignment of the 1850's," *Journal of American History* 44 (Mar. 1978): 961–66; Dale Baum, *The Civil War Party System: The Case of Massachusetts, 1848–1876* (Chapel Hill: University of North Carolina Press, 1984), pp. 27–31; George H. Haynes, "A Know Nothing Legislature," *Annual Report of the American Historical Association for 1896*, 2 vols. (Washington, D.C.: U.S. Government Printing Office, 1897) 1: 178–79; Robert Kelly, *The Cultural Pattern in American Politics* (New York: Knopf, 1979), pp. 190–91, argues that "there is a sense in which the Know-Nothing party was a precursor to the Progressive movement . . . voters in a fight to save pure and honest republican government."

30. Haynes, "Know Nothing Legislature," pp. 178–82; Henry J. Gardner, *Address of Henry J. Gardner to the Two Branches of the Legislature of*

Massachusetts, Jan. 9, 1855 (Boston: William White, 1855), pp. 5, 8–22; *Know Nothing and American Crusader* (Boston), 25 Nov. 1854.

31. Roy B. Basler, ed., *The Collected Works of Abraham Lincoln,* 9 vols. (New Brunswick, N.J.: Rutgers University Press, 1953), 2:316; Edward L. Pierce, *Effect of Proscriptive or Extreme Legislation against Foreigners in Massachusetts & New England* (Boston: Commercial Printing, 1857), pp. 1–6; Haynes, "Know Nothing Legislature," p. 187.

32. Elias Nason and Thomas Russell, *The Life and Public Services of Henry Wilson* (Boston: B. B. Russell, 1876), pp. 119, 134–45.

33. Baum, "Know-Nothingism," p. 985; Baum, *Civil War Party System,* pp. 33–54; Paul Kleppner, *The Third Electoral System, 1853–1892* (Chapel Hill: University of North Carolina Press, 1979), pp. 53–55.

34. Carroll John Noonan, *Nativism in Connecticut, 1829–1860* (Washington, D.C.: Catholic University of America Press, 1938), pp. 185–89, 194–95; Robert D. Parmet, "The Know Nothings in Connecticut" (Ph.D. dissertation, Columbia University, 1966), pp. 71–86, 121–26.

35. Parmet, "Know Nothings in Connecticut," pp. 155–65; Noonan, *Nativism in Connecticut,* pp. 201–31, 254–55.

36. Charles Stickney, "Know-Nothingism in Rhode Island," *Publications of the Rhode Island Historical Society* 1 (1894): 246–55; Larry Anthony Rand, "The Know-Nothing Party in Rhode Island," *Rhode Island History* 23 (Oct. 1964): 109–16.

37. Parmet, "Know Nothings in Connecticut," pp. 144–48, 172, 190, 275–80; Noonan, *Nativism in Connecticut,* pp. 223–24, 270–304; Susan E. Hirsch, *Roots of the American Working Class: Newark, 1800–1860* (Philadelphia: University of Pennsylvania Press, 1978), pp. 103–7, 121–22.

38. The most persuasive case for Know-Nothingism as a revolt against politics as usual in America has been made by Michael F. Holt. See, for example, Holt, "The Politics of Impatience," *Journal of American History* 40 (Sept. 1973), 310–22; Michael F. Holt, *The Political Crisis of the 1850's* (New York: Wiley, 1978), pp. 163–69; and Michael F. Holt, *Forging a Majority* (New Haven: Yale University Press, 1969), pp. 135–54, 167–74, 339–43. See also Kleppner, *Third Electoral System,* pp. 69–70; Ronald P. Formisano, "Political Character, Antipartyism, and the Second Party System," *American Quarterly* 21 (Winter 1969): 683–709; Joel H. Silbey, *The Transformation of American Politics, 1840–1860* (Englewood Cliffs, N.J.: Prentice-Hall, 1967), pp. 1–34; Warren F. Hewitt, "The Know Nothing Party in Pennsylvania," *Pennsylvania History* 11 (1 Apr. 1935): 73–74.

39. On voting patterns in the North in these years, see Kleppner, *Third Electoral System,* p. 54, Baum, "Know-Nothingism," pp. 961–62, 964–65; Kevin Sweeney, "Rum, Romanism, Representation, and Reform: Coalition Politics in Massachusetts, 1847–1853," *Civil War History* 22 (June 1976): 116–37.

CHAPTER 9

1. Frederick Jackson Turner, *The Frontier in American History* (New York: Holt, Rinehart and Winston, 1920), pp. 350–51.

2. U.S. Congress, Senate, *Reports of the Immigration Commission*, 8 vols., 61st Cong., 3d sess., Document 747 (1911), I: 76–77, 134.

3. Sister M. Evangeline Thomas, *Nativism in the Old Northwest, 1850–1860* (Washington, D.C.: Catholic University Press, 1936), pp. 19, 150, 164–74; John A. Hawgood, *The Tragedy of German-America* (New York: G. P. Putnam's Sons, 1940), pp. 33, 238; Marcus Lee Hansen, *The Atlantic Migration* (Cambridge, Mass.: Harvard University Press, 1940), pp. 301–2; Ray Allen Billington, *The Protestant Crusade, 1800–1860* (Chicago, Quadrangle Books, 1964), pp. 395–97; George M. Stephenson, "Nativism in the Forties and Fifties, with Special Reference to the Mississippi Valley," *Mississippi Valley Historical Review* 9 (Dec. 1922): 188–89.

4. Thomas, *Nativism in the Old Northwest*, p. 151; Hawgood, *Tragedy of German-America*, pp. 34–40. German immigrants found work in skilled trades—baking, apparel, tailoring, shoemaking—whereas the Irish usually found work as unskilled laborers. See Nora Faires, "Occupational Patterns of German-Americans in Nineteenth Century Cities," in Hartmut Keil and John B. Jentz, eds., *German Workers in Industrial Chicago* (De Kalb: Northern Illinois University Press, 1983), pp. 37–39.

5. Carl F. Brand, "The History of the Know Nothing Party in Indiana," *Indiana Magazine of History* 18 (Mar., June, Dec. 1922): 47, 58–61, 74. Brand, like other students of the Know Nothings, complained about the lack of council records (destroyed when the movement disbanded) and the compulsive secrecy that proved a problem to the organization's historians as well as to its contemporary enemies. See also George W. Julian, *Political Recollections, 1840–1872* (Chicago: Jansen, McClurg, 1884), pp. 140–42.

6. Brand, "History of the Know Nothing Party in Indiana," pp. 64, 66, 71–74; Richard H. Sewell, *Bullets for Freedom* (New York: Oxford University Press, 1976), pp. 272–73.

7. Brand, "History of the Know Nothing Party in Indiana," pp. 68, 79–80, 191–96, 200, 268–69, 282. On the ways the sectional and slavery controversy doomed the Know Nothings in Ohio, see Stephen E. Maizlish, "Know Nothing Movement in the Antebellum North," in William E. Gienapp, et al., *Essays on American Antebellum Politics, 1840–1860* (College Station: Texas A & M University Press, 1982), pp. 182–98.

8. Joseph Schafer, "Know-Nothingism in Wisconsin," *Wisconsin Magazine of History* 8 (Sept. 1924): 8–21; Hawgood, *Tragedy of German-America*, pp. 50–51; Ronald P. Formisano, "Ethnicity and Party in Michigan, 1854–1860," in Frederick C. Luebke, ed., *Ethnic Voters and the Election of Lincoln* (Lincoln: University of Nebraska Press, 1971), pp. 181–82; Harry J. Carman and Reinhard H. Luthin, "Some Aspects of the Know-Nothing Movement Reconsidered," *South Atlantic Quarterly* 39 (Apr. 1940): 223–26; Paul Kleppner, *The Cross of Culture* (New York: Free Press, 1970), pp. 40–42, 76.

9. John P. Senning, "The Know-Nothing Movement in Illinois, 1854–1856," *Journal of the Illinois State Historical Society* 7 (Apr. 1954): 9–13; *Illinois State Register*, 16 Aug. 1954.

10. Senning, "Know-Nothing Movement in Illinois," pp. 7, 18–29.

11. Peyton Hurt, "The Rise and Fall of the Know Nothings in California," *Quarterly of the California Historical Society* 9 (Mar. and June 1930): 36–37, 66.

12. Ibid., pp. 19–27.

13. Ibid., pp. 32–66.

14. Stephenson, "Nativism in the Forties and Fifties," pp. 199–201; Kleppner, *Cross of Culture*, p. 103; Paul Kleppner, *The Third Electoral System, 1853–1892* (Chapel Hill: University of North Carolina Press, 1959), pp. 71–72; Hansen, *Atlantic Migration*, p. 304; Sewell, *Bullets for Freedom*, pp. 274–75; Ronald P. Formisano, *The Birth of Mass Political Parties: Michigan, 1827–1881* (Princeton: Princeton University Press, 1971), pp. 242–65.

15. U.S. Senate, *Reports of the Immigration Commission*, 1:128–29; J. D. B. De Bow, *Statistical View of the United States: Compendium of the Seventh Census* (Washington, D.C.: Senate Printer, 1854), p. 61.

16. William G. Bean, "An Aspect of Know Nothingism: The Immigrant and Slavery," *South Atlantic Quarterly* 23 (Oct. 1924): 324–34; Billington, *Protestant Crusade*, pp. 241–42, 393–94; George M. Stephenson, *A History of American Immigration, 1820–1924* (Boston: Ginn, 1926), pp. 116–17.

17. W. S. Tisdale, *Know Nothing Almanac for 1856 or True American's Manual* (New York: DeWitt and Davenport, 1855), pp. 60–62; Arthur C. Cole, "Nativism in the Lower Mississippi Valley," *Proceedings of the Mississippi Valley Historical Association*, ed. Benjamin F. Shambaugh (Cedar Rapids, Iowa: Torch Press, 1913), 6:273–74; *Speech of the Honorable S. Adams of Mississippi, United States Senator, on Bill to Amend Naturalization Laws* (Washington, D.C., 1856), pp. 1–16.

18. *Congressional Globe*, 33d Cong., 1st sess., 15 Mar. 1854, p. 373; Bean, "Aspect of Know Nothingism," pp. 331–34; W. Darrell Overdyke, *The Know-Nothing Party in the South* (Baton Rouge: Louisiana State University Press, 1950), pp. 130–64.

19. Sister Agnes Geraldine McGann, *Nativism in Kentucky to 1860* (Washington, D.C.: Catholic University of America Press, 1944), pp. 21, 56–57; James R. Robertson, "Sectionalism in Kentucky from 1855 to 1865," *Mississippi Valley Historical Review* 4 (June 1917): 53–55.

20. Robertson, "Sectionalism in Kentucky," p. 55; McGann, *Nativism in Kentucky*, pp. 59–75; *Louisville Times*, 12 Jan. 1855.

21. McGann, *Nativism in Kentucky*, pp. 84–98; Brand, "History of the Know Nothing Party in Indiana," pp. 84–85; Reuben Maury, *The Wars of the Godly* (New York: Robert T. McBride, 1928), pp. 141–42; *Congressional Globe*, 34th Cong., 1st sess., 1 July 1856, p. 712.

22. McGann, *Nativism in Kentucky*, pp. 114–18; *Congressional Globe*, 34th Cong., 2d sess., 16 Aug. 1856, p. 2167.

23. *Speech of L. M. Cox of Kentucky, House of Representatives, Decem-*

ber 16 and 17, 1855 on *Principles of National American Party* (Washington, D.C., 1855), pp. 1–5.

24. Sister Paul of the Cross McGrath, *Political Nativism in Texas, 1825–1860* (Washington, D.C.: Catholic University of America Press, 1930), pp. 9–193.

25. Philip Morrison Rice, "The Know-Nothing Party in Virginia, 1854–1856," *Virginia Magazine of History and Biography* 55 (Jan., Apr. 1947): 61–73, 160–161; Bean, "Aspect of Know Nothingism," pp. 328–29. A southerner, Kenneth Raynor of North Carolina, had proposed the "third degree of membership," the "Union degree," at the National Council meeting in Cincinnati in November 1854. It was a pledge of fidelity to the Union, to "discourage and denounce any attempt coming from any quarter to destroy or subvert it or to weaken its bonds" (ibid.).

26. Henry A. Wise, *Religious Liberty: Equality of Civil Rights among Native and Naturalized Citizens (The Virginia Campaign of 1855) and Governor Wise's Letter on Know-Nothingism* (Richmond, 1855), pp. 3–31, 53–59. Other Virginia politicians made similar arguments. See, for example, *Speech of J. S. Millson, Virginia, House of Representatives, February 23, 1855 on The Know Nothings* (Washington, D.C., 1855), pp. 4–6.

27. Wise, *Religious Liberty*, pp. 64–67; M. W. Cluskey, ed., *The Political Text Book or Encyclopedia* 9 (Philadelphia: James Smith & Co., 1859): 283–98; Rice, "Know Nothing Party in Virginia," pp. 162–67.

28. Leon C. Soule, *The Know Nothing Party in New Orleans* (Baton Rouge: Louisiana Historical Association, 1961), pp. 3–4; Hansen *Atlantic Migration*, p. 9; Cole, "Nativism in the Lower Mississippi Valley," pp. 26–62, 268–69.

29. Soule, *Know Nothing Party in New Orleans*, pp. 3–75; *Daily Picayune* (New Orleans), 11 Nov. 1853; Earl F. Niehaus, *The Irish in New Orleans, 1800–1860* (Baton Rouge: Louisiana State University Press, 1965), pp. 59–92; Charles Gayarre, *Address to the People of Louisiana on the State of the Parties* (New Orleans: Sherman & Wharton, 1855), pp. 18–36.

30. Soule, *Know Nothing Party in New Orleans*, pp. 66–120; Gayarre, *Address*, pp. 20–28.

31. Lawrence F. Schmeckebier, *History of the Know Nothing Party in Maryland* (Baltimore: Johns Hopkins Press, 1899), pp. 23–25; Jean H. Baker, *Ambivalent Americans: The Know-Nothing Party in Maryland* (Baltimore: Johns Hopkins University Press, 1977), pp. 4–20.

32. Baker, *Ambivalent Americans*, pp. 20–25.

33. Benjamin Tuska, *Know-Nothingism in Baltimore, 1854–1860* (New York: 1925), pp. 4–15; Billington, *Protestant Crusade*, pp. 421–25; Schmeckebier, *History of the Know Nothing Party in Maryland*, pp. 40–42.

34. Baker, *Ambivalent Americans*, pp. 2–3; Tuska, *Know-Nothingism in Baltimore*, p. 3; Schmeckebier, *History of the Know Nothing Party in Maryland*, 17, 44–45.

35. *Speech of Augustus R. Sollers, Maryland, House of Representatives, on Defense of Americanism* (Washington, D. C., 1857), pp. 1–2; Schmecke-

bier, *History of the Know Nothing Party in Maryland*, p. 27, Baker, *Ambivalent Americans*, pp. 29–31, 38.

36. *Speech of Augustus R. Sollers*, pp. 2–7; Baker, *Ambivalent Americans*, pp. 62–68, 140–51.

37. Schmeckebier, *History of the Know Nothing Party in Maryland*, pp. 70–114; Tuska, *Know-Nothingism in Baltimore*, pp. 16–32.

38. Baker, *Ambivalent Americans*, pp. 97–107; Schmeckebier, *History of the Know Nothing Party in Maryland*, pp. 114–15.

39. Baker, *Ambivalent Americans*, pp. 152–54; Tuska, *Know-Nothingism in Baltimore*, pp. 32–33.

40. Royce McCrary, "John MacPherson Berrien and the Know-Nothing Movement in Georgia," *Georgia Historical Quarterly* 61 (Spring 1977): 35–42; Augustus B. Longstreet, *Know Nothingism Unveiled* (Washington, D.C., 1855), pp. 1–8; *Speech of the Honorable S. Adams*, pp. 13–16; *Speech of the Honorable James C. Jones of Tennessee, United States Senator on the American Party, August 9, 1856* (Washington, D.C., 1856), pp. 3–7; *Speech of Representative Smith of Alabama, House of Representatives, Jan. 15, 1855 on the American Party and Its Mission* (Washington, D.C., 1855), pp. 1–10; Mark W. Kruman, *Parties and Politics in North Carolina, 1836–1865* (Baton Rouge: Louisiana State University Press, 1983), pp. 159–79.

41. Billington, *Protestant Crusade*, pp. 428–29; Robert J. Rayback, *Millard Fillmore* (Buffalo: Buffalo Historical Society, 1959), pp. 407–9; Kirk H. Porter and Donald B. Johnson, eds., *National Party Platforms, 1840–1956* (Urbana: University of Illinois Press, 1956), pp. 22–23; *Plain Facts and Considerations in Favor of James Buchanan for President* (Boston: Brown, Bazin & Co., 1856), pp. 1–31; Carman and Luthin, "Some Aspects of the Know Nothing Movement," pp. 227–29; Humphrey J. Desmond, *The Know-Nothing Party* (Washington, D.C., New Century Press, 1904), pp. 112–21; John Bach McMaster, *With the Fathers* (New York: D. Appleton and Co., 1899), p. 105.

42. *Citizen* (New York), 28 July, 11, 18 Aug. 1855; Thomas J. Curran, "Know Nothings of New York State" (Ph.D. dissertation, Columbia University, 1963), pp. 266–85; Billington, *Protestant Crusade*, pp. 410–20; Carman and Luthin, "Some Aspects of the Know Nothing Movement," pp. 229–34; Charles Granville Hamilton, *Lincoln and the Know Nothing Movement* (Washington, D.C.: Public Affairs Press, 1954), pp. 8–11.

43. Desmond, *Know-Nothing Party*, pp. 22–40; Baker, *Ambivalent Americans*, 29–44, 61–79, 142–45, 155–58, 165–67; Michael F. Holt, "The Antimasonic and Know-Nothing Parties," in Arthur Schlesinger, ed., *History of U.S. Political Parties*, 4 vols. (New York: Chelsea House, 1973), 1: 600.

Jean Baker, in her careful study of the Know-Nothing party in Maryland, used a variety of analytic techniques familiar to practitioners of the new political history to confirm the middle-class character of many Maryland nativist voters, the passionate nature of nativist rhetoric in the state, and the social backgrounds of nativist leadership. Particularly interesting is her content analysis of Know Nothing speeches, the multiple regression analysis of the Maryland vote in 1856, and her use of tax assessment schedules to assess the relative wealth of Maryland's nativist leaders.

CHAPTER 10

1. John Higham, *Strangers in the Land: Patterns of American Nativism, 1860–1925* (1955; 2d ed. New York: Atheneum, 1963), pp. 15–19, 20–28. Since its appearance, this elegant, insightful book has been the standard work on American nativism after the Civil War.

2. U.S. Congress, Senate, *Reports of the Immigration Commission*, 8 vols., 61st Cong., 3d sess., Document 747 (1911), 1: 82–96, 134–37, 149–53, 167, 182; Philip Taylor, *The Distant Magnet: European Emigration to the U.S.A.* (New York: Harper & Row, 1971), pp. 48–65; National Industrial Conference Board, *The Immigration Problem in the United States*, Research Report 58 (New York: National Industrial Conference Board, 1923), pp. 6–17, 72, 123.

3. Roy L. Garis, *Immigration Restriction: A Study of Opposition to and Regulation of Immigration into the United States* (New York: Macmillan, 1927), pp. 86–89, 94–95, 191–93, 203–5, 292–315; Lucie Cheng and Edna Bonacich, eds., *Labor under Capitalism: Asian Workers in the United States* (Berkeley and Los Angeles: University of California Press, 1984), pp. 74–77; Robert D. Parmet, *Labor and Immigration in Industrial America* (Boston: Twayne, 1981), pp. 28–44, 160–68.

4. Jack Chen, *The Chinese in America* (San Francisco: Harper & Row, 1980), pp. 127–49, 160–69; Elmer Clarence Sandmeyer, *The Anti-Chinese Movement in California* (Urbana: University of Illinois Press, 1939), pp. 40–41, 84–85, 93, 109–11; Jules Alexander Karlin, "The Anti-Chinese Outbreaks in Seattle, 1885," and "The Anti-Chinese Outbreaks in Tacoma, 1885," William R. Locklear, "The Celestials and the Angels: Anti-Chinese Movements in Los Angeles, 1882," and Roy T. Wortman, "Denver's Anti-Chinese Riot, 1880," in Roger Daniels, ed., *Anti-Chinese Violence in North America* (New York: Arno Press, 1978), pp. 103–291; Rose Hun Lee, *The Chinese in the United States* (Hong Kong: Hong Kong University Press, 1960), pp. 73–75; Stanford M. Lyman, *Chinese Americans* (New York: Random House, 1974), pp. 70–85.

5. Roger Daniels, *The Politics of Prejudice: The Anti-Japanese Movement in California and the Struggle for Japanese Exclusion* (Berkeley and Los Angeles: University of California Press, 1962), pp. 16–30, 44–45; Yamato Ichihashi, "Anti-Japanese Agitation," in Roger Daniels and Spencer C. Olin, Jr., eds., *Racism in California* (New York: Macmillan, 1972), pp. 105–15.

6. Higham, *Strangers in the Land*, pp. 25–44; Seymour Martin Lipset and Earl Raab, *The Politics of Unreason: Right-Wing Extremism in America, 1790–1970*, pp. 76–79; Alvin P. Stauffer, "Anti-Catholicism in American

Politics, 1865–1900" (Ph.D. dissertation, Harvard University, 1933), pp. 2–80.

7. Woodrow Wilson, *A History of the American People*, 5 vols. (New York: Harper & Brothers, 1901–2), 5: 212–13; Garis, *Immigration Restriction*, pp. 216–20; Edward A. Ross, *The Old World in the New* (New York: Century Co., 1914), pp. 254–85, 287, 291, 296–304; Higham, *Strangers in the Land*, pp. 35–42, 49–53.

8. Joseph Arthur de Gobineau, *The Inequality of Human Races* (New York: G. P. Putnam's Sons, 1915), pp. 117–81, 205–12; Michael D. Biddis, *Father of Racist Ideology* (London: Weidenfeld and Nicolson, 1970), pp. 121–31, 265–71; Houston Stewart Chamberlain, *The Foundations of the Nineteenth Century*, 3 vols. (New York: John Lane, 1909), 1: 256–58, 269, 329–56; Ross, *Old World in the New*, pp. 95–167, 195–256; Higham, *Strangers in the Land*, pp. 35–42, 49–53.

9. Thomas E. Watson's *Life and Times of Andrew Jackson* is quoted in Richard Hofstadter, *The Age of Reform: From Bryan to F.D.R.* (New York: Knopf, 1955), p. 82. See also Ross, *Old World in the New*, pp. 127–40, 96–120.

10. Watson quoted in Hofstadter, *Age of Reform*, p. 82.

11. Higham suggests that the "pioneers of the nativist revival were not the appointed representatives of militant labor or the conscious spokesmen of adamant capital" because this movement would attract men not "securely attached to the congealing power groups that were straining the social fabric." Instead, it drew in those petty businessmen, nonunionized workers, and white-collar folk whose "very in-betweenness . . . left them easy victims of demoralization" (*Strangers in the Land*, p. 53).

12. Robert F. Foerster, *The Italian Emigration of Our Times*, (Cambridge, Mass.: Harvard University Press, 1924), pp. 98–105, 327–28; Humbert S. Nelli, *From Immigrants to Ethnics: The Italian Americans* (New York: Oxford University Press, 1983), pp. 19–72; Andrew Rolle, *The Italian Americans: Troubled Roots* (New York: Free Press, 1980), pp. 1–27; Nathan Glazer and Daniel Patrick Moynihan, *Beyond the Melting Pot* (Cambridge, Mass.: M.I.T. Press, 1963), pp. 184–86; Thomas Kessner, *The Golden Door* (New York: Oxford University Press, 1977), pp. 30–31; Joseph A. Wytrwal, *America's Polish Heritage* (Detroit: Endurance Press, 1961), pp. 109–10; William I. Thomas and Florian Zaniecki, "The Polish-American Community," in Leonard Dinerstein and Fred Cople Jaher, eds., *The Aliens* (New York: Appleton Century Crofts, 1970), pp. 254–57; George J. Prpic, *South Slavic Immigration in America* (Boston: Twayne, 1978), pp. 78–82; Irving Howe, *World of Our Fathers* (New York: Harcourt Brace Jovanovich, 1976), pp. 5–6, 26–29; Emily Greene Balch, "The Newer Slavic Immigration," in Philip Davis, ed., *Immigration and Americanization* (Boston: Ginn and Co., 1920), pp. 155–69.

13. Glazer and Moynihan, *Beyond the Melting Pot*, pp. 188–202; Rolle, *Italian Americans*, pp. 134–39; Nelli, *From Immigrants to Ethnics*, pp. 77–79, 144–47; Edward C. Banfield, *The Moral Basis of a Backward Society*

(Glencoe, Ill.: Free Press, 1958), pp. 7–161; Emily G. Balch, *Our Slavic Fellow Citizens* (New York: Charities Publication, 1919), pp. 317–20; Kessner, *Golden Door*, p. 172; Leonard Covello, *The Social Background of the Italo-American School Child* (Leiden: E. J. Brill, 1967), pp. 192–391; Foerster, *Italian Emigration*, pp. 371–73; Rudolph J. Vecoli, "Contadini in Chicago: A Critique of the Uprooted," *Journal of American History* 51 (Dec. 1964): 404–417; Richard Maxwell Brown, *Strain of Violence* (New York: Oxford University Press, 1975), p. 160.

14. Foerster, *Italian Emigration*, pp. 342–62; Prpic, *South Slavic Immigration*, p. 73; Wytrwal, *America's Polish Heritage*, pp. 84–85; quoted in Higham, *Strangers in the Land*, pp. 65–66, 160; Appleton Morgan, "What Shall We Do with the 'Dago'?" *Popular Science Monthly* 38 (1890): 177. On immigrant overcrowding in housing and the limited occupational opportunities available, see U.S. Senate, *Reports of the Immigration Commission*, 1: 430–31, 826–27.

15. John Higham, "Anti-Semitism in the Gilded Age: A Reinterpretation," *Mississippi Valley Historical Review* 43 (Mar. 1957): 577–78; George M. Stephenson, *A History of American Immigration* (Boston: Ginn and Company, 1926), p. 147; John Higham, *Send These to Me* (New York: Atheneum, 1975), pp. 113, 125–29, 130–35, 183–84; Worthington Chauncey Ford, ed., *Letters of Henry Adams, 1892–1918* (Boston: Houghton Mifflin, 1938), pp. 35, 338, 620; Ernest Samuels, *Henry Adams: The Major Phase* (Cambridge, Mass.: Harvard University Press, 1964), pp. 129, 167, 168, 356–57; Michael Selzer, ed., *"Kike": Anti-Semitism in America* (New York: World, 1972), pp. 50–76.

16. See Miscellaneous Letters and Papers, 1887–92, Morton House Conference Letters and Papers, 1889, and Philadelphia Conference Papers, 1890–91, in Henry Baldwin Papers, New York Public Library, Division of Manuscripts, New York (cited hereafter as Baldwin Papers). See also Scrapbook, 1891–92, in Baldwin Papers for the description of the National League for the Protection of American Institutions, dated 24 Dec. 1889; *Papers Presented to the Conference of American and Protestant Organizations* (Philadelphia: Camp News, 1889), pp. 5–6; *Constitution of the National Association of Loyal Men of American Liberty* (Boston: Loyal Men of American Liberty, 1890), pp. 3–4; *Ritual and Full Information Concerning the American Patriotic* (New York: 1891); *By Laws of the United Order of Native Americans* (San José: A. S. York, 1888); *How to Become a Member of the Order of United American Mechanics* (New York: G. H. Burton, 1882), pp. 1–5. For the list of organizations represented at Morton House, see Baldwin to Executive Officers of American and Protestant Organizations of the United States, 22 Feb. 1889, Baldwin Papers. See also Baldwin, circular letter, 25 Nov. 1887, in ibid.

17. *The Patriotic Order Sons of America: Something about the Order* (Philadelphia: State Camp, 1888–89), pp. 3–15; *The Patriotic Order Sons of America: Platform of Principles* (Cincinnati: Johns, Brumbeck, 1889), pp. 2–7; *Official Pocket Dictionary, Patriotic Order Sons of America*

(Philadelphia: H. Stager, 1889), pp. 1–69; *Papers Presented to the Conference*, pp. 13–18 (see remarks of Charles Hoyt of United Americans); Henry F. Bowers to Baldwin, 22 Dec. 1890, H. J. Deily to Baldwin, 5 June 1891, Charles L. Hoyt to Baldwin, 10 Nov. 1887, Baldwin to J. F. Hanlin, 20 Jan. 1888, H. C. Pake (national secretary of the American Patriotic League) to Baldwin, 3 Dec. 1892, Baldwin Papers; *Ritual and Full Information Concerning the American Patriotic League* (New York: American Patriotic League, 1891), pp. 4–9.

18. Baldwin to Harry Miner, 9 Mar. 1893, C. V. Haskins to Baldwin, 15 Oct. 1892, Baldwin to George A. Minor, 4 Oct. 1891, Baldwin Papers; *Papers Presented to the Conference*, p. 11.

19. Donald L. Kinzer, *An Episode in Anti-Catholicism: The American Protective Association* (Seattle: University of Washington Press, 1964), pp. 35–41; John Higham, "The Mind of a Nativist: Henry F. Bowers and the A.P.A.," *American Quarterly* 55 (Spring 1952): 16–20.

20. Kinzer, *Episode in Anti-Catholicism*, pp. 19–25; Higham, *Strangers in the Land*, pp. 58–60. On anti-Catholic feelings and their impact on Republican party politics, see Paul Kleppner, *The Third Electoral System, 1853–1892* (Chapel Hill: University of North Carolina Press, 1979), pp. 218–19, 228–37.

21. Humphrey J. Desmond, *The A.P.A. Movement* (Washington, D. C.: New Century Press, 1912), pp. 10–12, 63–66; Kinzer, *Episode in Anti-Catholicism*, pp. 58–82, 90–93, 95–139, 178–79; Higham, *Strangers in the Land*, pp. 80–81, 88–90; W. J. H. Traynor, "Policy and Power of the A.P.A.," *North American Review* 162 (June 1896): 658–66; W. J. H. Traynor, "The Menace of Romanism," *North American Review* 161 (Aug. 1895): 129–35; K. Gerald Marsden, "Patriotic Societies and American Labor: The American Protective Association in Wisconsin," *Wisconsin Magazine of History* 41 (Summer 1958): 288–89; Bowers to Baldwin, 12 June 1895, Baldwin Papers; Lipset and Raab, *Politics of Unreason*, p. 89. Donald Kinzer estimates the total size of all patriotic societies in the years of the APA's greatest strength at some 2.5 million, including 175,000 followers in California, 150,000 in New York, 165,000 in Pennsylvania, 163,000 in Ohio, 176,000 in Wisconsin, and 125,000 in Michigan.

22. "The Society of Jesus: Will It Seat the Next Pope in Washington," "The Moral Code of the Jesuits," "Satolli and the Jesuits Must Go," "Rome's Greed for Money," in *A.P.A. Magazine* (San Francisco) 1 (June 1895): 1–96; "The Confession Box," *A.P.A. Magazine* 2 (Dec. 1895): 713; R. W. Thompson, *The Footprints of the Jesuits* (New York: Hunt & Easton, 1894), pp. 3, 18–32; "The Black Pope," *Patriot: An Advocate of Americanism* (Chicago) 1 (Mar. 1891): 3–4; *Wisconsin Patriot* (Milwaukee), 12 Jan. 1894; W. J. H. Traynor, "The Aims and Methods of the A.P.A.," *North American Review* 159 (July 1894): 67–70; Desmond, *A.P.A. Movement*, pp. 18–26. There were foreign-born Americans in the APA, notably Scandinavians in Minnesota. Traynor endorsed their membership and even promoted APA units in Canada, on the curious grounds that "if we drive" the Catholics from

America, they will only retreat to Canada and threaten "our Republic's cherished institutions" from across the border. See "Annual Address by W. J. H. Traynor," *A.P.A. Magazine* 1 (July 1895): 166–68.

23. "This Country Is in Danger" and "President Lincoln's Assassination Is Traced Directly to the Doors of Rome," *A.P.A. Magazine* 1 (Nov. 1895): 547–72; "Pat's Grip on the Government," *A.P.A. Magazine* 1 (July 1895): 110–12; "The Pope's Irish in American Politics," *A.P.A. Magazine* 1 (Nov. 1895): 518–31; "Pat and His Church," *A.P.A. Magazine* 1 (Oct. 1895): 409–13; *Patriot* (Chicago) 1 (June 1891): 3–19; *Wisconsin Patriot*, 28 Dec. 1895. The movement's anti-Catholic attacks elicited an angry response. See, for example, J. J. Tighe's assessment of an "organization based on hatred of Christ and his Church" in Rev. J. J. Tighe, *The A.P.A.* (New York: D. P. Murphy, 1893), pp. 5–57; Elbert Hubbard's dismissal of the movement as "paranoia" in action in Elbert Hubbard, "A New Disease," *Arena* 10 (June 1894): 77–78; and Washington Gladden, "The Anti-Catholic Crusade," *Century Magazine* 48 (Mar. 1894): 789–95.

24. Desmond, *A.P.A. Movement*; Lipset and Raab, *Politics of Unreason*, pp. 81–82; Michael Williams, *Shadow of the Pope* (New York: McGraw-Hill, 1932), pp. 98–99; Traynor, "Annual Address," *A.P.A. Magazine* 1 (July 1895): 174; 3 (Feb. 1897): 1637; 3 (Apr. 1897): 1865, 1878; *American Patriot* (San Francisco), 11 Oct. 1894.

25. Joseph P. Camp (treasurer of the National Home Labor League of America) to Baldwin, 17 Feb. 1891, Baldwin Papers; *National Spirit* (published by the NHLL in Philadelphia), 1 Jan. 1891; Higham, *Strangers in the Land*, pp. 87–96. Some nativist publications attacked predatory big business and defended workers struggling against exploitation. See the *Wisconsin Patriot*, 25 Aug. 1894, 8 Aug. 1896. But if the Pullman Company could be assailed for mistreatment of the labor force, the APA editors were also fearful of "Jesuits" behind the radical unions, attacking the American Railway Union, and Eugene V. Debs, that "grand steerer of the Huns, the Slavs, the Micks and the Dagos" who were flooding the country (*Wisconsin Patriot*, 22, 29 Sept. 1896, 9 Oct. 1897, 18 Apr. 1896). See also Lipset and Raab, *Politics of Unreason*, pp. 83–88; Stauffer, "Anti-Catholicism in American Politics," pp. 186–223, 274, 348–49.

26. W. J. Phillips, "Convent's Horror," *A.P.A. Magazine* 2 (Mar. 1896): 949–52; ads for Maria Monk in ibid., pp. 943–44; "A Priestly Liar," *A.P.A. Magazine* 1 (June 1895): 32–33; Tighe, *A.P.A.*, p. 36; *Omaha American*, 25 Nov. 1892; *Wisconsin Patriot*, 10 Aug. 1895. Traynor, echoing the concerns of his Know Nothing predecessors, called for "nunneries open to public inspection" in his annual address in 1895 (*A.P.A. Magazine* 1 [July 1895]: 169).

27. Margaret L. Shepherd, *My Life in the Convent* (Toledo: L. J. King), pp. 5, 88–126, 162–79, 182–200, 234–56. But nativism in the 1890s did offer a slowly changing image of women. Although women were still portrayed as helpless victims in the convent literature, APA members pointed with pride at how much better they were treated in the United States than in the despised alien lands across the ocean. Women's nativist orders, sister

groups to the fraternities, emerged, among them the National Daughters of Liberty and the Women's American Protective Association. See *Constitution of the National Council Daughters of Liberty* (New York: G. Burton, 1887), pp. 1–36, and Jane Roy to Baldwin, 6 Jan. 1891, Baldwin Papers. Still, true equality of the sexes frightened the nativists and one newspaper printed a futuristic fantasy in which the "New Woman" came to power, emasculating men, usurping their power and authority. See "Women in the Next Century," (set in 1945), in *Wisconsin Patriot*, 18 May 1895. On the relationship between the treatment of women in the nativist movements of the 1840s and 1890s, see David H. Bennett, "Women and the Nativist Movement," in Carol V. R. George, ed., *"Remember the Ladies": New Perspectives on Women in American History* (Syracuse: Syracuse University Press, 1975), pp. 71–89.

28. Walter T. K. Nugent, *The Tolerant Populists* (Chicago: University of Chicago Press, 1963), pp. 153–67; Kinzer, *Episode in Anti-Catholicism*, pp. 119–20, 140–42, 157–69; Desmond, *A.P.A.*, pp. 31–34; Paul Kleppner, *The Cross of Culture* (New York: Free Press, 1970), pp. 251–56, 266–67; Higham, *Strangers in the Land*, pp. 84–85; Felix Wepost, "A.P.A. in Politics," *A.P.A. Magazine* 1 (Aug. 1895): 228. Catholic voters "of all types of ethnicity" were overwhelmingly Democratic.

29. Wepost, "A.P.A. in Politics," pp. 228–29; Kinzer, *Episode in Anti-Catholicism*, pp. 109–74.

30. Desmond, *A.P.A. Movement*, pp. 50–52, 77–87, 91–94; Kinzer, *Episode in Anti-Catholicism*, pp. 181–87, 205–12, 214–39; *A.P.A. Magazine* 2 (Aug. 1896): 1313. Some members of the movement continued to denounce McKinley after the election; the *Wisconsin Patriot*, 27 Feb. 1897, reported that "Archbishop Ireland was said to have helped in the selection of his Cabinet." Paul Kleppner in *The Cross of Culture*, p. 351, observes that "to be attacked by an anti-Catholic order" was "no liability to a candidate who sought to broaden the base of his party's support by attracting Catholic voters" disillusioned with the Democrats.

31. Higham, *Strangers in the Land*, pp. 82–87; Desmond, *A.P.A. Movement*, pp. 73, 91–94.

32. Ignatius Donnelly, *Caesar's Column*, ed. Walter B. Rideout (1890; rpt. Cambridge, Mass.: Harvard University Press, 1960), pp. 30–43, 123–31, 146–53; William H. Harvey, *Coin's Financial School* (1894; rpt. Cambridge, Mass.: Harvard University Press, 1963), pp. 58–60; Higham, *Send These to Me*, pp. 130–32; David Brion Davis, ed., *The Fear of Conspiracy* (Ithaca: Cornell University Press, 1971), pp. 195–200.

33. U.S. Senate, *Reports of the Immigration Commission*, 1: 23–48, 554–600, 41: 103–10; Higham, *Strangers in the Land*, pp. 158–93; Isaac A. Hourwich, *Immigration and Labor: The Economic Aspects of European Immigration to the United States* (1912; rpt. New York: Arno Press, 1969), pp. 48–102, 240–42, 360–62.

34. On the history of nativism in this period, see Higham, *Strangers in the Land*, pp. 106–93. The assault on the "great fallacy of the melting pot" is found in Henry Pratt Fairchild, *Immigration: A World Movement and Its*

American Significance (New York: Macmillan, 1913), pp. 133–34, 189–201, 306–7, 363, 409–21, 442–59. On Tom Watson and Leo Frank, see C. Vann Woodward, *Tom Watson: Agrarian Rebel* (Savannah, Ga.: Beehive Press, 1973), pp. 360–89. See also Higham, *Send These to Me,* p. 128; Gustave LeBon, *The Crowd* (London: Ernest Beim, 1896), pp. 42–43; Gustave LeBon, *The World in Revolt* (New York: Macmillan, 1921), pp. 19–21; Madison Grant, *The Passing of the Great Race: The Racial Basis of European History,* rev. ed. (New York: Charles Scribner's Sons, 1918), pp. 3–55; Lipset and Raab, *Politics of Unreason,* pp. 96–98, 102–3.

CHAPTER 11

1. John Higham, *Strangers in the Land: Patterns of American Nativism, 1860–1925* (1955, 2d ed. New York: Atheneum, 1963), pp. 194–204; *New York Times,* 1 Feb. 1915.

2. Emerson Hough, *The Web: A Revelation of Patriotism* (Chicago: National Directors of the American Protective League, 1919), pp. 63–69, 420–46; La Vern J. Rippley, *The German-Americans* (Boston: Twayne, 1976), pp. 185–86; John A. Hawgood, *The Tragedy of German-America* (New York: G. P. Putnam's Sons, 1940), pp. 296–97; Higham, *Strangers in the Land,* pp. 200–218; Earl E. Sperry, *The Tentacles of the German Octopus in America* (New York: National Security League, 1918), pp. 2, 7–12; Albert Bushnell Hart, ed., *America at War* (New York: National Security League, 1918), pp. 316–17; Frederick C. Luebke, *Bonds of Loyalty: German-Americans and World War I* (DeKalb: Northern Illinois University Press, 1974), pp. 57–307; Harold M. Hyman, *To Try Men's Souls: Loyalty Tests in American History* (Berkeley and Los Angeles: University of California Press, 1959), pp. 267–97. On Military Intelligence Division monitoring, see reports of "possible German activities in W.W.I." in Globe, Arizona, 11 May 1917, Italian anarchists in Sagamore, Massachusetts, 13 June 1917, and alleged sabotage plans for Great Lakes shipping, 18 June, 10 July 1917, in *U.S. Military Intelligence Reports: Surveillance of Radicals in the United States, 1917–1941,* a microfilm project (Frederick, Md.: University Publications of America, 1984), from Record Group 165, Film Series 101120, Reel 1, Numbers 11, 58, 60, National Archives (hereafter *Surveillance of Radicals*).

3. Mercer Green Johnston, *Patriotism and Radicalism* (Boston: Sherman, French, 1917), pp. 21–22; Archibald B. Roosevelt, comp. *Theodore Roosevelt on Race Riots, Reds, Crime* (Sayville, N.Y.: Probe Publishers, 1969), pp. 36–37 (this "compilation" of TR's comments and writings on a variety of subjects presents a distorted picture based on material taken out of context, but some passages do reflect the former president's views in 1918). See also Arthur L. Frothingham, *National Security League Handbook of War Facts and Peace Problems* (New York: Committee on Organized Education of National Security League, 1919), pp. 104, 190. The Military Intelligence

Division investigated "reports" of "German sources" funding the IWW and German spies encouraging Wobblies to secure work in shipyards and then slow down production through a "folded arms" strategy. See *Surveillance of Radicals,* Reel 1, No. 69, and Reel 9, No. 753.

4. Paul L. Murphy, "Sources and Nature of Intolerance in the 1920's," *Journal of American History* 51 (June 1964): 62–64; Higham, *Strangers in the Land,* pp. 202–4, 209–10, 220–22; Irving Howe and Lewis Coser, *The American Communist Party* (New York: Frederick A. Praeger, 1962), pp. 22–24; William Preston, Jr., *Aliens and Dissenters: Federal Suppression of Radicals, 1903–1933* (New York: Harper & Row, 1966), pp. 88–207; *New York Times,* 7 July, 11 Aug., 15, 21 Sept. 1918. See also *Surveillance of Radicals,* Reel 9, No. 753, "IWW Situation in Northwest, April 29, 1918"; Sidney Lens, *Radicalism in America* (New York: Crowell, 1969), pp. 254–55.

5. Robert K. Murray, *Red Scare* (Minneapolis: University of Minnesota Press, 1955), pp. 2–15; Clayton R. Lusk, "Radicalism under Inquiry," *American Review of Reviews* 61 (Feb. 1920): 167–68; Julian F. Jaffe, *Crusade against Radicalism: New York during the Red Scare, 1914–1924* (Port Washington, N.Y.: Kennikat Press, 1972), p. 119; Frothingham, *National Security League Handbook,* pp. 105–6; Higham, *Strangers in the Land,* p. 223. On the Creel Committee, see George Creel, *How We Advertised America* (New York: Harper & Brothers, 1920), pp. 16–221.

6. Murray, *Red Scare,* pp. 54–68, 114–66; Higham, *Strangers in the Land,* p. 226; Emerson Hough, "Round Our Town," *Saturday Evening Post* 192 (14 Feb. 1920): 18–19, 90, 192 (21 Feb. 1920): 106; David Brody, *Labor in Crisis* (New York: J. B. Lippincott, 1965), pp. 71, 152. On the Seattle strike, see reports from the Seattle Office of Military Intelligence, 4, 7, 8, 14 Feb. 1919, in *Surveillance of Radicals,* Reel 6, No. 362, and "A World Wave of Anarchy," a ninety-three-page report from the military representative, Postal Censorship Committee, Seattle, in *Surveillance of Radicals,* Reel 13, No. 1114.

7. Theodore Draper, *The Roots of American Communism* (New York: Viking Press, 1957), pp. 148–96; Howe and Coser, *American Communist Party,* pp. 31–46. See also *Surveillance of Radicals,* Reel 10, No. 853, and Reel 12, No. 920.

8. Stanley Coben, *A. Mitchell Palmer: Politician* (New York: Columbia University Press, 1963), pp. 197–209.

9. Ibid., pp. 200–207; *New York Times,* 1, 2 Apr., 4 May 1919; "May Day Riot in Cleveland," in Richard Hofstadter and Michael Wallace, eds., *American Violence: A Documentary History* (New York: Vintage Books, 1971), pp. 351–53; Murray, *Red Scare,* pp. 71–76; *Proceedings and Committees: Caucus of the American Legion, First National Convention* (St. Louis: American Legion, 1919), pp. 114–17. See also "Anarchist Bomb Plot, June 2, 1919" (Chicago) and "Bomb Plot, Aug. 4, 1919" (Boston) in *Surveillance of Radicals,* Reel 14, Nos. 1282, 1285.

10. *New York Times,* 17 Oct. 1919; Coben, *A. Mitchell Palmer,* pp. 207–

16; Murray, *Red Scare*, pp. 79–88, 195–98; "Weekly Bulletin on Radical Activities," 19–24, 25–31 Jan., 1–7 Feb., 7–13, 20–27 Mar. 1920, in *Surveillance of Radicals*, Reel 16, No. 1683.

11. Coben, *A. Mitchell Palmer*, pp. 217–22; Murray, *Red Scare*, pp. 183–98, 207–224; Marquis James, "A Verdict for God and Country," *American Legion Weekly* 1 (21 Nov. 1919): 7–9, 27–28; "Centralia 1919," in Hofstadter and Wallace, eds., *American Violence*, pp. 354–56; Ralph Chaplin, *The Centralia Conspiracy* (Chicago: Charles H. Kerr, 1973), pp. 29–70. On Wobblies in the Northwest, see *Surveillance of Radicals*, Reel 5, Nos. 230, 235. On Emma Goldman, see Military Intelligence Reports in ibid., Reel 7, No. 525, and Reel 15, No. 1688.

12. Murray, *Red Scare*, pp. 198–224; Coben, *A. Mitchell Palmer*, pp. 227–30; Howe and Coser, *American Communist Party*, pp. 51–55; Draper, *Roots of American Communism*, pp. 204–5; Frederick R. Barkley, "Jailing Radicals in Detroit," *Nation* 110 (31 Jan. 1920): 136–37; Murray B. Levin, *Political Hysteria in America* (New York: Basic Books, 1971), pp. 62–66; Preston, *Aliens and Dissenters*, pp. 205–37; *New York Times*, 3 Jan. 1920; "Who Is in Back of the Persecution," *One Big Union Monthly* 2 (Jan. 1920): 7, 60; "Raids on Radicals," Military Intelligence Reports, 6, 8, 12, 24 Jan. 1920 (Chicago), *Surveillance of Radicals*, Reel 15, No. 1584.

13. William T. Ellis, "The Fighting Quaker of the Cabinet," *American Review of Reviews* 61 (Jan. 1920): 35–38; Arthur Wallace Dunn, "The Reds in America," *American Review of Reviews* 61 (Feb. 1920): 161–66; A. Mitchell Palmer, "The Case against the Reds," *Forum* 63 (Feb. 1920): 174–185; *Annual Report of the Attorney General of the United States for 1920* (Washington, D.C.: U.S. Government Printing Office, 1920), pp. 172–81; A. Mitchell Palmer, ed., *Red Radicalism As Described by Its Own Leaders* (Washington, D.C.: U.S. Government Printing Office, 1920), pp. 3–18, 20–83; Charles S. Thomas, "The Evils in Our Democracy," *Forum* 61 (Jan. 1919): 50–52; W. L. Whittlesey, "Where Do the Reds Come From: Chiefly Imported, and So Are Their Red Theories," *American Legion Weekly* 2 (30 Jan. 1920): 12–13, 33–34.

14. Jaffe, *Crusade against Radicalism*, pp. 119–97; *Literary Digest*, 24 Jan. 1920, p. 19; New York State Legislature, Joint Legislative Committee Investigating Seditious Activities, Clayton R. Lusk, Chairman, *Revolutionary Radicalism: Its History, Purpose and Tactics* 4 vols. (Albany, N.Y., 1920), 1: 8–10; Lusk, "Radicalism under Inquiry," pp. 167–70.

15. *New York Times*, 16 Apr., 1, 8 May 1920; Louis F. Post, *The Deportations Delirium of Nineteen-Twenty* (Chicago: Charles H. Kerr, 1923), pp. 154–209, 327; Francis Fisher Kane, "The Communist Deportations," *Survey* 44 (24 Apr. 1920): 141–44, 157; Murray, *Red Scare*, pp. 251–56; Preston, *Aliens and Dissenters*, p. 230; Higham, *Strangers in the Land*, pp. 231–32; National Popular Government League, *To the American People: Report Upon the Illegal Practices of the United States Department of Justice* (Washington, D.C.: National Popular Government League, 1920), pp. 1–67; Sidney Howard, "In Judge Anderson's Court," *Survey* 44 (1 May 1920): 182–84. See also Zechariah Chafee, Jr., *Free Speech in the United*

States (Cambridge, Mass.: Harvard University Press, 1946), pp. 196–240, on the deportations.

16. Coben, *A. Mitchell Palmer,* pp. 235–36; Higham, *Strangers in the Land,* p. 233; Murray, *Red Scare,* pp. 256–60; *New York Times,* 1, 2 May 1920.

17. Draper, *Roots of American Communism,* p. 205; Howe and Coser, *American Communist Party,* p. 52; James Weinstein, *The Decline of Socialism in America, 1912–1925* (New York: Vintage Books, 1969), pp. 240–54.

18. Stanley Coben, "A Study in Nativism: The American Red Scare of 1919–1920," *Political Science Quarterly* 79 (Mar. 1964): 52–75; Anthony F. C. Wallace, "Revitalization Movements," *American Anthropologist* 58 (Apr. 1956): 264–81.

19. Robert D. Parmet, *Labor and Immigration in Industrial America* (Boston: Twayne, 1981), pp. 183–90; Alan M. Kraut, *The Huddled Masses: The Immigrant in American Society, 1880–1921* (Arlington Heights, Ill.: Harlan Davidson, 1982), pp. 177–78; Richard H. Easterlin, David Ward, William S. Bernard, and Reed Ueda, *Immigration* (Cambridge, Mass.: Harvard University Press, 1982), pp. 94–99.

CHAPTER 12

1. John Kenneth Galbraith, *The Great Crash, 1929* (New York: Houghton Mifflin, 1954), pp. 6–16.

2. Bruce Barton, *The Man Nobody Knows* (1925; rpt. New York: Bobbs-Merrill, 1962), pp. 32–45, 52–53, 71, 109–17.

3. F. Scott Fitzgerald, *The Great Gatsby* (1925; rpt. New York: Bantam Books, 1945), p. 106.

4. Robert S. Lynd and Helen Merrell Lynd, *Middletown: A Study in American Culture* (New York: Harcourt, Brace, 1929), pp. 500–502; Rowland Berthoff, *An Unsettled People: Social Order and Disorder in America* (New York: Harper & Row, 1971), pp. 444–45; John William Ward, "The Meaning of Lindbergh's Flight," *American Quarterly* 10 (Spring 1958): 3–16; Geoffrey Perrett, *America in the Twenties* (New York: Simon and Schuster, 1982), pp. 207–23.

The use of "celebrity" as a term almost interchangeable with "hero" in this context does not take account of the important distinction made by Daniel J. Boorstin in *The Image* (New York: Atheneum, 1961). In a brilliant and illuminating analysis, Boorstin describes a "celebrity" not as one whose achievement is heroic but as a person well known for his or her "well-knownness." But in the 1920s, perhaps some of the heroes of the age were also celebrities, as the term has come to be used in the 1980s.

5. Paul L. Murphy, "Sources and Nature of Intolerance in the 1920s," *Journal of American History* 51 (June 1964): 66–70; Ferdinand Tönnies, *Gemeinschaft and Gesellschaft,* trans. and ed. Charles P. Loomis (East Lansing: Michigan State University Press, 1957); Henry F. May, "Shifting Per-

spectives on the 1920's," *Mississippi Valley Historical Review* 63 (Sept. 1956): 424–27; Burl Noggle, *Into the Twenties* (Urbana: University of Illinois Press, 1974), pp. 152–56, 170–72.

6. Joseph R. Gusfield, *Symbolic Crusade: Status Politics and the American Temperance Movement* (Urbana: University of Illinois Press, 1966), pp. 139–51; Frederick Lewis Allen, *Only Yesterday* (New York: Harper & Row, 1964), pp. 204–15; Herbert Asbury, "The Noble Experiment of Izzie and Moe," in Isabel Leighton, ed., *The Aspirin Age, 1919–1941* (New York: Simon and Schuster, 1949), pp. 34–49; Paul A. Carter, *Another Part of the Twenties* (New York: Columbia University Press, 1977), pp. 86–102; Joseph R. Gusfield, "Prohibition: The Impact of Political Utopianism," in John Braeman, Robert A. Bremner, and David Brody, eds., *Change and Continuity in Twentieth-Century America: The 1920's* (Columbus: Ohio State University Press, 1968), pp. 257–308; Norman H. Clark, *Deliver Us from Evil: An Interpretation of American Prohibition* (New York: Norton, 1976), pp. 140–80; James A. Timberlake, *Prohibition and the Progressive Movement* (Cambridge, Mass.: Harvard University Press, 1963); Andrew Sinclair, *Prohibition: The Era of Excess* (Boston: Atlantic Monthly Press, 1962), p. 163. See also two contemporary works endorsing the movement: Harry S. Warner, *Prohibition: An Adventure in Freedom* (Westerville, Ohio: World League against Alcoholism, 1928), pp. 96–216, and Roy A. Haynes, *Prohibition Inside Out* (New York: Doubleday, Page, 1923), pp. 166–85.

7. *The International Jew: The World's Foremost Problem*, reprint of a series of articles appearing in the *Dearborn Independent* from 22 May to 2 Oct. 1920 (Dearborn, Mich.: Dearborn Publishing Co., 1920), pp. 9–75, 85–235; *Jewish Activities in the United States*, reprint from articles in the *Dearborn Independent*, 9 Oct. 1920 to 19 Mar. 1921 (Dearborn, Mich.: Dearborn Publishing Co., 1921), pp. 7–185, 197–255; *Jewish Influence in American Life*, reprint of a third selection from articles appearing in the *Dearborn Independent* (Dearborn, Mich.: Dearborn Publishing Co., 1921), pp. 7–166, 191–256.

8. Carey McWilliams, *A Mask for Privilege: Anti-Semitism in America* (Boston: Little, Brown, 1949), pp. 33–38; Emory S. Bogardus, *Immigration and Race Attitudes* (Boston: D. C. Heath, 1928), pp. 19–20; Rabbi Lee J. Levinger, *Anti-Semitism in the United States* (1925; rpt. Westport, Conn.: Greenwood Press, 1972), pp. 67–84.

9. There is a rich literature concerning fundamentalism and the fundamentalist controversy of the 1920s. Ernest Sandeen, *The Roots of Fundamentalism: British and American Millenarianism, 1800–1930* (Chicago: University of Chicago Press, 1970), pp. xi–xv, 103–31, argues that American fundamentalism was not a reaction to a social setting in which urban-industrial developments and status anxieties played the key role but was the product of a long-standing theological controversy, a tradition of millenarianism stretching back to the nineteenth century. Accepting Sandeen's insights but noting as well the complex social and cultural conditions serving as framework for the fundamentalist controversy is George M. Mars-

den, *Fundamentalism and American Culture* (New York: Oxford University Press, 1980), pp. 5–7, 118–23, 141–64, 199–211. On the religious debate between fundamentalists and modernists, the activities of the millenarians and the decline of the social gospel, the fundamentalist influence in different branches of American Protestantism, the role of World War I in stimulating fundamentalist fervor, the relationship—if any—between fundamentalism, nativism, and right-wing political activity, and the fundamentalist controversy at the Scopes trial, see Timothy P. Weber, *Living in the Shadow of the Second Coming: American Premillennialism, 1875–1925* (New York: Oxford University Press, 1979), pp. 5–12, 105–27, 154–57, 169–76; Ferenc Morton Szasz, *The Divided Mind of Protestant America, 1880–1930* (University, Ala.: University of Alabama Press, 1982), pp. 9–10, 84–125, 136–38; Robert Moats Miller, *American Protestantism and Social Issues, 1919–1939* (Chapel Hill: University of North Carolina Press, 1958), pp. 71, 154–59, 164–65; C. Allyn Russell, *Voices of American Fundamentalism* (Philadelphia: Westminster Press, 1976), pp. 14–17, 166–89; William Jennings Bryan, "Faith of Our Fathers," and Clarence Darrow, "In Defense of Reason," in John Tipple, ed., *Crisis of the American Dream* (New York: Pegasus, 1968), pp. 80–92; Norman P. Furniss, *The Fundamentalist Controversy, 1918–1931* (New Haven: Yale University Press, 1954), pp. 37–38, 76–100; Lawrence W. Levine, *Defender of the Faith: William Jennings Bryan, 1915–1925* (New York: Oxford University Press, 1965), pp. 256–57, 338–57; Ray Ginger, *Six Days or Forever: Tennessee vs John Thomas Scopes* (New York: Oxford University Press, 1958), pp. 1–3, 8–21, 128–29; Sandeen, *Roots of Fundamentalism*, pp. 233–69; Paul A. Carter, *The Decline and Revival of the Social Gospel* (Ithaca: Cornell University Press, 1954), pp. 47–48; Paul A. Carter, "The Fundamentalist Defense of the Faith," in Braeman, Bremner, and Brody, eds. *Change and Continuity*, pp. 179–214.

10. Robert L. Duffus, "Salesmen of Hate: The Ku Klux Klan," *World's Work* 46 (May 1923): 31–38; Winfield Jones, *Knights of the Ku Klux Klan* (New York: Tocsin Publishers, 1941), pp. 74–89; John Moffatt Mecklin, *The Ku Klux Klan: A Study of the American Mind* (New York: Harcourt, Brace, 1924), pp. 16–26, 53–72; David M. Chalmers, *Hooded Americanism* (Chicago, Quadrangle Books, 1968), pp. 24–30; Charles O. Jackson, "William J. Simmons: A Career in 'Ku Kluxism,'" *Georgia Historical Quarterly* 50 (Dec. 1966): 351–54.

11. Jackson, "William J. Simmons," pp. 358–59; Mecklin, *Ku Klux Klan*, pp. 5–6; Charles C. Alexander, *The Ku Klux Klan in the Southwest* (Lexington: University Press of Kentucky, 1966), pp. 5–7.

12. Duffus, "Salesmen of Hate," pp. 25–35; Alexander, *Ku Klux Klan in the Southwest*, pp. 6–9; Jones, *Knights of the Ku Klux Klan*, pp. 108–12; Mecklin, *Ku Klux Klan*, pp. 101–2.

13. Stanley Frost, *The Challenge of the Klan* (New York: Bobbs-Merrill, 1924), pp. 11–27; Henry P. Fry, *The Modern Ku Klux Klan* (1922, rpt. New York: Negro Universities Press, 1969), pp. 2–6; Frank Tannenbaum, *Darker Phases of the South* (New York: G. P. Putnam's Sons, 1924), pp. 60, 87;

Chalmers, *Hooded Americanism*, pp. 33–35, 115–17; "KKK: The Strangest Society in the World Today," *Wide World* 53 (Sept. 1924): 435–46; E. H. Laugher, *The Kall of the Klan in Kentucky* (Greenfield, Ind.: 1924), p. 13.

14. Editor of the *Imperial Night-Hawk*, "The Klan and the Press," in *Papers Read at the Meeting of Grand Dragons, 1923* (Atlanta: Ku Klux Klan, 1923), pp. 93–98; Duffus, "Salesmen of Hate," pp. 37–38; American Civil Liberties Union, *Archives* (Princeton University Library, microfilm in New York Public Library), vol. 190, *Ku Klux Klan, 1921–22; New York Times,* 27 July 1921; Robert L. Duffus, "How the Ku Klux Klan Sells Hate," *World's Work* 46 (June 1923): 174–83; *New York World,* 19 Sept. 1921; U.S. Congress, House of Representatives, Committee on Rules, *Hearings on the Ku Klux Klan,* 67th Cong., 1st sess.; Kenneth T. Jackson, *The Ku Klux Klan in the City, 1915–1930* (New York: Oxford University Press, 1967), pp. 11–12; "The Ku Klux Klan and the Next Election," *World's Work* 46 (Oct. 1923): 574–75; "The Reign of the Tar Bucket," *Literary Digest* 70 (27 Aug. 1921): 12–13.

15. Chalmers, *Hooded Americanism*, pp. 101–4; Jackson, "William J. Simmons," pp. 356–61; Duffus, "Salesmen of Hate," pp. 37–38; Frost, *Challenge of the Klan*, pp. 20–22.

16. William J. Simmons, *America's Menace or the Enemy Within* (Atlanta: Bureau of Patriotic Books, 1926), pp. 66–139; *Dawn* (Chicago), 17 Nov., 8 Dec. 1923; *Imperial Night-Hawk* (Atlanta), 4 Apr. 1923; Jackson, "William J. Simmons," pp. 363–64; Jones, *Knights of the Ku Klux Klan,* pp. 141–44.

17. *Imperial Night-Hawk* (Atlanta), 28 Mar. 1923; *New York Times,* 28 Dec. 1923; American Civil Liberties Union, *Archives,* vol. 228; Chalmers, *Hooded Americanism,* p. 105; Jackson, *Ku Klux Klan in the City,* pp. 16–18; Furniss, *Fundamentalist Controversy,* pp. 63–66; Marsden, *Fundamentalism and American Culture,* p. 189; Ginger, *Six Days,* pp. 211–12. See also *The Ku Klux Klan as Exposed by C. Anderson Wright, Ex Grand Goblin,* comp. George E. Whitehead (Atlanta: 1923), pp. 7–16; and Edgar I. Fuller, *The Visible of the Invisible Empire* (Denver: Maelstrom, 1925), pp. 7–111, an exposé by Clarke's former assistant, characterizing the Klan as a "monstrous and malformed thing."

18. Laugher, *Kall of the Klan,* p. 10; *Dawn,* 17 Nov. 1923; Hiram Wesley Evans, "The Klan's Mission—Americanism," *Kourier Magazine* (Atlanta) 1 (Sept. 1925): 16, and 1 (Nov. 1925): 4–12; *Fiery Cross,* National Edition (Indianapolis), 16, 30 Mar. 1923; Interview with H. W. Evans in Edward Price Bell, *Creed of the Klansmen* (Chicago: Daily News, 1924), pp. 4–12; Hiram Wesley Evans, *The Klan of Tomorrow and the Klan Spiritual,* Address Delivered at the Second Imperial Klonvokation, Kansas City, Sept. 1924 (Atlanta: Knights of the Ku Klux Klan, 1924), pp. 5–7.

19. "Jesus the Protestant," *Kourier Magazine* 1 (Feb. 1925): 3, 1 (Mar. 1925): 4–5, 1 (Dec. 1924): 8–9; *Fiery Cross,* 31 Oct. 1924; Hiram Wesley Evans, *The Rising Storm* (Atlanta: Buckland Publishing, 1930), pp. 20–128, 177–248; George Estes, *The Roman Catholic Kingdom and the Ku Klux Klan* (Portland, Ore.: Empire, 1923), p. 3; *Dawn,* 26 Jan. 1924; *American*

Standard (New York), 1 Jan. 1925; *National Kourier* (Washington, D.C.), 6 Mar. 1925.

20. John S. Fleming, *What Is Ku Kluxism: Let Americans Answer, Aliens Only Muddy the Waters* (Birmingham, Ala., 1923), pp. 13, 21–26; *American Standard* 1, 15 Jan. 1925; *National Kourier*, Eastern and Middle West Edition, 3 Apr. 1923; Estes, *Roman Catholic Kingdom*, pp. 6–7; *Fiery Cross*, 1 June 1923; "Citizenship and Fair Play," *Articles on the Klan and Elementary Klankraft* (Atlanta: Knights of the Ku Klux Klan, 1925), No. 3, ser. B; *Kourier Magazine* 1 (Mar. 1925): 1–5.

21. Bishop Alma White, *Klansmen: Guardians of Liberty* (Zarepath, N.J.: Good Citizen, 1926), pp. 11–15; C. Lewis Fowler, *The Ku Klux Klan: Its Origin and Meaning* (Atlanta: 1922), p. 22; Levinger, *Anti-Semitism in the United States*, p. 79; Blaine Mast, *KKK: Friend or Foe?* (Armstrong County, Pa.: 1924), pp. 16–29; Laugher, *Kall of the Klan*, pp. 51–52; *American Standard*, 1 Jan., 15 Apr., 1 May 1925.

22. *Imperial Night-Hawk*, 28 Mar., 25 Apr. 1923, 23 Jan. 1924; *National Kourier*, Southern Edition, 2 Jan. 1925; "Bramble Bush Government," *Articles on the Klan*, No. 1, ser. B; Grand Dragon of South Carolina, "Regulation of Immigration," *Papers Read*, pp. 69–74; *National Kourier*, Eastern and Middle West Edition, 3 Apr. 1925; "Americans Take Heed," *Articles on the Klan*, No. 8, ser. A; William J. Simmons, *The Klan Unmasked* (Atlanta: William F. Thompson Publishing, 1923), pp. 50–51, 113–17.

23. Hiram Wesley Evans, "Our Alien Crime Plague," *Kourier Magazine* 11 (Mar. 1926): 1–7; Hiram Wesley Evans, "Alienism in the Democracy," *Kourier Magazine* 3 (Apr. 1927): 1–8; Hiram Wesley Evans, "Aliens in the Democracy: For the People or for the Pope?" *Kourier Magazine* 3 (July 1927): 1–4; *Fiery Cross*, New Jersey State Edition, 14, 28 Dec. 1923; *National Kourier*, 10 July, 7 Aug. 1925; *Fiery Cross*, Ohio State Edition, 8 Jan. 1924; Laugher, *Kall of the Klan*, p. 57; *Inspirational Addresses Delivered at the Second Imperial Klonvokation* (Kansas City: Knights of KKK, 1924), pp. 1–8; *Imperial Night-Hawk*, 28 June 1923; *Fiery Cross*, 7, 30 Mar. 1923, 26 Sept. 1924; Hiram Wesley Evans, *The Public School Problem in America* (Atlanta: Ku Klux Klan, 1924), pp. 13–24.

24. W. C. Wright, *Religious and Patriotic Ideals of the Ku Klux Klan* (Waco, Texas: 1926), pp. 1–17; "Woman's Loyalty Will Fulfill a Manifest Destiny," *Fiery Cross*, 6 July 1923; "Rome Opposes Advancement of Womanhood," *National Kourier*, 14 Aug. 1925; *Imperial Night-Hawk*, 3 Oct. 1923; James A. Comer, Grand Dragon of Arkansas, "A Tribute and Challenge to the Wonderful American Women," *Papers Read*, pp. 89–92; "Women and the Romanists," *Dawn*, 8 Dec. 1923; "The Fate of the Nation Is in the Hands of Its Women," *Dawn*, 19 Jan. 1924. One role of women as spiritual leaders of the land was protecting the primacy of the Protestant Bible and the proper education of children. A Klan writer called on women to gather at Dayton, Tennessee, to provide the "spiritual aid of womanhood" in William Jennings Bryan's defense of biblical truth in the Scopes Trial. See *American Standard*, 15 May 1925.

25. Fry, *Modern Ku Klux Klan*, pp. 185–91; Alexander, *Ku Klux Klan in*

the Southwest, pp. 43, 52, 65; "Reign of the Tar Bucket," pp. 1–12; American Civil Liberties Union, *Archives,* vol. 231; *Chicago Defender,* 17 Feb. 1923; David H. Bennett, "Women and the Nativist Movement," in Carol V. R. George, ed., *"Remember the Ladies": New Perspectives on Women in American History* (Syracuse: Syracuse University Press, 1975), pp. 85–89. Of course, racism was another constant theme in the Klan call to protect women from sexual assault. See Tannenbaum, *Darker Phases of the South,* pp. 32–33, and W. C. Wright, *Religious and Patriotic Ideals,* p. 45.

26. *Dawn,* 2 June, 8 Dec. 1923; *National Kourier,* 1 Oct. 1925; White, *Klansmen,* pp. 127–38; Helen Jackson, *Convent Cruelties; or My Life in a Convent* (Detroit: 1919).

27. *Dawn,* 17 Nov. 1923, 2 Feb. 1924; *Imperial Night-Hawk,* 3 Oct. 1923; Alexander, *Ku Klux Klan in the Southwest,* pp. 100–106; *National Kourier,* Southern Edition, 2 Jan. 1925; Walter F. White, "Reviving the Ku Klux Klan," *Forum* 65 (Apr. 1921): 414–24; Robbie Gill, "American Women," in *Inspirational Addresses,* pp. 51–60. One Klansman argued that the United States flag symbolized women's place in America: "Red for the blood shed for women's protection, white for purity and virtue, blue for the loyalty of men to women and to home" ("American Women," *Kourier Magazine* 1 [Apr. 1925]: 11–15).

28. Duffus, "How the Ku Klux Klan Sells Hate," pp. 177–79; Robert L. Duffus, "Ancestry and the End of the Ku Klux Klan," *World's Work* 46 (Sept. 1923): 527–36; Tannenbaum, *Darker Phases of the South,* pp. 4–29; William Allen White, "Psychoanalyzing the Klan," *World Tomorrow* 7 (Mar. 1924): 87; American Civil Liberties Union, *Archives,* vol. 252; Frank Bohn, "The Ku Klux Klan Interpreted," *American Journal of Sociology* 30 (Jan. 1925): 385–407.

29. Frost, *Challenge of the Klan,* pp. 10, 41, 159–60; Alexander, *Ku Klux Klan in the Southwest,* pp. 20–21; John Higham, *Strangers in the Land: Patterns of American Nativism, 1860–1925* (1955; 2d ed. New York: Atheneum, 1963), pp. 291–95; Robert Moats Miller, "The Ku Klux Klan," in Braeman, Bremner, and Brody, eds., *Change and Continuity,* pp. 215–55.

30. Mecklin, *Ku Klux Klan,* p. 103; Alexander, *Ku Klux Klan in the Southwest,* pp. 18–19; Hiram Wesley Evans, "The Klan's Fight for Americanism," *North American Review* 123 (Mar. 1926): 33–63.

31. *Fiery Cross,* 15 June 1923, 4 Apr. 1924; American Civil Liberties Union, *Archives,* vols. 245, 252; Frost, *Challenge of the Klan,* p. 148; Stanley Frost, "When the Klan Rules," *Outlook* 136 (13 Feb. 1924): 261–64. At one picnic in Atlanta, old nativism and modern nativism joined forces when the Klan held a joint meeting with the Junior Order of American Mechanics. See *National Kourier,* 31 July 1925.

32. Miller, *American Protestantism,* pp. 137–46.

33. Frost, *Challenge of the Klan,* pp. 1–14; Robert L. Duffus, "The Ku Klux Klan in the Middle West," *World's Work* 46 (Aug. 1923): 363; *New York Times,* 28 Aug. 1925; Chalmers, *Hooded Americanism,* p. 202; Jackson, *Ku Klux Klan in the City,* pp. 233–39.

34. Jackson, *Ku Klux Klan in the City*, pp. 29–44, 237–39; Governor Clifford Walker, "Americanism Applied," in *Inspirational Addresses*, pp. 38–45; *New York Times*, 16 Sept. 1923; Chalmers, *Hooded Americanism*, pp. 70–77. The lynching of Leo Frank provided an additional setting for Klan nativist rhetoric.

35. Chalmers, *Hooded Americanism*, pp. 66–67, 78–84; *New York Times*, 26 May 1922, 9 Nov. 1923, 2 Oct. 1927; Jackson, *Ku Klux Klan in the City*, pp. 44, 60–61, 237–39. Kenneth T. Jackson's excellent study of the urban movement is essential reading for Klan activity in many areas. It is particularly good for the Tennessee cities where the movement left local chapter records.

36. John Rogers, *The Murders of Mer Rouge* (St. Louis: Security Publishing Co., 1923), pp. 14–64; *New York Times*, 30, 31 Dec. 1922, 6 Jan. 1923; "The Ku Klux Klan," *Catholic World* 116 (Jan. 1923): 433; Duffus, "How the Ku Klux Klan Sells Hate," pp. 174–83; Alexander, *Ku Klux Klan in the Southwest*, pp. 69–75, 80–81. In the *Fiery Cross*, 23 Feb. 1923, the Klan leaders charged that Klansmen in Mer Rouge were victims of a "frameup."

37. William D. McBee, *The Oklahoma Revolution* (Oklahoma City: Modern Publishers, 1956), pp. 40–51, 70–77, 96, 156, 171–76; "Quaint Customs and Methods of the Ku Klux Klan," *Literary Digest* 74 (5 Aug. 1922): 44–46; *New York World*, 11, 20 Sept., 1, 5 Oct., 15 Nov. 1923; American Civil Liberties Union, *Archives*, vols. 190, 228; *New York Times*, 7, 8, 17, 19 Sept., 10 Oct. 1923; Sheldon Neuringer, "The War on the Ku Klux Klan in Oklahoma," *Chronicles of Oklahoma* 45 (Summer 1967): 155–73; *National Anti-Klan Weekly: Jack Walton's Paper* (Oklahoma City), 9 Dec. 1923; Alexander, *Ku Klux Klan in the Southwest*, pp. 127–58; *Imperial Night-Hawk*, 30 May, 19 Sept. 1923. When the unmasking directives in Oklahoma were enacted, Klansmen were warned: "The laws of secrecy must be obeyed. Klansmen, keep your visors down!"

38. Jackson, *Ku Klux Klan in the City*, pp. 66–80; Chalmers, *Hooded Americanism*, pp. 39–48; *New York Times*, 26 July 1921, 24, 25, 31 Aug. 1924, 19 Jan. 1925; Charles C. Alexander, *Crusade for Conformity: The Ku Klux Klan in Texas, 1920–1930* (Houston: Texas Gulf Coast Historical Publications, 1962), pp. 1–80; Furniss, *Fundamentalist Controversy*, pp. 44, 87–88.

39. *National Kourier*, Western Edition, 15 May 1925; *New York Times*, 14 July 1921, 16 Dec. 1922, 11 Sept. 1923; George S. Turnbull, *An Oregon Crusader* (Portland: Binfords and Mort, 1955), pp. 65–71; Waldo Roberts, "The Ku-Kluxing of Oregon," *Outlook* 133 (14 Mar. 1923): 490–91; Eckard V. Toy, Jr., "The Ku Klux Klan in Tillamook, Oregon," *Pacific Northwest Quarterly* 53 (Apr. 1962): 60–64; *Harpoon* (Portland), Apr. 1924; Lem A. Dever, *Masks Off! Confessions of an Imperial Klansman* (Portland, 1924), pp. 1–64; American Civil Liberties Union, *Archives*, vol. 252; Chalmers, *Hooded Americanism*, pp. 85–91, 117–25; Jackson, *Ku Klux Klan in the City*, pp. 187–214.

40. Jackson, *Ku Klux Klan in the City*, pp. 215–31; James H. Davis,

"Colorado under the Klan," *Colorado Magazine* 42 (Spring 1965): 93–108; *New York Times*, 10 Jan. 1925; Chalmers, *Hooded Americanism*, pp. 216–34.

41. Chalmers, *Hooded Americanism*, pp. 236–65; *New York Times*, 1, 2 Nov. 1923, 24 Mar., 1 May, 27 July 1924; *Dawn*, 27 Oct. 1923; Stanley Coben, "The Failure of the Melting Pot," in Gary B. Nash and Ricard Weiss, eds., *The Great Fear: Race in the Mind of America* (New York: Holt, Rinehart and Winston, 1970), pp. 150–60; Donald A. Crownover, "The Ku Klux Klan in Lancaster County, 1923–1924," *Journal of the Lancaster County Historical Society* 68 (Spring 1964): 63–77; "The Klan Defies a State," *Literary Digest* 77 (9 June 1923): 12–13; Emerson Loucks, *The Ku Klux Klan in Pennsylvania: A Study in Nativism* (New York: Telegraph Press, 1936); Jackson, *Ku Klux Klan in the City*, pp. 170–84, 237–39.

42. Walter Johnson, *William Allen White's America* (New York: Henry Holt, 1947), pp. 375–85; *The Autobiography of William Allen White* (New York: Macmillan, 1966), pp. 625, 627, 629–34; Walter Johnson, ed., *Selected Letters of William Allen White, 1899–1943* (New York: Greenwood Press, 1968), pp. 242–46.

43. Jackson, *Ku Klux Klan in the City*, pp. 127–43; *Fiery Cross*, Michigan State Edition, 21 Sept. 1923; "The Ku Klux Klan and the Next Election," *World's Work* 46 (Oct. 1923): 573–75; Duffus, "Ku Klux Klan in the Middle West," 363–72; Chalmers, *Hooded Americanism*, pp. 141–48, 175–82.

44. Paul M. Angle, Collector, Bloody Williamson Papers, Chicago Historical Society [James M. Gillis], "The Ku Klux Klan," Folder 6; *Catholic World* 116: 443; *New York Times*, 9 Jan., 21 Oct. 1924, 27 Jan. 1925, 21 Aug. 1922; *Dawn*, 20 Oct., 10, 24 Nov. 1923; Duffus, "Ancestry and the End of the Ku Klux Klan," pp. 527–28. Jackson, *Ku Klux Klan in the City*, pp. 93–126, makes use of local Klan records and materials from *Tolerance* in an invaluable analysis of the Chicago Klans.

45. Morton Harrison, "Gentlemen from Indiana," *Atlantic Monthly* 141 (May 1928): 676–86; Jackson, *Ku Klux Klan in the City*, pp. 144–69; *Fiery Cross*, Indiana State Edition, 13, 30 July 1923; *New York Times*, 16 Aug., 7 Nov. 1923; Lynd and Lynd, *Middletown*, pp. 364–66, 480–84.

46. *Fiery Cross*, Indiana State Edition, 5 Oct. 1923, 25 Jan. 1924; Robert Coughlan, "Konklave in Kokomo," in Leighton, ed., *Aspirin Age*, pp. 105–29; *New York Times*, 7 June 1924; American Civil Liberties Union, Archives, vol. 231; *New York World*, 2 Sept. 1923; Chalmers, *Hooded Americanism*, pp. 161–70; Emma Lou Thornbourgh, "Segregation in Indiana during the Era of the 1920's," *Mississippi Valley Historical Review* 47 (Mar. 1961): 594–619. It was Stephenson who claimed two hundred thousand spectators at the Kokomo meeting. Other sources put the crowd at one hundred thousand.

47. Lee N. Allen, "The McAdoo Campaign for the Presidential Nomination in 1924," *Journal of Southern History* 29 (May 1963): 211–28; David B. Burner, "The Democratic Party in the Election of 1924," *Mid-America* 46 (1964): 92–113; John D. Hicks, *Republican Ascendancy, 1921–1933* (New

York: Harper & Row, 1960), pp. 96–98; *New York Times*, 22, 24 June, 12, 22 Sept. 1924; Donald R. McCoy, *Calvin Coolidge: The Quiet President* (New York: Macmillan, 1967), pp. 248–58, 328; Michael Williams, *Shadow of the Pope* (New York: McGraw-Hill, 1932), pp. 145–68; Chalmers, *Hooded Americanism*, pp. 202–15.

48. Coughlan, "Konklave at Kokomo," pp. 125–29; *Indiana Kourier* (Washington, D.C.), 10, 24 Apr. 1925; *New York Times*, 12 Aug. 1927, 5 Jan. 1928, 9 Jan. 1926; Harrison, "Gentlemen from Indiana," pp. 683–86; *National Kourier*, 10 July 1925.

49. Allan J. Lichtman, *Prejudice and the Old Politics: The Presidential Election of 1928* (Chapel Hill: University of North Carolina Press, 1979), pp. 68–76, 231–46; *New York Times*, 12 Oct. 1926, 5 June 1944; Edmund A. Moore, *A Catholic Runs for President: The Campaign of 1928* (New York: Ronald Press, 1956), pp. 108–10; William G. Carleton, "The Popish Plot of 1928: Smith-Hoover Presidential Campaign," *Forum* 112 (Sept. 1949): 141–47; Miller, *American Protestantism*, pp. 49–50; Frank Freidel, *Franklin D. Roosevelt: The Ordeal* (Boston: Little, Brown, 1954), p. 231; Chalmers, *Hooded Americanism*, pp. 279–324.

CHAPTER 13

1. See, for example, Arthur M. Schlesinger, Jr., *The Crisis of the Old Order, 1919–1933* (Boston: Houghton Mifflin, 1957), pp. 248–69; Walter Johnson, *1600 Pennsylvania Avenue: Presidents and the People, 1929–1959* (Boston: Little, Brown, 1960), pp. 3–48; Irving Bernstein, *Turbulent Years* (Boston: Houghton Mifflin, 1969), pp. 1–15.

2. Dixon Wecter, *The Age of the Great Depression* (New York: Macmillan, 1948), pp. 39–40; William E. Leuchtenburg, *Franklin D. Roosevelt and the New Deal* (New York: Harper & Row, 1963), pp. 24–25.

3. Milton Friedman and Anna Jacobson Schwartz, *The Great Contraction, 1929–1933* (Princeton: Princeton University Press, 1965), pp. i–ii, 3–5, 9–19, 38–48, 53–54, 67–70, 111–23; Murray N. Rothbard, *America's Great Depression* (Princeton: D. Van Nostrand, 1963), pp. 3–6, 54–125; Peter Temin, *Did Monetary Forces Cause the Great Depression?* (New York: Norton, 1976), pp. 7–12, 168–78; Charles P. Kindelberger, *The World in the Depression, 1929–39* (Berkeley and Los Angeles: University of California Press, 1973), pp. 19–23, 291–307; Peter Temin, "Money, Money Everywhere: A Retrospective Review of *A Monetary History of the United States*," *Reviews in American History* 5 (Mar. 1977): 151–59.

4. Norman Thomas, *America's Way Out* (New York: Macmillan, 1931), pp. 306–7; Johnson, *1600 Pennsylvania Avenue*, pp. 20–21; The Editors, "Wanted: A Dictator! A Solution of the National Difficulty," *Vanity Fair* 38 (June 1932): 32, 66; Henry Hazlitt, "Without Benefit of Congress," *Scribner's Magazine* 92 (July 1932): 13–18.

5. Central Committee, Communist Party, U.S.A., *Toward Revolutionary*

Mass Work (New York: Workers Library Publishers, 1932), pp. 3–4; Earl Browder, *Communism in the United States* (New York: International Publishers, 1935), pp. 14, 31, 66–71.

6. Georgi Dimitroff, *The United Front* (New York: International Publishers, 1938), p. 15; Earl Browder, *The People's Front* (New York: International Publishers, 1938), p. 198; A. B. Magil, "The New Deal, 1933–1938," *New Masses*, 5 July 1938, p. 6; Earl Browder, *The Democratic Front for Jobs, Security, Democracy and Peace* (New York: Workers Library Publishers, 1938), p. 10; Earl Browder, "The People's Front Moves Forward," *Communist*, Dec. 1937, p. 1095; District Communist Party, Washington, D.C., *We Do Not Propose to Let the President Down* (1938).

7. Edward Levison, ed., *A Plan for America: Official 1932 Campaign Handbook of the Socialist Party* (Chicago: Socialist Party of America, 1932), pp. 10–11; Norman Thomas, *Why I Am a Socialist* (Chicago: Socialist Party of America, 1932), pp. 9–10; Norman Thomas, *Is the New Deal Socialism? An Answer to Al Smith and the American Liberty League* (Chicago: Socialist Party of America, 1936), p. 7; Norman Thomas, *The Choice before Us: Mankind at the Crossroads* (New York: Macmillan, 1934), pp. 158–59; Bernard K. Johnpoll, *Pacifists' Progress: Norman Thomas and the Decline of American Socialism* (Chicago: Quadrangle Books, 1970), p. 177; Frank Warren III, *An Alternative Vision: The Socialist Party in the 1930's* (Bloomington: Indiana University Press, 1978), p. 5–19; Daniel Bell, "The Problem of Ideological Rigidity," in John M. Laslett and Seymour Martin Lipset, eds., *Failure of a Dream: Essays in the History of American Socialism* (Garden City, N.Y.: Doubleday Anchor Books, 1974), p. 89. On the mild Red Scare of the 1930s, see Elizabeth Dilling, *The Red Network: A Who's Who of Radicalism for Patriots* (Chicago: Privately published, 1934), with its list of five hundred organizations that "are part of a Communist conspiracy to take over America." During these years, college teachers were harassed at some institutions for espousing "radical" ideas and articles were published expressing fear that the anticommunist activity would mount. See Roger N. Baldwin, "Red Scare: 1935," *Common Sense* 4 (Mar. 1935): 8–10. For a careful recent assessment of the history of the House Un-American Activities Committee, see Kenneth O'Reilly, *Hoover and the Un-Americans* (Philadelphia: Temple University Press, 1983), pp. 21–74.

8. Donald L. Miller, *The New American Radicalism: Alfred M. Bingham and Non-Marxian Insurgency in the New Deal Era* (Port Washington, N.Y.: Kennikat Press, 1979), pp. 34–136; Stuart Chase, "The Age of Distribution," in Howard Zinn, ed., *New Deal Thought* (New York: Bobbs-Merrill, 1966), pp. 24–27; Frank Warren III, *Liberals and Communism* (Bloomington: Indiana University Press, 1966), pp. 23–25; "What Does Our Platform Mean," *Common Sense* 1 (29 Dec. 1932): 2.

9. Arthur M. Schlesinger, Jr., *The Politics of Upheaval* (Boston: Houghton Mifflin, 1960), pp. 80–81; Nathaniel Weyl, "The Khaki Shirts—American Fascists," *New Republic* 72 (21 Sept. 1932): 145–46; *New York Times*, 18 Sept., 17 Oct., 14 Dec. 1933.

10. Donald S. Strong, *Organized Anti-Semitism in America* (Washington, D.C.: American Council on Public Affairs, 1941), pp. 71–77, 83–106; Ralph Lord Roy, *Apostles of Discord* (Boston: Beacon Press, 1953), pp. 26–31; Robert Moats Miller, *American Protestantism and Social Issues, 1919–1939* (Chapel Hill: University of North Carolina Press, 1938), pp. 152, 160; *New York Times*, 23 July 1938; Leo P. Ribuffo, *The Old Christian Right: The Protestant Far Right from the Great Depression to the Cold War* (Philadelphia: Temple University Press, 1983), pp. 80–127; *Defender Magazine*, Apr. 1930, Dec. 1933, Aug. 1938, Sept. 1938; Seymour Martin Lipset and Earl Raab, *The Politics of Unreason: Right-Wing Extremism in America, 1790–1970* (New York: Harper & Row, 1970), pp. 160–67; Walter Johnson, ed., *Selected Letters of William Allen White, 1899–1943* (New York: Greenwood Press, 1968), pp. 383, 390. Richard Hofstadter, *Anti-Intellectualism in American Life* (New York: Vintage Books, 1962), p. 132, observes: "Although no one has ever tried to trace in detail the historic links between the radical right of the depression . . . and the fundamentalism of the 1920s, there are some suggestive continuities among the leaders."

11. John M. Werly, "The Millenarian Right: William Dudley Pelley and the Silver Shirt Legion of America" (Ph.D. dissertation, Syracuse University, 1972), pp. 133–40; *Silver Legion Ranger*, 8 Nov., 6 Dec. 1933; Strong, *Organized Anti-Semitism*, pp. 40–56; U.S. Congress, House of Representatives, *Report on the Investigation of Un-American Propaganda in the United States*, 76th Cong., 3d sess., 1940, Report 1476, p. 20.

12. William Dudley Pelley, "Seven Minutes in Eternity—The Amazing Experience That Made Me Over," *American Magazine* 107 (Mar. 1929): 7–9, 139–43; Avedis Derounian [John Roy Carlson], *Under Cover: My Four Years in the Nazi Underworld of America* (New York: Dutton, 1943), pp. 317–19; *Liberator*, 18 Feb., 22 Apr., 26 Aug. 1933.

13. *Pelley's Weekly*, 8 Aug. 1934, 22 Jan. 1936; Ribuffo, *Old Christian Right*, pp. 43–79; Geoffrey S. Smith, *To Save a Nation* (New York: Basic Books, 1973), pp. 53–86; *Liberator*, 4, 7 Sept. 1937. Perhaps the best work on Pelley and the Silver Legion is John M. Werly's "Millenarian Right." Another brief but probing treatment is offered in Geoffrey Smith's *To Save a Nation*. Werly views Pelley as a religious mystic turned political leader, a man who embraced the Jewish-Communist conspiracy thesis as a millenarian.

There is a different view in *Politics of Unreason*, pp. 164–67; Lipset and Raab argue that Pelley's Silver Shirts, compared to the nativist movements of the 1920s and earlier, represent a "bridge point of modern extremism," from "corporate status preservatism to disjunctive or anomic status preservatism." This comes, according to Lipset, when the individual seeks "some other symbolic identification" than found in trying to restore his declining group status. Thus Protestant townsmen shift from nativistic fundamentalism to a larger fundamentalist Christianity, for with their "ethnic identity disappearing," their status identification turns away from "old-fashioned Protestantism," to "old-fashioned Americanism." Lipset's larger point concerning the "break between old and new right-wing extremism" is provocative; his insistance that the Silver Legion foreshadowed this break is less persuasive.

14. Werly, "Millenarian Right," pp. 294–96; Morris Schonbach, "Native Fascism during the 1930's and 1940's" (Ph.D. dissertation, University of California at Los Angeles, 1958), pp. 337–39; Lipset and Raab, *Politics of Unreason*, pp. 157–59; Morris Janowitz, "Black Legions on the March," in Daniel Aaron, ed., *America in Crisis* (New York: Knopf, 1952), pp. 305–8.

15. Sander A. Diamond, *The Nazi Movement in the United States, 1924–1941* (Ithaca: Cornell University Press, 1974), pp. 193–95, 202–353; Smith, *To Save a Nation*, pp. 87–100; *New York Times*, 16 Oct. 1936; Strong, *Organized Anti-Semitism*, pp. 21–39.

16. Strong, *Organized Anti-Semitism*, pp. 136–37, 172; Schonbach, "Native Fascism," pp. 339–43; Werly, "Millenarian Right," pp. 290–93; Janowitz, "Black Legions," pp. 315–16; *Pelley's Weekly*, 1 July 1936. H. Arthur Steiner, "Fascism in America," *American Political Science Review* 29 (Oct. 1935): 823–30, calls these movements "at best quasi-fascist."

17. David H. Bennett, "The Year of the Old Folks' Revolt," *American Heritage* 16 (Dec. 1964): 48–51, 99–107; Richard Milne, *That Man Townsend* (Los Angeles: Prosperity Publishing, 1935), pp. 5–28; Abraham Holtzman, "The Townsend Movement: A Study in Old Age Pension Politics," (Ph.D. dissertation, Harvard University, 1952), pp. 8–38, 66–67; Francis E. Townsend, *New Horizons* (Chicago: J. L. Steward Publishing, 1943), pp. 132–42; Francis E. Townsend and Robert E. Clements, *The Townsend Plan* (Los Angeles: Old Age Revolving Pensions, Ltd., 1935), p. 10; Francis E. Townsend, *Old Age Revolving Pensions* (Long Beach: Old Age Revolving Pensions, Ltd., 1934), p. 4; Seymour J. Milliken, "$200 a Month at Sixty," *Forum* 92 (Nov. 1934): 326–28; Stuart A. Rice, "Is the Townsend Plan Practical?" *Vital Speeches of the Day* 2 (27 Jan. 1936): 254; Committee on Old Age Security of the Twentieth Century Fund, *The Townsend Crusade* (New York: Twentieth Century Fund, 1936), pp. 5–6, 32–35, 48–49; Harry D. Gideonse, ed., *The Economic Meaning of the Townsend Plan* (Chicago: University of Chicago Press, 1936), pp. 14–23; Donald Richberg, "The Townsend Delusion," *Review of Reviews* 93 (Feb. 1936): 27; Professor Edwin E. Witte to Merrill G. Murray, 11 Dec. 1935, Papers of Franklin D. Roosevelt, Franklin D. Roosevelt Library, Hyde Park, N.Y., Official File, 1542 (Dr. Francis E. Townsend); Richard L. Neuberger and Kelley Loe, *An Army of the Aged* (Caldwell, Idaho: Caxton Printers, 1936), pp. 175–76.

18. *Townsend National Weekly*, 8 July 1935; Duncan Aikman, "Townsendism: Old Time Religion," *New York Times Magazine*, 8 Mar. 1936, pp. 5, 25.

19. *Townsend National Weekly*, 2 Nov., 21 Dec. 1936; Townsend and Clements, *Townsend Plan*, pp. 6–7. Frederick A. Delano to Roosevelt, 25 Nov. 1935, and Dr. Stanley High to Roosevelt, 29 Aug. 1935, Roosevelt Papers, Official File 1542, sent the president descriptions of Townsend Club meetings. California was a fertile ground for other inflationary panaceas designed to end the depression, but none had the appeal of the Town-

send Plan. Among the others were End Poverty in California, Technocracy, and Thirty Dollars Every Thursday.

20. David H. Bennett, *Demagogues in the Depression: American Radicals and the Union Party, 1932–1936* (New Brunswick: Rutgers University Press, 1969), pp. 113–30; T. Harry Williams, "The Gentleman from Louisiana: Demagogue or Democrat," *Journal of Southern History* 26 (Feb. 1960): 4–21; Huey P. Long, *My First Days in the White House* (Harrisburg: Telegraph Press, 1935), pp. 3–6, 26–150; Huey P. Long, *Share Our Wealth* (Washington, D.C.: Huey P. Long, 1934), pp. 7–16; Hodding Carter, "How Come Huey Long? (I. Bogeyman)," *New Republic* 82 (13 Feb. 1935): 13; Gerald L. K. Smith, "How Come Huey Long? (II. Or Superman)," *New Republic* 82 (13 Feb. 1935): 14–15; Huey P. Long, *Every Man a King* (New Orleans: National Book Co., 1933), p. 297; *American Progress*, 4 Jan., 1 Feb., 4 May 1935; T. Harry Williams, *Huey Long* (New York: Knopf, 1969), pp. 679–706; Allan P. Sindler, *Huey Long's Louisiana* (Baltimore: Johns Hopkins Press, 1956), pp. 85–86; Forrest Davis, *Huey Long: A Candid Biography* (New York: Dodge Publishing, 1935), pp. 34, 37, 276–85; Raymond Gram Swing, *Forerunners of American Fascism* (New York: Julian Messner, 1935), pp. 62–107; Glen Jeansonne, "Challenge to the New Deal: Huey P. Long and the Redistribution of Wealth," *Louisiana History* 21 (Fall 1980): 331–39; Glen Jeansonne, "Huey P. Long's Share-Our-Wealth Society: Utopia Comes to the Masses," in Ralph M. Aderman, ed., *The Quest for Social Justice* (Madison: University of Wisconsin Press, 1983), 279–96. Alan Brinkley in *Voices of Protest: Huey Long, Father Coughlin and the Great Depression* (New York: Knopf, 1982), pp. 57–74, 80–81, offers a new analysis of Long, more sympathetic than many others. Brinkley argues that Share-Our-Wealth, "for all its faults . . . was not without elements of economic truth."

21. The argument over the nativist elements in Populism begins with Richard Hofstadter's enormously influential *Age of Reform: From Bryan to F.D.R.* (New York: Knopf, 1956), pp. 5, 23–130. Different perspectives are found in a number of works. See C. Vann Woodward, "The Populist Heritage and the Intellectual," *American Scholar* 29 (Winter 1959–60): 55–72; Walter T. K. Nugent, *The Tolerant Populists* (Chicago: University of Chicago Press, 1963); and Norman Pollack, *The Populist Response to Industrial America* (Cambridge, Mass.: Harvard University Press, 1962), for notable early responses.

22. U.S. Congress, House of Representatives, Committee on Un-American Activities, *Hearings, Investigation of Un-American Propaganda Activities in the United States* (Gerald L. K. Smith), 79th Cong., 2d sess. (1946), pp. 7–21; Harnett T. Kane, *Louisiana Hayride* (New York: Morrow, 1941), pp. 150–51; Herman B. Deutsch, "Huey Long, the Last Phase," *Saturday Evening Post* 208 (12 Oct. 1935): 27; Walter Davenport, "The Mysterious Gerald Smith," *Collier's* 113 (4 Mar. 1944): 15.

23. *American Progress*, 4 Jan. 1935; *New York Times*, 22 Sept. 1935; Gerald L. K. Smith, "The Huey Long Movement," in Rita James Simon, ed., *As We Saw the Thirties* (Urbana: University of Illinois Press, 1967), p.

61; Oral History Research Project, Columbia University, Reminiscences of Arthur Krock, No. 54; Gerald L. K. Smith to Roosevelt, 9, 16 Sept. 1936, Roosevelt Papers, Official File 1403 (Huey P. Long); *New Orleans Times Picayune*, 21 June 1936; James A. Farley, *Behind the Ballots* (New York: Harcourt, Brace, 1938), pp. 171, 249–50; Ribuffo, *Old Christian Right*, pp. 128–40; William Bradford Huey, "Gerald Smith's Bid for Power," *American Mercury* 55 (Aug. 1942): 147; Victor C. Ferkiss, "The Political and Economic Philosophy of American Fascism" (Ph.D. dissertation, University of Chicago, 1954), pp. 156, 287–88; Glen Jeansonne, "Partisan Parson: An Oral History Account of the Louisiana Years of Gerald L. K. Smith," *Louisiana History* 23 (Spring 1982): 149–58.

24. Louis B. Ward, *Father Charles E. Coughlin: An Authorized Biography* (Detroit: Tower Publications, 1933), pp. 3–35; Irving Kolodin, "Propaganda on the Air," *American Mercury* 35 (July 1939): 293–98.

25. Bennett, *Demagogues in the Depression*, pp. 29–37; Ward, *Coughlin*, pp. 5–35; Kolodin, "Propaganda on the Air," pp. 293–98; Wallace Stegner, "The Radio Priest and His Flock," in Isabel Leighton, ed., *The Aspirin Age, 1919–1941* (New York: Simon and Schuster, 1949), p. 234; Brinkley, *Voices of Protest*, pp. 82–106; Nick Arthur Masters, "Father Coughlin and Social Justice—A Case Study of a Social Movement" (Ph.D. dissertation, University of Wisconsin, 1955), p. 48.

26. Charles E. Coughlin to Franklin D. Roosevelt, 14 June, 1, 12, 16 Aug., 24 Sept., 13 Nov. 1933, Roosevelt Papers, Official File 306 (Charles E. Coughlin); Charles E. Coughlin, *The New Deal in Money* (Royal Oak, Mich.: Radio League of the Little Flower, 1933), pp. 5, 15, 86, 116; Charles E. Coughlin, *Driving Out the Money Changers* (Detroit: Radio League of the Little Flower, 1933), pp. 76, 80–93; Bennett, *Demagogues in the Depression*, pp. 37–57.

27. Charles E. Coughlin, *Money: Questions and Answers* (Royal Oak, Mich.: Social Justice Publishing Co., 1936), pp. 156–60; Charles E. Coughlin, "Inflation and Silver," *Today* 1 (6 Jan. 1934): 7, 22; Bennett, *Demagogues in the Depression*, pp. 43–53. On the influence of the papal encyclicals, see Forrest Davis, "Father Coughlin," *Atlantic Monthly* 156 (Dec. 1935): 661–63. For the Populist spokesmen, see John D. Hicks, *The Populist Revolt* (Minneapolis: University of Minnesota Press, 1931), p. 440; and Hofstadter, *Age of Reform*, pp. 64–65.

28. Bennett, *Demagogues in the Depression*, pp. 57–58; *Social Justice*, 3 Apr. 1936; Coughlin, *New Deal*, pp. 38–49; Charles E. Coughlin, *Eight Lectures on Labor, Capital and Justice* (Royal Oak, Mich.: Radio League of the Little Flower, 1934), pp. 30, 66, 81–127; Charles E. Coughlin, *A Series of Lectures on Social Justice, 1935–1936* (Royal Oaks, Mich: Radio League of the Little Flower, 1936), pp. 11–12, 17, 154; Charles E. Coughlin, "How Long Can Democracy and Capitalism Last?" *Today* 3 (29 Dec. 1934): 6–7.

29. Charles E. Coughlin, *A Series of Lectures on Social Justice, 1934–1935* (Royal Oak, Mich.: Radio League of the Little Flower, 1935), pp. 9–22; *New York Times*, 25 Apr. 1935, 6 Jan. 1936; *Social Justice*, 13 Mar. 1936.

30. James P. Shenton, "The Coughlin Movement and the New Deal,"

Political Science Quarterly 82 (Sept. 1958): 360–66; Schlesinger, *Politics of Upheaval*, p. 26; Bennett, *Demagogues in the Depression*, pp. 58–60; Brinkley, *Voices of Protest*, p. 202; Lipset and Raab, *Politics of Unreason*, pp. 172–78; Masters, "Father Coughlin and Social Justice," pp. 62–71; Samuel Lubell, *The Future of American Politics* (New York: Harper & Row, 1965), pp. 143–44; *Pilot* (Boston), 8 Apr. 1932; Charles E. Coughlin, *Series of Lectures on Social Justice, 1934–1935*, p. 70; Wilfred Parsons, "Father Coughlin: The Aftermath," *America* 53 (29 June 1935): 275–76.

31. Brinkley, *Voices of Protest*, pp. 144, 168, 201–3; "Dangers of Demagogy," *Commonweal* 19 (8 Dec. 1933): 144; Father Coughlin's Friends, *An Answer to Father Coughlin's Critics* (Royal Oak, Mich: Radio League of the Little Flower, 1940), p. 6.

32. Coughlin, *New Deal*, pp. 8–9; Coughlin, *Series of Lectures, 1934–35*, pp. 173–78; Bennett, *Demagogues in the Depression*, pp. 62–66.

33. *New York Times*, 16 Aug. 1936; *Cleveland Plain Dealer*, 16 Apr. 1936; Gerald Frank, "Father Coughlin's Fish Fry," *Nation* 143 (22 Aug. 1936): 208; Jonathan Mitchell, "Father Coughlin's Children," *New Republic* 87 (26 Aug. 1936): 73; Bennett, *Demagogues in the Depression*, pp. 16–18.

34. *Social Justice*, 9 June 1936; *Townsend National Weekly*, 7 Sept. 1936; *New York Times*, 23, 29 May, 1, 17, 19 June 1936; Charles E. Coughlin to William Lemke, 8 June 1936, in William Lemke Papers, University of North Dakota, Grand Forks; Holtzman, "Townsend Movement," pp. 442–43.

35. "Report on the Union Filing Situation," 7 Aug. 1936, Lemke Papers; *Social Justice*, 6 July 1936; Bennett, *Demagogues in the Depression*, pp. 200–207, 248–50.

36. James Roosevelt to James A. Farley, 17 Sept. 1936, Farley to William R. Thomas, 24 Aug. 1936, Democratic National Campaign Committee, 1936: Correspondence of James A. Farley, Chairman, in Franklin D. Roosevelt Library; *New York Times*, 17 July, 3, 5, 6, 15 Aug., 7, 12, 13, 27 Sept. 1936; *Social Justice*, 3 July 1936.

37. H. F. Swett (director of organization of the Union party) to William Skeels, 30 July 1936, Charlotte F. Jones to Lemke, 15 Feb. 1937, Lemke Papers; Kloeb to Farley, 4 Sept. 1936, National Committee Correspondence.

38. *New York Times*, 2, 3, 8, 12, 18, 19, 20, 21, 26 Aug., 1 Nov 1936; Henry B. R. Briggs to Farley, 27 July 1936, National Committee Correspondence; "Pensions and Ballots," *Literary Digest* 122 (22 Aug. 1936): 6; "Last-Minute Squabbles Weaken Coalition of Messiahs," *Newsweek* 8 (31 Oct. 1936): 9; Ribuffo, *Old Christian Right*, p. 147.

39. Many have analyzed the Union party vote, searching for evidence of religious, ethnic, ideological, class, or sectional feeling expressed through this ballot. But because of the nature of the campaign, the defections, and the problems of finding a place on the ballot of so many states, the final Union vote is an unsatisfactory data base for studying Coughlin's supporters or the followers of the other leaders. See, for example, Murray S. Stedman, Jr., and Susan W. Stedman, *Discontent at the Polls: A Study of*

Farmer and Labor Parties, 1927–1948 (New York: Columbia University Press, 1950), p. 52; Masters, "Father Coughlin and Social Justice," pp. 296–330; Lubell, *Future of American Politics*, pp. 150–54; Edward C. Blackorby, "William Lemke: Agrarian Radical and Union Party Presidential Candidate," *Mississippi Valley Historical Review* 49 (June 1962): 80; Louis H. Bean, *How to Predict Elections* (New York: Knopf, 1948), pp. 96–101; Bennett, *Demagogues in the Depression*, pp. 263–76; Michael Paul Rogin, *The Intellectuals and McCarthy: The Radical Specter* (Cambridge, Mass.: MIT Press, 1967), pp. 103, 131–33; Lipset and Raab, *Politics of Unreason*, pp. 184–89.

40. *Social Justice*, 18 Jan, 1 Feb. 1937, 25 July 1938, 27 Mar, 3 Apr. 1939; Craig A. Newton, "Father Coughlin and His National Union for Social Justice," *Southwestern Social Science Quarterly* 41 (Dec. 1960): 348–49; Charles J. Tull, *Father Coughlin and the New Deal* (Syracuse: Syracuse University Press, 1965), pp. 177–88; *New York Times*, 8 Oct. 1938, 16 Aug. 1939; George Seldes, *Facts and Fascism* (New York: New Union Press, 1943), pp. 129–30; Ferkiss, "Political and Economic Philosophy of American Fascism," pp. 242–52; Shenton, "Coughlin Movement," p. 372; Theodore Irwin, "Inside the Christian Front," *Forum* 103 (Mar. 1940): 102–8.

41. Marshall Sklare and Theodore Solotaroff, "Introduction," John Higham, "American Anti-Semitism Historically Reconsidered," Morton Keller, "Jews and the Character of American Life since 1930," and Robin Williams, Jr., "Changes in Value Orientation," in Charles Herbert Stember et al., *Jews in the Mind of America* (New York: Basic Books, 1966), pp. 19, 242–43, 261–63, 347.

42. Charles Herbert Stember, "The Recent History of Public Attitudes: Reaction to Anti-Semitic Appeals before and during the War" in Stember et al., *Jews in the Mind of America*, pp. 116–17, 121, 124–25, 128. The particular poll data were from Opinion Research Corporation surveys, March and May 1938. See also Carey McWilliams, *A Mask for Privilege: Anti-Semitism in the United States* (1925; rpt. Westport, Conn.: Greenwood Press, 1972), p. 193.

43. *Social Justice*, 11 Nov. 1940, 8, 22 Dec. 1941; William C. Kernan, *The Ghost of Royal Oak* (New York: Free Speech Forum, 1940), p. 22.

44. Roy, *Apostles of Discord*, pp. 62–74; Ribuffo, *Old Christian Right*, pp. 142–55, 162–70; Ferkiss, "Political and Economic Philosophy of American Fascism," pp. 287–88, 318; U.S. Congress, House, Committee on Un-American Activities, *Hearings: Investigation of Un-American Propaganda,"* pp. 19–22; Keller, "Jews and the Character of American Life," p. 266. Smith did receive 130,000 votes as a senatorial candidate in Michigan in 1942. See also Victor G. Reuther, *The Brothers Reuther and the Story of the U.A.W.* (New York: Houghton Mifflin, 1976), p. 215.

45. *Social Justice*, 9 Feb. 1942; *New York Times*, 5 May 1942; Francis Biddle, *The Fear of Freedom* (Garden City, N.Y.: Doubleday, 1952), p. 79.

46. John Morton Blum, *V Was for Victory: Politics and American Culture during World War II* (New York: Harcourt Brace Jovanovich, 1976), pp. 146–55; American Civil Liberties Union, "Freedom in Wartime," in

Richard Polenberg, ed., *America at War: The Home Front, 1941–1945* (Englewood Cliffs, N.J.: Prentice-Hall, 1968), pp. 90–91.

47. Carey McWilliams, *Prejudice: Japanese-Americans, Symbols of Racial Intolerance* (Boston: Little, Brown, 1944), pp. 156–80; Bill Hosokawa, *Nisei* (New York: Morrow, 1969), pp. 243–78; Blum, *V Was for Victory*, pp. 155–67.

48. Earl Warren, "Testimony on the Japanese Evacuation," in Polenberg, ed., *America at War*, pp. 90–91; John P. Roche, *The Quest for the Dream* (New York: Macmillan, 1963), pp. 193–200.

49. Allan R. Bosworth, *America's Concentration Camps* (New York: Norton, 1967), pp. 143–80; Morton Grodzins, *Americans Betrayed: Politics and the Japanese Evacuation* (Chicago: University of Chicago Press, 1949), pp. 38–50, 283–302; Arthur Zich, "Japanese Americans: Home at Last," *National Geographic* 169 (Apr. 1986): 518–33.

50. Ellen H. Posner, "Intergroup Relations," in Henry Schneiderman, ed., *The American Jewish Year Book*, 45 (Philadelphia: Jewish Publication Society of America, 1943), pp. 181–88; Dale Kramer, "The American Fascists," *Harper's Magazine* 181 (Sept. 1940), 380–93; Ribuffo, *Old Christian Right*, pp. 178–81, 190–216. See also Charles B. Hudson, "America in Danger!," Carl H. Mote, "The Ruling Oligarchy Wants to Engage in a Foreign War," Elizabeth Dilling, "The Roosevelt Red Record and Its Background," and Martin Dies, "Communist Influence in High Places," in David Brion Davis, ed., *Fear of Conspiracy: Images of Un-American Subversion from the Revolution to the Present* (Ithaca: Cornell University Press, 1971), pp. 251–57, 273–76, 282–84.

51. David S. Wyman, *The Abandonment of the Jews* (New York: Pantheon Books, 1984), pp. 10–15; Ellen H. Posner, "Anti-Jewish Manifestations," in Harry Schneiderman, ed., *The American Jewish Year Book*, 46 (Philadelphia: Jewish Publication Society of America, 1944), pp. 133–43; *New York Times*, 30 Dec. 1943, 11 Jan. 1944.

52. Wyman, *Abandonment of the Jews*, pp. 6–9, 56–57, 106–7, 190–91, 266–67, 279–87; David S. Wyman, *Paper Walls: America and the Refugee Crisis, 1938–1941* (New York: Pantheon Books, 1968), pp. 138–39, 146–47, 173, 178–79, 193; Stember, "Recent History of Public Attitudes," pp. 144–46. The surveys in question were made by the Elmo Roper organization in July and December 1938 and the National Opinion Research Center of the University of Chicago in January 1943.

53. Stember, "Recent History of Public Attitudes," pp. 115, 121–22, 159–61; Keller, "Jews and the Character of American Life," pp. 265–66; John Higham, *Send These to Me* (New York: Atheneum, 1975), pp. 191–92; Carey McWilliams, "The Zoot Suit Riots," *New Republic* 108 (21 June 1943): 818–20.

54. Richard Polenberg, *One Nation Divisible* (New York: Viking Press, 1980), pp. 53–78; Harvard Sitkoff, "The Detroit Race Riot of 1943," *Michigan History* 53 (Fall 1969): 183–206; Thurgood Marshall, "The Gestapo in Detroit," *Crisis* (Aug. 1943): 232–46.

CHAPTER 14

1. "X" [George F. Kennan], "The Sources of Soviet Conduct," *Foreign Affairs* 25 (July 1947): 566–82; Arthur H. Vandenberg, Jr., *The Private Papers of Senator Vandenberg* (Boston: Houghton Mifflin, 1952), pp. 390–91.

2. Loren Baritz, ed., *The Culture of the Twenties* (New York: Bobbs-Merrill, 1970), pp. xxii–xxiii, xxx–xli; Stanley Coben and Lorman Ratner, "Introduction," Loren Baritz, "The Culture of the Twenties," and Cushing Strout, "Individuals Well Organized," in Stanley Coben and Lorman Ratner, eds., *The Development of an American Culture* (Englewood Cliffs, N.J.: Prentice-Hall, 1970), pp. 8–11, 156–57, 225–26.

3. Warren Susman, "Introduction," in Warren Susman, ed., *Culture and Commitment, 1929–1945* (New York: George Braziller, 1973), pp. 1–12, 14–16; Studs Terkel, *Hard Times* (New York: Pantheon Books, 1970), pp. 78–81.

4. Robert E. Wiebe, *The Segmented Society* (New York: Oxford University Press, 1973), pp. 70–72.

5. John Higham, *Strangers in the Land: Patterns of American Nativism, 1860–1925* (1955; 2d ed. New York: Atheneum, 1963), p. 157; Lothrop Stoddard, *The Rising Tide of Color* (New York: Charles Scribner's Sons, 1925), pp. 198–310; Horace M. Kallen, *Culture and Democracy in the United States* (New York: Boni and Liveright, 1924), pp. 116–234; Stanley Coben, "Introduction," Horace Meyer Kallen, "Cultural Pluralism: An Alternative to the Melting Pot," and Madison Grant, "The Master Race," in Stanley Coben, ed., *Reform, War and Reaction, 1912–1932* (Columbia: University of South Carolina Press, 1972), pp. xiv, 147–65, 188–207; Milton M. Gordon, *Human Nature, Class and Ethnicity* (New York: Oxford University Press, 1978), pp. 99–201; Franz Boas, "Changes in Bodily Forms of Descendants of Immigrants" (1912), "Report on an Anthropometric Investigation of the Population of the United States" (1922), in Franz Boas, *Race, Language and Culture* (New York: Macmillan, 1948), pp. 28, 42–48, 60–85; Franz Boas, *Anthropology and Modern Life* (New York: Norton, 1928), pp. 26–27, 40–48, 59–61; Franz Boas, *Race and Democratic Society* (New York: J. J. Augustin, 1945), pp. 20–37; William S. Willis, Jr., "Skeletons in the Anthropological Closet," in *Reinventing Anthropology* (New York: Pantheon Books, 1972), pp. 134–41.

6. Ruth Benedict, *Race and Racism* (1942; rpt. London: Routeledge & Kegan Paul, 1983), pp. 64–68, 80–93, 141–87; Higham, *Strangers in the Land*, pp. 275–76; Peter I. Rose, *The Subject Is Race* (New York: Oxford University Press, 1968), pp. 37–41; Robert Ezra Park, "Racial Ideologies" (1943), in Park, *Race and Culture* (Glencoe, Ill.: Free Press, 1950), p. 315; George Eaton Simpson and J. Milton Yinger, *Racial and Cultural Minorities* (1953; rpt. New York: Harper & Row, 1965), pp. 109–238, 523–46. In the 1970s, William Shockley, Nobel Laureate in physics, would argue that there were hereditary intellectual deficits, racially genetic in origin, to be found among blacks and other minorities. Shockley's views were rejected by an overwhelming majority of biologists and psychologists who responded to his work.

7. Robert J. Donovan, *Conflict and Crisis: The Presidency of Harry S. Truman, 1945–1948* (New York: Norton, 1977), pp. 293–98; Kenneth O'Reilly, *Hoover and the Un-Americans: the FBI, HUAC and the Red Menace* (Philadelphia: Temple University Press, 1983), pp. 75–76, 102; Earl Latham, *The Communist Controversy in Washington* (Cambridge, Mass.: Harvard University Press, 1966), pp. 203–16; Richard M. Fried, *Men against McCarthy* (New York: Columbia University Press, 1976), p. 9; Harry S. Truman, *Years of Trial and Hope, Memoirs*, vol. 2, *1946–1952* (New York: Signet Books, 1956), pp. 321–22.

8. Alan D. Harper, *The Politics of Loyalty: The White House and the Communist Issue, 1946–1952* (Westport, Conn.: Greenwood Press, 1969), pp. 20–59; Francis Biddle, *Fear of Freedom* (Garden City, N.Y.: Doubleday, 1952), pp. 201–18, 238–41; David Caute, *The Great Fear: The Anti-Communist Purge under Truman and Eisenhower* (New York: Simon and Schuster, 1978), pp. 24–31; Alonzo L. Hamby, *Beyond the New Deal: Harry S. Truman and American Liberalism* (New York: Columbia University Press, 1973), pp. 170–72; Roger S. Abbott, "The Federal Loyalty Program: Background and Problems," *American Political Science Review* 42 (June 1948): 486–99.

9. Harper, *Politics of Loyalty*, p. 46; Peter H. Irons, "American Business and the Origins of McCarthyism: The Cold War Crusade of the United States Chamber of Commerce," in Robert Griffith and Athan Theoharis, eds., *The Specter: Original Essays on the Cold War and the Origins of McCarthyism* (New York: New Viewpoints, 1974), pp. 79–87.

10. Donald F. Crosby, S.J., "The Politics of Religion: American Catholics and the Anti-Communist Impulse," in Griffith and Theoharis, eds., *Specter*, pp. 28–35; Robert I. Gannon, S.J., *The Cardinal Spellman Story* (New York: Doubleday, 1962), pp. 336–38, 348–50; Eric F. Goldman, *The Crucial Decade and After* (New York: Vintage Books, 1960), pp. 129–31; Fulton J. Sheen, *Communism and the Conscience of the West* (New York: Bobbs-Merrill, 1948), pp. 48–158.

11. McGrath is quoted in Lawrence S. Wittmer, *Cold War America* (New York: Praeger, 1974), pp. 86–87; Hamby, *Beyond the New Deal*, pp. 467–69; "The Case of the Eleven Communists: Mr. Justice Jackson, Concurring, Mr. Justice Douglas, Dissenting," in John C. Wahlke, ed., *Loyalty in a Democratic State* (Boston: D. C. Heath, 1952), pp. 35–45; Nathaniel Weyl, *The Battle against Disloyalty* (New York: Thomas Y. Crowell, 1951), pp. 303–22; Caute, *Great Fear*, pp. 151–52; O'Reilly, *Hoover and the Un-Americans*, pp. 117–18; Latham, *Communist Controversy*, pp. 3, 350, 381.

12. U.S. Congress, House of Representatives, *Hearings Regarding Communist Espionage in the United States Government*, 80th Cong., 2d sess., pp. 975–1000; Harper, *Politics of Loyalty*, pp. 2, 71; Harry S. Truman Press Conference, 5 Aug. 1948, in Barton J. Bernstein and Allen J. Matusow, eds., *The Truman Administration: A Documentary History* (New York: Harper & Row, 1966), pp. 385–86.

13. Richard M. Nixon, "Plea for an Anti-Communist Faith," in Eric Bentley, ed., *Thirty Years of Treason* (New York: Viking Press, 1971), pp. 569–71; Goldman, *Crucial Decade*, pp. 101–12. The works on the Hiss-Chambers

case are numerous. Essential reading begins with Whittaker Chambers, *Witness* (New York: Random House, 1952), in which Chambers describes his background, discusses the case, and juxtaposes communism against religion: "Man without God is a beast." See also Alger Hiss, *In the Court of Public Opinion* (New York: Harper & Row, 1972). A psychoanalytic treatment is Meyer A. Zeligs, M.D., *Friendship and Fratricide: An Analysis of Whittaker Chambers and Alger Hiss* (New York: Viking Press, 1967). A post-Watergate assessment of two key actors is Morton Levitt and Michael Levitt, *A Tissue of Lies* (New York: McGraw-Hill, 1979), pp. 320–37, assailing Richard Nixon as "a liar" and attacking Hiss for lying at his trial.

14. *Congressional Record*, 81st Cong., 2d sess., 22 Sept. 1950, pp. 15629–32; Harper, *Politics of Loyalty*, pp. 144–63, 277–91; Caute, *Great Fear*, p. 21; Richard Freeland, *The Truman Doctrine and the Origins of McCarthyism* (New York: Knopf, 1970), p. 119; on balance, Freeland blames Truman for creating the atmosphere in which McCarthyism flourished (pp. 4–11, 87–100, 120–25, 359); Carey McWilliams, *Witch Hunt: The Revival of Heresy* (New York: Little, Brown, 1950), pp. 247–50; Weyl, *Battle against Disloyalty*, pp. 324–25.

15. The most important works on the Rosenberg affair, offering very different conclusions, are Ronald Radosh and Joyce Milton, *The Rosenberg File: A Search for the Truth* (New York: Holt, Rinehart and Winston, 1983), a persuasive analysis of the evidence, Walter Schneir and Miriam Schneir, *Invitation to an Inquest* (New York: Penguin Books, 1973), and Robert Meeropol and Michael Meeropol, *We Are Your Sons* (Boston: Houghton Mifflin, 1975). On Fuchs's arrest and confession and the subsequent arrest of the Americans, see Schneir and Schneir, *Invitation to an Inquest*, pp. 59–89. On Judge Kauffman's statement, see ibid., pp. 261–62, and Meeropol and Meeropol, *We Are Your Sons*, p. 34. Radosh and Milton suggest that the information on the implosion device might have saved the Soviet researchers time, for the uranium bomb (used at Hiroshima) was a dead end, as the Russian scientists might have deduced from the spy ring's evidence (see *Rosenberg File*, pp. 435–54).

16. For Julius Rosenberg's remarks, see Meeropol and Meeropol, *We Are Your Sons*, pp. 164–65. See also S. Andhil Fineberg, *The Rosenberg Case: Fact and Fiction* (New York: Oceana Publications, 1953), pp. viii, 147–48.

17. *Congressional Record*, 81st Cong., 2d sess., 20 Feb. 1950, pp. 1954–66.

18. Ibid., pp. 1956–57.

19. David Oshinsky, *A Conspiracy So Immense: The World of Joe McCarthy* (New York: Free Press, 1983), pp. 81–84, 109–111; Richard H. Rovere, *Senator Joe McCarthy* (New York: Harcourt, Brace, 1959), pp. 124–30; Michael O'Brien, *McCarthy and McCarthyism in Wisconsin* (Columbia: University of Missouri Press, 1980). The text of the Wheeling speech was inserted in the *Congressional Record* with the number 57. On another occasion, later in February, he said there were 81 "persons who I consider to be Communists in the State Department." The senator's charges were not only wildly erratic—as well as irresponsible and misleading—but as a

Washington Post reporter covering the story in these weeks noted, they were not even built on circumstantial evidence valid at the time. The "57" cited in later versions were people cleared by the FBI (over half the group) or in cases under investigation; the "205" had been subjected to the full procedures of the president's loyalty program, and only 65 remained in service in 1950. See Alfred Friendly, "The Noble Crusade of Senator McCarthy," *Harper's Magazine* 201 (Aug. 1950): 34–40.

The origins of the Wheeling speech and McCarthy's anticommunist crusade are matters of historical dispute. Richard Rovere, in his influential biography (pp. 122–24), described a dinner at the Colony restaurant in Washington on 7 January 1950. There, McCarthy asked three companions—a faculty member at Georgetown University, a Washington attorney, and Father Edmund A. Walsh, regent of the School of Foreign Service at Georgetown—to help him find a domestic issue for his 1952 reelection campaign. After considering the St. Lawrence Seaway and some "up to date variant of the Townsend Plan," McCarthy finally "seized upon" communism and its capacity for subversion: "That's it," he said, "the Government is full of communists. . . . We can hammer away at them." The "Dinner at the Colony" became the centerpiece of a chapter in Goldman's *Crucial Decade* (pp. 139–41), where once again Joe McCarthy was characterized as a latecomer to the anticommunist crusade, an unprincipled opportunist. This version has been challenged by Michael O'Brien, "McCarthy and McCarthyism: The Cedric Parker Case, November, 1949," in Griffith and Theoharis, eds., *Specter*, pp. 226–38, who points to the senator's earlier anti-communist activity in Wisconsin; Oshinsky (*A Conspiracy So Immense*, pp. 107–8), citing Father Walsh's denial that communism was discussed at the dinner and linking the entire incident to an erroneous report in Drew Pearson's syndicated column; and Donald F. Crosby, S.J., *God, Church, and Flag: Senator Joseph R. McCarthy and the Catholic Church, 1950–1952* (Chapel Hill: University of North Carolina Press, 1978), pp. 47–52.

20. Thomas C. Reeves, *The Life and Times of Joe McCarthy* (New York: Stein and Day, 1982), pp. 1–18; Oshinsky, *A Conspiracy So Immense*, pp. 2–15.

21. On McCarthy's early years, see Oshinsky, *A Conspiracy So Immense*, pp. 8–52; Reeves, *Joe McCarthy*, pp. 11–108; Rovere, *Senator Joe McCarthy*, pp. 87–104.

22. Rovere, *Senator Joe McCarthy*, pp. 104–18; Reeves, *Joe McCarthy*, pp. 161–200; Oshinsky, *A Conspiracy So Immense*, pp. 54–84; O'Brien, "Cedric Parker Case," pp. 228–38.

23. Reeves, *Joe McCarthy*, pp. 235–43; Fried, *Men Against McCarthy*, pp. 48–51.

24. Rovere, *Senator Joe McCarthy*, pp. 109–10, 139–53; Reeves, *Joe McCarthy*, pp. 235–49; Joseph Keeley, *The China Lobby Man* (New Rochelle: Arlington House, 1969).

25. Caute, *Great Fear*, pp. 305–21; Oshinsky, *A Conspiracy So Immense*, pp. 119–57; Joseph R. McCarthy, *McCarthyism: The Fight for America*

(New York: Devin-Adair, 1952), pp. 53–55; William F. Buckley, Jr., and L. Brent Bozell, *McCarthy and His Enemies* (Chicago: Henry Regnery, 1954), pp. 153–60; Rovere, *Senator Joe McCarthy*, pp. 147–55; Latham, *Communist Controversy*, pp. 270–316; Stanley I. Kutler, *The American Inquisition: Justice and Injustice in the Cold War* (New York: Hill and Wang, 1982), pp. 183–215. The persecution of Lattimore—he published a book titled *Ordeal by Slander* after the Tydings hearings—continued with a lengthy grilling by the Senate Internal Security Subcommittee in 1954. This was followed by a series of indictments for perjury. It was not until January 1955 that a federal judge finally threw out the case presented against Lattimore by the Justice Department and the FBI.

26. U.S. Congress, Senate, Committee on Foreign Relations, "State Department Employee Loyalty Investigations," Senate Report 2108, 81st Cong., 2d sess., 1 June 1950, *Congressional Record*, p. 7895.

27. James T. Patterson, *Mr. Republican: A Biography of Robert A. Taft* (Boston: Houghton Mifflin, 1973), pp. 444–46; William S. White, *The Taft Story* (New York: Harper & Row, 1954), p. 85. On another occasion, Taft called McCarthy "a fighting Marine who risked his life to preserve the liberties of the United States." The "greatest Kremlin asset in our history," he said, "has been the pro-Communist group in the State Department who surrendered to every demand of Russia at Yalta and Potsdam, and promoted at every opportunity the Communist cause in China until today Communism threatens to take over all of Asia."

28. Reeves, *Joe McCarthy*, pp. 314, 318–19, 359–61; Rovere, *Senator Joe McCarthy*, pp. 141–43; Edwin R. Bayley, *Joe McCarthy and the Press* (Madison: University of Wisconsin Press, 1981), pp. 25–26, 36–87. Some major syndicated columnists, including Drew Pearson and Marquis Childs, were outspoken McCarthy critics.

29. Fried, *Men against McCarthy*, pp. 122–53; McCarthy, *McCarthyism*; Reeves, *Joe McCarthy*, pp. 315–46. The most notorious campaign tactic in Maryland (cited by almost every student of the McCarthy years) was the use of a composite picture in which separate shots of Millard Tydings and Earl Browder, former general secretary of the Communist party of the United States, were placed side by side. The clear implication was that the senator and the well-known communist were old friends and associates. On the effect of anticommunist activity on academic freedom, see Alexander Meiklejohn, "Should Communists Be Allowed to Teach," and Sidney Hook, "Academic Freedom and Communism," in Wahlke, ed., *Loyalty in a Democratic State*, pp. 84–95; and Alan Barth, "The Loyalty of Free Men," in *American Association of University Professors Bulletin* 37 (Spring 1951): 5–16.

30. Rovere, *Senator Joe McCarthy*, pp. 170–77. Oshinsky, *A Conspiracy So Immense*, p. 200, suggests that the speech might have been written by right-wing journalist Forest Davis, who had worked for Kohlberg and Robert Taft. See "Proceedings and Debates of the Eighty-second Congress, First Session," vol. 97, p. 5, *Congressional Record*, 82d Cong., 1st sess., 14 June 1951, pp. 6594–6603 (also published as Joe McCarthy, *America's Retreat*

from Victory: The Story of George Catlett Marshall [New York: Devin-Adair, 1951]).

31. Truman, *Years of Trial and Hope*, p. 566; Leonard Mosley, *Marshall* (New York: Hearst Books, 1982), pp. 506–7; *New York Times*, 3, 4 Oct. 1952; Emmett John Hughes, *The Ordeal of Power* (New York: Atheneum, 1963), pp. 41–43; John Robert Greene, "The Crusade: The Presidential Election of 1952" (Ph.D. dissertation, Syracuse University, 1983), pp. 597–606.

32. Bernstein and Matusow, eds., *Truman Administration*, pp. 145–47; *Congressional Record*, 82d Cong., 2d sess. 25 June 1952, pp. 8082–85; Truman, *Years of Trial and Hope*, p. 542.

33. Herbert S. Parmet, *Eisenhower and the American Crusade* (New York: Macmillan, 1971), pp. 125–32; Greene, "Crusade," pp. 607–13; Allen J. Matusow, ed., *Joseph McCarthy* (Englewood Cliffs, N.J.: Prentice-Hall, 1970), pp. 61–64; *New York Times*, 28 Oct. 1952; Rovere, *Senator Joe McCarthy*, pp. 181–83; Stuart Gerry Brown, *Conscience in Politics: Adlai E. Stevenson in the 1950's* (Syracuse: Syracuse University Press, 1961), pp. 72–73; Walter Johnson, ed., *The Papers of Adlai Stevenson*, vol. 4, *1952–1958* (Boston: Little, Brown, 1974), pp. 164–65, 392–93.

34. *New York Times*, 5 Nov. 1952, 18 Jan. 1953; Reeves, *Joe McCarthy*, pp. 543–45; Angus Campbell, Philip E. Converse, William E. Miller, and Donald E. Stokes, *The Voter Decides* (Evanston: Row Peterson, 1954), p. 52.

35. Robert H. Ferrell, ed., *The Eisenhower Diaries* (New York: Norton, 1981), pp. 233–34; Parmet, *Eisenhower*, pp. 248–49.

36. Parmet, *Eisenhower*, pp. 127–28, 229; Rovere, *Senator Joe McCarthy*, pp. 189–90.

37. Rovere, *Senator Joe McCarthy*, pp. 201–5; Reeves, *Joe McCarthy*, pp. 463–64, 484–87, 507; Goldman, *Crucial Decade*, pp. 251–53.

38. Joseph B. Matthews, "Reds and Our Churches," *American Mercury* 77 (July 1953): 3–13; J. B. Matthews, "Communism and the Colleges," in David B. Davis, ed., *The Fear of Conspiracy* (Ithaca: Cornell University Press, 1971), pp. 298–302; Crosby, *God, Church and Flag*, pp. 126–32. Crosby argues that although Catholic liberals condemned McCarthy over the Matthews affair, many Protestants still "saw the Matthews attacks as a Catholic assault on their loyalty," and "the chasm between Protestants and Catholics" widened as a result.

39. U.S. Congress, Senate, Permanent Subcommittee on Investigations, *Communist Infiltration in the Army, Hearings*, 83d Cong. 2d sess., pp. 145–55; *New York Times*, 26, 28 Feb. 1954; Reeves, *Joe McCarthy*, pp. 530–31, 540–63; Bayley, *Joe McCarthy and the Press*, pp. 187–99.

40. *New York Times*, 4, 9, 10 Mar. 1954; Reeves, *Joe McCarthy*, pp. 555–63.

41. Edward Bliss, Jr., ed., *In Search of Light: The Broadcasts of Edward R. Murrow, 1938–1961* (New York: Avon Books, 1974), pp. 265–66; Erik Barnouw, *The Image Empire: A History of Broadcasting in the United States*, 3 vols. (New York: Oxford University Press, 1970), 3: 53; Robert Mertz, *CBS: Reflections in a Bloodshot Eye* (New York: Signet, 1975), pp. 286–88.

42. *New York Times*, 13–18 Mar. 1954.

43. Ibid., 15–16, 22–23 Apr. 1954; Bayley, *Joe McCarthy and the Press*, pp. 204–8.

44. U.S. Congress, Senate, Special Subcommittee on Investigation, *Special Senate Investigation on Charges and Countercharges Involving Secretary of the Army Robert T. Stevens, John G. Adams, H. Struve Hervel and Senator Joseph McCarthy, Roy M. Cohn and Francis P. Carr, Hearings*, 83d Cong., 2d sess., pp. 2426–30; Roy Cohn, *McCarthy* (New York: New American Library, 1968), pp. 200–204; Reeves, *Joe McCarthy*, pp. 628–72; Oshinsky, *A Conspiracy So Immense*, pp. 446–504; Goldman, *Crucial Decade*, pp. 272–77.

45. John G. Adams, *Without Precedent: The Story of the Death of McCarthyism* (New York: Norton, 1983), pp. 168–233; Arthur V. Watkins, *Enough Rope: The Inside Story of the Censure of Senator Joe McCarthy* (Englewood Cliffs, N.J.: Prentice-Hall, 1969), pp. 125–85.

46. Buckley and Bozell, *McCarthy and His Enemies*, pp. 311, 335; Irving Howe and Lewis Coser, *American Communist Party* (New York: Frederick A. Praeger, 1957), pp. 444–90; Latham, *Communist Controversy*, pp. 314–15.

47. Daniel Bell, ed., *The Radical Right: The New American Right Expanded and Updated* (Garden City, N.Y.: Doubleday, 1963). See, in particular, Daniel Bell, "Interpretations of American Politics (1955)," pp. 31, 47–48; Richard Hofstadter, "The Pseudo-Conservative Revolt (1955)," pp. 69–72; David Riesman and Nathan Glazer, "The Intellectuals and the Discontented Classes (1955)," pp. 95–96; Peter Viereck, "The Revolt against the Elite (1955)," pp. 150–54; Talcott Parsons, "Social Strains in America (1955)," pp. 189–92; Seymour Martin Lipset, "The Sources of the Radical Right (1955)," pp. 259–312. See also Daniel Bell, *The End of Ideology* (New York: Free Press, 1962), pp. 111, 123; Seymour Martin Lipset and Earl Raab, *The Politics of Unreason* (New York: Harper & Row, 1970), pp. 212–14; and Richard Hofstadter, *The Paranoid Style in American Politics* (New York: Alfred A. Knopf, 1965), pp. 66–92.

48. Nelson Polsby, "Toward an Explanation of McCarthyism," *Political Studies* 8 (Oct. 1960): 250–71; Latham, *Communist Controversy*, pp. 412–23; Michael Paul Rogin, *The Intellectuals and McCarthy: The Radical Specter* (Cambridge, Mass.: MIT Press, 1967), pp. 247–48; Robert Griffith, "American Politics and the Origin of McCarthyism," pp. 2–17, and Athan Theoharis, "The Politics of Scholarship: Liberals, Anti-Communism, and McCarthyism," pp. 264–80, in Griffith and Theoharis, eds., *Specter*. See also Samuel Lubell, *The Future of American Politics* (New York: Avon Books, 1955), pp. 164, 241–57.

49. Samuel A. Stouffer, *Communism, Conformity, and Civil Liberties* (1955; rpt. New York: Wiley, 1965), pp. 58–88, 156–87. Although Stouffer's polls led him to conclude that "very few are deeply worried about Communism," his data revealed that 43 percent of a national cross-section marked "very great danger" or "great danger" in response to the question: "How great a danger do you feel American Communists are to this country at the

present time?" Only a handful of respondents marked "hardly any danger" or "no danger." Few people had ever known a person they suspected of being a communist; the fear was of an unseen enemy that was "anti-religious" and believed in total "government ownership of property." It is clear that the Red specter was real enough to millions of Americans in the early 1950s.

50. Lipset and Raab, *Politics of Unreason*, pp. 230–38; Rogin, *Intellectuals and McCarthy*, pp. 238–39; Seymour Martin Lipset, "Three Decades of the Radical Right—1962," in Bell, ed., *Radical Right*, pp. 332–38. Crosby, *God, Church, and Flag*, pp. 228–54, challenges the notion that there was "a Catholic position on McCarthy." He argues that the polls also revealed a "remarkably large body of vague opinion on McCarthy" by Catholics as well as by other Americans. He concludes that "the Catholic population [was] not radically different from the rest of the nation in its views on the Senator." See also Hofstadter, *Paranoid Style*, p. 73.

51. Wiebe, *Segmented Society*, pp. 95–110.

52. Robert Welch, *The Blue Book of the John Birch Society* (Belmont, Mass., 1961), pp. ii, 1–5; Robert Welch, *What Is the John Birch Society* (Belmont, Mass.: American Opinion, n.d.), pp. 1–4, 10–11; Benjamin R. Epstein and Arnold Forster, *The Radical Right: Report on the John Birch Society and Its Allies* (New York: Vintage Books, 1967), pp. 87–88. Welch used the pages of the *Blue Book* to advance some old and some new conspiracy theories. He wrote of FDR's role in the bombing of Pearl Harbor, which should have "brought him impeachment," and revealed the "truth" about the Soviet A-bomb: "They had not built one," but just exploded ones stolen from "our plants" for "show off purposes" (*Blue Book*, pp. 99, 160).

53. Welch, *Blue Book*, pp. 21–22, 54–55, 74–77, 94–98, 110–111, 169. In the "footnotes" to the *Blue Book*, Welch explained his aversion to democratic procedures by appealing to "our founding fathers": they "gave us a republic" and "spurned democracy as probably the worst of all forms of government" (p. xv).

54. Ibid., pp. 77–112; *John Birch Society Bulletin*, Feb. 1964, pp. 4–16.

55. Robert Welch, "More Stately Mansions" in Davis, ed., *Fear of Conspiracy*, pp. 327–36; Welch, *Blue Book*, pp. 145, 168; Welch, *What Is the John Birch Society*, pp. 4–5; Epstein and Forster, *Radical Right*, pp. 128–37; "Christmas Card to Father Guider, Council Member," *John Birch Society Bulletin*, Dec. 1962, pp. 21–22; Lipset and Raab, *Politics of Unreason*, pp. 258–67, 297–300; Lipset, "Three Decades of the Radical Right," p. 356; "The Manion Forum," in Arnold Forster and Benjamin R. Epstein, *Danger on the Right* (New York: Random House, 1964), pp. 115–31; Clarence Manion, *The Conservative American* (New York: Devin Adair, 1964), pp. 162–80, 190–202.

56. *John Birch Society Bulletin*, Dec. 1962, pp. 13–17; Robert Welch, *The Time Has Come* (Belmont, Mass.: Privately printed, 1964), pp. 5–7; *John Birch Society Bulletin*, Feb. 1964, pp. 4–14; ibid., Nov. 1965, pp. 1–10.

57. Robert Welch, *The Politician* (Belmont, Mass.: Privately printed, 1963), pp. xi–xiii, 35–46, 95–97, 167, 222–23, 251, 259–72.

58. Alan F. Westin, "The John Birch Society—1962," in Bell, ed., *Radical Right*, pp. 206–14; Epstein and Forster, *Radical Right*, pp. 11, 187–88, 204; Welch, *Blue Book*, pp. 164–65.

59. Jay David, ed., *The Kennedy Reader* (New York: Bobbs-Merrill, 1967), pp. 7–11.

60. Lawrence H. Fuchs, *John F. Kennedy and American Catholicism* (New York: Meredith Press, 1967), pp. 1–2, 152–53; Berton Duke and Edward J. Richter, *Religion and the Presidency* (New York: Macmillan, 1962), pp. 122–48; Theodore H. White, *The Making of the President 1960* (New York: Atheneum, 1961), pp. 107–8; Arthur M. Schlesinger, Jr., *A Thousand Days* (Boston: Houghton Mifflin, 1965), p. 7.

61. Dulce and Richter, *Religion and the Presidency*, pp. 149–71; Fuchs, *John F. Kennedy and American Catholicism*, pp. 164–82.

62. Fuchs, *John F. Kennedy and American Catholicism*, pp. 182–88; Dulce and Richter, *Religion and the Presidency*, pp. 172–95.

63. Fuchs, *John F. Kennedy and American Catholicism*, pp. 1–2, 152–53, 158–62, 165–87; Schlesinger, *A Thousand Days*, p. 7; White, *The Making of the President 1960*, pp. 107–8, 237–41, 259–62, 356–57; Dulce and Richter, *Religion and the Presidency*, pp. 122–95.

64. Robert Welch, *The New American* (Boston: Western Island, 1966), pp. 4–5; Lipset and Raab, *Politics of Unreason*, pp. 295–300, 310–311; Scott G. McNall, *Career of a Radical Rightist* (Port Washington, N.Y.: Kennikat Press, 1975), pp. 106–7, 185; *John Birch Society Bulletin*, July 1967, pp. 16–18; Fred W. Grupp, Jr., "The Political Perspectives of Birch Society Members," in Robert A. Schoenberger, ed., *The American Right Wing* (New York: Holt, Rinehart and Winston, 1969), pp. 94–98, 102–18; "Beliefs and Principles of the John Birch Society," Extension of Remarks of Hon. John H. Rousselot of California in the House of Representatives, *Congressional Record*, 87th Cong., 2d sess., 12 June 1962, pp. 10186–90; Scott G. McNall, "Social Disorganization and Availability: Accounting for Radical Rightism," in Schoenberger, ed., *American Right Wing*, pp. 124–39; Ira S. Rohter, "The Righteous Rightists," *Trans-action* 4 (May 1976): 31–35.

65. John A. Stormer, *None Dare Call It Treason* (Florissant, Mo.: Liberty Bell Press, 1964), pp. 7–114, 216–36; Ezra Taft Benson, *An Enemy Hath Done This* (Salt Lake City: Parkhorst Publishers, 1969), pp. 189–208; Epstein and Forster, *Radical Right*, pp. 7–11, 67–68, 145–80; James Burnham, *The Web of Subversion* (Boston: Western Islands, 1965), pp. 137–202.

66. James H. Madole, "The Program of the National Renaissance Party," *National Renaissance Bulletin*, Oct. 1953, pp. 3–4; ibid., May 1953, pp. 2–4.

67. George Lincoln Rockwell, "Our Fascist Founding Fathers," *Rockwell Report*, May 1965, pp.2–7.

68. Dorval Janson and Bernard Eismann, *The Far Right* (New York: McGraw-Hill, 1963), pp. 116–25.

69. "Objectives, Policies and Program of the Minuteman Organization," *On Target*, 1 Mar. 1966, pp. 1–8; Lipset and Raab, *Politics of Unreason*,

pp. 265, 281, 328; T. Harry Jones, *The Minutemen* (New York: Doubleday, 1968).

70. Janson and Eismann, *Far Right*, pp. 146–47; Lipset and Raab, *Politics of Unreason*, pp. 267–77, 327–32; David M. Chalmers, *Hooded Americanism* (Chicago: Quadrangle Books, 1968), pp. 323–24; Forster and Epstein, *Danger on the Right*, pp. 1–10, 265–71, 279; U.S. Congress, House of Representatives, Committee on Un-American Activities, *Report*, 279; *The Present Day Ku Klux Klan Movement*, 90th Cong., 2d sess. (1967), Document 377, pp. 3–371.

71. Jonathan Martin Kolkey, *The New Right, 1960–1968, with Epilogue, 1969–1980* (Washington, D.C.: University Press of America, 1983), pp. 158–59; Arnold Forster and Benjamin R. Epstein, *The New Anti-Semitism* (New York: McGraw-Hill, 1974), pp. 17–48; Calvin Trillin, "U.S. Journal: Eureka Springs, Arkansas," *New Yorker* 41 (26 July 1969): 69–70, 75–79; *Cross and The Flag*, June 1962, Nov. 1966; Glen Jeansonne, "Oral History, Biography, and Political Demagoguery: The Case of Gerald L. K. Smith," *Oral History Review* 11 (1983): 87–102; *New York Times*, 16 Apr. 1976; Leo P. Ribuffo, *The Old Christian Right: The Protestant Far Right from the Great Depression to the Cold War* (Philadelphia: Temple University Press, 1983), pp. 230–34.

72. Smith died 15 April 1978. Forster and Epstein, *Danger on the Right*, pp. 100–114; Carl McIntire, *Servants of Apostasy* (Collingwood, N.J.: Christian Beacon Press, 1955); Erling Jorstad, *The Politics of Doomsday: Fundamentalists of the Far Right* (Nashville: Abingdon Press, 1970), pp. 25–69.

73. Dr. Fred Schwarz, *You Can Trust the Communists (To Be Communists)* (New York: Prentice-Hall, 1960), pp. 164–82; Raymond E. Wolfinger, Barbara Kaye Wolfinger, Kenneth Prewitt, Sheilah Rosenhack, "America's Radical Right: Politics and Ideology," in David E. Apter, ed., *Ideology and Discontent* (Glencoe, Ill.: Free Press, 1964), pp. 262–93; Sheilah R. Koeppen, "The Radical Right and the Politics of Consensus," in Schoenberger, ed., *American Right Wing*, pp. 72–82.

74. Billy James Hargis, *Communist America—Must It Be?* (Butler, Ind.: Highley Huffman Press, 1960), pp. 21–39, 96–97; John H. Redekop, *The American Far Right: A Case Study of Billy James Hargis and the Christian Crusade* (Grand Rapids: Eerdsmans, 1968), pp. 3–220; Harry Overstreet and Bonaro Overstreet, *The Strange Tactics of Extremism* (New York: Norton, 1964), pp. 189–203; Jorstad, *Politics of Doomsday*, pp. 72–134; Forster and Epstein, *Danger on the Right*, pp. 68–86; Ira S. Rohter, "Social and Psychological Determinants of Radical Rightism," in Schoenberger, ed., *American Right Wing*, pp. 208, 225–237.

CHAPTER 15

1. Seymour Martin Lipset and Earl Raab, *The Politics of Unreason: Right-Wing Extremism in America, 1790–1970* (New York: Harper & Row, 1970), pp. 340–41, 356–58.

2. Michael Novak, *The Rise of the Unmeltable Ethnics* (New York: Macmillan, 1972); Robert Sherill, *Gothic Politics in the Deep South* (New York: Grossman, 1968), p. 300.

3. *Washington Post*, 12 Oct. 1967; *New York Times*, 25 Aug., 3 Sept. 1968. Among the works assessing the attitudes and the anxieties of those who might be attracted to the Wallace movement, see Richard Rogin, "Joe Kelly Has Reached His Boiling Point," Jerome M. Rosow, "The Problem of the Blue Collar Worker," Peter Binsen, "The Schools of Whitetown," Andrew M. Greeley, "What is an Ethnic?," and David Danzig, "The Social Framework of Ethnic Conflict in America," in Murray Friedman, ed., *Overcoming Middle Class Rage* (Philadelphia: Westminster Press, 1971), pp. 66–85, 86–102, 105–31, 231–40, 241–56; Richard Lemon, *The Troubled American* (New York: Simon and Schuster, 1969), pp. 8–43; Robert E. Lane, "The Fear of Equality," in Louise Kapp Howe, *The White Majority: Between Poverty and Affluence* (New York: Random House, 1970), pp. 119–47; Robert Schrank and Susan Stein, "Yearning, Learning and Status," in Sar A. Levitan, ed., *Blue Collar Workers* (New York: McGraw-Hill, 1971), pp. 318–41.

4. Jerry Rubin, *Do It!* (New York: Simon and Schuster, 1970), pp. 57–68, 106, 113, 117, 161, 201–6. See also Seymour Martin Lipset and Earl Raab, *The Politics of Unreason: Right-Wing Extremism in America, 1790–1970*, 2d ed. (Chicago: University of Chicago Press, 1978), pp. 525–30.

5. Kirkpatrick Sale, *SDS* (New York: Vintage Books, 1974), pp. 505–650; *Communism and the New Left: What They're Up to Now* (Washington: U.S. News and World Report, 1969), pp. 13–40, 111–28, and a chapter titled "Marxism: Food for the New Left," pp. 173–82; Irwin Unger, *The Movement* (New York: Dodd and Mead, 1974), pp. 117–48.

6. On the wide range of protests in the Nixon years, see Thomas F. Parker, ed., *Violence in the United States*, 2 vols. (New York: Facts on File, 1974), 2: 3–230.

7. Some writers could see only the arrogant innocence and destructive intolerance of the student movements. John W. Aldridge, *In the Country of the Young* (New York: Harper & Row, 1970), pp. 3–128, viewed the rebels as the spoiled issue of a generation that had grown up in the depression and come of age in the war, parents embracing the private culture after the public crises of their youth, the fathers and mothers of this new "royal family of adolescence." For other critical assessments by some well-known intellectuals, see William P. Gerberding and Duane E. Smith, eds., *The Radical Left: The Abuse of Discontent* (Boston: Houghton Mifflin, 1970).

8. Norman Macrae, "The Neurotic Trillionaire," *Economist*, 10 May 1969 (Special Supplement: A Survey of Mr. Nixon's America), pp. 11–62, begins with the statement: "The United States in this last third of the

twentieth century is the place where man's long economic problem is ending. . . . It is almost certainly the most momentous news-story so far in the history of the world." See also Norman Macrae, "Pacific Century, 1975–2075?" *Economist*, 4 Jan. 1975, pp. 15–16, 18, 21–26, 28–32, 34–35.

9. Jack T. Chick, *Alberto* (Chico, Calif.: Chick Publications, 1979), pp. 1–23; Jack T. Chick, *Double Cross: Alberto, Part Two* (Chico, Calif.: Chick Publications, 1981), pp. 1–32; Gary Metz, "The Alberto Story," *Cornerstone* (1982): 29–31.

10. Ernest Volkman, *A Legacy of Hate: Anti-Semitism in America* (New York: Franklin Watts, 1982), pp. 125–29; Philip Finch, *God, Guts and Guns* (New York: Seaview Press, 1983), pp. 22–25, 184–87; Donald Alexander Downs, *Nazis in Skokie: Freedom, Communists and the First Amendment* (Notre Dame: University of Notre Dame Press, 1985), pp. 19–37, 150–53; David Hamlin, *The Nazi/Skokie Conflict: A Civil Liberties Battle* (Boston: Beacon Press, 1980), pp. 1–23, 71–98, 175–80. The Skokie affair has become a major case for students of freedom of speech and expression.

11. *New York Times*, 11 July 1977, 27 Apr. 1986; Arnold Forster and Benjamin R. Epstein, *The New Anti-Semitism* (New York: McGraw-Hill, 1974), pp. 303–7; Volkman, *Legacy of Hate*, pp. 123–28; Report of the Georgia State Advisory Commission of the United States Commission of Civil Rights, *Perceptions of Hate Group Activity in Georgia* (Commission on Civil Rights of Georgia, 1982), pp. 2–3, 12–14; Jerry Thompson, *My Life in the Klan* (New York: G. P. Putnam's Sons, 1982), pp. 173–81; Patsy Sims, *The Klan* (New York: Stein and Day, 1978), pp. 7, 9–32, 57–76, 100–128, 142, 173–224, 235–62, 280–92; Larry R. Gerlach, *Blazing Crosses in Zion: The Ku Klux Klan in Utah* (Logan: Utah State University Press, 1982), pp. 171–72.

12. *New York Times*, 5, 14, 21, 26 Apr., 9, 14 Sept. 1985, 7 Feb. 1986; NBC "Evening News," 12 Apr. 1985; *Washington Post*, 14 Apr. 1985; *Newsweek* 105 (4 Mar. 1985): 31.

13. *New York Times*, 21, 29 Sept., 11, 17 Dec. 1985; *Time* 126 (23 Sept. 1985): 32; Finch, *God, Guts and Guns*, pp. 66–85.

14. Gerlach, *Blazing Crosses in Zion*, pp. 171–72, 185–86, 227, 231; *New York Times*, 3 Oct. 1985, 21 Apr. 1986; "Neo-Nazis Out to Save the White Race," *Syracuse Herald-American* (UPI), 3 Mar. 1985.

15. Leonard Zeskind, *The "Christian Identity" Movement: A Theological Justification for Racist and Anti-Semitic Violence* (Atlanta: Division of Church and Society of the National Council of the Churches of Christ in the U.S.A., 1986), pp. 5–40; *New York Times*, 7 Feb., 5, 14 July 1986, 29 Apr. 1987; *Washington Post*, 29 Apr. 1987.

16. *New York Times*, 8 Feb., 18, 22, 23 Apr., 17, 18 July, 13 Aug., 6, 21, 26 Sept., 3 Oct. 1985; CBS "Evening News," 22 Apr. 1985; Finch, *Gods, Guts and Guns*, pp. 101–3; Zeskind, *"Christian Identity" Movement*, pp. 7, 36–38.

17. *New York Times*, 18 May, 4 June, 11 July 1983; *Washington Post*, 5, 8, 21 June 1983; Phillip Finch, "Renegade Justice: The Fury of the Posse

Commitatus," *New Republic* 188 (25 Apr. 1983): 9–11.

18. *New York Times*, 11 Mar. 1986; Finch, *God, Guts and Guns*, pp. 20, 103–5.

19. Finch, "Renegade Justice," pp 10–11; Zeskind, *"Christian Identity" Movement*, pp. 7, 30–31; *Washington Post*, 21 June 1983.

20. A. James Rudin, "Resisting Bigotry in Troubled Rural America," *Christian Science Monitor*, 25 Nov. 1985; "All Things Considered," National Public Radio, 30 July 1985; *New York Times*, 18 May, 11 June, 11 Mar. 1986.

21. Calvin Trillin, "I've Got Problems," *New Yorker* 61 (18 Mar. 1985): 109–18; *Christian Science Monitor*, 18 Dec. 1985.

Other small right-wing groups have been implicated in acts of violence. For example, the anti-Semitic Ryan cult in Nebraska engaged in farm robberies in 1984–85 in the name of Yahoweh (God). The Duck Club, a conservative organization based in Cocoa Beach, Florida, also has chapters in the Northwest. David L. Rice, who said he was an "anti-Communist soldier," had attended meetings sponsored by this club. Rice was convicted of murdering the Charles Goldmark family in Seattle in May 1986 because he believed the Goldmarks were Jews and communists. His attorney entered a plea of insanity. In Phoenix, several members of the Arizona Patriots were arrested in December 1986, accused of planning to blow up an Internal Revenue Service complex in Utah and rob an armored car in Nevada. See *New York Times*, 11 Mar., 28 May, 17 Dec. 1986.

22. Forster and Epstein, *New Anti-Semitism*, pp. 293–96; Volkman, *Legacy of Hate*, pp. 90–92, 134–37; Finch, *God, Guts and Guns*, pp. 22–25; *Christian Science Monitor*, 16 Sept. 1983; *Los Angeles Times*, 25 July 1985; *Washington Post*, 9, 18, 21, 26 Oct. 1985; *Spotlight*, 11 Oct. 1976. One exception to the Liberty Lobby's failure to attract media attention came with its lawsuit against William Buckley and the *National Review*. The Liberty Lobby claimed it had been libeled by a *National Review* article in 1979 suggesting the lobby was funneling money to Lyndon LaRouche. In a countersuit, the *National Review*, which is also on LaRouche's enemies list, was awarded the verdict.

23. Lyndon LaRouche, "Democrat for President," paid political presentations (one-half hour), WIXT, WTVH (Syracuse, N.Y.), 1 June 1984, WSTM, 3 June 1984, WTVH, 5 Nov. 1984.

24. *New York Times*, 20, 27, 31 Mar., 4 Apr. 1986; *Washington Post*, 25 Mar. 1986; *Time* 127 (31 Mar. 1986): 25–29; *Wall Street Journal*, 28 Mar. 1986.

25. L. Marcus, "The Third Stage of Imperialism," in K. T. Fann and Donald C. Hodges, eds., *Readings in U.S. Imperialism* (Boston: Porter Sargent Publishing, 1971), pp. 85–92; Lyn Marcus, *Dialectical Economics: An Introduction to Marxist Political Economy* (Lexington, Mass.: D. C. Heath, 1975), pp. v, 3–64, 377–413; Dennis King and Ronald Radosh, "The World According to LaRouche," *New Republic* 191 (19 Nov. 1984): 18; *Village Voice*, 11 Nov. 1981; *Guardian*, 14 Apr., 1 Sept. 1976; Finch, *God, Guts*

and Guns, pp. 22–28; *New York Times*, 7, 8, 9 Sept., 8 Oct. 1979, 2 Nov. 1984, 4 Apr. 1986; *Washington Post*, 13, 14, 15 Jan. 1985; "Lyndon La-Rouche: Beyond the Fringe," *Newsweek* 107 (7 Apr. 1986): 38–39, 41.

26. *Wall Street Journal*, 28 Mar. 1986; *Washington Post*, 14 Jan. 1985; *New York Times*, 8 Oct. 1979, 3 Oct. 1985, 4 Apr. 1986, 10, 11 Sept., 3, 7, 8, Oct. 1986; "Richard Burt Dangerous to West's Security," *New Solidarity*, 15 Mar. 1985; "Only SDI Crash Program Will Curb Soviet Threat, ibid., 14 Jan. 1985; "10,000 March to Feed Africa, Build SDI," (the Movement for the Inalienable Rights of Man sponsored by the Schiller Institute), ibid., 21 Jan. 1985; Dennis King and Ronald Radosh, "The LaRouche Connection," *New Republic* 191 (19 Nov. 1984): 15–25; *Newsweek* 103 (16 Apr. 1984): 31, 105; "LaRouche Arouses Fears in Rural Area of Virginia," *New York Times*, 3 Oct. 1985; "LaRouche: The Nut Next Door," *Syracuse Herald-American* (UPI), 13 Apr. 1986; "*Wall Street Journal* Joins Dope Lobby Attack on LaRouche," *New Solidarity*, 2 June 1986; "Burt, in Bonn, Is Sabotaging U.S. Interests," ibid., 9 Dec. 1985.

27. *Washington Post*, 15 Jan. 1985; *New York Times*, 14 Jan. 1985, 4 Apr. 1986; "Gary Hart's New Yalta Policy Selling Out to the Soviets," *New Solidarity*, 20 June 1986; "Liberals Plot Crises to Hand Russia World Power," ibid., 16 June 1986.

28. *New York Times*, 4 Apr., 8 Oct. 1986; King and Radosh, "The La-Rouche Connection," pp. 15–25; ABC "Nightline," 21 Mar. 1986; "ADL Extortion Racket Run through State Department," *New Solidarity*, 9 June 1986; "Trilaterals Meet, Push World Supergovernment," ibid., 26 May 1986; "Trilateral Stooges Declare War on President," ibid., 16 Aug. 1985; "Kissinger, Rockefeller Set Trap for Thailand," ibid., 7 Oct. 1985; "Trilateral Commission Plots to Wreck NATO," ibid., 6 Sept. 1985; "Eastern Liberal Establishment the Modern Day Descendants of the British East India Company," ibid., 17 Apr. 1985; "State Department Handing the Mideast to Moscow," ibid., 28 Oct. 1985; "Schultz in Moscow to Betray Western Allies," ibid., 4 Nov. 1985.

29. Janice Hart on "Nightline," ABC Television, 21 Mar. 1986; Mark Fairchild and Janice Hart, Press Conference (Congressional News Service), 21 Mar. 1986; Janice Hart, "Our Solutions Work, They're Not Far Out," *USA Today*, 2 Apr. 1986; "LaRouche Phenomenon Starts to Fizzle," *Syracuse Herald-Journal* (NNS), 8 May 1986; *New York Times*, 27, 31 Mar., 4, 10, 20 Apr., 25 May, 10, 11 Sept., 6, 7 Oct., 17 Dec. 1986, 22 Apr. 1987; *Los Angeles Times*, 7 Oct. 1986; *Washington Post*, 25 Mar. 1986; "Politics from the Twilight Zone," *Time* 127 (31 Mar. 1986): 28–29; Mike Royko, "Tale of a Political Sucker," *Syracuse Herald-Journal*, 2 May 1986.

On the "paranoid bigotry" of the LaRouche opponents, *New Solidarity*, 9 June 1986. On the "witch-hunt" nature of the Federal Election Commission investigation of alleged misuse of credit cards, ibid., 4 Jan. 1986.

In *New Solidarity* 17 (16 June 1986) there is a story titled "Tired of Reading the Same Old Smears about La Rouche?" It contains a call to become a "press watchdog" for the LaRouche "movement": "Send us copies of every article that mentions Lyndon La Rouche. In conjunction with our legal department, we will contact the press. . . . If they are lying, we will make sure they understand the implications."

30. *Boston Globe*, 11 Aug. 1984; *Congressional Record*, 98th Cong., 2d sess., 11 June 1984, p. H–5560.

31. Vernon M. Briggs, Jr., *Immigration Policy and the American Labor Force* (Baltimore: Johns Hopkins University Press, 1984), pp. 61–95; Elizabeth Midgley, "Comings and Goings in U.S. Immigration Policy," in Demetrious G. Papademetriou and Mark J. Miller, eds., *The Unavoidable Issue: U.S. Immigration Policy in the 1980's* (Philadelphia: ISHI, 1983), pp. 49–52; David M. Reimers, *Still the Golden Door* (New York: Columbia University Press, 1985), pp. 63–90; Charles B. Keely, "Current Status of U.S. Immigration and Refugee Policy," in Mary M. Kritz, ed., *U.S. Immigration and Refugee Policy* (Lexington, Mass.: D. C. Heath, 1983), pp. 339–59; Pastora San Juan Cafferty, Barry R. Chiswick, Andrew M. Greeley, and Teresa A. Sullivan, *The Dilemma of American Immigration* (New Brunswick, N.J.: Transaction Books, 1983), pp. 55–63; *New York Times*, 30 June 1986.

32. Letter from Alan E. Eliason, *New York Times*, 29 Apr. 1986; "Alien Surge at Border Hits Record," *USA Today*, 20 May 1986; Bill Moyers, "Whose America Is It?" "CBS Reports," 3 Sept. 1985; *New York Times*, 26, 27 June 1986.

33. Briggs, *Immigration Policy and the American Labor Force*, pp. 6–12, 128–37; Demetrios G. Papademetriou and Mark J. Miller, "U.S. Immigration Policy," in Papademetriou and Miller, eds., *Unavoidable Issue*, p. 23; Milton D. Morris, *Immigration—The Beleaguered Bureaucracy* (Washington, D.C.: Brookings Institution, 1985), pp. 51–55, 106–10; John Crewdson, *The Tarnished Door* (New York: Times Books, 1983), pp. 103–11; Governor Richard D. Lamm and Gary Imhoff, *The Immigration Time Bomb* (New York: Truman/Talley Books, 1985), pp. 5, 55–65; Reimers, *Still the Golden Door*, p. 216; *FAIR Immigration Report* 6 (Mar., Apr., 1986); Arthur F. Corwin, "The Numbers Game: Estimates of Illegal Aliens in the United States, 1970–1981," in Richard R. Hofstetter, ed., *U.S. Immigration Policy* (Durham: Duke University Press, 1984), pp. 223–91; David B. Levine, Kenneth Hill, and Robert Warren, eds., *Immigration Statistics: A Story of Neglect* (Washington, D.C.: National Academy Press, 1985), pp. 16–73, 110–48; W. Tim Dagodag, "Illegal Mexican Immigration to California from Western Mexico," in Richard C. Jones, ed., *Patterns of Undocumented Migration: Mexico and the United States* (Totowa, N.J.: Rowman and Allenheld, 1984), pp. 70–73.

34. Midgley, "Comings and Goings in U.S. Immigration Policy," pp. 43–60; Phillip L. Martin and Marion F. Houstoun, "European and American Immigration Policies," in Hofstetter, ed., *U.S. Immigration Policy*, pp. 46–50; Alex Stepick, "Haitian Boat People: A Study in Conflicting Forces Shaping U.S. Immigration Policy" in ibid., pp. 183–96.

35. Crewdson, *Tarnished Door*, pp. 307–22; Harris N. Miller, " 'The Right Thing to Do': A History of Simpson-Mazzoli," in Nathan Glazer, ed.,

Clamor at the Gates: The New American Immigration (San Francisco: ICS Press, 1985), pp. 49–63.

36. Vernon M. Briggs, Jr., "Foreign Labor Programs as an Alternative to Illegal Immigration: A Dissenting View," in Peter G. Brown and Henry Shue, eds., *The Border That Joins: Mexican Migrants and U.S. Responsibility* (Totowa, N.J.: Rowman and Allenheld, 1983), pp. 231–32; Miller, "'The Right Thing to Do': A History of Simpson-Mazzoli," pp. 49–71; Crewdson, *Tarnished Door,* pp. 307–43; Lamm and Imhoff, *Immigration Time Bomb,* pp. 230–34; *New York Times,* 18 Oct. 1984.

37. Wayne A. Cornelius, Leo R. Chavez, and Jorge G. Castro, *Mexican Immigrants and Southern California: A Summary of Current Knowledge* (San Diego: Center for U.S.-Mexican Studies, 1982), pp. 34–68; Michael J. Piore, *Birds of Passage: Migrant Labor and Industrial Societies* (Cambridge: Cambridge University Press, 1979), pp. 9, 186–90; Julian Simon in Julian Simon and Roger Conner, *Debate: How Immigration Affects Americans' Living Standard* (Washington, D.C.: Heritage Foundation, 1984), pp. 6–13, 24–25; Franklin S. Abrams, "American Immigration Policy: How Strait the Gate," in Hofstetter, ed., *U.S. Immigration Policy,* pp. 118–120, and Maxine S. Seller, "Historical Perspectives on American Immigration Policy" in ibid., pp. 158–60; Arthur F. Corwin and Walter A. Fogel, "Shadow Labor Force: Mexican Workers in the American Economy," in Arthur F. Corwin, ed., *Immigrants and Immigration: Perspectives on Mexican Labor Migration to the United States* (Westport, Conn.: Greenwood Press, 1978), pp. 285–95; Cafferty et al., *Dilemma of American Immigration,* pp. 16–18; Thomas Muller, "Economic Effects of Immigration," in Glazer, ed., *Clamor at the Gates,* pp. 127–28; Edward P. Reubens, "Immigration Problems, Limited Visa Programs and Other Options," in Brown and Shue, eds., *Border That Joins,* pp. 196–99.

38. Roger Conner, *Breaking down the Barriers: The Changing Relationship between Illegal Immigration and Welfare,* FAIR Immigration Paper IV (1982), pp. 9–35; Roger Conner in Simon and Conner, *Debate,* p. 18; *New York Times,* 27 April 1986; *FAIR Immigration Report* 6 (Feb. 1986); F. Ray Marshall, *Illegal Immigration: The Problem, the Solution,* FAIR Immigration Paper III, (1982), pp. 8–14; Walter Fogel, "Immigration and the Labor Market: Historical Perspectives and Current Issues," in Papademetriou and Miller, eds., *Unavoidable Issue,* pp. 88–91; Michael S. Teitelbaum, "Right versus Right: Immigration and Refugee Policy in the United States," *Foreign Affairs* 59 (Fall 1980): 37–41; Vernon M. Briggs, Jr., "Employment Trends and Contemporary Immigration Policy," in Glazer, ed., *Clamor at the Gates,* pp. 150–54; Briggs, *Immigration Policy and the American Labor Force,* pp. 156–65; Roger Waldinger, "The Occupational and Economic Integration of the New Immigrants," in Hofstetter, ed., *U.S. Immigration Policy,* pp. 206–13; Lamm and Imhoff, *Immigration Time Bomb,* pp. 154, 157–85; Briggs, "Foreign Labor Programs," pp. 235–47; Moyers, "Whose America Is It?"; Federation for American Immigration Reform, *Hispanic and Black Attitudes toward Immigration Policy: A National Survey,* Executive Survey in FAIR Position Paper, 1985 (the survey conducted by Peter

D. Hart Research Associates of Washington and V. Lance Tarrant and Associates of Houston); Reimers, *Still the Golden Door*, pp. 236–37, 281; Richard C. Jones, "Macro-Patterns of Undocumented Migration between Mexico and the U.S.," in Jones, ed., *Patterns of Undocumented Migration*, pp. 53–54; Rodolfo O. De La Garza, "Mexican Americans, Mexican Immigrants and Immigration Reform," in Glazer, ed., *Clamor at the Gates*, pp. 93–105.

39. Otis L. Graham, Jr., *Illegal Immigration and the New Reform Movement*, FAIR Immigration Paper II (1980), pp. 9–19.

40. Ibid., pp. 18–19, 26–27; Cornelius , Chavez, and Castro, *Mexican Immigrants and Southern California*, p. 26; Briggs, *Immigration Policy and the American Labor Force*, pp. 148–52, 231 (see quotation from Gene Lyons on Algeria and Zaire).

41. Lourdes Arizpe, "The Rural Exodus in Mexico and Mexican Migration to the United States," in Brown and Shue, eds., *Border That Joins*, pp. 179–81; Milton D. Morris and Albert Mayio, *Curbing Illegal Immigration* (Washington, D.C.: Brookings Institution, 1982), pp. 3–9; Nelson Gage Copp, *"Wetbacks" and Braceros: Mexican Migrant Laborers and American Immigration Policy, 1930–1960* (San Francisco: R & E Research Associates, 1971), pp. 26–78; Julian Samora, *Los Mojados: The Wet Back Story* (Notre Dame: University of Notre Dame Press, 1971), pp. 33–88, 131–38; Manuel Garcia Griego, "The Importation of Mexican Contract Laborers to the United States, 1942–1964," in Brown and Shue, eds., *Border That Joins*, pp. 49–84; Reimers, *Still the Golden Door*, pp. 39–62, 126–28; *New York Times*, 26, 27 June 1986.

42. Leon F. Bouvier, *Immigration and Its Impact on U.S. Society* (Washington, D.C.: Population Reference Bureau, 1981), pp. 1–26; Leon F. Bouvier, *The Impact of Immigration on U.S. Population Size* (Washington, D.C.: Population Reference Bureau, 1981), pp. 4–19; Piore, *Birds of Passage*, pp. 59–85; Graham, *Illegal Immigration and the New Reform Movement*, pp. 7–9; Briggs, *Immigration Policy and the American Labor Force*, pp. 246–60; Cafferty et al., *Dilemma of American Immigration*, pp. 181–86.

43. Lawrence H. Fuchs, "The Search for a Sound Immigration Policy," in Glazer, ed., *Clamor at the Gates*, p. 27; Graham, *Illegal Immigration and the New Reform Movement*, p. 24; Conner in Simon and Conner, *Debate*, pp. 4–7. Waldinger, "Occupation and Economic Integration," agrees that illegals "have gained access to the labor market at the very lowest levels" and that "upward movement ... can be most difficult" but argues that "there is little likelihood that the 'underclass' thesis can be sustained in its extreme version" (pp. 211–21).

44. Teitelbaum, "Right versus Right," pp. 58–59; Graham, *Illegal Immigration and the New Reform Movement*, pp. 12–14; Lamm and Imhoff, *Immigration Time Bomb*, pp. 99–124; Nathan Glazer, *Ethnic Dilemmas, 1964–1982* (Cambridge, Mass.: Harvard University Press, 1983), pp. 143–46; *New York Times*, 30 June, 13, 14, 15, 16, 17, 18, 20 Oct., 13 Nov., 4, 6, 7 Dec. 1986, 21 Apr., 3, 6, 8 May 1987; Moyers, "Whose Country Is It?"

45. *New York Times*, 4 Sept., 16, 17, 18 Oct. 1984, 30 Sept. 1985. For an assessment of anti-Semitism at the end of the 1960s, which concludes that "anti-Semitism is widespread and pervasive but not in a dangerous form," see Gertrude J. Selznick and Stephen Sternberg, *The Tenacity of Prejudice: Anti-Semitism in Contemporary America* (New York: Harper & Row, 1969), pp. 184–88. See also Harold E. Quintey and Charles Y. Glock, *Anti-Semitism in America* (New York: Free Press, 1979), pp. 184–86. Charles P. Sheldon, *The Bolshevization of the USA* (New York: Carlton Press, 1978), offers anti-Semitic, anticommunist arguments reminiscent of the conspiratorial fantasies of antialiens of the past, replete with descriptions of the "Jewish World Empire" and antielitist assessments of "Harvard University and the World"; see pp. 318–23, 557–63, 626–31.

46. *Syracuse Herald-Journal*, 18 Oct. 1984; *Syracuse Post-Standard*, 18 Oct. 1984; *New York Times*, 30 Aug. 1986.

47. Steve Chapple, "The Gospel According to Jimmy Lee Swaggart," *Mother Jones* 11 (July–Aug. 1986): 36–45; "Unholy Row," *Time* 129 (6 Apr. 1987): 63–64.

48. Jimmy Swaggart, "The Meaning of the Baptism," television crusade from Hartford, Connecticut, 23 June 1986; "Presidential Prospects," *Christian Century* 102 (20 Nov. 1985): 1057; "King of Honky Tonk Heaven," *Newsweek* 101 (30 May 1983): 89–91.

49. Jimmy Swaggart, "America and the Roman Empire," television crusade from Atlanta, Georgia, 23 June 1984; Jimmy Swaggart, "America at the Crossroads," television crusade from San Antonio, Texas, 5 Nov. 1984.

50. Swaggart, television crusade, 5 Nov. 1984; Jimmy Swaggart, national television crusade, 15 Oct. 1984; "Rise of Fundamentalism Is Cheered," *Broadcasting* 110 (10 Feb. 1986): 72–74. See direct mail appeal, Clergy and Laity Concerned, signed by Rev. John Collins.

51. Tim LaHaye, *The Battle for the Mind* (Old Tappan, N.J.: Fleming H. Revell, 1980), pp. 27–33, 37–46, 57–96, 125–79, 181–95; Charles Krauthammer, "The Humanist Phantom," *New Republic* 188 (25 July 1981): 20–25; Marlin Maddoux, *America Betrayed!* (2d ed. of *Humanism Exposed*) (Shreveport, La.: Huntington House, 1984), pp. 17–49, 52–153; Maxine Negri, "The Well-Planned Conspiracy," *Humanist* 42 (May–June 1986): 40–41; Sidney Blumenthal, "The Righteous Empire," *New Republic* 191 (22 Oct. 1984): 18–24; *New York Times*, 6, 16, 17 Oct. 1986.

52. Pat Robertson, "The 700 Club," television presentation, Christian Broadcasting Network, 26 Oct. 1984; Jeffrey K. Hadden and Charles E. Swann, *Prime Time Preachers: The Rising Power of Televangelism* (Reading, Mass.: Addison, Wesley, 1981), pp. 34–37, 60, 95–96, 113–14; Pat Robertson, *The Secret Kingdom* (New York: Bantam Books, 1984), pp. 28–34; William Barry Furlong, "The 700 Club: On Screen and Behind the Scenes," *Saturday Evening Post*, 254 (Nov. 1982): 56–59; Marion G. "Pat" Robertson on "McNeill-Lehrer News Hour," 11 Nov. 1985, Public Broadcasting System; "Pentecostal for President," *Newsweek* 106 (14 Oct. 1985): 77; Erling Jorstad, *The Politics of Moralism: The New Christian Right in American Life* (Minneapolis: Augsburg, 1981), pp. 28–37; Ben Armstrong, *The Elec-*

tric Church (Nashville: Thomas Nelson, 1979), pp. 106–8; "Power, Glory and Politics: Right-Wing Preachers Dominate the Dial," *Time* 127 (17 Feb. 1986): 62, 65–68.

53. Hadden and Swann, *Prime Time Preachers*, pp. 32–34; Jorstad, *Politics of Moralism*, pp. 38–45, 92–94.

54. "Heaven Can Wait," *Newsweek* 109 (8 June 1987): 60–62, 65, 69; Hadden and Swann, *Prime Time Preachers*, pp. 12, 42–43, 114–15; "Power, Glory and Politics," pp. 64–65.

55. C. F. H. Henry, "The Fundamentalist Phenomenon," *Christianity Today* 25 (Sept. 1981): 30–31; Ed Dobson, Ed Hindson, and Jerry Falwell, *The Fundamentalist Phenomenon: The Resurgence of Conservative Christianity*, 2d ed. (Grand Rapids, Mich: Baker Book House, 1986), pp. 6–7, 19–20, 88–89, 102–3, 116–22, 129, 142, 157–64; Gabriel Fackre, *The Religious Right and Christian Faith* (Grand Rapids, Mich.: Eerdmans, 1982), pp. 1–30; Gilliam Peele, *Revival and Reaction: The Right in Contemporary America* (Oxford: Clarendon Press, 1984), pp. 80–119; Hadden and Swann, *Prime Time Preachers*, pp. 155–56; George Marsden, "Introduction," in George Marsden, ed., *Evangelicalism and Modern America* (Grand Rapids, Mich.: Eerdmans, 1984), pp. viii–xvi.

56. The terms "pentecostal," "neopentecostal," and "charismatic movement" have been used "in a confusing number of ways," as one scholar, David Edwin Harrell, Jr., has observed. Falwell has written that "most Fundamentalists would not accept the Charismatic movement as a legitimate representation of Fundamentalism," but he also notes that there are "some Fundamentalists who are charismatic in their convictions." See Dobson, Hindson, and Falwell, *Fundamentalist Phenomenon*, pp. 103–8, and David Edwin Harrell, Jr., *Things Are Possible: The Healing and Charismatic Revivals in Modern America* (Bloomington: Indiana University Press, 1975), pp. ix–xi, 3–9, 214–16.

57. Frances FitzGerald, "A Disciplined, Charging Army: The Reverend Jerry Falwell," *New Yorker* 57 (18 May 1981): 54–60; Alan Crawford, *Thunder on the Right: The New Right and the Politics of Resentment* (New York: Putnam Books, 1980), pp. 160–61; *Christian Century*, 20 Nov. 1985, p. 1057; William Seletan, "Teflon Telepreacher," *New Republic* 194 (20 June 1986): 9–11; William Martin, "Television: The Birth of a Media Myth," *Atlantic* 247 (June 1981): 7, 10–16; Flo Conway and Jim Seligman, *Holy Terror* (Garden City, N.Y.: Doubleday, 1982), pp. 68–72; Hadden and Swann, *Prime Time Preachers*, pp. 48–49, 60–61; Armstrong, *Electric Church*, pp. 100–121; George H. Hill, *Airwaves to the Soul* (Saratoga, Calif.: R & E Publishers, 1983), pp. 51–63, 85–92; Peter G. Horsfield, *Religious Television* (New York: Longman, 1984), pp. 3–36, 89–110, 148–49; Tina Rosenberg, "How the Media Made the Moral Majority," *Washington Monthly* 14 (May 1982): 26–34.

58. Jerry Falwell, "Ministers and Marches," Sermon delivered at Thomas Road Baptist Church, 21 Mar. 1965, reprinted in Perry Deane Young, *God's Bullies* (New York: Holt, Rinehart and Winston, 1982), pp. 310–17.

59. FitzGerald, "Disciplined, Charging Army," pp. 59–60, 78–90; Jerry Falwell, "The Old Time Gospel Hour," television presentation, 23 June, 1984, 9 Feb. 1986, 22 June 1986; Tom Minnery, "The Man Behind the Mask," *Christianity Today* 25 (4 Sept. 1981): 28–29; "Jerry Falwell Spreads the Word," *Time* 126 (2 Sept. 1985): 58–61; Jerry Falwell, *Listen, America!* (Garden City, N.Y.: Doubleday, 1980), pp. 13, 121–37, 165–86, 197–240; *New York Times*, 16 Jan. 1986; "Thomas Road Baptist Church in the Fifth Dimension," *Christianity Today* 26 (12 Nov. 1982): 98–99; Hadden and Swann, *Prime Time Preachers*, pp. 27–29, 59. (Falwell also refers to his network as OTGHTV, Old Time Gospel Hour. His "Jerry Falwell" special in 1986 was aired on the larger Atlanta-based WTBS superstation, with the message that "this is a Liberty Television Network broadcast.") See also Mark Smith, "Porn Pollution: Obscene Lyrics Invade the Music Industry," *Moral Majority Report* 7 (Nov. 1985): 3–4, 6–8; Martin Mawyer, "Porn Kings Earning Billions," ibid. 7 (Aug. 1985): 3–6. *Moral Majority Report* claimed a readership of 1.11 million by January 1985 (ibid. 7 [Jan. 1985]: 1).

60. Swaggart, "America at the Crossroads," 5 Nov. 1984; FitzGerald, "Disciplined, Charging Army," pp. 59–69, 111–20, 129–31; Martin E. Marty, "Precursors of the Moral Majority," *American Heritage* 33 (Feb.– Mar. 1982): 98–99; Francis J. Flaherty, "The Creationist Controversy: The Social Stakes," *Commonweal* 119 (22 Oct. 1982): 555–59; "Guideposts for the Current Debate over Origins," *Christianity Today* 26 (8 Oct. 1982): 22– 26; Anna Brenner, "The Creationist Controversy: The Religious Issues," *Commonweal* 119 (27 Oct. 1982): 559; *New York Times*, 6 May 1986; Henry M. Morris, *History of Modern Creationism* (San Diego: Creation of Life Publishers, 1984), pp. 17–67, 273–334. On the historic opposition of fundamentalists to the theory of evolution, the roots of fundamentalism in the nineteenth and early twentieth centuries and the fundamentalist-modernist controversy, see Chapter 12 above and note 9 in that chapter concerning the work of Ernest Sandeen, George M. Marsden, Timothy P. Weber, Ferenc Morton Szasz, Lawrence W. Levine, et al.

61. Hal Lindsey, *The Late Great Planet Earth* (Grand Rapids, Mich.: Zondervan, 1970), pp. 34–35, 48–60, 83–102, 124–68.

62. Lindsey, *Late Great Planet Earth*, pp. 168–77; Arthur E. Bloomfield, *Before the Last Battle: Armageddon* (Minneapolis: Dimension Books, 1982), pp. 148–50; Robertson, *Secret Kingdom*, pp. 212–23; Timothy P. Weber, *Living in the Shadow of the Second Coming: American Premillennialism, 1875–1925*, 1st ed. (New York: Oxford University Press, 1979), pp. 9– 11, 156–57; Charles Krauthammer, "The Edge of the World," *New Republic* 188 (28 Mar. 1983): 12–15; Timothy P. Weber, *Living in the Shadow of the Second Coming*, enlarged ed. (Grand Rapids, Mich.: Academe Books, 1983), pp. 218–19, 222–23, 228–32; Michael Barkun, "Nuclear War and Millenarian Symbols: Premillenarians Confront the Bomb," paper presented at the Annual Meeting of the Society for the Scientific Study of Religion, 25– 27 Oct. 1985; Hal Lindsey, *There's a New World Coming* (Eugene, Ore.: Harvest Books, 1983), pp. 96–98.

63. "Religious Leaders Assail Armageddon Theory, Rightists Defend It," *New York Times,* 24 Oct. 1984; Hal Lindsey on "Crossfire," television presentation, Cable News Network, 31 Oct. 1984.

64. FitzGerald, "Disciplined Charging Army," pp. 111–20, 133; Blumenthal, "Righteous Empire," pp. 18–19; *Newsweek* (30 May 1983): 91; "Swaggart's One-Edged Sword," ibid. (9 Jan. 1984): 65; "Falwell's Follies," *New Republic* 192 (29 Apr. 1985): 10–11; "Unholy Row," p. 63.

65. "An Interview with the Lone Ranger of American Fundamentalism," *Christianity Today* 25 (4 Sept. 1981): 24–25; Richard John Neuhaus, "Mechanic of the New Right—With No Apologies" (on Paul Weyrich), *Commonweal* 108 (9 Oct. 1981): 555–57.

66. "Interview with the Lone Ranger of American Fundamentalism," pp. 24–25; "Jerry Falwell Objects," *Christianity Today* 26 (27 Jan. 1982): 16–17; FitzGerald, "Disciplined, Charging Army," pp. 114–15.

Of course, Falwell, the militant fundamentalist, limits his enthusiasm for Judaism. He has written: "The Jews are returning to their land of unbelief. They are spiritually blind and desperately in need of their Messiah and Savior." But this passage is immediately followed by the observation: "Yet they are God's people, and in the world today, Bible-believing Christians in America are the best friends the nation Israel has." For many on the New Christian Right, the enthusiasm for the state of Israel is in part a function of how its creation in 1948 was a signal to premillenarians that biblical prophecies were coming true. See Fackre, *Religious Right and Christian Faith,* pp. 61–63; Ruth Mouly, "Israel: Darling of the Religious Right," *Humanist* 42 (May–June 1982): 5–11; Young, *God's Bullies,* pp. 200–205; Falwell, *Listen America!,* pp. 93–96, 107–13 ("That Miracle Called Israel"); Daniel C. Maguire, *The New Subversives: Anti-Americanism of the Religious Right* (New York: Continuum, 1982), pp. 15–26.

67. Jerry Falwell introduced T. E. B. Hills, a black minister from Watts, on one of his OTGH shows, saying, "The Ku Klux Klan tried to run him out of Texas in his earlier years. I am proud to say that he is my friend" ("Old Time Gospel Hour," WTBS, 5 Jan. 1986). Of course, Ben Kinchlow, Pat Robertson's co-host on the "700 Club," is black.

68. FitzGerald, "Disciplined, Charging Army," pp. 70–73, 96–99, 110, 114.

Many more women than men make up the New Christian Right television audience. A Nielsen survey in 1979 indicated that women constituted between 52 and 61 percent of the viewers for Swaggart, Falwell, Bakker, Robinson, and Robertson. See Horsfield, *Religious Television,* pp. 112, 122–23. On the southern dimension of the televangelists' audience, see Hadden and Swann, *Prime Time Preachers,* p. 60.

69. Richard John Neuhaus, "Who, Now, Will Shape the Meaning of America," *Christianity Today* 26 (19 May 1984): 6–12; Bruce T. Grindal, "Creationism, Sexual Purity and the Religious Right," *Humanist* 43 (Mar.–Apr. 1983): 19–23, 37; Falwell, *Listen America!,* pp. 252–54; Max Stackhouse, "Fundamentalism around the World," *Christian Century* 102 (28 Aug.–4 Sept. 1985): 764–77; Robert N. Bellah, Richard Madsen, William N.

Sullivan, Ann Swidler, and Steven N. Tipton, *Habits of the Heart* (Berkeley and Los Angeles: University of California Press, 1985), pp. 238, 276–77, 280–81; Dean M. Kelly, *Why Conservative Churches Are Growing* (New York: Harper & Row, 1977), pp. 154–57. See also Jeremy Rifkin with Ted Howard, *The Emerging Order* (New York: G. P. Putnam's, 1979), pp. 47–96, 99, 178–84, 209–10.

70. The religious-political linkage on the right wing had been in decline with the weakening of the anticommunist activities of Billy James Hargis and Carl McIntire. Hargis had claimed a total income for his Christian Crusade of $3 million in 1970; his staff had grown to 104 and he was broadcasting "in living color" on forty television stations and on one hundred radio stations. He had moved to the Tulsa suburbs, into a spacious "Cathedral of the Christian Crusade." He was building the campus of his American College. His anticommunist rhetoric filled speeches, sermons, and a journal, the *Christian Crusade,* in addition to his media presentations. He continued to see the specter of communism everywhere, particularly in the activities of liberal leaders. He wrote ugly editorials after the deaths of Martin Luther King, Jr., and Robert F. Kennedy. But he would soon experience a shattering personal setback. In 1976, a national magazine reported that students—both male and female—had claimed to have had sex with Hargis. Billy James Hargis denied the charges, but his ministry was ruined.

See Dobson, Hindson, and Falwell, *Fundamentalist Phenomenon,* pp. 102–3; "It Isn't the First Time," *Newsweek* 104 (6 Apr. 1987): 6; Gary K. Clabaugh, *Thunder on the Right: The Protestant Fundamentalists* (Chicago: Nelson-Hill, 1974), pp. 3–14, 69–105; *New York Times,* 6 Aug. 1971; Billy James Hargis, "The Life and Death of Martin Luther King," *Christian Crusade* 20 (May 1968): 8, 20; Billy James Hargis, "The Assassination of Robert Kennedy and What It Means," ibid. (July 1968): 10–12; Billy James Hargis, "The Christian Crusade: A Look at the Future," ibid. (Nov. 1968): 4; David A. Noebel, "Biblical Christianity versus Atheistic Communism," ibid. 21 (Jan.–Feb. 1969): 28–30; Billy James Hargis, "Excesses That Undermine America," ibid. (July 1969): 5–7, 10–11; Billy James Hargis, "Liberal Churches Support Communist Goal of Disarming America," ibid. (Aug.–Sept. 1969): 10–12.

71. Kevin P. Phillips, *Post-Conservative America* (New York: Random House, 1982), pp. 46–49; Richard A. Viguerie, *The New Right: We're Ready to Lead* (Falls Church, Va.: Viguerie Co., 1981), pp. 6–8, 31–70, 90–99, 129; Frances FitzGerald, "The Triumphs of the New Right," *New York Review of Books* 27 (19 Nov. 1981): 19–21; Crawford, *Thunder on the Right,* pp. 55, 62–63; Conway and Seligman, *Holy Terror,* pp. 83–99; Young, *God's Bullies,* pp. 83–95.

72. Young, *God's Bullies,* pp. 107–16, 123–31, 139–52; Phillips, *Post-Conservative America,* pp. 48–49; Blumenthal, "Righteous Empire," pp. 20–24; *New York Times,* 13 May 1981; Neuhaus, "Mechanic of The New Right—with No Apologies" (on Paul Weyrich), p. 555; *Los Angeles Times,* 31 Dec. 1986.

73. Michael Lienesch, "Right Wing Religion: Christian Conservatism as a Political Movement," *Political Science Quarterly* 94 (Fall 1982): 407–10; Neuhaus, "Mechanic of the New Right," pp. 555–57.

74. *New York Times*, 21 Jan., 18 Aug. 1980, 31 May 1981; Lienesch, "Right Wing Religion," pp. 403–25; Richard Alvarez, "President Stirs Controversy over Star Wars," *Moral Majority Report* 7 (Oct. 1985): 20–21; Falwell, *Listen America!*, pp. 81–96 ("The Threat of Communism") and pp. 97–106 ("Faltering National Defense"); *Washington Post*, 25 Aug. 1979; Viguerie, *New Right*, p. 53; Blumenthal, "Righteous Empire," p. 24; LaHaye, *Battle for the Mind*, pp. 200–206; Phillips, *Post-Conservative America*, pp. 190–91; Young, *God's Bullies*, pp. 96–106, 117–22, 220–37; David W. Balsiger and Colonel V. Doner, *The Presidential Biblical Scoreboard* (Costa Mesa, Calif.: Biblical News Service, 1984), pp. 2–39; Paul M. Weyrich, "Archie Bunker Wants Cultural Conservatism," *Conservative Digest* 11 (June 1986): 107–12; Paul M. Weyrich, "The Pantheon of Our Sacred Groups," ibid. (Apr. 1986): 97–104; Christian Voice, *Strategy Guide for Reclaiming America* (Pacific Grove, Calif.: Christian Voice, 1984); Samuel S. Hill and Dennis E. Owen, *The New Religious Political Right in America* (Nashville: Abingdon, 1982), pp. 51–140; Neuhaus, "Mechanic of the New Right," pp. 555–57. It is Neuhaus who quotes Jerry Falwell on John Paul as "the best hope we Baptists ever had"; he reports that Weyrich told him that "if we didn't know that the Pope agrees with us . . . we Catholics of the New Right would have serious conscience problems."

75. Neuhaus, "Mechanic of the New Right," pp. 555–56; "Thunder on the Right," *Time* 124 (16 Aug. 1982): 24–25; Morton Kondrake, "Hard Times on the Hard Right," *New Republic* 187 (20 Dec. 1982): 20–23; *New York Times*, 26 June 1983; FitzGerald, "Disciplined, Charging Army," pp. 124–28; Hadden and Swann, *Prime Time Preachers*, pp. 127–33, 164–65; Carl T. Rowan quotes Howard Phillips on Reagan and Chamberlain, *Syracuse Herald-Journal*, 17 Nov. 1984; *Conservative Digest* 7 (Jan. 1981): 4–5; Jeffrey K. Hadden, "Televangelism and the New Christian Right" in Jeffrey K. Hadden and Theodore E. Long, eds., *Religion and Religiosity in America* (New York: Crossroad, 1983), pp. 117–27. Ronald Reagan's White House made an effort to inspire numerous books referring to Reagan as deeply religious and his coming to the presidency as the work of God, foretold in prophecy. See "Reagan Beginning to Get Top Billing in Christian Bookstores for Policies," *New York Times*, 28 Sept. 1984, and "Why President Reagan Does Not Attend Church," *Moral Majority Report* 7 (Feb. 1985): 21. On Reagan as a "creationist," see Joseph Kraft in *Newsday*, 10 Sept. 1984. But to the attack on the Reagan White House for weakening separation of church and state (see, for example, Anthony Lewis, "Abroad at Home," *New York Times*, 8 Oct. 1984), some writers respond in part that Falwell and others are only emulating Martin Luther King, Jr.'s SCLC in organizing grass-roots movements in the churches. See Leo P. Ribuffo, "Fundamentalism Revisited: Liberals and That Old Time Religion," *Nation* 231 (29 Nov. 1980): 570–73.

76. Richard Reeves, "The Republicans," *New York Times Magazine*,

9 Sept. 1984, pp. 57, 112; Hadden and Swann, *Prime Time Preachers*, pp. 137–38; Peele, *Revival and Reaction*, pp. 49–79; V. S. Naipaul, "Among the Republicans," *New York Review of Books* 21 (25 Oct. 1984): 8.

77. Naipaul, "Among the Republicans," pp. 14–15; Reeves, "Republicans," p. 117; LaHaye, *Battle for the Mind*, p. 156; Bill Moyers, CBS television commentary at the Republican National Convention, 21 Aug. 1984.

78. "Falwell in Town to Register Voters," *Syracuse Herald-Journal*, 1 Sept. 1984; "Religious Abuses in the Reagan Administration," *Christian Century* 102 (22 May 1985): 527; Colonel V. Doner, American Coalition for Traditional Values, on "Late Night America," television presentation on Public Broadcasting System, 29 Oct. 1984; "Playing Politics at Church," *Newsweek* 104 (9 July 1984): 52. Critics of the Moral Majority argue that most Americans reject its program and its tactics. For an empirical study, see Anson Shupe and William A. Stacey, *Born Again Politics and the Moral Majority: What Social Surveys Really Show* (New York: Edwin Mellen Press, 1982), pp. 103–8. Terry Dolan, New Right lobbyist, died at age thirty-six on 30 December 1986. He was an ardent advocate of "traditional family values," but his private life had been a source of rumors. Spokesmen put the "immediate cause of death" after a "long illness" as "congestive heart failure." See *Los Angeles Times*, 31 Dec. 1986; Young, *God's Bullies*, pp. 139–52.

79. Neuhaus, "Mechanic of the New Right," pp. 556, quotes Weyrich on "our background" and "third generation wealth." See also Naipaul, "Among the Republicans," p. 10; Phillips, *Post-Conservative America*, pp. 43, 48, 194–204.

80. Richard A. Viguerie, *The Establishment vs. the People: Is a New Populist Revolt on the Way?* (Chicago: Regnery Gateway, 1983), pp. vii, 1–12, 27–29, 40–42, 57, 59, 81–87, 97, 101, 111–12.

81. Lawrence Goodwyn, arguing that the Populist movement of the 1890s produced a "distinctively new vision of society," rejects "contemporary populism" as being only a "provincial rebellion by malcontents who do not understand the real world" ("The New Populism," *Progressive* 48 [June 1984]: 18–20). Eugene Litwak, Nancy Hooyman, and Donald Warren, "Ideological Complexities and Middle American Rationality," *Public Opinion Quarterly* 37 (Fall 1973), 320, describe what other analysts have called "center extremism" in a portrayal of "middle American radicals," who are not liberal or conservative, rejecting blacks and poor but suspicious of the rich as well, practitioners of a different brand of social conservatism.

In a review of a book on American attitudes toward civil liberties, *The Dimensions of Tolerance*, in which elites are described as much more tolerant, more committed to civil liberties than average Americans, Paul Brest asks: "Might civil libertarian norms serve the interests of their adherents more than . . . people with a lower level of tolerance?" Might "intolerance" help "maintain a sense of culture and community among citizens who do not share power with the elites?" See Paul Brest, "Civil Liberties for Some," *New York Times Book Review*, 1 Jan. 1984, p. 12.

82. "Bush Salutes Falwell Conservatism," *New York Times*, 26 Jan. 1986;

Jerry Falwell, "Don't Press a Friend or Undermine an Ally," *USA Today*, 7 Jan. 1986; Ronald S. Godwin, "South Africa: The Watergate of the American Media," *Moral Majority Report* 7 (Oct 1985): 3–4, 8; "Television Preachers Finding It Tougher to Pay the Bills," *Syracuse Herald-American* (UPI), 20 Apr. 1986; Murray Wa, "Falwell's New Name," *New Republic* 194 (31 Mar. 1986): 16–17.

83. Jerry Falwell on "Nightline," ABC Television, 4 Sept. 1985; *Newsweek* 107 (2 Sept. 1986): 4; *New York Times*, 1, 5, Apr., 5 Sept. 1986; Larry King, *USA Today*, 29 Oct. 1984; Jerry Falwell, "Old Time Gospel Hour," 22 June 1986, WTBS; Letter from Jerry Falwell, 21 Nov. 1986; "Where is Jerry Falwell Headed in 1986?" Interview in *Christianity Today* 30 (21 Feb. 1986): 39–41; Cal Thomas, "Falwell Vows to Curb Political Activism," *Syracuse Herald-Journal*, 5 Sept. 1986; Connaught Marshner, "Interview: How Jerry Falwell Is Driving the Left to an Early Grave," *Conservative Digest* 11 (June 1986): 93–104. In his interview with the *Conservative Digest*, Falwell insisted that the Moral Majority name had not been abandoned. The Moral Majority will continue as a subsidiary of Liberty Federation, "dealing with strictly moral issues [abortion, traditional family values, gay rights]. The Liberty Federation will address political questions such as SDI, Central America, and Angola."

On another front, New Right organizers heard accusations that the American Coalition for Traditional Values was receiving funds from Reverend Moon's Unification church. Associates of Moon, who has discussed the unification of the world under a Korean theocracy, allegedly were in contact with Tim LaHaye. See Carolyn Weaver, "The Unholy Alliance," *Mother Jones* 11 (Jan. 1986): 14.

84. David Brooks, "Richard Viguerie, Tycoon in Crisis," *National Review* 38 (20 June 1986): 28–32; Seletan, "Teflon Telepreacher," pp. 9–11.

85. *New York Times*, 15, 16 June, 18, 30 Sept. 1986; *Washington Post*, 28 May 1986; "Robertson Shows Political Clout in Michigan," *Syracuse Post Standard* (Knight-Ridder News Service), 2 June 1986; "Crusade for the White House," *Newsweek* 107 (2 June 1986): 27; *Syracuse Herald-Journal* (AP), 12, 23 Sept. 1986.

86. "Why is Pat Robertson Considering a Race for the Oval Office," interview in *Christianity Today* 30 (17 Jan. 1986): 34–38; Marhard Good Stoddard, "CBN's Pat Robertson: White House Next?" *Saturday Evening Post* 257 (Mar. 1985): 54; *New York Times*, 2, 10 Oct., 10 Dec. 1986.

87. "T.V. Evangelist Charges Bigotry by Democratic National Chairman," *Syracuse Herald-American* (AP), 21 Mar. 1986; Paul M. Weyrich, "Democrats Attack the Clergy," *Conservative Digest* 11 (May 1986): 53–60.

88. John Buchanan, "Pat Robertson for President?" *Dallas Morning News*, 6 Dec. 1985; Pat Robertson on "McNeill-Lehrer News Hour," PBS, 11 Nov. 1985; *Time* 127 (17 Feb. 1986): 62–66; Pat Robertson, "An Agenda for Public Action," *Saturday Evening Post* 257 (Mar. 1985): 57; Beth Spring, "Pat Robertson for President?" *Christianity Today* 29 (8 Nov. 1985): 48–81.

Critics of Robertson's presidential aspirations pointed to problems that could be caused by his claims as a faith healer. He told a newsmagazine of the "unusual blessing God has given me" physically "to heal the sick." In fact, "we have medical verification, our tv crews have taken their stories ...it is absolutely extraordinary." Political opponents have speculated on the fate of a faith healer in the presidential arena, on the use of videotapes of 1981 CBN testimonials to the miraculous cures for hemorrhoids and varicose veins. They also noted that the man who had talked in tongues once said he had preached in Shanghai in English but his listeners had heard him in their native Chinese. How would that play to a larger, nonsectarian audience?

89. *New York Times*, 20, 21 Mar., 7, 13, 27, 29, 30 April. 1987; *Philadelphia Inquirer*, 3, 5 Apr. 1987; Jerry Falwell on Cable News Network, 29 April 1987; Jim and Tammy Bakker on ABC *News*, 1 May 1987; Jimmy Swaggart on "Nightline," ABC Television, 24 Mar. 1987; Jerry Falwell on "Nightline," ABC Television, 29 Apr. 1987; Jimmy Swaggart on "Face the Nation," CBS Television, 26 Apr. 1987; "Bakker Was Cancer, Swaggart Contends," *Syracuse Herald-Journal* (AP), 25 Mar. 1987; "Unholy Row," pp. 60–67; "Holy Wars," *Newsweek* 109 (6 Apr. 1987): 16–23.

90. Jon Ankerberg on the "Jon Ankerberg Show," Christian Broadcasting Network, 25 Apr. 1987; *New York Times*, 1, 2, 26, 29, 31 May, 4 June 1987; "What Profits a Preacher," *Newsweek* 109 (4 May 1987): 68; Jon Ankerberg and Ken Woodward, "Nightline," ABC Television, 23 Apr. 1987; Cal Thomas, "Unholy Trinity: Money, Sex, Power," *USA Today*, 27 Mar. 1987; "Survey Finds Many Skeptics among Evangelists' Viewers," *New York Times*, 31 Mar. 1987; Jerry Falwell, "Doing God's Business Requires Giving Money," *USA Today*, 29 May 1987; *Washington Post*, 27, 28 May 1987.

91. William Schneider, "The New Shape of American Politics," *Atlantic* 259 (Jan. 1987): 50–54.

CHAPTER 16

1. Gary Burtless and Timothy Smeeding, "America's Tide: Lifting the Yachts, Swamping the Rowboats," *Washington Post*, June 25, 1995.

2. *New York Times*, 20 Feb., 4 Mar., 15 May, 1988; Edith L. Blumhofer, "Swaggart and the Pentecostal Ethos, *Christian Century*, 105 (6 Apr. 1988): 333–35; "More Troubles on the Broadcast Front," *Christianity Today*, 32 (18 Mar. 1988): 47–48; Michael D'Antonio, *Fall From Grace: The Failed Crusade of the Christian Right* (New York: Farrar Straus Giroux, 1989), pp. 235–37.

3. "Scandals and High TV Costs Leave Empty Pews in the Electronic Church," *New York Times*, 31 Mar. 1991.

4. "Politics, Not Religion, Trips Up Robertson," *Christian Century* 105 (6 Apr. 1988): 341–43; Kenneth D. Wild, "Ministering to the Nation: The campaigns of Jesse Jackson and Pat Robertson" in Emmett H. Buell, Jr. and Lee Sigelman, eds., *Nominating the President* (Knoxville: University of Tennessee Press, 1991), pp. 133–34; Allen D. Hertzke, "Harvest of Discontent: Religion and Populism in the 1988 Presidential Campaign" in James L. Guth and John C. Green, eds., *The Bible and the Ballot Box: Religion and Politics in the 1988*

Election (Boulder Col.: Westview Press, 1991), pp. 21–22; D'Antonio, *Fall From Grace*, pp. 228–230.

5. *New York Times*, 6 Mar., 9 May, 1988; D'Antonio, *Fall From Grace*, pp. 238–39.

6. Steve Bruce, *The Rise and Fall of the New Christian Right* (Oxford: Clarendon Press, 1988), pp. 172–75; Ted G. Jelen, *The Political Mobilization of Religious Beliefs* (New York: Praeger, 1991), pp. 146–147; D'Antonio, *Fall From Grace*, pp. 240–241; Joseph B. Tamney and Ronald Burton, "Pat Robertson: Who Supported His Candidacy for President?", *Journal for the Scientific Study of Religion* 28 (Dec. 1989): 387–89.

7. *New York Times*, 12 June 1989, 3 Mar. 1991; *Washington Times*, 29 Aug. 1989; *New Orleans Times Picayune*, 15 Mar. 1990, 15 Nov., 14 Dec. 1991; *Christianity Today* 36 (10 Feb. 1992): 46–47; *Christian Century* 108 (18–25 Dec. 1991): 1191

8. "Whatever Happened to the Religious Right," *Christianity Today* (15 Dec. 1989): 44–47. One study of the Robertson campaign in 1988 cited election survey data in the 1988 National Election Study to demonstrate that Pat Robertson's support was overwhelmingly female (70%) and composed of people with lower incomes than any other major candidate in the primary race for either party (62% with incomes under $30,000.) See Allen D. Hertzke, *Echoes of Discontent: Jesse Jackson, Pat Robertson and the Resurgence of Populism* (Washington, D.C.: CQ Press, 1993), pp. 217, 222.

9. Jeffrey H. Birnbaum, "The Gospel According to Ralph," *Time* 145 (15 May 1995): 28–35.

10. *Atlanta Journal*, 15 Jan. 1995; *Los Angeles Times*, 1 May, 1995; Robert E. Sullivan, "An Army of the Faithful," *New York Times Magazine*, (25, Apr. 1993): 32–35.

11. Seth Mydans, "Evangelicals Gain With Covert Candidates," *New York Times*, 27 Oct. 1992; Sidney Blumenthal, "Christian Soldiers," *New Yorker*, LXX (15 July, 1994): 31.

12. *Los Angeles Times*, 15 May 1990; 22 Mar., 1992; *New York Times*, 27 Oct. 1992

13. *New York Times*, 25 April, 1993; Gillian Liechtling, Jonathan Mazzochi, Steven Gardner, "The Covert Crusade," *The Covert Crusade: The Christian Right and Politics in the West* (Portland: Western States Center and Coalition for Human Dignity, 1994), pp. 3–11. For the quotations from Ralph Reed and Guy Rodgers see *The Religious Right: The Assault on Tolerance and Pluralism in America* (New York: Anti-Defamation League, 1994), pp. 27, 39. The Christian Coalition also began publishing its own newspaper, with Pat Robertson offering his views to the readership. See, for example, "Pat's View," *Christian American*, May/June, 1995.

14. S. L. Gardner, *Rolling Back Civil Rights* (Portland: Coalition for Human Dignity, 1992), p. 15; Thomas C. Atwood, "Through the Glass Darkly: Is the Christian Right Overconfident It Knows God's Will?," *Policy Review* 54 (Fall 1990): 44–52.

15. *Christian Century* 110 (11–18 Aug. 1993): 781–84; *New York Times*, 27 Oct., 1992, 26 April, 1993; Blumenthal, "Christian Soldiers," pp. 35–36.

16. *New York Times,* 27 Oct. 1992, 25 April, 1993, 12 June 1994; *Christian Century* 110 (6–13 Jan. 1993): 10, Blumenthal, "Christian Soldiers," p. 32; *Time* 145 (15 May 1995): 30–31.

17. Ralph Reed, *Politically Incorrect: The Emerging Faith Factor in American Politics* (Dallas: Word Publishing, 1994), pp. 2–8, 38–40, 130, 171–187; Blumenthal, "Christian Soldiers," p. 31.

18. *Atlanta Journal,* 5 June 1994; *Christian Century* 109 (26 Aug.–2 Sept. 1992): 770.

19. *Washington Post,* 18 May 1995; *Wall Street Journal,* 8 May 1995; *Atlanta Constitution,* 23 May 1995; *Los Angeles Times,* 18, 21 May 1995; *USA Today,* 18 May 1995; *New York Times,* 12 Nov., 1994, 15 May 1995; Ralph E. Reed, Jr., *Christian Coalition: An Agenda for the New Congress,* speech to The Economic Club of Detroit, Detroit, Mich., 17 Jan. 1995.

20. *Washington Post,* 11 Feb. 1995; *The Religious Right,* pp. 4–5; *Time* 145 (15 May 1995): 32–33; Blumenthal, "Christian Soldiers," p. 33; *San Francisco Chronicle,* 14 Sept. 1993.

21. *New York Times,* 13 May 1992, 26 Nov. 1993; *Washington Post,* 9 Oct. 1993; *Wall Street Journal,* 14 May 1992; "On God's Green Earth: A Glimpse Inside Pat Robertson's Sprawling Financial Empire," *U.S. News & World Report,* 118 (April 24, 1995): 31–32. In the spring of 1995, two national newsmagazines had cover stories on the Christian Right: *Time* (May 15) had Ralph Reed on the cover with the words, "The Right Hand of God;" *U.S. News & World Report* had Pat Robertson, with the words "For God's Sake."

22. Pat Robertson, *The New World Order* (Dallas: Word Publishing, 1991), pp. 1–14, 35–58, 64–73, 78–80, 92, 95–102, 177–125, 138–140, 158, 176–185, 197, 207–211, 257–268. Scattered through this book are Robertson's conservative views of "liberal" policies, including an attack on "the American and European welfare states" and their suffocating regulatory rules, which would become even worse under the "new world order" (see p. 210). In an earlier book, revised and reissued in 1992, he made related arguments: "Financial morality has been corrupted as the government, exalted by humanist philosophy, has become God and Provider." See Pat Robertson, *The Secret Kingdom* (Dallas: Word Publishing, 1992), p. 31.

23. Michael Lind, "Rev. Robertson's Grand International Conspiracy Theory," *The New York Review of Books* XLII (2 Feb. 1995): 21–25; Frank Rich, "Bait and Switch," *The New York Times,* 2 Mar. 1995; Gustav Niebuhr, "Pat Robertson Says He Intended No Anti-Semitism in Book He Wrote Four Years Ago," *New York Times,* 4 Mar. 1995. (Robertson's letter to *The Times* is printed next to this article.)

24. On the defense of Pat Robertson and the attacks on Michael Lind, the author of the critical essay review (as well as the responses to these attacks), see Michael Lind, "On Pat Robertson: His Defenders," and Jacob Heilbrunn, "On Pat Robertson: His Anti-Semitic Sources," *The New York Review of Books,* XLII (20 Apr. 1995): 67–71 and Norman Podhoretz "In the Matter of Pat Robertson," *Commentary,* 100 (Aug. 1995): 27–32. For an earlier defense of Robertson against charges of intolerance, see Midge Decter, "The ADL vs. The Religious Right," *Commentary,* 98 (Sept. 1994): 45–47.

25. *Christian Century* 110 (7 Apr. 1993): 325; *Newsweek* 124 (25 July 1994): 72; *Time* 144 (1 Aug. 1994): 21; *Christian Century* 111 (1–8 June 1994): 566–67; Sidney Blumenthal, "The Friends of Paul Jones," *New Yorker* 70 (20 June, 1994): 38–43

26. *The Religious Right*, pp. 109–111; Gardiner, *Rolling Back Civil Rights*, p. 38.

27. Gustav Niebuhr, "Advice for Parents, and for Politicians: Religious Group Speaks to Family Issues and to the Right," *New York Times*, 30 May 1995; *The Religious Right*, pp. 75–84, 113–18; *New York Times*, 15 May 1995; "The Heavy Hitter: James Dobson Speaks for a 'Parallel Culture' Washington Has Ignored," *U.S. News & World Report* (24 Apr. 1995): 38–39.

28. Michael Lienesch, *Redeeming America: Piety and Politics in the New Christian Right* (Chapel Hill: University of North Carolina Press, 1993) pp. 11–12, 248–49; Walter H. Capps, *The New Religious Right: Piety Patriotism, and Politics* (Columbia: University of South Carolina Press, 1990), pp. 165–66.

29. Lienesch, *Redeeming America*, pp. 94–138, 158–66. One writer argues that "the strong alignment of the religiously conservative segments of the electorate with the Republican party ... signals a 'Europeanization' of the American party system in which the parties become ideologically more homogeneous and, with regard to ideology and voter alignments, the party of the right becomes the party of religion whereas the party of the left becomes the more secular party." See Michael Minkenberg, *The New Right in Comparative Perspective: The USA and Germany* (Ithaca: Cornell Western Societies Paper, 1993), pp. 50–51.

30. Reed is quoted in Blumenthal, "Christian Soldiers," pp. 34–35.

31. John Kifner, "Bomb Suspect Felt at Home Riding the Gun Show Circuit, *New York Times*, 5 July 1995; "Oklahoma City: The Manhunt," *Newsweek* CXXV (1 May 1995): 30–47.

32. *Paroled: The La Rouche Political Cult Regroups* (New York: Anti-Defamation League, 1994), pp. 1–34.

33. John George & Lair Wilcox, *Nazis, Communists, Klansmen, and Others on the Fringe: Political Extremism in America* (Buffalo: Prometheus Books, pp. 255–265; Frank P. Mintz, *The Liberty Lobby and the American Right* (Westport, Conn.: Greenwood Press, 1985), pp. 104–05, 196–204; *Liberty Lobby: Network of Hate* (New York: Anti-Defamation League, 1990), pp. 1–13; *Washington Post*, 11 May 1995; *Paranoia as Patriotism: Far Right Influences on the Militia Movement* (New York: Anti-Defamation League, 1995) pp. 22–23.

34. George & Wilcox, *Nazis, Communists, Klansmen*, pp. 22–23; *The John Birch Society*, an internet webpage; Sidney Blumenthal, "Her Own Private Idaho," *New Yorker* LXXI (10 July 1995), pp. 31–32.

35. *Klanwatch Intelligence Report: Special Year-End Edition, 1994* 77 (Mar. 1995): 9–13; *Klanwatch Intelligence Report: Special Year End Edition, 1993* 71 (Feb. 1994): 3, 12, 15; *The Klan Splits: A Radical Breakaway* (New York: Anti-Defamation League, 1994), pp. 1–3; *The KKK Today: A 1991 Status Report* (New York: Anti-Defamation League, 1991), pp. 1–21; Michael Cox, "Be-

yond the Fringe: The Extreme Right in the United States of America," in Paul
Hainsworth, ed., *The Extreme Right in Europe and the USA* (New York: St.
Martin's Press, 1992), pp. 292–94; *Thom Robb: The Klansman's New Clothes*
(New York: Anti-Defamation League, 1991) pp. 1–2; George & Wilcox, *Nazis,
Communists, Klansmen*, pp. 405–406; *Time* 140 (6 July, 1992): 24–27; Mira
L. Boland, "Mainstream" Hatred, *The Police Chief* (June 1992): 30–31.

36. *Dukewatch 1995* (New York: Anti-Defamation League, 1995), pp. 2–37;
Elinor Langer, "The American Neo-Nazi Movement Today," *The Nation* 251
(16/23 July 1990): 94–106; *U.S. News & World Report* 109 (23 July 1990): 24–
25; Larry Cohler, "Republican Racist," *New Republic* 201 (18–25 Sept. 1989):
11–14.

37. On Tom Metzger's career, see Mark S. Hamm, *American Skinheads:
The Criminology and Control of Hate Crime* (Westport, Conn.: Praeger, 1993),
pp. 42–57; Langer, "The American Neo-Nazi Movement Today," pp. 84–89;
Young and Violent: The Growing Menace of America's Neo-Nazi Skinheads
(New York: Anti-Defamation League), pp. 3–4; David Van Biema, "When
White Makes Right," *Time* 142 (9 Aug. 1993): 40–42; *Extremism on the Right*
(New York: Anti-Defamation League, 1988), pp. 128–29; James Ridgeway,
*Blood in the Face: The Ku Klux Klan, Aryan Nations, Nazi Skinheads, and
the Rise of a New White Culture* (New York: Thunder's Mouth Press, 1990)
pp. 162–176.

38. Dan Korem, "Neo-Nazi Skinheads: Angry, Violent, Rebellious and
Reachable," *Klanwatch Intelligence Report: 1993*, pp. 8–9; *Sounds of Hate:
Neo-Nazi Rock Music From Germany* (New York: Anti-Defamation League,
1992), pp. 1–11; *Klanwatch Intelligence Report*, 54 (Feb. 1991): 1–2, 14–15;
Young Nazi Killers: The Rising Skinhead Danger (New York: Anti-Defamation
League, 1993), pp. 1–33; *Shaved for Battle: Skinheads Target America's Youth*
(New York: Anti-Defamation League, 1987) pp. 1–5; Hamm, *American Skin-
heads*, pp. 15–42, 126–32.

39. *Klanwatch Intelligence Report: 1994*, p. 3; *Young Nazi Killers: The
Rising Skinhead Danger*, pp. 31–34.

40. Morris Dees and Steve Fiffer, *Hate On Trial: The Case Against America's Most Dangerous Neo-Nazi* (New York: Villard Books, 1993), pp. 1–25,
250–80; *Klanwatch Intelligence Report* 54 (Feb. 1991): 1–3; *New York Times*,
20 Feb., 9 Sept., 2 Oct., 8 Nov., 12 Nov., 1993; *Time* 142 (26 July 1993): 49;
Jack Levin and Jack McDevitt, *Hate Crimes* (New York: Plenum Press 1993),
pp. 99–107; *Electronic Hate: Bigotry Comes to TV* (New York: Anti-Defamation League, 1991), pp. 2–3. Tom Metzger responded to the Portland verdict
in a letter to *The Nation*. He had been convicted, he argued, for "the advocacy
of ideas" and it was clear that the "system works against Skinheads exactly
as it did against Communists in the 50s or Black Panthers in the 60s. Don't
expect justice in America if you are poor or hold unpopular political views."
See Tom Metzger, "A Case of Aryan Self-Defense," *The Nation* 25 (8 Oct.
1990).

41. *Klanwatch Intelligence Report: 1993*, pp. 10–17; *Klanwatch Intelligence Report, 1994*, pp. 1–3, 9–13; *Young Nazi Killers: The Rising Skinhead
Danger*, p. 5.

42. *Gary "Gerhard" Lauck: A Nebraska Nazi's Global Reach* (Special Edition from the Anti-Defamation League: Feb. 1993), pp. 1–2; *Washington Post*, 11 May, 1995; "A Powerful Alliance," *Klanwatch Intelligence Report: 1994*, pp. 6–7, 12–13.

43. *New York Times*, 5 July 1995; *William L. Pierce: Novelist of Hate* (New York: Anti-Defamation League Research Report, 1995), pp. 3–11; *Klanwatch Intelligence Report: Militia Task Force Edition 78* (June 1995), pp. 4–5; *Klanwatch Intelligence Report: 1994;* pp. 1–9; Dr. William L. Pierce, "OKC Bombing and America's Future," *American Dissident Voices* broadcast, 19 Apr. 1995; Dr. William L. Pierce, "The New World Order, 'Free' Trade, and the Deindustrialization of America," from *National Vanguard* magazine (Hillsboro, W. Va.), distributed as well on the internet; Andrew Macdonald (William L. Pierce), *The Turner Diaries*, Second Edition (Washington, D.C.: National Vanguard Books, 1980), pp. 35–43; Andrew Macdonald [William L. Pierce], *Hunter*, (Hillsboro, West Va.: National Vanguard Books, 1989), pp. 157, 259; Brad Whitsel, "The Cosmotheist Community: Aryan Vision for the Future in the West Virginia Mountains," unpublished ms. to appear in *Journal of Terrorism and Political Violence.*

44. The best study of the origins and development of Christian Identity is found in Michael Barkun, *Religion and the Racist Right: The Origins of the Christian Identity Movement* (Chapel Hill: University of North Carolina Press, 1994), pp. 3–242.

45. Robert Crawford, S. L. Gardner, Jonathan Mozzochi, R. L. Taylor, *The Northwest Imperative: Documenting a Decade of Hate* (Portland: Coalition for Human Dignity, 1994), pp. 3.3–3.33. On Christian Identity in Idaho, see James A. Aho, *The Politics of Righteousness: Idaho Christian Patriotism* (Seattle: University of Washington Press, 1990), pp. 21–24, 51–67, 68–113, 161–84, 209–211.

46. *The Church of the Creator: Creed of Hate* (New York: Anti-Defamation League, 1993), pp. 1–16; *Klanwatch Intelligence Report: 1993*, p. 12.

47. *The Northwest Imperative*, pp. 3.27–3.30; *"Pastor" Pete Peters* (New York: Anti-Defamation League Special Edition), Feb. 1994, pp. 1–2; *New York Times*, 16 Nov. 1993; "Who is Pastor Peters?, Scriptures for American Ministries," internet announcement, 6 June, 1995.

48. *New York Times*, 20, 22, May 1995; Raphael S. Ezekiel, *The Racist Mind: Portraits of American Neo-Nazis and Klansmen* (New York: Viking, 1995), pp. 26–36; Brent L. Smith, *Terrorism in America* (Albany: State University of New York Press, 1994), pp. 88–89.

49. *New York Times*, 26 Apr. 1995; "Background on Louis Beam," (Portland: Coalition for Human Dignity, 12 May 1995), pp. 1–4; Louis Beam, "Leaderless Resistance" (1992), copy of an address supplied by Coalition for Human Dignity (Portland); *Klanwatch Intelligence Report; 1994*, p. 5; *Louis Beam* (New York: Anti-Defamation League Special Edition, 1990), pp. 1–2; James William Gibson, *Warrior Dreams: Paramilitary Culture in Post-Vietnam America* (New York: Hill and Wang, 1994), pp. 218, 226–27, 230.

50. *Klanwatch Intelligence Report: 1994*, pp. 1, 5–7; Michael Janofsky, "For

Aryan Congress, Stridency and Security: White Supremacists Convene in Idaho," *New York Times*, 23 July 1995.

51. On the fall of The Order, see Thomas Martinez with John Guinther, *Brotherhood of Murder* (New York: McGraw-Hill, 1988). On Gordon Kahl and his movement, see James Corcoran, *Bitter Harvest: Gordon Kahl and the Posse Comitatus* (New York: Viking, 1990). See also Smith, *Terrorism in America*, pp. 57–60, 77–79.

52. Conversation with Danny Welch, 29 June 1995. On political alternatives for Christian Identity and similar movements, see Barkun, *Religion and the Racist Right*, pp. 199–253.

53. On Christian Patriots and their beliefs, see *The Northwest Imperative*, pp. 2.3–2.7. See also *Washington Post*, 20 May 1995; Philip Weiss, "Off the Grid," *New York Times Magazine*, (8 Jan. 1995), pp. 26, 29.

54. *The Northwest Imperative*, pp. 2.9–2.39; Center for Democratic Renewal, "An Analysis of Militias in America," 25 Apr. 1995, p. 6; M. J. Red Beckman, *The Church Deceived* (Billings, Mont.: Common Sense Press, 1985); *New York Times*, 27 Sept. 1991, 26 May 1995; *Wall Street Journal*, 25 May 1995; *Los Angeles Times*, 5 Dec. 1993.

55. Robert Crawford, Steven Gardiner, Jonathan Mozzochi, *Almost Heaven! Bo Gritz, SPIKE and the Christian Covenant Communities* (Portland: Coalition for Human Dignity, 1994), pp. 1–9; Philip Weiss, "Off the Grid," pp. 36, 44, 48; *New York Times*, 12 June, 1993. Some members of human rights organizations studying such movements are not certain that Gritz truly has renounced racism. See *The Northwest Imperative*, pp. 2.21–2.26, and *Colonel James "Bo" Gritz: Patriot or Extremist?* (New York: Anti-Defamation League Special Edition, Jan. 1995), pp. 1–2. James A. Aho, *The Politics of Righteousness*, pp. 161–63, 209, 220, notes that for groups he categorizes (in Idaho) under Christian Patriots as Christian Constitutionalists, Issue-oriented Patriots, and even Identity Christians, "educational levels are about as high as the conventional majority" and that what distinguishes these patriots from ordinary Idahoans is "their access to and involvement in . . . a patriot 'opportunity structure' "; they were exposed through family, friends and church to the movement and then through the special movement media.

56. Richard Leiby, "Paranoia," *Washington Post*, 8 May 1995; *Detroit News*, 26 Apr. 1995; Timothy Egan, "Inside the World of the Paranoid," *New York Times*, 30 April, 1995; Michael Janofsky, "Demons and Conspiracies Haunt a 'Patriot' World," *New York Times*, 31 May 1995; "The View From the Far Right," *Newsweek* CXXV (1 May 1995): 36–39; "Enemies of the State" and "Calling All Paranoids," *Time* 145 (8 May 1995) 58–69; Spider Rybaak, "Onward, Christian Soldiers: New York's Militias Battle a Godless New World Order," *Syracuse New Times*, 5–12 July, 1995.

57. On the origins of paramilitary groups in modern American history, see *Klanwatch Intelligence Report: Special Militia Task Force Edition*, pp. 12–13; *Paranoia as Patriotism: Far-Right Influences on the Militia Movement* (New York: Anti-Defamation League, 1995) pp. 7–8, 29–30; Eckard V. Toy, Jr., "Right-Wing Extremism from the Ku Klux Klan to the Order," in Ted Robert

Gurr, Ed., *Violence in America*, Vol. 2 (Newbury Park: Sage Publications, 1989), pp. 144–46; Smith, *Terrorism in America*, pp. 79–87.

58. *Paranoia as Patriotism: Far-Right Influences on the Militia Movement*, p. 5; *Washington Post*, 20 May 1995; *New York Times*, 23 Nov. 1993; 13 Dec. 1994; 6 Jan., 6 July 1995. There were new developments involving the Weaver affair in the summer of 1995: Justice Department investigators uncovered evidence that a few FBI managers, apparently hoping to protect some agency officials at Washington headquarters from harsher discipline—such as the sanctions applied to the on-site commanders at Ruby Ridge—had blocked federal prosecutors from obtaining bureau records in the case and may have destroyed documents. (Of course, this had nothing to do with Weaver's illegal activities or the death of the federal agent, only the alleged concerns by some in the FBI to avoid responsibility for ordering a change in the rules of engagement.) The government in August agreed to pay $3.1 million to the surviving members of the Weaver family. While not admitting government wrongdoing, Federal attorneys apparently wanted to settle the case in which the government was charged with the wrongful death of Weaver's wife and son, before it came to an Idaho jury. See *New York Times*, 16 July, 16 Aug. 1995. See also "The Echoes of Ruby Ridge," *Newsweek* CXXVI (28 Aug. 1995): 24–28 and Jess Walter, " 'Every Knee Shall Bow,' " *Newsweek* (28 Aug. 1995): 29–33.

59. *Klanwatch Intelligence Report: Special Militia Task Force Edition*, pp. 1–2.

60. Ibid.

61. Michael Kelly, "The Road to Paranoia," *New Yorker* LXXI (19 July 1995): 67–73; *Armed & Dangerous: Militias Take Aim At The Federal Government* (New York: Anti-Defamation League, 1994), pp. 17–19; Kenneth S. Stern, *Militias: A Growing Danger*, (New York: The American Jewish Committee, 1995), pp. 7–10; *Washington Post*, 29 April, 1995; *Denver Post*, 22 April, 1995; *USA Today*, 24 April 1995.

62. Keith Schneider, "Manual for Terrorists Extols 'Greatest Coldbloodedness,' " *New York Times*, 29 April 1995; *Beyond the Bombing: The Militia Menace Grows* (New York: Anti-Defamation League, 1995), pp. 21–23; *Denver Post*, 22 Jan. 1995; Martha A. Bethel, "Terror in Montana," *New York Times*, 29 July 1995.

63. *The Militia Menace Grows*, pp. 22–23. For a description of the video *Invasion & Betrayal* and its influence on other militia groups, see Rybaak, "Onward, Christian Soldiers: New York's Militias Battle a Godless New World Order," 5–12 July 1995, in which the author—a militia admirer—approvingly describes these "scariest of all" scenarios. For a very different treatment of the conspiratorial vision of the leaders of the Militia of Montana, see Kelly, "The Road to Paranoia," pp. 61–67. In this *New Yorker* article, Michael Kelly offers what he calls a "fusion paranoia" thesis. In this approach, "there is no left and right." Extremists of the far right—like the MOM activists—embrace paranoid fantasies similar to those embraced by leftists in the past. Their paranoid vision "rejects the bipolar model (of the left and the right) for a more primal polarity:

Us versus Them." Thus, Kelly argues, for the fusion paranoid there is "only unanimity of belief in the boundless, cabalistic evil of the government and its allies."

64. *New York Times*, 26 Apr., 1995; *Seattle Times*, 19 Mar. 1995; Stern, *Militias: A Growing Danger*, Appendix I, pp. 15–16; "Why There Is A Need For The Militia In America," *Federal Lands Update* (Oct. 1994): 1–3; "Martial Law and Emergency Powers," *Federal Lands Update* (Nov. 1994): 1–7; "Too Close to Home," *New Yorker* LXXXI (24 July 1995) p. 29. The episode at the council meeting in Everett, Washington, was described by a witness at the unofficial forum on the militias conducted in July 1995 by Representative Charles Schumer (D.–New York). See also Paul Glastris, "Patriot Games," *Washington Monthly* (June 1995): 23–26.

65. *New York Times*, 25 June 1995; Stern, *Militias: A Growing Danger*, Appendix I, pp. 13–14; *Sixteenth American Jurisprudence (Second Edition)*.

66. Col. Curtis B. Dall and E. Stanley Rittenhouse, *Review and Commentary on Proposed New Constitution for the Newstates of America* (Washington: Liberty Lobby, n.d.), pp. 3–30; *First Amendment to the Constitution of the United States* (North American Patriots Free Network-Defenders of Liberty), pp. 1–20; Dirk Johnson, "Conspiracy Theories' Impact Reverberates in Legislatures," *New York Times*, 6 July 1995; *Wall Street Journal*, 9 May 1995.

67. "From the Editor," *Media Bypass* 3 (March 1995); Stern, *Militias: A Growing Danger*, pp. 16–17; *Bill of Rights Jury Handbook* (Phoenix: Whitten Printers, n.d.), pp. 2–14; "National Common Law Grand Jury" (June 4, 1995).

68. Beth Hawkins, "Patriot Games," *Detroit Metro Times*, 12–18 Oct. 1994; Keith Schneider, "Fearing a Conspiracy, Some Heed a Call to Arms," *New York Times*, 14 Nov. 1994.

69. *Detroit Free Press*, 13 Oct. 1994; Christopher John Farley, "Patriot Games," *Time* 144 (19 Dec. 1994); *Detroit Metro Times*, 12–18 Oct., 1994; *New York Times*, 14 Nov. 1994; *Los Angeles Times*, 6 May 1995; *Detroit News*, 1 May 1995; Jill Smolowe, "Enemies of the State," *Time* 145 (8 May 1995): 63–64; "The View From the Far Right," *Newsweek* CXXV (1 May 1995): 35–38.

70. *Detroit News*, 16 June, 1995; *Lansing State Journal*, 18 Oct. 1994; *New York Times*, 25 June 1995; *Los Angeles Times*, 22 Apr. 1995.

71. *The Michigan Minute Men: Michigan Militia Corps Handbook; Central Michigan Regional Militia Wolverines: Background, Mission, Purpose and Organization;* "New World Army," *The New American* 9 (Nov. 1993): 15–32; *Flashpoint: A Newsletter Ministry of Texe Marrs* (May 1995): 1–6; "Technotronic Surveillance: The Prohibition of Privacy," *Relevance* 1 (23 Nov. 1994): 1–12; "Death Of A Freedom: The Fight for the Fourth Amendment Turns Deadly," *Relevance* 1 (April 1995): 1–12; "Concentration Camp Plans for U.S. Citizens," (n.d.), pp. 1–19; "The Bombing of The Alfred P. Murrah Federal Building, Oklahoma City, Oklahoma," pp. 1–46.

72. *Wall Street Journal*, 1 May 1995; *Detroit News*, 8, 18 May, 1995; Smolowe, "Enemies of the State," pp. 61–66; *Spokane Spokesman Review*, 3 Dec. 1994; *Los Angeles Times*, 22 Apr. 1995. FEMA looms large in the imaginations of militia conspiracy theorists; the text of Public Law 94-412 (Sept. 14, 1976),

the National Emergencies Act, has been widely copied and circulated among members.

73. Adam Parfrey & Jim Redden, "Patriot Games: Linda Thompson," *Village Voice* 39 (11 Oct. 1994) :26–30; *Atlanta Constitution,* 18 May 1995; *Washington Post,* 11 May 1995; *USA Today,* 24 Apr. 1995; *Waco the Big Lie-Battle of Ideas,* video, 1994, American Justice Federation; *America Under Siege,* video, 1994, American Justice Federation.

74. Jason Vest, "The Spooky World of Linda Thompson," *Washington Post,* 11 May 1995; *Paranoia as Patriotism: Far-Right Influences on the Militia Movement,* p. 31. The John Birch Society was among other far Right groups attacking Thompson for her "deplorable call for an armed march on Washington . . . consistent with tactics often employed by conspiratorial forces." See Robert W. Lee, "An Insurrectionist Messenger," *The New American* (19 Sept. 1994) :29–32.

75. Judy Pasternak, "Ohio Town Lives in Fear of Militia Revenge," *Los Angeles Times,* 8 July 1995.

76. *Idaho Falls Post Register,* 3 Aug. 1994; Stern, *Militias: A Growing Danger,* Appendix 96, pp. 1–3; *Salt Lake Tribune,* 8 Feb. 1995.

77. Robert Crawford, S. L. Gardiner, Jonathan Mozzochi, *Patriot Games: Jack McLamb & Citizen Militias* (Portland: Coalition for Human Dignity Special Report, 1995), pp. 1–12; *Aid & Abet Newsletter* 1 (No. 3, n.d.) 3–5; *Arizona Republic* (Phoenix), 2 Feb. 1995.

78. *Denver Post,* 23 Jan. 1995; *Armed and Dangerous,* pp. 5–6; *Klanwatch Intelligence Report: Special Militia Edition,* pp. 7–11.

79. *Beyond the Bombing: The Militia Menace Grows,* pp. 10–11, 30–31; *Armed & Dangerous,* pp. 7–9; *Washington Post,* 22 May 1995; *USA Today,* 30 Jan. 1995; *Baltimore Sun,* 19 March 1995; *Sunday Telegraph,* 4 Dec. 1994; *Houston Chronicle,* 27 Nov. 1994; "Formation of a Texas Constitutional Militia" in Stern, *Militias: A Growing Danger,* Appendix 28; *The Militia News,* 94 (n.d.), pp. 1–7.

80. *Armed & Dangerous,* pp. 22–23, 25–26; *Washington Post,* 20 May 1995.

81. *Washington Post,* 18 May 1995; Richard Harwood, "The Anger Isn't Out There," *Washington Post,* 30 May 1995. The poll was a *Washington Post-ABC News Poll* conducted May 10–14, 1995; a total of 1,011 randomly selected adults were interviewed with a margin of sampling error for the overall results as plus or minus 3 percentage points.

82. *Washington Post,* 8 May 1995; *Detroit Free Press,* 6 June 1995; Kelly, "The Road to Paranoia," pp. 62–3; *New York Times,* 31 May 1995; *Wall Street Journal,* 28 April, 1995.

83. *Minneapolis Star-Tribune,* 24 Feb. 1995; *New York Post,* 27 April 1995; *Washington Post,* 25, 26 Apr. 1995; *New York Times,* 14 Feb., 6 May 1995; *St. Louis Post-Dispatch,* 19 May 1995; Patricia J. Williams, "Hate Radio," *Ms.* 4 (Mar./Apr. 1994): 25–29.

84. John Mintz, "Ideological War Pits NRA Hard-Liners Against More Moderate Staff," *Washington Post,* 29 May 1995; B. Drummond Ayres Jr., "NRA Official Is Wary of 'Hate Groups,' " *New York Times,* 22 May 1995; Jill Smolowe, "NRA: Go Ahead, Make Our Day," *Time* (29 May 1995): 18–22; *New*

York Times, 26 June 1995. (The poll of gun owners was a *Time/CNN Poll* of 600 adult American gun owners on May 17–18; sampling error was plus or minus 4 percent.)

85. David Johnston, "Waco Witness Says NRA Consultant Posed as a House Aide," *New York Times,* 17 July 1995; Frank Rich, "Smoking GOP Guns," *New York Times,* 24 June 1995; Michael Janofsky, "Accounts of Violence by Paramilitary Groups," *New York Times,* 12 July 1995; Senate Judiciary Committee, Subcommittee on Terrorism, Techonology and Government Information, Hearings on the Militias in the United States, June 15, 1995, *C-SPAN; New York Times,* 17 May, 15 June, 6 July 1995.

86. Timothy Egan, "Trying to Explain Support From Paramilitary Groups," *New York Times,* 2 May 1995; Don Morgan, "Militia Ties to GOP," *Washington Post,* 1 May 1995; *Los Angeles Times,* 28 Apr., 15 May, 1995; *Houston Chronicle,* 29 Apr. 1995; Blumenthal, "Her Own Private Idaho," pp. 28–29, 31; "The Movement's Sympathetic Ears on Capitol Hill," *Time* 145 (8 May 1995): 66; "The View From the Far Right," *Newsweek,* pp. 37–38.

87. James William Gibson, *Warrior Dreams: Paramilitary Culture in Post-Vietnam America,* pp. 9–10, 142–169, 212–230; James A. Aho, *This Thing of Darkness: A Sociology of the Enemy* (Seattle: University of Washington Press, 1994), pp. 52–54, 64–66; James L. Pate, "Gun Gestapo Gang-Bangers: Lamplugh Raid a New Low in BATF Terror Tactics," *Soldier of Fortune* (July 1995): 56–59, 72. The founder and editor/publisher of the magazine, Robert K. Brown, wrote in the same issue—after the bombing in Oklahoma City—"I am not comfortable with the idea of armed, organized paramilitary bodies not under any type of control." See Robert K. Brown, "Terrorism's Vicious Circle," p. 3.

88. Barkun, *Religion and the Racist Right,* p. 217. Gary Wills, "The New Revolutionaries," *New York Review of Books* LXII (10 Aug. 1995): 54, observes of the setting in which militia movements arise: "If the Government is only good for fighting Communists and it no longer fights Communists, then what is it good for?"

89. Sean Reilly, "The Case for Unions," *Washington Monthly* 27 (July/Aug. 1995): pp. 26–27; John Agnew, "Democracy and Human Rights After the Cold War," in R. Johnson, P. Taylor, M. Watts, eds., *Geographies of Global Change: Remapping the World in the Late Twentieth Century* (Oxford: Blackwell, 1994).

INDEX

★ ★

66; during World War II, 266–72;
the religious Right, in the 1960s,
328–30; publicity and educational
institutions, 329, 352, 356–67, 359–
61, 381, 384–85; New Right (1990s),
xvi–xviii, 409, 412, 413–45; the religious right, in the 1990s, xvi–xviii,
413–28. *See also* Facist organiza-
tions; Television and radio broad-
casting
Riis, Jacob, 165
Rivera, Alberto, 346, 363
Rivera, Geraldo, 435
Robb, Thom, 431–32, 439
Roberts, Rev. Oral, 381, 403–4
Robertson, A. Willis, 379, 404
Robertson, Rev. Marion G. ("Pat"), xiv,
xv, 361, 379–80, 382–83, 394–95,
399, 402–5, 407, 414–17, 419–20,
428, 464, 468, 474; *The New World
Order*, xvi, 422–25
Robison, Rev. James, 381, 388, 394–95
Robison, John, 24–25, 245, 317
Rockefeller, David, 348
Rockefeller, John D., 188
Rockefeller, Nelson, 393, 424
Rockefeller family, 357, 361, 423, 443
Rockefeller Foundation, 378, 423
Rockne, Knute, 203
Rockwell, George Lincoln, 324–25,
330, 337
Rodgers, Guy, 418
Rodino, Peter, 366, 373
Roemer, Buddy, 432
Roman Catholic church, and Catho-
lics, 3, 10, 18–22, 27, 29–30, 51–52,
54, 58–60, 62, 87–91, 114, 129–30,
148, 171–72, 256, 258–60, 287–88,
313, 317, 319–21, 395. *See also*
Anti-Catholicism; Coughlin, Father
Charles E.; Kennedy, John F.; Smith,
Alfred E.
Roosevelt, Franklin D., xiv, 190, 234,
242–43, 246, 255–57, 259–63, 266,
268, 274–76, 282, 412
Roosevelt, Theodore, 162, 164, 179,
184–85, 201, 283
Root, E. Merrill, 323
Root, Russell C., 105
Rosenberg, Ethel, 291–92
Rosenberg, Julius, 291–92

Ross, Edward Alsworth, 164–65, 283
Rothschild family, 348, 355, 423, 474
Rousseau, Jean-Jacques, 378
Rousselot, John H., 322, 396
Rovere, Richard, 297–98, 304
Rowan, Carl, 367
Rubin, Jerry, 333–34, 337–38, 339
Ruby Ridge affair, 445, 448–49, 469
Ruffin, Edmund, 96
Russell, Richard B., Sr., 223
Russian Workers, Union of, 291
Ruth, George Herman ("Babe"), 203
Ryan, Father John A., 258

Sacco-Vanzetti case, 196
St. Leopold, Society of, 40–41, 171
Sams, 138–39, 151
Sandburg, Carl, 317
Santorum, Rich, 420
Sapir, Edward, 284
Sartre, Jean-Paul, 291
Satolli, Francis (Archbishop), 172–
73
Saunders, Frederick, 80–81, 111
Savage, Fred, 212
Schade, Louis, 121
Schine, G. David, 305–6, 308
Schlafly, Phyllis, 395
Schools. *See* Educational issues
Schultz, George, 361
Schumer, Charles E., 373, 466, 467
Schwarz, Dr. Fred, 328–29
Scoggin, Robert, 347
Scott, Winfield, 112
Secret societies, 23–25, 44, 49–50, 90,
105, 107–8, 110–12, 114–15, 120–
22, 127, 137, 144, 147–47, 153, 155,
228, 325; proscriptions, unmaskings,
and exposés, 211–12, 225–31, 234;
voluntary unmaskings, 127, 133,
138, 144, 148. *See also* Fraternal or-
ganizations; Know Nothings: origin
and rise; Ku Klux Klan
Sectional differences, pre-Civil War,
11, 93–98, 102–3, 109–10, 112–13,
116, 122–33, 137–39, 141–55
Secular humanism, xv–xvi, 377–78,
380–81, 383, 385, 387, 389, 391, 399,
403, 405, 421, 427, 430
Sedition: World War I, 186; 1919–20s,
190–96; among fascist groups, 245,